Beginning
Access™ 2007 VBA

Beginning
Access™ 2007 VBA

Denise Gosnell

Wiley Publishing, Inc.

Beginning Access™ 2007 VBA

Published by
Wiley Publishing, Inc.
10475 Crosspoint Boulevard
Indianapolis, IN 46256
www.wiley.com

ISBN: 978-0-470-04684-5

Manufactured in the United States of America

10 9 8 7 6 5 4 3 2 1

Library of Congress Cataloging-in-Publication Data

Gosnell, Denise.
  Beginning Access 2007 VBA / Denise Gosnell.
    p. cm.
  ISBN-13: 978-0-470-04684-5 (paper/website)
  ISBN-10: 0-470-04684-8 (paper/website)
  1. Microsoft Access. 2. Database management. 3. Microsoft Visual Basic for applications. I. Title.
  QA76.9.D3G68 2007
  005.75'65—dc22
                    2007004985

About the Author

Denise Gosnell is a software patent attorney and technology consultant with Gosnell & Associates, Inc., which she founded in 2005. Denise has a unique background in both technology and law, and presently uses her deep technical and legal expertise to counsel hi-tech clients on intellectual property and technical matters. Denise was recognized in February 2005 with the *Indianapolis Business Journal* award: "Top 40 Under 40," which recognizes the top up-and-coming professionals under the age of 40 in the city of Indianapolis each year. She also appeared on the *Inside Indiana Business with Gerry Dick* television show in March 2005 to discuss hi-tech issues facing the business world.

Denise has over 12 years of experience in creating software applications, ranging from standalone and client-server to enterprise-wide applications. Denise has worked for leading software companies such as Microsoft and EDS, and has earned a worldwide reputation for her technology expertise. She received a bachelor of arts degree in Computer Science–Business (summa cum laude) from Anderson University, where she currently serves as an adjunct professor for the Computer Science Department. Denise obtained a doctor of jurisprudence degree from Indiana University School of Law in Indianapolis.

Denise has authored and coauthored seven other software development books to date, covering topics such as database development, Access, Visual Basic .NET, and web services. Most recently, Denise authored *Professional Development with Web APIs* (Wiley 2005) and *Beginning Access 2003 VBA* (Wiley 2004). Denise was a featured technology speaker at the Microsoft European Professional Developer's Conference in December 2001 and has on numerous occasions assisted Microsoft's Training and Certification group in creating new exams for their MCSD and MCSE certifications.

Denise can be reached at denisegosnell@yahoo.com or denise@denisegosnell.com.

Credits

Executive Editor
Chris Webb

Development Editor
Rosanne Koneval

Technical Editor
Auri Rahimzadeh

Production Editor
Elizabeth Kuball

Copy Editor
Foxxe Editorial Services

Editorial Manager
Mary Beth Wakefield

Production Manager
Tim Tate

Vice President and Executive Group Publisher
Richard Swadley

Vice President and Executive Publisher
Joseph B. Wikert

Graphics and Production Specialists
Denny Hager
Jennifer Mayberry
Barbara Moore
Ronald Terry

Quality Control Technicians
Laura Albert
John Greenough

Project Coordinator
Erin Smith

Proofreading
Aptara

Indexing
Potomac Indexing, LLC

Anniversary Logo Design
Richard Pacifico

This book is dedicated to my daughter, Victoria. You are too young to understand this now, but I hope to teach you that you can accomplish anything you set your mind to. The sky is truly the limit.

Acknowledgments

To my assistant Pam Woodsford, keep up your progress and aim high. You are only limited by your own imagination. I am proud of how fast you have grown in such a short amount of time and look forward to watching you reach your full potential.

I would like to offer a special thanks to my friend Jonathon Walsh for helping me update the content in this book for Access 2007, and for contributing the materials on SharePoint Lists. I always enjoy working with you and hope to get many more opportunities.

I had a great technical editor on this book too, quite possibly the best one I have ever had to date: Auri Rahimzadeh. Thanks Auri!

Last, but certainly not least, I would like to thank Rosanne Koneval, Chris Webb, and the staff at Wiley who played such an important role in producing this book. Thanks for putting up with me through all the delays. I hope the end result makes up for it!

Contents

Acknowledgments ix

Introduction xix

Chapter 1: Introduction to Access 2007 VBA 1

What Is Access 2007 VBA? 1

What's New in Access 2007 VBA? 2

Access 2007 VBA Programming 101 3

Requirements-Gathering Phase 3

Design Phase 4

Model the Application Design 4

Determine Application Architecture 11

Development Phase 18

The Visual Basic Editor 18

Testing Phase 24

Running and Debugging Code in the Visual Basic Editor 24

Implementation Phase 25

Summary 25

Exercises 26

Chapter 2: The Basics of Writing and Testing VBA Code 27

Creating Modules 27

Standard Modules versus Class Modules 29

Creating and Calling Procedures 33

Sub versus Function Procedure 33

Create and Call a New Sub Procedure 33

Create and Call a New Function Procedure 42

Scope and Lifetime of Sub Procedures and Functions 45

Using Built-In Functions 45

Macros versus Procedures 46

Using Variables and Constants to Store Values 49

Types of Variables 49

Declaring and Using Variables 51

Declaring and Using Arrays 51

Contents

Constants   53

     Declaring and Using Constants   53

     Using Built-In Constants   54

Scope and Lifetime of Variables and Constants   54

Naming Conventions   55

Controlling Program Flow   **56**

Decision Making   56

     If . . .Then   56

     IIf   59

     Conditional If   59

     Select . . . Case   59

Loops   61

     For . . . Next and For Each . . . Next   61

     Do . . . Loop   62

     While . . . Wend   63

Documenting Your Code   **63**

Error Debugging   **64**

Types of Errors   64

     Syntax Errors   64

     Compile Errors   64

     Runtime Errors   64

     Logic Errors   66

Debugging Your Code   66

     Using Breakpoints to Step through Code   66

     Using the Immediate Window   68

     Using the Locals Window   68

     Using the Watch Window   69

     Using the Call Stack   70

Error Handling   **71**

Default Error Messages   72

Handling Errors with an On Error Statement   72

     On Error Statement   72

     Resume Statement   72

The Err Object   74

     Raising an Error   74

Using the Errors Collection   75

Creating a Generic Error Handler   75

Summary   **78**

Exercises   **78**

Chapter 3: Programming Applications Using Objects 79

Elements of an Object 79
What Is a Property? 80
What Is a Method? 82
What Is an Event? 84
Viewing Objects Using the Object Browser 91
Ways to Refer to Objects 93
Using Access Collections and Objects 94
The Forms Collection and Form Object 94
The Reports Collection and Report Object 96
The CurrentProject Object 97
The DoCmd Object 97
The Screen Object 98
The Printers Collection and Printer Object 98
Other Objects 100
Summary 100
Exercises 100

Chapter 4: Creating Your Own Objects 101

Using Class Modules to Create Your Own Objects 101
Class Diagrams 102
Creating Properties 105
Using Public Variables 105
Using Property Let, Property Get, and Property Set 106
Creating Methods 111
Using Public Sub Procedures and Functions 111
Creating Events 113
Declaring and Raising Events 114
Creating the Event Sub Procedure or Function 114
Using the Class 115
Instantiating the Class 115
Initialize and Terminate Events 115
Advanced Techniques 121
Creating Multiple Instances of the Class 121
Creating Class Hierarchies 122
Working with Enumerated Types 122
Inheritance Using Implements Keyword 123

Contents

Create Custom Properties for Existing Objects   **124**

Using Existing Tag Property   124

Using Public Variables   124

Using Property Let, Property Get, and Property Set Routines   124

Create Custom Methods for Existing Objects   **125**

Using Public Sub Procedures and Functions   126

Summary   **127**

Exercises   **127**

Chapter 5: Interacting with Data Using ADO and SQL   **129**

Introduction to Data Access   **129**

Using ADODB to Work with Data   **130**

The ADO Object Model   130

The Connection Object   131

Connecting to Access Databases   132

Connecting to Other Databases   132

The Command Object   132

The Recordset Object   132

Creating a Recordset   133

Counting Records in a Recordset   140

Navigating through a Recordset   141

Adding, Editing, and Deleting Records in a Recordset   141

Sorting, Finding, and Filtering Records in a Recordset   156

Introduction to SQL   **159**

Retrieving Data Using SQL Select Statements   160

Select Clause   160

From Clause   160

Where Clause   161

Order By Clause   161

Subqueries   162

Union   162

Using SQL and ADO to Populate a Recordset   162

Inserting Data Using SQL Insert Statements   164

Inserting Results of a Select into a Table   165

Updating Data Using SQL Statements   165

Deleting Data Using SQL Statements   165

Using ADOX to Manipulate Data Objects   **177**
Creating a Table with ADOX   177
Summary   **179**
Exercises   **179**

Chapter 6: Building Interactive Forms   181

Form Navigation and Flow   **181**
Working with Controls   **187**
Combo Boxes versus List Boxes   188
Tab Controls and Subforms   193
Building User Interaction   **195**
The MsgBox Function   195
Validating User Input   196
Adding Polish to Your Forms   **197**
Summary   **198**
Exercises   **198**

Chapter 7: Importing, Linking, and Exporting Using External Data Sources   199

Linking, Importing, and Exporting Overview   **200**
Access and Other Databases   **200**
Transferring Complete SQL Server Database   **203**
Spreadsheets   **204**
Text Files   **205**
XML Files   **208**
E-mails and Outlook   **210**
Other Ways to Export Data   **211**
Summary   **211**
Exercises   **212**

Chapter 8: Using Access with Web Services and SharePoint Lists   213

Introduction to Web Services   **214**
Using Data from Web Services   **214**
Introduction to SharePoint Lists   **221**
Using Data from SharePoint Lists   **222**
Linking and Importing SharePoint Lists   222
Summary   **232**
Exercises   **233**

Contents

Chapter 9: Creating Reports and Web-Enabled Output — 235

Working with Reports from VBA — **235**
Setting the Report Data Source — 236
Creating Reports Programmatically — 237
    Creating an Empty Report — 238
    Adding Controls to the Report — 238
    Using the Printer Object to Designate Printing Options — 246
    Working with Report Events — 247
Exporting Access Data to Web Formats — **248**
Creating Static HTML Pages — 249
Summary — **251**
Exercises — **251**

Chapter 10: Building SQL Server Applications with Access Projects — 253

Access Projects — Using Access as a Front End to SQL server — **253**
Setting Up SQL Server — **254**
SQL Server Versions — 255
Obtaining and Installing SQL Server Express Engine — 255
    The Benefits of SQL Server Express Edition — 256
    Installing SQL Server Express Edition — 256
    Understanding What Was Installed — 257
Creating Access Projects (ADPs) — **259**
Using an Existing SQL Server Database — 260
Using a New SQL Server Database — 262
Working with SQL Server Objects from Access — **264**
SQL Server Tables — 264
SQL Server Stored Procedures — 267
SQL Server Views — 271
SQL Server Functions — 275
Migrating an Existing Access Database to an Access Project — **277**
Changes to an Existing Database — 277
Using the Upsizing Wizard — 277
Summary — **285**
Exercises — **285**

Chapter 11: Advanced Access Programming — 287

Using Dynamic Link Libraries (DLLs) — **287**
Standard DLLs — 287
Using External DLLs — 291

Automation   **294**
  Working with Automation Objects   294
  Controlling Microsoft Excel   295
  Controlling Microsoft Word   298
  Controlling Microsoft Outlook   302
ActiveX Controls   **305**
Libraries   **308**
Add-Ins   **312**
Transactions   **313**
Summary   **314**
Exercises   **314**

Chapter 12: Finishing the Application   **315**

Multiuser Considerations   **315**
  Record Locking and Update Conflicts   316
    Record Locking on Bound Forms   316
    Record Locking on Unbound Forms   317
  Multiuser Architecture Considerations   318
Optimizing Your Applications   **322**
  Improving Actual Performance   322
    General Design Guidelines   322
    Optimizing VBA Code   323
    Improving Data Access   324
  Improving Perceived Performance   325
  Running the Performance Analyzer   326
Securing Your Application   **327**
  Adding a Database Password   327
  Adding a Password for VBA Code   328
  Encrypting a Database   329
Distributing Your Application   **329**
  Distributing the Application to Users with the Full Version of Access 330
  Distributing the Application with the Access Runtime   330
  Distributing an Execute-Only Application   331
Maintaining the Application   **331**
  Compacting and Repairing the Database   331
  Making Backup Copies of the Database   331
Summary   **332**
Exercises   **332**

Contents

Chapter 13: Case Study 1: Project Tracker Application   333

Design Specifications   334
Building the Database   340
Building the User Interface   344
Building the Class Modules for the Objects   357
    The Project Class   358
    The Contact Class   372
Building the Standard Modules   383
Connecting the User Interface to the Code   410
    The Projects Form   410
    The Contacts Form   440
Touring the Finished Project Tracker Application   452
Summary   459

Chapter 14: Case Study 2: Customer Service Application   461

Design Specifications   461
Building the Database and Database Objects   465
Building the User Interface   475
Building the Class Module for the Objects   481
Building the Standard Modules   488
Connecting the User Interface to the Code   499
    The Customer Search Form   500
    The View/Manage Customer Accounts Form   504
Touring the Finished Customer Service Application   512
Summary   518

Appendix A: Exercise Answers   519

Index   527

Introduction

Microsoft Access 2007 is a powerful database application that allows you to build standalone and client-server database applications. Access applications are widespread in the enterprise. Access has powerful wizards and tools that make it relatively easy for users to build a database application that then grows in popularity and requirements that are beyond the capabilities of the relatively simple design. VBA is a powerful programming language that can be used in Access applications to expand the functionality in ways you never imagined. If you are hoping to take your current Access databases or future databases to a more robust level of functionality, then *Beginning Access 2007 VBA* is the book for you.

Whom This Book Is For

This book assumes that you have created Access databases in the past that have tables, forms, and possibly macros. You may have even written some VBA code in Access before, or you may have experience with Visual Basic or VBScript and want to learn how to write VBA code from within Access applications. No prior experience with VBA is required. As long as you have the ability to create Access tables and forms and the desire to learn VBA, this book will have a lot to offer you.

It is very possible that you have realized limitations with your current Access applications and now desire to build more sophisticated solutions. For example, your current application may need additional features included that must be programmed with VBA. Your current application may need to be improved to support more users or a client-server environment because it has been a great success and has outgrown the current design. Or, you may want to begin creating your new database applications with expanded functionality. The tools and techniques covered in this book will teach you how to take your Access applications to the next level.

What This Book Covers

Access 2007 is vastly different in many ways from Access 2003, such as the revamped user interface that uses "ribbons," among other differences. However, Access 2007 VBA has not changed a whole lot since the prior versions of Access. The VBA interface for Access 2007 still uses the same old user interface as before, not the ribbons that Access 2007 uses. The VBA language syntax has not changed very much either. Even if you are using a prior version of Access, you can still gain a lot from this book. However, there will be some examples that deal with features only supported in Access 2007.

After reading this book, you will learn:

❑ Basic programming life-cycle and architecture concepts

❑ How VBA can be used for professional application development

❑ The basics of programming using VBA

❑   Basic object-oriented programming techniques using VBA

❑   How to use existing objects

❑   How to create custom objects

❑   How to use ActiveX Data Objects (ADO) to retrieve and update data

❑   How to retrieve data from external data sources

❑   How to create reports and web content from the database

❑   How to integrate with Office applications

❑   How to integrate with SharePoint Lists

❑   How to build SQL Server solutions with Access projects

❑   How to fine-tune and distribute the application

How This Book Is Structured

Just as with the prior edition, the chapters are structured with standalone examples that do not require you to follow the chapters in order. This structure will allow you to go straight to a chapter that interests you, or to skip around among chapters as desired. Certainly, there are some chapters that will not make as much sense unless you have read the prior chapters or are already familiar with the topics covered therein. At least you will not be required to read the prior chapters that cover topics you already know just for the purpose of building parts of a solution that are prerequisites to the chapter you are really interested in.

Chapter 1 will provide an overview of Access 2007 VBA and the programming life cycle, and will introduce the Visual Basic editor environment to you. Chapter 2 teaches you several important VBA programming concepts, such as how to create code procedures, how to control the flow of execution of your code, how to make decisions in your code, how to handle errors, how to debug your application, and so on.

Chapters 3 and 4 will demystify the concept of object-oriented programming and will teach you how to use existing objects and to create your own custom objects. Chapter 5 will illustrate how to use ADO to retrieve and update data in databases. Chapter 5 will also illustrate how to create and execute SQL statements using ADO. Chapter 6 discusses how you can build interactive forms.

Chapter 7 covers various ways to import, link, and export data to and from external data sources, such as MDB files, SQL Server databases, XML files, and other data sources. Chapter 8 illustrates how to use VBA with web services and SharePoint Lists. Chapter 9 describes how you can use VBA to create reports programmatically, as well as how to export data in your Access 2007 application to various web formats, such as HTML, ASP, and data access pages.

Chapter 10 illustrates how to create a new Access project as a front end to SQL Server for more robust applications, and covers how to migrate an existing Access database to an Access project that uses SQL Server.

Chapter 11 covers various advanced VBA topics, such as how to work with external DLLs, how to use automation to control external programs such as Microsoft Word and Excel, as well as security, transactions, and multiuser considerations. Chapter 12 then rounds out the prior chapters by covering some finishing touches that you can apply to prepare your application for distribution.

Chapters 13 and 14 provide two comprehensive case studies that will give you hands-on experience in building real-world solutions using the concepts covered in the book. Chapter 13 focuses on building a standalone project-tracking application. The project-tracking application allows a user to track projects and related details, such as comments, contacts, and file attachments. A few examples of the user interface for the project tracking application you will create in Chapter 13 are shown in Figures I-1 and I-2.

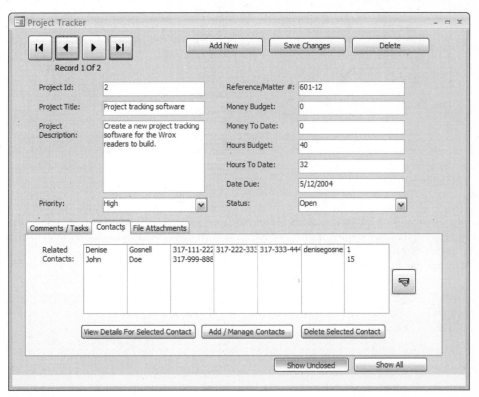

Figure I-1

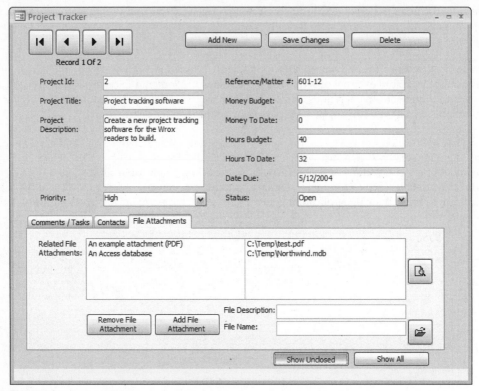

Figure I-2

Chapter 14 focuses on building a client-server customer service application that uses SQL Server as the database. The customer service application allows a customer service agent to locate a customer record based on search criteria and then view and modify the customer record details. An example of the user interface for this customer service application is shown in Figure I-3.

Solutions to the exercises provided at the end of each chapter are provided in the appendix.

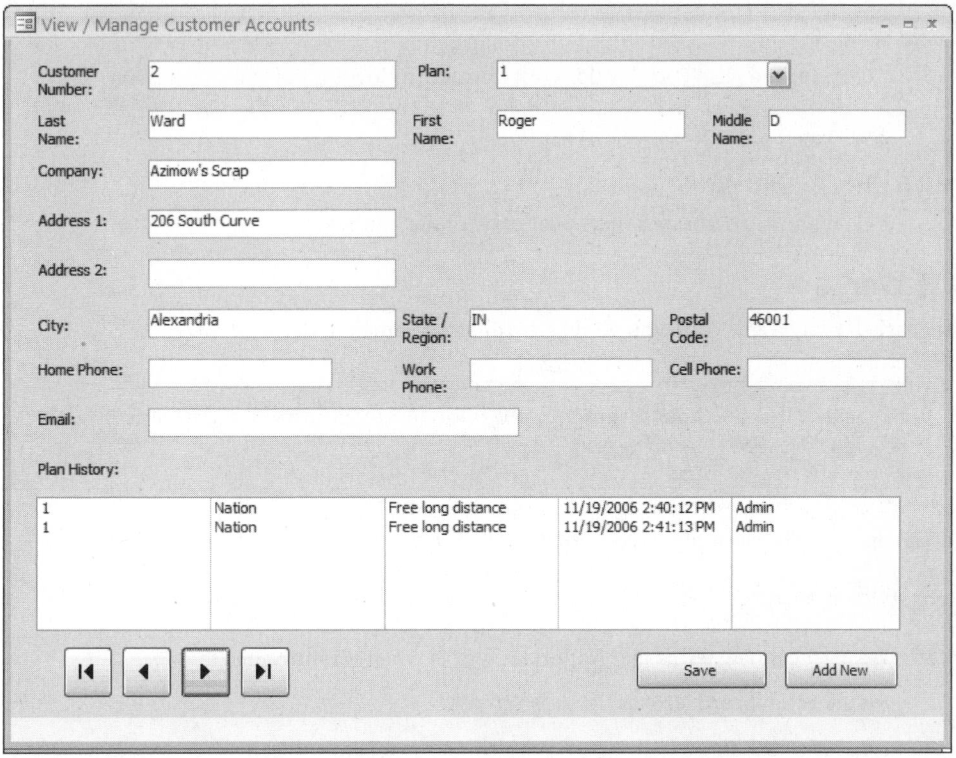

Figure I-3

What You Need to Use This Book

At a minimum, you need Access 2007 in order to implement the examples provided throughout the book. One topic covered in Chapter 8 is how to retrieve data from web services, which requires the Office Web Services toolkit. The Office Web Services toolkit is available for downloading from Microsoft's web site. Chapters 10 and 14 deal with examples based on SQL Server 2005 as the database, and thus a copy of SQL Server 2005 is needed to implement those examples. A free entry-level version of SQL Server 2005 is available for downloading from Microsoft's web site.

Conventions

To help you get the most from the text and keep track of what's happening, we've used a number of conventions throughout the book.

Try It Out

The *Try It Out* is an exercise you should work through, following the text in the book.

1. They usually consist of a set of steps.

2. Each step has a number.

3. Follow the steps through with your copy of the database.

How It Works

After each *Try It Out*, the code you've typed will be explained in detail.

> **Boxes like this one hold important, not-to-be forgotten information that is directly relevant to the surrounding text.**

Tips, hints, tricks, and asides to the current discussion are offset and placed in italics like this.

As for styles in the text:

❑ We *highlight* new terms and important words when we introduce them.

❑ We show keyboard strokes like this: Ctrl+A.

❑ We show file names, URLs, and code within the text like this: `persistence.properties`.

❑ We present code in two different ways:

```
In code examples we highlight new and important code with a gray background.
```

```
The gray highlighting is not used for code that's less important in the present
context, or has been shown before.
```

Source Code

As you work through the examples in this book, you may choose either to type in all the code manually or to use the source code files that accompany the book. All of the source code used in this book is available for downloading at `http://www.wrox.com`. Once at the site, simply locate the book's title (either by using the Search box or by using one of the title lists) and click the Download Code link on the book's detail page to obtain all the source code for the book.

Because many books have similar titles, you may find it easiest to search by ISBN; this book's ISBN is 978-0-470-04684-5.

Once you download the code, just decompress it with your favorite compression tool. Alternately, you can go to the main Wrox code download page at `www.wrox.com/dynamic/books/download.aspx` to see the code available for this book and all other Wrox books.

Errata

We make every effort to ensure that there are no errors in the text or in the code. However, no one is perfect, and mistakes do occur. If you find an error in one of our books, like a spelling mistake or faulty piece of code, we would be very grateful for your feedback. By sending in errata you may save another reader hours of frustration and at the same time you will be helping us provide even higher-quality information.

To find the errata page for this book, go to `www.wrox.com` and locate the title using the Search box or one of the title lists. Then, on the book details page, click the Book Errata link. On this page you can view all errata that has been submitted for this book and posted by Wrox editors. A complete book list including links to each's book's errata is also available at www.wrox.com/misc-pages/booklist.shtml.

If you don't spot "your" error on the Book Errata page, go to www.wrox.com/contact/techsupport .shtml and complete the form there to send us the error you have found. We'll check the information and, if appropriate, post a message to the book's errata page and fix the problem in subsequent editions of the book.

p2p.wrox.com

For author and peer discussion, join the P2P forums at p2p.wrox.com. The forums are a Web-based system for you to post messages relating to Wrox books and related technologies and interact with other readers and technology users. The forums offer a subscription feature to e-mail you topics of interest of your choosing when new posts are made to the forums. Wrox authors, editors, other industry experts, and your fellow readers are present on these forums.

At http://p2p.wrox.com you will find a number of different forums that will help you not only as you read this book but also as you develop your own applications. To join the forums, just follow these steps:

1. Go to p2p.wrox.com and click the Register link.

2. Read the terms of use and click Agree.

3. Complete the required information to join as well as any optional information you wish to provide and click Submit.

4. You will receive an e-mail with information describing how to verify your account and complete the joining process.

   You can read messages in the forums without joining P2P but in order to post your own messages, you must join.

Once you join, you can post new messages and respond to messages other users post. You can read messages at any time on the Web. If you would like to have new messages from a particular forum e-mailed to you, click the Subscribe to this Forum icon by the forum name in the forum listing.

For more information about how to use the Wrox P2P, be sure to read the P2P FAQs for answers to questions about how the forum software works as well as many common questions specific to P2P and Wrox books. To read the FAQs, click the FAQ link on any P2P page.

Introduction to Access 2007 VBA

This chapter will provide an introduction to the world of Access 2007 VBA and programming in general. More specifically, this chapter will cover:

❑ Introduction to Access 2007 VBA and new features

❑ Explanation of the stages in the Systems Development Life Cycle of software development

❑ Techniques for designing applications

❑ Writing and testing VBA code using the Visual Basic Editor

What Is Access 2007 VBA?

VBA is an acronym that stands for Visual Basic for Applications. VBA is included as part of several Microsoft products, including Access, Word, and Excel. For example, Access 2007 VBA uses VBA version 6.0, which is the same version of VBA used by Word 2007 VBA and Excel 2007 VBA. VBA is a programming language that can be used to add additional features to your applications. You are no doubt already aware that Access is a powerful database application that also enables you to create applications that include user interfaces. You can use VBA instead of or in addition to Access macros to provide advanced functionality to those Access applications. For example, you might use an AutoExec macro to control which form loads when the application begins, and then write the business logic that controls how the application works using VBA.

VBA should not be confused with the Microsoft Visual Basic (VB) or Visual Basic .NET (VB.NET) programming products. VB and VB.NET have their own syntaxes for the Visual Basic programming language. The VB syntax, the VB.NET syntax, and the VBA syntax are very similar, but they have some differences. Unlike Access, the VB and VB.NET products do not have a built-in database. The Visual Basic and Visual Basic .NET programming products are typically used in building more complex enterprise applications that use Access, SQL Server, or Oracle as the database. Access 2007 VBA is typically used to build small and simple Access database applications designed for a few users. The experience you gain writing VBA code in Access or other

Microsoft Office application products will certainly be helpful if you ever decide to use the Microsoft VB or VB.NET programming products. Microsoft has a development solution called Visual Studio Tools for Microsoft Office that allows Microsoft Office products, including Access 2007, to call code that is written in a .NET programming language.

What's New in Access 2007 VBA?

Access 2007, in general, has changed substantially from Access 2003, although Access 2007 VBA has not changed much from Access 2003 VBA. One significant change with Access 2007 is the introduction of a new ACCDB file format, instead of the MDB file format of the past. Another significant change to Access 2007 and all other Office 2007 programs in general is the new user interface design. The new user interface for Access 2007 uses ribbons on the toolbar that replace the layers of menus and toolbars found in earlier releases. Actions or options on the ribbons are grouped together in a logical fashion based on the task they accomplish. While the user interface for Access 2007 has changed significantly, the Visual Basic Editor for Access 2007 has remained mostly unchanged. The Visual Basic Editor opens in a separate window from Access 2007. In developing a VBA application, you will work with both Access 2007 and the Visual Basic Editor.

Some examples of the additional changes to Access 2007 in general (but not Visual Basic for Applications) include:

- ❏ **Templates** – Many prebuilt templates are included to get you started quickly with certain common applications.

- ❏ **Rich text in memo fields** – Text can now be formatted with options, such as bold, italic, colors, and the like.

- ❏ **Navigation pane** – The navigation pane replaces the old database window and contains all of the database objects, such as tables, forms, and so on. What is interesting about the navigation pane is that it also allows you to create custom groupings of objects, such as tables, forms, reports and so on to a particular meaningful grouping, such as Products.

- ❏ **Embedded macros** – Embedded macros support simple variables, some looping, and even some error handling. You can also embed a macro within a control's event property. For example, if you need a button to open a form, you can write a one-line embedded macro instead of using VBA code to accomplish this simple task. In other words, you can save VBA for the more complex coding tasks and can use macros for some of the simplest tasks.

- ❏ **Custom ribbons** – You can create custom ribbons for the toolbar, since ribbons are built dynamically from XML contained in hidden system tables in the Access database.

Another change that is likely of interest to an Access VBA developer is the change in user-level security. With the Access 2007 ACCDB file format, user-level security is not supported. A database password can still be used to protect the database, but it is no longer stored in the Access data file. If more comprehensive security is needed beyond a database password, then the ACCDE file format (which replaces MDEs) can be used to protect your code, forms, and reports. The ACCDE format, however, does not provide any specific security on the data stored in the application. In addition to removed user-level security, replication has also been removed for ACCDB files. In other words, you cannot replicate data and design changes between databases using the ACCDB file format. A workaround for user-level security and replication is to use the Access 2000 or Access 2002–2003 MDB format when working in Access 2007.

Note that user-level security is not the same concept as the security model you create for your Access applications. You can store user names, passwords, and credentials in your database and implement a security model for your application that uses these stored values. The prior section on Access security discusses the intrinsic security features of Access.

Access 2007 VBA Programming 101

Many people first enter the world of programming by creating simple Access applications that become a success and must be expanded. These programmers typically have little to no formal experience in designing software applications and have taught themselves how to write basic Access applications. They now need to use VBA to extend those applications. You may very well fall into this category. The rest of this chapter will provide you with a basic overview of general programming concepts such as the phases of the Systems Development Life Cycle and will explain how Access VBA fits into each of these phases.

All applications should be written according to a development methodology that provides guidelines for developing the application. A commonly followed development methodology is a *Systems Development Life Cycle (SDLC)*, which includes the following phases:

❑   Requirements gathering

❑   Designing

❑   Developing

❑   Testing

❑   Implementing

These phases are discussed in detail below.

Various other types of application development methodologies can be used in addition to, or instead of, the Systems Development Life Cycle as appropriate, such as Rapid Application Design (RAD) techniques, Extreme Programming techniques, and so on.

Requirements-Gathering Phase

In the requirements-gathering phase, your goal is to identify the objectives for the new application. The final output of the requirements-gathering phase should be a document describing the purpose of and features requested for the new application and any other helpful details you gathered during this phase.

You should determine the purpose of the application overall, who will use the application, from what locations the application will be accessed, and exactly what features the application should provide. Interview end users and other company employees as appropriate to determine what electronic or paper systems this application will replace. Ask them questions about the problems with the current systems, so you can better understand what will make your application successful. You should also find out from the end users what features they would like to see included in the application, which features they feel are critical, and which are less so. Also obtain copies of any current documents or screens of current applications or processes that are being used. Reviewing the existing applications that your application will replace is a very helpful strategy.

Interviewing end users is a critical part of developing a software application because if you expect some-one to use your application you have to first find out what he is looking for. If your application does not meet some need he has, he has no incentive to use it. You should also know, however, that end users often ask for many more features than you can or should include in the application. You have to learn how to prioritize the features and implement those that are required or helpful for meeting the needs of most users or that are required in order to comply with management orders.

For purposes of illustrating some concepts in the Systems Development Life Cycle, I use a hypothetical example. Suppose that you have the task of writing a Wrox Auto Sales Application that will be used by sales and other staff at the auto sales company. Applying these requirements-gathering techniques, you have determined that the application should allow the users to search inventory for available and sold cars, to view or edit details about a selected car, and to view or edit customer details. Currently this pro-cess is being implemented solely on paper and needs to be automated in an Access application that will be used by a few end users. You have written down extensive details about what data elements need to be tracked, the features that are desired, and other details that you learned in this process. You are ready to move into the design phase.

Design Phase

During the design phase, you analyze the requirements gathered in the prior phase and determine a sys-tem design. The final output of the design phase should be a written document describing the features your application will provide and, ideally, a prototype of each screen.

You can document your design for the hypothetical Wrox Auto Sales Application and any other applica-tion in various ways, but having some type of documentation on paper before writing the first line of code is very important. You will understand why momentarily.

Start the design phase by organizing the requirements into logical groupings and/or steps. They will help you determine the layout for screens and the code. Using the Wrox Auto Sales example, let's look at some ways you can use modeling to assist you with your design.

Model the Application Design

Modeling is best defined as the process of documenting one or more parts of an application on paper (or with an electronic tool). A variety of modeling techniques can be used to accomplish the end result: mod-eling the flow of activities through the system, modeling the way the code will be structured, and so on.

Regardless of the modeling techniques you decide to use, the objective is to come up with a complete *roadmap* for building the system before you write a single line of code. If you start coding a solution without a roadmap, you will find that it becomes extremely difficult and inefficient to make major adjustments. Think of the roadmap as a blueprint for building a house. You wouldn't want to build a house without a blueprint showing how it is supposed to be structured. Suppose that you have someone build a house for you without a blueprint, and you check up on the progress a few weeks later. When you walk into the house, you notice that it has no basement. The first and second floors have been framed, yet there is no basement (and you wanted one). Think of how much work is involved in having all of the framing for the first and second floors torn down just so the basement can be put in. The rework involved, the cost, and the delays are enormous.

This same concept applies to designing a computer application. If you plan up front how the application needs to look and what it will do, you have a detailed roadmap. You probably won't get deep into the process and discover some major unresolved issue. This is not to say that proper modeling will take away all risk of later problems, because that is impossible. However, you will, at least, get the major framework of the system (such as whether the house needs a basement) defined, and you can worry about finishing the very minor details (like paint colors) later. I hope you now see why documenting the system on paper before writing code is so important. Now you'll take a look at some of the most commonly used diagramming techniques — Use Case Diagrams and Activity Diagrams — and see how they can be used to help design your applications.

Use Case Diagrams

Use Case Diagrams show the services provided by the system to its users. I like to think of it as the actions a user can take in the system. For example, in the case of the Wrox Auto Sales hypothetical application, the auto sales staff will need some type of Search Inventory Screen to allow them to search the inventory of cars. From that screen, they need to be able to run searches, clear the search results, open a selected car detail record, open the car detail screen (empty), or open the customer screen (empty). Suppose that each of these is an action the user can take on the Search Inventory Screen in the system. Thus, each of these actions can map to an action in a Use Case Diagram.

First, let's look at how such a Use Case Diagram would appear on the screen (see Figure 1-1), and then you can study in more detail how it is structured.

Notice how the Use Case Diagram in Figure 1-1 lists the separate actions the Wrox Auto Sales Staff can take on the Search Inventory Screen in the system, as described previously. The stick figure representing a person is called an *Actor*. The actor represents the Wrox Auto Sales Staff member who is using the system. Lines are drawn to each of the actions the actor can perform. No special requirement exists for how you group Use Cases. In other words, whether you group Use Cases together by screens, major functionality, logically related concepts, and so on is up to you. In the preceding example, I have structured the Use Cases by a particular screen. This is the structure that I use most frequently, as it is typically easier to think of activities you can perform in an application from the perspective of the particular screens on which they can be invoked.

Notice how each of the Use Cases is numbered beginning with the Requirement Number followed by the Use Case Number (for example, 1.2 for representing the second Use Case in Requirement One). This is another technique that I myself follow because it makes numbering Use Cases much easier should you later insert or delete one in a particular section. For example, if you add a new action that the user is allowed to perform on the Search Inventory Screen, you don't have to renumber all the Use Cases for the entire system. You just add the next highest Use Case for that particular requirement (for example, the new one would be UC 1.6 for the preceding example).

This is the basic concept of the structure of Use Cases. So now, take a look at the Use Case Diagram for another screen in the system. Figure 1-2 shows the activities the user performs on some type of View/Manage Car Details Screen.

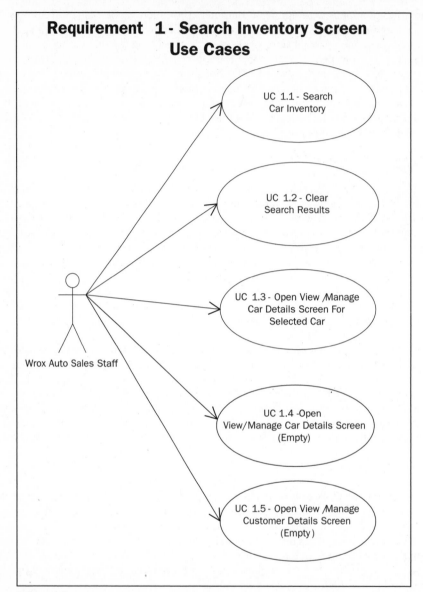

Figure 1-1

These two sample Use Case Diagrams cover several of the actions that our hypothetical Wrox Auto Sales Application will allow a user to take in the system. In Chapter 4, you will learn how the Use Case Diagrams can help create Class Diagrams to represent how source code should be structured into custom objects that you will create. Now, look at creating Activity Diagrams to portray the flow of actions in the system.

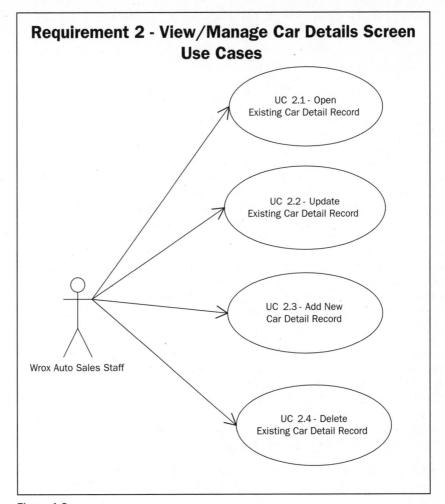

Figure 1-2

Activity Diagrams

Activity Diagrams are diagrams very similar to process Flow Diagrams, showing the flow from activity to activity and action to action. They provide a detailed view of the way a user (an actor) can operate within the system. Here are some basic steps for creating an Activity Diagram:

1. Determine the scope you want your Activity Diagram to portray (that is, a single Use Case, a series of Use Cases, a business process, a screen, and so on).

2. Add the *Starting Point* for the diagram.

3. Add the activities for each step users can take. This includes the initial step (opening the screen, and so on) plus any steps describing what they do next.

4. Add the *Connectors* from each activity to the next.

5.   Label alternative paths appropriately so you can tell that the user can take one or more paths. These are called *Decision Points*.

6.   Add any *Parallel Activities*, or activities that can happen simultaneously and must both finish before another action can be taken.

7.   Add the *Ending Points*, which are the one or more points in the flow that the actions may end.

Activity Diagrams are helpful for many reasons, including aiding in structuring your code for the system and aiding in the test cases for the functionality you must ensure the system provides.

You will now see how we can apply these concepts to creating an Activity Diagram for the Search Inventory Screen of the hypothetical Wrox Auto Sales application. Based on the requirements you have gathered and analyzed so far, you have enough information to describe the actions a user can take on this screen in plain English. First, the Search Inventory Screen opens. Next, the user can open the View/Manage Car Details Screen, open the View/Manage Customer Details Screen, or run a search against inventory. If she opens the View/Manage Car Details Screen, the flow on this Search screen ends. If she opens the View/Manage Customer Details Screen, the flow on this screen also ends. However, the user can also run a search, fill in the search criteria, click the Search button, and view the results. She can then clear the results, run the search again, or open the detail screen for a selected car. After she finishes searching (or if she opens a car detail record), the flow on this screen ends. Figure 1-3 shows how these steps can be depicted in an Activity Diagram.

Notice how the alternative paths the user can take are depicted using *OR*. Further, notice how each activity is connected with an arrow. The starting and ending circles depict the points where the flow starts and the points where the flow can end. That's really all there is to creating an Activity Diagram. You simply model the flow of the actions a user takes in the system electronically or on paper in the order they happen, indicating any alternative or parallel activities. I used Microsoft Visio to create these diagrams, but you can use various other tools or just diagrams written on paper. The tool you use is not important, just as long as you document the design in some fashion. Let's look at an Activity Diagram for another screen in our Wrox Auto Sales application.

Figure 1-4 demonstrates the actions a user can take in order on a View/Manage Car Details Screen. Notice how the user can either open a car detail record or add a new car detail record when the screen first opens. After a record is opened, it can be viewed, modified, or deleted.

Screen Prototypes

After creating Use Case and Activity Diagrams (or other appropriate design diagrams), you should also create screen prototypes that illustrate at a basic level how the user interface will look.

Turning now to the Wrox Auto Sales hypothetical, look at what the Search Inventory and Manage Cars screen prototypes might look like. From the Use Case Diagram for the Search Inventory screen (shown in Figure 1-1), you know there are five requirements:

❏   UC 1.1   Search Car Inventory

❏   UC 1.2   Clear Search Results

❏   UC 1.3   Open View/Manage Car Details for Selected Car

❏   UC 1.4   Open View/Manage Car Details Screen (Empty)

❏   UC 1.5   Open View/Manage Customer Details Screen (Empty)

**Requirement 1 - Search Inventory Screen
Activity Diagram**

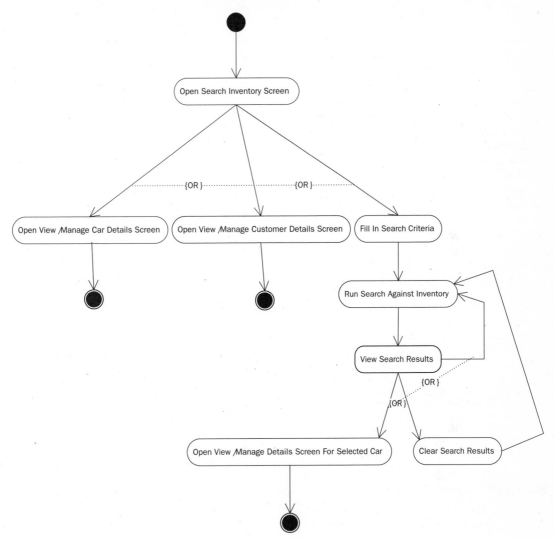

Figure 1-3

Use Cases can translate directly into menu options, buttons, and other controls on corresponding form(s).

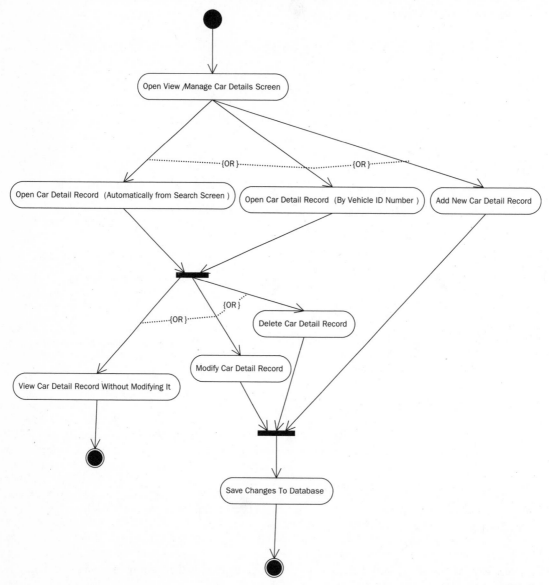

**Requirement 2 - View/Manage Car Details Screen
Activity Diagram**

Figure 1-4

Figure 1-5 shows an example of how these Use Cases were mapped to user interface elements for the Search Inventory Screen. Notice how the Use Cases are satisfied: Search button (UC 1.1), Clear button (UC 1.2), Manage Cars Screen option in View menu (UC 1.3 and UC 1.4), and Manage Customers Screen option in View menu (UC 1.5). Depending on whether a particular car is selected in the search results list, the Manage Cars Screen will open empty or containing data for the selected car. The other controls you see in Figure 1-5 are the data elements that the user can specify to run a search. These data elements include Vehicle ID Number, Year, Make, Color, Model, and Status. These data elements were originally determined in the requirements-gathering phase.

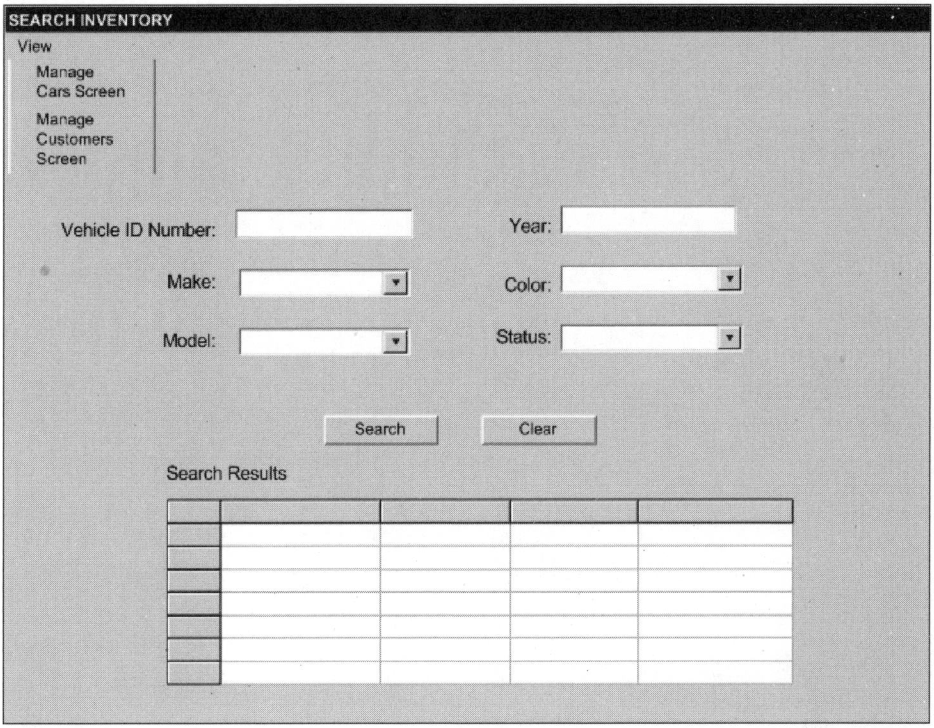

Figure 1-5

The same concepts apply to creating the View/Manage Car Details screen prototype for the hypothetical Wrox Auto Sales application. Recall that the Use Case Diagram in Figure 1-2 listed four requirements: UC 2.1 — Open Existing Car Detail Record, UC 2.2 — Updated Existing Car Detail Record, UC 2.3 — Add New Car Detail Record, and UC 2.4 — Delete Existing Car Detail Record. Figure 1-6 shows how these requirements can map to control buttons and other options on a screen. Notice how these Use Cases are satisfied in Figure 1-6: the Lookup button (UC 2.1), the Save button (UC 2.2), the Add New button (UC 2.3), and the Delete button (UC 2.4). Again, the data elements are also listed, such as Vehicle ID Number, Make, Model, and Year — all determined during the requirements-gathering phase.

Determine Application Architecture

During the design phase, you should have determined the architecture of your application. Let's now take a brief look at what application architecture actually is. *Application architecture* refers to the way you split up an application into smaller pieces. Just about all applications, including Access 2007 VBA applications, have the following elements:

❏ **User Interface** – The screens the user sees and interacts with

❏ **Business Rules** – The processing that takes place in response to the user's action, such as calculating some result, looking up information, and so on

❏ **Database** – A physical data store for certain information used by the application

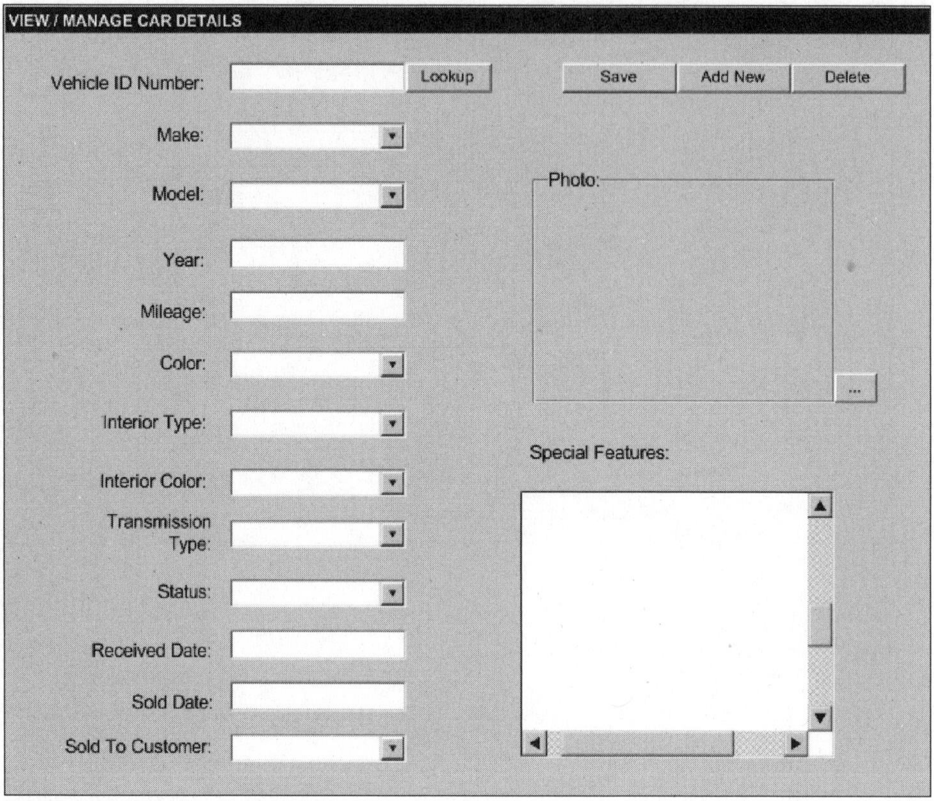

Figure 1-6

The architecture is the manner in which you put all the pieces together to form an application. Often, the architecture of an application is referred to by the number of *tiers* it contains. In this context, *tiers* refers to the number of machines that an application actually runs on. If any part of an application runs on a particular machine, that machine is counted in the tiers. This concept will be described in much more detail as you look at the different types of architecture: single-tier, two-tier, and three/n-tier.

> *Most of the examples in this book will be based on a single-tier standalone architecture for the sake of simplicity, although some two-tier client-server examples will also be covered.*

Single-Tier (Standalone)

Single-tier applications became common at the beginning of the PC era, but they have actually been around longer than that. A single-tier application is one where the entire application is contained and runs on a single computer. This is also referred to as a *standalone application*. An example of a standalone application is, of course, a Microsoft Access application that has the user interface, business logic, and data all within the same file on one computer.

An application need not be completely contained in a single file to be considered standalone. Take, for instance, a loan amortization program installed on your computer that has an .exe file that runs and reads information from one or more files on your hard drive. The entire application runs on a single computer even though more than one file is involved. This application is also a standalone application. Figure 1-7 illustrates a diagram of a typical standalone application.

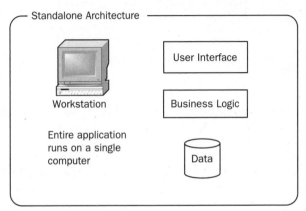

Figure 1-7

With a standalone application, everything is nicely self-contained. If you are the only person who will use the application and data, a standalone architecture is fine. In the case of Access applications, you may also put the single Access file containing both the user interface and the database on the network to allow multiple people to access the application. This works fine in many situations and also qualifies as a standalone architecture. As the number of users for a standalone Access application grows, the standalone architecture can become problematic because each user is accessing the same file on the network for the user interface and database. Many of the Access 2007 VBA examples covered in this book are based on a standalone architecture.

As applications grew and had to be shared more often, a client-server architecture was introduced to facilitate sharing. You will see how the client-server architecture can help address some of the limitations of the standalone architecture.

Two-Tier (Client-Server)

Client-server applications (applications that span *two-tiers*: a client machine and a server machine) solved the problem introduced by standalone applications and allowed multiple people to share the same data more easily. Client-server applications require a central server to hold the data store in a central location. The database server then processes requests for data from each of the client machines. Client-server applications first appeared in the early 1990s on the PC platform. A diagram of this architecture is depicted in Figure 1-8.

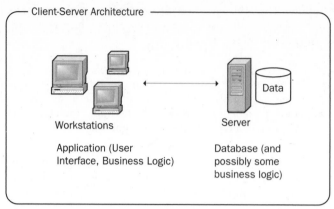

Figure 1-8

In this architecture, the data store is abstracted from the client. The client machine makes a request from the server to add, insert, update, or view data, and the server processes the request and returns the results to the client. A typical database server in such a scenario might be an Access, SQL Server, or Oracle database. In the case of an Access client-server application, the user interface may reside in one Access file, and the database may reside in a separate file or database application on a server, such as an Access or SQL Server database. Creating client-server applications using Access or SQL Server databases will be discussed in Chapters 7, 10, and 4.

In a client-server application, the main application is loaded on each client computer. The application includes the user interface and probably most or all of the business logic elements. In other words, the application contains code to create the user interface, process the user actions, perform any validations or calculations, and look up or modify data in the database. It is possible, however, to have some of the business logic on the database server, such as in stored procedures that are described in Chapters 10 and 14. For example, if you require a zip code to be five characters in length, you could put that logic in the insert or update stored procedure to raise an error instead of the code on the client. The bottom line with business logic in client-server applications is that it can be entirely on the client, entirely on the server, or you can use a combination of the two.

The advantages of client-server applications are that you can share data across multiple computers more easily than before and also separate the user interface from the database. Each client always updates the central repository.

At some point, however, the central database server is limited in terms of how many users it can handle. This might mean that a database server must *scale up* to a bigger server or beef up the resources of the existing server. To address some of these problems with growth and maintenance, the three-tier/n-tier architecture was introduced.

Three-Tier/N-Tier

The *three-tiered architecture* addresses the limitations imposed by the client-server architecture and allows you to architect solutions that can grow easily as your needs grow. The three-tiered architecture is sometimes called *n-tier* because it can have more than three tiers in certain situations. With three-tier and n-tier applications, you can simply add additional servers to handle the processing. Microsoft Access is not typically used to create three-tier applications, although with some complex coding it can be used as part of a three-tier application design. Access should not be used for three-tier applications because for such a large-scale application, Access is not the best user interface or database to use. It contains serious limitations.

Even though you will not use Access to develop three-tier applications, it is still worthwhile to understand what a three-tier application includes. I discuss this because, at some point, you may need to migrate your client-server Access application to a three-tier architecture.

So, how does a three-tier architecture create incredible growth potential? The idea is that application elements are physically compiled as separate elements, and they run on different computers. For example, the user interface elements are separate from the middle-layer business logic, which is separate from the database layer. In this case, the application is running on three different computers: the client, the middle-tier server, and the database server (hence the name three-tier). Figure 1-9 diagrams this.

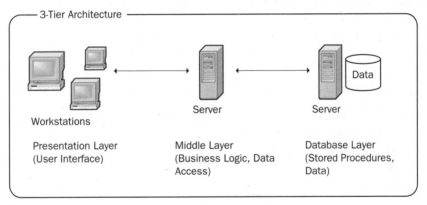

Figure 1-9

The three-tier/n-tier architecture takes client-server to the next level by abstracting all the various layers of processing from both the client and the server. It takes some practice to do this correctly. In plain English, what does this mean to you as a programmer? It means that you break the application into isolated pieces that call each other as appropriate. You no longer write a single program with intermixed code that creates the user interface, checks the business rules, performs calculations, and updates the database.

When these actions get split into separate functionalities, they can be thought of as separate source code projects. You create the part of the program that deals specifically with showing the graphical user interface in its own project (such as an .exe created using Visual Basic or Visual Basic .NET). You then create the business logic in its own project that will be compiled into a business logic component (such as a DLL created using Visual Basic or Visual Basic .NET). The business logic component will then be called by the client project to perform any calculations, business rules checks, and so on. The brief summary below states this idea another way.

The *presentation layer* is responsible for:

❑   Displaying the user interface

❑   Processing user requests

❑   Sending user requests to the middle (business) layer for processing

❑   Receiving results of the user requests from the middle (business) layer

❑   Presenting the results of the requests to the user

The presentation layer can be a Web browser interface (thin client) or a traditional non-Web-based (rich client) user interface. *Thin client* refers to the fact that very little, if any, compiled code is installed on the client for rendering the user interface. *Rich client* refers to the fact that a fair amount of compiled code is installed on the machine to make the interface richer to the user. Either way, thin or rich client, the user interface elements are still separated from the other layers.

The *middle (business) layer* is responsible for:

❑   Receiving requests from the presentation layer

❑   Performing any business logic checks or calculations

❑   Interacting with the data (database) layer

❑   Returning the processed results to the presentation layer

The *data (database) layer* is responsible for:

❑   Storing the data

❑   Returning data upon request to the middle layer

❑   Modifying data upon request from the middle layer

This three-tier/n-tier architecture allows each processing layer to be built as a set of components (sometimes called objects) that can be called very efficiently from a large number of clients.

In addition to isolating the business logic from the presentation and database layers, it is also very common to further separate any call to the database into its own layer, as shown in the diagram in Figure 1-10.

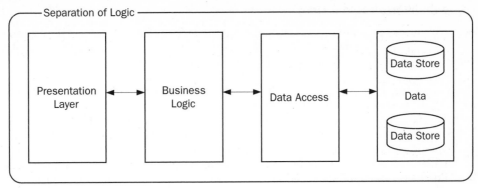

Figure 1-10

Using this approach, the summary of the actions performed by each layer is modified as follows:

The *presentation layer* is responsible for:

❑　Displaying the user interface

❑　Processing user requests

❑　Sending user inputs to the Business Logic Layer for processing

❑　Receiving results of the user requests from the Business Logic Layer

❑　Presenting the results of the requests to the user

The *business logic layer* is responsible for:

❑　Receiving requests from the presentation layer

❑　Performing any business logic checks or calculations

❑　Returning the processed results to the presentation layer

The *data access layer* is responsible for:

❑　Receiving requests from the business logic layer

❑　Interacting with the data (database) layer

❑　Returning the processed results to the business logic layer

The *data (database) layer* is responsible for:

❑　Storing the data

❑　Returning data upon request to the data access layer

❑　Modifying data upon request from the data access layer

Separating Code into Logical Tiers

Although the idea of separating your code into different tiers was just described in the context of design-ing three-tier enterprise applications, be aware that you can write your Access 2007 VBA applications in multiple logical tiers to make future migrations easier. I will show you why.

For example, if you isolate all code that will touch the database for an add, update, delete, or retrieval of data into its own separate component or module (totally separate from the business logic), it is much easier to change from one database platform to another. Suppose that you decide to switch from Access to SQL Server as the database. With the database access code isolated in a single module, you only have to modify the data access components and the database itself. You do not have to touch any of the pre-sentation (user interface) code or the business logic code. Imagine how much easier this is than weeding through dozens of procedures unrelated to database access to find what must be modified for the new database platform.

Although you organize the application into separate modules or components, you may not actually run them on separate servers. For example, you may have written a module (such as a VBA module) for all of the business logic and a separate module (such as a VBA module) for handling all data access calls to the database. Although those modules are in separate *logical tiers*, they may run on the same server (*the physical tier*). The beauty is that by structuring your Access code properly now, you prepare for future growth if later you decide to migrate to different servers or implementations. Various chapters through-out this book will illustrate these preferred design techniques in detail to make your future modifica-tions and migrations easier.

Now that I have covered how to document your application into a written specification and to deter-mine the appropriate architecture, let's move on to the next phase of the SDLC.

Development Phase

After you have completed the design phase and have a written specification for how your application should function and look, you enter the *development phase*. Here you begin using Access 2007 and Access 2007 VBA to create your application according to the design specifications you just created. As you are probably already aware, you use Forms in Access to create the user interface. You should use VBA to cre-ate the code for the business logic and data access logic. You should use a database such as Access or SQL Server to store the database tables and records.

Because this is a book about VBA, I show you how to write VBA code for the business logic and database access logic using the Visual Basic Editor. Let's take a look at some simple examples in the Visual Basic Editor.

The Visual Basic Editor

As previously mentioned, VBA code is written in Access using the *Visual Basic Editor*. You can get to the Visual Basic Editor in various ways. One way is to select the Database Tools ribbon, and then select the Visual Basic icon in the Macro group, as shown in Figure 1-11.

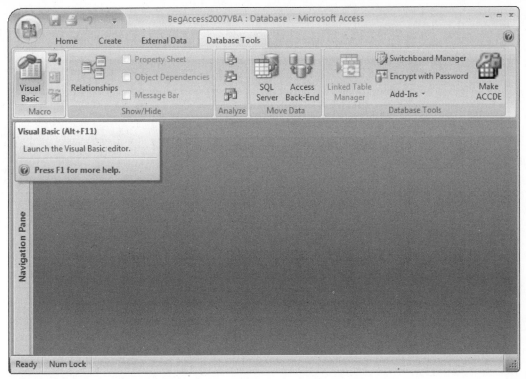

Figure 1-11

You can also select Alt+F11 to open the Visual Basic Editor. Yet another way to get to the Visual Basic Editor in Access is to select the Create ribbon, select the drop-down list for Macro, and then select Module from the list. This is shown in Figure 1-12.

Figure 1-13 shows an example of what the Visual Basic Editor looks like.

Notice that the Visual Basic Editor in Figure 1-13 contains a Code window on the right side, a Project window on the upper-left side, and a Properties module on the bottom-left side. The way these windows are arranged can be customized to suit your preferences. Additional windows can also be displayed by using the View menu.

What you see in the Visual Basic Editor depends on how you got there and what objects are part of the Access database already. The concept of Access objects will be described in detail in Chapter 3. For now, just think of forms, controls, modules, and examples of potential objects that may have VBA code associated with them. In the Project window of Figure 1-13, a new module called Module1 was just inserted. The cursor is flashing in the code window that is associated with Module1. When other objects are present in the Project window, you can navigate through the hierarchy and use the Code window to add or modify code that corresponds to the selected objects.

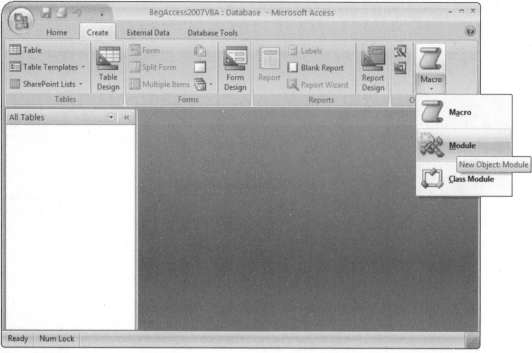

Figure 1-12

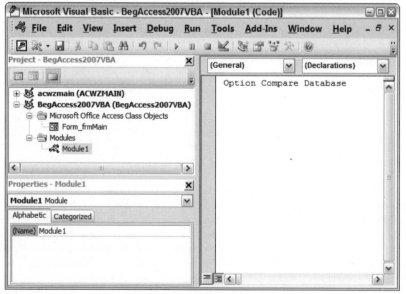

Figure 1-13

For example, suppose that you have a form in your Access database called `frmMain`. You have added a command button called `cmdText` to your `frmMain`. You can get to the Visual Basic Editor from within `frmMain` by first selecting the `cmdText` control and then selecting an event, such as `On_Click`, as shown in Figure 1-14.

Next, click the button with the ellipses (...) to open the screen shown in Figure 1-15.

On the Choose Builder screen shown in Figure 1-15, select the Code Builder option and then click OK. The Visual Basic Editor is then opened with a new empty procedure for the `cmdTest_click` event in the Code window, as shown in Figure 1-16.

Notice how you now see the `frmMain` Form in the Project window in the upper-left side of the screen as well. Let's look at a few examples of how you can add code to the Code window using the `cmdTest_click` event as an example. If you begin typing a command in the code window, such as the `msgbox` command, a tooltip appears (where available and appropriate) to provide you with details on the syntax required for that command. An example of this is displayed in Figure 1-17.

Another helpful feature of the Visual Basic Editor helps you complete a particular command by displaying a list of available options. An example of this feature is shown in Figure 1-18.

Notice in Figure 1-18 how the `docmd` command has been entered followed by a period. The moment you type the period, the available options for `docmd` are displayed. You can then select one of the available options from the list. In the development phase, you use the Visual Basic Editor to write the code to implement the business logic and database logic for your forms.

After you have developed all or part of your code, you enter the testing phase.

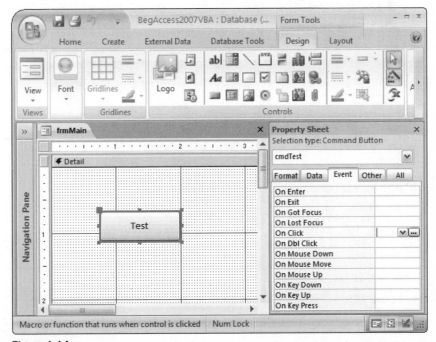

Figure 1-14

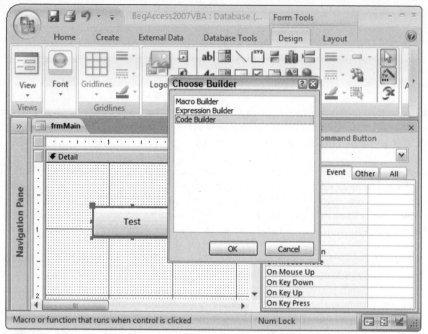

Figure 1-15

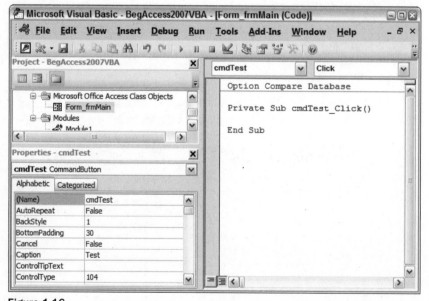

Figure 1-16

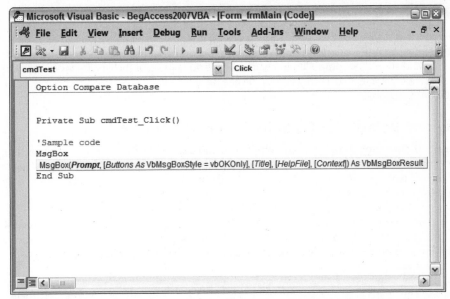

Figure 1-17

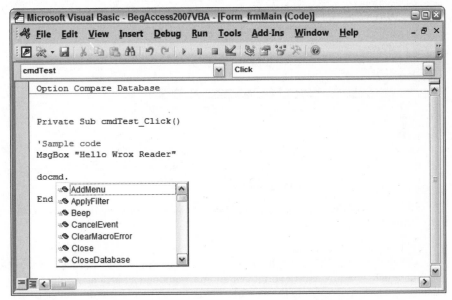

Figure 1-18

Testing Phase

In the *testing phase*, you test the application to ensure it works. Testing is an iterative process. For example, unit testing should be performed as different parts of the application are completed. Also, system tests at the end should be completed to ensure that various parts of the system work correctly together. To test the code you create using the Visual Basic Editor, you can use various techniques, as I describe in the following sections.

Running and Debugging Code in the Visual Basic Editor

The Visual Basic Editor allows you to compile, run and debug your VBA code. The steps involved in running and debugging your application are illustrated in detail in Chapter 2 in the Debugging section. However, to give you just a few examples of how the testing phase works, look at some of the types of techniques you can use to test your code.

As shown in Figure 1-19, breakpoints can be added to particular lines of code so that execution stops when that line is reached. Breakpoints can be set at various places in your code so that you can stop on selected lines of code to analyze various aspects of the application at that particular time.

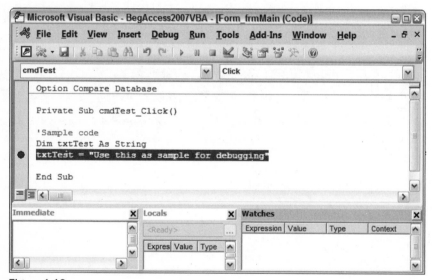

Figure 1-19

Notice how in Figure 1-19 and Figure 1-20, the screen includes Immediate, Locals, and Watches windows. The Immediate window allows you to obtain information at a particular point in time, such as when a breakpoint is encountered. In the example in Figure 1-20, the current value of the txtTest variable was retrieved using the Immediate window by typing ? txtTest in the window just after running the line of code that set the value of the variable. In the Locals window, you can see that all variables of the current procedure are displayed, which in this example is the txtTest variable. The Watches window is currently empty but allows you to establish rules for watching certain activities as they occur.

As mentioned previously, these testing techniques and several others will be covered in the debugging section of Chapter 2. For now, just be aware that you write your VBA code in the Visual Basic Editor according to your design specifications. The Editor has various features that allow you to run, test, and fix your VBA code for the application. You will be using the Visual Basic Editor throughout the entire book, so you will become very familiar with how it works.

Implementation Phase

After you complete the testing phase and have corrected your application, you enter the *implementation phase*. In this phase, you distribute the application to the end users. In Access, there are various ways to distribute your application, as I discuss in detail in Chapter 10.

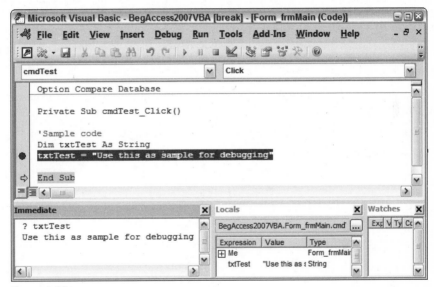

Figure 1-20

After you implement the application, some or all of the phases discussed herein can be repeated as necessary, for example when the existing features are being maintained or new features are being added.

Summary

Access 2007 VBA is an example of a programming language that can be used to extend your Access applications. As part of developing Access and other applications, you should follow a development methodology such as the Systems Development Life Cycle to facilitate the development process and reduce the amount of rework needed later.

The SDLC includes various phases, including the requirements gathering, design, development, testing, and implementation phases. In the requirements gathering phase, you determine the list of features that the application must include. In the design phase, you document the application on paper so that you know how to code it. Some examples of how you can document your design include using Use Cases, Activity Diagrams, and screen prototypes. As part of the design phase, you determine whether to use the standalone or client-server application architecture. In the development phase, you use Access to create your forms, and VBA from the Visual Basic Editor to create the business logic and data access code for your application. In the testing phase, you use the Visual Basic Editor to test and fix your application. In the implementation phase, you prepare and distribute your application to end users.

With this chapter under your belt, you now move on to Chapter 2, where you learn the basics of writing and testing VBA code using the Visual Basic Editor. Before you move on to Chapter 2, you may want to try out the exercises below to check your understanding of the concepts in this chapter. All answers to exercise questions can be found in Appendix A.

Exercises

1. What are the phases of the Systems Development Life Cycle (SDLC) and the purposes of each phase?

2. What are some examples of the ways you can document your design in the design phase of the SDLC?

3. What is the difference between a standalone application and a client-server application?

4. What are the advantages of separating your code into logical tiers in your Access applications?

The Basics of Writing and Testing VBA Code

Chapter 1 introduced the Access VBA programming environment and some general software development concepts. At this point, you are ready to learn the basics of writing and testing code using VBA. This chapter will cover:

❑   Creating code modules

❑   Creating and calling procedures

❑   Using variables to store values

❑   Controlling the flow of programs

❑   Debugging and handling errors

This chapter will serve as a building block for the more advanced VBA concepts covered in later chapters. The techniques covered in this chapter and in most of the remaining chapters are used during the development and testing phases of the Systems Development Life Cycle, as defined in Chapter 1.

Creating Modules

Modules are best described as containers for holding VBA code. Modules can contain declarations and procedures. VBA code that is placed in one or more modules can be called from an Access application to perform a specified task. I discuss this in greater detail throughout.

Figure 2-1 shows a sample module displayed in the Visual Basic Editor.

Note that the previous figure has four areas labeled. Each one will now be mentioned briefly.

1.   **Object navigation box** – Use to select the object to work with

2.   **Declarations/Procedure navigation box** – Use to navigate to the general declarations section or to a particular procedure

3. **Declarations** – Contains the declarations for the module

4. **Procedures** – Contains the sub procedures and functions for the module

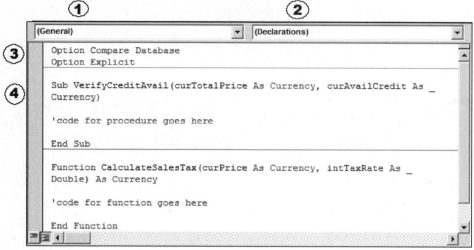

Figure 2-1

When you select the Declarations/Procedure navigation box, a list appears that displays the existing procedures of the module, as shown in Figure 2-2.

Now that you have a basic idea of what a module is (container for code), let's turn to the different types of modules.

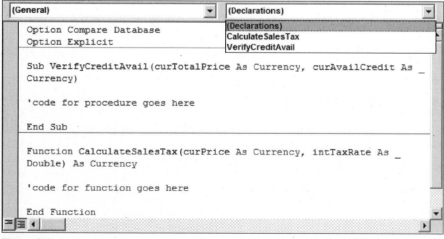

Figure 2-2

Standard Modules versus Class Modules

There are two types of modules: standard modules and class modules. *Standard modules* are modules that contain procedures that are not associated with any particular object. *Class modules* are modules that are associated with a particular object. Class modules can be used either for form or report modules or for custom objects accessible throughout your VBA application. For example, form and report modules can contain code that corresponds to a particular form or report. An example of a form module is an event procedure, such as the click event for a control on a form. Since Access 97, class modules can also be created independently of a form or report to create a definition for a custom object. The current chapter will focus on standard modules and class modules that are associated with a form or report. Custom objects are discussed in detail in Chapter 4.

> In general, it is a good programming practice to write most or all of your business logic and data access for the application in procedures that are contained in standard modules and keep the presentation logic in class modules associated with the form or report. This separation of code concept was briefly introduced in Chapter 1 in the architecture section.

One way to create a module is to select the Modules tab in the database window and click the New button. Another way to create a module is to select Insert ⇨ Module. Let's now create a sample database with a form and a module that can be used for the examples throughout this chapter. This will also illustrate how to create a new module. I will continue with the discussion on modules and procedures after the database has been created.

Try it Out   Create a Database to Use with Examples in the Chapter

Let's jump right in by creating the database that can be used with the examples in this chapter.

1.   Create a new database. To do so, the Office Button (where the File menu used to be) ⇨ New ⇨ Blank Database. Next, navigate to the path where you want to save the database and specify Ch2CodeExamples.accdb as the File Name field. Click the Create button and the new database will be created. An empty table is displayed on the screen. You can simply close the table view by selecting the X in the right corner, since a new table is not used in this example.

Note that the default format for databases in Access is 2007 (ACCDB file format), but if you need the compatibility with Access 2002 or 2003 (MDB file format), you should change it to 2002–2003 format. You can change this option by selecting the Office Button ⇨ Access Options, and on the Personalize Tab changing the Default File Format option from Access 2007 to Access 2002–2003.

2.   Add a new form to your database. To do so, select the Create ribbon and then select the Blank Form option.

3.   The form opens in Layout View. To switch to Design View, select a blank area of the form, right click, and choose Design View from the pop-up menu that appears. Alternatively, you can change the view by selecting View ⇨ Design View from the toolbar.

4.   Use the controls shown in the toolbar to select and draw two text boxes and one command button onto the form, as shown in Figure 2-3. You can select Cancel to exit the Button Wizard that appears after you draw the button on the form.

5. Select the Design ribbon, and then Property Sheet in the Tools area of the toolbar to display the Properties dialog box for the form. Alternatively, you can press Alt+ Enter to open the Properties dialog box. Change the Name properties of the first text box, second text box, and command button to `txtValue1`, `txtValue2`, and `cmdRun`, respectively. If you select a particular control, such as the first text box, you can set its properties in the Properties dialog box. Figure 2-4 provides an example of how to change the Name property of the selected control, which in this example is `txtValue1`.

6. Change the Name property of the first text box label to `lblValue1` and its Caption property to `Value 1`. Change the Name property of second text box label to `lblValue2` and the Caption property to `Value 2`. Change the cmdRun Caption property to `Run`. After these changes have been made, the finished form should look like that shown in Figure 2-5.

7. Save the form. Select Office Button ➪ Save, or click the Save icon on the top right, or click X in the upper-right corner of the form itself. When prompted, specify the name for the form as `frmTest`. Close the form by clicking the X in the upper-right corner of the form itself, if you have not already done so.

After `frmTest` is saved, it appears in the left navigation pane as an "Unrelated Object."

8. Create a new module. Select the Create ribbon from the toolbar, and then select Macro in the area of the toolbar labeled Other, as shown in Figure 2-6. The drop-down with the Create Module option displays Macro, Module, and Class Module as the options in the list.

9. The Visual Basic Editor window appears. Use the Properties window of the Visual Basic Editor to rename the module to `modBusinessLogic`, as shown in Figure 2-7. If the Properties Window is not already displayed, you can select View ➪ Properties Window to display it.

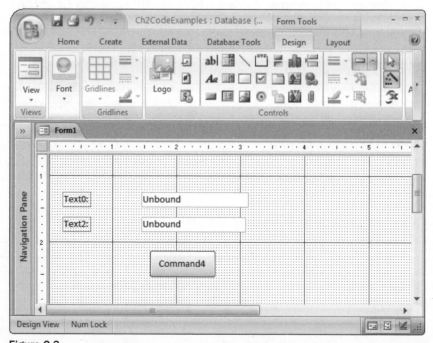

Figure 2-3

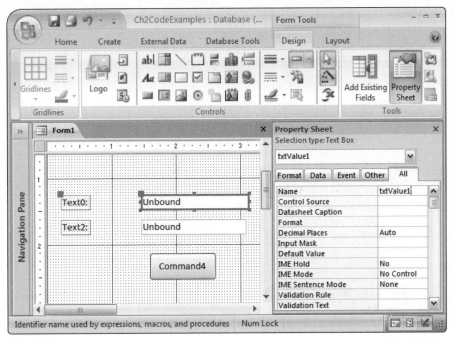

Figure 2-4

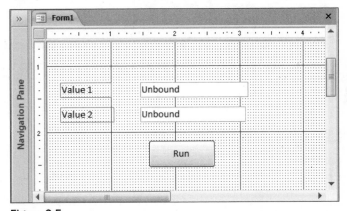

Figure 2-5

Figure 2-7 contains an Option Explicit *statement in the declarations section of the module. If the module you just created does not have the* Option Explicit *statement, you should select Tools ⇨ Options and select the Require Variable Declaration option in the Code Settings area of the Editor tab and then reinsert the module. The* Option Explicit *statement then appears. If it still doesn't appear, type "Option Explicit" after the line "Option Compare Database." This Option Explicit option requires variables to be defined before they can be used and promotes better coding habits.*

How It Works

You just created a new Access 2007 database, added a new form with three controls, and added a new module. No real code is written yet, so the database will not really do anything at this point. But you will be writing code in the new database throughout the rest of this chapter to illustrate various coding concepts.

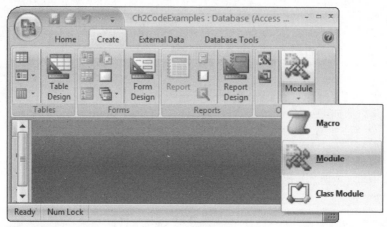

Figure 2-6

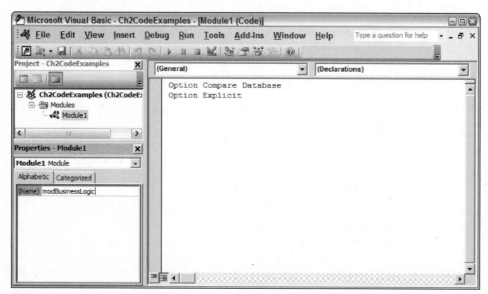

Figure 2-7

Creating and Calling Procedures

Now that you have a sample database, I return to a discussion of modules and procedures. You already saw a procedure inside the sample module illustrations provided previously, but let's now analyze what the procedures are and how they can be used.

Procedures are the building blocks of modules. Each module contains one or more sub procedures or functions, and each sub procedure or function contains one or more VBA code statements.

Sub versus Function Procedure

Procedures can either be sub procedures or function procedures. A *sub procedure* performs an action but does not return a particular result. A *function* performs an action and returns a particular result. I will provide various examples to illustrate these differences. Sub procedures and functions can be called both from within other procedures and functions and when an event associated with an object is triggered (for example, `button_click`), as I describe in more detail in Chapter 3.

Create and Call a New Sub Procedure

The syntax for declaring a new sub procedure without parameters is:

```
Sub ProcedureName
'code for the procedure
End Sub
```

The syntax for a new sub procedure that contains variables as parameters is:

```
Sub ProcedureName(Variables)
'code for the procedure
End Sub
```

Variables are containers for storing data. If a procedure must use the value stored in a particular variable, that variable can be passed as a parameter to the procedure. Let's create a new procedure to see how this works.

Try It Out   **Creating the VerifyCreditAvail Procedure**

Next, you will create a `VerifyCreditAvail` procedure that will compare two numbers to see if enough credit is available for the purchase.

1.   Insert the following code in the `modBusinessLogic` module underneath the declarations section (underneath `Option Explicit` statement). See Figure 2-2 for an example if you are unsure where to put the code.

```
Sub VerifyCreditAvail(curTotalPrice As Currency, curAvailCredit As Currency)

'inform user if not enough credit for purchase

If curTotalPrice > curAvailCredit Then
    MsgBox "You do not have enough credit available for this purchase."
End If
End Sub
```

2. Run the procedure from the Immediate Window. If the Immediate Window is not already open, select View ⇨ Immediate Window. Type the command (shown in Figure 2-8) in the Immediate Window and then click Enter.

   If you receive an error message that says "the Macros in this project are disabled," then you need to take a few steps to authorize the modules you just created to run. To do so, close the VBA Editor window you are in and return to Access. Locate the area underneath the ribbon toolbar that says "Security Warning – certain content in the database has been disabled." Click the Options button to the right of this warning. Select the "Enable this Content" option from the pop-up that appears, and click OK. Return to the VBA Editor and repeat step 2 above to run the procedure. It should run this time.

3. You should see a message box like the one shown in Figure 2-9.

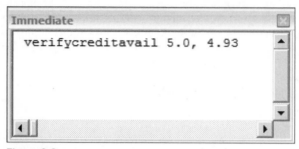

Figure 2-8

Figure 2-9

How It Works

The `VerifyCreditAvail` sub procedure accepts two variables as parameters, `curTotalPrice` and `curAvailCredit`:

```
Sub VerifyCreditAvail(curTotalPrice As Currency, curAvailCredit As Currency)
```

The procedure contains an `If` statement that compares the value of `curTotalPrice` to `curAvailCredit` to see if `curTotalPrice` is larger:

```
'inform user if not enough credit for purchase
If curTotalPrice > curAvailCredit Then
    MsgBox "You do not have enough credit available for this purchase."
End If
```

From the Immediate Window, you call the `VerifyCreditAvail` sub procedure and pass it the values `5.0` and `4.93`. The value `5.0` represents `curTotalPrice` and the value `4.93` represents `curAvailCredit`. When the preceding `If` statement was evaluated, Access determined that 5.0 was greater than 4.93, and thus the message box indicating insufficient available credit was displayed.

Call a Sub Procedure from Another Procedure

After a procedure has been created, it can be called from within another procedure if desired. Here's a simple example to illustrate the syntax:

```
Sub FirstProcedure
    'This code calls a procedure called SecondProcedure    SecondProcedure
End Sub
```

Now that you know the syntax for calling a procedure from within another procedure, you can write code to call the `VerifyCreditAvail` procedure you created previously from another procedure.

Try It Out   Calling VerifyCreditAvail from Another Procedure

You can now create a new procedure, called `FinalizeOrder`, that will call the `VerifyCreditAvail` procedure.

1. Add the following procedure, called `FinalizeOrder`, to the `modBusinessLogic` module underneath `VerifyCreditAvail`:

```
Sub FinalizeOrder()

'declare variables for storing Price and Credit Avail
Dim curPrice As Currency
Dim curCreditAvail As Currency

'give variables values here for illustration purposes
curPrice = 4.5
curCreditAvail = 3.75

'call VerifyCreditAvail procedure
VerifyCreditAvail curPrice, curCreditAvail

End Sub
```

2. Run the `FinalizeOrder` procedure from the Immediate Window as shown in Figure 2-10.

3. The same message box you received earlier is again displayed to indicate that available credit is not sufficient.

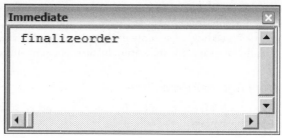

Figure 2-10

How It Works

The FinalizeOrder procedure uses two local variables: curPrice and curCreditAvail.

```
Sub FinalizeOrder()

'declare variables for storing Price and Credit Avail
Dim curPrice As Currency
Dim curCreditAvail As Currency
```

The variables are then assigned values for illustration purposes.

```
'give variables values here for illustration purposes
curPrice = 4.5
curCreditAvail = 3.75
```

Note that, in most cases, you would not hard-code the values in the procedure, but instead you would retrieve them from a database, another variable, or another source. After the variables were assigned values, you call the VerifyCreditAvail procedure, with those variables passed as parameters:

```
'call VerifyCreditAvail procedure
VerifyCreditAvail curPrice, curCreditAvail
```

You then run the FinalizeOrder procedure from the Immediate Window to test it. The FinalizeOrder procedure executes the code to declare the variables, assign the variable values, and call the VerifyCreditAvail procedure. Because the value of 4.5 specified for curPrice was greater than the value specified for curCreditAvail, the VerifyCreditAvail procedure caused a message box to be displayed, as in the prior example.

Call a Sub Procedure from an Event

In addition to being called from another procedure, sub procedures can also be called from an event. As discussed in detail in Chapter 4, events occur in response to an action taken by the user or the system. Recall that earlier I discussed the two types of modules: standard modules and class modules. The code examples you have written so far were written in the standard module called modBusinessLogic. You will now write code in a class module associated with a particular form.

Creating a Procedure for an Object Using the Code Builder

The first time you write code for a class module of a particular form or report, you must generate the empty procedure using the Code Builder. You may recall that in Chapter 1 there was an example of creating a new event procedure for cmdTest_Click using the Code Builder. We'll now revisit the Code Builder idea to further investigate how it works and to let you try it out for yourself. The concept of events and their associated objects is described in greater detail in Chapter 3.

Try It Out   Create New Procedure for frmTest Using Code Builder

Let's now create a new procedure for frmTest using the Code Builder.

1. Return to the database window and open frmTest in design view. To do so, select Object Type ⇨ Forms from the Objects list, select frmTest, right-click, and then click the Design View option. Alternatively, select the Home ribbon on the toolbar, and then select View ⇨ Design View from the drop-down menu.

2. Select the cmdRun button on the form. You should see the Properties window. If the Properties window is not visible, select the Design ribbon, and then Property Sheet in the Tools area of the toolbar and select the cmdRun button again.

3. Select the Event tab from the cmdRun Properties window. Click the On Click event from the list, as shown in Figure 2-11.

4. Click the ellipsis (...) button in the Event tab, and the screen in Figure 2-12 will appear.

5. Select the Code Builder option from the list, as shown in the previous figure, and click the OK button.

6. The Visual Basic Editor will now be displayed with the cursor flashing in a newly created empty procedure called cmdRun_Click (see Figure 2-13).

7. Add the following code to the newly created procedure:

```
Private Sub cmdRun_Click()

'declare variables to store price and avail credit
Dim curPrice As Currency
Dim curCreditAvail As Currency

'assign variables from current values in text boxes on Form
curPrice = txtValue1
curCreditAvail = txtValue2

'call VerifyCreditAvail procedure
VerifyCreditAvail curPrice, curCreditAvail

End Sub
```

8. After adding the preceding code to the cmdRun_Click procedure, click the Save button in the Visual Basic Editor to make sure all code so far has been saved. It is a good idea to select the Save option periodically to ensure you do not lose any of your work.

9. Return to the `frmTest` form and open it in View mode to run it. To do so, select the Home ribbon on the toolbar, and then click View ⇨ Form View from the toolbar menu with the form open. Input a value of 2000 for Value 1 and 1500 for Value 2, as shown in Figure 2-14.

10. You should see the same message box that appeared before, indicating that not enough credit is available (see Figure 2-15).

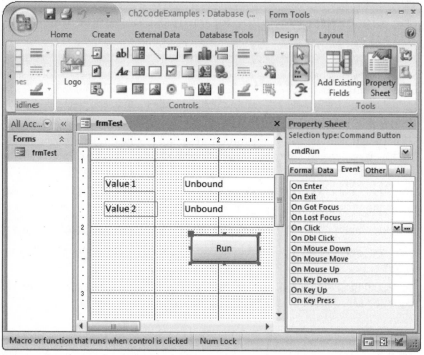

Figure 2-11

Figure 2-12

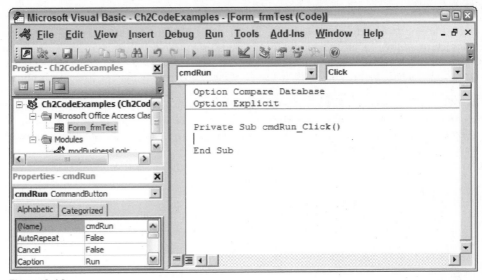

Figure 2-13

Figure 2-14

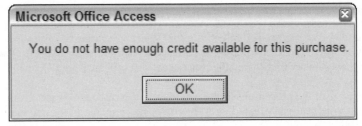

Figure 2-15

How It Works

To create the empty procedure, you used the Code Builder from the frmTest form. Because you selected the click Event on the Properties window for the cmdRun button and then chose the Code Builder option, Access automatically generated an empty event procedure called cmdRun_Click. This event procedure will be called anytime the cmdRun button is clicked when the frmTest form is running.

When the code in cmdRun_Click runs, it first declares some local variables and assigns values to the local variables that the user specified in the text boxes. For example, the value of 2000 specified for the first text box is assigned to the curPrice variable. The value of 1500 for the second text box is assigned to the curCreditAvail variable.

```
'declare variables to store price and avail credit
Dim curPrice As Currency
Dim curCreditAvail As Currency

'assign variables to current values in text boxes on Form
curPrice = txtValue1
curCreditAvail = txtValue2
```

The VerifyCreditAvail procedure is then called using the local variables as parameters.

```
'call VerifyCreditAvail procedure
VerifyCreditAvail curPrice, curCreditAvail
```

When the VerifyCreditAvail procedure executed, it evaluated the available credit and displayed the same error message you saw earlier because the value you input for curPrice was greater than the value for curCreditAvail.

Creating Additional Procedures for an Object Using the Code Window

After the first event procedure is created for a form or report, an associated form or report module is automatically created. You can then create additional procedures for that particular form easily from within the code window itself. For example, after you added the cmdRun_Click event, the Form_frmTest object appears in the Project window below. When you select Form_frmTest in the Project window and then the Object navigation drop-down list, all the objects associated with frmTest are displayed (see Figure 2-16).

In the preceding example, txtValue1 is selected. This is the name of the first text box on the frmTest form. After you select the txtValue1 value from the Object navigation list, the values in the declarations/procedures navigation list are then updated to correspond with those available for the txtValue1. Figure 2-17 displays some of these available procedures that can be created for the txtValue1 text box.

When you select any of the procedures in the list, such as BeforeUpdate, a corresponding empty procedure will automatically be created with the cursor flashing, ready for you to input your code (see Figure 2-18).

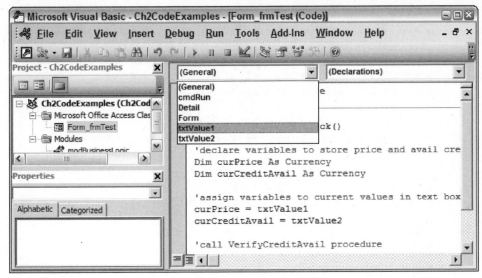

Figure 2-16

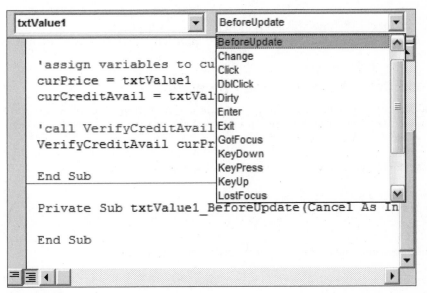

Figure 2-17

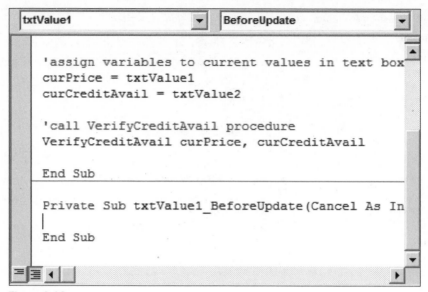

Figure 2-18

Writing code for object events will be explored in detail in Chapter 3, but at this point you should just know what a procedure is and that it can be called from various places, such as from an event or another procedure.

Create and Call a New Function Procedure

So far, all the examples you have reviewed have dealt with creating and calling sub procedures. Earlier, you learned that a function procedure is used to perform a particular action and also return a particular result. Let's look at that in more detail now.

The syntax for declaring a new function procedure without parameters is:

```
Function ProcedureName() As DataType
'code for the function
End Function
```

The syntax for a new sub procedure that contains variables as parameters is:

```
Function ProcedureName(Variables) As DataType
'code for the procedure
End Function
```

Note that in both the preceding cases, the Function keyword is used instead of the Sub keyword in two places. Also note that a data type is required as part of the function declaration. The data type should be specified to correspond to the type of the value you want the function to output.

Now you can create a new function to illustrate these procedures.

Creating the CalculateSalesTax Function

The `CalculateSalesTax` function you create next accepts a price and a tax rate as parameters and calculates the amount of tax.

1. In the `modBusinessLogic` standard module, add the following function, called `CalculateSalesTax`, after the `FinalizeOrder` sub procedure.

```
Function CalculateSalesTax(curPrice As Currency, dblTaxRate As Double) As Currency

    'declare variable for storing calculated tax
    Dim curTaxAmt As Currency

    'calculate amt of tax based on price and rate
    curTaxAmt = curPrice * dblTaxRate

    'return the calculated amt
    CalculateSalesTax = curTaxAmt

End Function
```

2. After the function has been added, the Visual Basic Editor window should look something like Figure 2-19.

3. Run the new function from the Immediate Window using the syntax shown in Figure 2-20 and press Enter. You can select View ➪ Immediate Window if it is not already displayed.

4. After you press Enter, the `0.25` value is displayed in the Immediate Window.

How It Works

The `CalculateSalesTax` function has a declaration containing two variables as parameters. It uses Currency as the return data type.

```
Function CalculateSalesTax(curPrice As Currency, dblTaxRate As Double) As Currency
```

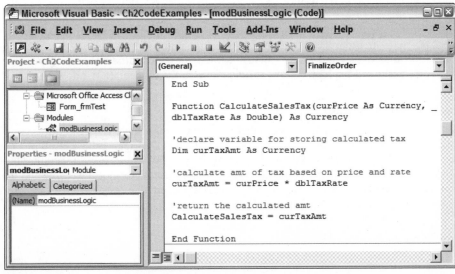

Figure 2-19

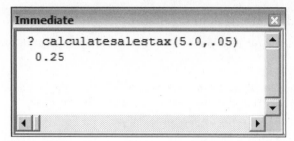

Figure 2-20

A variable is declared to store the calculated tax value.

```
'declare variable for storing calculated tax
Dim curTaxAmt As Currency
```

The amount of tax is calculated by multiplying the `curPrice` value by the `dblTaxRate` value.

```
'calculate amt of tax based on price and rate
curTaxAmt = curPrice * dblTaxRate
```

Because the procedure is a function procedure, a particular value should be returned. In this case, it is desirable to return the amount of sales tax that was calculated. The name of the function is assigned to the `curTaxAmt` value. This, in effect, returns the `curTaxAmt` value to the calling procedure for further use and processing.

```
'return the calculated amt
CalculateSalesTax = curTaxAmt
```

When the function procedure was tested using the Immediate Window, the preceding code was executed using the values `5.0` and `.05` you specified as the parameters. The value of `5.0` was assigned to the `curPrice` variable, and the value of `.05` was assigned to the `dblTaxRate` variable. The result of `0.25` was then displayed as the result.

Did you happen to notice that this time you had to use a question mark and put the parameters in parentheses? The prior examples did not use the question mark and parenthesis when calling sub procedures from the Immediate Window. As you just learned, the syntax differs slightly depending on whether you want to call a sub procedure or function from the Immediate Window.

Call a Function from Another Procedure

Just like sub procedures, functions can be called from other procedures. The procedures you follow are basically the same as those described in the prior example that illustrates calling a sub procedure from another sub procedure. The main difference is that when you call a function from another function or sub procedure, you typically assign the return value of the function to a local variable and then use it appropriately. For example, to call the `CalculateSalesTax` function from within another function or sub procedure, you could use the following code:

```
Dim curSalesTax As Currency

'call the CalculateSalesTax function and assign the result to the local variable
curSalesTax = CalculateSalesTax(100,.06)
```

Calling a Function from an Event

Again, just as with sub procedures, you can call a function from a class module associated with a form or report. The procedures are basically the same as those described in the prior example that illustrates calling a sub procedure from an event. A more detailed explanation of events can be found in Chapter 3.

Scope and Lifetime of Sub Procedures and Functions

Sub procedures and functions have a particular life cycle that determines how long they will live. They also have characteristics that determine from where they can be called. This is referred to as *scope*. How the procedure is declared determines how long the procedure will live and from where the procedure can be called.

First, let's look at the procedure life cycle. Traditionally, a procedure executes and then everything it contained — such as the values in the variables — are released from memory. In circumstances where you must preserve all the values within a procedure after it finishes executing, you can declare the procedure with the Static keyword.

Using the Static keyword in the declaration will basically keep the procedure in memory from the last time the procedure ran, including all associated values of the variables. As you may be aware, there are other ways to preserve particular values after a procedure ends. Examples include using public variables or storing certain values in a database for later retrieval.

Let's now look at how to determine and specify procedure scope from where a procedure is called. Event procedures are private by default, but all other procedures and functions are public by default. In the examples used so far in this chapter, all the procedures were standard public declarations. The sub and function declaration syntax did not always use the word "Public" per se, but those declarations were indeed private declarations. When a procedure is declared as private, it can only be called from within the same object. The Public keyword can be used with to make modules available from outside the same object.

Using Built-In Functions

You have looked at some examples of creating your own functions. You should also know that VBA has an extensive list of built-in functions that you can use instead of writing the code yourself for certain common actions. One example of a built-in function that you have already used is the MsgBox function. You can obtain a complete list of available functions in the VBA Help documentation, as in the help topic shown in Figure 2-21.

You can also view a list of available functions using the Expression Builder. Consult the VBA Help documentation for how to access the Expression Builder.

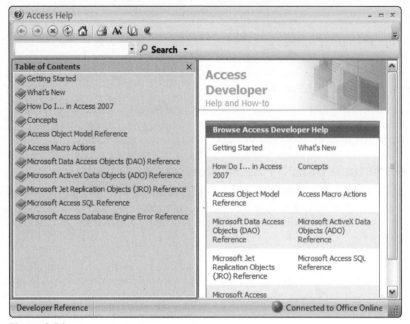

Figure 2-21

Macros versus Procedures

Now that you are familiar with procedures and functions, it is worth mentioning that you can use macros instead of procedures for some very basic tasks. Procedures provide you with much greater functionality and flexibility than do macros. Thus, in most cases, you should start using procedures instead of macros. However, with the many improvements in Access 2007 for macros, you may want to start using macros for some of the simpler programming-related tasks, and then use VBA for the more complex tasks. With Access 2007, macros now support simple variables, limited looping, and even some error handling. The applications you build in later chapters will use both macros and VBA code so you can get a better idea of when to use one versus the other. For now, let's look at a simple example of a macro.

The AutoExec macro is one example of a macro that you can use to control which form loads when the database opens. Let's create a new AutoExec macro to open the `frmTest` form you created earlier any time the `Ch2CodeExamples.ACCDB` file is opened. Create a new macro by selecting the Create ribbon on the toolbar, and then selecting Macro from the group called Macro, as shown in Figure 2-22.

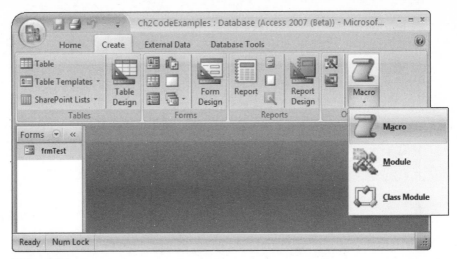

Figure 2-22

A new empty macro is displayed. To have a form load, select the OpenForm action from the action list, as shown in Figure 2-23. Next, to specify which form to open, select frmTest from the Form Name field, as shown in Figure 2-24.

Finally, you need to save the macro, such as by selecting the Save icon or by selecting the X in the right corner of the macro window (not of Access 2007 overall or you will close Access). You will be prompted to save the macro. Name the macro AutoExec, as shown in Figure 2-25, so it will run when the database opens. Whenever an Access database opens, it looks for a macro named AutoExec, and if one is found, the commands it contains are executed automatically.

Now, anytime you open the database, the AutoExec macro will load and open the frmTest form. Other types of macros will be illustrated throughout this book. Give it a try on your database. Close and reopen the database you created in this chapter and see if the form now loads automatically.

As mentioned earlier in the chapter, if a security warning appears, you may need to enable macros and VBA code when you open Access in order for the code to execute. The Trust Center can be used to further customize the security settings in Access. To access the Trust Center, click the Office Button, and then choose Access Options near the bottom. Select the group called Trust Center from the left navigation area.

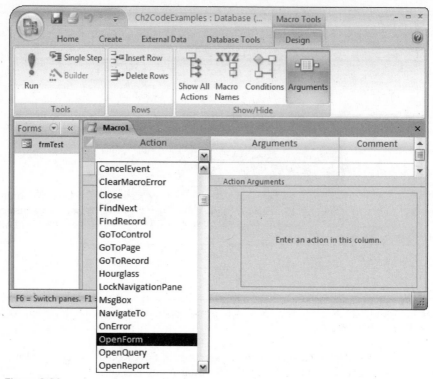

Figure 2-23

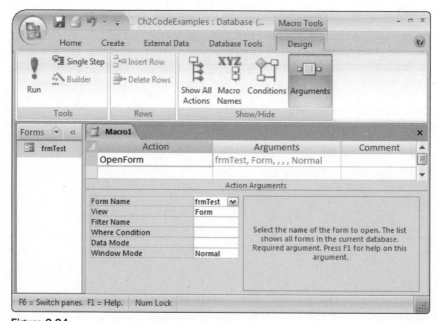

Figure 2-24

Using Variables and Constants to Store Values

Now that you have a basic understanding of how to create procedures, turn your attention to learning how to use variables and constants in those procedures. Variables and constants can be used to store values that are used by your Access program. You have already seen a few examples of using variables to store values. This chapter covers variables in a bit more detail because they are so important to writing VBA code.

Types of Variables

Various types of variables can be declared and used in your procedures. The most common variables are probably `String`, `Integer`, `Long`, `Currency`, and `Date`, although other variables are also commonly used. The following table illustrates the various data types that are available in VBA and offers an explanation of the type of value each can store.

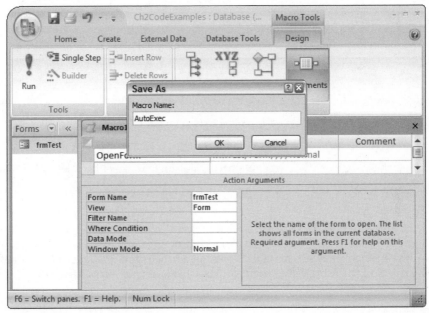

Figure 2-25

Data Type	What It Stores
Attachment	File attachment
Boolean	True or false
Byte	Positive integers from 0 to 255
Currency	Positive and negative currency values with four decimal places
Date	Date and time from 1/1/0100 to 12/31/9999
Double	8-byte decimal values
Hyperlink	URL for a hyperlink
Integer	2-byte integers from –32,768 to +32,768
Long	4-byte integers from –2 billion to +2 billion
Object	Access object reference
Single	4-byte decimal values

Data Type	What It Stores
String (variable length)	From 0 to 2 billion characters
String (fixed length)	From 1 to 65,000 characters
User-defined (with Type)	Same as its associated data type
Variant (numbers)	Numeric value up to range of Double
Variant (characters)	From 0 to 2 billion characters

Note that the VBA data type does not correspond perfectly to the field data types listed in database tables you create in Access. The following table shows examples of how each VBA data type maps to a particular Access field data type. This table is presented to help you evaluate which variable data types to use when reading and using values from particular fields in your Access databases.

Visual Basic Data Type	Corresponding Access Field Data Type
Attachment	Attachment
Boolean	Yes/No
Byte	Number (Byte)
Currency	Currency
Date	Date/Time
Double	Number (Double)

Visual Basic Data Type	Corresponding Access Field Data Type
Hyperlink	Hyperlink
Integer	Number (Integer)
Long	Number (Long Integer) or AutoNumber (Long Integer)
Single	Number (Single)
String	Text or Memo

Declaring and Using Variables

The previous examples briefly illustrated that variables can be declared using the Dim statement. Here are some additional examples:

```
Dim strMessage As String
Dim rsSales As Adodb.Recordset
Dim intCounter As Integer
Dim blnResponse As Boolean
```

After it is declared, a variable obtains its value (is assigned) by setting the variable equal to a value or to an expression that evaluates to a value. The expression can contain operators (such as = , > , or <), other variables, constants, key words, formulas, and so on.

Further examples illustrating variable assignments are provided at the end of this chapter.

Declaring and Using Arrays

Arrays are indexed elements that have the same data type. Each array element has a unique index number. Arrays can be static or dynamic. Static arrays have a fixed number of elements, whereas dynamic arrays have the option to grow in size. The lowest index of an array is 0 by default.

Here is an example of how to declare and use an array.

```
Sub DemoFixedArray()

'declare an array with 5 elements
Dim arstrPictureFile(4) As String

'populate each array element with a value
arstrPictureFile(0) = "Christmas.jpg"
arstrPictureFile(1) = "Thanksgiving.jpg"
arstrPictureFile(2) = "WinterVacation.jpg"
arstrPictureFile(3) = "SummerVacation.jpg"
arstrPictureFile(4) = "Anniversary.jpg"

End Sub
```

The preceding array illustrates how to declare a fixed-size array. In some cases, you may not know exactly how big the array needs to be. In such cases, you use a dynamic array. A dynamic array is declared without an upper bound index, as shown in the following example.

```
Sub DemoDynamicArray()

'declare an dynamic array
Dim arstrPictureFile() As String

'once you have determined how big the array needs to be
'then specify a size
'for the arrayReDim arstrPictureFile(50) As String

'populate the first 5 array elements with a value
arstrPictureFile(0) = "Christmas.jpg"
arstrPictureFile(1) = "Thanksgiving.jpg"
arstrPictureFile(2) = "WinterVacation.jpg"
arstrPictureFile(3) = "SummerVacation.jpg"
arstrPictureFile(4) = "Anniversary.jpg"

End Sub
```

The ReDim statement is used to define the size of the array when it has already been defined with an unknown size but now is known. Any values stored in the array when the ReDim statement are used are lost because the array is reset. The Preserve statement can be used in circumstances where you want to preserve the prior values in the array when using the ReDim statement.

Declaring and Using User-Defined Data Types

User-defined types allow you to create your own data types. User-defined types can contain various pieces of information of the same or varying data types. Here is an example:

```
Public Type typTripInfo
    strTripLocation As String
    dtTripStartDate As Date
    dtTripEndDate As Date
    strPhotoPath As String
End Type
```

The preceding code can be placed in the General Declarations section of the module. Now, let's look at a sample procedure that uses the typTripInfo user-defined type.

```
Sub TestUserDefinedType()

'declare a variable as the user defined type typTripInfo
Dim typRecentTrip As typTripInfo

'assign values to the typRecentTrip user defined type
typRecentTrip.strTripLocation = "Italy"
typRecentTrip.dtTripStartDate = "3-18-04"
typRecentTrip.dtTripEndDate = "3-27-04"
typRecentTrip.strPhotoPath = "c:\trips\Italy"

End Sub
```

In the preceding procedure, a local variable is declared as the custom data type `typTripInfo`. Then, values for each of the variables in the user-defined type are specified.

Declaring and Using Object Variables

Object variables are variables that reference objects, such as databases, recordsets, forms, or controls. Object variables allow you to create references with shorter names than the original object and to pass objects as parameters to procedures.

Here is an example of how to declare and use a text box object variable from a form module.

```
Sub TestObjectVariable()

'declare an object variable
Dim txtPrice As TextBox

'point the object to the txtValue1 text box
Set txtPrice = Me.txtValue1

'set the text value of the text box
txtPrice.Text = "2000"

End Sub
```

The preceding procedure declares a new variable as a text box object and then points the new variable to the existing `txtValue1` text box. A value of `2000` is then assigned to the new variable, which actually ends up physically setting the value in the original `txtValue1` text box on the form to which you have pointed the new variable.

Constants

VBA allows you to create your own constants or use built-in constants.

Declaring and Using Constants

A *constant* is a type of variable that maintains a constant value that does not change. Unlike traditional variables, constants are assigned values when you create them. Constants are declared with the `Const` statement instead of the `Dim` statement. Here are some examples:

```
Const conWelcomeMessage as String = "Welcome to my first VBA application."
Const conRate as Double = 5.5
```

Constants can help improve the readability of your code. For example, a line of code is much cleaner and more understandable if it uses the constant `conRate` than if it is hard-coded with a value of `5.5`:

```
dblTotalSales = conRate
```

Constants can also make your code easier to maintain. For example, because the constant is declared in one place, you do not have to search for every instance where the rate with a hard-coded value of `5.5` is used in the code. Instead, you simply use a constant to store the current rate and modify that one item if the rate later changes.

Using Built-In Constants

VBA has numerous intrinsic constants that can be used in your code to save you from writing the code yourself. For example, the msgbox function has various constants that can be used instead of the particular integers. The constant vbOK represents a value of 1 and is used to test or indicate that an OK button was clicked. The constant vbCancel represents a value of 2 and is used to indicate or test whether a Cancel button was clicked. Please refer to help documentation for more information on the constants available.

Scope and Lifetime of Variables and Constants

Variables and constants have a scope and life cycle and scope similar to procedures. With respect to life cycle, the variables within sub and function procedures generally *live* while the procedure is executing. The Static keyword can be used when necessary to alter this traditional lifetime and preserve the value of the variable after the last procedure that uses it finishes executing.

The scope of a variable determines from where the variable can be seen or used. A variable created locally within a procedure can be seen only by that procedure. A variable that is declared in the General Declarations section can be seen by all procedures in that particular module or by procedures in all modules, depending on whether it is declared as public or private. If the variable is declared with the Public keyword, all procedures in all modules can use and see it. If it is not, the variable is private and only the procedures in the particular module where the declaration is located can see it.

Try It Out   Declaring a Public Variable

Next, you can declare a public variable to illustrate how to make variables visible from procedures in any module.

1.   In the modBusinessLogic standard module, go to the General Declarations section (see Figure 2-26).

2.   Add a public constant called strTest to the General Declarations section, as shown in the previous figure.

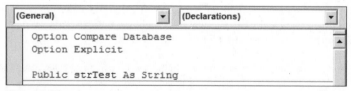

Figure 2-26

How It Works

Declaring the variable `strTest` as `Public` means that it can be used and seen from procedures in any module now. It is important that you make sure to only use the same public variable name once. The Option Explicit statement discussed earlier in this chapter will warn you if you use the same public variable name more than once.

Naming Conventions

You may have noticed that all the examples covered so far prefixed each variable and object declaration with a two- or three-character prefix, such as the variable `strTest` in the prior figure. These prefixes are used as a naming convention to provide a standardized way of naming objects and variables. Various types of naming conventions are in use today, and one may be just as good as the other.

Following some type of naming convention is a valuable practice. For example, if you name a variable with a prefix that indicates its data type, you do not have to weed through lines and lines of code looking for the place it was declared to see what data type it stores.

The following table illustrates some naming conventions that I like to use for my variables. Other conventions could also be used, as was mentioned previously.

Prefix	Data Type	Example
Bln	Boolean	blnResult
Byt	Byte	bytResponse
Cur	Currency	curTotalSales
Dt	Date	dtBirth
Dbl	Double	dblGPA
Int	Integer	intCount
Lng	Long	lngTrackingNum
Obj	Object	objControl
Sng	Single	sngResult
str	String	strMessage
typ	User-Defined Type	typExample
var	Variant	varOutput

The following table lists some naming conventions I like to use for objects. Some objects and variables are not listed in these naming convention tables, but these are the most common to give you the general idea.

Prefix	Object	Example
Cls	Class Module	clsProject
Frm	Form	frmMain
fsub	SubForm	fsubMainDetail
Mcr	Macro	mcrAutoExec
Mod	Module	modBusinessLogic
Qry	Query	qryCalculateSales
Rpt	Report	rptAnnualSales
Rsub	Subreport	rsubAccountExecutives
Tbl	Table	tblSales

If you would like additional ideas for naming conventions, Microsoft Consulting Services has a suggested list of prefixes at http://support.microsoft.com/kb/110264.

Controlling Program Flow

So far, you have learned how to create one or more modules to contain your code as well as how to create procedures within those modules. Now you will see how to write commands within procedures that control the flow of the program. The flow of a program can be controlled through decision-making, loops, and in other ways. We'll start by looking at writing decision-making code.

Decision Making

VBA has various statements you can use to make decisions in your code and then take an appropriate action depending on the result. The following gives you several decision-making examples to illustrate this concept.

If . . .Then

If...Then statements can be used to make decisions and perform certain actions depending on whether the conditions are met.

The syntax for an If...Then statement is:

```
If CONDITION Then
'code if the condition is met
End If
```

The syntax for an `If...Then...Else` statement is:

```
If CONDITION Then
'code if the condition is met
Else
'code if the condition is not met
End If
```

The syntax for an `If...Then...ElseIf` statement is:

```
If CONDITION Then
'code if the condition is met
ElseIf CONDITION Then
'code if the ElseIf condition is met
End If
```

`ElseIf` and `Else` can be used together as part of the same `If...Then` statement, or they can be used separately, as illustrated in the previous example. `If...Then` statements can also be nested within each other, as shown in the following example:

```
If intCounter < 0 Then
   'reset intCounter to 0
   intCounter = 0

ElseIf intCounter > 0 and intCounter < 50 Then
   If intCounter = 50 Then
      Msgbox "The maximum number of sessions has been reached."
   Else
      Msgbox "There are still sessions remaining."
   End If

   intCounter = intCounter + 1

End If
```

Try It Out   Creating TestIfStatement Procedure

Now, it's your turn to create a new procedure and makes uses of `If...Then` statements.

1. In the `modBusinessLogic` standard module, add the following `TestIfStatement` procedure:

```
Sub TestIfStatement()

'declare variable to store sales tax value
Dim curSalesTax As Currency
 'call function to calculate sales tax
curSalesTax = CalculateSalesTax(500, 0.05)

'evaluate sales tax and write proper message
'to debug window
If curSalesTax <= 10 Then
    Debug.Print "You are lucky - the amount of tax is nominal."
ElseIf curSalesTax > 10 And curSalesTax <= 50 Then
```

```
      Debug.Print "The amount of sales tax could have bought you a nice meal."
Else
      Debug.Print "You bought a really nice item for that tax amount."
End If

End Sub
```

2. From the Immediate Window, run the new `TestIfStatement` procedure. The result is displayed in Figure 2-27, in the Immediate Window.

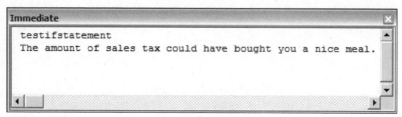

Figure 2-27

How It Works

The `TestIfStatement` procedure calls the `CalculateSalesTax` function that you created previously and evaluates the result in an `If...Then` statement to determine which message to display in the Immediate Window. The procedure begins by declaring a variable to store the calculated sales tax value.

```
Sub TestIfStatement()

'declare variable to store sales tax value
Dim curSalesTax As Currency
```

The `curSalesTax` variable is assigned to the result of the `CalculateSalesTax` function. In other words, the `CalculateSalesTax` procedure is called with the hard-coded values, and the resulting value is placed in the `curSalesTax` variable.

```
'call function to calculate sales tax
curSalesTax = CalculateSalesTax(500, 0.05)
```

An `If...` statement is then used to evaluate the `curSalesTax` value and write a particular message to the Immediate Window, depending on how the expression is evaluated.

```
'evaluate sales tax and write proper message
'to debug window
If curSalesTax <= 10 Then
    Debug.Print "You are lucky - the amount of tax is nominal."
ElseIf curSalesTax > 10 And curSalesTax <= 50 Then
     Debug.Print "The amount of sales tax could have bought you a nice meal."
Else
    Debug.Print "You bought a really nice item for that tax amount."
End If
End Sub
```

In the current example, because a value of 500 is specified for the sales amount parameter of the CalculateSalesTax function and .05 is specified for the tax rate parameter, the resulting tax amount is 25. Thus, when you run the procedure, the Immediate Window displays the corresponding message.

IIf

The IIf function can be used to return one of two possible values depending on whether the condition being tested is true or false. The syntax for the IIf function is:

```
IIf(expr, truepart, falsepart)
```

Here is an example:

```
strResult = IIf(intWeight > 25, "Heavy", "Light")
```

If the intWeight value is greater than 25, then the IIF function will return the value "Heavy" and assign it to the strResult variable. Otherwise, the strResult variable will be assigned to the value "Light".

Conditional If

Conditional If...Then statements enable you to selectively compile and execute certain blocks of code. Conditional If statements can be used in various scenarios, such as when you want certain blocks of code to execute during testing but not in the release version, or when you're distributing your application in different regions and want certain code to apply in some regions but not others. The following is an example of the general syntax:

```
#If conLanguage = "English" Then
   'The code specific to the English version of the software goes here.
#ElseIf conLanguage = "Spanish" Then
   'The code specific to the Spanish version of the software goes here.
#Else
   'The code specific to the remaining versions of the software goes here.
#End If
```

Select . . . Case

Another way to implement decision making in your VBA code is to use a Select...Case statement. Select...Case statements can be used to easily evaluate the same variable multiple times and then take a particular action depending on the evaluation.

The syntax for a Select...Case statement is:

```
Select Case VARIABLE
Case VALUE1
   'code to run if VARIABLE equals Value1
Case VALUE2
   'code to run if VARIABLE equals Value2
Case Else
   'code to run for remaining cases
End Select
```

Try It Out   **Create the TestCaseStatement Procedure**

Let's create a new procedure that makes use of a `Select...Case` statement to illustrate this in further detail.

1.   Add the following `TestCaseStatement` procedure to the `modBusinessLogic` standard module.

```
Sub TestCaseStatement(strCountry As String)

'evaluate the value of strCountry and display applicable result in debug window
Select Case strCountry
Case "Italy"
    Debug.Print "The buildings dating back to 400 BC are incredible."
Case "China"
    Debug.Print "Great bargains for shoppers."
Case "Russia"
    Debug.Print "A beautiful country with a growing democracy."
Case "Germany"
    Debug.Print "Fantastic food - you will not starve there."
Case Else
    Debug.Print "You should travel more when you have the chance."
End Select

End Sub
```

2.   Run the `TestCaseStatement` procedure from the Immediate Window and specify `"Italy"` as the parameter, as shown in Figure 2-28. Click Enter to run the procedure. The resulting value is then displayed in the Immediate Window.

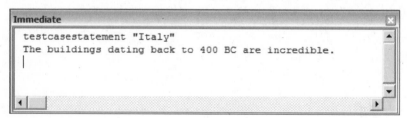

Figure 2-28

How It Works

The `TestCaseStatement` procedure accepts a string variable called `strCountry` as a parameter.

```
Sub TestCaseStatement(strCountry As String)
```

The `strCountry` variable is evaluated in the `Select...Case` statement to determine which one of a variety of messages should be displayed.

```
'evaluate the value of strCountry and display applicable result in debug window
Select Case strCountry
Case "Italy"
    Debug.Print "The buildings dating back to 400 BC are incredible."
```

```
Case "China"
    Debug.Print "Great bargains for shoppers."
Case "Russia"
    Debug.Print "A beautiful country with a growing democracy."
Case "Germany"
    Debug.Print "Fantastic food - you will not starve there."
Case Else        Debug.Print "You should travel more when you have the chance."
End Select
```

Because you ran the procedure using "Italy" as the value for Country, the message for Italy was displayed in the Immediate Window. Try running the procedure with different values for Country and see how the results differ.

Loops

Various types of loops can be used to iterate through a particular action until a particular scenario occurs. For example, loops can be used to run particular code a specified number of times. Now you will learn about a few different ways to declare loops using VBA code.

For . . . Next and For Each . . . Next

For...Next loops can be used to run the same code a particular number of times. For Each...Next loops can be used to run the same code for each object in a particular collection, such as for each form in the Forms collection. The basic syntax for a For...Next loop is shown here.

```
For counter = start To end
    'statements go here
Next [counter]
```

The basic syntax for a For Each...Next loop is shown here.

```
For Each element In Collection
    'statements go here
Next [element]
```

Try It Out   Creating a For . . . Next Loop

Let's jump right in by creating our own For...Next loop to see how this works.

1.   Place this code for the TestLoop procedure in the modBusinessLogic standard module.

```
Sub TestLoop()

'declare variable to store Counter
Dim intCounter As Integer

'increment intCounter from 1 to 5 and
'display output in debug window
For intCounter = 1 To 5
    Debug.Print intCounter
Next intCounter

End Sub
```

2. Run the `TestLoop` procedure from the Immediate Window. The results of running the procedure are shown in Figure 2-29.

Figure 2-29

How It Works

The `TestLoop` procedure begins by declaring an `intCounter` variable to store the number of times the loop has been iterated.

```
Sub TestLoop()

'declare variable to store Counter
Dim intCounter As Integer
```

The `For...Next` statement comes next, with code specifying that the loop should run with `intCounter` starting at 1 and repeat multiple times until `intCounter` reaches 5. The `Next` statement increments the `intCounter` value by one. When `intCounter` reaches 5, the `Debug.Print` statement will execute for the last time and then the loop is exited.

```
'increment intCounter from 1 to 5 and
'display output in debug window
For intCounter = 1 To 5
    Debug.Print intCounter
Next intCounter
```

Do . . . Loop

The `Do...Loop` statement can be used instead of `For...Next` to accomplish the same purpose. The two types of `Do...Loops` are `Do...While` and `Do...Until`. `Do...While` may never run any statements if the condition is not initially true, while `Do...Until` will always run at least once.

The generic syntax for `Do...Loop` is shown here.

```
Do [{While | Until} condition]
   'statements go here
Loop
```

Or, you can use this syntax:

```
Do
   'statements go here
Loop [{While | Until} condition]
```

The following code uses a Do...While statement to accomplish the same result as the For...Next loop described previously.

```
Do While intCounter <= 5
   Debug.Print intCounter intCounter = intCounter + 1
Loop
```

An example of a Do Until loop is shown here.

```
Do Until intCounter = 6
   Debug.Print intCounter   intCounter = intCounter + 1
Loop
```

If the condition in a Do Until *statement is never met, then the loop is known as an infinite loop, which will execute indefinitely.*

While . . . Wend

The While...Wend statement executes repeatedly while a certain condition is met. When the condition is no longer met, the loop terminates. Here is an example:

```
intCounter = 1
While intCounter <= 5
    Debug.Print intCounter intCounter = intCounter + 1
Wend
```

Documenting Your Code

It is a good idea to document your code very well so that you and others will be able to understand the purpose of each procedure and why it was written in a certain way. You can document your code in several ways. The ideal way to document your code is to use a general comment section at the beginning of each procedure and to use in-line comments to describe each segment of code. Here is an example of such a general comment section.

```
'*****************************************************************
'*
'* Procedure Name: TestProcedure
'*
'* Purpose: The purpose of this procedure is to illustrate why
'* documenting your code is so important.
'*
'* Parameters: None.
'*
'* Date Created: September 4, 2006
'* By:  Denise M. Gosnell
'*
'* Modification Log:
'* Date                Explanation of Modification      Modified By
'* -----------         --------------------------------  ------------------------
'*
'*****************************************************************
```

The preceding documentation style may be overkill if the procedure itself is only a few lines of code. Some type of general comment section should be used with all procedures, even if it is not as detailed as the one in the preceding code.

You have seen in-line comments in all the code examples throughout this chapter. Here is another example:

```
'display a message to the user
Msgbox "Demonstration of In-Line commenting"
```

It is always better to write too many comments than too few. As you gain more experience writing VBA code, you will see how difficult it can be to follow what is happening in a particular procedure. This is especially true if you go back to the code at a later date and no longer remember the details about why you wrote it a particular way, or if you are reviewing code that someone else wrote. Code comments make this process much easier.

Error Debugging

Now that I have covered several basic ways to write VBA code and to control the flow of the program, let's look at the types of errors you may encounter, how to debug them, and how to write error handlers to handle them.

Types of Errors

The types of errors include: syntax errors, compile errors, runtime errors, and logic errors, each of which will be discussed in turn.

Syntax Errors

Syntax errors are errors that occur because the code you wrote does not comply with the required syntax. Figure 2-30 illustrates a syntax error that occurred because the As part of the Dim statement is missing.

Compile Errors

Compile errors are errors discovered on compilation that may have a correct code syntax, but for some reason will not compile. Figure 2-31 illustrates a compiler error that has occurred because a CalculateTax function cannot be located. In this particular example, the reason for the compile error is that the function is incorrectly listed as CalculateTax instead of CalculateSalesTax.

Runtime Errors

Runtime errors occur at runtime when the code executes. Runtime errors can include errors that occur because of something that it not allowed or supposed to happen. For example, a line of code that tries to assign a variable of one data type to an incompatible value could result in a runtime error. The example in Figure 2-32 runs the CalculateSalesTax function and passes string values as parameters, instead of the required currency and double values. The result is a runtime error, which in this example is a Type Mismatch error.

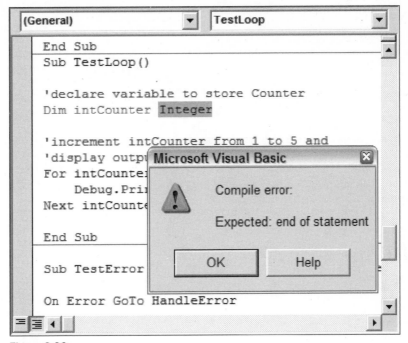

Figure 2-30

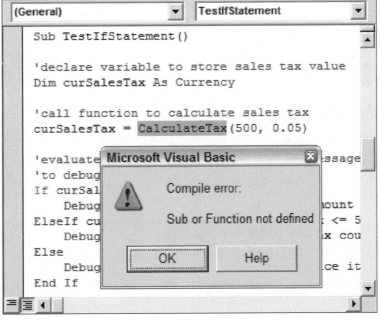

Figure 2-31

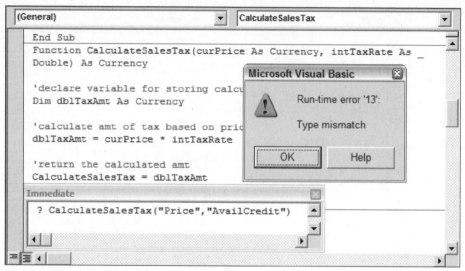

Figure 2-32

Logic Errors

Logic errors are flaws in the logic of your code. Logic errors can be the hardest to find because they are syntactically correct but can only be discovered by testing your code and ensuring it produces the desired and appropriate result.

Debugging Your Code

You certainly need the capability to debug and correct your VBA code as you encounter errors. As you may recall from Chapter 1, the Visual Basic Editor provides several ways to help you debug and correct your code. Now we'll look at some of these methods in more detail.

Using Breakpoints to Step through Code

Breakpoints can be set on one or more lines of code. When a line of code that has an associated break-point is reached, code execution stops and you can then choose to Step Into, Step Over, or Step Out of the code. Selecting the Step Into option from the Debug menu will run the current line of code at the breakpoint. The Step Over option will skip the current line of code at the breakpoint and move on to the next line of code.

Try It Out   **Setting and Using Breakpoints**

It's your turn to set a breakpoint and use it to step through code.

1. Navigate to the TestLoop procedure you created previously in the modBusinessLogic stan-dard module.

2. Set a breakpoint on the Debug.Print and the Next intCounter lines of code, as shown in Figure 2-33. You can set a breakpoint by pointing and clicking the cursor just to the left of the line of code where you want to add a breakpoint.

3. Next, open the Immediate Window and run the `TestLoop` procedure. The code will stop execution at the first breakpoint, as shown in Figure 2-34.

4. While at the breakpoint, use the Immediate Window to inquire about the current value of the `intCounter` variable. To do so, type `? intCounter` and press Enter, as shown in Figure 2-35.

5. The current value of `intCounter` is displayed in the Immediate Window. You should press F5 or select Run ⇨ Continue to keep executing the lines of code. Execution will stop on each breakpoint.

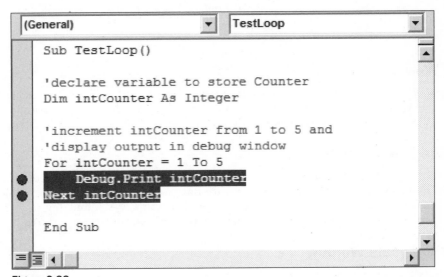

Figure 2-33

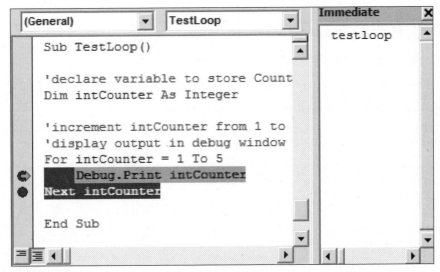

Figure 2-34

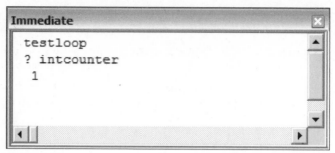

Figure 2-35

How It Works

The breakpoint enables you to closely monitor and determine the values of variables and take other actions that will allow you to test and review your code most effectively. This example allows you to see how the value of intCounter increments as the loop repeats.

Using the Immediate Window

As you are well aware at this point, you can use the Immediate Window to call procedures and to display the results of a line of code. You can also use the Immediate Window to assign new values to variables. You have already learned that the Debug.Print statement writes output directly to the Immediate Window. The Debug.Print statement can be used for your testing purposes.

Using the Locals Window

The Locals Window can be used to see a list of all the objects and variables that are used in the current procedure. The values in the list are updated every time you suspend execution with a breakpoint or step through code.

Try It Out   Using the Locals Window

Now, let's walk through an example of using the Locals Window.

1. Display the Locals Window by selecting View ⇨ Locals Window.

2. Run the TestLoop procedure again from the Immediate Window.

3. The code execution will again stop when the first breakpoint is reached. Notice that the values in the Locals Window are updated with the current value of intCounter.

4. Press F5 or select Run ⇨ Continue to keep executing the lines of code. You should see that the values of intCounter in the Locals window change as you walk through the code, as shown in Figure 2-36.

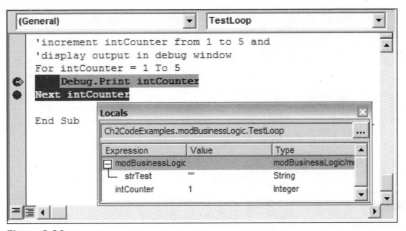

Figure 2-36

How It Works

The Locals Window allows you to closely monitor and determine values of variables. This example allows you to see how the value of `intCounter` increments as the loop repeats.

Using the Watch Window

The Watch Window can be used to see a list of objects and variables in the current procedure. The Watch Window can be used to monitor the value of variables as breakpoints are encountered, just as the Immediate and Locals Windows can. The Watch Window also provides additional features, such as allowing you to add a Watch that will cause the code execution to break when a certain event or value occurs. This enables you to have the system break for you automatically when the certain event occurs without having to set a predetermined breakpoint.

Try It Out   Adding a Watch

Let's look at an example of adding a watch using the Watch Window.

1. From the Debug menu in the Visual Basic Editor, choose Add Watch, as shown in Figure 2-37.

2. On the Add Watch dialog box, specify `intCounter` as the Expression, `TestLoop` as the procedure, and `modBusinessLogic` as the Module.

3. Click the OK button on the Add Watch dialog box, and a Watch Window will appear.

4. Run the `TestLoop` procedure again from the Immediate Window. You should see the values in the Watch Window change when the first breakpoint is encountered.

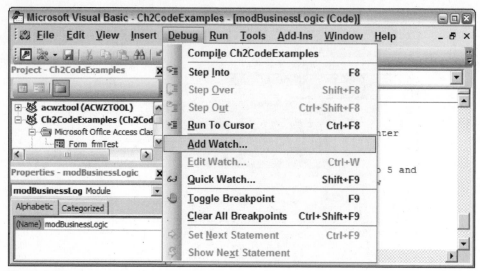

Figure 2-37

How It Works

The Watch Window allows you to closely monitor and determine values of variables and also to cause code to automatically enter a break mode when certain events happen. The example shown in Figures 2-38, 2-39, and 2-40 illustrates how the value of intCounter increments as the loop repeats, just as the prior examples did.

Using the Call Stack

A call stack can be used to trace through the process of nested procedures. You can use the call stack window when VBA is in break mode by selecting View ⇨ Call Stack. However, you have to create your own call stack if you are not in Debug Mode. You have various ways to create your own call stack, such as to write various messages to the Immediate Window as you enter certain procedures to see the order in which they were called.

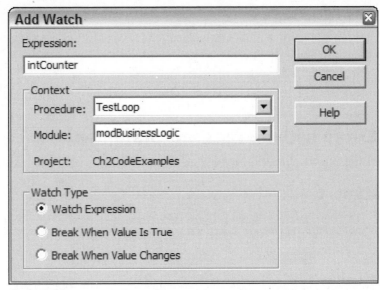

Figure 2-38

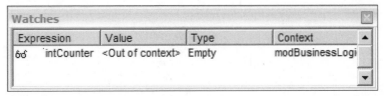

Figure 2-39

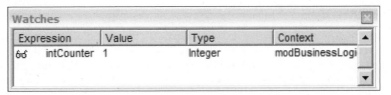

Figure 2-40

Error Handling

Now that you are familiar with various types of errors that can occur in your VBA code and how to debug them, it's time to look at how to write error-handling code in your procedures so that your application performs well for users.

Default Error Messages

You have all used applications that did not have very good error handling and found yourself getting booted out of the application without warning or faced with unfriendly messages like the ones you saw earlier in this chapter. You do not want such problems to happen when users interact with your application. Errors will always occur, but if you design error handlers correctly, at least they can be handled reasonably well.

Handling Errors with an On Error Statement

Errors can be handled in VBA procedures using the On Error statement, as I show you next.

On Error Statement

The On Error statement can be placed on your procedure to specify a section in the procedure to which the execution should jump when an error occurs. Here is an example:

```
Sub Test()

On Error GoTo HandleError
'normal code for the procedure goes hereExit Sub

HandleError:
'code for handling the error goes here
Exit Sub

End Sub
```

If you want to make sure your own error handler doesn't kick in when you're debugging your code, select Tools ⇨ Options ⇨ General and enable the Break On All Errors option. This will allow you to see the root of the error and not your own error handler.

Resume Statement

The Resume and Resume Next statements can be used with the On Error statement. The Resume statement will cause code execution to resume at the line that caused the error, and the Resume Next statement will cause code execution to resume at the line following the one that caused the error. Resume statements are commonly added within the error-handler routines, such as the one shown here.

```
Sub Test()

On Error GoTo HandleError
'normal code for the procedure goes hereExit Sub

HandleError:
'code for handling the error goes here

Resume Next
Exit Sub

End Sub
```

Try It Out   Creating an Error Handler

It is your turn to try your hand at creating an error handler.

1. Place the following code for a new procedure called `TestError` in the `modBusinessLogic` standard module:

```
Sub TestError(intValue1 As Integer, intValue2 As Integer)

On Error GoTo HandleError

    'declare variable to store result
    Dim intResult As Integer

    'calculate result by dividing first value by second value
    intResult = intValue1 / intValue2

Exit Sub

HandleError:
    MsgBox "An error has occurred in your application: " & Err.Description
    Exit Sub
End Sub
```

2. Run the `TestError` procedure from the Immediate Window, as shown in Figure 2-41.

3. The following error message (shown in Figure 2-42) is displayed.

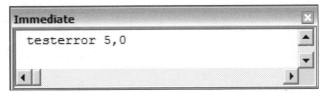

Figure 2-41

Figure 2-42

How It Works

The `TestError` procedure accepts two variables as parameters.

```
Sub TestError(intValue1 As Integer, intValue2 As Integer)
```

The `On Error` statement indicates that the `HandleError` section of code should execute when an error occurs.

```
On Error GoTo HandleError
```

A variable is declared that will be used to store the result of an upcoming mathematical calculation.

```
'declare variable to store result
Dim intResult As Integer
```

The `intValue1` value is then divided by the `intValue2` value.

```
'calculate result by dividing first value by second value
intResult = intValue1 / intValue2
```

Because the `intValue2` value you specified when calling the procedure was set to 0, a divide by 0 error occurs when the preceding line of code executes. Thus, the execution of code then jumps to the error handler `HandleError` at the bottom of the procedure.

```
HandleError:
    MsgBox "An error has occurred in your application: " & Err.Description
    Exit Sub
End Sub
```

A message box is then displayed to indicate that an error has occurred and to provide a description of the error.

The Err Object

The `Err` object contains information about runtime errors that occur when your code executes. Error handlers can use it to provide useful information to users or to the system to help determine what action should be taken. For example, in the error-handling example you just looked at, the `Description` property of the `Err` object (`Err.Description`) was used to include a description of the error to the user.

The `Err` object has a global scope. You need not declare it. Some examples of the properties available for the `Err` object include `Number`, `Description`, `HelpContext`, `HelpFile`, and `Source`. `Number` and `Description` are the most commonly used properties of the `Err` object.

Raising an Error

The `Err` object has a `Raise` method that allows runtime errors to be raised when necessary. Here is the syntax:

```
Err.Raise number, source, description, helpfile, helpcontext
```

The number argument is required for raising an error, but the other arguments are optional. Here's an example to illustrate how you can raise an error in your code.

```
Sub TestErrRaise(intValue1 As Integer, intValue2 As Integer)

    On Error GoTo HandleError

    'declare variable to store result
    Dim intResult As Integer

    If intValue2 <> 0 Then
        'calculate result by dividing first value by second value
        intResult = intValue1 / intValue2
    ElseIf intValue2 = 0 Then
        'raise a custom divide by 0 error
        Err.Raise vbObjectError + 513, "TestErrRaise", _
                        "The second value cannot be 0."
    End If
Exit Sub

HandleError:
    MsgBox "An error has occurred in your application: " & Err.Description
    Exit Sub

End Sub
```

When the error is raised, the code then jumps to the error handler just as if the error had occurred in the traditional fashion.

Using the Errors Collection

The `Errors` collection stores the most recent ActiveX Data Objects (ADO) database errors that have occurred. Chapter 5 covers ADO in detail. For now, just be aware that the `Errors` collection can be used to loop through each error that was generated by one database operation. Only a few instances require that you implement such an error-handling feature.

Creating a Generic Error Handler

One way of handling errors is to create a generic error handler that gets called from every sub procedure or function.

Try It Out   **Creating a Generic Error Handler**

Create a generic error handler now.

1.   Add the `GeneralErrorHandler` procedure that follows to the `modBusinessLogic` standard module:

```
Public Sub GeneralErrorHandler(lngErrNumber As Long, strErrDesc As String,
strModuleSource As String, strProcedureSource As String)
Dim strMessage As String

    'build the error message string from the parameters passed in
```

```
strMessage = "An error has occurred in the application."
strMessage = strMessage & vbCrLf & "Error Number: " & lngErrNumber
strMessage = strMessage & vbCrLf & "Error Description: " & strErrDesc
strMessage = strMessage & vbCrLf & "Module Source: " & strModuleSource
strMessage = strMessage & vbCrLf & "Procedure Source: " & strProcedureSource

'display the message to the user
MsgBox strMessage, vbCritical

End Sub
```

2. Add the procedure `TestError2` to the `modBusinessLogic` standard module:

```
Sub TestError2(intValue1 As Integer, intValue2 As Integer)
On Error GoTo HandleError

    'declare variable to store result
    Dim intResult As Integer

    'calculate result by dividing first value by second value
    intResult = intValue1 / intValue2

Exit Sub

HandleError:
    GeneralErrorHandler Err.Number, Err.Description, "modBusinessLogic", _
                "TestError2"
    Exit Sub
End Sub
```

3. Call the `TestError2` procedure from the Immediate Window with the values shown in Figure 2-43.

4. The message box shown in Figure 2-44 is displayed.

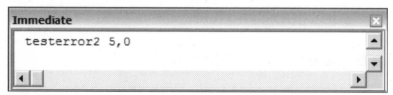

Figure 2-43

How It Works

The `TestError2` procedure operates nearly identically to the `TestError` procedure. `TestError2` has two parameter variables.

```
Sub TestError2(intValue1 As Integer, intValue2 As Integer)
```

Figure 2-44

An `On Error` statement specifies that the `HandleError` section of code should be executed when an error occurs.

```
On Error GoTo HandleError
```

A variable is declared to store the result of the division, and then the values that were passed in as parameters to the procedure are used for the division. Because the values passed in cause a divide by 0 error, the code execution skips down to the `HandleError` section of code.

```
'declare variable to store result
Dim intResult As Integer

'calculate result by dividing first value by second value
intResult = intValue1 / intValue2
```

This time, the `HandleError` section includes a call to the `GeneralErrorHandler` procedure you just added. The error number, error description, module name, and procedure name are passed as parameters to the `GeneralErrorHandler` procedure.

```
HandleError:
    GeneralErrorHandler Err.Number, Err.Description, "modBusinessLogic", _
        "TestError2"
```

Now let's turn to the `GeneralErrorHandler` procedure, since it runs next to handle the error. The `GeneralErrorHandler` procedure accepts the `Error Number`, `Error Description`, `Module Source`, and `Procedure Source` as parameters.

```
Public Sub GeneralErrorHandler(lngErrNumber As Long, strErrDesc As String,
    strModuleSource As String, strProcedureSource As String)
```

A variable is declared to store the error message, and the error message is created based on the various values passed in to the procedure.

```
Dim strMessage As String

'build the error message string from the parameters passed in
strMessage = "An error has occurred in the application."
strMessage = strMessage & vbCrLf & "Error Number: " & lngErrNumber
strMessage = strMessage & vbCrLf & "Error Description: " & strErrDesc
strMessage = strMessage & vbCrLf & "Module Source: " & strModuleSource
strMessage = strMessage & vbCrLf & "Procedure Source: " & strProcedureSource
```

The error message is then displayed to the user:

```
'display the message to the user
MsgBox strMessage, vbCritical
```

This generic error handler can be called from every procedure you write, changing only those variables that specify the current module and procedure. Errors can also be logged to a table, written to a file, or e-mailed, but those options are beyond the scope of this book.

Summary

This chapter covered the basic VBA programming concepts. You learned that code can be placed in standard modules or class modules and that various coding statements can be placed in the modules for controlling the flow of execution, storing values, and so on. You also learned how to test and run your VBA code and to capture errors. These basic VBA coding techniques will serve as a foundation for all remaining chapters in the book. Now that you have a basic understanding of how to write VBA code statements, let's move on to Chapter 3, where you will explore the world of object-oriented programming.

Exercises

1. What is a module, and what are the different types of modules?

2. What is the difference between a sub procedure and a function? When should you use each one?

3. Describe at least three ways you can control the flow of code execution. Also describe how variables fit into controlling the flow of code execution.

4. Implementing naming conventions and code documentation are both good habits to practice. What value do they provide?

5. Describe the types of errors that you might encounter in your application and how to resolve them so that the program will operate and will provide users with informative error messages.

Programming Applications Using Objects

This chapter explains the basic concepts of the object-oriented programming environment, such as using objects in your programs. You will learn the definition of properties, methods, and events, and when to use each one. Because the code is encapsulated into objects with properties, methods, and events available for the objects — a concept called *object-oriented programming (OOP)* — you can build reusable objects that save a lot of development time. Coding is simplified because the system is organized into smaller sets of interrelated objects, instead of one huge object. Your code will be easier to maintain because it will be easier to understand.

Object-oriented programming is a scary concept for most people, but this chapter demonstrates that it's really not that complicated. After covering basic object-oriented programming concepts, you will also learn about several Microsoft Access objects and how to use them. Chapter 4 covers cover object-oriented programming in greater detail.

You may want to create a new database for use with examples in this chapter. From within Access, click the Office Button on the top left and select New. Enter the database file name as Ch3CodeExamples *in the panel on the far right side, and click Create. You can also simply click the New Database link when you first launch Access.*

Note that the file menu no longer says the word "File," but has a circular graphic in the upper-left corner of the screen called the Office Button.

Elements of an Object

Objects are all the things that make up your Access database, such as forms, reports, modules, macros, and tables. Each object has *properties* that determine its behavior or appearance, as well as *methods* that determine which actions can be taken upon it. Objects also respond to *events* that are triggered by actions taken by the user or caused by the system.

Some people tend to confuse a collection with an object. A *collection* comprises multiple objects. Thus, an object can be a member of a collection. Sometimes you may want to manipulate a specific object (for example, a particular form), whereas other times you may want to manipulate a collection of objects (all the forms in your database). Let's now turn to some of the most important concepts in the object-oriented programming world: properties, methods, and events.

What Is a Property?

Properties are characteristics of an object that determine its behavior or appearance. Examples of properties include the name, caption, or size of a control. Figure 3-1 shows various properties of a Form. This dialog box can be displayed when the Form is in design view and you select the Design ribbon ⇨ Property Sheet or press Alt+Enter. Note that some of the properties listed in the figure have selectable Yes/No values, some are text input fields like the Caption property, and others have different choices you can select from a drop-down list.

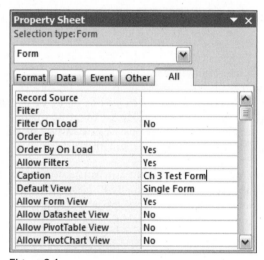

Figure 3-1

After setting the preceding Caption property to Ch 3 Test Form for this particular form and running the form, notice how the caption of the form (shown in Figure 3-2) is now set to the value that was in the Properties dialog box.

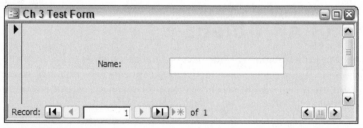

Figure 3-2

You can also select other objects on the form in the object drop-down list of the Properties Window, such as text box controls or labels, as shown in Figure 3-3.

As shown earlier, selecting another object from the list in the Properties dialog box allow you to view and modify its properties. Various objects share many of the same properties. For example, forms, text boxes, and labels all have a `Caption` property, as well as a `Name` property.

The Properties Window can be used to view and modify properties as well as events. This concept will be discussed later in the chapter.

Property Sheet	▼ ✕
Selection type: Section	
Detail	⌄
Detail	
Form	
lblName	
txtName	
Force New Page	None
New Row Or Col	None
Keep Together	No
Visible	Yes
Display When	Always
Can Grow	No
Can Shrink	No
Height	5.25"
Back Color	#FFFFFF
Alternate Back Color	No Color
Special Effect	Flat

Figure 3-3

The property values that are set in the Properties dialog box, such as the `Caption` property shown previously, are called *design time settings*. Design time settings are those you specify at design time that become the starting value settings for that object. The starting value can be modified at runtime in your VBA code, or at a later time in design view. For example, to change the `Caption` property of the preceding form at *runtime* while the program executes, you could use the following VBA command:

```
Forms.Item("frmTestProperties").Caption = "New caption goes here."
```

In addition to the Properties dialog box, another way to see the available properties for an object is by typing VBA code in the Visual Basic Editor. Figure 3-4 shows that as you type the name of an existing object and press the period key, the list of properties available for that object is displayed.

This feature is very helpful because it keeps you from having to memorize the exact syntax of every property. You just look up a property as you write your code.

The values in the list on Figure 3-4 are all properties, as is indicated by the icon showing a hand holding a card:

Other items can be present in the drop-down list as well, as I discuss later in this chapter. For now, be aware that you can see a list of properties available for an object within the Code window in the Visual Basic Editor (VBE).

Some objects are visual—such as forms, text boxes, labels, and reports. Other objects are not visual. The user sees nothing when those objects are used. An example of a nonvisual object is a recordset that holds data from a database. Although you may later display data from the recordset on a form, the object itself does not have a visual presence. Both visual and nonvisual objects can have properties.

Yet another way to view the properties available for an object is by using the Object Browser, discussed later in this chapter.

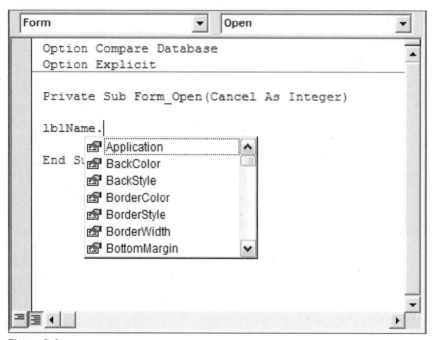

Figure 3-4

What Is a Method?

Methods are actions that can be taken on an object. They are really sub procedures or functions that are called to perform a particular action. You do not see the code behind sub procedures or functions when using existing Access objects, but they are there. An example of a method you have already used is:

```
Debug.Print
```

The programmers who wrote Microsoft Access created a `Debug` object to allow you to interact with the Immediate Window, as you have already done to test your code. Somewhere in the source code for the Debug object is a sub procedure or function called Print that receives the message to print as a parameter and then has code for displaying the message in the Immediate Window. Because Microsoft does not give you the source code for Microsoft Access, you do not see this code—but it's there. This is also true for objects created by other third parties—a sub procedure or function is behind the method.

Let's look at an example of how you can see what methods are available for an object. In the code window in the VBE (see Figure 3-5), you can type the object name followed by a period, just as you did before. You get a drop-down list that shows the available methods. Recall from the prior section, you can also use this feature to view the properties available for an object.

In the preceding example, you can see that the Recordset object has properties such as Name and NoMatch, but it also has various methods, such as MoveLast and MoveNext. You can tell whether the item in the list is a property or method based on the icon displayed to the left. You might say the icon for methods looks like a brick in motion:

You might describe the icon differently, but the point is that this icon indicates that the item in the list is a method. Recall that the hand holding the card is the icon for the Properties window. Another way to see the methods and properties available for an object is to use the Object Browser, as you will see later in this chapter.

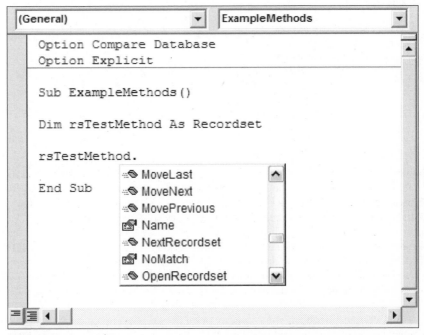

Figure 3-5

What Is an Event?

Events are triggered by actions taken by the user and the application, such as changes to data, mouse movements, or the opening of a form. You use VBA code or macros to respond to events. In other words, you link up the code you write with the user interface of your application through events. For example, you specify which VBA procedure or function to run when a particular event happens. This concept was illustrated briefly in Chapter 2 when you created new procedures and functions. Remember that you tied an event to a procedure so that the procedure would run? Let's look at some additional examples so this important concept will become totally clear.

One way to view a list of events available for a control is from the Properties dialog box that you saw earlier. As you recall, you can select the Design ribbon ⇨ Property Sheet from a designer, such as the form or report designer, to view the Properties dialog box. Events for form and report objects, such as controls, can be located by selecting the object and then viewing the Event tab of the Properties dialog box. Figure 3-6 shows the Event tab of the Properties dialog box for a form.

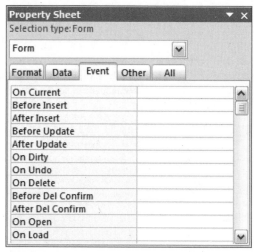

Figure 3-6

Notice how various types of events are listed. These events allow you to specify when the VBA code you write should execute. You actually have three options for how the event can execute. When you select a particular event from the list and click the Ellipsis button (...), a dialog box appears that gives you the option to use the Expression Builder, the Macro Builder, or the Code Builder.

In all the examples so far, you have used the Code Builder because this is a book about VBA code. If you choose Expression Builder, the value displayed in the Properties dialog box will be `"=expression"`, where *expression* is the expression that was entered in the Expression Builder window. If Macro Builder is chosen, the value is the name of the macro. If Code Builder is chosen, the value will be `"[Event Procedure]"`.

Like properties, various objects often have many or all the same events in common. For example, suppose that you have a form with a text box named `txtName` (that is, with the `Name` property set to `txtName`) that you will use to display a message to the user anytime the `On Key Press` event occurs. First, select the `txtName` text box on the form, and then select the Event tab of the Properties dialog box for the text box. Because you want to create an event procedure, select the Event Procedure option from the list that is shown in Figure 3-7 and then click the Ellipsis (...) button. If you click the Ellipsis (...) button without selecting the Event Procedure option, you will be prompted to select Code Builder from the list of three options.

When you click the Ellipsis button (...), the VBE opens with a new empty procedure created for the KeyPress event. Suppose that the following code is added to the KeyPress event for the txtName text box object:

```
Private Sub txtName_KeyPress(KeyAscii As Integer)

MsgBox "The KeyPress event just fired"
End Sub
```

When the form runs and something is typed into the txtName field, the message in Figure 3-8 is displayed.

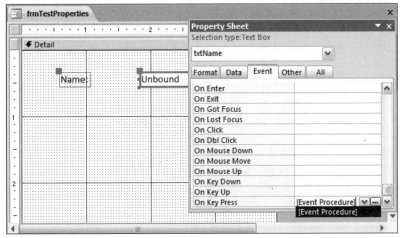

Figure 3-7

Figure 3-8

Notice that the event fires before you see the value in the text box on the form. Other examples of events commonly used are On Click, On Double Click, and On Open. So many types of events are available for a particular object that it is impossible to cover them all in this chapter. However, I hope you understand that an event allows you to hook up your forms and reports with the VBA code that you write based on certain events that occur in the application. I present another example momentarily, just to make sure you are clear on the difference between properties, methods, and events.

Try It Out   Using Properties, Methods, and Events

It's your turn now to try your hand at an example that uses properties, methods, and events. As you work, try to keep track of which items are properties, which are methods, and which are events. You can check your answers when I explain the example.

1. If you have not already done so, create a new database for use with examples in this chapter. To do so, select Office Button ⇨ New ⇨ Blank Database. Specify the file name as Ch3CodeExamples and click the Create button. You can close the empty table that opens by default, as you will not be using a table in this example.

2. Add a new form to the database. Select the Create ribbon and then the Blank Form icon to create a new form. To switch to design view, select the Format ribbon, and then Design View from the View list.

3. On the new form, use the ToolBox to select and draw a text box control and a command button on the form, as shown in Figure 3-9. The ToolBox is displayed on the Design ribbon, in the Controls area. You can select Cancel to the wizard dialog boxes that appear.

4. Select the text box control. Select the Design ribbon ⇨ Property Sheet to view the Properties dialog box if it is not already displayed. From the Properties dialog box for the text box control, select the All tab, and change the Name property to txtDateOfBirth.

5. Select the label. From the Properties dialog box, change the Name property of the label to lblDateOfBirth. Change the Caption property of the label to Enter Date of Birth:

    You may need to resize the label to display all its contents.

6. Select the Command button. From the Properties dialog box, change the Name property of the Command button to cmdCalculate, and change the Caption property to Calculate. The form should now look like the one shown in Figure 3-10.

7. Close the form to save it, and when prompted, specify the name frmTestObjects for the form. Reopen the form by selecting it in the Navigation Pane, and switch back to design view by selecting Home ribbon, and then Design View from the View list.

8. Select the txtDateOfBirth text box again. Select the Event tab of the Properties dialog box, and locate the On Exit event. Select the Code Builder option to open VBE to write code for the event. One way to do so is to choose Event Procedure in the drop-down list and then click the ellipsis (...). You can also select the Ellipsis button and then choose Code Builder from the dialog box that appears. In either case, add the following code to the Exit event:

```
Private Sub txtDateOfBirth_Exit(Cancel As Integer)

'if the user did not enter a date, then
'display an error and set the focus back
'to the date of birth text box control.
If Not IsDate(txtDateOfBirth.Text) Then
    MsgBox "You must enter a date for the Date of Birth field."
    txtDateOfBirth.SetFocus
    Cancel = True
End If

End Sub
```

9. Select the cmdCalculate command button. On the Event tab of the Properties dialog box, select the On Click event, then click the ellipsis, then Code Builder, and add the following code to the newly created event procedure as shown here:

```
Private Sub cmdCalculate_Click()

'declare local variable for month of birth
Dim intMonthOfBirth As Integer

'convert the value in the text box to a
'month and assign the value to the month
'of birth variable
intMonthOfBirth = DatePart("M", CDate(txtDateOfBirth))

'display a message to the user regarding
'the month of birth
MsgBox "Month you were born: " & intMonthOfBirth

End Sub
```

10. Click the Save button from the toolbar to save all the changes. Return to the frmTestObjects form in Access and click the Save button to save all changes on the form. Run the form by clicking the Home ribbon and clicking the Form View item on the View list.

11. Enter something in the text box other than a date (see Figure 3-11).

12. Now, click the Calculate button. The message should be similar to the one shown in Figure 3-12.

13. After you click the OK button, focus returns to the Date of Birth text box field. Type your date of birth (as shown in Figure 3-13).

14. Click the Calculate button. You should get a message box similar to the own shown in Figure 3-14.

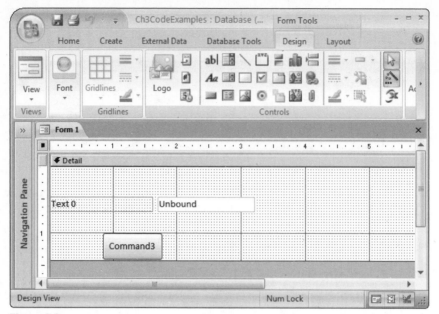

Figure 3-9

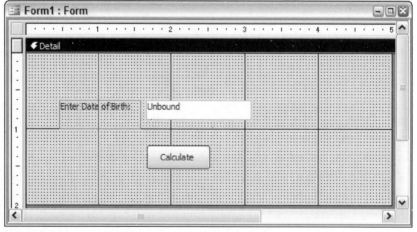

Figure 3-10

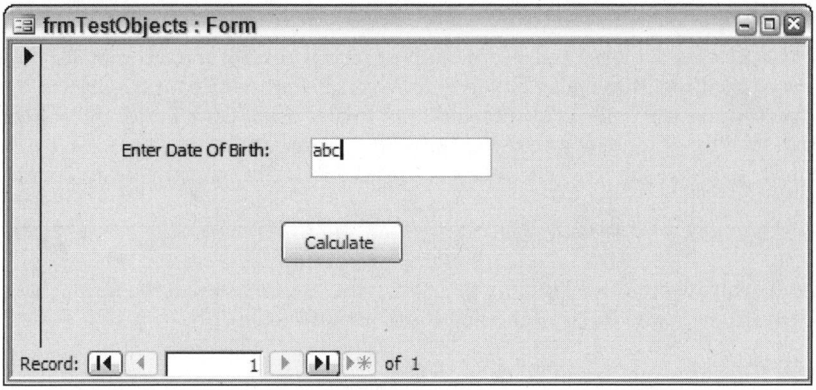

Figure 3-11

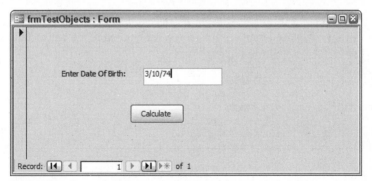

Figure 3-12

Figure 3-13

Figure 3-14

How It Works

You first created a new database and a form with a text box control and a command button control. Next, you used the Properties dialog box to specify various properties for the objects. You then created two event procedures, also called "event handlers," in the Visual Basic Editor by launching the Code Builder from the Properties dialog box. The first event procedure was for the `Exit` event of the txtDateOfBirth text box. The `Exit` event procedure accepts a `Cancel` variable as a parameter by default.

```
Private Sub txtDateOfBirth_Exit(Cancel As Integer)
```

The code will evaluate the value input by the user in the text box, and, if the format is not in a date format, a message is displayed to the user using the `msgbox` function.

```
'if the user did not enter a date, then
'display an error and set the focus back
'to the date of birth text box control.
If Not IsDate(txtDateOfBirth.Text) Then
    MsgBox "You must enter a date for the Date of Birth field."
```

The focus is then set back to the txtDateOfBirth text box, using the `SetFocus` method of the text box:

```
txtDateOfBirth.SetFocus
```

The `Cancel` parameter is then set to `True` to indicate that the event processing should stop because a problem exists. If you forget to set the `Cancel` parameter to `True`, other events that you may not want to fire will do so because the error occurred.

```
Cancel = True
```

The next event you added was the `Click` event for the cmdCalculate command button. The `Click` event first declares a local variable and then converts the value entered in the txtDateOfBirth text box to a month and stores that value in the local variable.

```
Private Sub cmdCalculate_Click()
'declare local variable for month of birth
Dim intMonthOfBirth As Integer

'convert the value in the text box to a
'month and assign the value to the month
'of birth variable
intMonthOfBirth = DatePart("M", CDate(txtDateOfBirth))
```

The code for displaying a message to the user is then listed. In this case, the message is created by concatenating the phrase `"Month you were born: "` with the value in the variable.

```
'display a message to the user regarding
'the month of birth
MsgBox "Month you were born: " & intMonthOfBirth
```

When you ran the form, you first entered an invalid date value in the text box and then clicked the Calculate button. The Exit event for the text box ran first and evaluated the value that you entered. Because the value was not a date, the error message was displayed, indicating that a date is required, and the mouse was positioned by the set focus event back to the txtDateOfBirth text box.

The second time, you entered a correct date value in the text box field and clicked the Calculate button. This time, the Exit event for the text box ran again but did not have any problems, so the application continued and processed the Click event for the Calculate button. The Click event procedure extracted the month from the date value you entered and then displayed that month to you in a message box.

It's now time for the quiz. Did you keep track of all the properties, methods, and events used in the example? If so, compare your list to the one that follows.

Type	Object	Property, Method, or Event
Property	txtDateOfBirth (text box)	Name
Property	lblDateOfBirth (label)	Name
Property	lblDateOfBirth (label)	Caption
Property	cmdCalculate (command button)	Name
Property	cmdCalculate (command button)	Caption
Event	txtDateOfBirth (text box)	On Exit
Event	cmdCalculate (command button)	On Click
Method	txtDateOfBirth (text box)	Set Focus

See, that wasn't so difficult, was it?

Viewing Objects Using the Object Browser

Now that you understand what objects and their respective properties, methods, and events are, let's look at another way to view objects. The *Object Browser* is a tool that allows you to view and manage the objects in your application. You can use the Object Browser to learn about the objects available in Access 2007 as well as objects available from almost any Windows program.

The Object Browser can be opened from the Visual Basic Editor in one of three ways: by choosing the Object Browser button on toolbar, by selecting View ➪ Object Browser, or by pressing F2. Any of these will result in a screen such as the one shown in Figure 3-15.

Notice how the Libraries drop-down list currently displays All Libraries. The values displayed in the Classes list are for the Classes of All Libraries. You can select a particular Library, such as Access, to limit the list of Classes and corresponding Class Members that are displayed (see Figure 3-16).

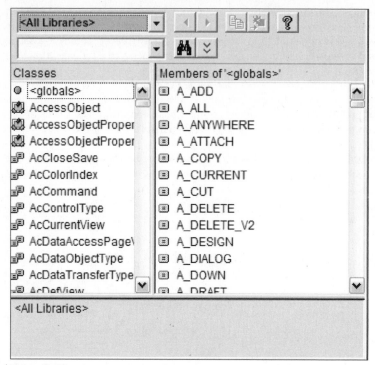

Figure 3-15

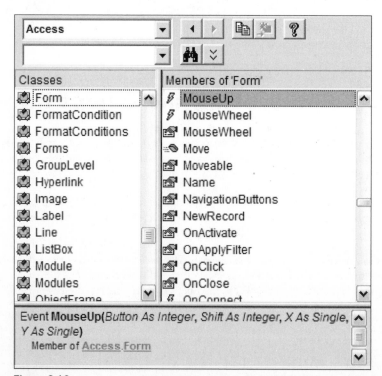

Figure 3-16

Notice how you can drill down into the Classes and view the properties, methods, and events available for the selected class. In the previous example, the Access Form class is selected, and you can see `MouseUp` and `MouseWheel` events (as indicated by the lightening bolt icon), various properties such as `MouseWheel`, and various methods such as `Move`. Notice how in this example the `MouseUp` event is selected, and you can see the syntax for the event in the bottom portion of the display. You can see why the Object Browser is a very useful tool for viewing and working with objects.

If you change the Libraries list to the current project (such as `Ch3CodeExamples`), you see the `frmTestObjects` form (see Figure 3-17).

Double-click on the `Form_frmTestObjects` class name to display a Code window showing the sub procedures and functions for that class module. In this example, you see the event procedures you created earlier in this chapter for the `frmTestObjects` form.

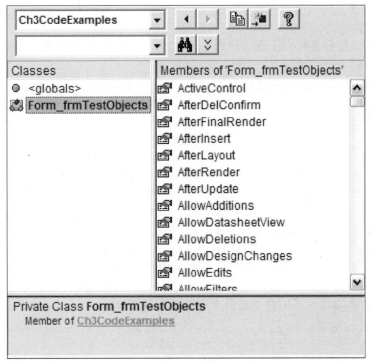

Figure 3-17

Ways to Refer to Objects

You should also know the various ways to refer to an object. Here are some examples:

```
Forms.frmTestObjects
Forms!frmTestObjects
Forms("frmTestObjects")
Forms(0)
```

Using the period (`Forms.frmTestObjects`) is my personal preference for most situations because you can see the list of available properties, methods, events, and constants as you type. You already saw this used with objects earlier in this chapter.

You can also refer to objects using the `Me` keyword as a shortcut. `Me` refers to the current object. So if you use `Me` in a form module, it refers to the form. Here is an example:

```
Me.txtDateOfBirth
```

An equivalent, but longer, version of the same statement is:

```
Forms.frmTestObjects.txtDateOfBirth
```

Only use the `Me` keyword when you want to refer to the existing object (not to a totally different object).

Using Access Collections and Objects

Earlier in this chapter, you briefly explored the difference between an object and a collection. To recap, collections can contain multiple objects. For example, you might use a forms collection to loop through all forms in the project, whereas you would refer to a particular form object when you wanted to deal with that specific form only.

Now that you have mastered the basic concepts of object-oriented programming and understand that objects are different from collections, let's look at some of the most useful collections and objects that come with Access. The examples in this section are by no means an exhaustive list, but they provide you with the most common collections. A complete list can be obtained in the Visual Basic help documentation from the Visual Basic Editor.

The `Application` object is at the top of the Access object model and refers to the active Access application. It contains all other objects and collections. The `Application` object contains several child objects that are very useful. Several `Application` object examples will now be described.

The Forms Collection and Form Object

The `Forms` collection of the `Application` object contains all forms in the application. A `Form` object refers to a specific form in the `Forms` collection. Let's look at an example.

Try It Out   **Using the Forms Collection and Form Object**

You can use the `Forms` collection and `Form` object to obtain a list of all the open forms in the application.

1. Create a new form for your database and switch to design view. Use the ToolBox shown in the Controls area of the Design ribbon to drag a list box control and a command button control onto the new form. You can select Cancel to any wizards that appear when you draw the controls.

2. Change the `Name` property of the list box control to `lstForms`.

3. Select the label for the list box. Set the Name property of the list box to lblForms and the Caption property to All forms in project:. Set the RowSourceType property of the list box to Value List.

4. Next, select the command button control. Set the Name property to cmdGetForms and the Caption property to Get List of Forms.

5. At this point, the form should look similar to the one shown in Figure 3-18.

6. Make sure to save the form by clicking the Save button and, when prompted, give the form the name frmTestForms.

7. Select the cmdGetForms command button and view the Properties dialog box. Select the Design ribbon ⇨ Property Sheet if the Properties dialog box is not already displayed. Select the Events tab of the Properties dialog box, and select the Code Builder option to add the new On Click event. Add the code below to the newly created On Click event procedure.

```
Private Sub cmdGetForms_Click()

Dim frmForms As Form

'loop through forms collection and
'add name of each open form to list box
For Each frmForms In Forms
    Me.lstForms.AddItem (frmForms.Name)
Next frmForms
End Sub
```

8. Save the code in the Visual Basic Editor and return to the design view of the form.

9. Run the form by selecting View from the toolbar. Click the Get List of Forms command button. You should see the names of all open forms displayed in the list box control, as shown in Figure 3-19.

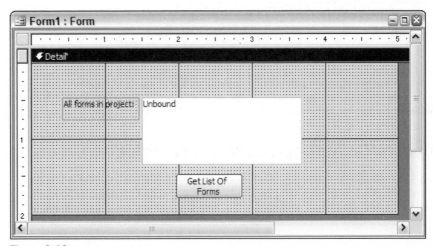

Figure 3-18

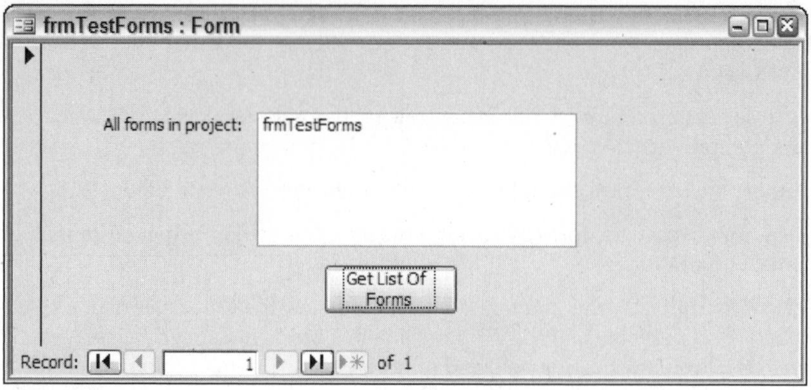

Figure 3-19

How It Works

First, you created a new form and added a list box object and a command button object to the form. You then set several properties of the list box and command button objects using the Properties dialog box. Next, you created an event procedure to run whenever the user clicks the cmdGetForms command button. The event procedure looped through the Forms collection to obtain a list of all open forms in the application and added the name of any open form to the list box.

```
Private Sub cmdGetForms_Click()

Dim frmForms As Form

'loop through forms collection and
'add name of each open form to list box
For Each frmForms In Forms
    Me.lstForms.AddItem (frmForms.Name)
Next frmForms

End Sub
```

More forms are included in the database than the one displayed. Is this an error? No, it is not. The reason you see the name of only one form in the list box is that it is the only form that is open. You can use the other collections and objects, whether or not they are open, as you will see in a later example.

The Reports Collection and Report Object

The Reports collection contains all the open reports in the application, and a Report object refers to a specific report. Look at another example. The modBusinessLogic standard module can be added to the database to store the sub procedures used in the remaining examples. Suppose that you have the following TestReports procedure in the modBusinessLogic standard module in your database.

```
Sub TestReports()

Dim rptReport As Report

'loop through each open report in the reports collection
```

```
'and display the name in the Immediate window
For Each rptReport In Reports
    Debug.Print rptReport.Name
Next rptReport

End Sub
```

Notice how a local variable called `rptReport` is first declared as a `Report` object, and then the program loops through each `Report` object in the `Reports` collection to print the name of the report to the Immediate Window. If any report is currently open in your database, you see the report name in the Immediate Window (after you run the preceding code) if you type `TestReports` and press Enter. Otherwise, you get a blank response to indicate that no reports are currently open.

The CurrentProject Object

The `CurrentProject` object of the `Application` object returns a reference to the current project. The `CurrentProject` object has various properties, such as `FullName` and `ProjectType`, as shown here:

```
Debug.Print Application.CurrentProject.FullName
Debug.Print Application.CurrentProject.ProjectType
```

These two lines of code will print the `FullName` and `ProjectType` properties of the current project to the Immediate Window. The `CurrentProject` object also has several collections, such as: `AllForms`, `AllReports`, `AllMacros`, and others. When you want to obtain a list of all forms in the project, regardless whether the form is open, you can use the `AllForms` collection. Here is an example:

```
Sub TestAllForms()

Dim objAccObj As AccessObject
Dim objTest As Object

'set the object equal to the Current Project
Set objTest = Application.CurrentProject

'loop through each form in the AllForms collection
'and print information about each Form to the
'Immediate Window.

For Each objAccObj In objTest.AllForms
    Debug.Print objAccObj.Name
Next objAccObj

End Sub
```

The preceding code declares a new instance of the `CurrentProject` object called `objTest`. Then, the name of each object that is a form in the `AllForms` collection of the `objTest` object is written to the Immediate Window.

The DoCmd Object

The `DoCmd` object can be used to perform nearly any macro command or menu option from VBA code. You have seen the `DoCmd` object in earlier chapters in examples that opened forms, such as the one that follows:

```
DoCmd.OpenForm "frmTestObjects"
```

The DoCmd object can also be used to open reports, go to a particular record, and obey numerous other commands that you issue from a menu option or a macro.

The Screen Object

The Screen object is used to refer to the form, datasheet, report, control, or data access page that currently has the focus. For example, to refer to the active control, you could use the following:

```
Screen.ActiveControl.Name
```

Let's look at another example.

Try It Out   Using the Screen Object

In this example, use the Screen object to obtain the name of the currently active form.

1. Open the frmTestForms form that was created earlier. Switch to the Visual Basic Editor and in the Immediate Window type the following:

```
? Screen.ActiveForm.Name
```

2. The name of the currently active form is displayed in the Immediate Window (see Figure 3-20).

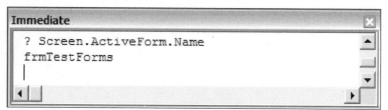

Figure 3-20

How It Works

In the current example, you used the Immediate Window to find the name of the active form on the screen, using the ? Screen.ActiveForm.Name command.

The Printers Collection and Printer Object

Another useful collection in the Application object is the Printers collection. The Printers collection is a collection of Printer objects and contains all printers available to an application. You can walk through an example to see how this works.

Try It Out   Using the Printers Collection and Printer Object

In this example, you use the Printers collection and Printer object to display the name of each printer device in the Debug window.

1. Add the following procedure to the `modBusinessLogic` standard module. If you have not yet created `modBusinessLogic`, do so by inserting a new module. Then add the following code to the new module:

```
Sub TestPrinter()

Dim prtAvailPrinters as Printer

For Each prtAvailPrinters In Application.Printers
    With prtAvailPrinters
        Debug.Print "Printer name: " & .DeviceName & "Printer driver: " & _
        .DriverName
    End With
Next prtAvailPrinters

End Sub
```

2. Run the `TestPrinter` procedure from the Immediate Window, and you will see a list of printers available on your computer, similar to Figure 3-21.

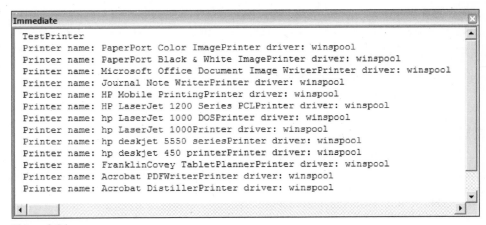

```
Immediate                                                                    ☒
TestPrinter                                                                  ▲
Printer name: PaperPort Color ImagePrinter driver: winspool
Printer name: PaperPort Black & White ImagePrinter driver: winspool
Printer name: Microsoft Office Document Image WriterPrinter driver: winspool
Printer name: Journal Note WriterPrinter driver: winspool
Printer name: HP Mobile PrintingPrinter driver: winspool
Printer name: HP LaserJet 1200 Series PCLPrinter driver: winspool
Printer name: hp LaserJet 1000 DOSPrinter driver: winspool
Printer name: hp LaserJet 1000Printer driver: winspool
Printer name: hp deskjet 5550 seriesPrinter driver: winspool
Printer name: hp deskjet 450 printerPrinter driver: winspool
Printer name: FranklinCovey TabletPlannerPrinter driver: winspool
Printer name: Acrobat PDFWriterPrinter driver: winspool
Printer name: Acrobat DistillerPrinter driver: winspool               ▼
◄                                                                    ►
```

Figure 3-21

How It Works

In this example, you created a new procedure to output a list of all printers on your computer. You started by creating a `TestPrinter` sub procedure in `modBusinessLogic` module.

```
Sub TestPrinter()
```

Next, you declared a local variable as a `Printer` object.

```
Dim prtAvailPrinters as Printer
```

Then, you used a `For Each` loop to iterate through all the `Printer` objects in the `Printers` collection and printed the device name and driver name of each `Printer` object to the Immediate Window.

```
For Each prtAvailPrinters In Application.Printers
    With prtAvailPrinters
        Debug.Print "Printer name: " & .DeviceName & "Printer driver: " & _
        .DriverName
    End With
Next prtAvailPrinters
```

The results of all printers on your computer were then displayed in the Immediate Window when you executed the procedure from the Immediate Window. It may take a few seconds for the complete list of printers to appear.

Other Objects

At this point, you should have an idea of the various ways you can use objects in your Access applications to perform various tasks. The `Application` objects that you are most likely to use as a beginning VBA programmer were illustrated. However, other `Application` objects in Access were not described in this chapter. Consult the Visual Basic help documentation from the Visual Basic Editor for more information.

Furthermore, numerous other libraries that contain useful objects are available for use in your Access applications. One example in Chapter 10 includes using Microsoft Office objects (such as the `CommandBar` object) that are common to all Microsoft Office programs. Chapter 10's example uses the Microsoft Office `CommandBar` object to customize the command bar you see in your applications. If you want to learn more about the objects that are available for use in your applications, consult the Object Browser to view them or review the Help documentation.

Summary

In the world of object-oriented programming, objects refer to all the things that make up your database, such as forms, reports, controls, and so on. By encapsulating code into objects, you make programs easier to maintain and code easier to reuse. Microsoft Access has several collections and objects that can be used to manipulate the objects contained in your database. For example, you can determine all the forms in your project for some useful purpose, or you can work with a particular form. With these object-oriented concepts in mind, turn to Chapter 4, where you will create custom objects.

Exercises

1. What are properties, methods, and events?

2. Name at least two ways that you can view the properties, methods, or events available for a given object.

3. What is the difference between the `Forms` collection and the `AllForms` collection?

Creating Your Own Objects

Now that you understand basic object-oriented programming concepts, you can turn your attention to the topic of creating your own objects. This chapter will provide a brief summary of what you have learned so far and will then teach you why and how to create custom class modules with associated properties, methods, and events. It will also cover how to extend existing objects, such as forms or controls, by adding custom properties, methods, and events. As with most other chapters, you can download the database containing the code for this chapter from Wrox.com.

Using Class Modules to Create Your Own Objects

As you have already learned, an object refers to all the things that make up your database, including forms, reports, and controls. By encapsulating code into objects, you make programs easier to maintain and code easier to reuse. You also have learned that objects can have properties, methods, and events. Properties are characteristics of the object, and methods are actions you take upon the object. Events are triggered when a user or application performs an action. These objects, which you worked with in Chapter 3, were created using class modules, although you did not see the proprietary source code for the Access objects.

You may remember from Chapter 2 that a class module is only one of the two types of modules; the other type is a standard module. Standard modules are modules that contain procedures that are not associated with any particular object. The procedures you wrote in the modBusinessLogic module in Chapter 2 were placed in a standard module. Class modules are modules that are associated with a particular object. Class modules can be used either for form or report modules or for custom objects. For example, form and report class modules can contain code that corresponds to a particular form or report, such as the event procedures for forms and controls that you wrote in the corresponding form class module in an earlier chapter. Since Access 97, class modules can also be created independently of a form or report and, in such cases, are used to create a definition for a custom object. This chapter will focus on using class modules for creating custom objects, as well as extending the class modules of existing objects with custom properties, methods, and events.

Go ahead and create a new database to use with the examples in this chapter. Select the Office Button ⇨ New ⇨ Blank Database and specify `Ch4CodeExamples` as the file name.

You can insert a new class module in three ways. One way is to select the Create ribbon from the toolbar, and then select Class Module in the area of the toolbar labeled Macro. The drop-down with the Create Module option displays Macro, Module, and Class Module as the options in the list. Another way to insert a new class module is from the Visual Basic Editor by selecting Insert ⇨ Class Module. A final way is to right-click on the Project Explorer from within the Visual Basic Editor and select Insert ⇨ Class Module from the pop-up menu.

Now that you have the empty database created, let's temporarily divert your attention to learn how custom objects should be documented using Class Diagrams during the design phase. I'll then give you the details on how to create custom objects.

Class Diagrams

Before jumping into the techniques for coding custom objects, you must understand how custom objects fit into the Systems Development Life Cycle and how to identify and document what custom objects you should create. You learned in Chapter 1 that during the design phase of your application you generate a written specification for how your application should be coded. Activity Diagrams, Use Case Diagrams, and screen prototypes are examples of some techniques that can be used to document your design. Class Diagrams are another documentation technique.

You are already well aware that an object can have properties, methods, and events. Your application should certainly make use of existing Access objects where possible, so that you do not have to rewrite code that the Microsoft programmers have already written for you. However, as appropriate, you should also take advantage of custom objects to maximize the unique features of your application. During the design phase, you should identify the custom objects for your application and document the custom objects using Class Diagrams.

Class Diagrams are critical in object-oriented system designs. They show the classes, relationships within the classes, and the way the code should be structured. In a Class Diagram, the properties and methods that make up an object are portrayed graphically. For example, in the case of the hypothetical Wrox Auto Sales Application described in Chapter 1, you deal with cars. Figure 4-1 shows the sample prototype screen for managing cars, as discussed in Chapter 1.

An object that you might want to create is a `Car` object. You could use a `Car` class to represent the `Car` object. The user interface is often a good starting point for determining properties and methods of an object. The `Car` object can have certain properties: Make, Model, Year, and so on, as the fields on the user interface indicate. In addition to these properties, the `Car` object needs methods that allow for retrieving, adding, updating, and deleting a specific record. These methods correlate to the Lookup, Add New, Save, and Delete buttons on the user interface.

Figure 4-2 shows an example Class Diagram for the Car `object`.

Notice that the properties for the Car class are listed first, followed by a divider line and then by the methods it contains. The Class Diagram in Figure 4-2 contains the tracked properties and the methods for which you must write code. When you create a new system, create a Class Diagram that depicts all objects in the entire system. This is not an easy task and requires effort and time to learn. For the sake of simplicity, I focus on writing custom properties, methods, and events for the Car class of the hypothetical Wrox Auto Sales.

A complete solution would contain other class modules as well, such as one for a Customer object or a SearchInventory object. The comprehensive case studies in Chapters 13 and 14 will include complete Class Diagrams for the respective systems and are excellent resources for refining your understanding of documenting and creating custom objects.

In Chapter 1, I mentioned that your code can be separated into three different logical tiers, even though Access is not used for physical three-tier applications. In most cases, it is a good idea to separate your code into different logical tiers. This makes it easier to update a particular portion of the application and migrate it to other platforms.

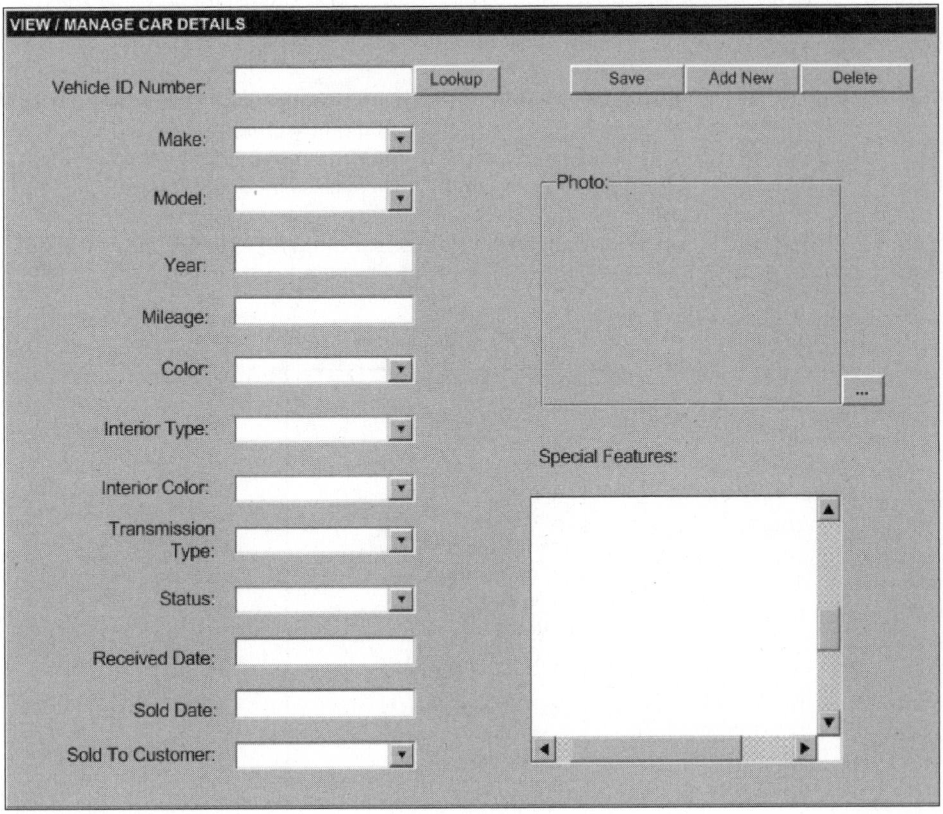

Figure 4-1

Returning to the Car class example, I will walk you through adding additional Class Diagrams based on the separation of tiers concept. You can actually create the Class Diagrams in any order you choose, but my personal preference is to start with the business logic layer first. The business logic layer is where you put your main classes like Car, and everything else revolves around it.

The Class Diagram in Figure 4-2 fits into the business logic layer. Now that you have created the business logic layer of the application, the other two remaining layers are really easy to create. Any call to the database will be included in a class in the data access layer. For each business logic layer class module that has a method requiring data from the database, you create a corresponding class module in the data access layer. Thus, the business logic layer (the Car class) will not make any calls directly to the database to get data. Instead, the Car class calls a method in a CarDb class in the data access layer, which, in turn, gets the data from the database, as you can see in Figure 4-3.

After creating the business logic layer and data access layer Class Diagrams, you create the diagrams for the presentation (user interface) layer. This is probably the easiest of the three to create, because you simply put each of your use cases on the diagram. Remember the use cases you created in Chapter 1 that defined each of the independent actions the user can take in the Wrox Auto Sales Application from the user interface? As Figure 4-3 illustrates, you can just list the use cases for the presentation layer class modules because the use cases define the user interface services to be performed.

Notice how each of the layers is connected appropriately to the others in the instances where they communicate with each other. For example, the Open Car action on the presentation layer calls the Retrieve method on the Car class, which in turn calls the RetrieveCarDb method on the CarDb class. The code to implement the presentation layer usually goes in class modules associated with the related form or report. The code to implement the business logic layer and data access layer ideally goes in custom class modules, although other variations are also possible and acceptable. I hope you are starting to see how this isolation of application logic into tiers works.

Car
-VehicleIdNumber
-MakeId
-ModelId
-Year
-Mileage
-ColorId
-InteriorTypeId
-InteriorColorId
-TransmissionTypeId
-StatusId
-ReceivedDate
-SoldDate
-SoldToCustomerId
-Photo
-Special Features
+Retrieve ()
+Add ()
+Update ()
+Delete()

Figure 4-2

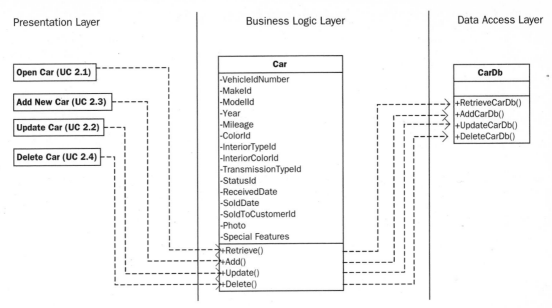

Presentation Layer · Business Logic Layer · Data Access Layer

Figure 4-3

At this point, don't worry about understanding the complex details of designing class modules for an entire application. You should just understand that Class Diagrams can be used to model the custom objects that you want to create. I now return to the discussion of creating custom objects, and show you how to write the code to implement the properties and methods listed on the `Car` object in Figures 4-2 and 4-3.

Creating Properties

To recap, properties are characteristics of an object. Properties for custom classes can be implemented using public variables or using `Property Let`, `Property Get`, and `Property Set` procedures, which are discussed next.

Using Public Variables

One way to create properties for a class is to use a public variable declaration in a class module. In Chapter 2, you learned how to write a public variable declaration. When you place a public variable declaration in the Declarations section of a class module, it becomes a property for that class. Here is an example:

```
Public VehicleIdNumber As Double
```

I do *not* recommend creating properties using public variables for several reasons. First, you cannot manipulate the value because the property is set. Second, you cannot create read-only and write-only properties. Third, you cannot easily validate what is assigned to public variables. The better way to create properties is discussed next and does not have these drawbacks.

Using Property Let, Property Get, and Property Set

Property Let, Property Get, and Property Set procedures enable you to create properties in a more flexible way than by using public variables. Property Let procedures determine what happens when you assign a value to the property. Here is a simple example showing the general syntax for a Property Let procedure:

```
Public Property Let TestProperty(ByVal strMessage As String)
    'code for assigning the property goes here
    strTestPropertyVal = strMessage
End Property
```

In many cases, you assign the value of the parameter passed to the property procedure to a variable that is declared in the Declarations section of the class. The Property Let procedure is a special type of procedure that is executed whenever you assign the property to another value in your code. For example, suppose that you have the following line of code:

```
TestProperty = "This is a new value for the property."
```

Because you are assigning the TestProperty property to a new value, the Property Let procedure will execute. In the current example, the string value listed in quotation marks is passed to the Property Let procedure as the strMessage parameter and is assigned to a strTestPropertyVal variable.

You can include much more than just a single assignment statement in a Property Let procedure. For example, you can perform validation checks or call other methods from within the Property Let procedure. The following example illustrates performing validation checks before assigning the property value.

```
Public Property Let TestProperty(ByVal strMessage As String)
    'if the length of the message is less than 25 then set the value
    If Len(strMessage) < 25 Then
        'code for assigning the property goes here
        strTestPropertyVal = strMessage
    Else
        Msgbox "The message for Test Property cannot exceed 25 characters!"
    End If
End Property
```

You can see in this example how using the Property Let procedure gives you greater flexibility than if you had declared the property as a public variable.

The Property Get procedure is used to specify what should happen upon retrieval of the property's value. Here is an example of the syntax used for a Property Get procedure:

```
Public Property Get TestProperty As String
    TestProperty = strTestPropertyVal
End Property
```

Notice how the name of the property is assigned to the local variable `strTestPropertyVal` that is being used to store the current value of the property. This is, in effect, a function that returns the value in the local variable upon request. Just like the `Property Set` procedure, the `Property Get` procedure can include additional code.

The `Property Set` procedure is used only to specify what should happen when the value of an object data type is assigned. In all other cases, you should use the `Property Let` procedure to specify what happens when properties are assigned values.

> *You can create read-only properties by eliminating the `Property Let` procedure and including only the `Property Get` procedure.*

It's time to try your hand at creating all the properties for the `Car` class of the Wrox Auto Sales Application that was analyzed earlier. You may want to refer to Figure 4-2 to see how the Class Diagram maps to the code you write.

Try It Out   Creating the Properties for the Car Class

1. If you have not already done so, create a new database for use with the examples in this chapter. To do so, select File ⇨ New ⇨ Blank Database. Specify the file name as `Ch4CodeExamples` and click the Create button.

2. Add a new class to the database. Open the Database Window and select the Create ribbon from the toolbar, then select Class Module in the area of the toolbar labeled Other. The drop-down with the Create Module option displays Macro, Module, and Class Module as the options in the list. In the Properties Window in the Visual Basic Editor, change the name of the class to `clsCar`.

3. Add the following declarations to the General Declarations section of the `clsCar` class:

```
Dim dblVehicleIdNumberVal As Double
Dim intMakeIdVal As Integer
Dim intModelIdVal As Integer
Dim intModelYearVal As Integer
Dim intMileageVal As Integer
Dim intColorIdVal As Integer
Dim intInteriorTypeIdVal As Integer
Dim intInteriorColorIdVal As Integer
Dim intTransmissionTypeIdVal As Integer
Dim intStatusIdVal As Integer
Dim dtReceivedDateVal As Date
Dim dtSoldDateVal As Date
Dim intSoldToPersonIdVal As Integer
Dim strPhotoVal As String
Dim strSpecialFeaturesVal As String
```

4.   Add the property procedures for `VehicleIdNumber` to the `clsCar` class:

```
Public Property Get VehicleIdNumber() As Double
    VehicleIdNumber = dblVehicleIdNumberVal
End Property

Public Property Let VehicleIdNumber(ByVal Value As Double)
    dblVehicleIdNumberVal = Value
End Property
```

5.   Add the property procedures for `MakeId` to the `clsCar` class:

```
Public Property Get MakeId() As Integer
    MakeId = intMakeIdVal
End Property

Public Property Let MakeId(ByVal Value As Integer)
    intMakeIdVal = Value
End Property
```

6.   Add the property procedures for `ModelId` to the `clsCar` class:

```
Public Property Get ModelId() As Integer
        ModelId = intModelIdVal
End Property

Public Property Let ModelId(ByVal Value As Integer)
    intModelIdVal = Value
End Property
```

7.   Add the property procedures for `ModelYear` to the `clsCar` class:

```
Public Property Get ModelYear() As Integer
        ModelYear = intModelYearVal
End Property

Public Property Let ModelYear(ByVal Value As Integer)
    intModelYearVal = Value
End Property
```

8.   Add the property procedures for `Mileage` to the `clsCar` class:

```
Public Property Get Mileage() As Integer
    Mileage = intMileageVal
End Property

Public Property Let Mileage(ByVal Value As Integer)
    intMileageVal = Value
End Property
```

9. Add the property procedures for `ColorId` to the `clsCar` class:

```
Public Property Get ColorId() As Integer
    ColorId = intColorIdVal
End Property

Public Property Let ColorId(ByVal Value As Integer)
    intColorIdVal = Value
End Property
```

10. Add the property procedures for `InteriorTypeId` to the `clsCar` class:

```
Public Property Get InteriorTypeId() As Integer
    InteriorTypeId = intInteriorTypeIdVal
End Property

Public Property Let InteriorTypeId(ByVal Value As Integer)
    intInteriorTypeIdVal = Value
End Property
```

11. Add the property procedures for `InteriorColorId` to the `clsCar` class:

```
Public Property Get InteriorColorId() As Integer
    InteriorColorId = intInteriorColorIdVal
End Property

Public Property Let InteriorColorId(ByVal Value As Integer)
    intInteriorColorIdVal = Value
End Property
```

12. Add the property procedures for `TransmissionTypeId` to the `clsCar` class:

```
Public Property Get TransmissionTypeId() As Integer
    TransmissionTypeId = intTransmissionTypeIdVal
End Property

Public Property Let TransmissionTypeId(ByVal Value As Integer)
    intTransmissionTypeIdVal = Value
End Property
```

13. Add the property procedures for `StatusId` to the `clsCar` class:

```
Public Property Get StatusId() As Integer
    StatusId = intStatusIdVal
End Property

Public Property Let StatusId(ByVal Value As Integer)
    intStatusIdVal = Value
End Property
```

14. Add the property procedures for `ReceivedDate` to the `clsCar` class:

```
Public Property Get ReceivedDate() As Date
    ReceivedDate = dtReceivedDateVal
End Property

Public Property Let ReceivedDate(ByVal Value As Date)
    dtReceivedDateVal = Value
End Property
```

15. Add the property procedures for `SoldDate` to the `clsCar` class:

```
Public Property Get SoldDate() As Date
    SoldDate = dtSoldDateVal
End Property

Public Property Let SoldDate(ByVal Value As Date)
    dtSoldDateVal = Value
End Property
```

16. Add the property procedures for `SoldToPersonId` to the `clsCar` class:

```
Public Property Get SoldToPersonId() As Integer
    SoldToPersonId = intSoldToPersonIdVal
End Property

Public Property Let SoldToPersonId(ByVal Value As Integer)
    intSoldToPersonIdVal = Value
End Property
```

17. Add the property procedures for `Photo` to the `clsCar` class:

```
Public Property Get Photo() As String
    Photo = strPhotoVal
End Property

Public Property Let Photo(ByVal Value As String)
    strPhotoVal = Value
End Property
```

18. Add the property procedures for `SpecialFeatures` to the `clsCar` class:

```
Public Property Get SpecialFeatures() As String
    SpecialFeatures = strSpecialFeaturesVal
End Property

Public Property Let SpecialFeatures(ByVal Value As String)
    strSpecialFeaturesVal = Value
End Property
```

19. Click the Save button on the toolbar to save your changes to the class.

How It Works

First, you created a new class module in the database and named it `clsCar`. You then added the local variables that are used later by the `Property Get` and `Property Set` procedures for each property, as shown in the following code.

```
Dim dblVehicleIdNumberVal As Double
Dim intMakeIdVal As Integer
Dim intModelIdVal As Integer
Dim intModelYearVal As Integer
Dim intMileageVal As Integer
Dim intColorIdVal As Integer
Dim intInteriorTypeIdVal As Integer
Dim intInteriorColorIdVal As Integer
Dim intTransmissionTypeIdVal As Integer
Dim intStatusIdVal As Integer
Dim dtReceivedDateVal As Date
Dim dtSoldDateVal As Date
Dim intSoldToPersonIdVal As Integer
Dim strPhotoVal As String
Dim strSpecialFeaturesVal As String
```

Next, you added `Property Get` and `Property Let` procedures for each property in the class. For example, you added `Property Get` and `Property Let` procedures to the `VehicleIdNumber` property to specify what happens whenever the property value is retrieved or assigned, respectively.

```
Public Property Get VehicleIdNumber() As Double
    VehicleIdNumber = dblVehicleIdNumberVal
End Property

Public Property Let VehicleIdNumber(ByVal Value As Double)
    dblVehicleIdNumberVal = Value
End Property
```

You can use this class later on in the chapter to see one or more of these properties in action.

Creating Methods

As you are aware, methods are actions that can be taken on an object. Methods for custom classes are implemented using public sub procedures and functions.

Using Public Sub Procedures and Functions

To implement a method for a custom class, you simply add a public sub procedure or function to the class itself. You are already familiar with creating new procedures, so creating a custom method will be really easy for you. To add a method called `TestMethod` to a class module, you simply add the following code:

```
Public Sub TestMethod()
    'code for the method goes here
End Sub
```

Now, create the four methods for the clsCar class: Retrieve, Add, Update, and Delete. You may wish to refer to Figure 4-2 to see how the Class Diagram maps to the code you write.

Try It Out   Creating the Methods for the Car Class

1.   Add the Retrieve method to the clsCar class:

```
Public Function Retrieve(ByVal VehicleId As Integer) As Recordset

    'Retrieve the detail record for the car from the database
    'code to call the data access layer that retrieves the record from
    'the database
    Debug.Print "clsCar.Retrieve method"
    Debug.Print "VehicleID: " & VehicleId & " will be retrieved from the database."

End Function
```

2.   Add the Add method to the clsCar class:

```
Public Sub Add()

    'Add the current values in the Car object to the database

    'code to call the data access layer that adds the record to the database

    Debug.Print "clsCar.Add method"
    Debug.Print "New record being added for VehicleId: " & Me.VehicleIdNumber
End Sub
```

Did you notice that when you typed Me and a period, all of your properties, class variables, and functions appeared? This command completion feature in Access and other Microsoft programming products is called Microsoft IntelliSense.

3.   Add the Update method to the clsCar class.

```
Public Sub Update()

    'Update the database with the current contents of the Car object

    'Code to call the data access layer that updates the existing
    'record in the database
    Debug.Print "clsCar.Update method"

    Debug.Print "Record being updated for VehicleId: " & Me.VehicleIdNumber

End Sub
```

4.   Add the Delete method to the clsCar class:

```
Public Sub Delete()

    'Delete the Car record from the database

    'Code to call the data access layer that deletes the record from the
    'database. Pass the VehicleId value as a parameter.
```

```
        Debug.Print "clsCar.Delete method"
        Debug.Print "Record being deleted for VehicleId: " & Me.VehicleIdNumber
    End Sub
```

5. Click the Save button on the toolbar to save your changes to the class.

How It Works

First, you created the `Retrieve` method of the `clsCar` class. The `Retrieve` method is responsible for calling the data access layer to look up a particular car record.

```
Public Function Retrieve(ByVal VehicleId As Integer) As Recordset
    'Retrieve the detail record for the car
    'from the database

    'code to call the data access layer that retrieves the record from
    'the database
```

For illustration purposes, the method includes code to print a message to the Immediate Window to let you know that the method executed.

```
        Debug.Print "clsCar.Retrieve method"
        Debug.Print "VehicleID: " & VehicleId & " will be retrieved from the database."

    End Function
```

Next, you created the `Add` method to handle adding a new car record to the database.

```
Public Sub Add()

    'Add the current values in the Car object to the database
    'code to call the data access layer that adds the record to the database
```

Again, the method includes code to print a message to the Immediate Window to let you know that the method executed.

```
        Debug.Print "clsCar.Add method"
        Debug.Print "New record being added for VehicleId: " & Me.VehicleIdNumber

    End Sub
```

The `Update` and `Delete` methods are created in similar ways. One or more of these methods will be used in later examples. Now turn your attention to events.

Creating Events

Events occur in response to an action taken by the user or the system. Custom events can be created in class modules, but they must also be *raised* (fired) in code or the event will never happen.

Declaring and Raising Events

First, you must declare and raise the event. An event declaration can be added to the General Declarations section of the class module as shown here:

```
Public Event EventName(VariableName As DataType)
```

After the event has been declared, you add code to a procedure in your class module to raise the event when a certain action happens. Events are raised with the RaiseEvent statement. To see how this works, create an event for the Car class.

Try It Out   **Creating an Event for the Car Class**

1.   Declare the event with the PublicEvent statement in the General Declarations section of the clsCar class module.

```
Public Event ActionSuccess(strMessage As String)
```

2.   Modify the existing Update method in clsCar to include the following additional code:

```
Public Sub Update()
    'Update the database with the current contents of the Car object

    'Code to call the data access layer that updates the existing
    'record in the database

    Debug.Print "clsCar.Update method"
    Debug.Print "Record being updated for VehicleId: " & Me.VehicleIdNumber

    'raise the ActionSuccess event
    RaiseEvent ActionSuccess("Updates to existing record saved successfully!")
End Function
```

How It Works

First, the event was declared in the class module by using the Public Event statement. Next, code was added to the existing Update method to raise the event. At this point, the code will not result in any action when the event fires. To create the action, take the following additional steps.

Creating the Event Sub Procedure or Function

You must write code that executes when an event is raised. In Chapter 3, you had to create event procedures to specify what should happen when an event occurs. You now use the same process for custom objects.

In the General Declarations section of the object where you wish to handle the event, you declare the object variable for the class that causes the event using the WithEvents keyword:

```
Dim WithEvents objCar As clsCar
```

After the object has been declared using WithEvents, the Visual Basic Editor displays the object in the list of objects and displays the event in the procedure drop-down list, just as it would for any other object. You can select the object and event from the list, and the code template is automatically specified. You then add the code that you want to run when the event occurs.

```
Private Sub objCar_ActionSuccess(strMessage As String)

'code to execute when event occurs goes here

End Sub
```

You will actually create the event in the sample database momentarily, but first I want to cover a few other topics necessary to write the sample code to handle the event.

Using the Class

After writing the code for the class module, you can use the class from other places in your application.

Instantiating the Class

To use a class module in your application, you first must use the `Dim` statement to declare the class and a `Set` statement to create a new instance of the class, as shown here:

```
Dim objCar As clsCar

Set objCar = New clsCar
```

As you will see in a moment, the preceding lines of code do not have to be contained in the same procedure. After the class has been instantiated, it becomes an object in memory.

Initialize and Terminate Events

Each class has `Initialize` and `Terminate` events that can be used. These events should be used when you want certain code to run each time the class is created or destroyed. Now return to the hypothetical Wrox Auto Sales application example and try out the properties, methods, and event of the `clsCar` class.

Try It Out	Using the Properties, Methods, and Events of the Car Class

1. Return to the database window and create a new form. To do so, select the Create ribbon, and then New Form. Switch to design view by selecting the Home ribbon, and then Design View from the View drop-down list. Use the controls on Design ribbon to select and draw one text box and four command buttons on the new form, as shown in Figure 4-4. Click cancel on the wizards that open as you draw the buttons on the form, as you do not need them.

2. Change the `Name` property of the text box to `txtVehicleId`. Change the `Name` property of the label to `lblVehicleId` and the `Caption` property to `Vehicle Id:`. Change the `Name` properties of the command buttons to `cmdLookup`, `cmdSave`, `cmdAddNew`, and `cmdDelete`, respectively. Change the `Caption` properties of the command buttons to `Lookup`, `Save`, `Add New`, and `Delete`, respectively. Figure 4-5 shows how the form should look at this point.

3. Select the Save button on the Toolbar of the Form Designer to save the form. Name the form `frmCarDetails`.

4. From the Properties dialog box of the Form, select the On Load event on the Events tab. Use the Code Builder to add an empty event procedure for the On Load event, as shown here:

```
Private Sub Form_Load()
End Sub
```

5. For the moment, leave the Form_Load event empty and add the following code to the General Declarations section of the frmCarDetails class:

```
Dim WithEvents objCar As clsCar
```

6. Return to the Form_Load event and add the following code:

```
Private Sub Form_Load()

'create a new instance of the car class to use while the form is open
Set objCar = New clsCar

End Sub
```

7. Add the following Click event to the frmCarDetails class:

```
Private Sub cmdLookup_Click()

'set the value of the VehicleId in the car object
'to the current value in the text box on the form
objCar.VehicleIdNumber = txtVehicleId

'call the Retrieve method
objCar.Retrieve (objCar.VehicleIdNumber)

End Sub
```

8. Add the following Save event to the frmCarDetails class:

```
Private Sub cmdSave_Click()

'add the values in the car object to the database
objCar.Update

End Sub
```

9. Add the following ActionSuccess event to the frmCarDetails class:

```
Private Sub objCar_ActionSuccess(strMessage As String)

    'display the message to the user
    MsgBox strMessage

End Sub
```

10. Save all your changes by clicking the Save button on the Visual Basic Editor. Also, return to your form and click the Save button on the Form Designer toolbar.

11. Run the form by selecting the Home ribbon, and then Form View from the View area. Enter a value for the VehicleId text box on the form, as shown in Figure 4-6.

12. Click the Lookup button. The Immediate Window of the Visual Basic Editor will display information similar to that shown in Figure 4-7.

13. Return to the form and click the command button labeled Save. The Immediate Window of the Visual Basic Editor will display information similar to that shown in Figure 4-8.

If the Immediate Window is not open, then go to the View Menu and select Immediate.

14. A message box similar to the one shown in Figure 4-9 is then displayed.

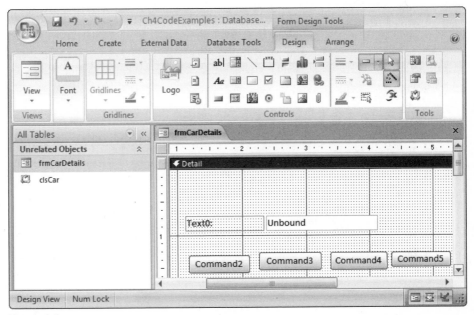

Figure 4-4

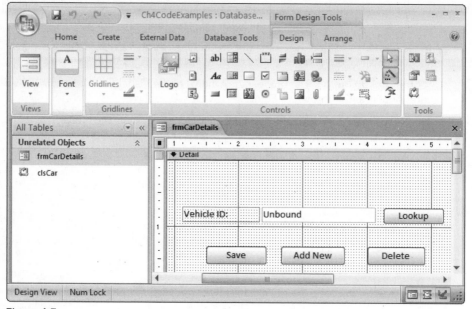

Figure 4-5

Figure 4-6

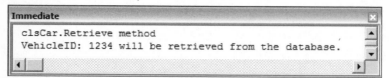

Figure 4-7

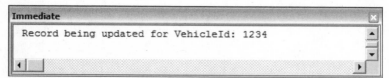

Figure 4-8

Figure 4-9

How It Works

You started by creating a new form called `frmCarDetails` and adding a text box control and four command buttons. The text box control is used to enter and display the Vehicle ID, and the four command buttons are used for Lookup, Save, Add New, and Delete functionality. After modifying various properties for the controls, you declared an `objCar` variable to store an instance of the `clsCar` class. Notice that the `WithEvents` keyword is used as part of the declaration so that the form can detect the custom event when it occurs.

```
Dim WithEvents objCar As clsCar
```

As shown in Figure 4-10, as you typed the declaration for the object, the name of the `clsCar` class that you created appeared in the drop-down list along with existing objects that you did not create.

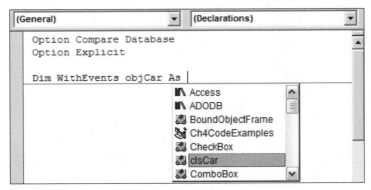

Figure 4-10

The code to instantiate the class was then added to the `Form_Load` event of the `frmCarDetails` class.

```
Private Sub Form_Load()

'create a new instance of the car class to use while the form is open
Set objCar = New clsCar

End Sub
```

You then added code for the `Click` event of the `cmdLookup` button of the `frmCarDetails` class. In this event, when the user clicks the Lookup button on the form, the `VehicleIdNumber` property of the `objCar` class is assigned the value from the text box on the form. The `Retrieve` method is then called.

```
Private Sub cmdLookup_Click()

'set the value of the VehicleId in the car object
'to the current value in the text box on the form
objCar.VehicleIdNumber = txtVehicleId

'call the Retrieve method
objCar.Retrieve (objCar.VehicleIdNumber)
End Sub
```

As you entered the code to set the `VehicleIdNumber` property, a drop-down list (as shown in Figure 4-11) appeared and displayed all the properties and methods for your custom class. Pretty cool, huh? Those are properties and methods that you created.

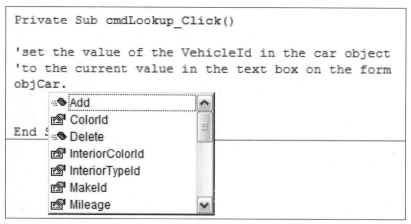

Figure 4-11

You then added the `Save` event to the `frmCarDetails` class to call the `Update` method when you click the Save button on the form.

```
Private Sub cmdSave_Click()

'add the values in the car object to the database
objCar.Update

End Sub
```

Next, you added the `ActionSuccess` event to the `frmCarDetails` class. This is a custom event that is raised in the `clsCar` class from the `Update` method. After the event is raised, the following code runs:

```
Private Sub objCar_ActionSuccess(strMessage As String)

'display the message to the user
MsgBox strMessage
End Sub
```

Next, you ran the form, entered a value for the VehicleId text box on the form, and selected the Lookup button. The Immediate Window then displayed the messages indicating that the Retrieve method of the clsCar object had executed. After you clicked the Save button on the form, the Immediate Window displayed messages indicating the Update method had executed, and displayed a message box indicating that the record was successfully updated. Remember that this is the code you previously added to the Update method to raise the custom event ActionSuccess. In just these few steps, you not only tested the properties, methods, and event for your custom object, but you also used several properties, methods, and events for the existing objects.

Note that the example used for the frmCarDetails form illustrated just a partial set of the controls that would be included on the production version of the Manage Cars screen. Only the VehicleIdNumber field was used for sake of simplicity.

Advanced Techniques

Now that you have a basic idea of how to use class modules to create your own objects with properties, methods, and events, you can delve into some advanced techniques.

Creating Multiple Instances of the Class

You already learned how to declare and create an instance of a class using the Dim and Set statements. The following example illustrates how you can create multiple instances of the same class when adding this code to the class module for frmCarDetails.

```
Public Sub TestMultipleInstances()

'declare both clsCar objects
Dim objCar1 As clsCar
Dim objCar2 As clsCar

'instantiate new instances for each
Set objCar1 = New clsCar
Set objCar2 = New clsCar
'set the VehicleId property for the first instance
'of clsCar and then call the previously created
'update method as an example
objCar1.VehicleIdNumber = "98765"
objCar1.Update

'set the VehicleId property for the second instance
'of clsCar and then call the previously created
'update method as an example
objCar2.VehicleIdNumber = "12345"
objCar2.Update

End Sub
```

Notice how two different `clsCar` objects are declared and instantiated. The `VehicleIdNumber` property of each instance of the class is assigned, and the `Update` method of each instance of the class is called.

As shown in Figure 4-12, the Immediate Window displays the messages generated from the `Update` method indicating that the record was being updated for each respective instance of the class.

```
Immediate                                              ☒
    Form_frmCarDetails.TestMultipleInstances      ▲
    clsCar.Update method
    Record being updated for VehicleId: 98765
    clsCar.Update method
    Record being updated for VehicleId: 12345     ▼
 ◀ |                                            | ▶
```

Figure 4-12

Creating Class Hierarchies

Classes can be related to each other in parent-child class relationships called *class hierarchies*. Suppose that you have an object called `Orders` that contains overall details about a particular order placed for products, and you also have an object called `OrderDetails` that contains details about a particular individual product within that order. The `Orders` object can contain multiple `OrderDetails` objects. To relate the `Orders` object to the `OrderDetails` object, place a declaration of the child class in the General Declarations section of the `Orders` object, as shown here:

```
Public ItemDetails As OrderDetails
```

You then use the `Set` statement to instantiate the `OrderDetails` class just as you do for the `Orders` class.

Working with Enumerated Types

Enumerated types can be used when you want to require a property value to be limited to a specified list of constants. Suppose that you have the following code in the General Declarations section of a `clsCar` object:

```
Public Enum SpecialFeaturesList
    SunRoof
    MoonRoof
    NavigationSystem
    IntegratedPhone
    Other
End Enum
```

In the property declarations, you see the `SpecialFeaturesList` enumerated type in the list of objects available, as shown in Figure 4-13.

The `Property Get` and `Property Let` procedures using the `SpecialFeaturesList` enumeration look like this:

```
Public Property Get SpecialFeatures() As SpecialFeaturesList
    SpecialFeatures = SpecialFeaturesVal
End Property

Public Property Let SpecialFeatures(ByVal Value As SpecialFeaturesList)
    SpecialFeaturesVal = Value
End Property
```

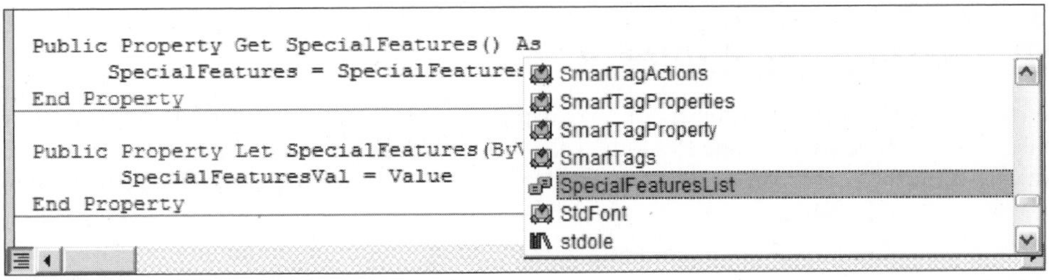

Figure 4-13

Now anytime you try to set that property using an assignment statement, you are limited to those values specified in the enumeration declaration, as shown in Figure 4-14.

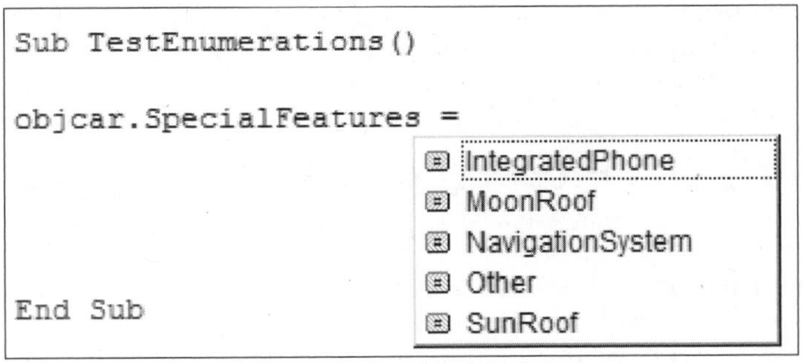

Figure 4-14

Inheritance Using Implements Keyword

Access allows for a type of inheritance called *interface inheritance*. Interface inheritance allows you to adopt the properties and methods of another object. This feature is implemented using the `implements` keyword, as shown here:

```
Implements clsCar
```

If the preceding code is placed in the General Declarations section of a new class module, you will see the clsCar object in the Object drop-down list, as well as the properties and methods of the clsCar object. You can then select a particular property or method and write the code for that property or method. This is a big drawback to interface inheritance — it requires you to write the code to implement those properties and methods. True inheritance (supported in more advanced programming languages, such as Visual C++, Visual Studio .NET, and Visual Studio Tools for Office) enables you to inherit all the properties and methods from another class, including all the code that goes with it.

Create Custom Properties for Existing Objects

Now that you have worked with existing objects and created your own objects, you will see a few ways to extend existing objects, giving them additional properties, methods, or events. Start by looking at how to create custom properties for existing objects.

Using Existing Tag Property

One way to create a custom property for an existing object is to use the Tag property. The Tag property is only used when you write code to set the value and then use that value later for some specified purpose. For example, you might use the Tag property to hold a value and then retrieve that value at a later time.

Using Public Variables

As described earlier, when you create properties for your custom objects, you can also create properties for existing objects, using public variables. To do so, just add the public variable declaration to the class module of the existing object, such as an existing class for a form. Again, this is *not* the recommended way to create properties. As discussed previously, I do not recommend this approach for three primary reasons. First, you cannot manipulate the value because the property is set; second, you cannot create read-only and write-only properties; third, you cannot easily validate what is assigned to public variables. A better way to create properties, discussed next, does not have these drawbacks.

Using Property Let, Property Get, and Property Set Routines

You can use the Property Let, Property Get, and Property Set procedures to create properties for existing objects. Again, you can do this just as you did for your own objects, only you add the PropertyLet and PropertyGet procedure to the existing object. Now add a new property to the frmCarDetails form to see how this works.

Try It Out   **Adding New Property for frmCarDetails Form**

1.   From the Visual Basic Editor, select the frmCarDetails class module. Add the following declaration to the General Declarations section of the class:

```
Dim strTestPropertyVal As String
```

2.   Also from the frmCarDetails class module, add the following property procedures:

```
Public Property Get TestProperty() As String
    TestProperty = strTestPropertyVal
End Property

Public Property Let TestProperty(ByVal Value As String)
    strTestPropertyVal = Value
End Property
```

3.   In the `frmCarDetails` class module, add a new procedure called `ShowTestProperty` and type the `Me` keyword followed by a period, as shown in Figure 4-15. Note that the `TestProperty` that you just added in Step 2 now appears, and you can select it from the list and assign it a value if desired. You can delete the `ShowTestProperty` procedure, as it was just used to show you that the new property you just added is now available.

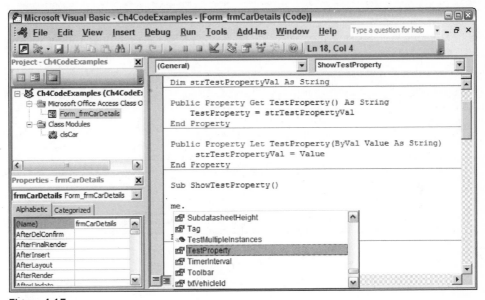

Figure 4-15

How It Works

First, you added the property procedures to the existing `frmCarDetails` form. Then, when you referred to `frmCarDetails` in code, you saw that the custom property you just added was in the drop-down list along with the other original properties.

Properties can be added to nearly any existing object. Custom properties that you add are not illustrated in the Properties panel, but are visible in the Code window as shown in Figure 4-15.

Create Custom Methods for Existing Objects

In addition to custom procedures, custom methods can also be created for existing objects by using public sub procedures or functions.

Using Public Sub Procedures and Functions

Custom methods can be created just as you created methods for your own objects, only you add a public sub procedure or function to the existing object. Now add a new method for the `frmCarDetails` form to see how this works.

Try It Out   **Adding New Method for the frmCarDetails Form**

1. From the Visual Basic Editor, select the `frmCarDetails` class module. Add the following method to the class:

```
Public Sub TestMethod()

MsgBox "This is a test method added to an existing object"

End Sub
```

2. From the `frmCarDetails` class module, add a new procedure called `DemonstrateCustomMethods` and type the `me` keyword followed by a period, as shown in Figure 4-16.

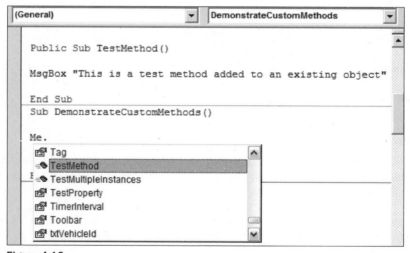

Figure 4-16

How It Works

First, you added the new method to the existing `frmCarDetails` form. Then, when you referred to `frmCarDetails` in code using the `me` keyword, you saw that the custom method you just added was in the drop-down list along with the custom property you just created and the original properties and methods. Just like properties, methods can be added to nearly any existing object.

Summary

In this chapter, you learned how to create a Class Diagram to model the classes and their relationships. Class diagrams provide a roadmap of your code structure. Ideally, Class Diagrams should be separated into a presentation layer, business logic layer, and data access layer. The presentation layer can map to your Use Case Diagrams. The business logic layer is the heart of your Class Diagram and contains the class modules that are the heart of your application. The business logic layer calls the data access layer for any activities that need communication with the database.

You then looked at several examples of how to create properties, methods, and events for custom objects. Custom properties can be created using public variable declarations in a class module. A preferred way of creating custom properties is to write public `Property Get` and `Property Let` procedures in the class module. `Property Get` procedures determine what happens when the property value is retrieved, and `Property Let` procedures determine what happens when the property is assigned. After you write the code for a custom object, the object can be used from other class modules or procedures by declaring the object and instantiating the object. The properties, methods, and events can be accessed in the custom object from the Visual Basic Editor Code window just like existing objects. You create custom methods by adding public procedures or functions to the class module. You can also add additional properties and methods to existing objects in the same way that you create your own properties and methods for objects. The only difference is that you place the code in the class module for the existing object, such as a form.

Now that you have learned how to work with existing objects and how to create your own objects, it's time to learn how ActiveX Data Objects (ADO) can be used in your applications to interact with data in your database.

Exercises

1.   What is a Class Diagram and why is it useful?

2.   Explain how you can create custom properties and methods.

3.   How can you add additional properties and methods to existing objects?

Interacting with Data Using ADO and SQL

In this chapter, you turn your attention to one of the most important concepts in Access programming: working with data in databases. Data is, after all, at the heart of almost every application. Programmers typically write applications to enable users to interact with data in meaningful ways. You have probably created Access applications yourself that retrieve data using forms that are bound directly to tables.

This chapter expands your knowledge of working with data by covering the basics of retrieving and modifying data from VBA code using ActiveX Data Objects (ADO). You will create the same contact form in three different ways so that you can see the various approaches to interaction with the same underlying data source. I will also cover the basics of writing SQL statements to interact with the database. The chapter ends with a brief section on the ADOX object model that can be used to manage database objects such as tables, users, and groups.

Introduction to Data Access

ADO is an acronym for ActiveX Data Objects. DAO stands for Data Access Objects. Both ADO and DAO allow you to manipulate databases from your Access 2007 VBA code.

The prior editions of this book with Access 2002 and earlier covered DAO in detail. DAO has been around since the earliest versions of Access and has always been an excellent data access method for working with native Access data.

ADO is a better choice for building sophisticated, multiuser applications or applications that interact with databases other than Access. It appears that DAO is being phased out, and most books and other resources you find on the topic recommend that ADO be used for all new development. I agree with this recommendation and have, therefore, in both the prior 2003 edition of the book and now with this 2007 edition continued to focus the examples on ADO. If you are dealing with older Access applications that have DAO code, consult the 2002 or prior editions of this book for a comprehensive explanation of DAO, or the online help documentation built into Access and the VBA Editor.

> *ADO should not be confused with ADO.NET. ADO.NET is a version of ADO that is designed to work with the Microsoft Visual Studio .NET development environment. Although ADO and ADO.NET have a lot of features in common, they are also different in numerous ways. In the future, it is possible that Microsoft will integrate the ADO.NET functionality into Microsoft Access to replace ADO, but such integration is not a certainty. Visual Studio Tools for Office (VSTO) uses ADO.NET. If you plan to use .NET in the future for your development or are already a .NET developer, then you should concentrate on ADO.NET.*

Using ADODB to Work with Data

In this section, you will explore the ADO object model and how to use the objects therein to work with data in underlying databases.

The ADO Object Model

Figure 5-1 provides an overview of the ADO object model. At the highest level of the object model, several collections exist: `Connection`, `Recordset`, `Command`, `Record`, and `Stream`.

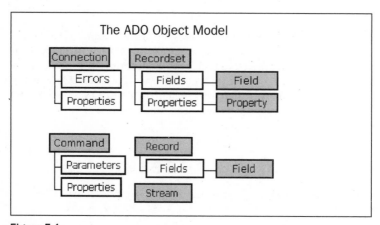

Figure 5-1

The ADO object library is sometimes referred to as the ADODB library. In order to use the features of ADO, you must have a reference to one of the ADO library versions in your project. You can add a reference to an ADO library by selecting Tools ➪ References from Visual Basic Editor and choosing a library from the list. Figure 5-2 shows an example with a reference set to version ADO version 2.7.

Several versions of ADO may exist on your computer, such as 2.1, 2.5, 2.7, and 2.8. The version you choose for your project depends on the version of Access that others in your organization are using.

If everyone is using Access 2007 or higher, you should use version 2.8. If everyone is using Access 2002 or higher, you should use version 2.7. If some people are using Access 2000, then you may want to use ADO version 2.5. If some are using Access 97, you may want to use ADO version 2.1.

The examples in this book use ADO 2.8 and earlier. There may be other releases of ADO that come with later versions of Windows and/or Office in the near future. The code examples used herein should still work in the same or similar fashion if you are using one of these later releases.

The Connection Object

The Connection object is the highest level of the ADO object model. The Connection object allows you to establish a connection to a data source. You must declare a Connection object before you can use it, as shown here:

```
Dim cnConnection as ADODB.Connection
```

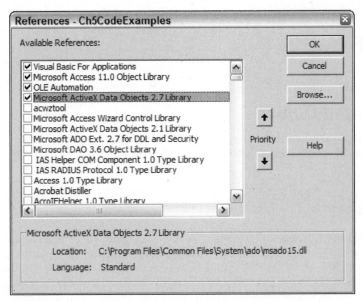

Figure 5-2

After declaring a Connection object, you must then instantiate a new Connection object, as follows:

```
Set cnConnection = New ADODB.Connection
```

Once instantiated, a Connection object can be opened to connect to Access and other databases. You open a connection by using the Open method of the Connection object. The Open method accepts various parameters, including a connection string, user id, password, and options.

Connecting to Access Databases

You specify the data source for the connection using a connection string. The connection string is then used in the Open method to open the data source. In the following example, the connection string connects to the Microsoft Access database for the current project called Ch5CodeExamples.mdb:

```
Dim strConnection As String
strConnection = "Provider=Microsoft.ACE.OLEDB.12.0;" & _
                "Data Source=" & CurrentProject.Path & "\Ch5CodeExamples.accdb;"
cnConnection.Open strConnection
```

Connecting to Other Databases

Access can be used as a front end to various other databases, such as SQL Server. The example that follows shows a connection string that you might use to connect to a SQL Server database called Pubs on an instance named SQLServerName using integrated Windows security:

```
Dim strConnection As String

strConnection = "Provider=sqloledb;Data Source=SQLServerName;" & _
                "Integrated Security=SSPI;Initial Catalog=Pubs"

cnConnection.Open strConnection
```

The Command Object

The Command object represents a SQL statement, query, or stored procedure that is executed against a data source. Just like a Connection object, you must declare and instantiate a Command object before you can use it:

```
Dim cmdCommand As ADODB.Command
Set cmdCommand = New ADODB.Command
```

After a new Connection object is instantiated, you can assign the Command object to an open connection and call the Execute method to execute a SQL statement, query, or stored procedure against the data source. This concept will be illustrated in more detail later in this chapter when you create SQL statements and use ADO to execute them. In addition, the comprehensive case study in Chapter 14 that deals with SQL Server will illustrate how to use the Command object to pass parameters to SQL Server stored procedures.

The Recordset Object

The Recordset object allows you to retrieve a set of records from a data source based on specified criteria. Recordsets can either be connected or disconnected. With connected recordsets, a connection to the database is maintained, and changes to the recordset are made to the underlying data source. With disconnected recordsets, the connection from the database is closed, and you work with a local copy of the information. You can use both connected and disconnected recordsets to display data to a user on a form, for example. Examples later in this chapter will illustrate the difference between connected and disconnected recordsets.

Creating a Recordset

As you did with a `Connection` object, you have to declare and instantiate a `Recordset` object before you can use it:

```
Dim rsRecordset As ADODB.Recordset
Set rsRecordset = New ADODB.Recordset
```

Next, you use the `Open` method to populate the recordset with a particular set of records:

```
rsRecordset.Open "SELECT * FROM tblSupplier", cnConnection
```

The `Open` method has various parameters that determine how the recordset will be created, such as `CursorType`, `CursorLocation`, `LockType`, and `Options`. These parameters must be set prior to opening the recordset for them to be effective.

CursorType Property

The `CursorType` property of the `Recordset` object indicates what type of movement you can take within a recordset. By default, the `CursorType` property is set to `adOpenForwardOnly`, which means that you can only move forward through the records. A forward-only cursor does not allow you to count how many records are in the recordset or navigate back and forth through the recordset. The following code is an example of setting the `CursorType` property:

```
rsRecordset.CursorType = adOpenStatic
```

The following table summarizes the four possible choices for the `CursorType` property.

Value	Explanation
adOpenForwardOnly	This cursor is read-only and is the fastest type of cursor. However, it allows only for forward movement through the records.
adOpenStatic	This cursor allows forward and backward movement through the records and also allows bookmarks. It doesn't show changes made by other users. This is a client-side cursor.
adOpenKeyset	This cursor allows forward and backward movement through the records and also allows bookmarks. It does not show new or deleted records. It points back to the original data.
adOpenDynamic	This cursor provides complete access to a set of records by showing additions and deletions. It also allows for forward and backward movement through the records.

The CursorLocation Property

The `CursorLocation` property of the `Recordset` object specifies where the set of records or record pointers are returned when you open a recordset. ADO supports two values for the `CursorLocation` property: `adUseServer` and `adUseClient`. These return records to the server and client, respectively.

You should generally use server cursors except when client cursors are specifically needed. An example of the syntax of this property is shown below:

```
rsRecordset.CursorLocation = adUseServer
```

The LockType Property

The LockType property of the Recordset object is what determines whether a recordset is updatable. The following table summarizes the four possible choices for the LockType property.

Value	Explanation
adLockReadOnly	The recordset is read-only and no changes are allowed.
adLockPessimistic	The record in the recordset will be locked as soon as editing begins.
adLockOptimistic	The record in the recordset will be locked when the Update method is issued.
adLockBatchOptimistic	The records will not be locked until a batch update of all records is performed.

An example of the syntax of this property is shown in the following code:

```
rsRecordset.LockType = adLockReadOnly
```

The Options Parameter

The Options parameter of the Recordset object allows you to specify how the provider should evaluate the source argument. If the Options property is not specified, it will be determined at runtime, which is slower. Here is an example showing how to specify the Options parameter:

```
rsRecordset.Open "SELECT * FROM tblSupplier", cnConnection, _
    Options:=adCmdText
```

Try It Out   Building a Contacts Form Bound to a Recordset

Now that you have a basic idea of various ADO settings, you can put the concepts into practice by building a contacts form that connects to and displays data from a recordset. Assume that the contacts form will be used by a U.S. company that does not deal with foreign addresses.

1. Create a new database by selecting Office Button ⇨ New ⇨ Blank Database and specifying Ch5CodeExamples as the file name.

2. Create a new table in the database by selecting the Create ribbon on the toolbar and then choosing Table from the Tables grouping. The table should be named tblContacts and should have the fields illustrated in Figure 5-3. Note that the field sizes are listed as part of the description for convenience purposes only, so that, when creating the table, you can see what size to set for each field.

3. Open the table from the Database Window and add at least one record to the table.

4. Create a new Blank Form named `frmContactsBound`. Use the ToolBox to drag and drop 12 text box controls onto the form. Modify the `Name` property for each text box to the following: `txtLastName`, `txtFirstName`, `txtMiddleName`, `txtTitle`, `txtAddress1`, `txtAddress2`, `txtCity`, `txtState`, `txtZip`, `txtWorkPhone`, `txtHomePhone`, and `txtCellPhone`, respectively. Also rename the `Caption` property for the corresponding label of each text box, as shown in Figure 5-4.

5. Add the following code to the `Form_Load` procedure of the `frmContactsBound` form. You can do so by selecting the form in the Designer Window, viewing the Properties dialog box for the form, selecting the Events tab, and then selecting the Code Builder option from the `On Load` event. Make sure that you also add the reference to ADO from the Tools, References menu option in the VB Editor.

Field Name	Data Type	Description
intContactId	AutoNumber	Unique Id for the contact
txtLastName	Text	Last Name (Field size 50)
txtFirstName	Text	First Name (Field size 50)
txtMiddleName	Text	Middle Name (Field size 50)
txtTitle	Text	Title (Field size 30)
txtAddress1	Text	Address 1 (Field size 100)
txtAddress2	Text	Address 2 (Field size 100)
txtCity	Text	City (Field size 50)
txtState	Text	State (Field size 2)
txtZip	Text	Zip (Field size 5)
txtWorkPhone	Text	Work Phone (Field size 12)
txtHomePhone	Text	Home Phone (Field size 12)
txtCellPhone	Text	Cell Phone (Field size 12)

tblContacts : Table

Figure 5-3

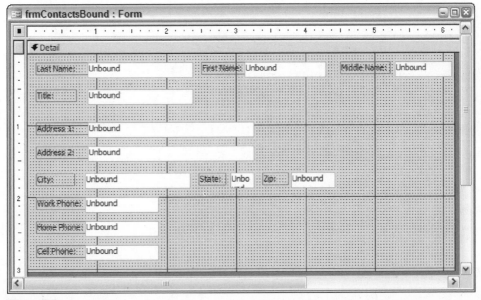

Figure 5-4

```
Private Sub Form_Load()

Dim cnCh5 As ADODB.Connection
Dim rsContacts As ADODB.Recordset
Dim strConnection As String

'specify the connection string for connecting to the database
strConnection = "Provider=Microsoft.ACE.OLEDB.12.0;" & _
                "Data Source=" & CurrentProject.Path & "\Ch5CodeExamples.accdb;"
'create a new connection instance and open it using the connection string
Set cnCh5 = New ADODB.Connection
cnCh5.Open strConnection

'create a new instance of a recordset
Set rsContacts = New ADODB.Recordset
'set various properties of the recordset
With rsContacts

    'specify a cursortype and lock type that will allow updates
    .CursorType = adOpenKeyset
    .CursorLocation = adUseClient
    .LockType = adLockOptimistic
    'open the recordset based on tblContacts table using the existing connection
    .Open "tblContacts", cnCh5
End With

'if the recordset is empty
If rsContacts.BOF And rsContacts.EOF Then
    MsgBox "There are no records in the database."
    Exit Sub
'if the recordset is not empty, then bind the
'recordset property of the form to the rsContacts recordset
Else
    Set Me.Recordset = rsContacts
End If

'bind the controls of the form to the proper field in the recordset (which has
'the same field names as the tblContacts table from which it was generated)
Me.txtLastName.ControlSource = "txtLastName"
Me.txtFirstName.ControlSource = "txtFirstName"
Me.txtMiddleName.ControlSource = "txtMiddleName"
Me.txtTitle.ControlSource = "txtTitle"
Me.txtAddress1.ControlSource = "txtAddress1"
Me.txtAddress2.ControlSource = "txtAddress2"
Me.txtCity.ControlSource = "txtCity"
Me.txtState.ControlSource = "txtState"
Me.txtZip.ControlSource = "txtZip"
Me.txtWorkPhone.ControlSource = "txtWorkPhone"
Me.txtHomePhone.ControlSource = "txtHomePhone"
Me.txtCellPhone.ControlSource = "txtCellPhone"

End Sub
```

6. Save the VBA code from the Visual Basic Editor by selecting the Save button from the toolbar.

7. Save the form from the Form Designer by selecting the Save button from the toolbar.

8. Open the form. You should see a screen similar to Figure 5-5.

9. Modify one of the existing records.

10. Click the Add New navigation button (right arrow with asterisk) to add a new record similar to the one shown in Figure 5-6.

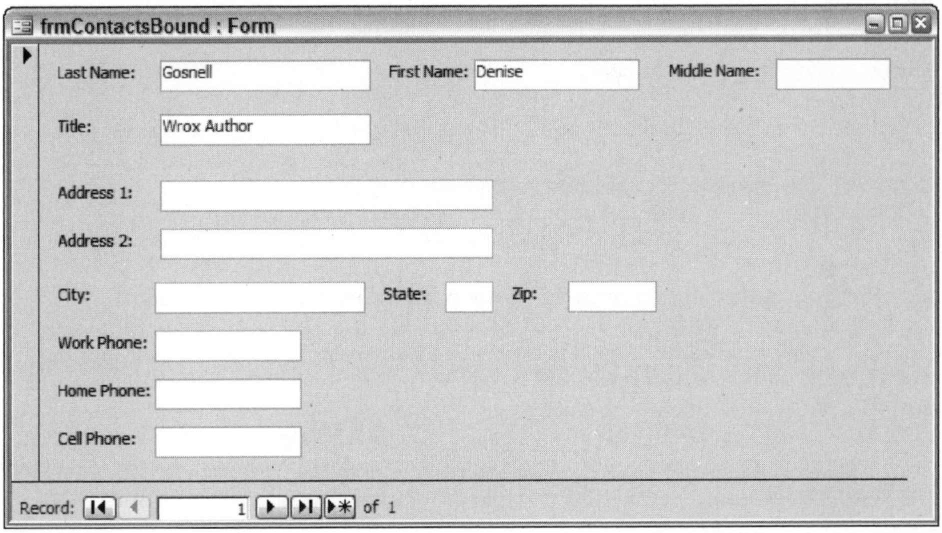

Figure 5-5

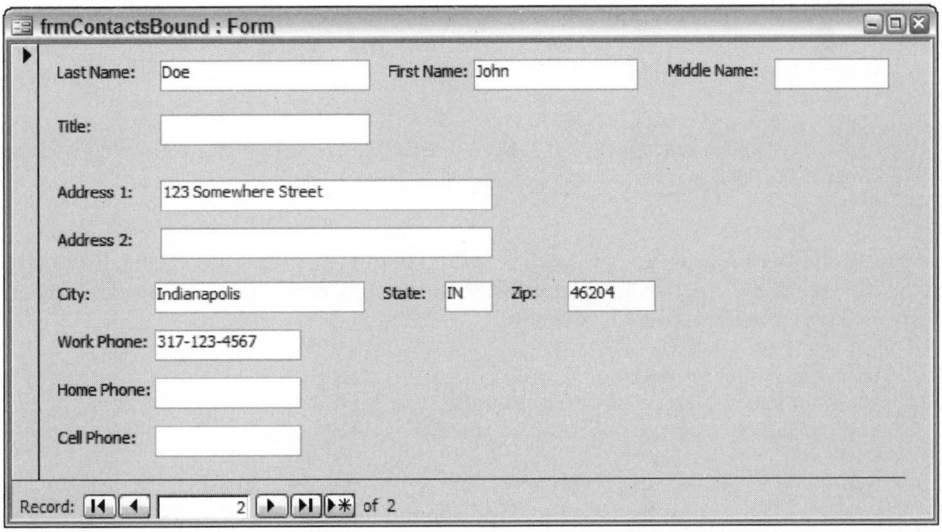

Figure 5-6

How It Works

This example binds the `frmContactsBound` form to an ADO recordset. Now I will show you how it works. All the code to make this application work is in the `Form_Load` event.

```
Private Sub Form_Load()
```

First, you declared new `Connection` and `Recordset` objects, along with a variable to store the connection string:

```
Dim cnCh5 As ADODB.Connection
Dim rsContacts As ADODB.Recordset
Dim strConnection As String
```

Next, you specified a value for the connection string that points to the current Access database:

```
'specify the connection string for connecting to the database
strConnection = "Provider=Microsoft.ACE.OLEDB.12.0;" & _
                "Data Source=" & CurrentProject.Path & "\Ch5CodeExamples.accdb;"
```

At this point, you created a new connection instance and opened the connection:

```
'create a new connection instance and open it using the connection string
Set cnCh5 = New ADODB.Connection
cnCh5.Open strConnection
```

The next set of code instantiated a new `Recordset` object and sets various properties that affect how the Recordset is populated:

```
'create a new instance of a recordset
Set rsContacts = New ADODB.Recordset
'set various properties of the recordset
With rsContacts
    'specify a cursortype and lock type that will allow updates
    .CursorType = adOpenKeyset
    .CursorLocation = adUseClient
    .LockType = adLockOptimistic
    'open the recordset based on tblContacts table using the existing connection
    .Open "tblContacts", cnCh5
End With
```

After you set the `CursorType`, `CursorLocation`, and `LockType` properties, the recordset was opened with the contents of the `tblContacts` table, using the existing connection. If the recordset did not contain any records, a message would be displayed.

```
'if the recordset is empty
If rsContacts.BOF And rsContacts.EOF Then
    MsgBox "There are no records in the database."
    Exit Sub
```

If the recordset was not empty, the next set of code bound the `Recordset` property of the form to the ADO recordset called `rsContacts`:

```
'if the recordset is not empty, then bind the
'recordset property of the form to the rsContacts recordset
Else

    Set Me.Recordset = rsContacts
End If
```

When you bound the recordset to the form, all the fields in the recordset became available for binding to the appropriate controls. However, the form does not know which controls should be bound to which recordset fields until you set the `ControlSource` property of the applicable controls. The next set of code assigned the `ControlSource` property of each text box to the respective field in the recordset, which was generated from the underlying `tblContacts` table:

```
'bind the controls of the form to the proper field in the recordset (which has
'the same field names as the tblContacts table from which it was generated)
Me.txtLastName.ControlSource = "txtLastName"
Me.txtFirstName.ControlSource = "txtFirstName"
Me.txtMiddleName.ControlSource = "txtMiddleName"
Me.txtTitle.ControlSource = "txtTitle"
Me.txtAddress1.ControlSource = "txtAddress1"
Me.txtAddress2.ControlSource = "txtAddress2"
Me.txtCity.ControlSource = "txtCity"
Me.txtState.ControlSource = "txtState"
Me.txtZip.ControlSource = "txtZip"
Me.txtWorkPhone.ControlSource = "txtWorkPhone"
Me.txtHomePhone.ControlSource = "txtHomePhone"
Me.txtCellPhone.ControlSource = "txtCellPhone"
End Sub
```

Next, you opened the form in View mode and updated and added records. If you open the underlying `tblContacts` table, you will see that the changes you made were correctly saved, as shown in Figure 5-7.

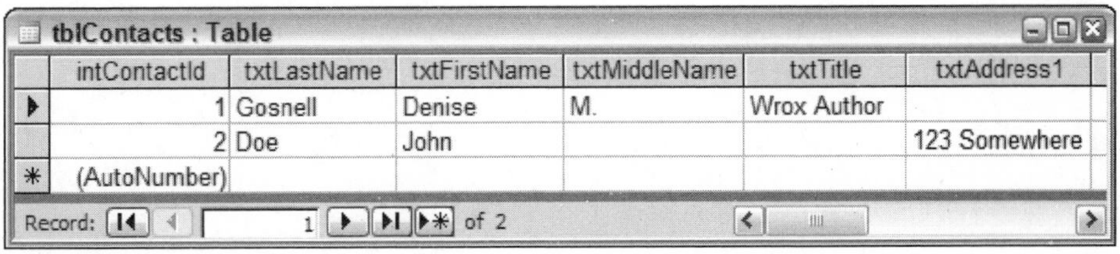

intContactId	txtLastName	txtFirstName	txtMiddleName	txtTitle	txtAddress1
1	Gosnell	Denise	M.	Wrox Author	
2	Doe	John			123 Somewhere
(AutoNumber)					

Record: 1 of 2

Figure 5-7

Did you notice that you did not have to write any of the code for the navigation and update features? Access handled this code for you automatically because the form was bound to the recordset. Binding a form to a recordset is a very quick and easy way to implement a basic user interface and does not require you to write code for navigation and database updates.

However, using bound forms presents some serious drawbacks. One drawback is that a database connection remains open the entire time you are working with the application. In applications with multiple users but limited licenses, this can be a problem. Another drawback is that records may remain locked longer than necessary because you are always maintaining the open database connection. If you walk away from your desk with the program open to a particular record, you might keep someone else from updating that same record because you have it locked. In a later example, you will explore how to create a disconnected recordset to help eliminate some of these problems.

You also need to make sure to close the table and form views before working on other portions of code because those views hold an exclusive lock on the database. You will receive an Access Denied error if you try to perform an operation needing to access the database when the database is locked by another operation.

Counting Records in a Recordset

The RecordCount property of the Recordset object returns the number of records in the recordset. Suppose that you have the following procedure:

```
Sub TestRecordCount()

Dim cnCh5 As ADODB.Connection
Dim rsContacts As ADODB.Recordset
Dim strConnection As String

'specify the connection string for connecting to the database
strConnection = "Provider=Microsoft.ACE.OLEDB.12.0;" & _
                "Data Source=" & CurrentProject.Path & "\Ch5CodeExamples.accdb;"

'create a new connection instance and open it using the connection string
Set cnCh5 = New ADODB.Connection
cnCh5.Open strConnection

'create a new instance of a recordset
Set rsContacts = New ADODB.Recordset
'set various properties of the recordset
With rsContacts

    .CursorType = adOpenStatic
    'open the recordset based on tblContacts table using the existing connection
    .Open "tblContacts", cnCh5
End With

'print the number of records to the Immediate Window
Debug.Print "The total number of records is: " & rsContacts.RecordCount

'close the database connection
cnCh5.Close

'set the recordset and connection to nothing
Set rsContacts = Nothing
Set cnCh5 = Nothing

End Sub
```

After the recordset is created, the code determines how many records are in the recordset using the RecordCount property. The number of records is then displayed in the Immediate Window, as shown in Figure 5-8.

If you remove the line specifying the CursorType, *then a* -1 *will be returned as the record count since the recordset will default to a forward-only recordset.*

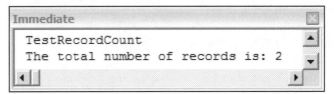

Figure 5-8

Navigating through a Recordset

The Recordset object has various methods that allow you to navigate among the records, assuming of course that the recordset is set to a CursorType that can be navigated. The following list contains four methods for navigation that can be used:

```
rsRecordset.MoveFirst
rsRecordset.MoveLast
rsRecordset.MoveNext
rsRecordset.MovePrevious
```

Before using the preceding record navigation methods, check the BOF and EOF properties of the Recordset. If the BOF property of the recordset is True, no current record exists and the current position is one prior to the first record. If the EOF property is True, no current record exists and the current position is one past the last record. If both BOF and EOF are True, the recordset is completely empty. You have to make sure the recordset is not at BOF or EOF before attempting to access the recordset contents, such as the recordset navigation, or you will get an error. The following shows you how to avoid such errors:

```
If NOT rsRecordset.BOF and NOT rsRecordset.EOF Then
rsRecordset.MoveFirst
End If
```

Adding, Editing, and Deleting Records in a Recordset

After you create a recordset, you can add, edit, and delete records. You already learned in the prior example that if the recordset is bound to the Recordset property and corresponding controls on a form, the moment you change the record on the form, it is updated in the underlying database. You did not have to write the update code to make this work.

ADO also has several methods that allow you to perform adds, edits, and deletions from within your code with the AddNew, Update, and Delete methods of the Recordset object. I will briefly introduce each of these methods, and then I will explain each in detail by using a hands-on example.

Adding a New Record with the AddNew Method

The AddNew method of the Recordset object adds an empty record to the recordset that can then be filled in with additional information:

```
rsRecordset.AddNew
```

141

If the recordset is connected to a data source, then the record is added to the underlying data source. Otherwise, the new record is saved in the local recordset and must be updated with the underlying data source or the new record will be lost. This is called working with a disconnected recordset and is explained in detail in an upcoming example.

Updating an Existing Record with the Update Method

The Update method of the Recordset object updates the current record. If the Update method is used in conjunction with the AddNew method, the information from the empty record is moved to the end of the recordset.

```
rsRecordset.Update
```

If the recordset is connected to a data source, the changes are saved in the underlying data source. If the recordset is disconnected from the data source, the changes are saved in the local recordset and must be updated in Batch or other mode with the underlying data source or the changes will be lost.

Deleting an Existing Record with the Delete Method

The Delete method of the Recordset object deletes the current record:

```
rsRecordset.Delete
```

Again, if the recordset is connected to a data source, then the deletion occurs on the underlying data source. If the recordset is disconnected from the data source, the record is deleted from the local recordset and must later be removed from the underlying data source.

Try It Out   **Building an Unbound Contacts Form Using a Disconnected Recordset**

Now, it's time to build a contacts form that is based on a disconnected recordset.

1. Select the frmContactsBound form you created previously, right-click, and select Copy from pop-up menu. Then, click Paste and name the new form frmContactsUnbound.

2. Open frmContactsUnbound. Delete the current code in the On Load event of the Form from the Event tab of the Properties dialog box or from the Visual Basic Editor.

3. Set the Record Selectors, Navigation Buttons, and Dividing Lines properties of the form to No, as shown in Figure 5-9.

4. Add seven command buttons to the form. Set the Name properties of each command button to cmdMoveFirst, cmdMovePrevious, cmdMoveNext, cmdMoveLast, cmdAddNew, cmdDelete, and cmdSaveAll, respectively. Change the Caption property of each command button to Move First, Move Previous, Move Next, Move Last, Add New, Delete, and Save Changes To Database, respectively. Change the Picture property of the four navigation buttons to existing pictures called Go To First 1, Go Previous, Go To Next 1, and Go To Last 1, respectively. Instead of the picture buttons, you can just use text as the caption if desired. The form should look similar to the form illustrated in Figure 5-10.

5. Add the following code to the General Declarations section of the form:

```
Dim rsContacts As ADODB.Recordset
Dim cnCh5 As ADODB.Connection
Dim strConnection As String
```

6. Add the following code to the Form_Load event of the form:

```
Private Sub Form_Load()

strConnection = "Provider=Microsoft.ACE.OLEDB.12.0;" & _
                "Data Source=" & CurrentProject.Path & "\Ch5CodeExamples.accdb;"

'create a new connection instance and open it using the connection string
Set cnCh5 = New ADODB.Connection
cnCh5.Open strConnection

'create a new instance of a recordset
Set rsContacts = New ADODB.Recordset

'set various properties of the recordset
With rsContacts
    'specify a cursortype and lock type that will allow updates
    .CursorType = adOpenKeyset
    .CursorLocation = adUseClient
    .LockType = adLockBatchOptimistic
    'open the recordset based on tblContacts table using the existing connection
    .Open "tblContacts", cnCh5
    'disconnect the recordset
    .ActiveConnection = Nothing
End With

'if the recordset is empty
If rsContacts.BOF And rsContacts.EOF Then
    Exit Sub
Else
    'move to the first record
    rsContacts.MoveFirst
    'populate the controls on the form
    Call PopulateControlsOnForm
End If

'close the database connection and release it from memory
cnCh5.Close
Set cnCh5 = Nothing

End Sub
```

7. Add the following event procedures to the class module for the Form.

```
Private Sub cmdAddNew_Click()

'add a new record to the local disconnected recordset
Call AddRecord

End Sub

Private Sub cmdDelete_Click()

'delete the current record from the local disconnected recordset
Call DeleteRecord
```

```
End Sub

Private Sub cmdMoveFirst_Click()

'move to the first record in the local disconnected recordset
Call MoveToFirstRecord

End Sub

Private Sub cmdMoveLast_Click()

'move to the last record in the local disconnected recordset
Call MoveToLastRecord

End Sub

Private Sub cmdMoveNext_Click()

'move to the next record in the local disconnected recordset
Call MoveToNextRecord

End Sub

Private Sub cmdMovePrevious_Click()
'move to the previous record in the local disconnected recordset
Call MoveToPreviousRecord

End Sub

Private Sub cmdSaveAll_Click()

'save all changes made to the local disconnected recordset
'back to the database
Call SaveAllRecords

End Sub
```

8. Add the following procedures to the class module for the form:

```
Sub AddRecord()

'add a new record to the local disconnected recordset
rsContacts.AddNew

'commit the new empty record to the local disconnected recordset
rsContacts.Update

'clear the current controls on the form so the
'user can fill in values for the new record
Call ClearControlsOnForm

End Sub

Sub DeleteRecord()

'delete the record from the local disconnected recordset
```

```
rsContacts.Delete

'commit the deletion to the local disconnected recordset
rsContacts.Update

'move to the first record since the current one has been deleted
rsContacts.MoveFirst

'populate the controls on the form
Call PopulateControlsOnForm

End Sub
```

9. Add the following navigation procedures to the class module for the form:

```
Sub MoveToFirstRecord()

'before performing move operation, save the current record
Call SaveCurrentRecord

'move to the first record in the local disconnected recordset
If Not rsContacts.BOF And Not rsContacts.EOF Then
    rsContacts.MoveFirst
    'populate the controls on the form with the current record
    Call PopulateControlsOnForm

End If

End Sub

Sub MoveToLastRecord()

'before performing move operation, save the current record
Call SaveCurrentRecord

'move to the last record in the local disconnected recordset
If Not rsContacts.BOF And Not rsContacts.EOF Then
    rsContacts.MoveLast
    'populate the controls on the form with the current record
    Call PopulateControlsOnForm

End If

End Sub

Sub MoveToPreviousRecord()

'before performing move operation, save the current record
Call SaveCurrentRecord

'move to the previous record in the local disconnected recordset
'if not already at the beginning
If Not rsContacts.BOF Then
    rsContacts.MovePrevious
    'populate the controls on the form with the current record
    Call PopulateControlsOnForm
```

```
    End If

    End Sub

    Sub MoveToNextRecord()

    'before performing move operation, save the current record
    Call SaveCurrentRecord

    'move to the next record in the local disconnected recordset
    'if not already at the end
    If Not rsContacts.EOF Then
        rsContacts.MoveNext
        'populate the controls on the form with the current record
        Call PopulateControlsOnForm
    End If

    End Sub
```

10. Add the following procedures to the class module for the form:

```
Sub PopulateControlsOnForm()

    'Populate the controls on the form with the values of the
    'current record in the local disconnected recordset.
    'Use the same field names as the tblContacts table from
    'which it was generated.
    If Not rsContacts.BOF And Not rsContacts.EOF Then
        Me.txtLastName = rsContacts!txtLastName
        Me.txtFirstName = rsContacts!txtFirstName
        Me.txtMiddleName = rsContacts!txtMiddleName
        Me.txtTitle = rsContacts!txtTitle
        Me.txtAddress1 = rsContacts!txtAddress1
        Me.txtAddress2 = rsContacts!txtAddress2
        Me.txtCity = rsContacts!txtCity
        Me.txtState = rsContacts!txtState
        Me.txtZip = rsContacts!txtZip
        Me.txtWorkPhone = rsContacts!txtWorkPhone
        Me.txtHomePhone = rsContacts!txtHomePhone
        Me.txtCellPhone = rsContacts!txtCellPhone
    ElseIf rsContacts.BOF Then
        'past beginning of recordset so move to next record
        rsContacts.MoveNext
    ElseIf rsContacts.EOF Then
        'past end of recordset so move back to previous record
        rsContacts.MovePrevious

    End If

End Sub

Sub ClearControlsOnForm()

'clear the values in the controls on the form
Me.txtLastName = ""
```

```vb
    Me.txtFirstName = ""
    Me.txtMiddleName = ""
    Me.txtTitle = ""
    Me.txtAddress1 = ""
    Me.txtAddress2 = ""
    Me.txtCity = ""
    Me.txtState = ""
    Me.txtZip = ""
    Me.txtWorkPhone = ""
    Me.txtHomePhone = ""
    Me.txtCellPhone = ""

End Sub

Sub SaveCurrentRecord()

'save the values in the controls on the form to the current record
'in the local disconnected recordset.
If Not rsContacts.BOF And Not rsContacts.EOF Then
    rsContacts!txtLastName = Me.txtLastName
    rsContacts!txtFirstName = Me.txtFirstName
    rsContacts!txtMiddleName = Me.txtMiddleName
    rsContacts!txtTitle = Me.txtTitle
    rsContacts!txtAddress1 = Me.txtAddress1
    rsContacts!txtAddress2 = Me.txtAddress2
    rsContacts!txtCity = Me.txtCity
    rsContacts!txtState = Me.txtState
    rsContacts!txtZip = Me.txtZip
    rsContacts!txtWorkPhone = Me.txtWorkPhone
    rsContacts!txtHomePhone = Me.txtHomePhone
    rsContacts!txtCellPhone = Me.txtCellPhone
End If

End Sub

Sub SaveAllRecords()

'Save current record to local disconnected recordset
Call SaveCurrentRecord

'create a new connection instance and open it using the connection string
Set cnCh5 = New ADODB.Connection
cnCh5.Open strConnection

'set the disconnected recordset to the reopened connection
Set rsContacts.ActiveConnection = cnCh5

'save all changes in the local disconnected recordset back
'to the database
rsContacts.UpdateBatch

'disconnect the recordset again
Set rsContacts.ActiveConnection = Nothing

'close the database connection and release it from memory
```

```
cnCh5.Close
Set cnCh5 = Nothing

End Sub
```

11. Add the following event procedure to the form:

```
Private Sub Form_Unload(Cancel As Integer)

Dim intResponse As Integer

'prompt the user to save changes
intResponse = MsgBox("Save All Changes To Database?", vbYesNo)

If intResponse = vbYes Then
    'save all local records in disconnected recordset back
    'to the database in a batch update
    Call SaveAllRecords
ElseIf intResponse = vbNo Then
    MsgBox "Unsaved changes were discarded."
    End If

'release the recordset from memory
Set rsContacts = Nothing

End Sub
```

12. Save all changes in the Visual Basic Editor by selecting Save from the toolbar.

13. Save all changes in the form from design view by selecting Save from the toolbar.

14. Open the form in View mode so that a screen like that in Figure 5-11 appears and displays some data.

15. Make changes to the values on the screen and then navigate to another record. When you return to the record, note whether the value is still changed.

16. Close the form without saving changes. See if the changes you previously made are present.

17. Make changes to the values on the screen and then select the Save All Changes To Database option.

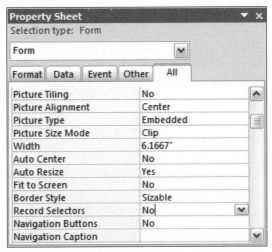

Figure 5-9

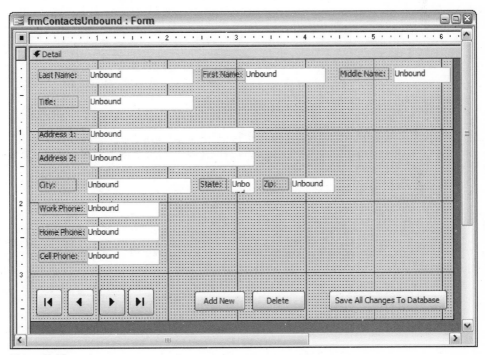

Figure 5-10

How It Works

First, you made a copy of the existing `frmContactsBound` and renamed it to `frmContactsUnbound`. You then added some additional controls, namely seven command buttons to the form. The command buttons were labeled for record navigation, add, delete, and save functionality.

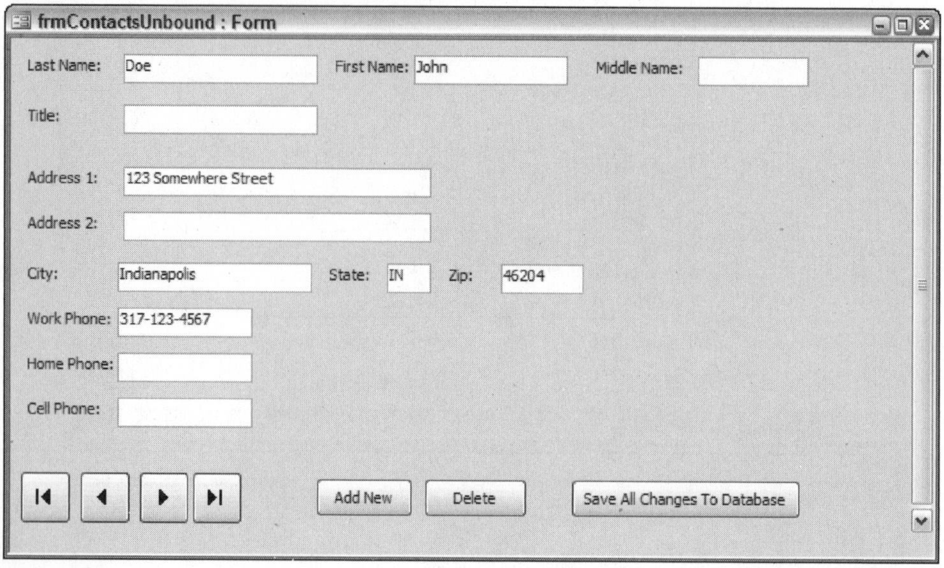

Figure 5-11

Next, you added code to the General Declarations section of the form for a `Recordset` object, `Connection` object, and connection string variable. These were placed in the General Declarations section because they need to remain in scope as long as the form is open.

```
Dim rsContacts As ADODB.Recordset
Dim cnCh5 As ADODB.Connection
Dim strConnection As String
```

Next, you added the `Form_Load` event of the form where the connection was opened and a new recordset instantiated:

```
Private Sub Form_Load()

strConnection = "ProviderProvider=Microsoft.ACE.OLEDB.12.0;" & _
                "Data Source=" & CurrentProject.Path & "\Ch5CodeExamples.accdb;"

'create a new connection instance and open it using the connection string
Set cnCh5 = New ADODB.Connection
cnCh5.Open strConnection

'create a new instance of a recordset
Set rsContacts = New ADODB.Recordset
```

You then set various properties of the `Recordset` object, such as the `CursorType` to specify that the cursor should be client side and the `LockType` to specify the recordset should be batch optimistic. The recordset was then opened and disconnected from the data source by setting the `ActiveConnection` property to nothing.

```
'set various properties of the recordset
With rsContacts
    'specify a cursortype and lock type that will allow updates
    .CursorType = adOpenKeyset
    .CursorLocation = adUseClient
    .LockType = adLockBatchOptimistic
    'open the recordset based on tblContacts table using the existing
     connection
    .Open "tblContacts", cnCh5
    'disconnect the recordset
    .ActiveConnection = Nothing
End With
```

With the recordset disconnected from the data source, the recordset is simply stored in local memory. Any changes made to a disconnected recordset are not automatically saved in the original data source.

Next, you added code to call a procedure to populate the controls on the form with the values in the recordset:

```
'if the recordset is empty

If rsContacts.BOF And rsContacts.EOF Then
    Exit Sub
Else
    'move to the first record
    rsContacts.MoveFirst
    'populate the controls on the form
    Call PopulateControlsOnForm
End If
```

The database connection was then closed and released from memory:

```
'close the database connection and release it from memory
cnCh5.Close
Set cnCh5 = Nothing
End Sub
```

You then added various event procedures to call the rest of the code when the user selects different options on the form. For example, the `cmdAddNew_Click` event was added to call the `AddRecord` procedure when the user clicks the Add New button on the form. A similar procedure was added for Delete.

```
Private Sub cmdAddNew_Click()
'add a new record to the local disconnected recordset
Call AddRecord
End Sub
```

Various event procedures were added to handle navigation through the recordset. For example, the cmdMoveFirst_Click event was added to call the procedure to move to the first record:

```
Private Sub cmdMoveFirst_Click()

'move to the first record in the local disconnected recordset
Call MoveToFirstRecord

End Sub
```

Other similar procedures were added for Move Last, Move Next, and Move Previous. An event procedure was also added for Save to cause the SaveAllRecords procedure to execute when the Save button on the form is clicked:

```
Private Sub cmdSaveAll_Click()

'save all changes made to the local disconnected recordset
'back to the database
Call SaveAllRecords

End Sub
```

Next, you added the procedures that really implement the heart of the functionality for the unbound form. The AddRecord procedure is called from the button's OnClick event after the user clicks the Add New button on the form. The AddRecord procedure uses the AddNew method to add a new record to the local disconnected recordset and then commits the new empty record to the local disconnected recordset using the Update method.

```
Sub AddRecord()

'add a new record to the local disconnected recordset
rsContacts.AddNew

'commit the new empty record to the local disconnected recordset
rsContacts.Update
```

The controls on the form are then cleared so that the user can enter values for the new record:

```
'clear the current controls on the form so the
'user can fill in values for the new record
Call ClearControlsOnForm

End Sub
```

The DeleteRecord procedure is called when the Click event of the cmdDelete button runs. This procedure deletes the current record in the local recordset using the Delete method and then commits the change to the local recordset using the Update method.

```
Sub DeleteRecord()

'delete the record from the local disconnected recordset
```

```
rsContacts.Delete

'commit the deletion to the local disconnected recordset
rsContacts.Update
```

The procedure then repositions the recordset to the first record and displays that record on the form to the user:

```
'move to the first record since the current one has been deleted
rsContacts.MoveFirst

'populate the controls on the form
Call PopulateControlsOnForm

End Sub
```

Various navigation procedures were then added to handle moving through the disconnected recordset. For example, the `MoveToFirstRecord` gets called when the `Click` event of the cmdMoveFirst button is fired. This procedure saves the current record in the local recordset before moving to the first record.

```
Sub MoveToFirstRecord()

'before performing move operation, save the current record
Call SaveCurrentRecord

'move to the first record in the local disconnected recordset
If Not rsContacts.BOF And Not rsContacts.EOF Then
    rsContacts.MoveFirst

    'populate the controls on the form with the current record
    Call PopulateControlsOnForm

End If

End Sub
```

Again, remember that the saves so far are just updating the local copy of the recordset but not the underlying database table that the records came from. You will see in a moment how the updates can be saved back to the original data source.

The `PopulateControlsOnForm` procedure set the text box controls on the form to the current values in the recordset. In other words, this code displays the values in the recordset to the user on the form:

```
Sub PopulateControlsOnForm()

    'Populate the controls on the form with the values of the
    'current record in the local disconnected recordset.
    'Use the same field names as the tblContacts table from
    'which it was generated.
    If Not rsContacts.BOF And Not rsContacts.EOF Then
        Me.txtLastName = rsContacts!txtLastName
        Me.txtFirstName = rsContacts!txtFirstName
        Me.txtMiddleName = rsContacts!txtMiddleName
```

```
              Me.txtTitle = rsContacts!txtTitle
              Me.txtAddress1 = rsContacts!txtAddress1
              Me.txtAddress2 = rsContacts!txtAddress2
              Me.txtCity = rsContacts!txtCity
              Me.txtState = rsContacts!txtState
              Me.txtZip = rsContacts!txtZip
              Me.txtWorkPhone = rsContacts!txtWorkPhone
              Me.txtHomePhone = rsContacts!txtHomePhone
              Me.txtCellPhone = rsContacts!txtCellPhone
        ElseIf rsContacts.BOF Then
              'past beginning of recordset so move to next record
              rsContacts.MoveNext
        ElseIf rsContacts.EOF Then
              'past end of recordset so move back to previous record
              rsContacts.MovePrevious
        End If

    End Sub
```

The `ClearControlsOnForm` empties out the data entry controls to allow a user to add a new record:

```
Sub ClearControlsOnForm()

    'clear the values in the controls on the form
    Me.txtLastName = ""
    Me.txtFirstName = ""
    Me.txtMiddleName = ""
    Me.txtTitle = ""
    Me.txtAddress1 = ""
    Me.txtAddress2 = ""
    Me.txtCity = ""
    Me.txtState = ""
    Me.txtZip = ""
    Me.txtWorkPhone = ""
    Me.txtHomePhone = ""
    Me.txtCellPhone = ""
End Sub
```

The `SaveCurrentRecord` procedure saves the values that are in the controls on the form into the current record in the local disconnected recordset.

```
Sub SaveCurrentRecord()

    'save the values in the controls on the form to the current record
    'in the local disconnected recordset.
    If Not rsContacts.BOF And Not rsContacts.EOF Then
        rsContacts!txtLastName = Me.txtLastName
        rsContacts!txtFirstName = Me.txtFirstName
        rsContacts!txtMiddleName = Me.txtMiddleName
        rsContacts!txtTitle = Me.txtTitle
        rsContacts!txtAddress1 = Me.txtAddress1
```

```
        rsContacts!txtAddress2 = Me.txtAddress2
        rsContacts!txtCity = Me.txtCity
        rsContacts!txtState = Me.txtState
        rsContacts!txtZip = Me.txtZip
        rsContacts!txtWorkPhone = Me.txtWorkPhone
        rsContacts!txtHomePhone = Me.txtHomePhone
        rsContacts!txtCellPhone = Me.txtCellPhone
    End If

    End Sub
```

The SaveAllRecords procedure is executed from the Click event of the cmdSaveAll button on the form. This procedure is responsible for updating the database with the current version of all records in the disconnected recordset. First, changes are saved to the current record in the local recordset, and a connection is reestablished with the database:

```
Sub SaveAllRecords()

'Save current record to local disconnected recordset
Call SaveCurrentRecord

'create a new connection instance and open it using the connection string
Set cnCh5 = New ADODB.Connection
cnCh5.Open strConnection
```

To reconnect the recordset to the underlying data source, the ActiveConnection property is assigned to the current open connection:

```
'set the disconnected recordset to the reopened connection
Set rsContacts.ActiveConnection = cnCh5
```

After it is reconnected to the underlying data source, the UpdateBatch method is executed to cause all the local changes to be updated in the original data source:

```
'save all changes in the local disconnected recordset back
'to the database
rsContacts.UpdateBatch
```

With the updates completed, the recordset is again disconnected to save an open connection and the database connection is again released:

```
'disconnect the recordset again
Set rsContacts.ActiveConnection = Nothing

'close the database connection and release it from memory
cnCh5.Close
Set cnCh5 = Nothing

End Sub
```

As an additional feature, code was placed under the Form_Unload event to make sure that the reader knows to save changes before closing the form:

```
Private Sub Form_Unload(Cancel As Integer)

Dim intResponse As Integer

'prompt the user to save changes
intResponse = MsgBox("Save All Changes To Database?", vbYesNo)

If intResponse = vbYes Then
    'save all local records in disconnected recordset back
    'to the database in a batch update
    Call SaveAllRecords
ElseIf intResponse = vbNo Then
    MsgBox "Unsaved changes were discarded."
    End If

'release the recordset from memory
Set rsContacts = Nothing

End Sub
```

Notice how in this instance, you had to write the code to perform record navigation and record updates because the recordset was disconnected from the underlying data source. This is certainly more time-consuming than the prior bound recordset example, which handled record navigation and record updates automatically. However, I recommend that you use disconnected recordsets and handle data interaction without keeping a connection open to the database. This helps you write an application that can support more users and that can more easily migrate to more advanced databases like SQL Server. Later in this chapter, you will see another example of using a disconnected recordset as well as SQL statements to handle unbound forms.

Sorting, Finding, and Filtering Records in a Recordset

The Recordset object has various properties and methods that allow you to sort, filter, and find records. Some examples of these properties will now be discussed.

The Sort Property

The Sort property allows you to modify the order in which the records appear in the recordset.

Try It Out	Sorting Records for the Unbound Contacts Form

Look at an example of how to sort the rsContacts recordset that you used previously.

1. In the code for the Form_Load event procedure of frmContactsUnbound, immediately following the line setting the ActiveConnection property, add the following Sort command:

```
With rsContacts
    'specify a cursortype and lock type that will allow updates
    .CursorType = adOpenKeyset
    .CursorLocation = adUseClient
```

```
    .LockType = adLockBatchOptimistic
    'open the recordset based on tblContacts table using the existing connection
    .Open "tblContacts", cnCh5
    'disconnect the recordset
    .ActiveConnection = Nothing

    'sort the recordset

    .Sort = "txtLastName, txtFirstName, txtMiddleName"
End With
```

2.   Now reopen the form and navigate through the records.

How It Works

The Sort method of the Recordset object allows you to specify one or more fields by which to sort the recordset. The preceding example sorts the contacts by last name, first name, and middle name. I hope you noticed that when you ran the form again, the order of the records was now alphabetical based on those three fields.

The Find Method

The Find method of the Recordset object allows you to navigate to a particular record that matches certain criteria. Here is a sample procedure that uses the Find method to locate a record that has a value for intContactId of 2.

```
Sub TestFind()

Dim rsContacts As ADODB.Recordset

'create a new instance of a recordset
Set rsContacts = New ADODB.Recordset
'set various properties of the recordset
With rsContacts
    .CursorType = adOpenStatic
    'open the recordset based on tblContacts table using the existing connection
    .Open "tblContacts", CurrentProject.Connection
End With

'find a contact with the intContactId value of 2

rsContacts.Find "[intContactId] = 2"


'output a message to the Immediate Window regarding find results
If rsContacts.EOF Then
    Debug.Print "Specified record not found"
Else
'record was found - display some info
    Debug.Print "Contact Id: " & rsContacts!intContactId & _
            " Last Name: " & rsContacts!txtLastName & _
```

```
                        " First Name: " & rsContacts!txtFirstName

        End If

        'close the recordset
        rsContacts.Close

        'set the recordset and connection to nothing
        Set rsContacts = Nothing


        End Sub
```

The Find method does not remove any records from the database, but instead just navigates you to a different record. Notice how the preceding example does not use a separate connection object but uses the existing connection for the project to create the recordset. This is an acceptable approach if you will always be working with the same database of your current project.

When you run the preceding procedure from the Immediate Window, you see results similar to those shown in Figure 5-12.

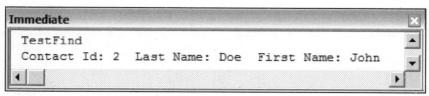

Figure 5-12

The Filter Property

The Filter property allows you to filter the recordset to a smaller subset that meets a certain criteria. For example, you might want to filter your recordset to last names starting with a certain letter.

```
        Sub TestFilter()
        Dim rsContacts As ADODB.Recordset
        'create a new instance of a recordset
        Set rsContacts = New ADODB.Recordset
        'set various properties of the recordset
        With rsContacts
            .CursorType = adOpenStatic
            'open the recordset based on tblContacts table using the existing connection
            .Open "tblContacts", CurrentProject.Connection
        End With

        'filter the recordset to contain only records with
        'last names starting with D
        rsContacts.Filter = "txtLastName Like 'D*'"

        'output a message to the Immediate Window regarding find results
        If rsContacts.EOF Then
```

```
        Debug.Print "No records met that criteria."
    Else
    'record was found - display some info for each record
        Do Until rsContacts.EOF
            Debug.Print "Contact Id: " & rsContacts!intContactId & _
                " Last Name: " & rsContacts!txtLastName & _
                " First Name: " & rsContacts!txtFirstName
            rsContacts.MoveNext
        Loop
    End If
```

```
    'close the recordset
    rsContacts.Close
    'set the recordset and connection to nothing
    Set rsContacts = Nothing
```

```
    End Sub
```

The preceding example uses the `Filter` property to filter the recordset down to records that start with D. To prove the filter worked, all the records remaining are displayed in the Immediate Window, as shown in Figure 5-13.

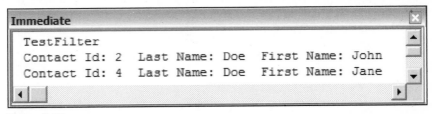

Figure 5-13

Using Bookmarks to Mark and Locate Data

Bookmarks allow you to mark a location in a recordset and return to that location later. For example, suppose that you have a variable called `varPosition` that has been declared as a variant. You can save the location of the current record in a bookmark:

```
    varPosition = rsContacts.Bookmark
```

And then return to it later by setting the `Bookmark` property equal to the saved position:

```
    rsContacts.BookMark = varPosition
```

Introduction to SQL

Structured Query Language (SQL) is a special language for structuring commands that can communicate with databases. Various dialects of SQL statements include Jet SQL, ANSI SQL, and the vendor specific implementations of ANSI SQL such as T-SQL for SQL Server. The syntax of SQL you use varies slightly depending on underlying database. In this section, I cover SQL that is common to most databases.

SQL statements can be used with and without ADO. For example, a SQL statement can be specified as the `RecordSource` property to which a form can be bound. The examples in this section will illustrate using SQL statements with ADO.

Note that you can also view SQL statements in the Query Designer and have the Query Designer help you create SQL. If you select View ⇨ SQL View from within a Query window, you can see the SQL statement that Access created for your statement. You'll learn how to write SQL statements without using a designer.

Retrieving Data Using SQL Select Statements

The `Select` statement allows you to retrieve records from one or more tables in a database and has a basic syntax as follows:

```
SELECT columns FROM tables WHERE where-clause ORDER BY columns
```

Select Clause

The `Select` clause specifies what columns in the underlying table or tables you want to retrieve. To retrieve all records in a certain table, use:

```
SELECT *
```

To select particular columns in a table, such as `txtLastName` and `txtFirstName`, list each name separated by commas:

```
SELECT txtLastName, txtFirstName
```

Predicates can also be used as part of the `Select` statement to further restrict what records get returned. For example, you can use the `DISTINCT` predicate to limit the results to unique records:

```
SELECT DISTINCT txtLastName
```

The `TOP` predicate allows you to restrict the number of records returned to a certain number or percent. For example, the following statement limits the number of records to be returned to five:

```
SELECT TOP 5 intSalesAmt from tblOrders
```

From Clause

The `FROM` clause specifies the tables from which the records should be selected. A basic `FROM` clause is:

```
FROM tblContacts
```

You can also specify a new name for the table, or a table alias, using the AS predicate, as shown here:

```
FROM tblContacts As Contacts
```

To retrieve data from more than one table, you use an Inner, Left, or Right Join to join the tables together. Here is the basic join syntax:

```
FROM <left table name> <join type> <right table name> ON <left join field name> =
<right join field name>
```

The following shows the differences in each type of join:

❑ INNER JOIN – Combines the records from the two tables where the joined values in both tables match.

❑ LEFT JOIN – Includes all records from the table on the left side of the clause even if there are no matching records from the table on the right side.

❑ RIGHT JOIN – Includes all records from the table on the right side of the clause even if there are no matching records from the table on the left side.

An example of an inner join is:

```
FROM tblContacts INNER JOIN tblSuppliers ON tblContacts.LastName =
tblSuppliers.LastName
```

The previous example returns records from the tblContacts table and from the tblSuppliers table where a match exists on the joined values in both tables.

An example of a left join is:

```
FROM tblContacts LEFT JOIN tblSuppliers ON tblContacts.LastName =
tblSuppliers.LastName
```

The left join example above returns all records from the tblContacts table, even if there are no matching records in the tblSuppliers table.

Where Clause

The Where clause is used to limit the rows the SQL Statement will retrieve. The Where clause is optional. If the Where clause is included, it can be followed by comparison operators, such as =, >, <, BETWEEN, IN, and string expressions such as Is Null. What follows is an example of a Where clause that uses comparison operators:

```
WHERE LastName = 'Doe' AND FirstName = 'John'
```

Expressions in a Where clause are separated by And statements. If the Where clause is omitted, you will get all records in the select without restriction. There are times when this is exactly what you want.

Order By Clause

The Order By clause allows you to specify in what order the records should be sorted when they are retrieved. For example, suppose that you want to sort the results by last name and then first name. You could use the following Order By clause:

```
ORDER BY txtLastName, txtFirstName
```

The previous example will return records in ascending order, which is the default. To return the records in descending order, use the DESC keyword:

```
ORDER BY txtLastName, txtFirstName DESC
```

Subqueries

Subqueries enable you to nest one Select statement within another Select statement. The following example selects those records in tblContacts that do not have the same last name in the tblContactsArchive table:

```
SELECT txtLastName, txtFirstName FROM tblContacts WHERE txtLastName Not In (SELECT txtLastName FROM tblContactsArchive)
```

Union

The Union statement allows you to combine data from two tables that have similar structures into the output. For example, suppose that you have a tblContacts table containing active contacts and a tblContactsArchive table that contains archived contacts. To retrieve a set of records that combines data from both of these tables, you use the Union statement:

```
SELECT txtLastName, txtFirstName
FROM tblContacts
UNION ALL SELECT txtLastName, txtFirstName
FROM tblContactsArchive
```

Using SQL and ADO to Populate a Recordset

Now that you have learned the basic syntax for Select statements, let's look at an example that uses a SQL statement along with ADO. The following example opens a new recordset and uses a SQL statement as the source for the Open method:

```
Sub TestSQLSelect()

Dim rsContacts As ADODB.Recordset

'create a new instance of a recordset
Set rsContacts = New ADODB.Recordset
'set various properties of the recordset
With rsContacts
    .CursorType = adOpenStatic
    'open the recordset based on SQL statement using the existing connection
    .Open "SELECT * FROM tblContacts", CurrentProject.Connection
End With

'loop through the recordset and display some info for
'each record
Do Until rsContacts.EOF
    Debug.Print "Contact Id: " & rsContacts!intContactId & _
        " Last Name: " & rsContacts!txtLastName & _
        " First Name: " & rsContacts!txtFirstName
    rsContacts.MoveNext
```

```
Loop

'close the recordset
rsContacts.Close

'set the recordset and connection to nothing
Set rsContacts = Nothing

End Sub
```

A portion of each record that is returned in the recordset is then printed in the Immediate Window, as shown in Figure 5-14 to demonstrate that the SQL statement selected what you expected it to select.

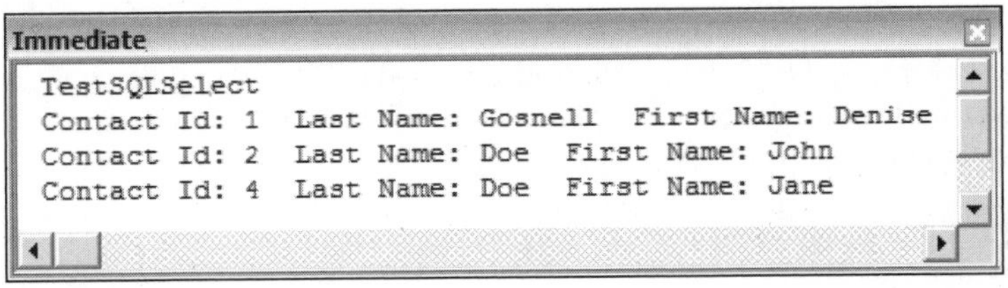

```
Immediate                                                    ☒
TestSQLSelect
Contact Id: 1   Last Name: Gosnell   First Name: Denise
Contact Id: 2   Last Name: Doe   First Name: John
Contact Id: 4   Last Name: Doe   First Name: Jane
```

Figure 5-14

The prior example retrieves data from a common data source: a database table. However, ADO enables you to connect to various data sources, and it can treat those data sources as *virtual tables*. For example, you can connect to Microsoft Outlook using a SQL statement and ADO to populate a recordset. Here is an example of how you can retrieve data from an Outlook Calendar on Microsoft Exchange and print the results to the Immediate Window:

```
Sub RetrieveCalendar()

    Dim strConnection As String
    Dim cnConn As ADODB.Connection
    Dim rsCalendar As ADODB.Recordset

        Set cnConn = New ADODB.Connection
    Set rsCalendar = New ADODB.Recordset

    With cnConn
        .Provider = "Microsoft.ACE.OLEDB.12.0"
        .ConnectionString = "Exchange 4.0;" _
                        & "MAPILEVEL=Mailbox - Gosnell, Denise|;" _
                        & "PROFILE=DMG;" _
                        & "TABLETYPE=0;DATABASE=C:\WINDOWS\TEMP\;"
        .Open
    End With

    With rsCalendar
        .Open "Select * from Calendar", cnConn, adOpenStatic, _
                adLockReadOnly
        'print all records in calendar
```

```
            Do While Not rsCalendar.EOF
                Debug.Print rsCalendar(3).Name & ": " & rsCalendar(3).Value
                Debug.Print rsCalendar(10).Name & ": " & rsCalendar(10).Value
                Debug.Print vbCrLf
                rsCalendar.MoveNext
            Loop
            .Close
        End With

        Set rsCalendar = Nothing
        cnConn.Close
        Set cnConn = Nothing

    End Sub
```

In the preceding example, the Mailbox and Profile as used by your Outlook database should be specified. When you run the preceding code with a valid Mailbox and Profile, you see results similar to the following in the Immediate Window:

```
Subject: Doctor's Appointment
Received: 5/24/2004 2:30:18 PM

Subject: Meet Benita for lunch
Received: 5/25/2004 10:06:52 AM

Subject: Jazz Fest Training Meeting
Received: 6/10/2004 2:28:51 PM
```

Inserting Data Using SQL Insert Statements

The Insert statement is used to insert data into a table. The syntax for an Insert statement is:

```
INSERT INTO tablename (fieldname1, fieldname2, ... fieldnameN) VALUES (value1,
value2, ... valueN)
```

The Insert clause can be used to insert all or part of a record into the database. For example, suppose that the tblContacts table only has txtLastName, txtFirstName, txtWorkPhone, and txtHome Phone fields. To insert all of the record into the database in such a scenario, you could use the following:

```
INSERT INTO tblContacts (txtLastName, txtFirstName, txtWorkPhone, txtHomePhone)
VALUES ('Doe', 'Jane', '317-123-4567', '317-987-6543')
```

When adding a partial row for a table, you must specify at least the required fields in the table. Otherwise, the syntax is the same as the example shown previously.

As I will illustrate in detail in a later example, you can use SQL statements as part of a Command object that gets executed against the database to insert new records.

Inserting Results of a Select into a Table

Sometimes you must insert the results from a Select statement into an existing table. As long as the data types correspond to each other, data from one or more tables can easily be inserted into another table. The basic syntax is shown here:

```
INSERT INTO destination (fieldname1, fieldname2, ... fieldnameN)
SELECT fieldname1, fieldname2, ... fieldnameN
FROM source
[WHERE criteria]
```

If you wanted to insert the entire contents of the tblContacts table into a tblContactsArchive table, you could use the following statement:

```
INSERT INTO tblContactsArchive
SELECT * FROM tblContacts
```

Alternatively, you could list each field.

Updating Data Using SQL Statements

Update statements can be used to update existing records in the database. The basic syntax for Update statements is:

```
UPDATE tablename
SET column = value
WHERE criteria
```

Suppose, for example, that Jane Doe got married again and must now update her last name to Dawson. You could issue the following Update statement to update her existing record:

```
UPDATE tblContacts
SET txtLastName = 'Dawson'
WHERE txtLastName = 'Doe' AND txtFirstName = 'Jane'
```

As I will illustrate in detail in a later example, you can use SQL statements as part of a Command object that gets executed against the database to update existing records.

Deleting Data Using SQL Statements

Delete statements can be used to delete existing records from the database. The basic syntax for Delete statements is:

```
DELETE
FROM tablename
WHERE criteria
```

To delete Jane Doe's record from the database altogether, you could use the following statement:

```
DELETE from tblContacts WHERE txtLastName = 'Doe' AND txtFirstName = 'Jane'
```

As I will illustrate in the following example, you can use SQL statements as part of a `Command` object that gets executed against the database to delete existing records.

Try It Out   **Modify the Unbound Contacts Form to Use SQL**

Now turn your attention to the final example of working with disconnected recordsets. In this case, you will modify our existing Contacts form to use SQL statements.

1. Select `frmContactsUnbound` and right-click and select Copy. Select the Paste option, and name the new copy of the form `frmContactsUnboundSQL`.

2. Modify the `cmdSaveAll` Caption property to `Save Current Record`. The form should look similar to the one shown in Figure 5-15.

3. Add an additional variable declaration to the General Declarations section of the form, as shown here:

```
Dim rsContacts As ADODB.Recordset
Dim cnCh5 As ADODB.Connection
Dim strConnection As String
```

```
Dim blnAddMode As Boolean
```

4. Delete the existing `SaveAllRecords` procedure.

5. Delete the existing `Form_Unload` procedure.

6. Replace the existing `AddRecord` procedure with the following:

```
Sub AddRecord()

'set add mode to true
blnAddMode = True
'clear the current controls on the form so the

'user can fill in values for the new record
Call ClearControlsOnForm
End Sub
```

7. Replace the existing `DeleteRecord` procedure with the following:

```
Sub DeleteRecord()

'don't let the user issue a delete command if in add mode
If blnAddMode = True Then

    Exit Sub
End If

Dim intResponse As Integer

'confirm that user really wants to delete record
intResponse = MsgBox("Are you sure you want to delete this record?", vbYesNo)

'if the user cancels delete, then exit this procedure
```

```vba
If intResponse = vbNo Then
    Exit Sub
End If

'declare and create new command object
Dim cmdCommand As ADODB.Command
Set cmdCommand = New ADODB.Command

'create a new connection instance and open it using the connection string
Set cnCh5 = New ADODB.Connection
cnCh5.Open strConnection

'declare variable to store current contact
Dim intCurContact As Integer
intCurContact = 0

'generate SQL command to delete current record
Dim strSQL As String
strSQL = "DELETE FROM tblContacts WHERE intContactId = "
& rsContacts!intContactId

'set the command to the current connection
Set cmdCommand.ActiveConnection = cnCh5
'set the delete SQL statement to the command text
cmdCommand.CommandText = strSQL
'execute the delete command against the database
cmdCommand.Execute

'move to the next record in the local recordset since the
'current one is being deleted
If Not rsContacts.EOF Then
    rsContacts.MoveNext
    'save the id of the current (next) record
    intCurContact = rsContacts!intContactId
End If

'while connected to the database, go ahead and
'repopulate the recordset to make sure it contains
'the most current values from the database.
Set rsContacts.ActiveConnection = cnCh5
rsContacts.Requery
Set rsContacts.ActiveConnection = Nothing

'move back to the contact that was current before the
'requery

rsContacts.Find "[intContactId] = " & intCurContact

'populate the controls on the form
Call PopulateControlsOnForm

End Sub
```

8. Replace the existing `SaveCurrentRecord` procedure with the following:

```
Sub SaveCurrentRecord()

Dim cmdCommand As ADODB.Command
Set cmdCommand = New ADODB.Command
Dim strSQL As String

If Not rsContacts.BOF And Not rsContacts.EOF Then

    'create a new connection instance and open it using the connection string
    Set cnCh5 = New ADODB.Connection
    cnCh5.Open strConnection

    Dim intCurContact As Integer
    intCurContact = 0

    'if adding a new record
    If blnAddMode = True Then

            'create SQL to insert a new record into the database
        'containing the values on the form
        strSQL = "INSERT INTO tblContacts(" & _
            "txtLastName, txtFirstName, txtMiddleName, " & _
            "txtTitle, txtAddress1, txtAddress2, " & _
            "txtCity, txtState, txtZip, " & _
            "txtWorkPhone, txtHomePhone, txtCellPhone) " & _
            "VALUES (" & _
            "'" & Me.txtLastName & "', " & _
            "'" & Me.txtFirstName & "', " & _
            "'" & Me.txtMiddleName & "', " & _
            "'" & Me.txtTitle & "', " & _
            "'" & Me.txtAddress1 & "', " & _
            "'" & Me.txtAddress2 & "', " & _
            "'" & Me.txtCity & "', " & _
            "'" & Me.txtState & "', " & _
            "'" & Me.txtZip & "', " & _
            "'" & Me.txtWorkPhone & "', " & _
            "'" & Me.txtHomePhone & "', " & _
            "'" & Me.txtCellPhone & "') "

    Else
        'create SQL to update the existing record in the
        'database with the values on the form
        strSQL = "UPDATE tblContacts SET " & _
            "txtLastName = '" & Me.txtLastName & "', " & _
            "txtFirstName = '" & Me.txtFirstName & "', " & _
            "txtMiddleName = '" & Me.txtMiddleName & "', " & _
            "txtTitle = '" & Me.txtTitle & "', " & _
            "txtAddress1 = '" & Me.txtAddress1 & "', " & _
            "txtAddress2 = '" & Me.txtAddress2 & "', " & _
            "txtCity = '" & Me.txtCity & "', " & _
            "txtState = '" & Me.txtState & "', " & _
            "txtZip = '" & Me.txtZip & "', " & _
            "txtWorkPhone = '" & Me.txtWorkPhone & "', " & _
```

```
                        "txtHomePhone = '" & Me.txtHomePhone & "', " & _
                        "txtCellPhone = '" & Me.txtCellPhone & "' " & _
                        "WHERE intContactId = " & rsContacts!intContactId

            'save the id of the current record
            intCurContact = rsContacts!intContactId

        End If

    'set the command to the current connection
    Set cmdCommand.ActiveConnection = cnCh5
    'set the insert or update SQL statement to the command text
    cmdCommand.CommandText = strSQL
    'execute the delete command against the database
    cmdCommand.Execute

    'while connected to the database, go ahead and
    'repopulate the recordset to make sure it contains
    'the most current values from the database.
    Set rsContacts.ActiveConnection = cnCh5
    rsContacts.Requery
    Set rsContacts.ActiveConnection = Nothing

    'move back to the contact that was current before the
    'requery
    If intCurContact > 0 Then
        'move back to the contact that was just updated
        rsContacts.Find "[intContactId] = " & intCurContact
    Else
        'if just added new record, move to the beginning of
        'the recordset
        rsContacts.MoveFirst
    End If

    'reset add mode flag to false
    blnAddMode = False

    'populate the controls on the form
    Call PopulateControlsOnForm

    End If

End Sub
```

9. Replace the existing `MoveToFirstRecord`, `MoveToNextRecord`, `MoveToPreviousRecord`, and `MoveToLastRecord` procedures with the following:

```
Sub MoveToFirstRecord()

'move to the first record in the local disconnected recordset
If Not rsContacts.BOF And Not rsContacts.EOF Then
    rsContacts.MoveFirst
    'populate the controls on the form with the current record
    Call PopulateControlsOnForm
    blnAddMode = False
```

```
End If

End Sub

Sub MoveToLastRecord()
'move to the last record in the local disconnected recordset
If Not rsContacts.BOF And Not rsContacts.EOF Then
    rsContacts.MoveLast
    'populate the controls on the form with the current record
    Call PopulateControlsOnForm
    blnAddMode = False

End If

End Sub

Sub MoveToPreviousRecord()
'move to the previous record in the local disconnected recordset
'if not already at the beginning
If Not rsContacts.BOF Then
    rsContacts.MovePrevious
    'populate the controls on the form with the current record
    Call PopulateControlsOnForm
    blnAddMode = False
End If

End Sub

Sub MoveToNextRecord()

'move to the next record in the local disconnected recordset
'if not already at the end
If Not rsContacts.EOF Then
    rsContacts.MoveNext
    'populate the controls on the form with the current record
    Call PopulateControlsOnForm
    blnAddMode = False
End If

End Sub
```

10. Run the form and you should see a screen similar to Figure 5-16.

11. Select the Delete button on the form, and you should see a screen similar to Figure 5-17.

12. Select the Yes option to delete the record.

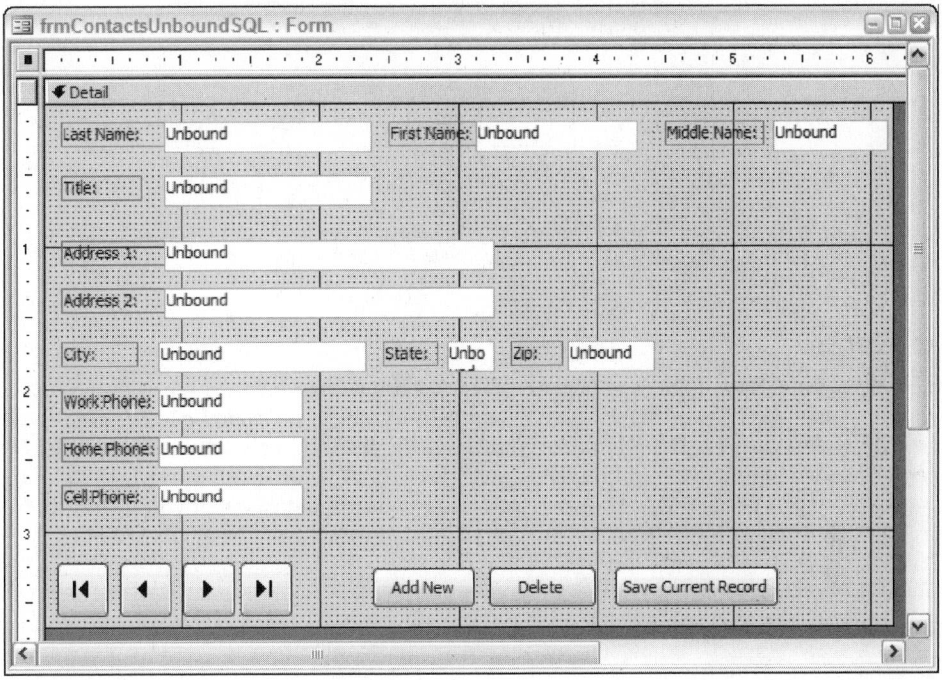

Figure 5-15

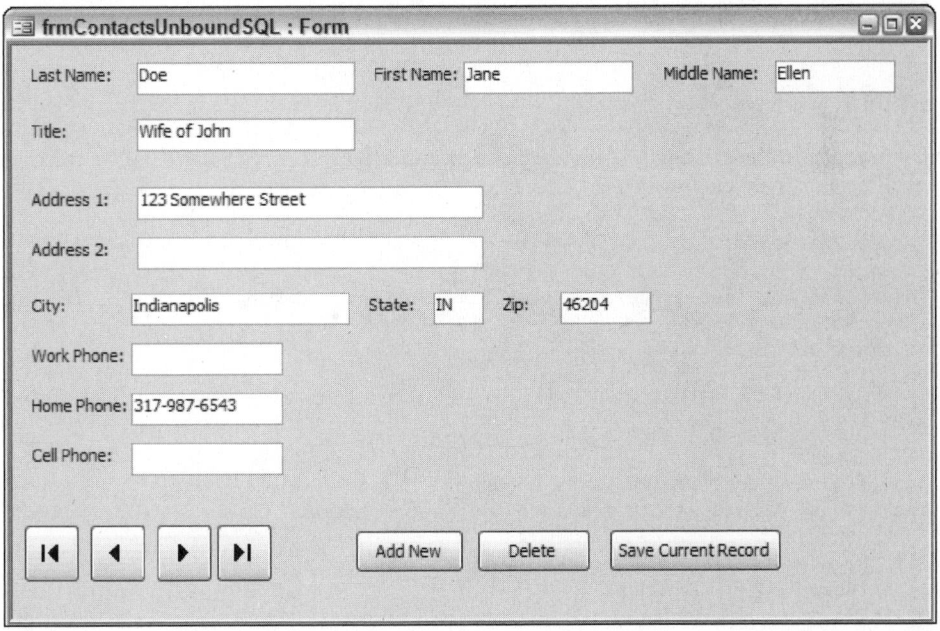

Figure 5-16

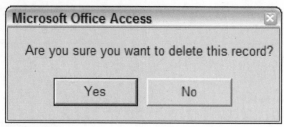

Figure 5-17

How It Works

First, you created a copy of the frmContactsUnbound and named it frmContactsUnboundSQL. You can now make changes to this version and still retain the prior one as an example to review as well. Next, you modified the Caption property of the cmdSaveAll button and deleted a few procedures that are no longer needed for the current example. Then, you replaced a few procedures, starting with AddRecord. The AddRecord procedure now sets a Boolean value to True to indicate that you're in Add mode. The controls on the form are then cleared so the user can input values into the empty controls.

```
Sub AddRecord()

'set add mode to true
blnAddMode = True

'clear the current controls on the form so the
'user can fill in values for the new record
Call ClearControlsOnForm


End Sub
```

Next, you replaced the existing DeleteRecord procedure with code that starts with confirming that the user really wants to delete the record:

```
Sub DeleteRecord()

'don't let the user issue a delete command if in add mode
If blnAddMode = True Then
    Exit Sub
End If

Dim intResponse As Integer

'confirm that user really wants to delete record
intResponse = MsgBox("Are you sure you want to delete this record?", vbYesNo)

'if the user cancels delete, then exit this procedure
If intResponse = vbNo Then
    Exit Sub
End If
```

Assuming that the user did not cancel the delete operation, you declared a new Command object and opened a new connection:

```
'declare and create new command object
Dim cmdCommand As ADODB.Command
Set cmdCommand = New ADODB.Command
'create a new connection instance and open it using the connection string
Set cnCh5 = New ADODB.Connection
cnCh5.Open strConnection
```

The current contact location was stored to be used later:

```
'declare variable to store current contact
Dim intCurContact As Integer
intCurContact = 0
```

You then created the SQL statement for the Delete command to delete the record based on the intContactId value of the current record:

```
'generate SQL command to delete current record
Dim strSQL As String
strSQL = "DELETE FROM tblContacts WHERE intContactId = " & rsContacts!intContactId
```

You then set the Command object to the existing connection, and the CommandText property was assigned to the SQL statement. When the Execute method executed, the SQL statement ran against the database:

```
'set the command to the current connection
Set cmdCommand.ActiveConnection = cnCh5
'set the delete SQL statement to the command text
cmdCommand.CommandText = strSQL
'execute the delete command against the database
cmdCommand.Execute
```

Next, the code moved to the next record because the prior one was just deleted:

```
'move to the next record in the local recordset since the
'current one is being deleted
If Not rsContacts.EOF Then
    rsContacts.MoveNext
    'save the id of the current (next) record
    intCurContact = rsContacts!intContactId
End If
```

Although connected to the database, the Requery method of the recordset was executed to refresh the recordset with the current values in the database:

```
'while connected to the database, go ahead and
'repopulate the recordset to make sure it contains
'the most current values from the database.
Set rsContacts.ActiveConnection = cnCh5
rsContacts.Requery
Set rsContacts.ActiveConnection = Nothing
```

The contact that was current before the requery was then located:

```
'move back to the contact that was current before the
'requery
rsContacts.Find "[intContactId] = " & intCurContact
```

At the end of the `DeleteRecord` procedure, the controls on the form were populated with the current record:

```
'populate the controls on the form
Call PopulateControlsOnForm

End Sub
```

After replacing the `DeleteRecord` procedure, you next replaced the `SaveCurrentRecord` procedure. The procedure began by declaring a `Command` object and a variable for the SQL statement:

```
Sub SaveCurrentRecord()

Dim cmdCommand As ADODB.Command
Set cmdCommand = New ADODB.Command
Dim strSQL As String
```

If records existed in the recordset, the connection was opened:

```
If Not rsContacts.BOF And Not rsContacts.EOF Then

    'create a new connection instance and open it using the connection string
    Set cnCh5 = New ADODB.Connection
    cnCh5.Open strConnection

        Dim intCurContact As Integer
    intCurContact = 0
```

If the `SaveAll` procedure was being called because you're in Add New Record mode, you created a SQL statement that inserted the current values on the form into the database:

```
'if adding a new record
If blnAddMode = True Then

    'create SQL to insert a new record into the database
    'containing the values on the form
    strSQL = "INSERT INTO tblContacts(" & _
        "txtLastName, txtFirstName, txtMiddleName, " & _
        "txtTitle, txtAddress1, txtAddress2, " & _
        "txtCity, txtState, txtZip, " & _
        "txtWorkPhone, txtHomePhone, txtCellPhone) " & _
        "VALUES (" & _
        "'" & Me.txtLastName & "', " & _
        "'" & Me.txtFirstName & "', " & _
        "'" & Me.txtMiddleName & "', " & _
        "'" & Me.txtTitle & "', " & _
        "'" & Me.txtAddress1 & "', " & _
```

```
                        "'" & Me.txtAddress2 & "', " & _
                        "'" & Me.txtCity & "', " & _
                        "'" & Me.txtState & "', " & _
                        "'" & Me.txtZip & "', " & _
                        "'" & Me.txtWorkPhone & "', " & _
                        "'" & Me.txtHomePhone & "', " & _
                        "'" & Me.txtCellPhone & "') "
```

If, however, you were in update mode in order to save changes to an existing record, you must create the SQL statement that will update the existing record in the database with the values in the controls on the form:

```
Else
    'create SQL to update the existing record in the
    'database with the values on the form
    strSQL = "UPDATE tblContacts SET " & _
        "txtLastName = '" & Me.txtLastName & "', " & _
        "txtFirstName = '" & Me.txtFirstName & "', " & _
        "txtMiddleName = '" & Me.txtMiddleName & "', " & _
        "txtTitle = '" & Me.txtTitle & "', " & _
        "txtAddress1 = '" & Me.txtAddress1 & "', " & _
        "txtAddress2 = '" & Me.txtAddress2 & "', " & _
        "txtCity = '" & Me.txtCity & "', " & _
        "txtState = '" & Me.txtState & "', " & _
        "txtZip = '" & Me.txtZip & "', " & _
        "txtWorkPhone = '" & Me.txtWorkPhone & "', " & _
        "txtHomePhone = '" & Me.txtHomePhone & "', " & _
        "txtCellPhone = '" & Me.txtCellPhone & "' " & _
        "WHERE intContactId = " & rsContacts!intContactId
        'save the id of the current record
    intCurContact = rsContacts!intContactId
End If
```

Whether you were in Add New or Update mode, you were now ready to execute the SQL statement against the database by assigning the CommandText property to the SQL statement and executing the Execute method:

```
'set the command to the current connection
Set cmdCommand.ActiveConnection = cnCh5
'set the insert or update SQL statement to the command text
cmdCommand.CommandText = strSQL
'execute the delete command against the database
cmdCommand.Execute
```

While still connected to the database, you repopulated the recordset with the most current values and then disconnected the recordset again:

```
'while connected to the database, go ahead and
'repopulate the recordset to make sure it contains
'the most current values from the database.
Set rsContacts.ActiveConnection = cnCh5
rsContacts.Requery
Set rsContacts.ActiveConnection = Nothing
```

Next, you moved back to the current record if you were in Update mode:

```
'move back to the contact that was current before the
'requery
If intCurContact > 0 Then
    'move back to the contact that was just updated
    rsContacts.Find "[intContactId] = " & intCurContact
Else
    'if just added new record, move to the beginning of
    'the recordset
    rsContacts.MoveFirst
End If
```

Finally, you reset the Add mode flag to `False` because you were no longer in Add mode under any circumstance. You set the controls on the form to display the values in the current record of the recordset.

```
'reset add mode flag to false
blnAddMode = False

'populate the controls on the form
Call PopulateControlsOnForm

End If

End Sub
```

You made a few minor changes to the `MoveToFirstRecord`, `MoveToNextRecord`, `MoveToPreviousRecord`, and `MoveToLastRecord` procedures to remove calls to `SaveCurrentRecord` and to add a statement setting the `blnAddMode` flag to `False`. These procedures were just replaced again for simplicity, but not a lot changed.

```
Sub MoveToFirstRecord()

'move to the first record in the local disconnected recordset
If Not rsContacts.BOF And Not rsContacts.EOF Then
    rsContacts.MoveFirst
    'populate the controls on the form with the current record
    Call PopulateControlsOnForm
    blnAddMode = False
End If

End Sub
```

You then ran the form and manipulated the database, including deleting an existing record. These procedures ran to issue SQL statements against the database to insert, update, and delete records, and then the disconnected recordset was repopulated with the current values in the database. This is yet another way to write code that allows your forms to interact with data in underlying data sources in a disconnected fashion.

Using ADOX to Manipulate Data Objects

The ADOX library has an object model that allows you to create database objects such as tables, indexes, and keys, as well as to control security, establish referential integrity in a database, and perform cascade updates and deletions. The `Catalog` object is at the top of the ADOX object model, with `Tables`, `Groups`, `Users`, `Procedures`, and `Views` collections. Please consult the online help for the complete ADOX object model.

Just as with the ADODB library, if you want to make use of the ADOX library in your Access solutions, you must add a reference. You can add references by selecting Tools ➪ References in the Visual Basic Editor. Figure 5-18 shows a reference to the ADOX library as part of the current project.

Let's look at a few examples of what you can do with the ADOX library.

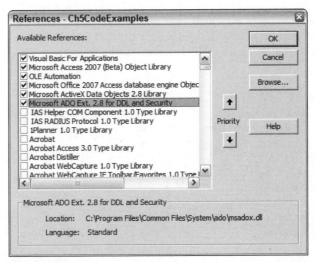

Figure 5-18

Creating a Table with ADOX

For starters, you can create new databases, tables, and other objects using the ADOX library. The following procedure is an example of how you can create a new table in an existing database.

```
Sub TestCreateTable()

    Dim catCatalog As ADOX.Catalog
    Dim tblSupplier As ADOX.Table

    Set catCatalog = New ADOX.Catalog
    Set catCatalog.ActiveConnection = CurrentProject.Connection

    ' Create and name the new table
    Set tblSupplier = New ADOX.Table
    With tblSupplier
```

```
            .Name = "tblSupplier"
            .Columns.Append "CompanyName", adVarWChar, 50
            .Columns.Append "CompanyPhone", adVarWChar, 12
        End With

        'append the new table to the database
        catCatalog.Tables.Append tblSupplier

        'release memory
        Set catCatalog.ActiveConnection = Nothing
        Set catCatalog = Nothing
        Set tblSupplier = Nothing

    End Sub
```

First, a new `Catalog` object is declared and is assigned to the current open connection. Then, a new table called `tblSupplier` is created, and a name and new columns are assigned to it. The new table is then appended to the `Catalog.Tables` collection, which added it to the database. After running the preceding procedure, you can see (in Figure 5-19) that a new table called `tblSupplier` has been added to the database.

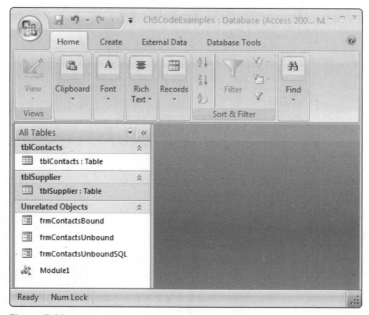

Figure 5-19

These and many other features can be manipulated using the ADOX library. This section is not meant to be exhaustive, but just to provide you with a few examples of how you might use the ADOX library.

Summary

This chapter covered one of the most important concepts in Access programming—working with data in databases. You should now understand the basics of retrieving and modifying data from VBA code using ActiveX Data Objects (ADO) and using the ADO object model—namely the `Connection`, `Command`, and `Recordset` objects. You also learned how to work with recordsets that are bound to the form and maintain an open connection and those that are disconnected. When recordsets are disconnected from the data source, changes made locally are not saved to the underlying database unless you take additional steps. You also learned how to use `Select`, `Insert`, `Update`, and `Delete` statements in the SQL language to interact with the database. Finally, you learned that the ADOX object model allows you to manipulate database tables and so on.

The next chapter discusses various techniques you can use to build interactive forms. It provides you with some useful approaches for improving user interaction.

Exercises

1. What is ADO, and why do you use it?

2. Why should you use a disconnected (unbound) recordset instead of a connected (bound) recordset?

3. What is SQL, and why do you use it?

4. What is the ADOX object model? Give some examples of what it will allow you to do.

Building Interactive Forms

Chapter 5 covered the basics of using ADO and SQL to work with data sources and showed you how to display the data retrieved from the database on a form. In this chapter, you will explore ways to build interactive forms and to control the operation of those forms programmatically using VBA code. Many of the topics covered in this chapter are illustrated in various examples throughout the book, but some also deserve a separate discussion.

The chapter will cover:

- ❑ Navigating between forms
- ❑ Opening, closing, and hiding forms
- ❑ Choosing the right type of control to use for data
- ❑ Populating controls
- ❑ Displaying messages to the user
- ❑ Validating data entered into controls
- ❑ Setting control alignment and tab stops

Form Navigation and Flow

You can control the order and manner in which forms can be opened within your Access applications in various ways. For example, you can design switchboard forms that allow the user to select which form to open. Another option is to open a main form and allow a user to open separate forms from the main form. The style of navigation you choose depends on the type of system and the manner in which users will interact with the various forms.

During the design phase, you should consider the flow of forms and how users will navigate from one form to the next. It is very simple to control how forms are displayed. The following is an example that illustrates how to open, hide, minimize, and close forms.

```
'open a form
DoCmd.OpenForm "FormName"
'close a form

DoCmd.Close acForm, "FormName"

'minimize the current form
DoCmd.Minimize

'hide a form
FormName.Visible = False

'make the form visible again
FormName.Visible = True
```

A well-designed application allows a user to interact with the application without having to use Access to open the form manually from the database window. An easy way to have a form open automatically is to use the AutoExec macro to specify which form should open automatically when the application opens.

Try It Out   Building a Switchboard Form

In this example, you will build a simple switchboard form that opens automatically when the application opens. The switchboard form enables the user to open multiple forms from a menu of choices.

1. Create a new database by selecting the Office Button ➪ New ➪ Blank Database. Specify Ch6CodeExamples for the file name and click the Create button.

2. Add four new forms to the application. Name the forms frmMain, frmAccounts, frmPayments, and frmRegister, respectively.

3. Open frmMain in design view and add three command buttons. Name the command buttons cmdAccounts, cmdPayments, and cmdRegister. Set the caption of the command buttons to View/Manage Accounts, Make Payments, and View/Manage Register, respectively. Also, set the Record Selectors, Navigation Buttons, and Dividing Lines properties of the form to No. An example of the form at this point is shown in Figure 6-1.

4. Select the cmdAccounts command button and add the following code to the Click event.

```
Private Sub cmdAccounts_Click()

'open the Accounts form
DoCmd.OpenForm "frmAccounts"

'hide the main switchboard form
Forms.Item("frmMain").Visible = False

End Sub
```

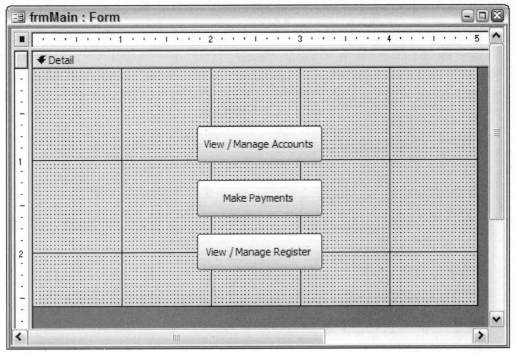

Figure 6-1

5. Select the cmdPayments command button and add the following code to the Click event:

```
Private Sub cmdPayments_Click()

'open the Accounts form
DoCmd.OpenForm "frmPayments"

'hide the main switchboard form
Forms.Item("frmMain").Visible = False

End Sub
```

6. Select the cmdRegister command button and add the following code to the Click event:

```
Private Sub cmdRegister_Click()

'open the Accounts form
DoCmd.OpenForm "frmRegister"

'hide the main switchboard form
Forms.Item("frmMain").Visible = False

End Sub
```

7. Open the `frmAccounts` form. Add a command button to the form. Change the `Name` property of the command button to `cmdMenu` and change the `Caption` property to `Menu`. Add a label to the form and type `View/Manage Accounts` in the label. The form should be similar to that shown in Figure 6-2.

8. Select the `cmdMenu` command button and add the following code to the `Click` event:

```
Private Sub cmdMenu_Click()

'display the switchboard main form
Forms.Item("frmMain").Visible = True

'close the current form
DoCmd.Close acForm, "frmAccounts"

End Sub
```

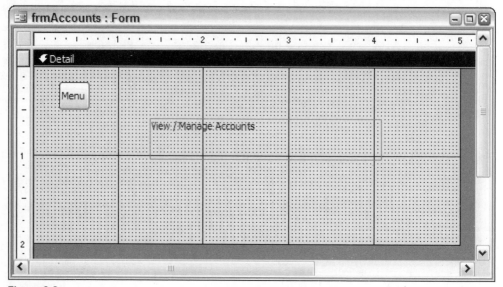

Figure 6-2

9. Open the `frmPayments` form. Add a command button to the form. Change the `Name` property of the command button to `cmdMenu` and change the `Caption` property to `Menu`. Add a label to the form and set the caption to `Make Payment`.

10. Select the `cmdMenu` command button and add the following code to the `Click` event:

```
Private Sub cmdMenu_Click()

'display the switchboard main form
```

```
Forms.Item("frmMain").Visible = True

'close the current form
DoCmd.Close acForm, "frmPayments"

End Sub
```

11. Open the `frmRegister` form. Add a command button to the form. Change the `Name` property of the command button to `cmdMenu` and change the `Caption` property to `Menu`. Add a label to the form and type `Check Register` in the label.

12. Select the `cmdMenu` command button and add the following code to the `Click` event:

```
Private Sub cmdMenu_Click()

'display the switchboard main form
Forms.Item("frmMain").Visible = True


'close the current form
DoCmd.Close acForm, "frmRegister"

End Sub
```

13. From the database window, create a new macro named `AutoExec` that contains the `OpenForm` command for `frmMain`, as shown in Figure 6-3.

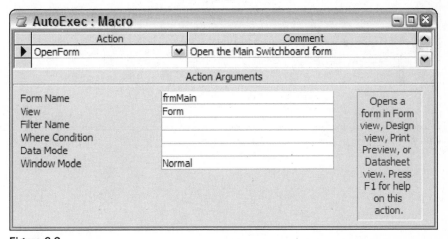

Figure 6-3

14. Save all changes to the forms and VBA code.

15. Close the entire database by selecting Office Button ⇨ Close Database, and then reopen the same database. A screen like the one shown in Figure 6-4 should load automatically.

16. Select the View/Manage Accounts button, and a screen like the one shown in Figure 6-5 should open.

How It Works

In this example, you created a switchboard form with three command buttons. Under each command, you added code to open the respective form, using the OpenForm method, and then you hid the switchboard form by setting its Visible property to False.

```
Private Sub cmdAccounts_Click()

'open the Accounts form
DoCmd.OpenForm "frmAccounts"

'hide the main switchboard form
Forms.Item("frmMain").Visible = False

End Sub
```

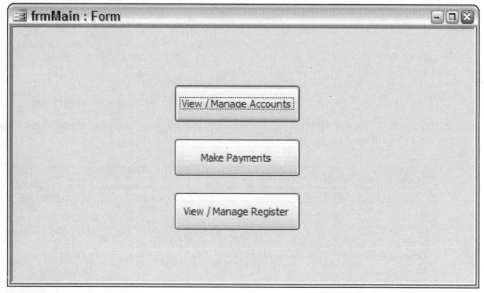

Figure 6-4

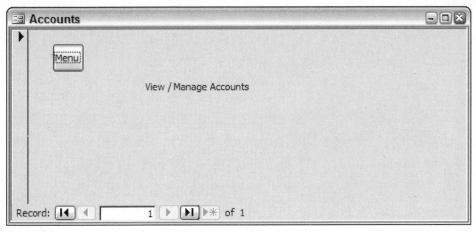

Figure 6-5

You also created the three forms that can be opened from the switchboard. On each of those forms, a command button was added to allow the user to return to the switchboard menu. Code was then added to the `Click` event of each menu button to unhide the switchboard form by setting the `Visible` property to `True`, and to close the current form by using the `Close` method of the `DoCmd` object:

```
Private Sub cmdMenu_Click()

'display the switchboard main form
Forms.Item("frmMain").Visible = True


'close the current form
DoCmd.Close acForm, "frmAccounts"

End Sub
```

You then added an `AutoExec` macro to cause the switchboard form to open when the database opens. When the database opens, Access automatically runs any commands in the macro named `AutoExec`.

From the switchboard, any one of the three other forms can be opened. You can then return to the switchboard to select a different form by using the Menu button on the respective form. Although this is a simple example, you can apply the concepts to any application for navigating among forms.

Working with Controls

Prior to reading this book, you probably worked with a variety of controls on Access forms, such as labels, text boxes, command buttons, and combo boxes. As you are already aware, controls can be added to a form using the Controls from the Design ribbon on the toolbar, as shown in Figure 6-6. Now turn your attention to a related topic: working with controls.

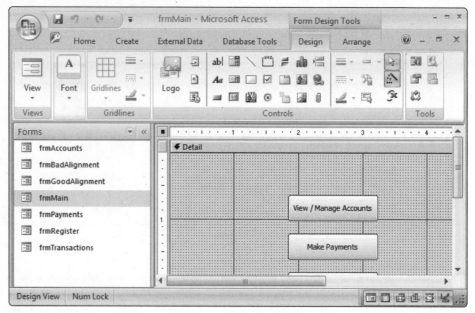

Figure 6-6

In this section, you'll explore a few ways to work with these controls through VBA code. You learned in Chapter 3 that objects have properties and methods that can be displayed in the Properties window in design view. You also learned that the properties, methods, and events of an object can be managed using VBA code. Controls are examples of objects that can be managed in these ways.

For example, you learned from the ADO examples in Chapter 5 that you can display data in a text box. An example of code that displays a value in a text box is shown here:

```
Me.txtLastName = rsContacts!txtLastName
```

Although text boxes are great for simple data entry and the displaying of a single and small value, at times you will require more sophisticated ways to display data. In the next few sections, you will look at some examples of more sophisticated controls that you can use to build more robust applications.

Combo Boxes versus List Boxes

Combo boxes and list boxes enable you to display various choices in a list. They also allow you to display multiple columns of data in the single listing.

Combo boxes and list boxes have a lot in common, but they also differ in some ways, as is illustrated in the comparison table that follows.

Feature	Combo Box	List Box
Values accepted from user	Allows the user to select a value from the list or to add a new value that is not on the list, depending on the setting for the Limit to List property.	Allows the user to select only a value in the list.
Locating values as user types	Matches the pattern as you type so that the value in the list that matches the letters you have typed appears as the selection.	Takes you to the first item in the list that starts with the letter you type.
Selection of values in a list	Allows a user to select only a single value.	Allows a user to select one or more values in the list.

You can programmatically add and remove items to and from combo boxes and list boxes by using the AddItem and RemoveItem methods. The below example uses the AddItem method to add values in a recordset to a combo box named cboPlan.

```
Dim rsPlans As New ADODB.Recordset

'populate the list of plans from the database
Set rsPlans = ExecuteSPRetrieveRS("spRetrievePlans", 0)

cboPlan.RowSource = ""
cboPlan.LimitToList = True
cboPlan.ColumnCount = 2
cboPlan.RowSourceType = "Value List"
cboPlan.BoundColumn = 0

Do While Not rsPlans.EOF
    'populate the priority combo box
    cboPlan.AddItem rsPlans!PlanId & ";" & rsPlans!PlanName
    rsPlans.MoveNext
Loop
```

In this example, for each entry in the combo box, the PlanId and PlanName are displayed because the AddItem method received values separated a by semicolon (;). The semicolon is used to designate that multiple columns should be created. For example, the following code adds values for both last and first name columns to the list:

```
cboName.AddItem "Doe;John"
```

Try It Out   Populating Combo and List Boxes

You will now populate a combo box and a list box with the same values and illustrate how to retrieve the selection from the user.

1. Open the `frmAccounts` form of the current Ch6CodeExamples database.

2. Add a combo box and a list box control to the form, using the ToolBox.

3. Set the `Name` property of the combo box to `cboAccounts` and the `Name` property of the list box control `lstAccounts`. Set each of the labels to `Accounts`. The form should look similar to the one shown in Figure 6-7.

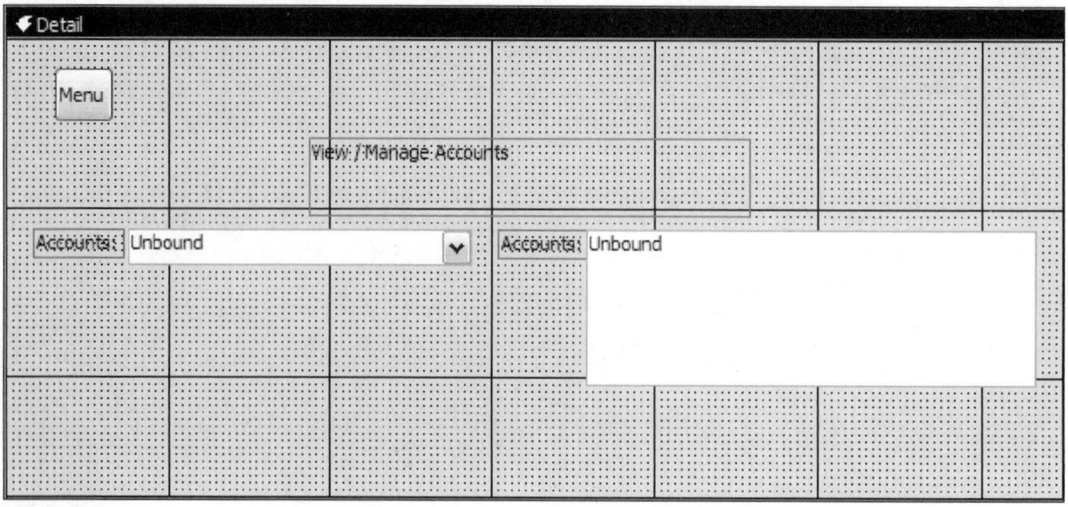

Figure 6-7

4. Add the following code to the `Load` event for the form:

```
Private Sub Form_Load()

    'populate the combo box with values from a
    'specified list
    With cboAccounts
        .RowSource = ""
        .ColumnCount = 2
```

```
        .RowSourceType = "Value List"
        .LimitToList = True
        .BoundColumn = 0
        .AddItem "Old National Bank;Car Payment"
        .AddItem "Chase Manhattan;MasterCard"
        .AddItem "Countrywide Home Loans;House Payment"
    End With

    'populate the list box with values from a
    'specified list

    With lstAccounts
        .RowSource = ""
        .ColumnCount = 2
        .RowSourceType = "Value List"
        .BoundColumn = 0
        .AddItem "Old National Bank;Car Payment"
        .AddItem "Chase Manhattan;MasterCard"
        .AddItem "Countrywide Home Loans;House Payment"
    End With

End Sub
```

5. Add the following code to the `Change` event of the combo box:

```
Private Sub cboAccounts_Change()

'display a message to the user of the selected valueMsgBox cboAccounts.Text

End Sub
```

6. Add the following code to the `Click` event of the list box:

```
Private Sub lstAccounts_Click()

'display a message to the user of the first value in
'the selected column
MsgBox lstAccounts.Column(0)

End Sub
```

7. Open the form in view mode to run the form. You should see a screen similar to Figure 6.8.

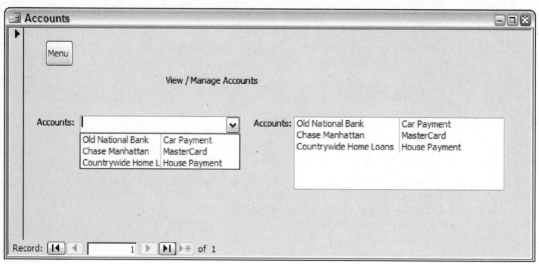

Figure 6-8

8. Type the letter C in the combo box. The text should jump to Chase Manhattan. Then, type an O in the combo box, and the text should jump to Countrywide Home Loans (because it starts with a CO). Repeat these steps for the list box. You should find that when you type C, Chase Manhattan is selected, and when you type O, Old National Bank is selected.

9. You should see message boxes displaying the value selected.

How It Works

Using the AddItem method, you added the same values to the combo box and the list box so that you could see the differences between the two controls side by side:

```
Private Sub Form_Load()

    'populate the combo box with values from a
    'specified list
    With cboAccounts
        .RowSource = ""
        .ColumnCount = 2
        .RowSourceType = "Value List"
        .LimitToList = True
        .BoundColumn = 0
        .AddItem "Old National Bank;Car Payment"
        .AddItem "Chase Manhattan;MasterCard"
        .AddItem "Countrywide Home Loans;House Payment"
```

```
        End With

        'populate the list box with values from a
        'specified list    With lstAccounts
            .RowSource = ""
            .ColumnCount = 2
            .RowSourceType = "Value List"
            .BoundColumn = 0
            .AddItem "Old National Bank;Car Payment"
            .AddItem "Chase Manhattan;MasterCard"
            .AddItem "Countrywide Home Loans;House Payment"
        End With

    End Sub
```

The LimitToList property of the combo box was set to True, so only values in the list could be selected. Various properties such as RowSource and RowSource type were specified to indicate that the values would be coming from a value list, as opposed to a table or other source.

You also added code to display the selected value from the combo box and list box. You changed the value in the combo box so that a message box shows users the value displayed in the text field.

```
    Private Sub cboAccounts_Change()

    'display a message to the user of the selected value
    MsgBox cboAccounts.Text

    End Sub
```

When you select a value from the list box, a message box shows users the value contained in the first selected column:

```
    Private Sub lstAccounts_Click()

    'display a message to the user of the first value in
    'the selected columnMsgBox lstAccounts.Column(0)

    End Sub
```

Tab Controls and Subforms

When you have a lot of data that needs to be displayed on a single form, tab controls provide one way or organizing data on a single form into separate components. A tab control allows you to place separate controls on each tab. For example, you may have one tab that contains checking account information and another tab that contains savings account information, as shown in Figure 6-9.

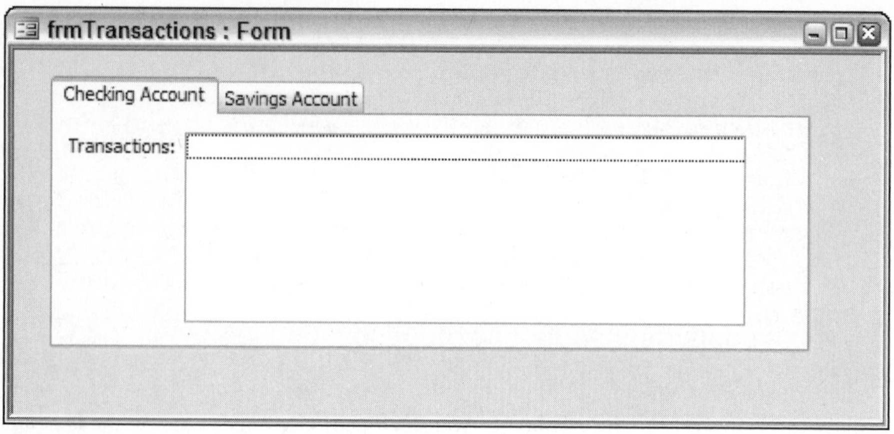

Figure 6-9

The case study in Chapter 13 illustrates using a tab control for different portions of the project record.

You can then refer to the pages of the tab control in VBA code, as shown here:

```
'show the checking account register
Page1.Visible = True

'hide the savings account register
Page2.Visible = False
```

In the preceding code example, the checking account register is displayed to the user and the savings account is not. This may be useful in a scenario when one user is named on both accounts, but another user is named on only one of the accounts. You could, for example, control the visibility of the tabs based on the specified user ID.

Another way to handle forms that include complex amounts or types of data is to use a subform. A subform is a form within a form. To insert a subform, you simply drag and drop the Subform control from the ToolBox just as you would any other control. You then change the Source Object property of the subform to the name of the form you wish to display. An example of a subform is shown in Figure 6-10.

Figure 6-10 shows a transactions form displayed within an accounts form. Any form that you create can be displayed within another form. You then tie the subform to the parent form so that the data it displays relates to the data on the parent form (for example, for the same account). One way to tie a subform to a parent form is using the Link Child Fields and Link Master Fields properties.

Whenever you make changes to a subform you are changing the original form, so be careful.

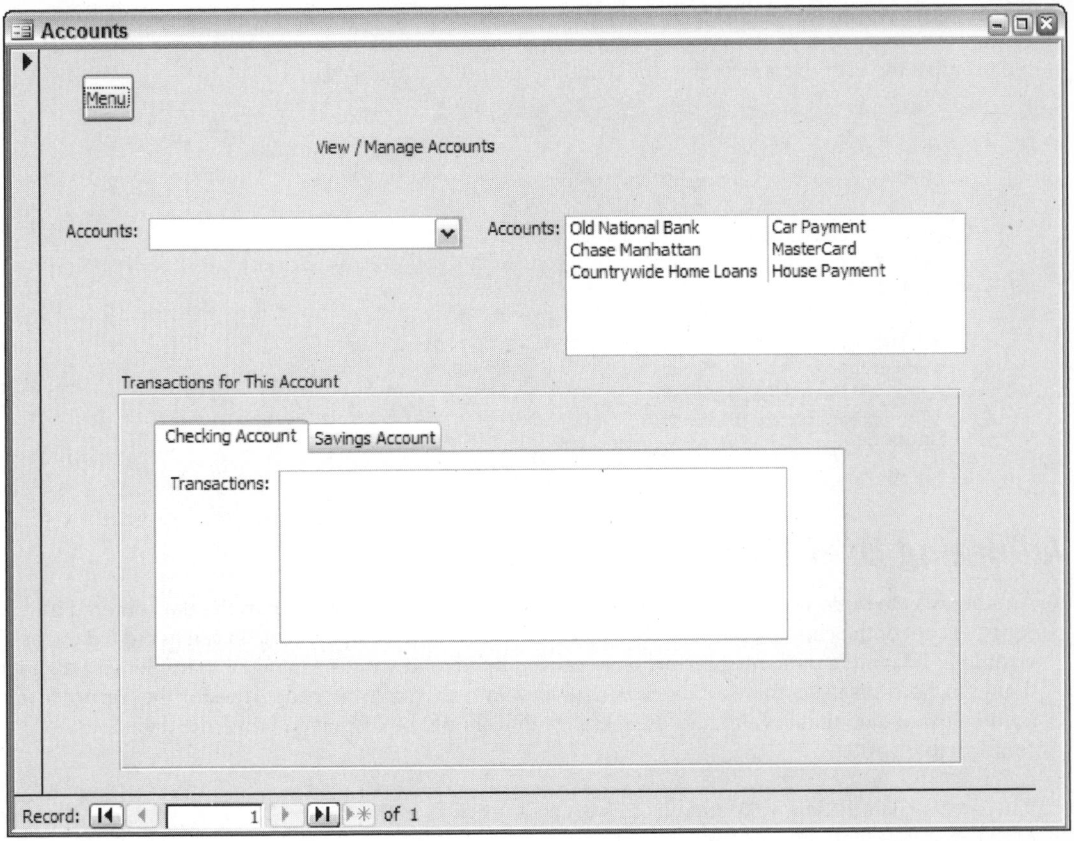

Figure 6-10

Building User Interaction

After you have chosen the right controls, you must program ways for users to interact with those controls. You can program the application to interact with a user in various ways. For example, you have already learned how to write event procedure code that executes when the user takes a particular action on the form. In this section, you will look at a couple of additional examples of how you can improve user interaction in your applications. You will look at using the MsgBox function for more complex scenarios and at validating user input.

The MsgBox Function

You have already seen examples of the MsgBox function to display a message. The MsgBox function is a lot more powerful than the simple examples I have illustrated so far. You can actually ask questions with multiple-choice answers and then process those choices to take the appropriate action.

For example, to ask the user a Yes/No question and then take a different action depending on the response, you can specify the vbYesNo value for the message box style parameter. The following example prompts the user to confirm that the deletion should be processed:

```
Dim intResponse As Integer

'display a Yes/No message box to the user
intResponse = MsgBox("Are you sure you want to delete this record?", vbYesNo,
"Delete?")

'determine how the user responded and act accordingly
If intResponse = vbYes Then
    MsgBox "Delete confirmed."
ElseIf intResponse = vbNo Then
    MsgBox "Delete cancelled."
End If
```

Validating User Input

Another way to build user interaction is to provide feedback to the user when the data entered into a control is not of the correct data type. By correcting the data error up front, you can avoid a database error later or avoid a data integrity problem caused by invalid values. One way to implement data validation in Access is to set the ValidationRule and ValidationText properties for the control to specify the type of data that is valid and the message that should be displayed when the data does not conform to the rule.

You can also handle data validation from VBA code, such as in the BeforeUpdate event or AfterUpdate event of the control.

Try It Out   Adding Data Validation to the frmPayments Form

Here you modify the sample application to implement a validation event for the frmPayments form.

1.   Open frmPayments in design view.

2.   Add a text box control to the form and name it txtValue.

3.   In the BeforeUpdate event for the text box, add the following code:

```
Private Sub txtValue_BeforeUpdate(Cancel As Integer)

If txtValue = "" Or IsNull(txtValue) Then
    MsgBox "You must specify a value for this field."
    Cancel = True
ElseIf Len(txtValue) > 10 Then
    MsgBox "The value for this field must be 10 characters or less."
    Cancel = True
End If

End Sub
```

4. Run the form, select the field and enter a value with more than 10 characters, and then press the tab key to leave the field. You should see a message indicating that the value must be 10 characters or less.

5. Delete the value entirely so that the field is blank. Then tab to another field. You should see a message indicating that a value must be specified for the field.

How It Works

In this example, you added a text box control to the form. You then added code for the `BeforeUpdate` event to make sure that the user entered a valid value in this required field.

Adding Polish to Your Forms

You can take several actions to make sure that your forms are polished. For example, you should always make sure to align the controls on the form and try to space them evenly to provide a clean appearance. Look at the difference between the forms shown side by side in Figure 6-11.

Figure 6-11

The second form has a much better appearance than the first one. To align the controls easily, you can hold down the `Shift` key to select the multiple controls to align. Then, right-click, select `Align`, and select the desired alignment direction from the list that appears.

Another nice finishing touch is to make sure that the tab stops are in the desired order. You have no doubt used an application where you tried to tab through the fields to fill in information quickly and found yourself in a field that was out of order. To provide a better user experience and make data entry and navigation as easy as possible, you should make sure the tab stops have a logical order. Access makes it very easy to view and modify tab stops. To view and modify the current tab stops for a form, simply select the Arrange ribbon ➪ Tab Order. A screen like the one shown in Figure 6-12 will be displayed where you can modify the order.

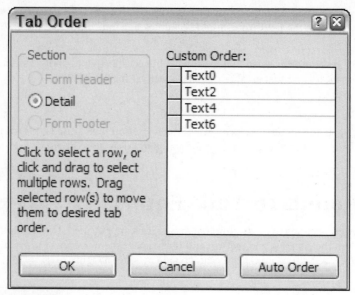

Figure 6-12

You can also select the `Auto Order` option to have Access automatically order the controls from top to bottom, left to right. These few basic tips will help you make your application appear more polished.

Summary

This chapter covered the basics of building interactive applications, including how to navigate among forms using VBA code and how to use some of the more complex controls to display data and receive user input. At this point, you have a basic understanding of how to design forms to display and manage data from a database. Chapter 7 covers the various ways to use VBA code to link, import, and export data to and from external data sources.

Exercises

1. What is the `AutoExec` macro, and why should you use it?

2. Describe at least two differences between combo boxes and list boxes.

3. What is the `MsgBox` function, and how can you use it?

Importing, Linking, and Exporting Using External Data Sources

Chapter 5 covered the basics of using ADO and SQL to work with data sources. All the ADO and SQL examples dealt with data stored in tables in a database. However, in today's world of technology, you will often work with data and applications in a variety of formats, such as text files and spreadsheets. You may need to import or link data from various sources into your database to avoid having to retype all the information that is already stored electronically in another format. At some point, another application might need the data in your application or you may want to get data out of your application for another reason. In that case, you can export information from your application into another format.

In this chapter, you will explore the various ways to use VBA code to link, import, and export to external data sources. The chapter will cover:

- ❑ The difference between linking, importing, and exporting
- ❑ Linking, importing, and exporting to external Access databases (MDB files)
- ❑ Linking, importing, and exporting to SQL Server databases
- ❑ Linking, importing, and exporting to other files such as spreadsheets and text files
- ❑ Creating and sending an e-mail programmatically

These techniques will enable you to build robust applications that interact with various applications and formats.

Linking, Importing, and Exporting Overview

Linking to external data means creating a pointer to an external data source that allows you to interact directly with the underlying data. *Importing* external data literally imports a copy of the data into your application. *Exporting* data refers to the idea of extracting data from your application to an external file or format.

Here are some situations when you should consider linking:

❑ The data resides on a database server that your application and others can use.

❑ The data is used by another program that requires the native file format.

❑ The underlying data needs to be updated on a regular basis in its native format.

Here are some instances when you should consider importing:

❑ An existing system is being migrated to a new application and the data from the old system will be used in the new application. (In some cases, you may be able to migrate to another system but keep the data on a database server without needing to import the data.)

❑ Numerous data operations must be run against the data from another source. You can obtain performance improvements by importing the data, but the underlying data will be out of sync if you make any changes to the data after it is imported.

Access allows you to link to and import from data sources such as Access (Jet) databases, SQL Server databases, other ODBC databases, dBase, Paradox, Microsoft Sharepoint, XML documents, HTML documents, text files, Microsoft Exchange, Microsoft Outlook, and spreadsheets such as Microsoft Excel and Lotus.

> *Many of the techniques covered in this chapter can also be implemented using menus and wizards in Access. To import or link data using the menus and wizards, select the External Data tab and then select the type of data you would like to use from the available options. You can export data by selecting a particular object (table, for example) in the Database Window, right-clicking, and selecting the Export option from the pop-up box.*

Now that you understand the high-level concept of importing, linking, and exporting, you can jump right in to learning the techniques that will allow you to work with some of these supported data sources.

Create a blank database to use for the examples in this chapter. To do so, select the Office Button ➪ New. From the list of available templates, select "Blank Database," provide the file name `Ch7CodeExamples.accdb` and path, and press the Create button.

Access and Other Databases

You can use the `TransferDatabase` method of the `DoCmd` object to import from, link to, and export data to Access and several other databases, including SQL Server and Oracle. The basic syntax of the `TransferDatabase` method is shown in the following code:

```
DoCmd.TransferDatabase TransferType, DatabaseType, DatabaseName, ObjectType,
Source, Destination, StructureOnly, StoreLogin
```

Various parameters are used to specify how the method should execute. The following table explains the use of each parameter.

Parameter	Description
TransferType	Type of transfer to be performed. Valid choices are acImport (default), acLink, and acExport.
DatabaseType	Type of database being used. Access is the default. See the help documentation for a complete list and for the exact syntax for a particular database.
DatabaseName	The full name, including the path, of the database being used.
ObjectType	The type of object that has data you want to work with. The default is acTable.
Source	Name of the object whose data you want to work with.
Destination	Name of the object in the destination database.
StructureOnly	Use True to work with the structure only and False to work with the structure and data. False is the default.
StoreLogin	Whether to store the login and password. False is the default.

Let's look at an example. Suppose that you want to import data from an Access database called SampleDb. The data you want to import is in a table called Sales, and you want it to be imported to your current database under the name tblSales. You could run the following command from your current Access application:

```
DoCmd.TransferDatabase acImport, "Microsoft Access",_
    "SampleDb.mdb", acTable, "Sales", "tblSales"
```

Here's an example that shows linking to a table called Sales in an ODBC database called Wrox:

```
DoCmd.TransferDatabase acLink, "ODBC Database", _
    "ODBC;DSN=DataSourceName;UID=username;PWD=pwd;
        LANGUAGE=us_english;" _
    & "DATABASE=Wrox", acTable, "Sales", "dboSales"
```

The ODBC data source name can point to any database that ODBC supports, including SQL Server and Oracle, to name a few examples. As with any linking operation, you see the table or tables from the Database Window in Access.

> WARNING: There is no Undo option for database transfers. Make sure that you have a current backup of both databases before you begin. Furthermore, be very sure to verify the correctness of the Source and Destination parameters.

Try It Out   Importing Data from the Sample Northwind Database

Now it's your turn to try this out. Let's import data from the sample Northwind database that comes with Access.

1. Insert a new module into your `Ch7CodeExamples` database.

2. Add the following code to the module:

```
Sub TestTransferDatabase()

'import from Northwind

DoCmd.TransferDatabase acImport, "Microsoft Access", _
    "C:\Program Files\Microsoft Office\OFFICE12\SAMPLES\Northwind.accdb", _
acTable, "Employees", "tblEmployees"

End Sub
```

3. Modify the preceding path to the location on your hard drive where `Northwind.mdb` is located. If you do not have the sample Northwind database installed, change the previous parameters to reference the Access database that you do have.

4. From the Immediate Window in the Visual Basic Editor, type `TestTransferDatabase` and press Enter to run the procedure. You may receive a warning message similar to that in Figure 7-1, in which case you should click the Open button.

Figure 7-1

5. Open the Database Window and you should see a screen similar to Figure 7-2.

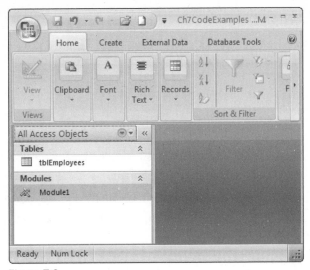

Figure 7-2

How It Works

In this example, you used the `TransferDatabase` method to import data from the Northwind sample database. The parameters of the `TransferDatabase` method specified the various bits of information Access needed to perform the import:

```
Sub TestTransferDatabase()

'import from Northwind
DoCmd.TransferDatabase acImport, "Microsoft Access", _
    "C:\Program Files\Microsoft Office\OFFICE12\SAMPLES\Northwind.accdb", _
        acTable, "Employees", "tblEmployees"

End Sub
```

After you ran the procedure, you should have noticed in the Database Window that the new table was inserted into your database.

Transferring Complete SQL Server Database

The `TransferSQLDatabase` method allows you to transfer an entire SQL Server database to another database. In effect, this method imports the entire SQL Server database into your Access database. Here is the basic syntax:

```
DoCmd.TransferSQLDatabase Server, Database, UseTrustedConnection, Login, Password,
TransferCopyData
```

Various parameters are used to specify how the method should execute. The following table explains the use of each parameter.

Parameter	Description
Server	Name of the SQL Server.
Database	Name of new database on specified SQL Server.
UseTrustedConnection	True if account has Administrator privileges, False otherwise and must specify Login and Password.
Login	Login name. Ignored if UseTrustedConnection is True.
Password	Login password. Ignored if UseTrustedConnection is True.
TransferCopyData	Use True to work with the data and schema and False to work with the schema only.

For example, to transfer the entire contents of a database called Pubs to the current database, you can use a command similar to the following:

```
DoCmd.TransferSQLDatabase _
    Server:="ServerName", _
    Database:="Pubs", _
    UseTrustedConnection:=True, _
    TransferCopyData:=False
```

Spreadsheets

The TransferSpreadsheet method is very similar to the TransferDatabase method in that it enables you to import, link, and export, only in this case it deals with spreadsheets. The syntax is shown in the following code:

```
DoCmd.TransferSpreadsheet TransferType, SpreadsheetType, TableName, FileName,
HasFieldNames, Range, UseOA
```

Various parameters are used to specify how the method should execute. The following table explains the use of each parameter.

Parameter	Description
TransferType	Type of transfer to be performed. Valid choices are acImport (default), acLink, and acExport.
SpreadsheetType	Type of spreadsheet. The default is acSpreadsheet TypeExcel12Xml. See the help documentation for a complete list and explanation.
TableName	String expression that contains a table name or a SQL statement if you want to export data based on a SQL statement.
FileName	File name and path of your spreadsheet.
HasFieldNames	Use True to use the first row of the spreadsheet as field names and False to treat the first row as data. False is the default.
Range	Valid range of cells or named range in the spreadsheet that you want to import from. Leave blank to import an entire spreadsheet. Using with Export will cause an error.
UseOA	Optional variant.

Now we'll walk through an example of how you might use the TransferSpreadsheet method to export data to a spreadsheet. Suppose that you want to export the contents of the Employees table you just imported from Northwind into a spreadsheet so that you can e-mail or send it to a colleague. The following code will create a new spreadsheet called Employees.xls in the temp directory.

```
DoCmd.TransferSpreadsheet acExport, acSpreadsheetTypeExcel12Xml, _
    "tblEmployees", "C:\Temp\Employees.xlsx"
```

An example of the spreadsheet created from the preceding command might look like the one shown in Figure 7-3.

You can also use ADO to select, insert, update, and delete the underlying data in most of the data sources in this chapter by specifying the correct ADO provider (in this case Excel).

Text Files

The TransferText method allows you to import from, link to, and export to text files. It has the following syntax:

```
DoCmd.TransferText TransferType, SpecificationName, TableName, FileName,
HasFieldNames, HTMLTableName, CodePage
```

As you would expect, various parameters can be used to specify how the method should execute. These parameters are similar to the TransferDatabase and TransferSpreadsheet methods you have already seen. The following table explains the use of each parameter.

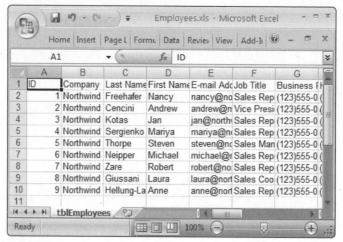

Figure 7-3

Parameter	Description
TransferType	Type of transfer to be performed. The default is acImportDelim. See the Access help documentation for a complete list and explanation.
SpecificationName	Name of import or export specification you have saved in the current database. This argument can be left blank for text files that are delimited with certain characters or spacing to indicate the location of the fields. The example text file in the next section is a comma-delimited file.
TableName	String expression that contains a table name you want to work with or a query you want to export.
FileName	File name and path of the text file you want to work with.
HasFieldNames	Use True to use the contents of first row of the spreadsheet as field names and False to treat the first row as data. False is the default.
HTMLTableName	Use with acImportHTML or acLinkHTML. Name of table or list in HTML file you want to work with. If blank, the first one is assumed.
CodePage	Long value indicating the character set of the code page.

Next, we'll jump right into importing data from a text file.

Try It Out   **Importing Data from a Text File**

Now, you import data from a text file into a new table, called tblEmails, in your Access database.

1. Create a text file as shown in Figure 7-4 and save it in C:\temp.

2. Add the following procedure to the module in your database:

```
Sub TestTransferText()

DoCmd.TransferText acImportDelim, , _
    "tblEmails", "C:\Temp\emails.txt", True

End Sub
```

3. Run the procedure from the Immediate Window in Visual Basic Editor.

4. Return to the database window and you should see a screen similar to that shown in Figure 7-5.

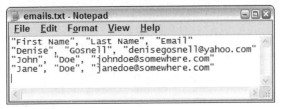

Figure 7-4

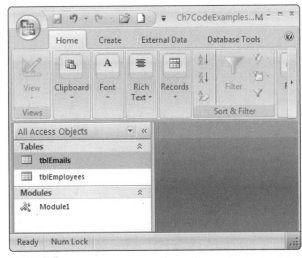

Figure 7-5

How It Works

First, you created a text file that contained comma-delimited records. You then created a procedure to import the comma-delimited file to your database:

```
Sub TestTransferText()

DoCmd.TransferText acImportDelim, , _
    "tblEmails", "C:\Temp\emails.txt", True

End Sub
```

The `TransferText` method imported the comma-delimited file into a new table called `tblEmails`, as shown in Figure 7-5. Note that the parameter for the `SpecificationName` was left blank because it is not required when working with delimited files.

XML Files

XML stands for eXtensible Markup Language. You have likely heard the XML buzzword, but you may not know what XML files really are. XML is a syntax that enables systems to create simple text documents with various tags that identify how the text should be interpreted. At the end of this section, you will create an XML document from a table so that you can see what one looks like.

The idea behind XML is to give various types of operating systems on different platforms a meaningful way of communicating with one another. As the use of XML has grown in popularity, the need to write Access applications that can import and export to XML text files has increased. Recent versions of Microsoft products incorporate extended XML functionality, including the `ImportXML` and `ExportXML` methods that Access provides to enable users to import from and export to XML databases. You will now look at each of these in turn.

The syntax for the `ImportXML` method is:

```
Application.ImportXML DataSource, ImportOptions
```

The `DataSource` is the name and path of the XML file to import. The `ImportOptions` parameter can be `acStructureAndData` (default), `acAppendData`, or `acStructureOnly`. Thus, to import an XML document into a table in your Access database, you might use the following code:

```
Application.ImportXML "employees.xml", acStructureAndData
```

The `ExportXML` method allows you to export data in your Access database to XML files to exchange data with other applications. Here is the syntax:

```
Application.ExportXML ObjectType, DataSource, DataTarget, SchemaTarget,
PresentationTarget, ImageTarget, Encoding, OtherFlags, WhereCondition,
AdditionalData
```

The following table explains what the various parameters of the `ExportXML` object are used for.

Parameter	Description
ObjectType	The type of Access object to export
DataSource	The name of the Access object to export
DataTarget	The file name and path for the exported data
SchemaTarget	The file name and path for the exported schema
PresentationTarget	The file name and path for the exported target information
ImageTarget	The path for exported images
Encoding	The text encoding to use
OtherFlags	Additional flags that can be used
WhereCondition	Subset of records to be exported
AdditionalData	Additional tables to export

I said earlier that I would provide a sample XML file so that you could see what it looks like. Well, it's now time to use the ExportXML method to export one of your tables to XML so that you can see how it works.

Suppose that you have the following procedure:

```
Sub TestExportXML()

Application.ExportXML acExportTable, "tblEmployees", _
    "c:\Temp\Employees.xml", _
    "c:\Temp\EmployeesSchema.xml"

End Sub
```

The procedure uses the ExportXML method to export the Employees table in your database to an XML file called Employees.xml. After you run the preceding procedure, you create the XML file that looks similar to the one shown in Figure 7-6.

Notice in Figure 7-6 how the tags describe the data in detailed ways. This is a more detailed and structured way of organizing and describing data than HTML, which is just designed for displaying data.

That's all it takes to export data from your Access application to another system. You're now ready to learn how to send an e-mail from VBA code.

Figure 7-6

E-mails and Outlook

One way you can send an e-mail from VBA code is using the SendObject method, as shown here:

```
DoCmd.SendObject ObjectType, ObjectName, OutputFormat, To, Cc, Bcc, Subject,
MessageText, EditMessage, TemplateFile
```

The ObjectType, ObjectName, and OutputFormat parameters are used to specify a file created from the database to include as an attachment. Remember that earlier I said you had exported the tblEmployees table to Excel so that you could e-mail it to a coworker. The SendObject method allows you to attach certain database objects in one of a variety of formats as part of the e-mail. Thus, to generate a new e-mail that also attaches the tblEmployees table as an Excel attachment, you could use something similar to the following:

```
'Send the Employees file
DoCmd.SendObject acSendTable, "tblEmployees", acFormatXLS, _
     "someone@yahoo.com", , , "Employee List", "For your review.", False
```

If you do not want to send an attachment, but just want to send an e-mail telling me how much you like the book so far, you can use the following command. Please do this — I would love to get this test e-mail from you!

```
'Send the author of this book an email
DoCmd.SendObject acSendNoObject, , , "denisegosnell@yahoo.com", , , _
    "This is cool!", _
    "I just sent an email from VBA. Really am enjoying your book.", False
```

If you want to learn more about controlling Outlook from your VBA applications, consult Chapter 11, where I cover automation with various Office programs such as Outlook. The SendObject method I just discussed is not specific to any e-mail program.

Other Ways to Export Data

Yet another way to export data can be implemented using the OutputTo method. The OutputTo method can export data to various formats: ASP, DAP, HTML, IIS, RTF, SNP, TXT, and XLS. The syntax for OutputTo is shown here:

```
DoCmd.OutputTo(ObjectType, ObjectName, OutputFormat, OutputFile, AutoStart,
TemplateFile, Encoding)
```

Please consult Chapter 9 for more information on the OutputTo method, as the entire chapter is dedicated to creating reports and Web-enabled output, including those created with the OutputTo method.

In addition to all the ways you can integrate with external data sources discussed so far, there are two more technologies that have not been touched on. Those two technologies are web services and the SharePoint product family. These two topics will be covered in Chapter 8.

Summary

In today's world of technology, it has become commonplace for companies to expect systems to communicate with each other in ways that were not possible just a decade ago. In this chapter, you explored ways to work with external data to facilitate communications between various systems. You learned VBA techniques for linking, importing, and exporting data to various sources, such as databases, spreadsheets, and text files. You also learned how to handle more advanced scenarios, such as sending e-mails programmatically with and without attachments.

Chapter 8 will build on this chapter by exploring some advanced linking and importing techniques using web services and the SharePoint product family.

Exercises

1. What are some reasons you would choose linking versus importing?

2. What is the difference between the `TransferDatabase` and `TransferSQLDatabase` methods?

3. How can you programmatically generate an e-mail to send to someone?

Using Access with Web Services and SharePoint Lists

In Chapter 5, I covered the basics of using ADO and SQL to work with data sources. All the ADO and SQL examples dealt with data stored in tables in a database. However, in today's world of technology, you often work with data and applications in a variety of formats, such as text files and spreadsheets. You may need to import or link data from various sources into your database to avoid having to retype all the information that is already stored electronically in another format. At some point, another application might need the data in your application or you may want to get data out of your application for another reason. In that case, you can export information from your application into another format.

In this chapter, you will explore the various ways to use VBA code to consume web services, as well as to link to and import SharePoint Lists. The chapter will cover:

❑   The definition of a web service and how you can use data returned from a web service

❑   The definition of SharePoint and SharePoint Lists

❑   Linking to SharePoint Lists

❑   Linking and importing SharePoint Lists using VBA

❑   Creating SharePoint list entries from VBA

These techniques will enable you to build applications that can interact with other systems throughout your organization and beyond.

Introduction to Web Services

A common topic of discussion in the high-tech sector these days is web services. *Web services* are reusable components that are based on standard Internet protocols. They enable systems on different platforms to talk to each other. In the simplest terms, I like to describe a web service as some procedure or function that someone has made available over Internet protocols so that you can use it for free or for a cost. Web services can be called (*consumed*) by Web and non-Web-based applications as long as the application can communicate using standard Internet protocols. Web services typically return a response in XML format that can then be used appropriately in the consuming program.

Although web services communicate using Internet protocols, you can still use web services for private purposes within a company. For example, some companies are better integrating legacy mainframe and other applications into their current environment by *exposing* parts of the old application as a web service. After the old application is made accessible using a web service, it can be called from other platforms that, traditionally, could not communicate easily. Although I could write a whole chapter or even a book on web services alone, I want you, at least, to learn the basic concept of what a web service is. I also want to give you a simple example of how you can use someone else's web service in your Access applications. The first part of this chapter will show you how to locate and consume web services from Access.

Using Data from Web Services

Before you can consume a web service, you must download and install the Microsoft Office 2003 Web Services Toolkit. Further, the toolkit requires that you have at least one product from Microsoft Office 2003 installed on your machine. As of this book's writing Microsoft has not indicated whether a newer 2007 version will be released or not. At the time of this book's writing, the easiest way to obtain the toolkit is to go to `www.microsoft.com/downloads/details.aspx?familyid=fa36018a-e1cf-48a3-9b35-169d819ecf18&displaylang=en`

Once you get the toolkit installed, the example in this section will work with Access 2007. If you cannot install the Toolkit, move on to the next section.

If you cannot locate the toolkit at the preceding link, you can go to the downloads area of Microsoft.com: `www.microsoft.com/downloads`. Then, select the Office and Home Application Download Category in the left navigation pane and then run the following search: Select Office System for Product/Technology and type `Web Services Toolkit` in the Keywords text box. Click the Search button. You will see a link to the Microsoft Office 2003 Web Services Toolkit 2.01 or later.

You can then follow the instructions on the page to download and run the setup program or just launch the setup directly from the Web site. Follow the onscreen instructions to complete the installation.

After you have the Web Services Toolkit installed, you can use web services from your Access applications.

Try It Out   **Adding a Reference to a Web Service**

Now, let's confirm that the Web Services Toolkit installation was successful and then add a reference to your Access project to an existing web service.

1.   Confirm that the Web Services Toolkit installation was successful. To do so, open the Visual Basic Editor and select Tools to confirm that you have a Web Services References option, as shown in Figure 8-1.

2.   Select Tools ⇨ Web Services References. Select the WebServiceURL option, and type the following URL into the box: http://terraserver-usa.com/TerraService2.asmx. Click the Search button. A screen similar to that shown in Figure 8-2 will be displayed.

   You will need a connection to the Internet, or the web services examples shown here will not function.

3.   Select the TerraService web services in the upper-right pane so that a check box appears. Also, expand the list so you can see the procedures available, including the procedures shown in Figure 8-3.

4.   Select the Add button to add a reference to the Terra Web Service to your form.

5.   When you return to the Visual Basic Editor, you can see that several class modules were added to your project, as shown in Figure 8-4.

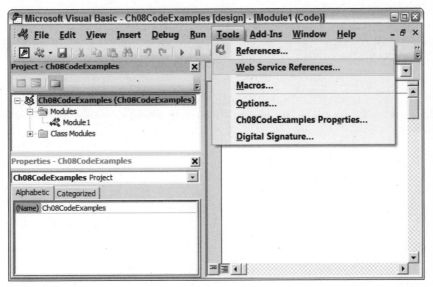

Figure 8-1

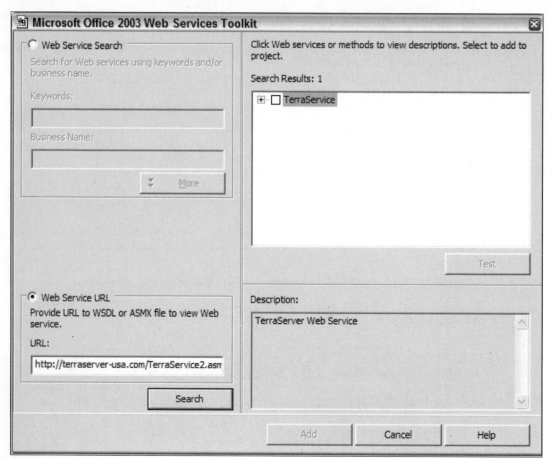

Figure 8-2

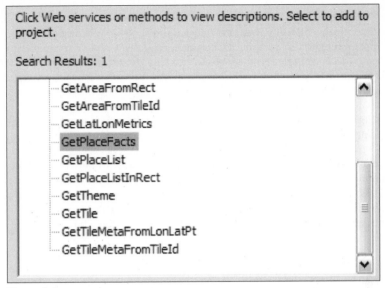

Figure 8-3

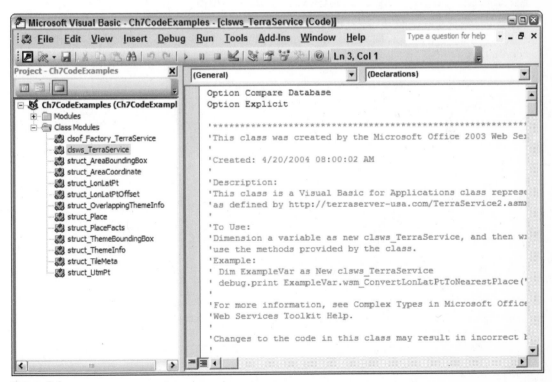

Figure 8-4

How It Works

To add a reference to a web service, you first selected the Tools ➪ Web Services References option. Because you're planning to use a service located at `http://terraserver-usa.com/TerraService2.asmx`, you selected the Web Service URL option and specified the Terra Server path in the URL field of Figure 8-2. You also could have searched for available web services using certain keywords or specified the location of another web service.

You then selected the Terra Server web service and clicked the Add button. Several class modules were added to the database to make the procedures you saw in Figure 8-3 available to your Access project.

You can add a reference to any web service that is available on your network over the Internet, or on your local computer, by navigating to its location. For example, Microsoft, Amazon, Google, and others have created web services that you can use. More information about these web services can be found at `http://msdn.microsoft.com/webservices/building/livewebservices/`. Many of these web services, although they are free, require that you obtain an ID. Other companies may charge for use of web services they offer.

Now that you have a reference to the Terra Server web service, you can consume one of its procedures from within your application.

Try It Out   Consuming the GetPlaceFacts Method

In this example, you will call one of the procedures in the Terra Server web service. The web service procedure you will call accepts latitude and longitude values and returns the city that is located at those coordinates.

1. Add the following procedure to your class module:

```
Sub TestWebService()

    'declare a new instance of the web service
    Dim ts As clsws_TerraService
    Set ts = New clsws_TerraService

    'declare a structure to hold the latitude and longitude values
    Dim objLonLatPt As New struct_LonLatPt

    'declare a variable to store the result from the web service
    Dim strResult As String

    'assign the latitude and longitude values
    objLonLatPt.Lat = "37.7875671"
    objLonLatPt.Lon = "-122.4276"

    'Call the web service to return the place for that latitude
    'and longitude
    strResult = ts.wsm_ConvertLonLatPtToNearestPlace(objLonLatPt)

    'display the result
    MsgBox "The city at that latitude and longitude is: " & strResult

End Sub
```

2. Run the procedure from the Immediate Window by typing `TestWebService` and pressing Enter. You should receive a message similar to the one in Figure 8-5.

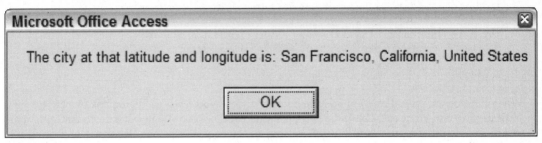

Figure 8-5

How It Works

To call the web service from your application, you created the `TestWebService` procedure:

```
Sub TestWebService()
```

You declare a new instance of the web service, just as you would declare any other object:

```
'declare a new instance of the web service
Dim ts As clsws_TerraService
Set ts = New clsws_TerraService
```

You declare a structure variable to store the latitude and longitude values. You created the structure definition in the code that was generated when adding the web service, so all you had to do was declare the variable:

```
'declare a structure to hold the latitude and longitude values
Dim objLonLatPt As New struct_LonLatPt
```

Next, you declared a local string variable to store the result of the web service:

```
'declare a variable to store the result from the web service
Dim strResult As String
```

You also set the latitude and longitude parameters of the `objLonLatPt` that will be passed to the web service as parameters:

```
'assign the latitude and longitude values
objLonLatPt.Lat = "37.7875671"
objLonLatPt.Lon = "-122.4276"
```

This line below actually calls the web service on the Terra Server over the Internet and returns the result into the `strResult` variable. If you do not have an Internet connection, this line will raise an error.

```
'Call the web service to return the place for that latitude
'and longitude
strResult = ts.wsm_ConvertLonLatPtToNearestPlace(objLonLatPt)
```

As you typed the line of code, you should have noticed that the tooltip displayed to show you what parameters the web service required. Figure 8-6 shows an example of this.

The last line of code displays the result that was retrieved from the web service:

```
'display the result
MsgBox "The city at that latitude and longitude is: " & strResult

End Sub
```

When running the procedure from the Immediate Window, you receive a dialog box like Figure 8-5 that indicates that San Francisco, California, USA is located at those coordinates. It is really amazing that you just executed a remote procedure that was located on someone else's computer and used the result in the application. Hopefully, you realize that it is almost as easy to call a web service as it is to call any other procedure. The only difference is that you have to locate and add a reference to the web service and familiarize yourself with the parameters it expects.

```
Sub TestWebService()

'declare a new instance of the web service
Dim ts As clsws_TerraService
Set ts = New clsws_TerraService

'declare a structure to hold the latitude and longitude values
Dim objLonLatPt As New struct_LonLatPt

'declare a variable to store the result from the web service
Dim strResult As String

'assign the latitude and longitude values
objLonLatPt.Lat = "37.7875671"
objLonLatPt.Lon = "-122.4276"

'Call the web service to return the place for that latitude
'and longitude
strResult = ts.wsm_ConvertLonLatPtToNearestPlace(objLonLatPt)
        wsm_ConvertLonLatPtToNearestPlace(ByVal obj_point As struct_LonLatPt) As String
'display the result
MsgBox "The city at that latitude and longitude is: " & strResult


End Sub
```

Figure 8-6

Introduction to SharePoint Lists

With Access 2007 you are now able to interact with SharePoint functionality; you can link, import, and export data to and from Office SharePoint Server 2007. Office SharePoint Server 2007 is built on Windows SharePoint Services 3.0 and brings together several products into one platform, including Microsoft SharePoint Portal Server 2003 and Microsoft Content Management Server 2002. This section will focus only on SharePoint functionality, specifically working with lists.

SharePoint lists are collections of items that are grouped together in a logical fashion. These items are then available to other SharePoint users to view. You can also create new lists based on an existing list type. The following are the different types of lists that can be created:

❑ **Announcements** – Used to broadcast short pieces of information to the rest of the SharePoint site users and can include an expiration date when the announcement will cease to be displayed.

❑ **Contacts** – A list of people and typical contact information including name, e-mail address, various phone numbers, address, and other miscellaneous information.

❑ **Events** – Used to capture specific point-in-time occurrences like meetings and deadlines. Information that can be captured with an event includes beginning date and time, ending date and time, descriptive information, and recurrence settings.

❑ **Issues** – Used to manage problems and issues. Information that can be captured with an issue includes name, to whom the issue is assigned, priority, status, and other miscellaneous information.

❑ **Links** – Used to capture links to network, intranet, and Internet resources.

❑ **Tasks** – Used to manage work assignments. Information that can be captured with an issue includes name, to whom the task is assigned, priority, status, and other miscellaneous information.

In addition to the built-in types, you can create custom lists. When creating custom lists you may use several different data types. The follow table is a list of the SharePoint data types and the corresponding Access data type.

SharePoint Column Type	Access Data Type	Comments
ID	AutoNumber	Read-only
Single line of text	Text	
Multiple lines of text	Memo	
Number	Number	
Currency	Currency	
Date or Time	Date/Time	
Lookup and Person or Group	Number or Memo	When importing, data type will be determined by retrieving IDs or display values. When linking, Number will be used.

Table continued on following page

SharePoint Column Type	Access Data Type	Comments
Choice (single)	Text	
Choice (multiple)	Text	
Yes/No	Yes/No	
Hyperlink	Hyperlink	
Attachment	Attachment	
Calculated	Determined by the resulting value	Read-only, formula is ignored
Rich Text	Memo	Displays only the first 64K of text
Enhanced Rich Text	Memo	Read-only
Displays only the first 64K of text		

Using Data from SharePoint Lists

Before you start using Access with SharePoint, you need to have a SharePoint instance available to you. If you do not have an instance of SharePoint available, you can download a trial version from Microsoft. At the time of writing, you could download a trial version from `http://office.microsoft.com/en-us/sharepointserver/FX100492001033.aspx`. As one further caveat, SharePoint can only be installed on Microsoft Windows Server 2003 Service Pack 1 or later. If you prefer not to host the SharePoint software yourself, there are many Internet hosting companies that offer SharePoint hosting on their servers for a small monthly fee. One example of such a company is 1&1 Internet (`www.1and1.com`). Some of these Internet hosting companies offer a free trial.

Now that you know what a SharePoint List is and what the different types are, it is time to start working with them.

Linking and Importing SharePoint Lists

Importing a SharePoint list is very similar to importing data from other external sources, as described in Chapter 7. There are two ways to import a SharePoint list: using the Access menus and through VBA. This section will demonstrate both.

Try It Out   **Importing Lists Using the Wizard**

1. Create a new database by selecting the Office Button ⇨ New. From the list of available templates, select "Blank Database," provide the file name and path, and press the Create button.

2. Click on the External Data tab and click on the SharePoint List Button, as shown Figure 8-7.

3. The Get External Data – SharePoint Site Wizard will pop up, as shown in Figure 8-8. Specify the URL of your SharePoint site and select the Import the source data into a new table in the current database option, then click the Next button.

4. The next step in the wizard is selecting which lists you want to import. Select all the lists, as shown in Figure 8-9. Click the OK button, and the tables will be imported into your database. Your database should look similar to Figure 8-11 when you are finished.

5. After the import is completed you are given the option to save the actions you just performed so that you can perform them again in the future as shown in Figure 8-10. Click the close button and you are finished.

Home
Create
External Data
Saved Imports
Access
Excel
SharePoint List
Text File
XML File
More
Import

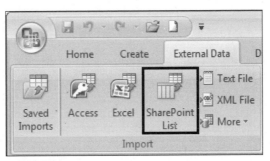

Figure 8-7

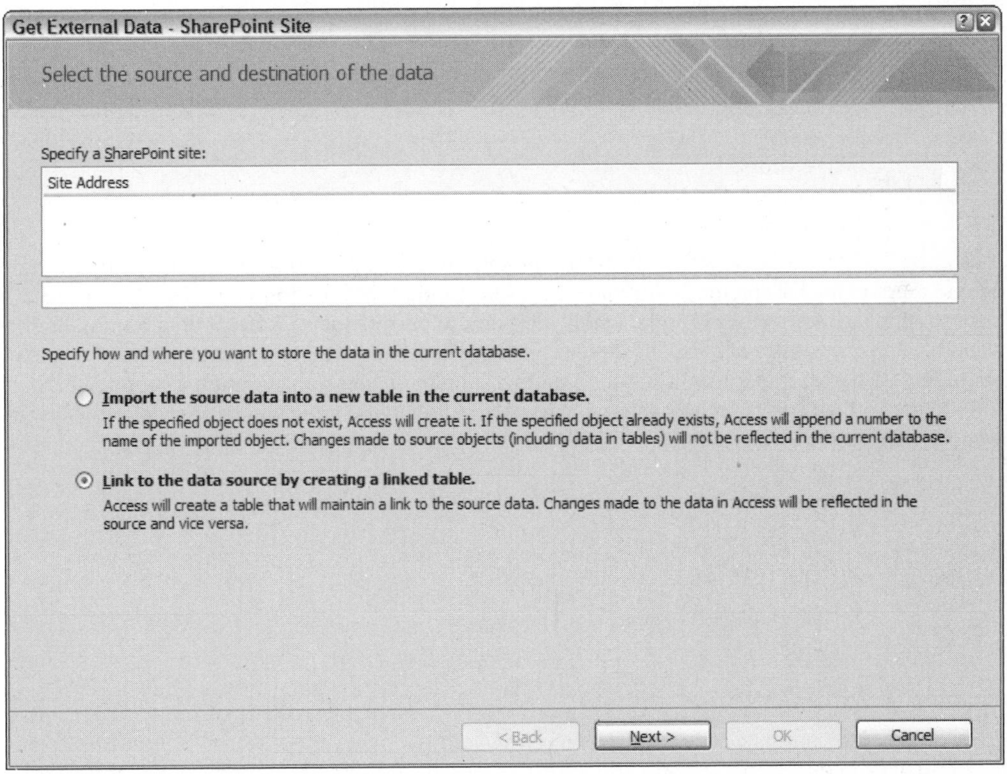

Get External Data - SharePoint Site
Select the source and destination of the data
Specify a SharePoint site:
Site Address
Specify how and where you want to store the data in the current database.
Import the source data into a new table in the current database.
If the specified object does not exist, Access will create it. If the specified object already exists, Access will append a number to the name of the imported object. Changes made to source objects (including data in tables) will not be reflected in the current database.
Link to the data source by creating a linked table.
Access will create a table that will maintain a link to the source data. Changes made to the data in Access will be reflected in the source and vice versa.
< Back
Next >
OK
Cancel

Figure 8-8

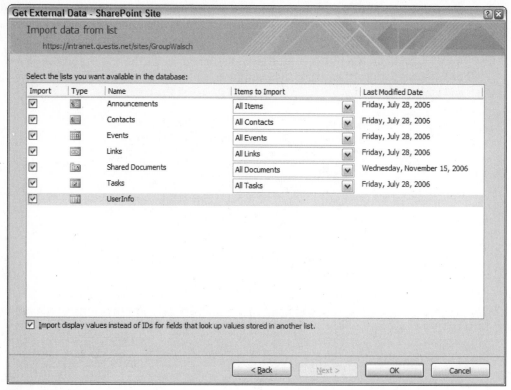

Figure 8-9

As shown in Figure 8-11, now that the tables are imported you can open each of them and compare the data in them to the lists on the SharePoint site to ensure that they are the same. There are times when importing makes sense; for example, when you want to perform some kind of data mining that looks back through the history of a list. However, it is more likely that you will want to simply link to a SharePoint list. Remember from Chapter 7 that with linked tables you maintain a connection to the data source (the list), and any changes you make to data in the linked table will be moved to the original data source.

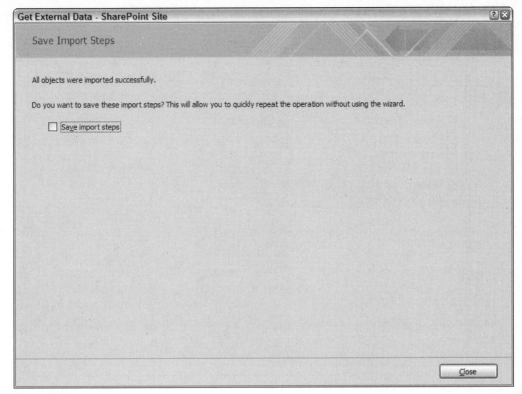

Figure 8-10

There are two different ways to programmatically link to SharePoint lists within Access. The first is the `TransferSharePointList` method of the `DoCmd` object. The basic syntax of the `Transfer SharePointList` method is:

```
DoCmd.TransferSharePointList TransferType, SiteAddress, ListID, [ViewID],
[TableName], [GetLookupDisplayValues]
```

Various parameters are used to specify how the method should execute. The following table explains the use of each parameter.

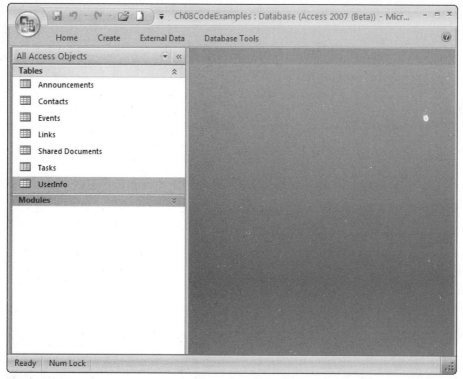

Figure 8-11

Parameter	Description
TransferType	Type of transfer to be performed. Valid choices are acImportSharePointList and acLinkSharePointList.
SiteAddress	The fully qualified URL of the SharePoint instance you are connecting to.
ListID	The ID of the list you are going to link to or import.
ViewID	Optional. The ID of the SharePoint view you would like to use when the list is imported or linked.
TableName	Optional. Name of the table as it will be seen within Access.
GetLookupDisplayValues	Optional. Whether to get the associated lookup values when attaching the data or use the IDs. The default is True.

Try It Out   **Programmatically Linking a List Using DoCmd Object**

Let's look at an example. Suppose that you want to link to the Contacts list in your SharePoint instance and you want the linked table to be name `LinkedContacts`.

1. Insert a new module into the database you created earlier.

2. Add the following code to the module

```
Public Sub LinkToContacts()

    Dim strSiteAddress As String
    Dim strListID As String
    Dim strTableName As String

    strSiteAddress = "https://SharePointServer/sites/Site"
    strListID = "{F1601AA2-D5BF-439D-B6E9-F0223667E827}"
    strTableName = "LinkedContacts"

    DoCmd.TransferSharePointList acLinkSharePointList, strSiteAddress, _
strListID, , strTableName

End Sub
```

3. Modify the value of `strSiteAddress` and `strListID` to your SharePoint instance and the ID of the Contacts list. To find the ID of the list you want use in SharePoint, open the list in SharePoint and click on the Modify Columns and Settings link (highlighted in Figure 8-12). In the Address Bar of your browser will see a URL similar to Figure 8-13. The part that comes directly after the `List=` portion is the ID you should use. Finally, in some cases the URL will be encoded, and you will need to decode it, which simply means replacing the characters `%7B` with a left brace ({), `%7D` with a right brace (}), and `%2D` with a hyphen (-).

4. From the Immediate Window in the Visual Basic Editor, type `LinkToContacts` and press Enter to run the procedure.

5. Open the Database Window, and you should see a screen similar to Figure 8-14.

Figure 8-12

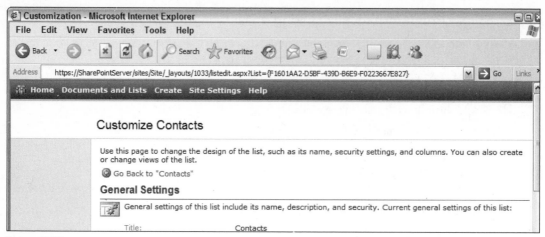

Figure 8-13

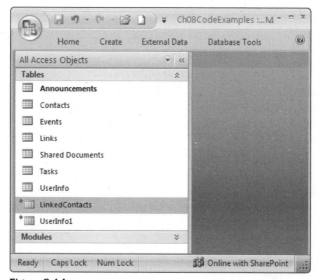

Figure 8-14

How It Works

In this example, you used the `TransferSharePointList` method to link to the Contact list of your SharePoint instance. The parameters of the `TransferSharePointList` method specified the various bits of information Access needed to perform the import:

```
Public Sub LinkToContacts()

    Dim strSiteAddress As String
    Dim strListID As String
```

```
   Dim strTableName As String

   strSiteAddress = "https://SharePointServer/sites/Site"
   strListID = "{F1601AA2-D5BF-439D-B6E9-F0223667E827}"
   strTableName = "LinkedContacts"

   DoCmd.TransferSharePointList acLinkSharePointList, strSiteAddress, _
strListID, , strTableName

End Sub
```

After you ran the procedure, you should have noticed in the Database Window that the new table was inserted into your database. You may have noticed an additional table that was linked that you hadn't specified, the `UserInfo1` table (as shown in Figure 8-14). This table was automatically linked because it had a relationship to the Contact list.

If you had wanted to import the table directly, instead of linking to it, you could have specified `acImportSharePointList` instead of `acLinkSharePointList`, which would have resulted in the Contact list being imported into the database as table `LinkedContacts` (along with the `UserInfo1` table).

The second method of linking to SharePoint lists is a bit more advanced but just as effective. It involves creating a new `TableDef` object with the SharePoint list as its source. You then append the new `TableDef` object to the current collection of TableDefs.

Try It Out   Programmatically Linking a List Using a TableDef Object

In this example, we will link to the Announcements list in SharePoint. In our database we shall name it `LinkedAnnouncements`.

1.   Open the same module you created earlier.

2.   Add the following code to the module:

```
Public Sub LinkToAnnouncements()

   'declare the TableDef object we will use
   Dim tdAnnouncements As TableDef

   'create the TableDef object, naming the table LinkedAnnouncements
   Set tdAnnouncements = CurrentDb.CreateTableDef("LinkedAnnouncements")

   'set the DSN to SharePoint site and correct List ID
   tdAnnouncements.Connect = "WSS;HDR=NO;IMEX=2;ACCDB=YES;" & _
                 "DATABASE=https://SharePointSite/sites/Site;" & _
                 "LIST={649C1EDF-2482-419A-9360-3BE7B8E19155};" & _
                 "VIEW=;RetrieveIds=Yes"

   'Set the source table name
   tdAnnouncements.SourceTableName = "Announcements"

   'include it in the current list of this DB's TableDefs
   CurrentDb.TableDefs.Append tdAnnouncements

End Sub
```

3. This method of linking to tables requires that we use a DSN. Although it looks quite a bit different than other DSNs it holds the same basic information. Replace the value of the DATABASE portion to your SharePoint instance and replace the value for List with the correct ID from your Announcement list.

4. From the Immediate Window in the Visual Basic Editor, type LinkToAnnouncements and press Enter to run the procedure.

5. Open the Database Window, and you should see a screen similar to Figure 8-15. (It may take a few minutes for the table to appear as Access refreshes its table definitions and attaches to the data source.)

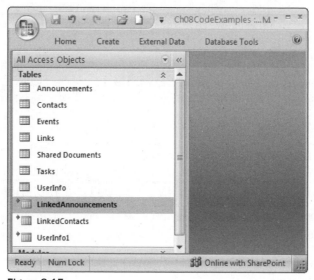

Figure 8-15

How It Works

In this example, you created a TableDef to connect to the SharePoint instance. The first thing you need to do is to create a TableDef object to use. The two code bits below do just that. The first code line declares an object of type TableDef. The second code line instantiates that variable and sets the name to LinkedAnnouncements.

```
'declare the TableDef object we will use
Dim tdAnnouncements As TableDef

'create the TableDef object, naming the table LinkedAnnouncements
Set tdAnnouncements = CurrentDb.CreateTableDef("LinkedAnnouncements")
```

The next thing to do is to tell the TableDef object where to get the object. This is done by setting the Connect property of the TableDef object to the DSN of the Announcement list. The SharePoint DSN looks a bit like other types of DSNs discussed in earlier chapters but with some differences.

```
'set the DSN to SharePoint site and correct List ID
tdAnnouncements.Connect = "WSS;HDR=NO;IMEX=2;ACCDB=YES;" & _
                "DATABASE=https://SharePointSite/sites/Site;" & _
                "LIST={649C1EDF-2482-419A-9360-3BE7B8E19155};" & _
                "VIEW=;RetrieveIds=Yes"
```

Note that the DSN for this example begins with WSS, which indicates that a SharePoint instance will be used. The DATABASE portion is the fully qualified URL to the SharePoint site. The LIST portion is the ID of the list to connect to. The last bit of the DSN is some options relating to using a view and whether to retrieve lookup IDs or not.

Next, the SourceTableName property is set to the name of the list:

```
'Set the source table name
tdAnnouncements.SourceTableName = "Announcements"
```

Finally, we append the new TableDef object to the current database's collection of TableDefs. This action is what initiates the link between the Access database and SharePoint, thus making it appear in the Database Window.

```
'include it in the current list of this DB's TableDefs
CurrentDb.TableDefs.Append tdAnnouncements
```

The previous two examples accomplish the same thing in that both attach a SharePoint list to your database. The first is easier than the second, so why would you want to use the second? Imagine a scenario where you did not want to keep the link open, but rather you wanted to connect briefly to insert some entries and then disconnect. The second method makes this a fairly painless process. Consider the following example:

```
Public Sub InsertAnnouncements()

    'declare the TableDef object we will use
    Dim tdAnnouncements As TableDef

    'create the TableDef object, naming the table LinkedAnnouncements
    Set tdAnnouncements = CurrentDb.CreateTableDef("LinkedAnnouncements")

    'set the DSN to SharePoint site and correct List ID
    tdAnnouncements.Connect = "WSS;HDR=NO;IMEX=2;ACCDB=YES;" & _
                "DATABASE=https://SharePointSite/sites/Site;" & _
                "LIST={649C1EDF-2482-419A-9360-3BE7B8E19155};" & _
                "VIEW=;RetrieveIds=Yes"

    'Set the source table name
    tdAnnouncements.SourceTableName = "Announcements"

    'include it in the current list of this DB's TableDefs
    CurrentDb.TableDefs.Append tdAnnouncements

    'create the sql to create an entry
    Dim sql As String
    sql = "INSERT INTO LinkedAnnouncements ( Title, Body, Expires )"
```

```
        sql = sql & " VALUES ( 'Access 2007 Released!', "
        sql = sql & "'Access 2007 has been released...', '2/1/2007')"

        'execute the sql
        DoCmd.RunSQL sql

        'now we detatch the linked table, we do not need it anymore
        CurrentDb.TableDefs.Delete "LinkedAnnouncements"

    End Sub
```

The first part of this method is exactly the same as the second example. You will notice though that once the table has been attached we insert a new announcement and then remove the linked table from the database. If you open the target SharePoint instance, you will see that the new entry is there, as shown in Figure 8-16.

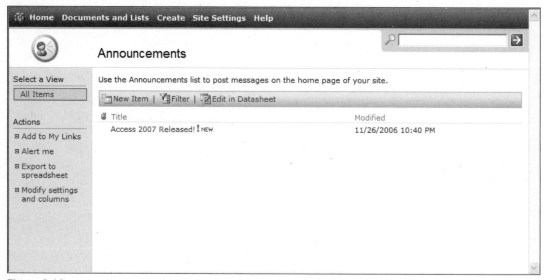

Figure 8-16

Summary

In today's world of technology, it has become commonplace for companies to expect systems to communicate with each other in ways that were not possible just a decade ago. In this chapter, you explored ways to work with external data to facilitate communications between various systems. You learned VBA techniques for consuming web services from your application. Web services allow applications on various platforms to exchange data upon request and have become an increasingly popular communication technique between systems. You learned how to import and link to SharePoint lists by using both the built-in wizard and using VBA. Chapter 9 will build on this chapter by explaining how to export data in your application to reports and Web-enabled output.

Exercises

1. What is a web service, and how do you use one?

2. What is the difference between the `acImportSharePointList` and `acLinkSharePointList` parameters when using the `TransferSharePointList` method?

3. Under what circumstances would you want to link to a SharePoint list by creating a `TableDef` object?

Creating Reports and Web-Enabled Output

Chapter 8 explored techniques to consume information from web services and the SharePoint product family. This chapter covers:

❑   Creating reports programmatically and how to output data from Access databases in ways that can be used over the Web. For example, you will explore how to set the record source for a report dynamically, so you can use the same report across different data sources.

❑   Using the OutputTo method to export data to various formats, such as HTML.

Working with Reports from VBA

Reports can be manipulated in numerous ways from VBA code. For example, you can change the data source on which the report is based from within VBA code. You can also create reports from scratch or modify existing reports from within VBA code. Let's look at a few examples to further illustrate these concepts.

Many of the examples in this chapter that deal with manipulating existing reports use the Northwind database. If you want to create those particular examples yourself, open the Northwind database and add a new module. Only the code for the Try It Out examples is included in the sample code available on Wrox.com for this chapter. If you do not have the Northwind database installed, you can install it and the other sample databases from the Microsoft Access setup program, or you can download it from Microsoft's web site in the Microsoft Office section that contains Access sample databases.

Setting the Report Data Source

The `DataSource` property of a `Report` object can be specified as a SQL statement. Suppose that you have an existing report called `Alphabetical List of Products`. The following procedure illustrates one way you can modify the `DataSource` of the report:

```
Sub ModifyExistingReport()

'declare a variable to store the SQL string
Dim strSQL As String

'set the SQL statement value to show only the top 5 orders
strSQL = "SELECT DISTINCTROW TOP 5 Orders.[Order ID], Orders.[Order Date]," & _
         "[Order Subtotals].Subtotal AS SaleAmount, " & _
         "[Customers Extended].Company AS CompanyName, Orders.[Shipped Date] " & _
         "FROM [Customers Extended] " & _
         "INNER JOIN (Orders INNER JOIN [Order Subtotals] ON " & _
         "Orders.[Order ID] = [Order Subtotals].[Order ID]) " & _
         "ON [Customers Extended].ID = Orders.[Customer ID] " & _
         "ORDER BY [Order Subtotals].Subtotal DESC;"

'access the report's design (hidden from the user)
DoCmd.Echo False
DoCmd.OpenReport "Top Ten Biggest Orders", acViewDesign

'set the source of the report to the SQL statement
Reports("Top Ten Biggest Orders").RecordSource = strSQL

'close the report's design and save changes
DoCmd.Close , , acSaveYes

'now open the report for the user in preview mode
DoCmd.OpenReport "Top Ten Biggest Orders", acViewPreview
DoCmd.Echo True

End Sub
```

Notice first how a SQL statement is created to specify which fields the report should be based upon. The report's design view is then accessed in hidden mode (DoCmd.Echo False) so that the user does not see the modifications. The `RecordSource` is then assigned to the `strSQL` variable. The report is then closed and the changes saved. Finally, the report is opened in preview mode, so you can see the changes.

> **When you make changes to report properties (such as the `RecordSource` property),
> you actually permanently change the report to those settings, just as if you had done
> so in the designer. You don't just make a temporary change that is undone after the
> code executes.**

You can also specify an ADO recordset as a report's data source. You could modify the prior example as follows:

```
Sub ModifyExistingReport()

'declare a variable to store the SQL string
Dim strSQL As String

'set the SQL statement value to show only the top 5 orders
strSQL = "SELECT DISTINCTROW TOP 5 Orders.[Order ID], Orders.[Order Date]," & _
        "[Order Subtotals].Subtotal AS SaleAmount, " & _
        "[Customers Extended].Company AS CompanyName, Orders.[Shipped Date] " & _
        "FROM [Customers Extended] " & _
        "INNER JOIN (Orders INNER JOIN [Order Subtotals] ON " & _
        "Orders.[Order ID] = [Order Subtotals].[Order ID]) " & _
        "ON [Customers Extended].ID = Orders.[Customer ID] " & _
        "ORDER BY [Order Subtotals].Subtotal DESC;"
'declare and instantiate a new recordset
Dim rsDiscontinued As ADODB.Recordset
Set rsDiscontinued = New ADODB.Recordset

'open the recordset based on the SQL statement
rsDiscontinued.Open strSQL, CurrentProject.Connection

'access the report's design (hidden from the user)
DoCmd.Echo False
DoCmd.OpenReport "Top Ten Biggest Orders", acViewDesign


'set the source of the report to the recordset source
Reports("Top Ten Biggest Orders").RecordSource = rsDiscontinued.Source

'close the report's design and save changes
DoCmd.Close , , acSaveYes

'now open the report for the user in preview mode
DoCmd.OpenReport "Top Ten Biggest Orders", acViewPreview
DoCmd.Echo True


'close the recordset and free the memory
rsDiscontinued.Close
Set rsDiscontinued = Nothing

End Sub
```

Notice how this example uses the SQL statement to create the ADO recordset and then assigns the RecordSource property of the report to the recordset's Source property.

Creating Reports Programmatically

Just as you can work with forms and other Access objects programmatically, you can also work with reports programmatically. You can create reports from scratch and modify existing reports. Let's look at how to create a report from scratch.

Creating an Empty Report

To create a new report, you use the `CreateReport` method. Here is the basic syntax:

```
Dim rptReport as Access.Report
Set rptReport = CreateReport
```

Below is an example that creates a new empty report and deletes any existing report with the same name before creating the new report:

```
Sub CreateNewReport()

Dim rptCustomers As Access.Report
Dim strReportName As String
Dim aoAccessObj As AccessObject


'set the name of the new report
strReportName = "Customers"

'delete any existing report with that name
For Each aoAccessObj In CurrentProject.AllReports
    If aoAccessObj.Name = strReportName Then
        DoCmd.DeleteObject acReport, strReportName
    End If
Next aoAccessObj

'create a new Customers Report
Set rptCustomers = CreateReport

'save and close the new report
DoCmd.Save , strReportName
DoCmd.Close

End Sub
```

First, the code loops through the `AllReports` collection to delete any existing report with the same name. Then, the Access report object `rptCustomers` is assigned to the `CreateReport` method. The report is then saved with the name specified. At this point, the report is empty and contains no controls. Let's look at how to add controls to the report.

Adding Controls to the Report

The `CreateReportControl` method allows you to add new controls to a report. The `CreateReport Control` method has the following basic syntax:

```
Set Object = CreateReportControl(ReportName, ControlType, Section, Parent,
ColumnName, Left,  Top, Width, Height)
```

This procedure is called with parentheses because a value, which in this case is a new control, is returned. Now, let's modify the prior code to add four fields to the report: CompanyName, ContactName, Title, and Phone. Each field needs a corresponding text box and label. The following modified procedure is one way to accomplish this:

```
Sub CreateNewReport()

    Dim rptCustomers As Access.Report
Dim strReportName As String
    Dim aoAccessObj As AccessObject

    Dim txtTextBox As Access.TextBox
    Dim lblLabel As Access.Label

    Dim strSQL As String
    Dim intPosition As Integer

    'set the name of the new report
    strReportName = "Customers"

    'set the source of the report to this SQL
    strSQL = "SELECT Customers.Company, " & _
    "Customers.[First Name] & ' ' & Customers.[Last Name] AS ContactName, " & _
    "Customers.[Job Title], Customers.[Business Phone] FROM Customers;"

    'delete any existing report with that name
    For Each aoAccessObj In CurrentProject.AllReports
        If aoAccessObj.Name = strReportName Then
            DoCmd.DeleteObject acReport, strReportName
        End If
    Next aoAccessObj

    'create a new Customers Report and set properties
    Set rptCustomers = CreateReport

    'set the report record source to the SQL Statement
    rptCustomers.RecordSource = strSQL

    'set the height, caption, and other report options
    rptCustomers.Section("Detail").Height = 500
    rptCustomers.Caption = "Client Contact List"

    'add a Company Name label and text box to the report
    intPosition = 0
    Set txtTextBox = CreateReportControl(rptCustomers.Name, acTextBox, _
                    acDetail, , "Company", intPosition)

    txtTextBox.Name = "txtCompanyName"
    txtTextBox.Width = 1800

    Set lblLabel = CreateReportControl(rptCustomers.Name, acLabel, _
```

```
                    acPageHeader, , , intPosition)

lblLabel.Name = "lblCompanyName"
lblLabel.Caption = "Company Name"
lblLabel.Height = txtTextBox.Height
lblLabel.Width = txtTextBox.Width
lblLabel.FontBold = True

'add a Contact Name label and text box to the report
intPosition = txtTextBox.Width + txtTextBox.Left + 350
Set txtTextBox = CreateReportControl(rptCustomers.Name, acTextBox, _
                    acDetail, , "ContactName", intPosition)

txtTextBox.Name = "txtContactName"
txtTextBox.Width = 1800

Set lblLabel = CreateReportControl(rptCustomers.Name, acLabel, _
                    acPageHeader, , , intPosition)

lblLabel.Name = "lblContactName"
lblLabel.Caption = "Contact Name"
lblLabel.Height = txtTextBox.Height
lblLabel.Width = txtTextBox.Width
lblLabel.FontBold = True


'add a Contact Title label and text box to the report
intPosition = txtTextBox.Width + txtTextBox.Left + 500

Set txtTextBox = CreateReportControl(rptCustomers.Name, acTextBox, _
                    acDetail, , "Job Title", intPosition)

txtTextBox.Name = "txtTitle"
txtTextBox.Width = 1800

Set lblLabel = CreateReportControl(rptCustomers.Name, acLabel, _
                    acPageHeader, , , intPosition)

lblLabel.Name = "lblTitle"
lblLabel.Caption = "Title"
lblLabel.Height = txtTextBox.Height
lblLabel.Width = txtTextBox.Width
lblLabel.FontBold = True


'add a Contact Phone label and text box to the report
intPosition = txtTextBox.Width + txtTextBox.Left + 1000

Set txtTextBox = CreateReportControl(rptCustomers.Name, acTextBox, _
                    acDetail, , "Business Phone", intPosition)

txtTextBox.Name = "txtPhone"

Set lblLabel = CreateReportControl(rptCustomers.Name, acLabel, _
```

```
                    acPageHeader, , , intPosition)

    lblLabel.Name = "lblPhone"
    lblLabel.Caption = "Phone"
    lblLabel.Height = txtTextBox.Height
    lblLabel.Width = txtTextBox.Width
    lblLabel.FontBold = True

    'save and close the new report
DoCmd.Save , strReportName
DoCmd.Close

End Sub
```

In the code example shown again in the following section, notice how a text box and label control are declared and then used to create each of the fields on the report. For example, txtTextBox is assigned to the result of the CreateReportControl method, which specifies the report name, type of control, section to add the control, name of the control, and the position in which to place the control. Various other properties of the text box control are specified, such as the Name and Width properties. The corresponding label control is also created and various settings specified.

```
'add a Company Name label and text box to the report
intPosition = 0
Set txtTextBox = CreateReportControl(rptCustomers.Name, acTextBox, _
                acDetail, , "Company", intPosition)
txtTextBox.Name = "txtCompanyName"
txtTextBox.Width = 1800
Set lblLabel = CreateReportControl(rptCustomers.Name, acLabel, _
                acPageHeader, , , intPosition)
lblLabel.Name = "lblCompanyName"
lblLabel.Caption = "Company Name"
lblLabel.Height = txtTextBox.Height
lblLabel.Width = txtTextBox.Width
lblLabel.FontBold = True
```

The same basic steps are then repeated to create each control for the report.

Try It Out   Creating a Report Programmatically

Now it's your turn to create a report programmatically. This example creates a report based on a new table that you create and uses a SQL statement as the report's RecordSource property.

1. Create a new database by selecting the Office Button ⇨ New. From the list of available templates, select Blank Database. Specify Ch9CodeExamples as the file name and path, and press the Create button.

2. Add a new tblComplaints table to the database, as shown in Figure 9-1.

Field Name	Data Type	Description
ComplaintID	AutoNumber	Unique Identified (Long Integer, Primary Key)
ComplaintDate	Date/Time	Date of Complaint
CustomerName	Text	Name of Customer (Field Size 50)
CustomerDayPhone	Text	Day Phone (Field Size 12)
CustomerEveningPhone	Text	Evening Phone (Field Size 12)
IssueDescription	Memo	Description of Issue
Resolved	Yes/No	Resolved (Boolean - Yes or No)
ResolutionDescription	Memo	Description of Resolution

Figure 9-1

3. Open the table and add some records, such as those shown in Figure 9-2.

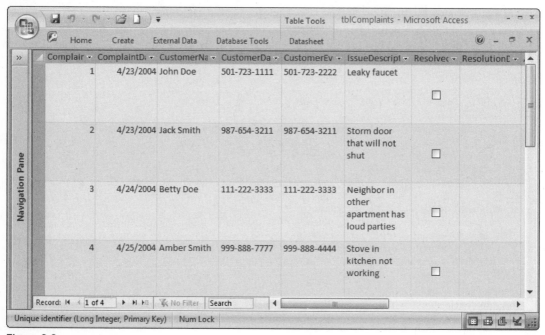

Figure 9-2

4. Insert a new module into the database. To do so, choose the Create ribbon, click on Macro, and select Module.

5. Add the following `CreateComplaintsReport` procedure to the module:

```
Sub CreateComplaintsReport()

Dim rptComplaints As Access.Report
Dim strReportName As String

Dim txtTextBox As Access.TextBox
```

```
Dim lblLabel As Access.Label
Dim strSQL As String

Dim intPosition As Integer

'set the name of the new report
strReportName = "Unresolved Customer Complaints"

strSQL = "SELECT * FROM tblComplaints WHERE Resolved=False"

'create a new Unresolved Customer Complaints Report
Set rptComplaints = CreateReport

With rptComplaints
    'set the report record source to the SQL Statement
    .RecordSource = strSQL

    'set the height, caption, and other report options
    .Section("Detail").Height = 500
    .Caption = "Unresolved Customer Complaints"
End With

'add a Customer Name label and text box to the report
intPosition = 0
Set txtTextBox = CreateReportControl(rptComplaints.Name, acTextBox, _
                    acDetail, , "CustomerName", intPosition)
txtTextBox.Name = "txtCustomerName"
txtTextBox.Width = 1800
Set lblLabel = CreateReportControl(rptComplaints.Name, acLabel,    _
                acPageHeader, , , intPosition)
lblLabel.Name = "lblCustomerName"
lblLabel.Caption = "Customer Name"
lblLabel.Height = txtTextBox.Height
lblLabel.Width = txtTextBox.Width
lblLabel.FontBold = True

'add a Customer Day Phone label and text box to the report
intPosition = txtTextBox.Width + txtTextBox.Left + 350
Set txtTextBox = CreateReportControl(rptComplaints.Name, acTextBox, _
acDetail, , "CustomerDayPhone", intPosition)
txtTextBox.Name = "txtCustomerDayPhone"
txtTextBox.Width = 1800
Set lblLabel = CreateReportControl(rptComplaints.Name, acLabel, _
            acPageHeader, , , intPosition)
lblLabel.Name = "lblCustomerDayPhone"
lblLabel.Caption = "Day Phone"
lblLabel.Height = txtTextBox.Height
lblLabel.Width = txtTextBox.Width
lblLabel.FontBold = True

'add a Customer Evening Phone label and text box to the report
intPosition = txtTextBox.Width + txtTextBox.Left + 500
Set txtTextBox = CreateReportControl(rptComplaints.Name, acTextBox,
    _               acDetail, , "CustomerEveningPhone", intPosition)
txtTextBox.Name = "txtCustomerEveningPhone"
```

```
txtTextBox.Width = 1800
Set lblLabel = CreateReportControl(rptComplaints.Name, acLabel, _
                acPageHeader, , , intPosition)
lblLabel.Name = "lblCustomerEveningPhone"
lblLabel.Caption = "Evening Phone"
lblLabel.Height = txtTextBox.Height
lblLabel.Width = txtTextBox.Width
lblLabel.FontBold = True

'add an Issue Description label and text box to the report
intPosition = txtTextBox.Width + txtTextBox.Left + 1000
Set txtTextBox = CreateReportControl(rptComplaints.Name, acTextBox, _
                acDetail, , "IssueDescription", intPosition)
txtTextBox.Name = "txtIssueDescription"
txtTextBox.Width = 2000
txtTextBox.Height = 750
Set lblLabel = CreateReportControl(rptComplaints.Name, acLabel, _
                acPageHeader, , , intPosition)
lblLabel.Name = "lblIssueDescription"
lblLabel.Caption = "Issue Description"
lblLabel.Height = txtTextBox.Height
lblLabel.Width = txtTextBox.Width
lblLabel.FontBold = True

'save and close the new report
DoCmd.Save , strReportName
DoCmd.Close

End Sub
```

6. Run the procedure from the Immediate Window by typing the procedure name.

How It Works

First, you created a new database and a table called tblComplaints. You then added some sample data to the tblComplaints table so the report would have data to display. Next, you created a new module and added the CreateComplaintsReport procedure to the module.

```
Sub CreateComplaintsReport()
```

The procedure declares some variables for use in the procedure, such as a Report object for creating the new report and the text box and label controls for adding to the report:

```
Dim rptComplaints As Access.Report
Dim strReportName As String

Dim txtTextBox As Access.TextBox
Dim lblLabel As Access.Label
Dim strSQL As String
Dim intPosition As Integer

'set the name of the new report
```

```
strReportName = "Unresolved Customer Complaints"

strSQL = "SELECT * FROM tblComplaints WHERE Resolved=False"
```

The new report was created using the `CreateReport` method, and properties such as `RecordSource`, `Height`, and `Caption` were specified. The `RecordSource` property assigned the source of data to the SQL statement. The Detail section's `Height` property specified the size of the report's detail section.

```
'create a new Unresolved Customer Complaints Report
Set rptComplaints = CreateReport

With rptComplaints
    'set the report record source to the SQL Statement
    .RecordSource = strSQL

    'set the height, caption, and other report options
    .Section("Detail").Height = 500
    .Caption = "Unresolved Customer Complaints"
End With
```

Next, you added code to create the report controls. For example, to create a new Customer Name label and text box, you used the `CreateReportControl` method. The parameters of `CreateReportControl` specified, among other things, where to include the field (in the report or detail section), what data source field the new field should be based on, and what position it should start in.

```
'add a Customer Name label and text box to the report
intPosition = 0
Set txtTextBox = CreateReportControl(rptComplaints.Name, acTextBox, _
                acDetail, , "CustomerName", intPosition)
txtTextBox.Name = "txtCustomerName"
txtTextBox.Width = 1800
Set lblLabel = CreateReportControl(rptComplaints.Name, acLabel, _
                acPageHeader, , , intPosition)
lblLabel.Name = "lblCustomerName"
lblLabel.Caption = "Customer Name"
lblLabel.Height = txtTextBox.Height
lblLabel.Width = txtTextBox.Width
lblLabel.FontBold = True
```

The same basic code was repeated for each of the remaining controls on the report, namely the labels and text boxes for Customer Day Phone, Customer Evening Phone, and Issue Description. The final lines of the procedure saved and closed the report.

```
'save and close the new report
DoCmd.Save , strReportName
DoCmd.Close

End Sub
```

When you ran the new procedure, the report was created and appeared in the Database Window, as shown in Figure 9-3. The report was then opened in preview mode, as shown in Figure 9-4, so you could see the final result of your efforts.

Figure 9-3

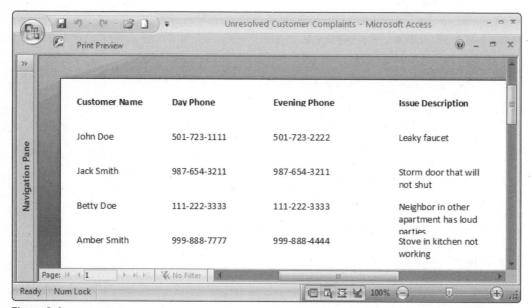

Figure 9-4

Using the Printer Object to Designate Printing Options

In Chapter 3, you learned about the `Printers` collection and `Printer` object. This collection and object are again important if you want to modify the margins or other printer characteristics of a report. For example, if you wanted to modify the margins and number of copies for the first printer, you could use code similar to the following:

```
Dim prtPrinter As Printer

Set prtPrinter = Application.Printers(0)

prtPrinter.TopMargin = 500
prtPrinter.BottomMargin = 250
prtPrinter.LeftMargin = 500
prtPrinter.RightMargin = 500
prtPrinter.Copies = 5
```

The example shown above for setting printer margins and copies is just a simple example for illustration purposes. In order to follow good programming practices, you would typically want to avoid hard-coding such values into the code. You would instead allow these values to be set by a user in a user interface or in a settings file and then set the values in the code above to the user-specified settings.

As another printer example, you could use the AllPrinters collection to loop through all printers on the computer and take some particular action, such as displaying the printer name in a printer dialog box. See Chapter 3 for additional examples.

Working with Report Events

At this point, you should be very familiar with how to add events to forms, such as the Click event of a button. Reports have events just as forms do, but not as many, as you can see in Figure 9-5.

You can also write VBA code behind report events, such as Open, Close, Activate, and Deactivate. For example, you might want to display a message to users when the report opens to inform them that the report will take a long time to load. You may want to add a custom toolbar to be displayed from the Activate event and then remove that toolbar when the Deactivate event fires.

The following is an example of adding and removing a custom toolbar from the report's Activate and Deactivate events.

```
Private Sub Report_Activate()
  DoCmd.ShowToolbar "CustomComplaints", acToolbarYes
End Sub

Private Sub Report_Deactivate()
  DoCmd.ShowToolbar "CustomComplaints", acToolbarNo
End Sub
```

Now that you have a basic idea of how to create reports programmatically and how to create report events, you can move on to the topic of exporting Access data to various Web formats.

Figure 9-5

Exporting Access Data to Web Formats

As you learned in Chapter 7, you have various ways to export data from Access to other formats. The OutputTo method allows exporting to various formats: HTML, RTF, TXT, XLS, and XLSB. The examples in this section will focus on a Web-centric example using HTML, but you could also use the OutputTo method to export to text files or other supported formats. Consult the Access Help documentation for additional information on these formats. The basic syntax for the OutputTo method is shown in the following code:

```
DoCmd.OutputTo ObjectType, ObjectName, OutputFormat, OutputFile, AutoStart,
TemplateFile, Encoding
```

Various parameters can specify how the method should execute. The following table explains the use of each parameter.

Parameter	Description
ObjectType	Type of object to be exported. See the help documentation for the complete list of objects.
ObjectName	Name of the object being exported.
OutputFormat	The format to which the object should be exported.
OutputFile	The full name, including the path, of the file to which the object should be exported.
AutoStart	Indication of whether the destination program is to start immediately. False is the default.
TemplateFile	The full name, including the path, of the file to use as a template.
Encoding	The type of character encoding format to use when outputting the text or HTML data.
OutputQuality	Type of output device to optimize for. The AcExportQuality constant specifies the type, and the default value is acExportQualityPrint.

Now that you are familiar with the basic syntax of the OutputTo method, let's look at how to use it to export data to HTML.

Creating Static HTML Pages

You have no doubt heard of *HTML* pages and are probably aware that they are typically used to display Web pages. You can use the OutputTo method to export a database table, query, results of a SQL statement, or other data to a static HTML document. A static HTML document is disconnected from the original data source and does not change as the underlying data changes — hence the name *static*.

To export the results of a report to an HTML document, you might use a statement similar to the following:

```
DoCmd.OutputTo acOutputReport, "ReportName", acFormatHTML,
    "c:\temp\tempReportName.html"
```

Now, try it out so you can see how this works.

Try It Out   **Exporting the tblComplaints Table to HTML**

This example will export the data contained in the tblComplaints table you created earlier in the chapter to an HTML file.

1. Add the following procedure to the module you created earlier:

```
Sub OutputToHTML()

DoCmd.OutputTo acOutputTable, "tblComplaints", acFormatHTML,
"c:\temp\tempcomplaints.html", True

End Sub
```

2. Run the OutputToHTML procedure from the Immediate Window by typing OutputToHTML and then pressing Enter.

3. The exported HTML document should open automatically in a Web browser, as shown in Figure 9-6.

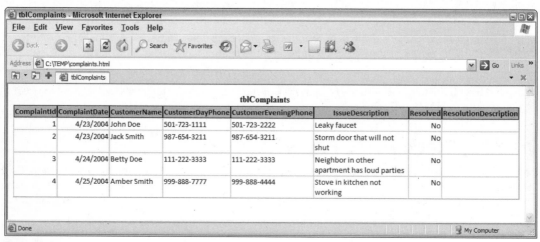

Figure 9-6

How It Works

The OutputToHTML procedure uses the OutputTo method with various parameters that indicate what should be exported, in what format, and to where. In this example, the tblComplaints table is exported to an HTML format into a new file called tempcomplaints.html. The True parameter at the end of the statement that follows is for the AutoStart parameter to indicate that the Web browser should automatically launch to display the file.

```
Sub OutputToHTML()

DoCmd.OutputTo acOutputTable, "tblComplaints", acFormatHTML,
"c:\temp\tempcomplaints.html", True

End Sub
```

After you run the preceding procedure, the Web browser does indeed launch and displays the newly created HTML file in a screen similar to Figure 9-6.

Summary

In this chapter, you learned various ways to display data programmatically from Access. You looked at several examples, such as creating new reports programmatically and exporting data to various formats. I hope you are beginning to see that there is much more to Access than just tables, forms, and reports. You have seen in this and prior chapters how to work with data in various sources, and to perform many advanced operations using VBA code.

I have talked a lot so far about SQL Server, but you have not seen any examples. The next chapter will focus on building Access solutions that use SQL Server as the database. You will learn that Access has many features that make working with SQL Server databases much easier.

Exercises

1. What is the difference between the `CreateReport` method and the `CreateReportControl` method?

2. How do report events differ from form events?

3. What is the purpose of the `AutoStart` parameter of the `OutputTo` method?

Building SQL Server Applications with Access Projects

So far, all the examples in this book have dealt with standard Access database files (ACCDB files). An *Access Project* (ADP file) is another type of Access database file that is designed specifically for working with SQL Server databases. In this chapter, you will explore how to create and manage SQL Server databases using Access Projects. You'll learn how to create new Access Projects from scratch and explore the various SQL Server objects that you can create and manage from an Access Project, such as tables, stored procedures, views, and functions. You will also migrate an existing Access database to SQL Server and provide guidelines for resolving any problems that occur during the migration.

This chapter focuses on using Access Projects to work with features that are specific to SQL Server, but it does not cover forms and modules. You still write forms and modules in Access Projects as you have done in prior chapters.

Access Projects — Using Access as a Front End to SQL server

As a quick recap, you are already familiar with standard Access database files: the ACCDB files. The ACCDB file is typically used in a standalone manner, meaning that all the tables, forms, modules, macros, and reports for the application are stored within the single file. In Chapter 7, you learned that it is also possible to use a standard Access ACCDB file in a client-server environment by linking to external database tables such as SQL Server. An example of a client-server architecture is shown in Figure 10-1, which illustrates a case where the user interface resides on the client and the database resides on the server.

When linking to a SQL Server database from a standard Access database, you can only work graphically with SQL Server tables from the Access environment. You cannot view and modify stored procedures, views, and functions from within the Access environment.

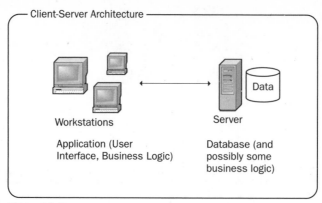

Figure 10-1

Access Projects are a special type of Access file designed to work specifically with SQL Server databases. Access Projects provide you with additional graphical tools for manipulating various SQL Server objects — not just the tables. When you are designing client-server applications that use SQL Server as the database, you should consider using an Access Project instead of a standard database so that you will have these additional design features.

The following table shows where the various objects that you can see from within the Access Project are actually stored.

Object	Location	Comments
Tables	SQL Server	SQL Server uses different data types.
Queries	SQL Server	These can be stored as stored procedures, views, or functions.
Database Diagrams	SQL Server	
Forms	Access file	
Reports	Access file	
Macros	Access file	
Modules	Access file	

Setting Up SQL Server

Now that you are aware that you can use Access Projects to work with SQL Server databases, I will take a moment to cover the different versions of SQL Server and explain how to install SQL Server. You must install one of the versions of SQL Server in order to perform the examples used throughout this chapter.

SQL Server Versions

As you are probably aware by now, Microsoft SQL Server is a relational database management system for storing, analyzing, and reporting data. Currently, seven versions of Microsoft SQL Server are available with SQL Server 2005. Each is briefly described here:

❑   **SQL Server 2005 Enterprise Edition** – This is the most comprehensive version of SQL Server 2005 and supports all the SQL Server 2005 features. This version is most appropriate for large organizations that are required to manage immense amounts of data quickly and efficiently.

❑   **SQL Server 2005 Standard Edition** – This version of SQL Server 2005 supports many of the available features, but it doesn't support the features that enable management of immense amounts of data quickly and efficiently. This version is primarily for small or medium-sized organizations that do not have the complex database requirements of a large organization. SQL Server 2005 Standard Edition is still an extremely powerful version of SQL Server and supports Analysis Services (with a few exceptions), Replication, Full-Text Search, Integration Services (Basic Transforms only), the Common Language Runtime and .NET Integration, and other advanced SQL Server features.

❑   **SQL Server 2005 Workgroup Edition** – This version of SQL Server 2005 supports basically the same features as the Standard Edition with some exceptions, most notably Notification Services and Integration Services. Additionally, Analysis Services and Full-Text Search are only available on certain operating systems with this edition. This version is most appropriate for small organizations or small business units.

❑   **SQL Server 2005 Mobile Edition** – This version of SQL Server 2005 runs on mobile devices — Windows CE. This compact version of SQL Server 2005 allows relational databases to be stored and managed on Windows CE devices for later synchronization. Plus, it gives users the capability to manage a SQL Server database remotely over the Internet from their CE devices.

❑   **SQL Server 2005 Developer Edition** – This version of SQL Server 2005 supports all the available features (just like the Enterprise Edition), except it prohibits deployment on production servers. This version is designed for developers, consultants, and solution providers to use while developing and testing their applications.

❑   **SQL Server 2005 Evaluation Edition** – This version is a fully functional version of SQL Server 2005 Enterprise Edition, but it will stop working after 120 days. It is available as a free trial to give organizations a chance to try out SQL Server 2005 Enterprise Edition before purchasing it.

❑   **SQL Server 2005 Express Edition (formerly called "Desktop Edition")** – This version is a free and redistributable version of the SQL Server database engine. This means that you can include it in your setup programs for applications that use SQL Server to store data. This release of Express Edition is similar to prior releases in that graphical user interface tools to manipulate the database are not included, thus, other products (such as Access or SQL Server 2005 APIs) must be used to manage data stored in this version of SQL Server. Also, Microsoft has created an Express Edition of its new database management tool, SQL Server Management Studio. Finally, please note that Express Edition requires that .NET Framework Version 2.0 be installed.

Obtaining and Installing SQL Server Express Engine

If you do not have SQL Server already installed, you should obtain a copy. You have a couple of options to get it up and running. You can download or order a free trial version of SQL Server (that expires after a trial period) from Microsoft. Another option is to install SQL Server 2005 Express Edition, which is free. The setup program for the Express Edition is on the Microsoft Office CDs, as I will explain momentarily.

The Benefits of SQL Server Express Edition

You may be wondering why Microsoft would offer a free version of SQL Server. Express Edition was introduced by Microsoft to bridge the gap between Microsoft Access and Microsoft SQL Server. A large segment of existing applications use Microsoft Access as both the front end and the database platform. As those applications become increasingly popular, they start outgrowing the capabilities of Access. Many people may find themselves modifying code to port the applications to a SQL Server database. This can be a monumental task in many instances, with several data type and SQL syntax differences.

Express Edition is actually a small-scale version of SQL Server, with a 4GB limitation. If your application does not need the capability to handle large databases or many users, the Express Edition version of SQL Server is a good choice. Some exceptions to this free licensing rule can be found in the licensing agreement that accompanies Express Edition and other versions of SQL Server.

Express Edition allows companies to create demo CDs of their products much more easily. In the past, many companies had to write an Access version of their SQL Server application to include on the demo CD so that they would not violate the licensing agreement of SQL Server. Alternatively, they included links or files to download trial versions of SQL Server in order for their demo to work. Because Express Edition is a free distribution version of SQL Server, you can now easily create CDs for demonstration purposes without rewriting any code.

The biggest advantage of using Express Edition is that you don't have to make any modifications to your code (SQL statements, table structures, and so on) when you upsize later because of an increase in database size or concurrent users. You just purchase the more powerful version of SQL Server and import the prior database to the new installation without modification. Thus, when your application becomes extremely popular and needs the power of the higher, nonfree versions of SQL Server, you will be ready.

Installing SQL Server Express Edition

You can obtain the setup program for Express Edition from the Microsoft web site. At the time of publication, the URL for download is `http://msdn.microsoft.com/vstudio/express/sql/download/`. Further, if service packs are available it is wise to download and install them as well.

1. Download the installer program to a location on your hard drive. The download gives you an option of saving the file to your local hard drive or simply running it. It is recommended that you save it to disk. The file is in excess of 50MB, so it may take a while depending on your Internet connection.

2. Launch the Express Edition Setup Program. Navigate to the folder on your hard drive where you saved the download. From that folder, double-click on the setup program to launch the setup program. You may be prompted to update some files on your system before setup can continue. If so, follow the prompts on the screen to update your system with the necessary files. This may require that you reboot your machine and restart the setup program again.

3. The Windows Installer or some other such program will flash for a few seconds to let you know that it is launching the setup program. After you double-click on the setup program, it should just automatically install Express Edition with all the default settings. If any prompts appear on the screen, follow the instructions to complete the setup.

4. It is also a good idea to download and install the latest service pack for whatever version of SQL Server you are running.

Now that you have successfully installed SQL Server Express Edition, take a look at what actually got installed.

Understanding What Was Installed

Unlike previous versions which installed three services, SQL Server 2005 Express Edition installs two services on your machine: SQL Server Agent and SQL Server browser.

The *SQL Server Configuration Manager* is installed with Express Edition to enable you to manage these two services. The SQL Server Configuration Manager window, shown in Figure 10-2, displays the settings for Server, Services, and the status of the Service

Figure 10-2

To start, stop, pause, continue, or restart the service, highlight the SQL Server service and right-click and select the desired action from the pop-up menu. Note that menu items are enabled or disabled as appropriate, based on the current status. Figure 10-3 shows the status of the SQL Server Service, with Pause, Stop, Resume, and Restart disabled.

If you select the Start menu item, the SQL Server Service starts running (see Figure 10-4).

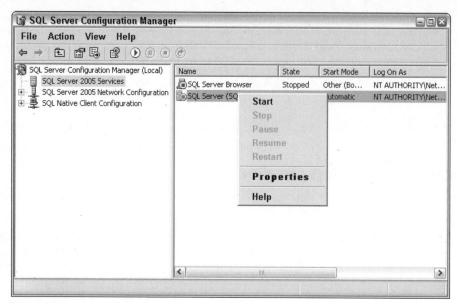

Figure 10-3

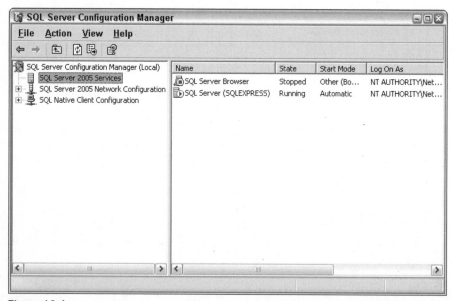

Figure 10-4

The *SQL Server Service* is the core of Express Edition and all other versions of SQL Server, for that matter. It consists of the SQL Server storage engine and the query processor. The storage engine is responsible for reading and writing the data to the database, and the query processor is responsible for receiving and executing SQL statements. The SQL Server Service must be running in order for data to be retrieved, inserted, updated, or deleted from Express Edition. The default installation of Express Edition sets this service to automatically run on startup of the computer where Express Edition is installed.

The SQL Server Service, shown in Figure 10-4, is running on a server called Goz_Tablet1100 and a database instance called SQLDEV. Notice how the indicator to auto-start the service when the OS starts is checked. This means that the SQL Server Service will start anytime the operating system boots. It is a good idea to have this setting turned on for the SQL Server Service so that database inserts, updates, deletes, reads, and so on will be allowed automatically. User intervention is not required to manually start the service each time.

The other service installed with Express Edition is the *SQL Server Browser Service*. This service receives incoming requests for resources and provides information about the database instances installed on the local machine. These examples illustrate how easy it is to manage the two services that are installed with Express Edition by using the SQL Server Configuration Manager utility. Now that I have covered the basics of setting up Express Edition and starting and stopping the services, let's return to the discussion of using Access Projects to work with SQL Server databases.

Creating Access Projects (ADPs)

Now that you have SQL Server installed, you can return to the discussion of using Access Projects to work with SQL Server databases. To create a new Access Project for a SQL Server database, you first select the Office Button ⇨ New. On the right side of the window, you will see the Blank Database section, as shown in Figure 10-5. Click on Browse (the folder icon to the right of the file name) and a window similar to the one shown in Figure 10-6 will be displayed.

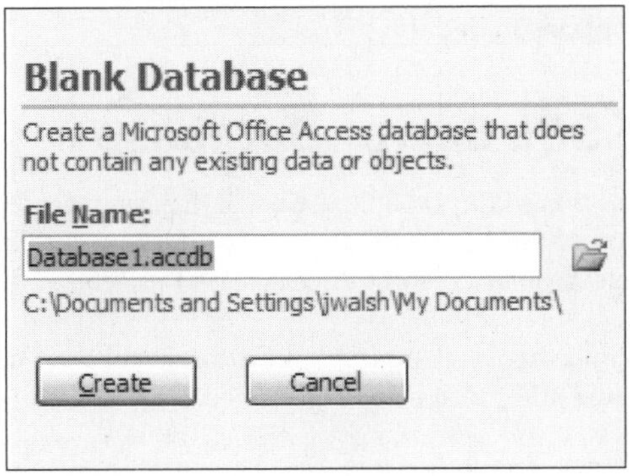

Blank Database

Create a Microsoft Office Access database that does not contain any existing data or objects.

File Name:

Database1.accdb

C:\Documents and Settings\jwalsh\My Documents\

[Create]   [Cancel]

Figure 10-5

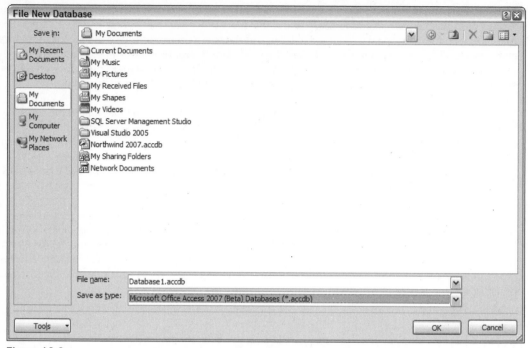

Figure 10-6

In the Save As Type drop-down list, select the Microsoft Office Access Projects (* .adp) option, select a location for the Access Project, specify a file name, and press the OK button. You will be returned to the original window and press the Create button. You will be asked if you want to connect to an existing SQL Server database. Selecting Yes will allow you to create a new Access Project using an existing SQL Server database. Selecting No will create a new Access Project and a new SQL Server database. You will now look at each of these options in detail.

Using an Existing SQL Server Database

To create a new Access Project based upon an existing SQL Server database, select the Office Button ⇨ New, browse for the location of the Access Project, and a window similar to that in Figure 10-6 is displayed, Provide a name, select the Microsoft Office Access Projects (* .adp) option, and then click on OK.

Click on the Create button and then click on the Yes button in the pop-up window. You are then prompted (as shown in Figure 10-7) to specify details necessary to connect to your SQL Server database.

In the example of Figure 10-7, a database called pubs on the goz_tablet1100\sqldev server is being used. The option to use integrated Windows security is checked, so no SQL Server user name or password has to be filled in.

If you have trouble connecting to SQL Server using integrated Windows security, try specifying a user name of sa *and a blank password, which may have been installed by default.*

You can click the Test Connection button to test the connection to make sure it works. You can create the new Access Project based on this database by clicking OK. The new Access Project will look similar to the screen shown in Figure 10-8.

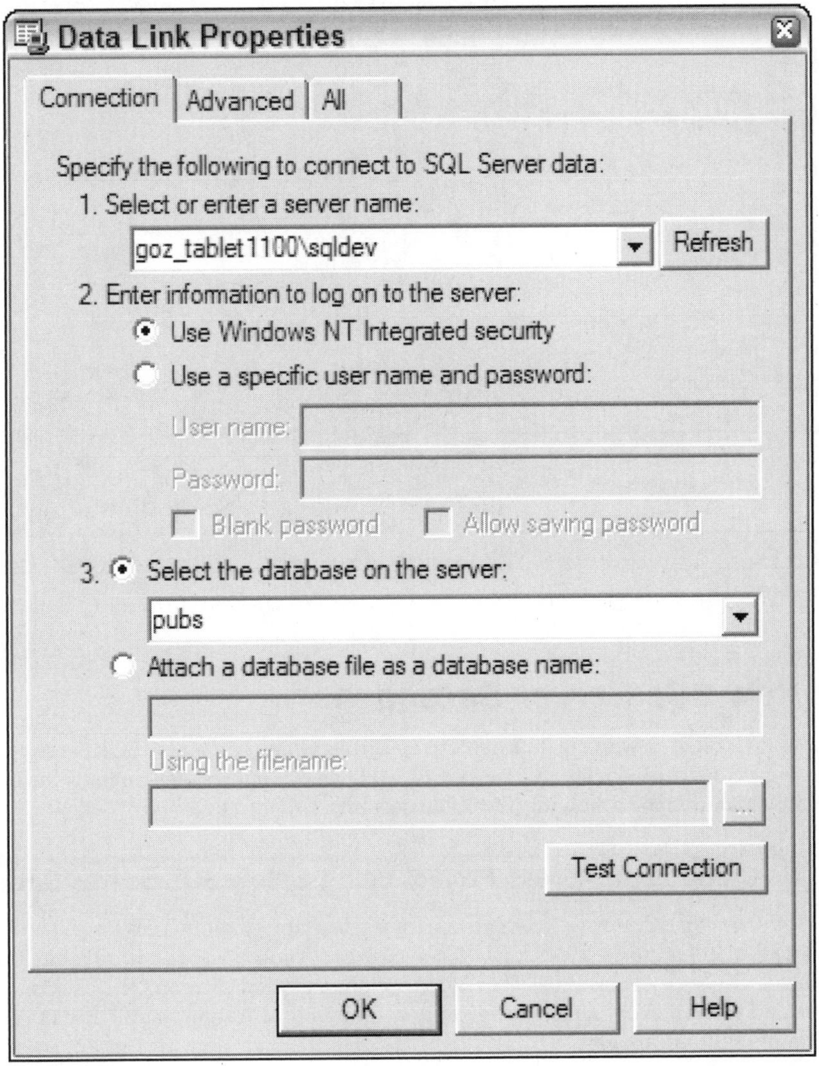

Figure 10-7

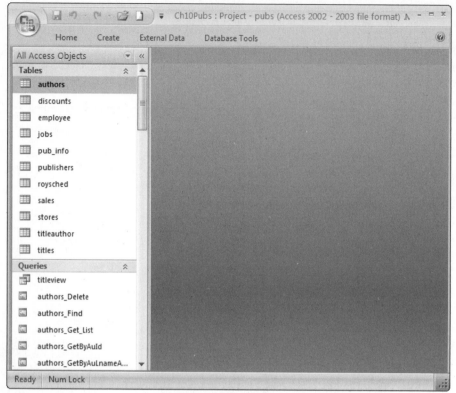

Figure 10-8

Using a New SQL Server Database

Let's now take a look at how to create a new Access Project based on a new SQL Server database. For your convenience, I included a text file for download from Wrox.com that contains the code for the SQL Server objects created in the following Try It Out sections.

Try It Out   **Creating an Access Project Using a New SQL Server Database**

1.   Select the Office Button ➪ New, browse for the location of the Access Project and a window similar to that in Figure 10-6 is displayed, Specify Ch10CodeExamples for the file name, select the Microsoft Office Access Projects (*.adp) option, and then click on OK. Click on the Create button and then click on the No button in pop-up window. A screen similar to the one shown in Figure 10-9 then appears.

2.   Specify the name of your SQL Server instance, or select one from the list. Specify whether to use a Trusted Connection or a specific SQL Server login account, depending on how security for your SQL Server instance is set up. Also, specify the name for the new SQL Server database as Ch10CodeExamplesSQL. Click the Next button.

3.   A screen similar to Figure 10-10 will appear. Click the Finish button to create the new SQL Server database.

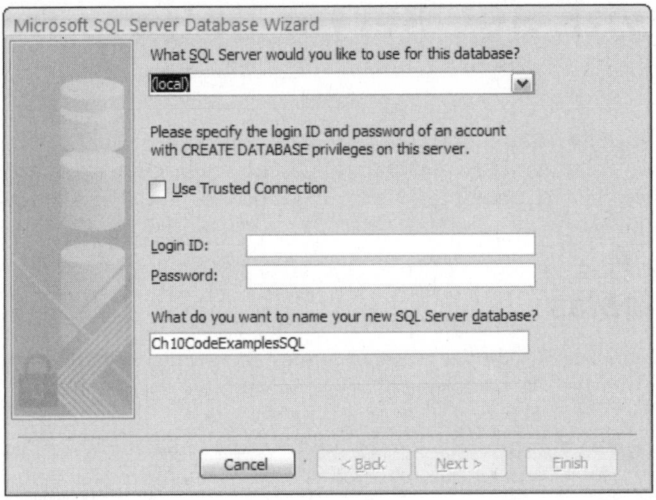

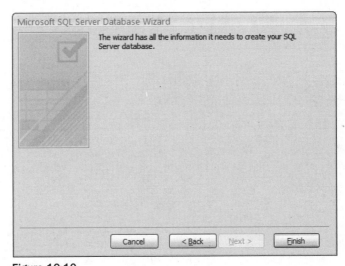

Figure 10-9

Figure 10-10

How It Works

The wizard walked you through the steps of creating a new Access Project and a new SQL Server database. The end result of performing the preceding steps is that you now have an Access Project (Ch10CodeExamples.ADP) on your hard drive, and you have a new database called Ch10CodeExamplesSQL in your SQL Server database. At this point, the SQL Server database and Access Project are both empty. Let's look at some examples of how to work with SQL Server objects from within Access so your project does not remain empty.

Working with SQL Server Objects from Access

The advantage of using an Access Project to work with SQL Server is that you can use various graphical designer tools from within Access to manipulate SQL Server objects. For example, you can view and create SQL Server tables, stored procedures, views, and functions. You'll look at each of these in detail in the sections that follow.

SQL Server Tables

You can view and manage SQL Server tables from the Tables category of the Navigation Pane in your Access Project. Figure 10-11 is an example of a SQL Server table opened from within Access.

From looking at the data in Figure 10-11, you would not know that it physically resides in a SQL Server database. This screen looks very similar to the other screens you have seen before with local Access tables. Now, if you open a SQL Server table in design view, a screen similar to the one shown in Figure 10-12 appears.

The table designer is a bit different from the one you have worked with before. Notice how some additional columns for Length and Allow Nulls have been added. SQL Server also has some data types other than the standard Access tables.

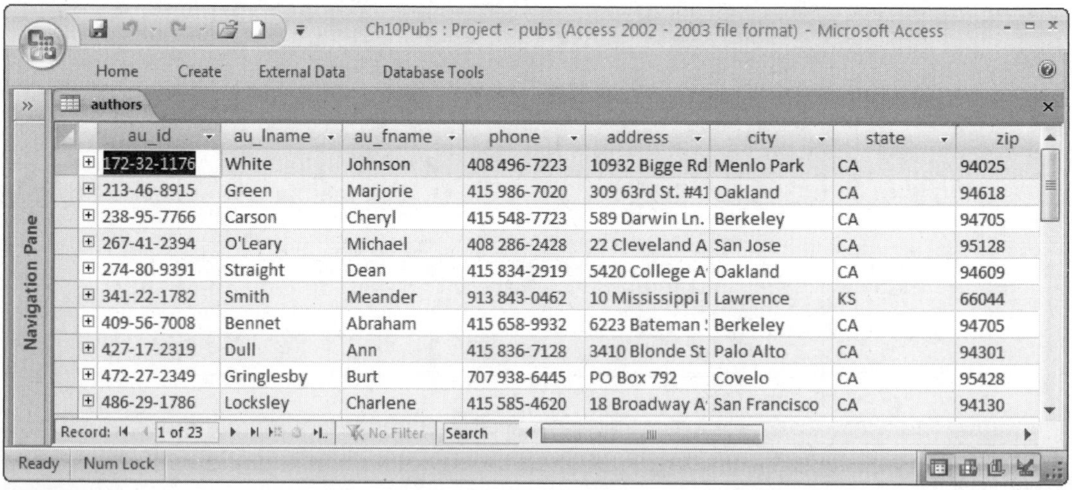

Figure 10-11

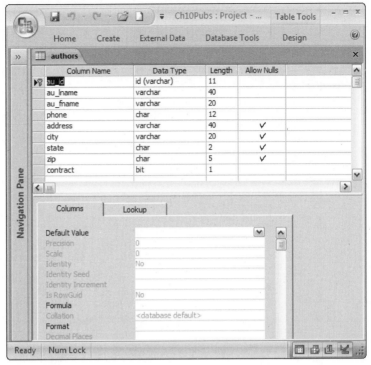

Figure 10-12

Try It Out   Creating a New SQL Server Table

It's your turn to try your hand at creating a new SQL Server table.

1. Create a new table, named `tblProducts`. To do so, select the Create tab and click on Table Design in the Tables ribbon. Fill in the table elements as shown in Figure 10-13.

2. After adding all the table columns and their respective data types, set the `ProductId` to the primary key. To set the primary key, select the `ProductId` field, right-click, and select the Primary Key option in the pop-up list.

3. Now, add some data to the table, such as that shown in Figure 10-14.

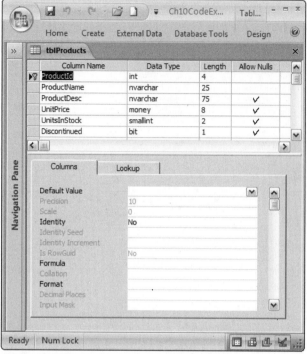

Ch10CodeEx...
Tabl...
Home
Create
External Data
Database Tools
Design
tblProducts
Navigation Pane
Column Name
Data Type
Length
Allow Nulls
ProductId
int
4
ProductName
nvarchar
25
ProductDesc
nvarchar
75
UnitPrice
money
8
UnitsInStock
smallint
2
Discontinued
bit
1
Columns
Lookup
Default Value
Precision
10
Scale
0
Identity
No
Identity Seed
Identity Increment
Is RowGuid
No
Formula
Collation
Format
Decimal Places
Input Mask
Ready
Num Lock

Figure 10-13

Ch10CodeExamples : Project - Ch10CodeExamplesSQL (Access 2002 - 2003 file format) ..!
Home
Create
External Data
Database Tools
tblProducts
Navigation Pane
ProductId
ProductName
ProductDesc
UnitPrice
UnitsInStock
Discontinue
123456
ABC Co. Wireless Speakers
Indoor/Outdoor wireless speakers and transmitter. 300 ft range
$129.00
5
234567
XYZ Co. Marble Table
Marble Patio table. 54 in dia.
$1,850.00
10
345678
XYZ Co. Umbrella
Umbrella for patio table. White color.
$199.50
30
345987
XYZ Co. Umbrella
Umbrella for patio table. Green color.
$199.50
0
True
345876
XYZ Co. Umbrella
Umbrella for patio table. Yellow color.
$199.50
0
True
456789
XYZ Co. Patio Chair
Patio chair. Swivel.
$399.99
25
Record: 1 of 6
No Filter
Search
Ready
Num Lock

Figure 10-14

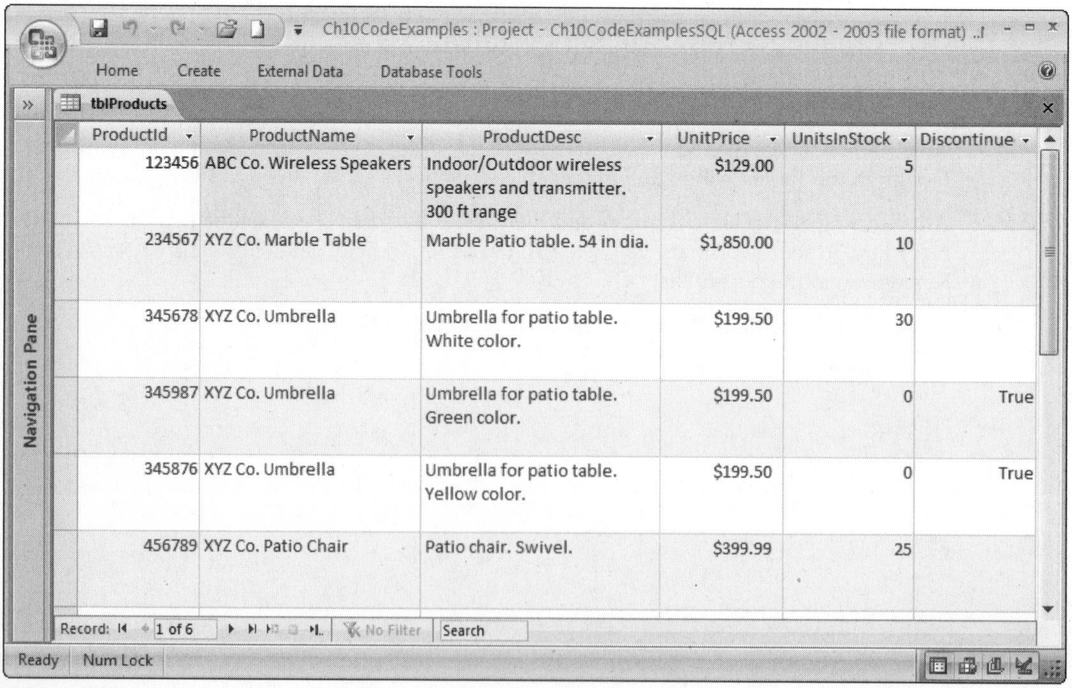

How It Works

The preceding example illustrates how to create a new table from the Access table designer that physically resides in the SQL Server database. You will now learn how to create stored procedures.

SQL Server Stored Procedures

Stored procedures are procedures that are stored in the SQL Server database. Their purpose is to enable you to take frequently used SQL statements and save them for reuse. You can then execute a stored procedure when you need it. A stored procedure is similar in concept to the VBA procedures and SQL statements you have written so far in this book. However, stored procedures (stored in the SQL Server database) are more efficient than passing SQL statements to the database on the fly because they are precompiled.

You can view stored procedures from the Queries category in the Navigation Pane. In fact, the Queries node will display all stored procedures, views, and functions that are stored in the SQL Server database. Figure 10-15 illustrates several stored procedures, as well as one view called `titleview`.

When you open the `byroyalty` stored procedure in Figure 10-15, a designer window like the one shown in Figure 10-16 appears.

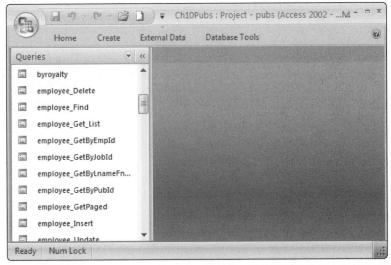

Figure 10-15

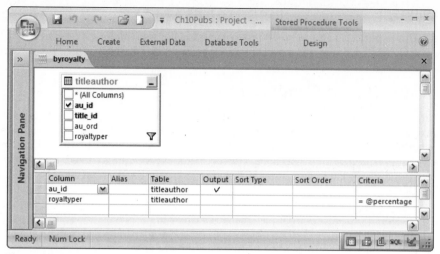

Figure 10-16

Notice how a table is displayed as well as a grid showing the columns to be output when the stored procedure executes. You can view the SQL code for the stored procedure by clicking the SQL button in the lower right-hand corner of the window; a screen similar to the one shown Figure 10-17 will appear.

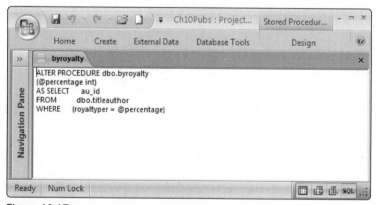

Figure 10-17

In the example of Figure 10-17, the stored procedure accepts a parameter called @percentage. When you call the stored procedure from VBA code, you must specify the parameter. You might call the stored procedure using the following code:

```
Dim cmdCommand As ADODB.Command
Dim prmPercent As ADODB.Parameter

'Create a new command object
Set cmdCommand = New ADODB.Command
cmdCommand.ActiveConnection = CurrentProject.Connection

'Specify the stored procedure to run
cmdCommand.CommandType = adCmdStoredProc
cmdCommand.CommandText = "byroyalty"

'Create the percentage parameter
Set prmPercent = cmdCommand.CreateParameter("@percentage", adInteger, adParamInput)
prmPercent.Value = 100
cmdCommand.Parameters.Append prmPercent

'execute the Stored Procedure
cmdCommand.Execute
```

In the preceding example, notice how the ADO Command object is used to specify that a stored procedure should be executed. The ADO Parameter object is used to specify the parameters that should be passed to the stored procedure. The Execute method of the Command object is then executed to run the stored procedure.

Try It Out   Creating a New SQL Server Stored Procedure

Let's create a new stored procedure in your Ch10CodeExamples Access Project.

1. Select the Create tab and then click on the Stored Procedure button on the Other ribbon.

2. Select the Add button on the Add Table window to add tblProducts. Click the Close button.

3. Fill in the columns and values as shown in Figure 10-18. The stored procedure outputs all but the discontinued column based on criteria where discontinued equals 1.

4. Save the stored procedure, and name it spDiscontinuedProducts.

5. Click on the SQL button to see the SQL statement for the procedure. A screen similar to the one shown in Figure 10-19 is displayed.

6. To run the stored procedure, select the View icon on the toolbar. A screen similar to the one shown in Figure 10-20 is displayed.

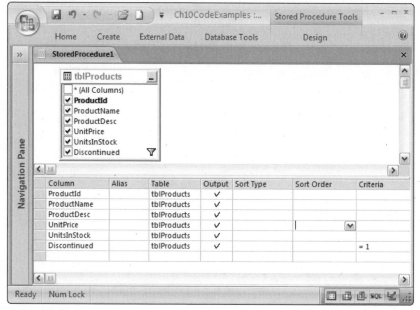

Figure 10-18

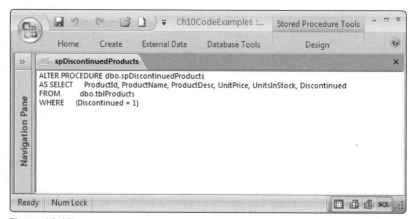

Figure 10-19

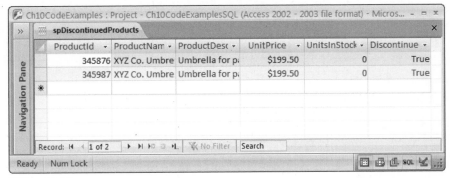

Figure 10-20

How It Works

In this example, you created a new stored procedure using the Access designer to specify the criteria for the procedure. You then viewed the SQL statement that Access created automatically from the criteria specified in the designer. You could have alternatively started with the SQL statement and Access would have generated the table and grid elements automatically from the SQL statement. You will see how to create a view in this manner momentarily.

SQL Server Views

Views are virtual tables that allow you to view information in a different way than you see it in the underlying tables. They are really just queries that have been saved to the SQL Server database that can be accessed in the same way as you would a table — only by specifying the view name instead of the table name. The capability to create an easily retrievable virtual table out of your most commonly used SQL statements is one advantage to using views.

Another advantage of views is that they provide the capability to implement row- and column-level security. Row-level security means restricting the values that a particular user can see down to the record level. Column-level security means restricting which fields a user can see. A common example of row-level security is the case where an employee can see his own personal information but not anyone else's. A common example of column-level security is a case where no one outside of the Personnel Department is permitted to see any columns that contain personal information, such as salary, but employees can see the nonpersonal information, such as job title.

Figure 10-21 illustrates the design view that retrieves data from multiple tables in a database.

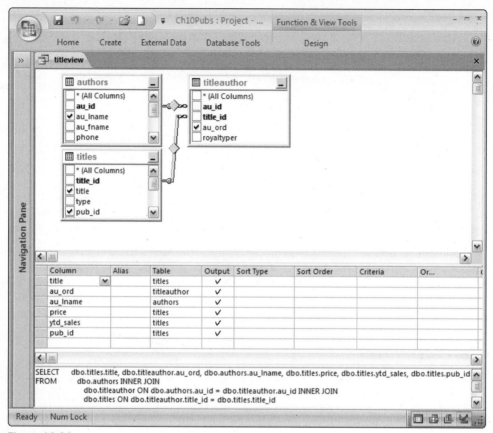

Figure 10-21

To view all three portions of the display shown in Figure 10-21, you must first click on the Design tab and select enable the Diagram, Grid, and SQL statement icons in the tool ribbon.

After a view has been created, you can reference it in all the places where you could otherwise use a table. For example, you could have an ADO recordset that is based on a SQL statement such as the following:

```
SELECT * FROM titleview
```

The previous SQL statement causes the SQL behind the view (as shown in Figure 10-21) to run and to return the various columns selected. The view of Figure 10-21 will be similar to the screen shown in Figure 10-22 if opened in view mode from within Access.

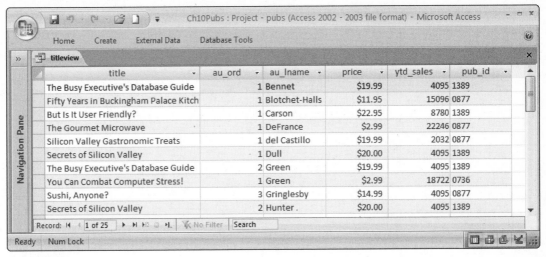

Figure 10-22

Try It Out   Creating a New View

It's your turn to create a view.

1. From the Database Window, click on the Create tab and then click on Query Wizard in the Other ribbon. Select Design View and click OK. Select the Close button to close the Add Tables dialog. Click the Design tab and select the SQL button on the tool ribbon to ensure that the SQL view is displayed. Add the following SQL statement:

```
SELECT      ProductName, ProductDesc, UnitPrice
FROM        dbo.tblProducts
```

2. Select the Save button on the toolbar to save the view and name it vwProductPrice. Close and reopen the view in design view. Notice that from the SQL statement you typed that Access determines and displays the table diagram and column grid that corresponds to the SQL statement, as shown in Figure 10-23.

3. Select the Save button on the toolbar to save the view. Name the view vwProductPrice.

4. Select the View button on the toolbar to execute the view. A screen similar to that shown in Figure 10-24 is displayed to show you the result of running the SQL statement behind the view.

Do not confuse the View button on the toolbar with the concept of a view. The View button on the tool-bar allows you to open various objects, including stored procedures, tables, and views to see the data. This is a different concept than a view itself.

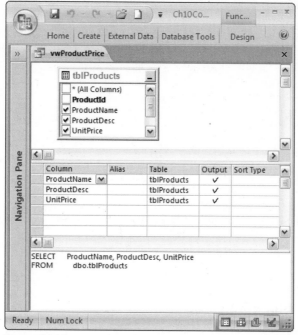

Figure 10-23

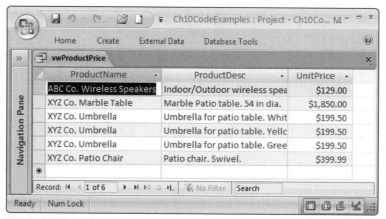

Figure 10-24

How It Works

In the preceding example, you created a new view by starting with a SQL statement. Microsoft Access then updated the designer to display the table and grid to graphically represent the SQL statement. The SQL statement selects the ProductName, ProductDesc, and UnitPrice fields from the tblProducts table.

SQL Server Functions

SQL Server comes with many built-in functions such as RTrim, GetDate, and many others. You can also create user-defined functions and call those functions as if they were built-in functions of SQL Server. User-defined functions can return a single value, such as the result of a calculation, or they can return an entire table of results.

You may be wondering how functions differ from stored procedures. User-defined functions have a lot in common with stored procedures because both are just SQL statements stored on the SQL Server. However, a user-defined function, unlike a stored procedure, can be embedded within a basic SQL statement, such as the following:

```
SELECT FormatDescription(ProductDesc) FROM tblProducts
```

In this instance, the function is called FormatDescription and will be called for each record selected in the SQL statement. If this code were contained in a stored procedure, a loop would have to be executed to call the stored procedure for each record.

When you open the designer from Access to add a Function, the Add Table dialog box appears, as shown in Figure 10-25. In this example, the function is based on the vwProductPrice view that you created in the prior example.

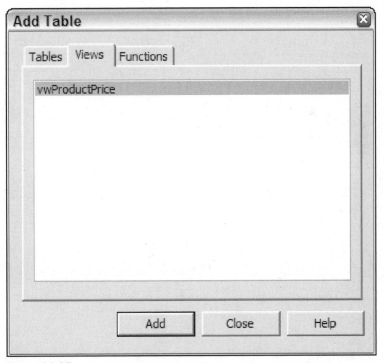

Figure 10-25

A designer similar to the other designers you have seen so far appears, as shown in Figure 10-26. In this example, the function will select the products that have a unit price greater than $500.

When you run the preceding function, all products that are greater than $500 are displayed, as shown in Figure 10-27.

At this point, you do not have to be an expert on determining when to use SQL Server stored procedures, view, or functions. It is a complicated topic that is beyond the scope of this introductory chapter. However, if you want to see more examples of how to use stored procedures, views, and functions in your applications, please consult the comprehensive case study in Chapter 14 that uses an Access Project with a SQL Server database.

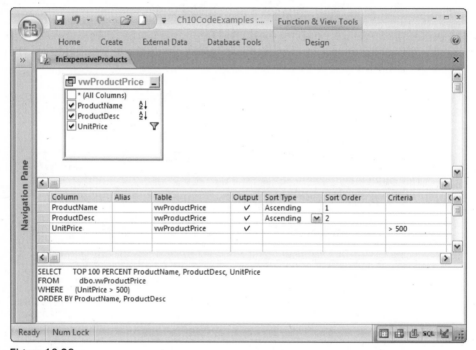

Figure 10-26

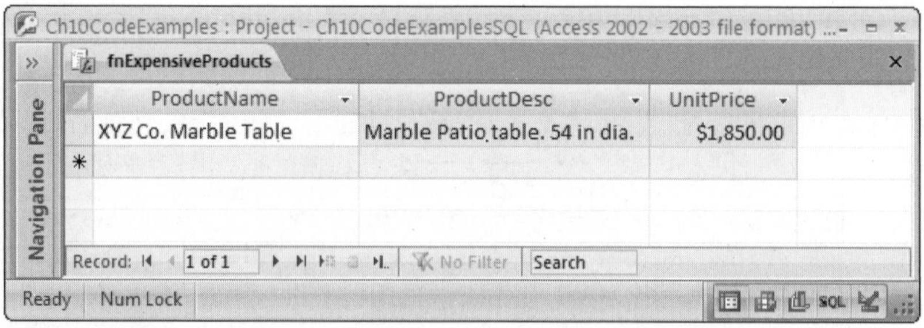

Figure 10-27

Now that you have a basic familiarity of Access Projects, you can walk through the several steps involved in upsizing an existing Access database to an Access Project and SQL Server database.

Migrating an Existing Access Database to an Access Project

Microsoft Access has an Upsizing Wizard to help you migrate existing Access databases to SQL Server. In this section, I cover some tips for making the migration smoother. You will then upsize the Northwind sample database that comes with Microsoft Access so you can see how the process works.

Changes to an Existing Database

Before migrating your existing Access application to an Access Project that uses SQL Server, here are some tips that will make the migration go more smoothly:

❑ Consider removing any spaces in your table names and, of course, if you change the name, also change all the places that reference the table name. If you do not remove them, you will later have to use brackets to refer to SQL Server tables with spaces in their names (for example, [Table Name]).

❑ Make sure that each table has a unique index. If you have established primary keys, that should be sufficient.

❑ Make a backup copy of the ACCDB file in case things go wrong.

❑ Check the dates in your Access tables. Most problems with upsizing occur with date conversions. For example, Access and SQL Server have different date ranges that are acceptable. SQL Server covers only the period from Jan 1, 1753 to Dec 31, 9999. Access allows dates in the range from Jan 1, 100 to Dec 31, 9999.

With these tips in mind, let's walk through using the Upsizing Wizard to see how this works.

Using the Upsizing Wizard

As previously mentioned, you can use the Upsizing Wizard to convert an existing Access database to an Access Project for the client and SQL Server for the database. You'll walk through the numerous steps involved in this process to upsize the sample Northwind database to a SQL Server database.

1. Open the database you want to upsize, which in this example is the Northwind database in the Samples directory of Office. To start the Wizard, click on Database Tools and then click on SQL Server on the Move Data ribbon. A screen similar to that shown in Figure 10-28 will appear.

2. Select the option Create New Database and click the Next button.

3. A screen similar to the one shown in Figure 10-29 appears next. Specify the SQL Server instance that should hold the new database. Also, fill in the security information, such as whether to use a trusted connection or a login and password. Then, provide the name of the new SQL Server database. Click Next.

4. As shown in Figure 10-30, you are then prompted to specify which tables to upsize. Figure 10-30 has selected all tables in the database, and they appear in the Export to SQL Server area of the screen. After selecting the tables to be upsized, click the Next button.

5. A screen similar to Figure 10-31 appears, allowing you to specify which table attributes to upsize. Select the options that you want included and click Next.

6. A screen, like the one shown in Figure 10-32, allows you to specify the name of the new Access Project file that should store the client user interface and business logic. After specifying the ADP file name, click Next.

7. The final screen of the wizard, as shown in Figure 10-33, allows you to specify whether to open the new ADP file or keep the ACCDB file open. After selecting your preference, click the Finish button.

8. The Upsizing Wizard then displays a progress bar and works its way through each object in the database that is being converted.

9. As shown in Figure 10-34, a report is displayed when the Upsizing Wizard completes. The report provides numerous details about exactly which objects were upsized, any errors that were encountered, and so on.

10. Figure 10-35 shows an example of a table that was upsized to SQL Server and illustrates how the data types were changed from Access data types to the equivalent SQL Server data types.

11. Figure 10-36 illustrates the fact that the existing Queries were converted to stored procedures, functions, and views depending on their purposes.

12. Figure 10-37 illustrates errors that occurred in upsizing two different queries. Any errors that prevent Access from upsizing certain elements will need to be corrected by using the correct SQL Server syntax. Even if Access could successfully upsize the query, you should review the query to make sure the modification still serves the intended purpose.

13. After the upsizing is completed, the new Access Project is displayed, as shown in Figure 10-38. If you had instead selected the option to keep the existing ACCDB open, that database would have been displayed instead.

14. If you navigate to the Queries objects in the Database Window, you can see that the previous queries were upsized to various stored procedures, views, and functions. This is illustrated in Figure 10-39.

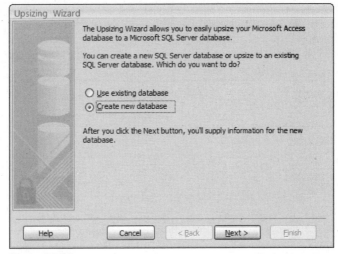

Figure 10-28

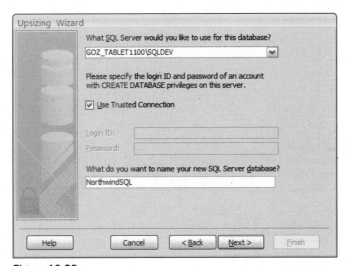

Figure 10-29

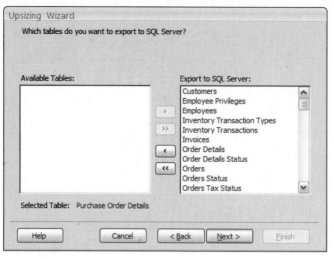

Figure 10-30

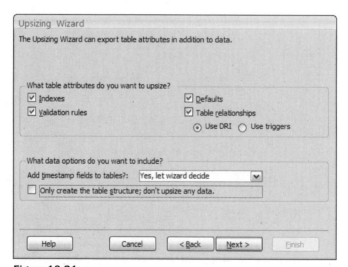

Figure 10-31

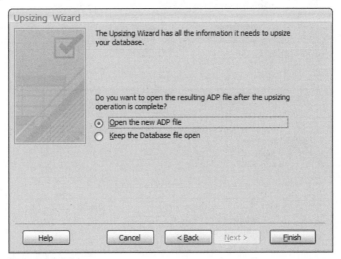

Figure 10-32

Figure 10-33

Upsizing Wizard Report

Database

Microsoft Access Database:	C:\Program Files\Microsoft Office\Office12\SAMPLES\Northwind.accdb
SQL Server Database:	NorthwindSQL

Upsizing Parameters

Table Attributes to Export

☑ Indexes

☑ Validation rules

☑ Defaults

☐ Structure only, no data

Table relationships:

Upsized using DRI

Timestamp fields added:

Some tables

Modifications to Existing Database

☐ Attach newly created SQL Server tables

☐ Save password and user ID with attached tables

Client/Server Modifications

☑ Create a new Access client/server application.

☐ Save password and user ID with application

Figure 10-34

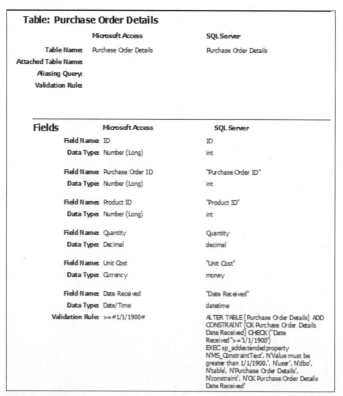

Table: Purchase Order Details

	Microsoft Access	SQL Server
Table Name:	Purchase Order Details	Purchase Order Details
Attached Table Name:		
Aliasing Query:		
Validation Rule:		

Fields

	Microsoft Access	SQL Server
Field Name:	ID	ID
Data Type:	Number (Long)	int
Field Name:	Purchase Order ID	"Purchase Order ID"
Data Type:	Number (Long)	int
Field Name:	Product ID	"Product ID"
Data Type:	Number (Long)	int
Field Name:	Quantity	Quantity
Data Type:	Decimal	decimal
Field Name:	Unit Cost	"Unit Cost"
Data Type:	Currency	money
Field Name:	Date Received	"Date Received"
Data Type:	Date/Time	datetime
Validation Rule:	>=#1/1/1900#	ALTER TABLE [Purchase Order Details] ADD CONSTRAINT [CK Purchase Order Details Date Received] CHECK ("Date Received">='1/1/1900') EXEC sp_addextendedproperty N'MS_ConstraintText', N'Value must be greater than 1/1/1900.', N'user', N'dbo', N'table', N'Purchase Order Details', N'constraint', N'CK Purchase Order Details Date Received'

Figure 10-35

Queries

Query Name   Customers Extended

This query is not upsizeable

Query Name   Employees Extended

This query is not upsizeable

Query Name   Inventory Purchased

Upsized using SQL:

```
CREATE VIEW "Inventory Purchased"
AS
SELECT "Inventory Transactions"."Product ID", sum("Inventory Transactions".Quantity) AS
"Quantity Purchased"
FROM "Inventory Transactions"
WHERE ((("Inventory Transactions"."Transaction Type")=1))
GROUP BY "Inventory Transactions"."Product ID"
```


Query Name   Inventory on Hold

Upsized using SQL:

```
CREATE VIEW "Inventory on Hold"
AS
SELECT "Inventory Transactions"."Product ID", sum("Inventory Transactions".Quantity) AS
"Quantity On Hold"
FROM "Inventory Transactions"
WHERE ((("Inventory Transactions"."Transaction Type")=3))
GROUP BY "Inventory Transactions"."Product ID"
```

Figure 10-36

Query Name   Product Orders

Failed to upsize. Attempted to use SQL:

```
CREATE FUNCTION "Product Orders" ()
RETURNS TABLE
AS RETURN (SELECT TOP 100 PERCENT "Order Details"."Product ID", Orders."Order ID",
Orders."Order Date", Orders."Shipped Date", Orders."Customer ID", "Order Details".Quantity,
"Order Details"."Unit Price", "Order Details".Discount, 'Sale' AS "Transaction", "Customers
Extended".Company AS "Company Name", "Order Details"."Status ID"
FROM ([Customers Extended]() "Customers Extended" INNER JOIN Orders ON ([Customers
Extended]() "Customers Extended".ID = Orders."Customer ID")) INNER JOIN "Order Details" ON
(Orders."Order ID" = "Order Details"."Order ID")
ORDER BY Orders."Order Date")
```

Figure 10-37

After the database has been upsized, you must correct any errors that were encountered and retest the functionality of the database to ensure that the objects were converted correctly. After these issues have been resolved and the application has been tested, you are ready to let your users work with your new SQL Server application from the Access Project.

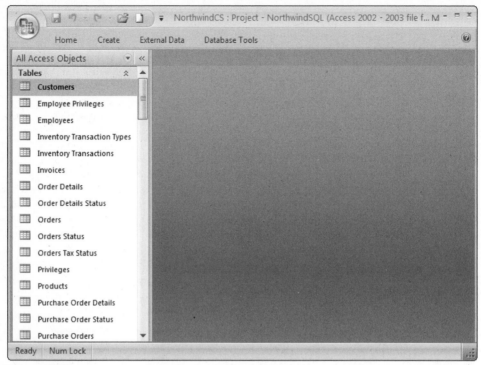

Figure 10-38

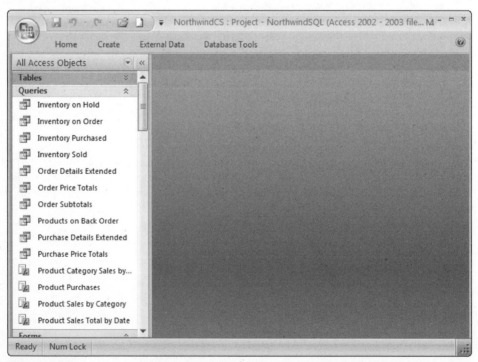

Figure 10-39

Summary

In this chapter, you explored how to use Access Projects to work with SQL Server databases. SQL Server is a very powerful enterprise database tool that should be used for more sophisticated applications. You can start with a free version of SQL Server called SQL Server 2005 Express Edition if you want to write your Access application using SQL Server to begin with. If you do so, you will not have to make extensive changes at a later date when your application has become successful and must be migrated to a more powerful database than Access. Access Projects allow you to create client-server applications with Access as the front end and SQL Server as the database. Access includes an Upsizing Wizard to help you transition an existing Access database to SQL Server. If you want more information on using Access Projects to work with SQL Server databases, consult the comprehensive case study in Chapter 14.

In prior chapters, you have learned how to create code in VBA, such as code that executes when certain events happen. You have also learned how to retrieve and export data from databases in various formats. In this chapter, you expanded your knowledge of working with other data sources by learning about Access Projects and SQL Server. In the next chapter, I will cover some advanced techniques to use in your Access applications.

Exercises

1. What is the difference between a standard Access database (ACCDB file) and an Access Project (ADP file)?

2. What are some advantages of using SQL Server for your applications now instead of waiting to migrate later?

3. What are stored procedures, views, and functions? How do you view them from Access Projects?

Advanced Access Programming

We covered a lot of ground in prior chapters exploring how to use VBA to extend your Access applications. This chapter will discuss some advanced programming techniques, but it is not meant to provide exhaustive coverage. This chapter covers the following techniques:

❏ Declaring and using standard and external DLLs

❏ Using automation to control Excel, Word, and Outlook from your Access applications

❏ Adding ActiveX controls to your forms

❏ Creating custom code libraries

❏ Using add-ins

❏ Implementing transactions in your code

For your convenience, I have included the database file and code generated during this chapter for download from Wrox.com.

Using Dynamic Link Libraries (DLLs)

Dynamic Link Libraries (DLLs) are simply compiled code libraries. You already used a DLL when adding a reference to the ADO library (Chapter 5) so that you could work with the ADO object model and the properties, methods, and events for the objects it contains. In this section, you will look at another example of how to use a standard DLL by just adding a reference in your project. You will also look at how to manually declare an external DLL and use it within your code.

Standard DLLs

You can reference libraries such as DLLs by selecting Tools ➪ References from the Visual Basic Editor and then selecting the particular library that you want to work with. After a reference has been added, you can then manipulate the functionality contained in the library from within your VBA code.

Try It Out **Using the Microsoft Office Object Library to Create a Custom Command Bar**

Let's look at an example of creating custom command bars for your application using the Microsoft Office 12.0 Object Library. The CommandBars property of the Application object allows you to access the CommandBars collection. The CommandBars collection enables you to manage and create toolbars, menu bars, and shortcut menus.

1. Create a new database. Select the Office Button ⇨ New. From the list of available templates, select "Blank Database." Name the database Ch11CodeExamples and click the Create button.

2. Set a reference to Microsoft Office 12.0 Object Library in the References dialog box, if one is not already set. From the Visual Basic Editor, select Tools ⇨ References and scroll down the list. Select Microsoft Office 12.0 Object Library, as shown in Figure 11-1. Click the OK button to add the reference.

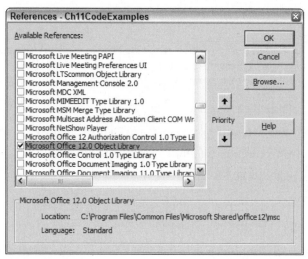

Figure 11-1

3. Add a new module to your database.

4. Add the following procedures to your module:

```
Sub CreateCommandBar()

Dim cbReport As CommandBar
Dim btnButton As CommandBarButton
'delete the command bar and continue if it does not exist
On Error Resume Next
CommandBars("Wrox Report").Delete
On Error GoTo 0
'add the new command bar to the collection
```

```
Set cbReport = CommandBars.Add("Wrox Report", msoBarFloating)

'add Zoom button to the toolbar
Set btnButton = cbReport.Controls.Add(msoControlButton, _
    CommandBars("Print Preview") _
    .Controls("Zoom").Id)

'add 2 pages button to the toolbar
Set btnButton = cbReport.Controls.Add(msoControlButton, _
    CommandBars("Print Preview") _
    .Controls("Two Pages").Id)

'add copy button to the toolbar
Set btnButton = cbReport.Controls.Add(msoControlButton, _
    CommandBars("Database") _
    .Controls("Copy").Id)

'add a custom button to the toolbar
Set btnButton = cbReport.Controls.Add(msoControlButton)
btnButton.Caption = "Test Button"
btnButton.Style = msoButtonCaption

'list the name of the procedure to call when the button is clicked
btnButton.OnAction = "DisplayMessage"
'display the new command bar by setting visible
cbReport.Visible = True

End Sub

Sub DisplayMessage()

MsgBox "The new button was clicked."

End Sub
```

5. From the Immediate Window, execute the `CreateCommandBar` function by typing `CreateCommandBar` and pressing Enter. A new toolbar (as shown in Figure 11-2) is added to the Add-Ins tab on the Custom Toolbars ribbon.

6. Click Test Button on the toolbar. You should see a screen similar to the one shown in Figure 11-3.

Figure 11-2

Figure 11-3

How It Works

After adding a reference to the Microsoft Office 12.0 Object Library, you created two new procedures to make use of the `CommandBar` and `CommandBarButton` objects that are contained in the library. The `CreateCommandBar` procedure creates a new section in the Add-Ins tab on the Custom Toolbars ribbon.

```
Sub CreateCommandBar()

Dim cbReport As CommandBar
Dim btnButton As CommandBarButton

'delete the command bar and continue if it does not exist

On Error Resume Next
CommandBars("Wrox Report").Delete
On Error GoTo 0

'add the new command bar to the collection
Set cbReport = CommandBars.Add("Wrox Report", msoBarFloating)
```

After creating the new command bar, you can add various buttons with predefined functionality to it, including `Zoom`, `2 page`, and `Copy` buttons:

```
'add Zoom button to the toolbar
Set btnButton = cbReport.Controls.Add(msoControlButton, _
    CommandBars("Print Preview") _
    .Controls("Zoom").Id)

'add 2 pages button to the toolbar
Set btnButton = cbReport.Controls.Add(msoControlButton, _
    CommandBars("Print Preview") _
    .Controls("Two Pages").Id)
 'add copy button to the toolbar
Set btnButton = cbReport.Controls.Add(msoControlButton, _
    CommandBars("Database") _
    .Controls("Copy").Id)
```

A custom button called "Test Button" is then added, which calls the DisplayMessage procedure when clicked:

```
'add a custom button to the toolbar
Set btnButton = cbReport.Controls.Add(msoControlButton)
btnButton.Caption = "Test Button"
btnButton.Style = msoButtonCaption

'list the name of the procedure to call when the button is clicked
btnButton.OnAction = "DisplayMessage"
```

The new command bar is displayed by setting the Visible property to True:

```
'display the new command bar by setting visible
cbReport.Visible = True

End Sub
```

The DisplayMessage procedure was also created and gets called when the new Test Button is clicked because it is assigned to the OnAction property of the Test Button:

```
Sub DisplayMessage()

MsgBox "The new button was clicked."

End Sub
```

When you run the DisplayMessage procedure from the Immediate Window, the custom command bar is displayed. When you click the Test button, a message box is displayed to indicate that the new button was clicked. You could, for example, assign this command bar to display when a report opens by setting the Visible property to True in the OnOpen event of the desired report.

This is just one of numerous examples of how you can work with functionality provided by various libraries. You will look at some additional examples of working with other standard libraries later in this chapter in the discussion on automation.

Using External DLLs

In the prior section, you looked at how to add a reference to an existing library and then to use the features provided by the library from VBA code. By adding an explicit reference as you did before, you were able to see the available properties, methods, and events for each object as you typed code in the code window.

At times, however, you need to reference external DLLs from within your code. External DLLs do not provide the help feature that allows you to see what properties, methods, and events are available. You have to know the object and how to work with it. To use an external DLL, you must declare the function in VBA, call the function, and use the result.

Try It Out   **Using an External DLL to Get System Information**

Let's walk through an example of referencing an external DLL to get information about your system.

1.   First, declare the external DLL. To do so, add the following code to the General Declarations section of your module:

```
Private Declare Sub GetSystemInfo Lib "kernel32" (lpSystemInfo As SYSTEM_INFO)
```

2.   Next, add the SYSTEM_INFO type definition to the General Declarations section of the module:

```
Type SYSTEM_INFO
    dwOemID As Long
    dwPageSize As Long
    lpMinimumApplicationAddress As Long
    lpMaximumApplicationAddress As Long
    dwActiveProcessorMask As Long
    dwNumberOfProcessors As Long
    dwProcessorType As Long
    dwAllocationGranularity As Long
    dwReserved As Long
End Type
```

3.   Add the following procedure to the module:

```
Sub DisplaySystemInfo()

Dim strMessage As String
Dim lpSysInfo As SYSTEM_INFO

'call the external function and populate the SYSINFO user defined type
'with the results
GetSystemInfo lpSysInfo

'use the results from the function to build a string
strMessage = "Number of processors: " & lpSysInfo.dwNumberOfProcessors & vbCrLf
strMessage = strMessage & "Processor type: " & lpSysInfo.dwProcessorType

'display the number of processors and processor type to the user
MsgBox strMessage

End Sub
```

4.   From the Immediate Window, execute the DisplaySystemInfo procedure by typing DisplaySystemInfo and pressing Enter.

5.   You should see a message similar to the one shown in Figure 11-4.

Figure 11-4

How It Works

First, you added a declaration for the external library to the General Declarations section of the module. The declaration is case-sensitive and must be typed exactly as shown below.

```
Private Declare Sub GetSystemInfo Lib "kernel32" (lpSystemInfo As SYSTEM_INFO)
```

Next, you added the SYSTEM_INFO type declaration to the General Declarations section of the module. This data type contains the parameters in the exact format expected by the GetSystemInfo external library.

```
Type SYSTEM_INFO
    dwOemID As Long
    dwPageSize As Long
    lpMinimumApplicationAddress As Long
    lpMaximumApplicationAddress As Long
    dwActiveProcessorMask As Long
    dwNumberOfProcessors As Long
    dwProcessorType As Long
    dwAllocationGranularity As Long
    dwReserved As Long
End Type
```

You then added the DisplaySystemInfo procedure to call the external procedure and use the result:

```
Sub DisplaySystemInfo()
```

The procedure first declared a string variable and a variable to hold the result of the external function call:

```
Dim strMessage As String
Dim lpSysInfo As SYSTEM_INFO
```

The external function was then called and passed the local variable to hold the results:

```
'call the external function and populate the SYSINFO user defined type
'with the results
GetSystemInfo lpSysInfo
```

Part of the values returned from the function were added to the string variable:

```
'use the results from the function to build a string
strMessage = "Number of processors: " & lpSysInfo.dwNumberOfProcessors & _
        vbCrLf
strMessage = strMessage & "Processor type: " & lpSysInfo.dwProcessorType
```

The msgbox function then displayed the contents of the string variable to the user:

```
'display the number of processors and processor type to the user
MsgBox strMessage

End Sub
```

Upon executing the `DisplaySystemInfo` procedure from the Immediate Window, you called the external function, which retrieved information about the current system, and displayed the number of processors and the processor type for the current system in a message box on the screen. As you can see, working with external DLLs is a bit more complicated than adding a reference using the Tools ⇨ Add References feature. Working with external DLLs requires you to be very precise in your syntax or the function will not operate.

Automation

Automation refers to the capability to control one program from within another. For example, you can control Microsoft Excel from within your Access applications. In such a case, Access would be the *automation client* and Excel the *automation server*.

In order to use automation, you must first add a reference to the object library for the application that you want to automate. As you learned before, you can add references using Tools ⇨ References from the Visual Basic Editor.

Go ahead and add a reference to Excel, Word, and Outlook, as shown in Figure 11-5. You will be looking at examples of each of these next.

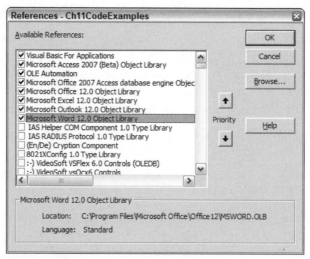

Figure 11-5

Working with Automation Objects

Before you can automate external applications, you need to declare an object variable. The following example shows how you declare an object variable for Excel:

```
Dim objExcel As New Excel.Application
```

The preceding line of code declares a new object and creates a new instance of Excel in a single line of code. If you want to control the point when a new instance of Excel is created, you can separate the declaration and instantiation into two lines of code, as shown next.

```
Dim objExcel As Excel.Application
Set objExcel = New Excel.Application
```

After you have created an instance of the automation object, you can work with the object's properties, methods, and events. You have already worked with properties, methods, and events of other objects in earlier chapters. Working with the properties, methods, and events of automation objects is not any different. For example, you can set the Visible property of the objExcel object to True so that it will be visible, as shown here:

```
objExcel.Visible = True
```

The preceding example implements a technique called *early binding*. Early binding occurs when you declare the type of object explicitly within your code. Several advantages result from using early binding. For example, when all lines of code referencing the object are resolved at compile time, the code executes faster, and you can view the available properties, methods, and events of the object as you type your code. For these reasons, you should use early binding whenever possible.

Although early binding is preferable, you can also use a technique called *late binding*. Late binding enables you to instantiate objects at runtime without referencing them at design time. In other words, your VBA application doesn't know what type of object you want and what you plan to do with the object until it runs the code and works with the object. Below is an example of using late binding with Excel:

```
'declare a new generic object
Dim objExcel as Object

'instantiate the new object as an Excel object
Set objExcel = CreateObject("Excel.Application")

objExcel.Visible = True
```

Notice that the CreateObject method is used to create a new instance of Excel. If you already have an open instance of the Excel object that you need to work with, use the GetObject method, as shown in the following code:

```
Set objExcel = GetObject(, "Excel.Application")
```

Now that you are familiar with the high-level concepts of declaring and instantiating new instances of automation objects, let's walk through some actual examples of controlling Excel, Word, and Outlook from Access.

Controlling Microsoft Excel

You have already seen a few examples of how to declare and instantiate Excel objects. Let's jump right into learning how you can control Excel from your Access application.

Try It Out **Controlling an Excel Spreadsheet from Access**

In this example, you will create a new Excel workbook and populate some of the cells with data.

1. Add the following code to your module:

```
Sub ControlExcel()

Dim objExcel As New Excel.Application
Dim objWorksheet As New Excel.Worksheet

'add a new workbook to the spreadsheet
objExcel.Workbooks.Add

'point the worksheet variable at the active sheet
Set objWorksheet = objExcel.ActiveSheet

'add various values to the cells
With objWorksheet
    .Cells(1, 1).Value = "First Name"
    .Cells(1, 2).Value = "Middle Initial"
    .Cells(1, 3).Value = "Last Name"
    .Cells(2, 1).Value = "John"
    .Cells(2, 2).Value = "A."
    .Cells(2, 3).Value = "Doe"
    .Cells(3, 1).Value = "Jack"
    .Cells(3, 2).Value = "D."
    .Cells(3, 3).Value = "Smith"
End With

'show Excel to the user
objExcel.Visible = True

End Sub
```

2. Execute the `ControlExcel` procedure from the Immediate Window by typing `ControlExcel` and pressing Enter.

3. You should see an Excel screen similar to that shown in Figure 11-6.

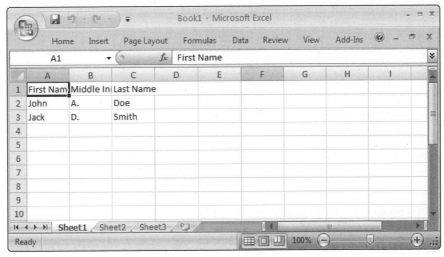

Figure 11-6

How It Works

The `ControlExcel` procedure uses an Excel `Application` object and an Excel `Worksheet` object:

```
Sub ControlExcel()

Dim objExcel As New Excel.Application
Dim objWorksheet As New Excel.Worksheet
```

After you declare the objects, a new workbook is added to the Excel object:

```
'add a new workbook to the spreadsheet
objExcel.Workbooks.Add
```

The new workbook is then pointed to the active sheet:

```
'point the worksheet variable at the active sheet
Set objWorksheet = objExcel.ActiveSheet
```

Using the `Cells` property of the `Worksheet` object, you assign values to various cells:

```
'add various values to the cells
With objWorksheet
    .Cells(1, 1).Value = "First Name"
    .Cells(1, 2).Value = "Middle Initial"
    .Cells(1, 3).Value = "Last Name"
    .Cells(2, 1).Value = "John"
    .Cells(2, 2).Value = "A."
    .Cells(2, 3).Value = "Doe"
    .Cells(3, 1).Value = "Jack"
    .Cells(3, 2).Value = "D."
    .Cells(3, 3).Value = "Smith"
End With
```

The last line of code displays the Excel instance to the user:

```
'show Excel to the user
objExcel.Visible = True

End Sub
```

When you run the procedure from the Immediate Window, you see an instance of Excel with the values populated in the cells as specified in the preceding code.

Controlling Microsoft Word

You can control Word from Access in the same way you can control Excel. The Word object model is, of course, different because you are working with documents instead of spreadsheets. Let's walk through how this works.

Try It Out   Creating Word Letters from Access

In this example, you will create a contacts table and then a Word document that contains a letter to be sent to each of the contacts in the contacts table.

1.   In your `Ch11CodeExamples` database, create a new table, as shown in Figure 11-7.

Field Name	Data Type	Description
ContactId	AutoNumber	Long Integer
FirstName	Text	Size 30
LastName	Text	Size 30
Address	Text	Size 50
City	Text	Size 50
Region	Text	Size 25
PostalCode	Text	Size 25
Email	Text	Size 75

tblContacts

Figure 11-7

2. Next, add some sample data to the table, such as the data shown in Figure 11-8.

Figure 11-8

3. Add the following `ControlWord` procedure to the existing module:

```
Sub ControlWord()

Dim objWord As New Word.Application
Dim rsContacts As New ADODB.Recordset

Dim strLtrContent As String

rsContacts.ActiveConnection = CurrentProject.Connection
rsContacts.Open "tblContacts"

objWord.Documents.Add

'for each record in the tblContacts table, create a letter in Word
Do While Not rsContacts.EOF

  strLtrContent = rsContacts("FirstName") & " " & rsContacts("LastName")
  strLtrContent = strLtrContent & vbCrLf & rsContacts("Address") & vbCrLf
  strLtrContent = strLtrContent & rsContacts("City") & ", " & rsContacts("Region")
  strLtrContent = strLtrContent & " " & rsContacts("PostalCode") & vbCrLf & vbCrLf
  strLtrContent = strLtrContent & "Dear " & rsContacts("FirstName") & " "
  strLtrContent = strLtrContent & rsContacts("LastName") & ":" & vbCrLf & vbCrLf
  strLtrContent = strLtrContent & "Please note we have moved to a new " & _
                                  "location. "
  strLtrContent = strLtrContent & "Our new address is 4 Somewhere, Avon, " & _
                                  "IN 46060."
  strLtrContent = strLtrContent & vbCrLf & vbCrLf & "Sincerely," & vbCrLf &
strLtrContent = strLtrContent & vbCrLf & "Your Favorite Store"

  'insert the content at the end of the document (which is the beginning
  'if it is the first one)
  objWord.Selection.EndOf
  objWord.Selection.Text = strLtrContent

  'insert a page break
  objWord.Selection.EndOf
  objWord.Selection.InsertBreak

  'get the next contact record
```

```
        rsContacts.MoveNext

Loop

'show word in Print Preview mode
objWord.Visible = True
objWord.PrintPreview = True

End Sub
```

4. Run the `ControlWord` procedure from the Immediate Window by typing `ControlWord` and pressing Enter. A screen similar to the one shown in Figure 11-9 should be displayed.

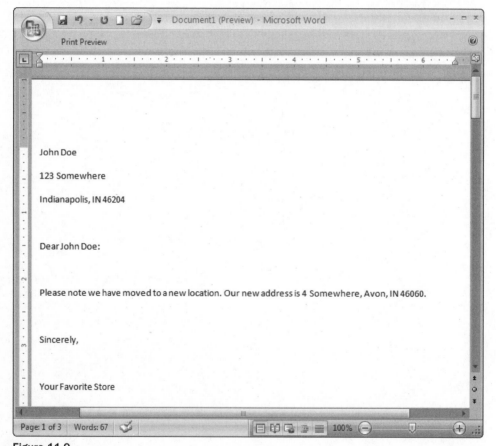

Figure 11-9

How It Works

First, you created a table called `tblContacts` and populated the table with some records. Next, you initiated a new procedure that created a new Word document and then you populated the document with specified text. The procedure began by declaring a new Word `Application` object and an ADO recordset.

```
Sub ControlWord()

Dim objWord As New Word.Application
Dim rsContacts As New ADODB.Recordset

Dim strLtrContent As String
```

The ADO recordset was opened and populated with the `tblContacts` table:

```
rsContacts.ActiveConnection = CurrentProject.Connection
rsContacts.Open "tblContacts"
```

A new document was then added to the `Word` object:

```
objWord.Documents.Add
```

For each contact record in the ADO recordset, a string containing the contents of the letter was populated. Each string contained the contents of the letter to the particular contact.

```
'for each record in the tblContacts table, create a letter in Word
Do While Not rsContacts.EOF

    strLtrContent = rsContacts("FirstName") & " " & rsContacts("LastName")
    strLtrContent = strLtrContent & vbCrLf & rsContacts("Address") & vbCrLf
    strLtrContent = strLtrContent & rsContacts("City") & ", " & rsContacts("Region")
    strLtrContent = strLtrContent & " " & rsContacts("PostalCode") & vbCrLf & vbCrLf
    strLtrContent = strLtrContent & "Dear " & rsContacts("FirstName") & " "
    strLtrContent = strLtrContent & rsContacts("LastName") & ":" & vbCrLf & vbCrLf
    strLtrContent = strLtrContent & "Please note we have moved to a new " & _
                                    "location. "
    strLtrContent = strLtrContent & "Our new address is 4 Somewhere, Avon, " & _
                                    "IN 46060."
    strLtrContent = strLtrContent & vbCrLf & vbCrLf & "Sincerely," & vbCrLf &
    strLtrContent = strLtrContent & vbCrLf & "Your Favorite Store"
""",,"","Content & "Your Favorite Store"
```

The contents were then placed at the end of the Word document:

```
'insert the content at the end of the document (which is the beginning
'if it is the first one)
objWord.Selection.EndOf
objWord.Selection.Text = strLtrContent
```

A page break was then inserted into the Word document so the next letter appeared on a separate page:

```
'insert a page break
objWord.Selection.EndOf
objWord.Selection.InsertBreak
```

The next record in the recordset was retrieved:

```
'get the next contact record
rsContacts.MoveNext
```

```
Loop
```

After all the records in the recordset were processed, the following code displayed Word in Print Preview mode:

```
'show word in Print Preview mode
objWord.Visible = True
objWord.PrintPreview = True
```

```
End Sub
```

When you run the procedure from the Immediate Window, the Print Preview Mode of the newly created Word document is displayed, and a letter addressed to each contact from the tblContacts table is displayed.

Controlling Microsoft Outlook

You can control Microsoft Outlook in various ways in order to manipulate contacts, e-mails, or calendar appointments. In this section, you will look at an example of sending an e-mail through Outlook from Access.

Try It Out   Sending an Outlook E-mail from Access

Using the tblContacts table that was created in the prior example, you will now walk through how to send an Outlook e-mail from Access.

1.   Revise the data in the tblContacts table so that only one record exists and the record points to your e-mail address. This ensures that you do not send e-mails to people by mistake based on the dummy data that you typed in the table.

2. Add the following `ControlOutlook` procedure to your module.

```
Sub ControlOutlook()

Dim objOutlook As New Outlook.Application
Dim objEmail As Outlook.MailItem

Dim strLtrContent As String
Dim rsContacts As New ADODB.Recordset

rsContacts.ActiveConnection = CurrentProject.Connection
rsContacts.Open "tblContacts"

'for each record in the tblContacts table, send an email
Do While Not rsContacts.EOF

  strLtrContent = "Dear " & rsContacts("FirstName") & " "
  strLtrContent = strLtrContent & rsContacts("LastName") & ":" & vbCrLf & vbCrLf
  strLtrContent = strLtrContent & "Please note we have moved to a new
                            location. "
  strLtrContent = strLtrContent & "Our new address is 4 Somewhere, Avon,
                            IN 46060."
  strLtrContent = strLtrContent & vbCrLf & vbCrLf & "Sincerely," & vbCrLf   &
vbCrLf
  strLtrContent = strLtrContent & "Your Favorite Store"

  'create an email regarding the new business location
  Set objEmail = objOutlook.CreateItem(olMailItem)
  objEmail.Recipients.Add rsContacts("Email")
  objEmail.Subject = "Our address has changed."
  objEmail.Body = strLtrContent

  'send the message
  objEmail.Send

  'move to the next contacts record
  rsContacts.MoveNext
Loop

End Sub
```

3. Run the procedure from the Immediate Window by typing `ControlOutlook` and pressing Enter. You should receive an e-mail similar to the one shown in Figure 11-10 in your Inbox at the account you specified in the `tblContacts` e-mail field.

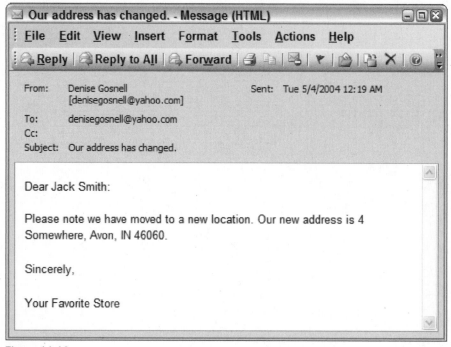

Figure 11-10

How It Works

First, you modified the values in the `tblContacts` table so that only you received an e-mail from running this test procedure. Then, you added the `ControlOutlook` procedure to your module:

```
Sub ControlOutlook()
```

The procedure used an Outlook `Application` object and an Outlook `MailItem` object to create and manipulate e-mail messages:

```
Dim objOutlook As New Outlook.Application
Dim objEmail As Outlook.MailItem
```

Next, a new ADO recordset was created based on the values in the `tblContacts` table:

```
Dim strLtrContent As String
Dim rsContacts As New ADODB.Recordset

rsContacts.ActiveConnection = CurrentProject.Connection
rsContacts.Open "tblContacts"
```

For each record in the recordset, a string message was generated using the e-mail field and some text that indicated the business had changed addresses:

```
'for each record in the tblContacts table, send an email
Do While Not rsContacts.EOF

    strLtrContent = "Dear " & rsContacts("FirstName") & " "
    strLtrContent = strLtrContent & rsContacts("LastName") & ":" & vbCrLf    & vbCrLf
    strLtrContent = strLtrContent & "Please note we have moved to a new " & _
                                    "location. "
    strLtrContent = strLtrContent & "Our new address is 4 Somewhere, Avon, " & _
                                    "IN 46060."
    strLtrContent = strLtrContent & vbCrLf & vbCrLf & "Sincerely," & vbCrLf &
    strLtrContent = strLtrContent & vbCrLf & "Your Favorite Store"
""""""Content & "Your Favorite Store"
```

An e-mail was generated that was addressed to the e-mail address in the current record in the recordset. The subject of the e-mail was specified and the body assigned to the string message created in the preceding code:

```
'create an email regarding the new business location
Set objEmail = objOutlook.CreateItem(olMailItem)
objEmail.Recipients.Add rsContacts("Email")
objEmail.Subject = "Our address has changed."
objEmail.Body = strLtrContent
```

The Send method of the MailItem object sent the e-mail to the recipient:

```
'send the message
objEmail.Send
```

The process repeated for each record in the recordset, which in this case should have been only one record:

```
'move to the next contacts record
rsContacts.MoveNext
Loop

End Sub
```

When you ran the procedure from the Immediate Window, an e-mail message was sent to the e-mail address you specified in the Email field in the tblContacts table. If your address was specified, you should have received a new e-mail message in your inbox containing the text shown in Figure 11-10, which indicated the business had a new address.

ActiveX Controls

ActiveX controls are additional controls that you can use in your Access forms. You have already worked with built-in controls such as text boxes and command buttons. What if you need a control that is not listed in the standard ToolBox? Numerous additional controls are available, including those already installed on your computer, from Microsoft and other vendors. You can take advantage of them by adding a reference to the control and using the control in your application.

For example, to use a Calendar control, create a new form and, with the form still open, select the Design tab and then click on the ActiveX Controls button on the Controls ribbon. A screen similar to the one shown in Figure 11-11 is displayed. To add the Calendar Control or any other desired control, simply select it in the list of controls and click OK.

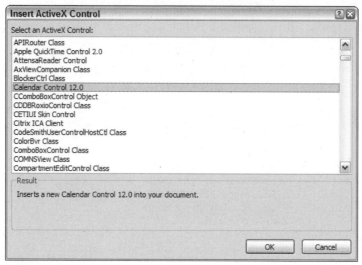

Figure 11-11

When you click OK, the Calendar Control is automatically placed on the new form, as shown in Figure 11-12.

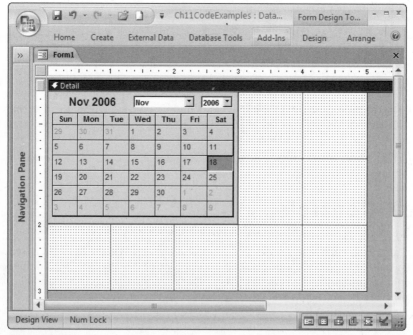

Figure 11-12

The Calendar Control has properties and events just like any other control, as you can see from the Properties Window shown in Figure 11-13.

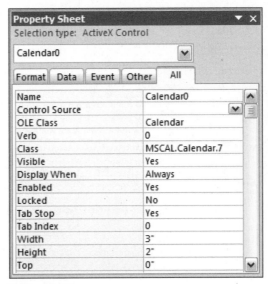

Figure 11-13

Suppose that you want to use the value of the selected date in the calendar, inserting the value into a field in order to spare the user from having to type out the date. Assume in this case that your form contains a text box control.

The following code example illustrates how you would display the selected date in the calendar control in the text box control when the calendar control loses the focus (such as when you click in the text box):

```
Private Sub Calendar0_LostFocus()

'set the text box value to the selected calendar value
txtSelectedDate = Calendar0.Value

End Sub
```

When you run the form and select a date in the calendar control, the value in the text box is updated. This is illustrated in Figure 11-14.

You can apply these concepts to any other ActiveX control that you want to work with. You simply add a reference to the control and then drag and drop the control onto the form if Access does not do so for you automatically. You can then work with the control just as you do with any other standard control.

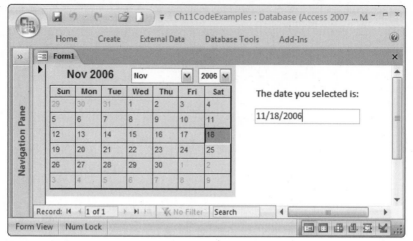

Figure 11-14

Libraries

So far, all the code you have written works only from within the database where you created it. There may be times when you want to reuse code across multiple Access projects, such as when performing a common task that multiple databases might need to perform. You can create libraries based on a specific Access databases that can then be referenced from and used by other Access databases. However, in order to be a good candidate for a library, the database should contain only generic procedures and functions, and not specific references to forms or other objects that may not be present in the other applications or databases from which the library might be used.

Try It Out   Creating and Using a Code Library

In this example, you will create a new Access database containing a sample error-handling procedure that you will make available to other Access databases. This error-handling procedure was described in Chapter 2. You will add the new database as a Library and then use the Library from another database.

1. Create another new database, by selecting the Office Button ⇨ New. From the list of available templates, select "Blank Database." Name the new database ErrorHandlerLibrary and click the Create button.

2. Insert a new module into the ErrorHandlerLibrary database. Name the module modError.

3. Add the following procedure to the new `modError` module:

```
Public Sub GeneralErrorHandler(lngErrNumber As Long, strErrDesc As String,
strModuleSource As String, strProcedureSource As String)

Dim strMessage As String

'build the error message string from the parameters passed in
strMessage = "An error has occurred in the application."
strMessage = strMessage & vbCrLf & "Error Number: " & lngErrNumber
strMessage = strMessage & vbCrLf & "Error Description: " & strErrDesc
strMessage = strMessage & vbCrLf & "Module Source: " & strModuleSource
strMessage = strMessage & vbCrLf & "Procedure Source: " & strProcedureSource

'display the message to the user
MsgBox strMessage, vbCritical

End Sub
```

4. Save the procedure by selecting the Save button on the toolbar.

5. Select Debug ⇨ Compile `ErrorHandlerLibrary` to make sure there are no compiler errors.

6. Close the `ErrorHandlerLibrary` database.

7. Reopen the `Ch11CodeExamples` database. From the Visual Basic Editor, select Tools ⇨ References and click the Browse button. Change the Files of Type filter to Microsoft Office Access Databases (*.mdb). Navigate to the location of the `ErrorHandlerLibrary` database, as shown in Figure 11-15. Click the Open button.

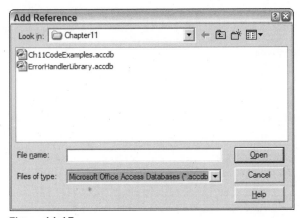

Figure 11-15

8. You should now see the new `ErrorHandlerLibrary` in the list of available references, as shown in Figure 11-16. Click the OK button to add a reference to this library to the `Ch11CodeExamples` database.

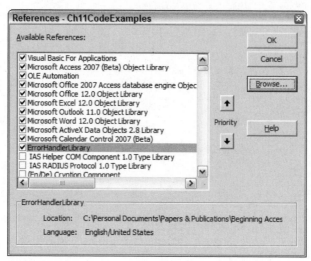

Figure 11-16

9. Add the following procedure to the existing module in the `Ch11CodeExamples` database and replace the word module1 on the next to last code line below with whatever your module is named.

```
Sub TestLibrary()

On Error GoTo HandleError

    'declare variable to store result
    Dim intResult As Integer

    Dim intValue1 As Integer
    Dim intValue2 As Integer

    intValue1 = 5
    intValue2 = 0

    'calculate result by dividing first value by second value
    intResult = intValue1 / intValue2

Exit Sub

HandleError:
    GeneralErrorHandler Err.Number, Err.Description, "module1", "TestLibrary"
    Exit Sub
End Sub
```

10. Execute the `TestLibrary` procedure from the Immediate Window by typing `TestLibrary` and pressing Enter.

11. You should see a screen similar to that shown in Figure 11-17 displaying an error message.

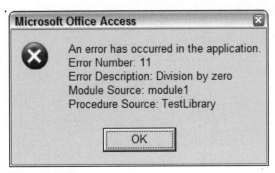

Figure 11-17

How It Works

First, you created a new Library by placing a `GeneralErrorHandler` error-handling procedure into a new database called `ErrorHandlerLibrary`. The procedure accepted some parameters regarding the error and then used the parameters to display a meaningful message to the user.

```
Public Sub GeneralErrorHandler(lngErrNumber As Long, strErrDesc As String, _
strModuleSource As String, strProcedureSource As String)
Dim strMessage As String


'build the error message string from the parameters passed in
strMessage = "An error has occurred in the application."
strMessage = strMessage & vbCrLf & "Error Number: " & lngErrNumber
strMessage = strMessage & vbCrLf & "Error Description: " & strErrDesc
strMessage = strMessage & vbCrLf & "Module Source: " & strModuleSource
strMessage = strMessage & vbCrLf & "Procedure Source: " & strProcedureSource

'display the message to the user
MsgBox strMessage, vbCritical

End Sub
```

After creating and saving the new procedure, you closed the `ErrorHandlerLibrary` database. You then returned to the `Ch11CodeExamples` database and added a reference to the `ErrorHandlerLibrary` database. After adding a reference to the library, you then added the `TestLibrary` procedure to make use of the `GeneralErrorHandler` procedure contained in the library. The `TestLibrary` procedure simply caused a divide-by-zero error so the error-handling code executed.

```
Sub TestLibrary()

On Error GoTo HandleError

    'declare variable to store result
    Dim intResult As Integer

    Dim intValue1 As Integer
    Dim intValue2 As Integer

    intValue1 = 5
    intValue2 = 0

    'calculate result by dividing first value by second value
    intResult = intValue1 / intValue2

Exit Sub
```

The error handler code that follows called the `GeneralErrorHandler` procedure that is contained in the separate `ErrorHandlerLibrary` Access database that you added as a Library.

```
HandleError:
    GeneralErrorHandler Err.Number, Err.Description, "module1", "TestLibrary"
    Exit Sub
End Sub
```

That's all there is to creating a new code library and using the library from other Access databases! You could extend the above example by adding additional error-handling procedures to the library. For example, you may want to create a logging procedure that logs all or certain errors to the database. You may want to create a procedure that e-mails the administrator when certain types of errors occur. These procedures are beyond the scope of this chapter, but I wanted to give you some additional ideas on how to expand the `ErrorHandlerLibrary` for use in your other projects.

Add-Ins

Add-ins are tools that provide additional functionality but are not part of the standard Microsoft Access product. Add-ins are provided with Access, obtained from third parties, or are custom designed. Several add-ins come with Access, such as the Performance Analyzer, Linked Table Manager, control wizards, and various others.

Three examples of some types of add-ins are menu add-ins, wizards, and builders. *Menu add-ins* can be accessed by selecting the Add-ins button on the Database Tools ribbon and generally operate on Access itself or multiple objects. You can use the existing menu add-ins, such as the Database Splitter, or create your own custom add-ins.

Wizard add-ins consist of a series of modal dialog boxes that walk you step by step through a particular process. You have, no doubt, used wizards in Access before to perform various tasks. In Chapter 10, you used the Upsizing Wizard to upsize the Northwind database to SQL Server. You can also create your own custom wizards.

Builder add-ins can help users construct a data element such as a SQL expression. Again, you can create your own custom builder add-ins or use the existing ones.

After you create one of these types of add-ins, you then register the add-in so that your application can use it. One way to register an add-in is using the Add-in Manager in Access. Another way is to have the setup program register the add-in automatically. Yet another way to register an add-in is directly, using the Windows Registry.

Transactions

This section details what a transaction is and how to implement a transaction from VBA code.

A *transaction* implements a series of changes in a single batch. The entire batch of changes either succeeds or fails as a group. Here is a simple example. Suppose that you want to make a series of updates to the database. You are updating a person's records because of a name and address change due to marriage. You may need to update two or more tables with the new information. If one or more of the updates fails, you want the entire set of updates to fail as a group. Otherwise, you might have an incomplete set of data in the database.

The ADO `Connection` object allows you to implement transactions. The `BeginTrans` method of the `Connection` object begins the transaction, whereas the `CommitTrans` method commits the transaction to make the changes final. If the transaction fails, the `RollbackTrans` method of the `Connection` object rolls back all the changes to the underlying data that were made as part of the transaction.

Here is an example of some code you could use to implement a transaction:

```
Sub TestTransaction()

Dim cnConnection As New ADODB.Connection
Dim cmdCommand As New ADODB.Command

'set the connection and command objects to the current connection
Set cnConnection = CurrentProject.Connection
cmdCommand.ActiveConnection = cnConnection

On Error GoTo HandleError

'begin the transaction
cnConnection.BeginTrans

'specify the first SQL Statement to execute that should not cause an error
cmdCommand.CommandText = _
    "UPDATE tblContacts SET FirstName = 'Test' WHERE ContactId = 1"

'execute the first SQL Statement which should not cause an error
cmdCommand.Execute

'specify the second SQL Statement to execute that will cause an error
cmdCommand.CommandText = _
    "UPDATE tblContacts SET ContactId = 'A' WHERE ContactId = 1"

'execute the second SQL Statement which should cause an error
```

```
cmdCommand.Execute

'commit the transaction if both updates were successful
cnConnection.CommitTrans

Exit Sub

HandleError:

    'rollback the transaction so all updates fail
    cnConnection.RollbackTrans

    MsgBox "An error occurred: " & Err.Description

End Sub
```

The preceding procedure uses the ADO `Command` and `Connection` object to execute a series of SQL statements against the database. The `BeginTrans` method indicates the beginning of the transaction. The `CommitTrans` method indicates that the transaction was processed without errors, and thus all the changes should be committed in the underlying data source. The `RollbackTrans` method is in the error handler and will roll back all changes in the event of an error, so all the updates fail together. In the previous example, the first SQL statement executed successfully, whereas the second one caused an error. The result is that the first successful change is rolled back because the second one failed.

Summary

This chapter introduced several advanced topics, including declaring and using standard and external DLLs, using automation to control other applications, and adding ActiveX controls to forms. I also covered how to create custom code libraries, how to use add-ins, and how to implement transactions in your code. Each one of these topics could warrant an entire chapter. For more information on these topics, please consult *Access 2007 VBA Programmer's Reference* (Wiley, 2007). In this chapter, I just wanted to provide you with some ideas of the advanced features available to your Access applications without giving you a detailed tutorial on how to actually implement each of them.

At this point you're ready to move on to Chapter 12, which covers various steps you should take to finish up your Access application, including improving performance and multiuser considerations, adding security to the application, and distributing the application. I will then finish the book with two comprehensive case studies that will bring all the concepts discussed throughout the book together into two real-world applications.

Exercises

1. What is the difference between a standard library and an external library?

2. What is automation, and what are some examples of ways to use automation?

3. How do you create a code library, and what are some advantages of doing so?

4. What is a transaction, and how do you implement one?

Finishing the Application

After working so hard to develop an advanced Access application using VBA, it is important to make sure that the application is capable of performing well and handling the number of users you expect. You also want to make sure that the end users are not able to modify the database source code and design without the proper permission. After you have fine-tuned, secured, and tested the application, you are ready to implement the application by distributing it to end users. However, after you distribute the application to end users, your job is still not finished. Access applications need to be backed up and compacted periodically to ensure that they remain in good working order and that they can be recovered from a backup if corruption or deletion occurs.

This chapter covers:

- ❑   Writing applications to handle multiple users
- ❑   Improving actual and perceived performance of the application
- ❑   Using the Performance Analyzer to help improve performance
- ❑   Adding security to prevent unauthorized access or modification
- ❑   Distributing applications to end users
- ❑   Backing up, compacting, and repairing applications

Multiuser Considerations

Various coding approaches can affect how well your application will handle multiple users. For example, the type of record lock that is used on records retrieved from the database will affect what happens when multiple users try to access the same record. When the application does not handle the scenario correctly, update conflicts can occur because one user overwrites the changes made by another user. If your application uses the proper type of record lock and handles update conflicts, it will be more capable of supporting multiple users. Another way to help your application better handle multiple users is to separate the data tables from the other objects by using two separate Access database files. Both of these techniques are discussed in the sections that follow.

Record Locking and Update Conflicts

Prior to reading this book, you likely worked with bound forms in your Access applications. Bound forms are connected directly to a table and keep an open connection to the database so all changes are made at that moment. Then, in Chapter 5, you learned how to populate an ADO recordset with data from a database and how to display records from the recordset on both bound and unbound forms.

Let's now look at how record locking is handled on bound and unbound forms and the ways you can modify record-locking settings to better handle multiple users.

Record Locking on Bound Forms

The type of record locking that is used for bound forms is determined by the Options settings. To modify the record locking options for bound forms, select the Office button, and at the button on the pop-up menu click on Access Options, and the select Advanced on the left menu. A dialog box like the one shown in Figure 12-1 is displayed. You may have to scroll down to see the options shown in Figure 12-1.

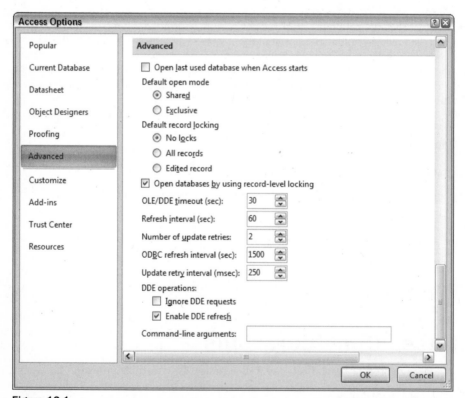

Figure 12-1

The three options for default record locking are No Locks, All Records, and Edited Record. If the No Locks option is selected, no records will be locked and all users will be able to make edits. This can result in one user stepping on the toes of another user by overwriting his changes without realizing it. If the All Records option is selected, all records in the underlying table of the form you're editing will be locked. This option is generally not good for multiuser applications except for the specific situations where you want to keep everyone else out while one user has the table open. A third option is to select the Edited Record option. This option locks only the specific record that the user is editing and is the preferred setting for most multiuser instances. However, it is not the default setting in Access. If the Open Databases Using Record-Level Locking option is enabled, record locking will be the default for the current database. If the option is unchecked, then page-level locking will be the default for the current database.

Your code will always override Access's default settings.

Record Locking on Unbound Forms

With unbound forms, the type of locking used depends on locking the source where the data comes from. For example, if your form is based on an ADO recordset, the lock type of the recordset is what determines locking. As you may recall from Chapter 5, the LockType property of the Recordset object can be one of four settings, shown in the following table.

Value	Explanation
adLockReadOnly	The recordset is read-only, and no changes are allowed.
adLockPessimistic	The record in the recordset will be locked as soon as editing begins.
adLockOptimistic	The record in the recordset will be locked when the Update method is issued.
adLockBatchOptimistic	The records will not be locked until a batch update of all records is performed.

An example of the syntax of this property is shown here:

```
rsRecordset.LockType = adLockReadOnly
```

Read-only locks should be used whenever the users do not need to update the data because they are faster and do not lock records unnecessarily. For multiuser applications, pessimistic and optimistic options are the best when users must update the data. With pessimistic locking, the record in the recordset is locked as soon as editing begins. This prevents any other user from changing that record until the first user has finished editing it.

With optimistic locking, the record is not locked until the very moment that the update command is processed. This option allows all users to interact with the same record even if someone else has it open. However, optimistic locking also presents the potential problem of having update conflicts. By default, you should use pessimistic locking when editing records in code, unless otherwise necessary.

Update Conflicts

An update conflict can occur when a first user is updating a record while a second user still has the old data on the screen. When the second user saves the changes to the database, some of the values being updated are old values that overwrite the changes made by the first user.

If you want to use optimistic locking, you should write code to handle update conflicts. You do so to avoid the possibility of one user overwriting another user's changes. One way to handle update conflicts in VBA code is to add a timestamp or version number value to each table so that you can tell the last time a record was updated. If you use this approach, you must keep track of the original value of the version number or timestamp when the record is first open, and then before updating the database you must check to see if the version number or timestamp has changed. Another way to handle update conflicts is to check for changes on a field-by-field basis and then notify the user of exactly which fields changed so that he can decide whether to overwrite the record.

The topic of update conflicts could take an entire chapter, but you should at least be aware of what it means and some ways to handle it. You can obtain more information about handling update conflicts by searching the articles on msdn.microsoft.com. Let's turn now to another consideration for improving multiuser applications.

Multiuser Architecture Considerations

One way to improve the capability of multiple users to work with an Access application is to separate the data tables from the user-interface aspects. If you put a single Access database that contains the entire application on a file server and allow multiple users to access it simultaneously, you are asking for trouble. A better solution is to separate the user interface from the data tables so that each user has his own copy of the user interface. The data tables can be stored in a separate database file on a server and accessed from each copy of the user interface. This approach is illustrated in Figure 12-2.

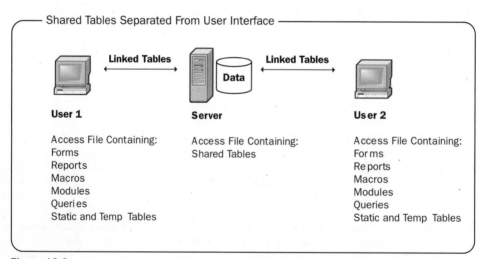

Figure 12-2

Notice that there is one central database for the data tables, and all users have a copy of the user-interface database with objects/code on their computers. The user-interface database is then linked to the database containing the tables.

This approach also improves the performance of the application as the number of users grows, as I discuss in the performance section later in this chapter.

Ideally, you should design your database using this approach from the very beginning. Simply create the database containing the tables in one database, create the database containing the user-interface objects in another database, and then link to the database containing the tables. To link to the database containing the tables, select the External Data ribbon ⇨ Access option from the Import ribbon, specify the database containing the tables to link, and select the Link The Data Source option. Follow the prompts to complete the linking. See Chapter 7 for more information on how to link to another database using VBA code.

Another option is to build the application in one database first and then perform the separation manually or by using the Database Splitter. To do so manually, you simply export the data tables to another database, delete the tables from your original database so that only the linked tables remain, and add a link to that external database. Now let's look at how to use the Database Splitter Wizard.

Try It Out   **Using the Database Splitter Wizard to Separate Database Tables from the User Interface**

Using the Database Splitter, you can easily separate an existing Access database into two database files: one containing the tables and the other for the user interface. Let's walk through an example of how to do this.

1. Open the existing database you want to split. Open the `Northwind.accdb` sample database if you have it on your computer. If not, open one of the databases created in the prior chapters. The steps are the same in either case.

It is recommended that you make a backup copy of the database before proceeding.

2. Select Database Tools, and the Access Database from the Move Data ribbon, as shown in Figure 12-3.

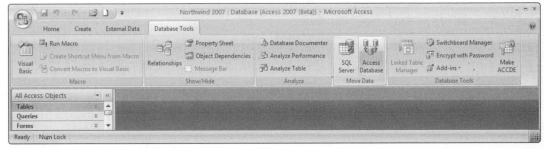

Figure 12-3

3. A screen like the one shown in Figure 12-4 is displayed. Select the Split Database button.

4. The Create Back-End Database dialog box is displayed, as shown in Figure 12-5. Specify the name and location of the database where you want the data tables to be stored. If you are splitting the Northwind database, specify a file name of `Northwind_be.accdb`. Then, click the Split button.

5. After the data is split into the separate database, you receive a message confirming the database was successfully split. Click OK on the dialog box.

6. You are then returned to the original database, which in this case is `Northwind.accdb`. As shown in Figure 12-6, you now see that the tables are linked to the newly created `Northwind_be.accdb`.

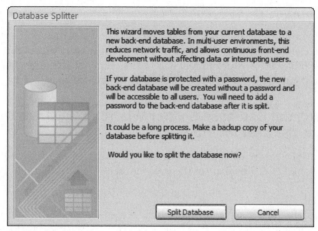

Figure 12-4

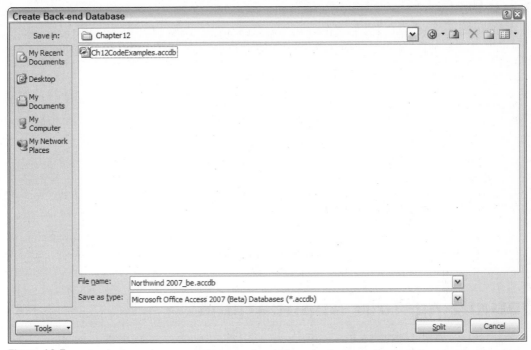

Figure 12-5

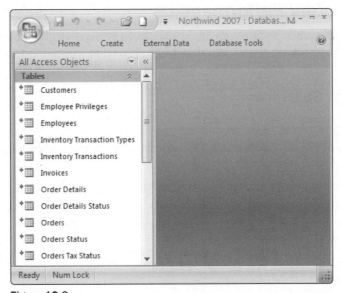

Figure 12-6

How It Works

The Database Splitter Wizard allowed you to convert a single Access database into two separate databases: one with the user interface and the other with the data tables. After you ran the Database Splitter, the data tables were moved to a new database and a link was added to the original database to point to the tables in the new database.

After the split is completed, you can copy the new database with the tables to a file server or other location where multiple client computers can access it. You can then copy the user-interface database to each user workstation.

> *Make sure that the links that are created will work from each computer where you plan to load the user-interface database. For example, if the tables are linked as the C: drive, that same location may be a different drive letter on a different client computer. If that is the case, you need to modify the links from the second computer so that it finds the data.*

Now that you have a few ideas on how to improve the multiuser capabilities of your application, let's turn to the various ways you can optimize your application.

Optimizing Your Applications

As part of the testing process, you should fine-tune the application to make it run faster and better. You can apply various techniques to improve the real speed, as well as the speed as perceived by users.

Improving Actual Performance

The speed at which your application actually performs can be improved by applying some general design guidelines, coding techniques, and data access techniques. You will now look at each of these in turn.

General Design Guidelines

Here are several general guidelines to help improve the actual performance of your applications:

- ❑ Minimize the code and objects in a form. Move the code to a standard module. The more complicated a form is, the longer it takes to load.

- ❑ Minimize the use of subforms because two forms are in memory.

- ❑ Write reusable modules that so you are not rewriting the same code in slightly different ways multiple times. This reduces the amount of code in your application and helps improve speed. For example, instead of having one procedure that enables all controls in one form, another that disables all controls in another form, and two others that disable controls in each of those same forms, write a generic module that enables or disables all controls on the specified form based on whether the enable or disable flag is passed as a variable.

- ❑ Eliminate code that is not used.

- ❑ Make sure that your application is compiled. Also, consider compiling your application into an ACCDE file as described later in this chapter.

❑ If you have all the user-interface objects in one database and the data tables in another (Access or other) database, open the database with the user interface exclusively for faster performance. On the File ➪ Open dialog box, you can specify the Open Exclusive setting to open the database exclusively, as shown in Figure 12-7.

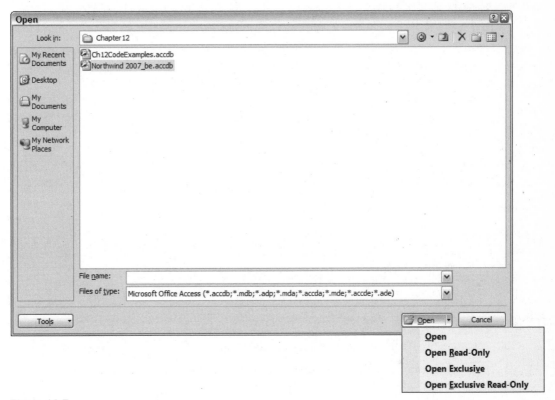

Figure 12-7

Let's now look at some ways you can improve performance by writing better VBA code.

Optimizing VBA Code

You have various ways to accomplish the same task using VBA code, some of which are faster than others. Here are some examples:

❑ Use With...End With when dealing with multiple settings for the same object. Otherwise, the process may be slow because the object has to be located each time. It is generally better to use:

```
With txtName
    .Text = "Hello"
    .Visible = True
    .Enabled = True
End With
```

than the following:

```
txtName.Text = "Hello"
txtName.Visible = True
txtName.Enabled = True
```

❏ Use the correct data type and make it only as large as you really need. For example, if you need an integer, do not use a double. Minimize the use of variants because they are the slowest. They must take time to determine a data type because one was not explicitly designated.

❏ When you are working with automation, as I described in Chapter 11, use early binding so references are resolved at compile time instead of runtime. For example, early binding to Excel like this:

```
Dim objExcel As Excel.Application
Set objExcel = New Excel.Application
```

is better than late binding to Excel like this:

```
'declare a new generic object
Dim objExcel as Object

'instantiate the new object as an Excel object
Set objExcel = CreateObject("Excel.Application")
```

❏ If...Then...Else is faster than IIF() statements.

❏ Instead of testing a Boolean variable for True, use the value explicitly. For example, use:

```
If blnValue Then
```

instead of:

```
If blnValue = True Then
```

❏ Use SQL queries to do batch inserts, updates, and deletes instead of looping through recordsets.

Improving Data Access

The performance of Access applications can be degraded because of improper data access. To make your applications run faster, keep the following guidelines in mind:

❏ Minimize the number of database connections open. For example, if you use a bound form, it maintains a constant connection to the database. Consider switching to an unbound form that connects to the database to retrieve the data, disconnects, and reconnects when it needs to update the data. See Chapter 5 on ADO for more information.

❑ Use a query as the source of a form, control, or ADO recordset that returns only the rows you need to work with instead of opening an entire table.

❑ Make sure that your query is written correctly. For example, make sure to retrieve only the columns that are being used. Also make sure that you are using the correct type of join.

❑ Make sure the type of cursor being used is not more than you really need. For example, if you are not modifying the data, use a read-only cursor.

❑ Use proper indexes on the tables to reduce the number of table scans. Add indexes to the fields that are used to join tables together and are frequently used to retrieve data. This will save Access from having to perform a scan of the entire database to find the desired record. However, do not add indexes on every field in the database. This will actually degrade performance more than having no indexes at all.

Improving Perceived Performance

The prior sections focused on how to improve the actual performance of your application. In this section, you look at a few ways to improve the performance as perceived by the end users. In other words, you are not really speeding up the application by implementing these features, but you make the user feel like the application is running faster or that progress is being made.

❑ Use an hourglass to indicate that the application is performing a task that may take a while. The hourglass can be turned on and off, respectively, with the following code:

```
DoCmd.Hourglass True
DoCmd.Hourglass False
```

❑ Hide forms that need to be reopened later. Instead of constantly opening and closing the same form, consider opening the form once and hiding it until it is needed again. Forms that remain in memory are faster than forms that are reloaded frequently, although they both take up resources. You use the `Visible` property of the form to hide and redisplay the form. For example, the following code hides a form:

```
frmName.Visible = False
```

❑ Use a splash screen when the application loads to indicate that something is happening. The splash screen should be a very simple screen with as few controls as possible. The idea is to get something in front of the user quickly while the rest of the application loads. To create a splash screen, just create a simple form and have that form load when the application begins. You then close the splash screen from code when you are ready to display the main form.

❑ Use a progress bar or percent meter to indicate the progress of an operation. For example, if you are performing an operation that is going to take some time iterating through multiple steps, you want to inform the user as the operation progresses. Think of a file copy operation. As the files are copied, you see the progress bar to see how many files remain. You can either create your own form to display the progress of an operation, or you can use the percent meter built into Access. The following is an example of using the percent meter that displays progress in the bottom-left corner of Access:

```
Dim intCounter As Integer
Dim intResult As Integer
Dim intPause As Long

intResult = SysCmd(acSysCmdInitMeter, "Copying 2000 files", 2000)
For intCounter = 1 To 2000
    intResult = SysCmd(acSysCmdUpdateMeter, intCounter)
    'Create pause so user can see progress bar
    For intPause = 1 To 20000
    Next intPause
Next intCounter

intResult = SysCmd(acSysCmdRemoveMeter)
```

Running the Performance Analyzer

Access comes with a Performance Analyzer utility that will analyze the selected objects and make suggestions to help improve the speed. You must have the database you wish to analyze open in order to run the analyzer.

Try It Out   **Using the Performance Analyzer**

Let's walk through an example of using the Performance Analyzer to analyze all the objects in the Northwind database for suggested ways to improve speed.

1.   Select Database Tools and then click on Analyze Performance in the Analyze ribbon. A screen similar to the one shown in Figure 12-8 is displayed.

2.   Select the All Object Types tab, as shown in Figure 12-8. Click the Select All button and then select OK. This selects all the objects in the database to analyze. The analyzer runs, and a screen similar to the one shown in Figure 12-9 is displayed, which makes various suggestions on ways to improve the performance of the application.

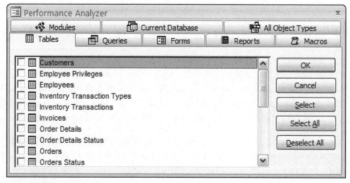

Figure 12-8

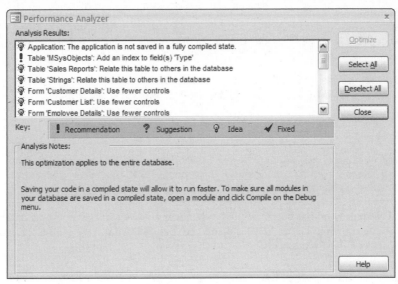

Figure 12-9

How It Works

The Performance Analyzer is a wizard you can use to let Access provide some suggestions on how to improve the performance of the application. In the example, you ran the wizard against the Northwind database and discovered that some additional improvements can still be made to make the application run even faster.

Securing Your Application

You have various ways to add security to your application. You can implement one or more of these techniques, depending on the type of security that is required for your application. For example, you can assign passwords to the database and/or to the code, and you can encrypt the database. Let's look at each of these concepts in more detail.

Adding a Database Password

One way to add security to your database is to require a user to input a password before the database can be opened. This is called file-level security. After the database file has been opened by specifying the correct password, the user can do anything to the database unless the other security features are implemented.

You have at least two ways to set a database password. One way is to select the Database Tools ribbon ⇨ Encrypt with Password option. You will be prompted to enter a password for the database. Another way to set a database password is programmatically using VBA code. For example, you can execute SQL statements against the database to set, change, and remove a database password. Here are sample SQL statements for each of these options:

```
'SQL statement for setting password for first time (from NULL to some value)
strSQL = "ALTER DATABASE PASSWORD [newpassword] NULL"

'SQL statement for changing the database password
strSQL = "ALTER DATABASE PASSWORD [anotherpassword] [newpassword]"

'SQL statement for setting password back to NULL (no password)
strSQL = "ALTER DATABASE PASSWORD NULL [anotherpassword]"

'For any of these statements, would also need code to execute the SQL statement
'against the database. For example, you could use ADO to execute these statements
'against the database.
```

After a database password has been assigned, whenever any user tries to open the database, a dialog similar to the one shown in Figure 12-10 is displayed. Before the database can be opened, the user must specify the correct database password.

Figure 12-10

Adding a Password for VBA Code

Adding a password to the database as described in the prior section does not keep the user from seeing your source code. Since Access 2000, you have to secure the VBA source code separately by locking the project from viewing and providing a password. To add a password for the VBA code, open the Visual Basic Editor. Then, select Tools ⇨ *ProjectName* Properties. Select the Protection tab, as shown in Figure 12-11.

Specify the Lock Project For Viewing option, and fill in a password that must be specified in order to view the source code. After you click OK, the specified password will be required in the future before the source code can be viewed or modified.

Another way to improve security through various file security features includes creating an ACCDE file. Please see the section later in this chapter that discusses ACCDE files.

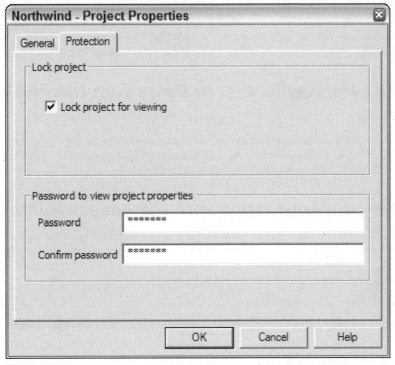

Figure 12-11

Encrypting a Database

Even after you add to your application the security features discussed so far, your application is still not totally secure. Someone could still view the contents of the database with a tool that can view partitions on disk and decipher data. If you are worried about someone being able to decipher the data from a disk utility, you should consider encrypting the database.

To do so, select the Database Tools ribbon and then Encode Database in the Database Tools group. Access then prompts you to specify a password. After you click OK, the entire database will be encrypted. In order for you to use the application after it has been encrypted, Access will have to decrypt the information. This means that encrypting the database will slow down performance as much as 20%. If this performance degradation is a problem for your application, decryption is not a good option.

Distributing Your Application

Now that you have tested and optimized your application, you are ready to compile and distribute the application to end users. You have various distribution options, such as distributing the database to users with the full-blown version of Access, distributing the application using the Access runtime, and distributing ACCDE files. Each of these will now be discussed.

Before distributing your application, you should first compile the application. You do not want end users dealing with compiler errors that could have been avoided by compiling prior to deployment. Compiling will also help the application run faster. One way to compile an application is from the Visual Basic Editor, by selecting the Debug ⇨ Compile DatabaseName option.

Distributing the Application to Users with the Full Version of Access

In some cases, you may be distributing the application to users who already have the full version of Access installed. Other than making the ACCDB file(s) accessible to each user, you do not have to take any other steps in order to deploy the application to those users.

Distributing the Application with the Access Runtime

If you have end users who do not have Access installed, you can distribute the application to them using the Access runtime. The runtime is a limited feature version of Access that has the following limitations:

❑ You cannot view or modify the object designs.

❑ The database window is hidden.

❑ Built-in toolbars and some menu items are not supported, so you may have to include your own menus in your application.

❑ Some keys are disabled.

You can create a setup program using the Packaging Wizard that will enable you to deploy your application with the Access runtime. In order to use the Packaging Wizard, you first have to have the Office Access 2007 Developer Extensions installed. Contact Microsoft for more information on how to obtain this extension. At the time of this book's writing, the developer extensions were only available as part of the Visual Studio Tools for the Microsoft Office System.

After you have installed a copy of the developer extensions, you must load the Packaging Wizard to your project. From the Visual Basic Editor, select Add-Ins ⇨ Add-In Manager ⇨ Packaging Wizard and check the Loaded/Unloaded box. Click OK. The wizard should now appear under the Add-In menu.

After it is installed, the wizard can be used to help you build a distribution solution based on the Access runtime. If you want to test your application to see how it will look in the Access runtime, you can open the database by using the /runtime switch, as shown in the following code:

```
msaccess.exe c:\bstempbsnorthwind.accdb /runtime
```

If you plan to distribute your application using the Access runtime, you should test it in this manner to ensure your users will be able to navigate correctly. You should also test the installer in the various environments to which you will be distributing your application to make sure the install goes smoothly.

Note that if you are using any third-party ActiveX controls in your application, you will need to include the installer for those before you distribute the application. Many computers you distribute to will not have the third-party components you have on your development machine.

Distributing an Execute-Only Application

An ACCDE is a compiled and compacted database file that has all editable source code removed. Because the source code is removed, additional security is provided for your application. Furthermore, because the code is removed, the size of the application is smaller and thus performance is improved. Because of the limitations of ACCDE files, you should keep the original database with the source code so that you will be able to make changes later.

To create an ACCDE file, open the database from which you want to create the ACCDE file. Select the Database Tools tab, and then click on the Make ACCDE icon in the Database Tools ribbon. Specify a name for the ACCDE file on the dialog box that appears, and click the OK button.

Maintaining the Application

Just because you have deployed your application to end users does not mean that your job is finished. It is important that you periodically compact the database to keep it in good working order and that you make periodic backup copies.

Compacting and Repairing the Database

You can compact and repair Access databases to reduce the amount of space they take up and to repair problems if Access discovers any. Because Access databases are file-based, records are being deleted and added to the system over time. A large amount of space may have been taken up by an operation that has already been completed or by database records that were already deleted. Compacting the database will recover that space and reduce the file size.

To compact and repair an Access database, select the Office Button ⇨ Manage ⇨ Compact and Repair Database. If you have the database open that you want to compact, selecting this option will automatically compact that one. If no databases are open, you will be prompted to specify the name and location of the database to compact.

Making Backup Copies of the Database

If you are like most people, you have probably lost data from some program before. It was certainly frustrating to lose the data and have to recreate it again. The same concept holds true for your Access applications. Access databases are file-based, which means that a lot of the information is contained in the single ACCDB file. Because so much is contained in a single file, and because it would be easy for a user to delete the database file from the network, it is *extremely* important that you make periodic backups of both the database tables and the user interface. The concept of backups is important for any application, but it is especially true for file-based applications like Access.

To back up an Access database, select the Office Button ⇨ Manage ⇨ Backup Database. You will be prompted to specify a file name and path where you want the backup saved. Click OK, and the backup copy will be created.

Summary

In this chapter, I discussed several techniques that will help ensure that your Access applications are capable of handling multiple users and performing well. You also explored various ways to fine-tune, secure, and test Access applications. You looked at various implementation options, as well as some maintenance issues that should be addressed to ensure that your hard work in building the application is not wasted. The concepts covered up to this point have illustrated the basics of building applications and have prepared you for the final two chapters. Chapters 13 and 14 are hands-on case studies that will allow you to build real-world applications, while solidifying the concepts covered in all the prior chapters.

Exercises

1. Describe two ways you can improve support for multiple users in your application.

2. Describe two ways you can improve the performance of your application.

3. What is involved in building a help system for your application?

4. Describe some ways you can add security to your application.

5. What is an ACCDE file? How does deploying your application using an ACCDE file differ from using the Access runtime version?

Case Study 1: Project Tracker Application

So far in this book, you have learned various ways to use VBA code to extend your Access applications. This chapter is the first of two case studies that will illustrate all the concepts covered to this point in a real-world and comprehensive example. It involves the Project Tracker application that allows users to track their projects and related contacts and document attachments. You will:

❑ Review the important design specifications

❑ Separate the code into different logical layers

❑ Use two separate Access database files for the application: one for the user interface and the other for the data

❑ Implement custom objects using class modules

❑ Launch an external file or program from your application

❑ Send an e-mail from your application

❑ Work with disconnected recordsets to minimize database connections and improve multiuser capabilities

❑ Learn how to handle errors

In this chapter, you are tasked with creating the Project Tracker application from start to finish. I will walk you through each step, and at the end many of the concepts covered in prior chapters will make a lot more sense. For your convenience I included the two database files with the source code and table structures available for download from Wrox.com. However, I recommend that you work through the chapter yourself — at least in the beginning — before using the source code I provide. The best way to learn Access is hands-on.

Design Specifications

Let's turn straight to the task of learning the requirements for the Project Tracker application. As discussed in Chapter 1, before you ever write a single line of code you should carefully plan your application on paper. Start this design process by determining exactly what the new application needs to do, who will use it, and what they are currently using. Go on a fact-finding mission to determine what needs the new application must meet. Many applications fail because coding was done too early and it was hard to retrofit changes. You may recall the house building analogy: If you wait until the first two floors have been framed to tell your builder you want a basement, you incur a lot of expense to get it at that point. The same concept applies in the world of programming. The more you plan up front, the better off you will be.

In the present case study, you have already talked to users and determined that each person needs a way to track his own personal projects. Corporate systems are in place to manage contacts, billing, and even projects for the company. However, the users are complaining that they need a simpler way to track their own little tasks in a coherent way. This system is not meant to replace the existing systems. The users will still have to maintain the projects in the master system. However, the personal details for each user's daily work do not need to be maintained in the master system, nor does management want them to be.

With that in mind, you determine that the application should, at least, allow users to track simple details about their projects, as well as store related contact information for each project. The user interface format should allow the user to navigate through the records one at a time. Preferably, only open projects should be displayed on the screen when the application opens, but the users must also have some way to see all projects, including those that are closed.

The Use Case Diagram, shown in Figure 13-1, illustrates these basic requirements.

Eight use cases are shown in Figure 13-1. Users can open the Project Tracker application with only unclosed records displayed (U.C. 1.1) but have the option to see all project records (U.C. 1.2). Buttons allow navigation among the records (U.C. 1.3). In addition, the application enables users to update existing (U.C. 1.4), add new (U.C. 1.5), and delete existing (U.C. 1.6) records. From the Project Tracker screen, a user can open the Contacts screen to see contact details for a particular contact that is associated with the project (U.C. 1.7). A user can also open the Contacts screen and manage existing contacts (U.C. 1.8) and add/associate a particular contact with the current project.

From the Contacts screen, you determine that the user should be able to view and manage contacts in a manner similar to the way the Project Tracker screen does, with record navigation and update capabilities. In addition, the user needs an option to associate a selected contact with the currently open project. Figure 13-2 shows these features represented in a Use Case Diagram.

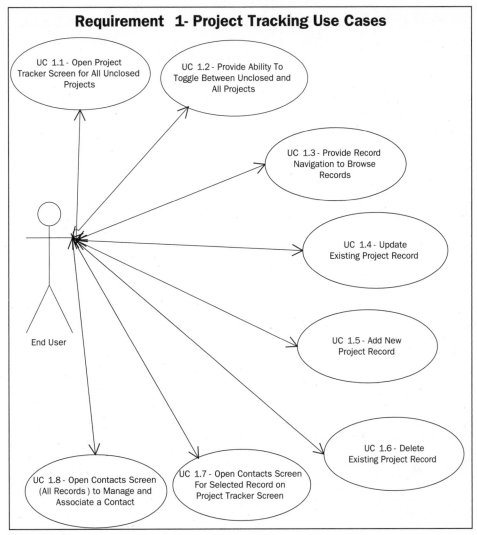

Figure 13-1

Again, the user can open contacts records (U.C. 2.1), and update (U.C. 2.2), add new (U.C. 2.3), and delete (U.C. 2.4) contact records. Record navigation is provided (U.C. 2.5) to enable viewing and maintenance of contacts. Furthermore, a user can associate a contact record with the currently open project on the project form (U.C. 2.6).

You may determine that although it is not required, it would also be desirable to add enhanced features, such as the capability to create a new e-mail to send to a selected contact from the project record. Users also want to associate external files, such as related documents and spreadsheets, with a project record. You might decide to include these features in the application because they will add a lot of additional value to the users, and management has approved of this approach.

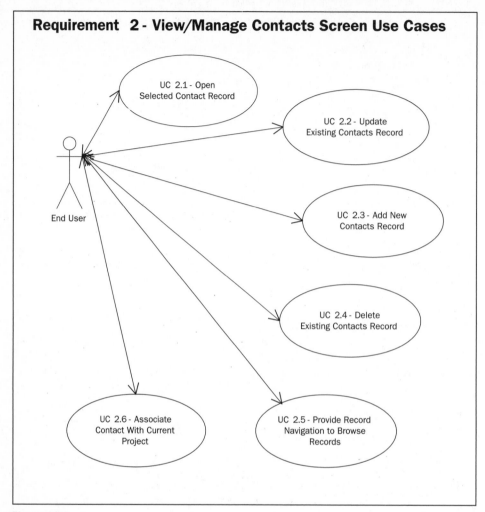

Figure 13-2

As discussed in Chapter 1, you have various other ways to document the application, including activity diagrams, other flow charts, network diagrams, object diagrams, and so on. Exactly what you do is not so important, as long as you arrive at a coherent design on paper before you begin writing the application. In Access, I typically generate prototype screens by using Access forms, because the work of drawing the forms can be reused when you actually start coding the forms. I sometimes use Visio to generate prototype screens as well. In any event, when you analyze the requirements previously discussed, you might determine that two main screens make sense: a Project Tracker screen and a Contacts screen. The Project Tracker screen can be further divided into tabs, such as a first tab for Comments/Tasks, a second tab for related contacts, and a third tab for file attachments. This design is illustrated in Figures 13-3, 13-4, and 13-5.

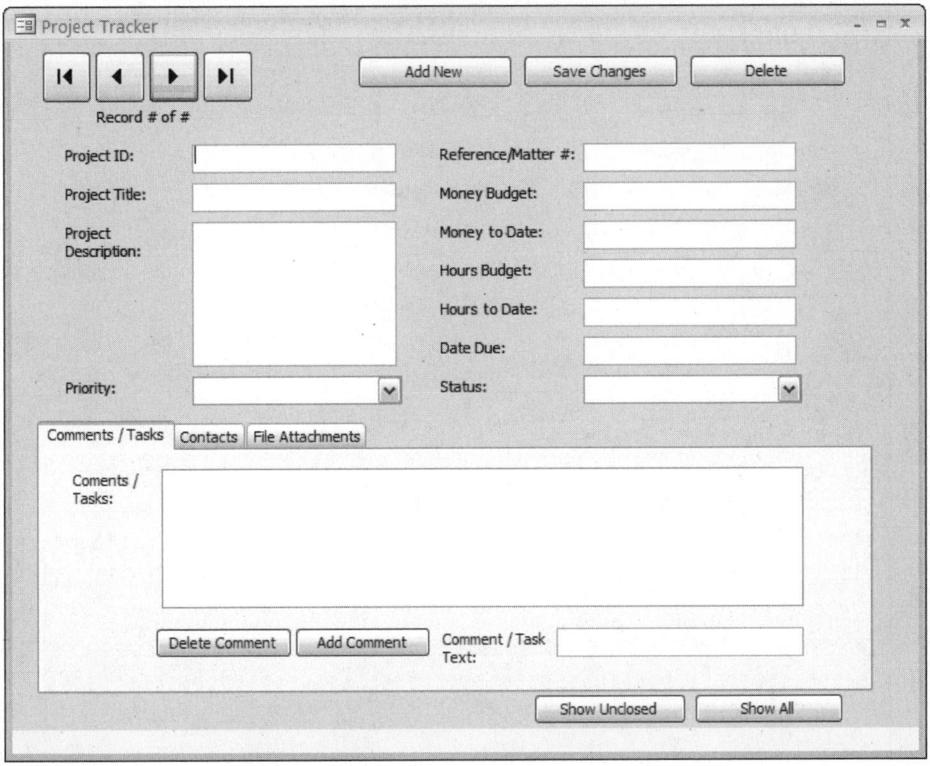

Figure 13-3

Figure 13-3 shows the general information for the project as well as the Comments tab where the user can enter tasks or comments about the project. The user can enter a comment or task in the Comment/Task Text field and then click the Add Comment button to add it to the project. Because you are planning to implement a disconnected recordset scenario as described in detail in Chapter 5 on ADO, you will not actually be saving the changes to the underlying database until the user clicks the Save Changes button. The Delete Comment button removes the comment from the list on the form but does not remove the comment from the database until the Save Changes button is later clicked.

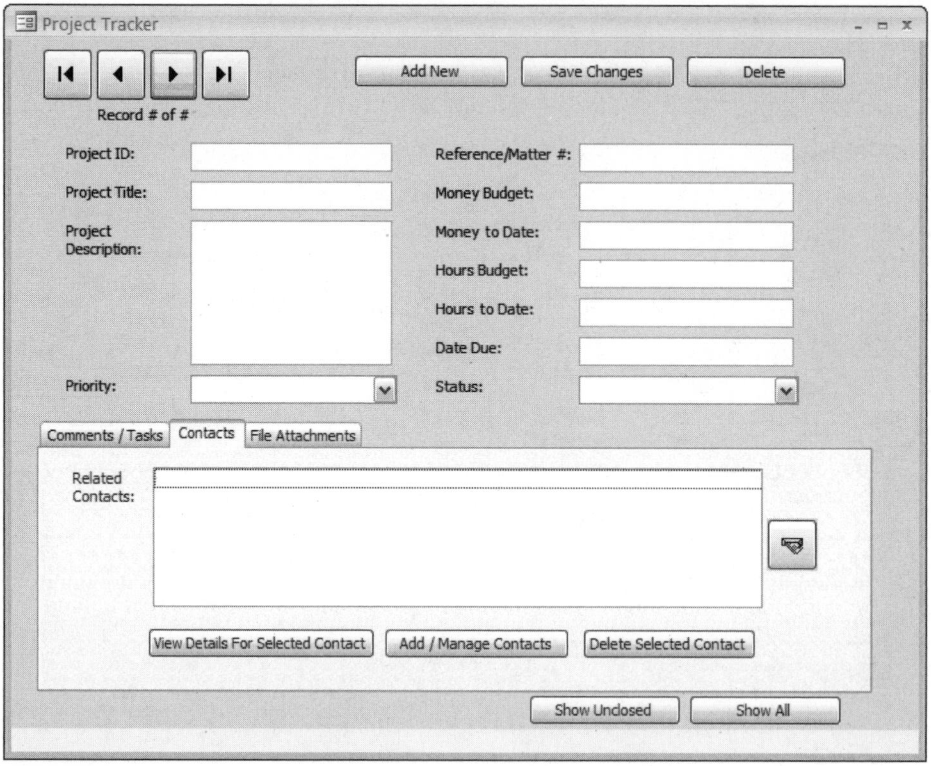

Figure 13-4

Figure 13-4 shows the same general project information at the top portion of the screen and has a Contacts tab where related contact records can be managed. Notice the button with the mail icon on the right of the contact list. You intend for a button such as this to enable a user to generate an e-mail to the currently selected contact in the list. This tab is where users launch the Contacts screen to view more information about the selected contact, manage existing contacts, and associate them with the current contact. The Delete Selected Contact button simply removes the contact from this project but not from the database until Save Changes is clicked.

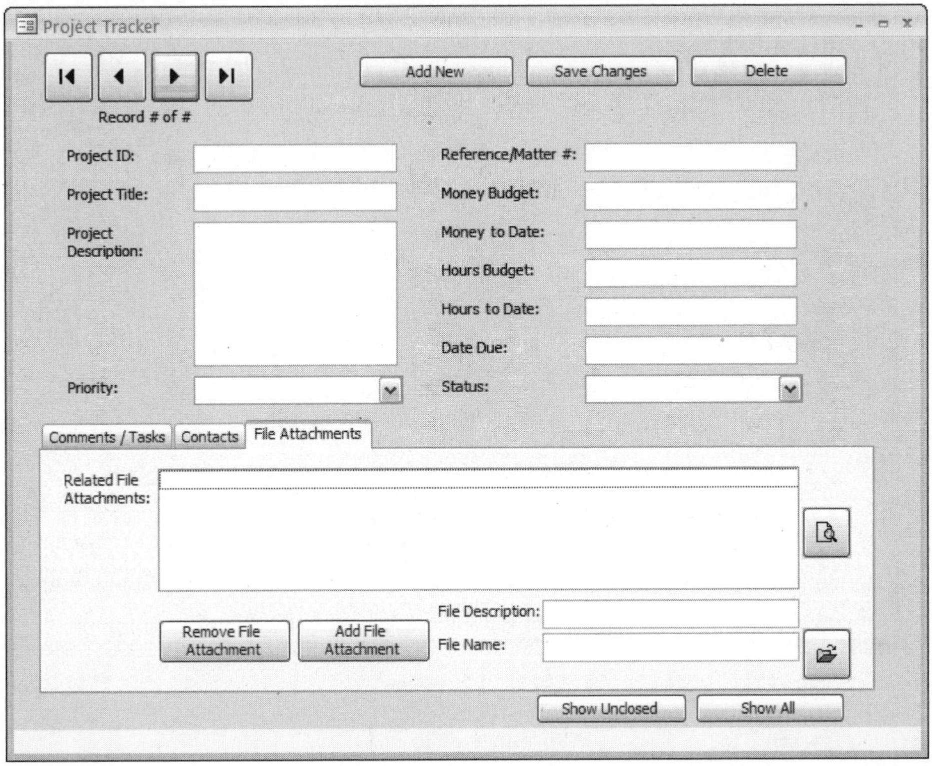

Figure 13-5

Figure 13-5 includes a File Attachments tab where users can associate separate files with the current project. The Preview button to the right of the list will allow a user to open a selected file attachment in a separate window in its native application. A File Open button allows a user to search on the file system for an attachment and includes any selected file name in the File Name field to be added to the project. After the user fills in a file description and file name and selects the Add File Attachment button, the file is added to the list.

Figure 13-6 is a prototype screen for Contacts. Notice how various data elements related to the contact are included, as well as navigation buttons and buttons for saving changes to records. The Add Current Contact To Project button allows a user to put the current contact back on the project form for the currently open project. Now that you have a written plan detailing what you want the application to do, it's time to get your hands dirty creating the database and the code!

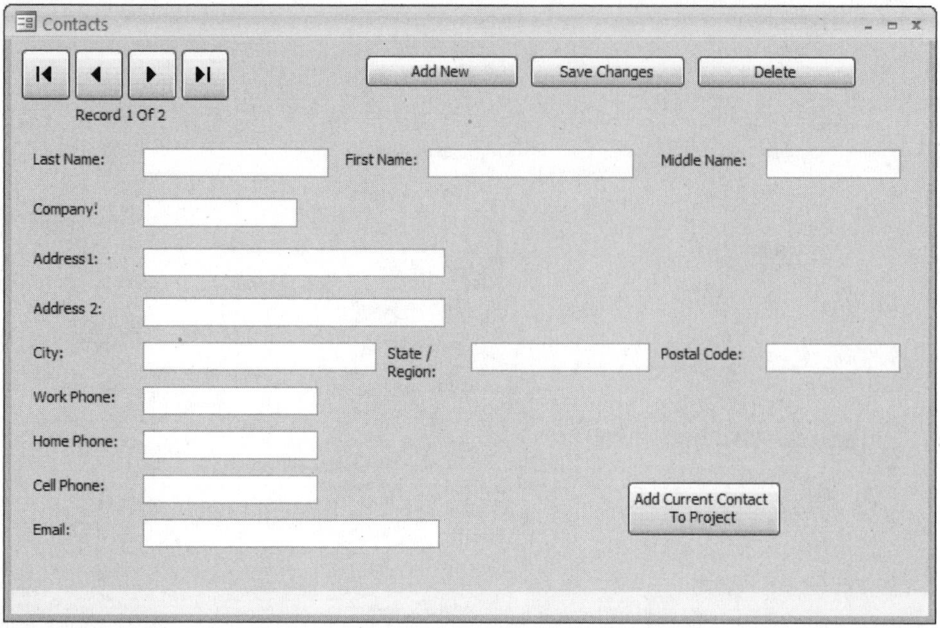

Figure 13-6

Building the Database

In this section, you will build the database in an Access file separately from the user interface. You learned in Chapter 11 that you can realize performance improvements by separating the user interface from the underlying data. The database containing the data tables can be placed on the same or a different computer than the one containing the user interface. If you are the only user, then having both files on the same computer is fine. If you have others with whom you must share the application, then putting the database with the data tables on a file server and the user interface on each user's workstation makes the most sense. In either case, you can make the database location configurable, so you can change the setup as your needs scale. This chapter will not discuss this option, but it is easily implemented in VBA.

Try It Out   Building the ProjectTrackerDb Database

Let's now build the database that will store the data tables.

1. Create a new database by selecting the Office Button ⇨ New. From the list of available templates, select "Blank Database." Specify ProjectTrackerDb for the file name, and click the Create button.

2. The tables for this database are shown in Figures 13-7 through 13-11. Note that for each table, the field size is specified in the Description field for your convenience. You also need to add primary keys as indicated in each table by the key icon.

3. Add the `tblProjects` table as shown in Figure 13-7. This table is the master project table for storing project information. Note that the fields in this table map to the fields on the prototype screen that are not on the tabs.

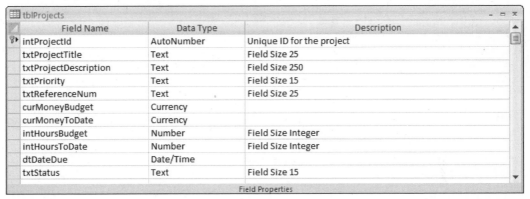

tblProjects

Field Name	Data Type	Description
intProjectId	AutoNumber	Unique ID for the project
txtProjectTitle	Text	Field Size 25
txtProjectDescription	Text	Field Size 250
txtPriority	Text	Field Size 15
txtReferenceNum	Text	Field Size 25
curMoneyBudget	Currency	
curMoneyToDate	Currency	
intHoursBudget	Number	Field Size Integer
intHoursToDate	Number	Field Size Integer
dtDateDue	Date/Time	
txtStatus	Text	Field Size 15

Field Properties

Figure 13-7

4. Add the `tblContacts` table as shown in Figure 13-8. This table maps to the fields on the Contacts prototype form.

tblContacts

Field Name	Data Type	Description
intContactId	AutoNumber	Unique ID for the contact
txtLastName	Text	Field Size 50
txtFirstName	Text	Field Size 50
txtMiddleName	Text	Field Size 50
txtCompany	Text	Field Size 50
txtAddress1	Text	Field Size 100
txtAddress2	Text	Field Size 100
txtCity	Text	Field Size 50
txtRegion	Text	Field Size 50
txtPostalCode	Text	Field Size 25
txtWorkPhone	Text	Field Size 12
txtHomePhone	Text	Field Size 12
txtCellPhone	Text	Field Size 12
txtEmail	Text	Field Size 50

Figure 13-8

5. Add the `tblProjectsComments` table as shown in Figure 13-9. This table is used to store the multiple comments that can be entered for a given project. This table maps to the first tab of the Project Tracker screen prototype. The reason a separate table has to be used for the tabs is that multiple entries can be included. You cannot simply put a field in the main table that holds multiple contacts. In the world of database design; you illustrate these relationships (one to many, many to many, and so on) in separate tables for various reasons.

Field Name	Data Type	Description
tblProjectsComments		
intCommentId	AutoNumber	Unique ID for the Comment
intProjectId	Number	Field Size Long Integer
txtComment	Text	Field Size 250

Figure 13-9

6. Add the `tblProjectsContacts` table as shown in Figure 13-10. This table maps to the second tab of the Project Tracker screen prototype.

Field Name	Data Type	Description
tblProjectsContacts		
intProjectId	Number	Long Integer
intContactId	Number	Long Integer

Figure 13-10

7. Add the `tblProjectsFileAttachments` table as shown in Figure 13-11. This table maps to the third tab of the Project Tracker screen prototype.

Field Name	Data Type	Description
tblProjectsFileAttachments		
intFileId	AutoNumber	Unique ID for the Project File Attachment
intProjectId	Number	Field Size Long Integer
txtFileDescription	Text	Field Size 50
txtFileName	Text	Field Size 250

Figure 13-11

8. At this point, your `ProjectTrackerDb` database should look like the one shown in Figure 13-12.

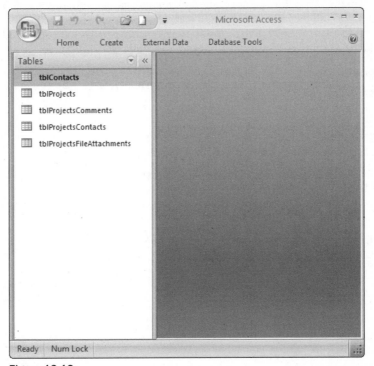

Figure 13-12

How It Works

You created five tables that will store the data for the Project Tracker application. These tables were created in a separate database from the user interface database to provide better support for multiple users. The `tblContacts` table is used to store data about each individual contact. The `tblProjects` table stores data about each project record. The `tblProjectsComments`, `tblProjectsContacts`, and `tblProjectsFileAttachments` tables can store multiple records for a particular project record.

Building the User Interface

Now that the tables have been created, it's time to move on to creating the empty forms for the user interface. You can then write the code in class modules and standard modules, and finish off by adding code to each form to call the class modules and standard modules. The example in this chapter uses ADO to connect to the `ProjectTrackerDb` database, but you can alternatively or additionally add an explicit link to the separate database so you can see the tables from within your user interface project.

Try It Out   **Building the frmProjects and frmContacts Forms**

Now let's create the separate database file that will store the user interface objects:

1. Select the Office Button ➪ New. From the list of available templates, select "Blank Database" and specify `ProjectTrackerUI` for the file name. Click the Create button.

2. Create a new form called `frmProjects`. First, open the form in design view. From the ToolBox, double-click the tab control and size it appropriately on the form. Select the tab control and right-click, so you can insert a third tab if one is not already present by using the Insert Page option. You add additional tabs/pages as illustrated in Figure 13-13.

3. Next, drag and drop the numerous other controls onto the form and page 1 of the tab, as shown in Figure 13-14.

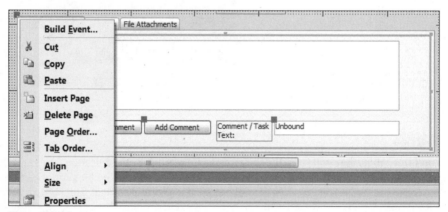

Figure 13-13

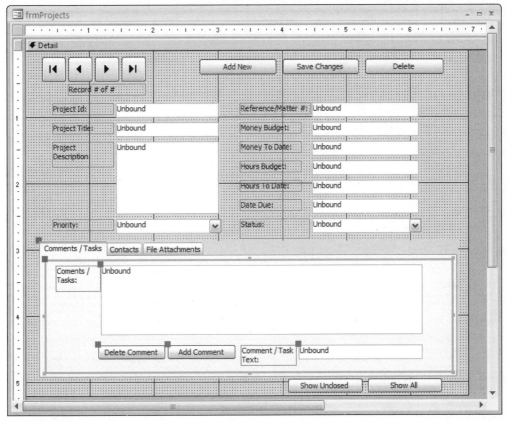

Figure 13-14

4. The following table will help ensure that you have all the correct objects on the form. Rename the controls and change other properties for each object as shown in the table.

Default Name in Figure 13-14	Name	Type of Control	Other Properties to Set from the Properties Dialog
Form1	frmProjects	Form	Record Selectors = No; Navigation Buttons = No; Dividing Lines = No; Pop up = Yes; Caption = "Project Tracker"
Text5	txtProjectId	Text Box	Set corresponding label caption to "Project ID:"
Text7	txtProjectTitle	Text Box&	Set corresponding label caption to "Project Title:"
Text9	txtProjectDesc	Text Box	Set corresponding label caption to "Project Description:"

Table continued on following page

Default Name in Figure 13-14	Name	Type of Control	Other Properties to Set from the Properties Dialog
Combo25	cboPriority	Combo Box	Set corresponding label caption to "Priority:"
Text11	txtReferenceNum	Text Box	Set corresponding label caption to "Reference/Matter #:"
Text13	txtMoneyBudget	Text Box	Set corresponding label caption to "Money Budget:"
Text15	txtMoneyToDate	Text Box	Set corresponding label caption to "MoneyToDate:"
Text17	txtHoursBudget	Text Box	Set corresponding label caption to "Hours Budget:"
Text21	txtHoursToDate	Text Box	Set corresponding label caption to "Hours to Date:"
Text23	txtDateDue	Text Box	Set corresponding label caption to "Date Due:"
Combo27	cboStatus	Combo Box	Set corresponding label caption to "Status:"
Toggle31	togShowUnclosed	Toggle Button	Caption = "Show Unclosed"
Toggle32	togShowAll	Toggle Button	Caption = "Show All"
Command33	cmdMoveFirst	Command Button	Caption = "Move First"; Picture = select Go to First 1 from list
Command34	cmdMovePrevious	Command Button	Caption = "Move Previous"; Picture = select Go to Previous 1 from list
Command35	cmdMoveNext	Command Button	Caption = "Move Next"; Picture = select Go to Next 1 from list
Command36	cmdMoveLast	Command Button	Caption = "Move Last"; Picture = select Go to Last 1 from list
Command37	cmdAddNew	Command Button	Caption = "Add New"
Command38	cmdSave	Command Button	Caption = "Save Changes"
Command39	cmdDelete	Command Button	Caption = "Delete"
Page1	pgComments	Page of Tab Control	Caption = "Comments/Tasks"
List41	lstComments	List Box	Set corresponding label caption to "Comments/Tasks:"
Command47	cmdDeleteComment	Command Button	Caption = "Delete Comment"
Command48	cmAddComment	Command Button	Caption = "Add Comment"

Default Name in Figure 13-14	Name	Type of Control	Other Properties to Set from the Properties Dialog
Text45	txtAddComment	Text Box	Set corresponding label caption to "Comment/Task Text:"
Label66	lblRecordNum	Label	Caption = "Record # of #"

5. Next, select Page 2 of the tab control and drag the additional controls onto that tab, as shown in Figure 13-15.

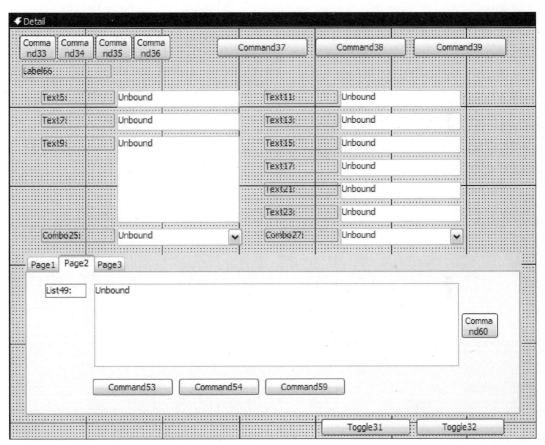

Figure 13-15

6. The following table will help ensure that you have all the correct objects on Page 2 of the tab control on frmProjects. Rename the controls and change other properties for each object as shown in the table.

Default Name on Figure 13-15	Name	Type of Control	Other Properties to Set from the Properties Dialog
Page2	pgContacts	Page of Tab Control	Caption = "Contacts"
List49	lstContacts	List Box	Set corresponding label caption to "Related Contacts:"
Command53	cmdViewContact	Command Button	Caption = "View Details for Selected Contact"
Command54	cmdManageContacts	Command Button	Caption = "Add/Manage Contacts"
Command59	cmdDeleteContact	Command Button	Caption = "Delete Selected Contact"
Command60	cmdEmailContact	Command Button	Caption = "Email Selected Contact"; Picture = select Mailbox from list of pictures

7. Next, select Page 3 of the tab control and drag the additional controls onto that tab, as shown in Figure 13-16.

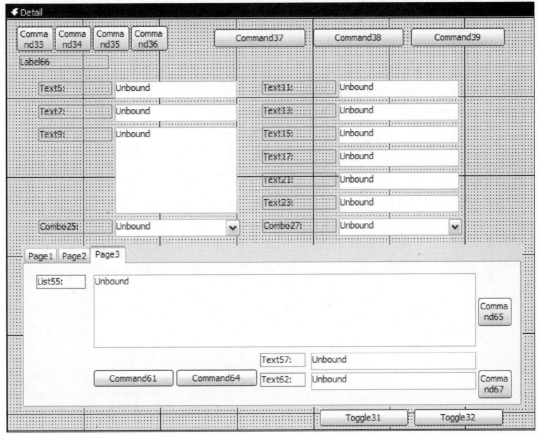

Figure 13-16

8. The following table will help ensure you have all the correct objects on Page 3 of the tab control on `frmProjects`. Again, rename the controls and change other properties for each object as shown in the table that follows.

Default Name on Figure 13-16	Name	Type of Control	Other Properties to Set from the Properties Dialog
Page3	pgFileAttachments	Page of Tab Control	Caption = "File Attachments"
List55	lstFileAttachments	List Box	Set corresponding label caption to "Related File Attachments:"
Command61	cmdRemoveAttachment	Command Button	Caption = "Remove File Attachment"
Command64	cmdAddAttachment	Command Button	Caption = "Add File Attachment"
Text57	txtFileDesc	Text Box	Set corresponding label caption to "File Description:"
Text 62	txtFileName	Text Box	Set corresponding label caption to "File Name:"
Command65	cmdOpenFile	Command Button	Caption = "Open Selected File"; Picture = select Preview Document from list
Command67	cmdFileBrowse	Command Button	Caption = "File Browse"; Picture = select Open Folder from list

9. Verify that each control on `frmProjects` has the correct name and other property settings as listed in the prior tables. If any of these are misspelled, later code referencing them will produce an error you will need to fix. The form should now appear similar to those shown in Figures 13-17 to 13-19.

10. Make sure to save all your changes to frmProjects.

11. Next, create a new form called frmContacts. Drag and drop the controls onto the form, as shown in Figure 13-20.

12. The following table will help ensure that you have all the correct objects on the form. Rename the controls and change other properties for each object as shown in the table.

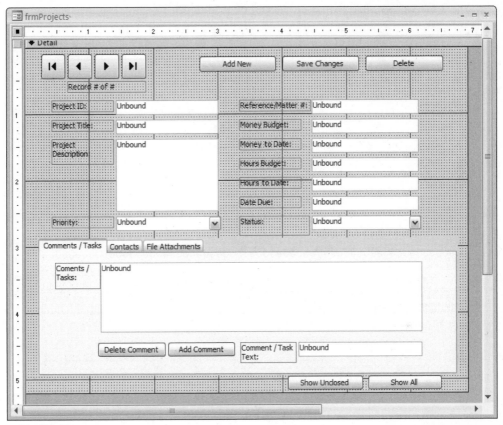

Figure 13-17

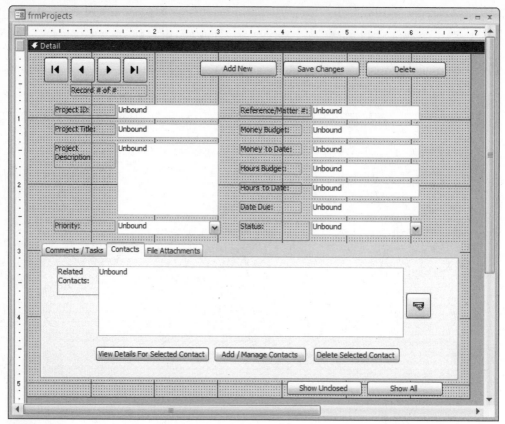

Figure 13-18

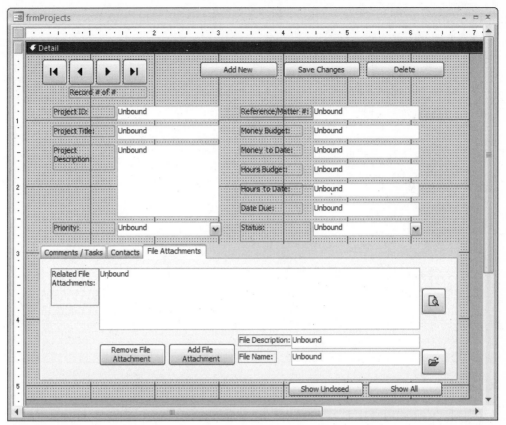

Figure 13-19

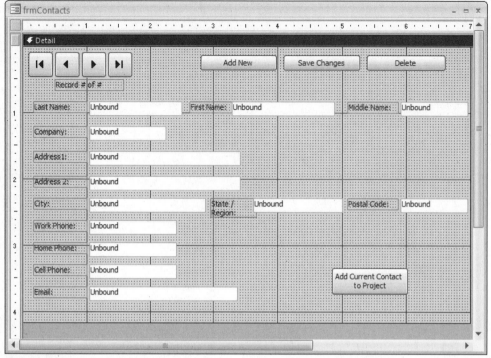

Figure 13-20

Default Name on Figure 13-20	Name	Type of Control	Other Properties to Set from the Properties Dialog
Form2	frmContacts	Form	Record Selectors = No; Navigation Buttons = No; Dividing Lines = No; Pop up = Yes; Caption = "Contacts"
Text0	txtLName	Text Box	Set corresponding label caption to "Last Name:"
Text2	txtFName	Text Box	Set corresponding label caption to "First Name:"
Text4	txtMName	Text Box	Set corresponding label caption to "Middle Name:"
Text6	txtCompany	Text Box	Set corresponding label caption to "Company:"
Text8	txtAddress1	Text Box	Set corresponding label caption to "Address1:"
Text10	txtAddress2	Text Box	Set corresponding label caption to "Address2:"

Default Name on Figure 13-20	Name	Type of Control	Other Properties to Set from the Properties Dialog
Text12	txtCity	Text Box	Set corresponding label caption to `"City:"`
Text14	txtRegion	Text Box	Set corresponding label caption to `"State/Region:"`
Text16	txtPostalCode	Text Box	Set corresponding label caption to `"Postal Code:"`
Text18	txtWorkPhone	Text Box	Set corresponding label caption to `"Work Phone:"`
Text20	txtHomePhone	Text Box	Set corresponding label caption to `"Home Phone:"`
Text22	txtCellPhone	Text Box	Set corresponding label caption to `"Cell Phone:"`
Text24	txtEmail	Text Box	Set corresponding label caption to `"E-mail:"`
Command26	cmdAddToProject	Command Button	Caption = `"Add Current Contact to Project"`
Command33	cmdMoveFirst	Command Button	Caption = `"Move First"`; Picture = select Go to First 1 from list
Command34	cmdMovePrevious	Command Button	Caption = `"Move Previous"`; Picture = select Go to Previous 1 from list
Command35	cmdMoveNext	Command Button	Caption = `"Move Next"`; Picture = select Go to Next 1 from list
Command36	cmdMoveLast	Command Button	Caption = `"Move Last"`; Picture = select Go to Last 1 from list
Command37	cmdAddNew	Command Button	Caption = `"Add New"`
Command38	cmdSave	Command Button	Caption = `"Save Changes"`
Command39	cmdDelete	Command Button	Caption = `"Delete"`
Label27	lblRecordNum	Label	Caption = `"Record # of #"`

13. After setting all the properties, `frmContacts` should now appear as shown in Figure 13-21.

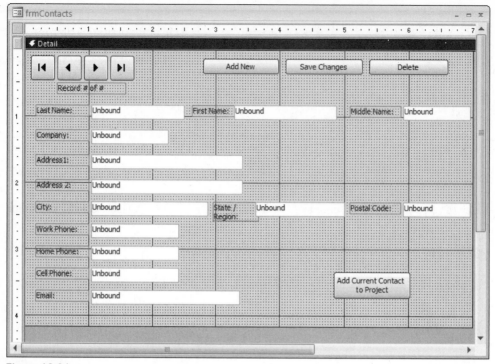

Figure 13-21

14. Save all the changes for `frmContacts`.

15. A Database Window showing how the `ProjectTrackerUI` database should appear at this point is illustrated in Figure 13-22.

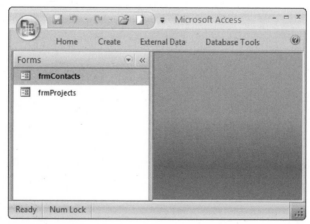

Figure 13-22

How It Works

The `frmProjects` form will be used to display project records. You added various controls to this form, including several text boxes and other controls that will be used to display data and accept input from a user. The primary data for the `frmProjects` form will come from the `tblProjects` table. Additional data for the tabs on the tab control will come from the `tblProjectsComments`, `tblProjectsContacts`, and `tblProjectsFileAttachments` tables.

The `frmContacts` form will be used to display contact records for all contacts or for a selected contact. You also added various controls to this form that will be used to display the contact data and accept input from a user. The data for the `frmContacts` form will come from the `tblContacts` table.

Building the Class Modules for the Objects

Throughout this book you learned that VBA code can be written in various places, such as class modules that are independent or associated with a form, as well as in standard modules. Next, you turn your attention to writing the code that will implement the desired features of the Project Tracker application. You will be creating the custom class modules first, then the standard modules, and finally the code for the forms to call the other modules. An example of how the Project Explorer will look in the Visual Basic Editor when you're finished is shown in Figure 13-23.

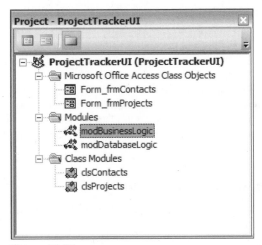

Figure 13-23

Chapter 4 introduced the idea of creating custom classes. In the current application, you will create two logical custom class modules. One is a class for a `Project` object that will represent the current project in memory on the Project Tracker screen. The other will be a `Contact` object that will represent any current contact in memory from the Contacts screen.

The Project Class

An object diagram for the Project class is shown in Figure 13-24.

The Contact class will be illustrated later in this chapter.

Project
-ProjectID
-ProjectTitle
-ProjectDescription
-Priority
-ReferenceNum
-MoneyBudget
-MoneytoDate
-HoursBudget
-HourstoDate
-DateDue
-Status
+Save ()
+Delete()
+RetrieveProjects ()
+RetrieveComments ()
+RetrieveContacts ()
+RetrieveAttachments ()
+PopulatePropertiesFromRecordset ()
+PopulatePropertiesFromForm ()
+ClearObject ()

Figure 13-24

The properties are represented in the top portion of the diagram, and the methods are shown in the bottom section. These correspond to the data elements on the form for the most part, except that the tabs with multiple records are not listed here. The methods represent various actions that you must take on the object. You will also write numerous other procedures that are not in the class module, as you will see later.

Try It Out   Building the clsProjects Class

Let's begin building the clsProjects class module that will implement the object illustrated in Figure 13-24.

1. Before building the class, you first need to add a reference to ADO (preferably 2.6 or higher) by selecting Tools, References, and then selecting ADO 2.6 from the list.

2. Add a new class module called clsProjects. In the General Declarations section of the class, add the following code:

```
Option Compare Database
Option Explicit

Const CLS_PROJECTS As String = "clsProjects"
```

```
Dim intProjectIdVal As Integer
Dim strProjectTitleVal As String
Dim strProjectDescriptionVal As String
Dim strPriorityVal As String
Dim strReferenceNumVal As String
Dim curMoneyBudgetVal As Currency
Dim curMoneyToDateVal As Currency
Dim intHoursBudgetVal As Integer
Dim intHoursToDateVal As Integer
Dim dtDateDueVal As Date
Dim strStatusVal As String
```

3. Add the various property procedures shown in the following code to `clsProjects` class module:

```
Public Property Get ProjectId() As Integer
    On Error Resume Next
    ProjectId = intProjectIdVal
End Property

    Public Property Let ProjectId(ByVal Value As Integer)
    On Error Resume Next
    intProjectIdVal = Value
End Property

  Public Property Get ProjectTitle() As String
    On Error Resume Next
    ProjectTitle = strProjectTitleVal
End Property

    Public Property Let ProjectTitle(ByVal Value As String)
    On Error Resume Next
    strProjectTitleVal = Value
End Property
Public Property Get ProjectDescription() As String
    On Error Resume Next
    ProjectDescription = strProjectDescriptionVal
End Property

    Public Property Let ProjectDescription(ByVal Value As String)
    On Error Resume Next
    strProjectDescriptionVal = Value
End Property

  Public Property Get Priority() As String
    On Error Resume Next
    Priority = strPriorityVal
End Property

    Public Property Let Priority(ByVal Value As String)
    On Error Resume Next
```

```vb
        strPriorityVal = Value
End Property

 Public Property Get ReferenceNum() As String
    On Error Resume Next
    ReferenceNum = strReferenceNumVal
End Property

Public Property Let ReferenceNum(ByVal Value As String)
    On Error Resume Next
    strReferenceNumVal = Value
End Property

Public Property Get MoneyBudget() As Currency
    On Error Resume Next
    MoneyBudget = curMoneyBudgetVal
End Property

    Public Property Let MoneyBudget(ByVal Value As Currency)
    On Error Resume Next
    curMoneyBudgetVal = Value
End Property

Public Property Get MoneyToDate() As Currency
    On Error Resume Next
    MoneyToDate = curMoneyToDateVal
End Property

    Public Property Let MoneyToDate(ByVal Value As Currency)
    On Error Resume Next
    curMoneyToDateVal = Value
End Property

Public Property Get HoursBudget() As Integer
    On Error Resume Next
    HoursBudget = intHoursBudgetVal
End Property
Public Property Let HoursBudget(ByVal Value As Integer)
    On Error Resume Next
    intHoursBudgetVal = Value
End Property

 Public Property Get HoursToDate() As Integer
    On Error Resume Next
    HoursToDate = intHoursToDateVal
End Property

    Public Property Let HoursToDate(ByVal Value As Integer)
    On Error Resume Next
    intHoursToDateVal = Value
```

```
End Property

Public Property Get DateDue() As Date
    On Error Resume Next
    DateDue = dtDateDueVal
End Property

Public Property Let DateDue(ByVal Value As Date)
    On Error Resume Next
    dtDateDueVal = Value
End Property

Public Property Get Status() As String
    On Error Resume Next
    Status = strStatusVal
End Property

    Public Property Let Status(ByVal Value As String)
    On Error Resume Next
    strStatusVal = Value
End Property
```

4. Add the `RetrieveProjects` function shown in the following code to the `clsProjects` class module:

```
Function RetrieveProjects(blnAllRecords As Boolean) As ADODB.Recordset

    On Error GoTo HandleError

    Dim strSQLStatement As String
    Dim rsProj As New ADODB.Recordset

    'build the SQL statement to retrieve data
    strSQLStatement = BuildSQLSelectProjects(blnAllRecords)

    'generate the recordset
    Set rsProj = ProcessRecordset(strSQLStatement)

    'return the populated recordset

    Exit Function

HandleError:
    GeneralErrorHandler Err.Number, Err.Description, CLS_PROJECTS, _
        "RetrieveProjects"

    Exit Function

End Function
```

5. Add the `RetrieveComments` function shown in the following code to the `clsProjects` class module:

```
Function RetrieveComments(intId As Integer) As ADODB.Recordset

    On Error GoTo HandleError

    Dim rsComments As New ADODB.Recordset
    Dim strSQL As String
    strSQL = "SELECT txtComment FROM tblProjectsComments WHERE " & _
            "intProjectId = " &_intId

    'retrieve the comments for tab 1 from the database
    Set rsComments = ProcessRecordset(strSQL)

        Set RetrieveComments = rsComments

        Exit Function

    HandleError:
    GeneralErrorHandler Err.Number, Err.Description, CLS_PROJECTS, _
            "RetrieveComments"
    Exit Function

End Function
```

6. Add the `RetrieveContacts` function shown in the following code to the `clsProjects` class module:

```
Function RetrieveContacts(intId As Integer) As ADODB.Recordset

    On Error GoTo HandleError

    Dim rsContacts As New ADODB.Recordset
    Dim strSQL As String
    strSQL = "SELECT txtFirstName, txtLastName, txtWorkPhone, txtHomePhone, " & _
        "txtCellPhone, txtEmail, tblcontacts.intContactId FROM tblContacts " & _
        "INNER JOIN tblProjectsContacts ON " & _
        "tblContacts.intContactId = tblProjectsContacts.intContactId " & _
        "WHERE tblProjectsContacts.intProjectId = " & intId

    'retrieve the comments for tab 2 from the database
    Set rsContacts = ProcessRecordset(strSQL)

    Set RetrieveContacts = rsContacts

        Exit Function
    HandleError:
    GeneralErrorHandler Err.Number, Err.Description, CLS_PROJECTS, _
```

```
        "RetrieveContacts"

    Exit Function

End Function
```

7. Add the `RetrieveAttachments` function shown in the following code to the `clsProjects` class module:

```
Function RetrieveAttachments(intId As Integer) As ADODB.Recordset
    On Error GoTo HandleError

    Dim rsAttachments As New ADODB.Recordset
    Dim strSQL As String
        strSQL = "SELECT txtFileDescription, txtFileName " & _
        "FROM tblProjectsFileAttachments WHERE intProjectId = " & intId

    'retrieve the comments for tab 3 from the database
    Set rsAttachments = ProcessRecordset(strSQL)

        Set RetrieveAttachments = rsAttachments
        Exit Function

    HandleError:
    GeneralErrorHandler Err.Number, Err.Description, CLS_PROJECTS, _
        "RetrieveAttachments"
    Exit Function

End Function
```

8. Add the `PopulatePropertiesFromRecordset` procedure shown in the following code to the `clsProjects` class module:

```
Sub PopulatePropertiesFromRecordset(rsProj As ADODB.Recordset)

    On Error GoTo HandleError

    'Populate the object with the current record in the
    'recordset
    Me.ProjectId = rsProj!intProjectId
    Me.ProjectTitle = rsProj!txtProjectTitle
    Me.ProjectDescription = rsProj!txtProjectDescription
    Me.Priority = rsProj!txtPriority
    Me.ReferenceNum = rsProj!txtReferenceNum
    Me.MoneyBudget = rsProj!curMoneyBudget
    Me.MoneyToDate = rsProj!curMoneyToDate
    Me.HoursBudget = rsProj!intHoursBudget
    Me.HoursToDate = rsProj!intHoursToDate
    Me.DateDue = rsProj!dtDateDue
```

```
    Me.Status = rsProj!txtStatus

  Exit Sub

HandleError:
    GeneralErrorHandler Err.Number, Err.Description, CLS_PROJECTS, _
        "PopulatePropertiesFromRecordset"
    Exit Sub

  End Sub
```

9. Add the `PopulatePropertiesFromForm` procedure shown in the following code to the `clsProjects` class module:

```
Sub PopulatePropertiesFromForm()

    On Error GoTo HandleError

  'Populate the object with the current record in the
  'form

  If Forms("frmProjects")!txtProjectId <> "" Then
      Me.ProjectId = CInt(Forms("frmProjects")!txtProjectId)
  End If

  Me.ProjectTitle = Forms("frmProjects")!txtProjectTitle
  Me.ProjectDescription = Forms("frmProjects")!txtProjectDesc
  Me.Priority = Forms("frmProjects")!cboPriority
  Me.ReferenceNum = Forms("frmProjects")!txtReferenceNum
  If Forms("frmProjects")!txtMoneyBudget <> "" Then
      Me.MoneyBudget = CCur(Forms("frmProjects")!txtMoneyBudget)
  End If

  If Forms("frmProjects")!txtMoneyToDate <> "" Then
      Me.MoneyToDate = CCur(Forms("frmProjects")!txtMoneyToDate)
  End If

  If Forms("frmProjects")!txtHoursBudget <> "" Then
      Me.HoursBudget = CInt(Forms("frmProjects")!txtHoursBudget)
  End If

  If Forms("frmProjects")!txtHoursToDate <> "" Then
      Me.HoursToDate = CInt(Forms("frmProjects")!txtHoursToDate)
  End If

  If Forms("frmProjects")!txtDateDue <> "" Then
      Me.DateDue = CDate(Forms("frmProjects")!txtDateDue)
  End If
  Me.Status = Forms("frmProjects")!cboStatus

  Exit Sub

HandleError:
```

```
        GeneralErrorHandler Err.Number, Err.Description, CLS_PROJECTS, _
            "PopulatePropertiesFromForm"
    Exit Sub

End Sub
```

10. Add the `ClearObject` procedure shown in the following code to the `clsProjects` class module:

```
Sub ClearObject()

    On Error GoTo HandleError

    'clear the values in the projects object
    Me.ProjectId = 0
    Me.ProjectTitle = ""
    Me.ProjectDescription = ""
    Me.Priority = 0
    Me.ReferenceNum = ""
    Me.MoneyBudget = 0
    Me.MoneyToDate = 0
    Me.HoursBudget = 0
    Me.HoursToDate = 0
    Me.DateDue = "01-01-1900"
    Me.Status = 0

    Exit Sub

HandleError:
    GeneralErrorHandler Err.Number, Err.Description, CLS_PROJECTS, "ClearObject"
    Exit Sub

End Sub
```

11. Add the `Delete` procedure shown in the following code to the `clsProjects` class module:

```
Sub Delete(intCurProjId As Integer, blnAddMode As Boolean, rsProj As _
        ADODB.Recordset)

    On Error GoTo HandleError

    Dim strSQLStatement As String
    Dim intResponse As Integer

    'make sure delete should be processed
    If Not ProceedWithDelete(blnAddMode) Then
        Exit Sub
    End If

    'build the SQL statement to delete the project
```

```
    strSQLStatement = BuildSQLDeleteProjects(intCurProjId)

    'perform the delete
    Call ProcessUpdate(strSQLStatement, rsProj)

        Exit Sub

HandleError:
    GeneralErrorHandler Err.Number, Err.Description, CLS_PROJECTS, "Delete"
    Exit Sub

End Sub
```

12. Add the `Save` procedure shown in the following code to the `clsProjects` class module:

```
Sub Save(blnAddMode As Boolean, rsProj As ADODB.Recordset)

    On Error GoTo HandleError

    Dim strSQLStatement As String
    'if adding a new record
    If blnAddMode = True Then
        strSQLStatement = BuildSQLInsertProjects(Me)
    Else
        'if updating a record
        strSQLStatement = BuildSQLUpdateProjects(Me)
    End If

    'perform the insert or update
    Call ProcessUpdate(strSQLStatement, rsProj)

    Exit Sub

HandleError:
    GeneralErrorHandler Err.Number, Err.Description, CLS_PROJECTS, "Save"
    Exit Sub

End Sub
```

How It Works

To build the `clsProjects` class module that implements the object illustrated in Figure 13-24, you first added code to the General Declarations section of the new class. For example, you declared various local variables for storing the current value of each property:

```
Dim intProjectIdVal As Integer
Dim strProjectTitleVal As String
Dim strProjectDescriptionVal As String
Dim strPriorityVal As String
Dim strReferenceNumVal As String
Dim curMoneyBudgetVal As Currency
Dim curMoneyToDateVal As Currency
Dim intHoursBudgetVal As Integer
```

```
Dim intHoursToDateVal As Integer
Dim dtDateDueVal As Date
Dim strStatusVal As String
```

Next, you added various `Get` and `Let` property procedures that will allow retrieving and setting the values in the respective property. A few of these property procedures are shown again in the following code:

```
Public Property Get ProjectId() As Integer
    On Error Resume Next
    ProjectId = intProjectIdVal
End Property

Public Property Let ProjectId(ByVal Value As Integer)
    On Error Resume Next
    intProjectIdVal = Value
End Property

Public Property Get ProjectTitle() As String
    On Error Resume Next
    ProjectTitle = strProjectTitleVal
End Property

Public Property Let ProjectTitle(ByVal Value As String)
    On Error Resume Next
    strProjectTitleVal = Value
End Property
```

After the properties for the class module were added, you added various sub procedures and functions to serve as the methods for the class. For example, the `RetrieveProjects` function is used to retrieve the project records from the database that will be displayed on the `frmProjects` form.

```
Function RetrieveProjects(blnAllRecords As Boolean) As ADODB.Recordset

    On Error GoTo HandleError

    Dim strSQLStatement As String
    Dim rsProj As New ADODB.Recordset

    'build the SQL statement to retrieve data
    strSQLStatement = BuildSQLSelectProjects(blnAllRecords)

    'generate the recordset
    Set rsProj = ProcessRecordset(strSQLStatement)

    'return the populated recordset
    Set RetrieveProjects = rsProj
    Exit Function
HandleError:
    GeneralErrorHandler Err.Number, Err.Description, CLS_PROJECTS, _
        "RetrieveProjects"
    Exit Function

End Function
```

Functions were also added to retrieve the comments, contacts, and attachment records associated with a particular project from the `tblProjectsComments`, `tblProjectsContacts`, and `tblProjectsFile Attachments` tables. For example, the `RetrieveComments` function declares a new recordset to store the results from the database. It then specifies the SQL statement that should be used to retrieve the records for the particular project and calls a `ProcessRecord` function that will actually populate the recordset by executing the SQL statement against the database. The `RetrieveContacts` and `RetrieveAttachments` functions work in a similar fashion.

```
Function RetrieveComments(intId As Integer) As ADODB.Recordset

On Error GoTo HandleError

    Dim rsComments As New ADODB.Recordset
    Dim strSQL As String
    strSQL = "SELECT txtComment FROM tblProjectsComments WHERE intProjectId = " & _
            intId

    'retrieve the comments for tab 1 from the database
    Set rsComments = ProcessRecordset(strSQL)

    Set RetrieveComments = rsComments

    Exit Function

    HandleError:
    GeneralErrorHandler Err.Number, Err.Description, CLS_PROJECTS, _
            "RetrieveComments"
    Exit Function


    End Function
```

Next, you added two procedures that populate the properties of the class. The first procedure, `PopulatePropertiesFromRecordset`, populates the properties of the class from values in the `rsProj` recordset. After the recordset has been populated with the project records, the values for the current project must be loaded into the `clsProject` object and ultimately displayed on the form to the user.

```
Sub PopulatePropertiesFromRecordset(rsProj As ADODB.Recordset)

    On Error GoTo HandleError

    'Populate the object with the current record in the
    'recordset
    Me.ProjectId = rsProj!intProjectId
    Me.ProjectTitle = rsProj!txtProjectTitle
    Me.ProjectDescription = rsProj!txtProjectDescription
    Me.Priority = rsProj!txtPriority
    Me.ReferenceNum = rsProj!txtReferenceNum
    Me.MoneyBudget = rsProj!curMoneyBudget
    Me.MoneyToDate = rsProj!curMoneyToDate
    Me.HoursBudget = rsProj!intHoursBudget
```

```
          Me.HoursToDate = rsProj!intHoursToDate
          Me.DateDue = rsProj!dtDateDue
          Me.Status = rsProj!txtStatus

              Exit Sub

     HandleError:
          GeneralErrorHandler Err.Number, Err.Description, CLS_PROJECTS, _
                "PopulatePropertiesFromRecordset"

              Exit Sub


          End Sub
```

Similarly, the `PopulatePropertiesFromForm` procedure populates the properties of the object with the values currently in the controls on the form. To avoid a data conversion error, some statements first test to make sure the field on the form is not blank before assigning a value.

```
     Sub PopulatePropertiesFromForm()

        On Error GoTo HandleError

        'Populate the object with the current record in the
        'form

        If Forms("frmProjects")!txtProjectId <> "" Then
             Me.ProjectId = CInt(Forms("frmProjects")!txtProjectId)
        End If

        Me.ProjectTitle = Forms("frmProjects")!txtProjectTitle
        Me.ProjectDescription = Forms("frmProjects")!txtProjectDesc
        Me.Priority = Forms("frmProjects")!cboPriority
        Me.ReferenceNum = Forms("frmProjects")!txtReferenceNum

        If Forms("frmProjects")!txtMoneyBudget <> "" Then
             Me.MoneyBudget = CCur(Forms("frmProjects")!txtMoneyBudget)
        End If

        If Forms("frmProjects")!txtMoneyToDate <> "" Then
             Me.MoneyToDate = CCur(Forms("frmProjects")!txtMoneyToDate)
        End If

        If Forms("frmProjects")!txtHoursBudget <> "" Then
             Me.HoursBudget = CInt(Forms("frmProjects")!txtHoursBudget)
        End If

        If Forms("frmProjects")!txtHoursToDate <> "" Then
             Me.HoursToDate = CInt(Forms("frmProjects")!txtHoursToDate)
        End If
        If Forms("frmProjects")!txtDateDue <> "" Then
             Me.DateDue = CDate(Forms("frmProjects")!txtDateDue)
```

```
        End If

        Me.Status = Forms("frmProjects")!cboStatus

        Exit Sub

    HandleError:
        GeneralErrorHandler Err.Number, Err.Description, CLS_PROJECTS, _
                "PopulatePropertiesFromForm"
        Exit Sub


    End Sub
```

In addition to adding procedures that populate the object, you also added a procedure that clears all of the values in the object. The ClearObject procedure changes all the values in the object to initialization values so that the object can be reused for another project record.

```
    Sub ClearObject()

        On Error GoTo HandleError

        'clear the values in the projects object
        Me.ProjectId = 0
        Me.ProjectTitle = ""
        Me.ProjectDescription = ""
        Me.Priority = 0
        Me.ReferenceNum = ""
        Me.MoneyBudget = 0
        Me.MoneyToDate = 0
        Me.HoursBudget = 0
        Me.HoursToDate = 0
        Me.DateDue = "01-01-1900"
        Me.Status = 0

        Exit Sub

    HandleError:
        GeneralErrorHandler Err.Number, Err.Description, CLS_PROJECTS, "ClearObject"
        Exit Sub

    End Sub
```

The final two procedures you added to the clsProjects class module included the Delete and Save procedures. The Delete procedure is responsible for deleting a particular project record from the database after confirming the user wishes to continue.

```
    Sub Delete(intCurProjId As Integer, blnAddMode As Boolean, rsProj As _
            ADODB.Recordset)

        On Error GoTo HandleError
        Dim strSQLStatement As String
```

```
      Dim intResponse As Integer

      'make sure delete should be processed
      If Not ProceedWithDelete(blnAddMode) Then
        Exit Sub
      End If

      'build the SQL statement to delete the project
      strSQLStatement = BuildSQLDeleteProjects(intCurProjId)

      'perform the delete
      Call ProcessUpdate(strSQLStatement, rsProj)

          Exit Sub

  HandleError:
      GeneralErrorHandler Err.Number, Err.Description, CLS_PROJECTS, "Delete"
      Exit Sub


  End Sub
```

The Save procedure is responsible for saving the new or updated record to the database:

```
  Sub Save(blnAddMode As Boolean, rsProj As ADODB.Recordset)
      On Error GoTo HandleError
        Dim strSQLStatement As String
```

If a new record is being added, the appropriate SQL insert statement is generated:

```
  'if adding a new record
  If blnAddMode = True Then
      strSQLStatement = BuildSQLInsertProjects(Me)
  Else
```

If an existing record is being updated, the appropriate SQL update statement is generated:

```
  'if updating a record
      strSQLStatement = BuildSQLUpdateProjects(Me)
  End If
```

The ProcessUpdate procedure is then executed so the SQL statement for the insert or update will be executed against the database:

```
      'perform the insert or update
      Call ProcessUpdate(strSQLStatement, rsProj)

          Exit Sub

  HandleError:
```

```
        GeneralErrorHandler Err.Number, Err.Description, CLS_PROJECTS, "Save"
        Exit Sub


    End Sub
```

The Contact Class

An object diagram for the Contacts class is shown in Figure 13-25. The Contacts class has properties that correspond to those data elements, such as those shown on the Contacts form, as well as some methods that can be executed upon it.

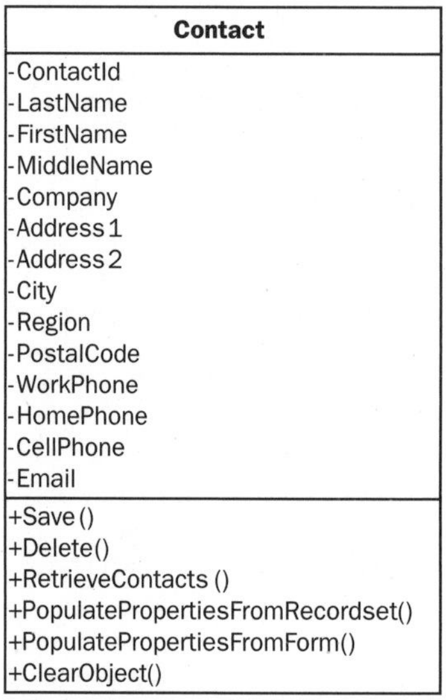

Contact
-ContactId
-LastName
-FirstName
-MiddleName
-Company
-Address1
-Address2
-City
-Region
-PostalCode
-WorkPhone
-HomePhone
-CellPhone
-Email
+Save ()
+Delete()
+RetrieveContacts ()
+PopulatePropertiesFromRecordset()
+PopulatePropertiesFromForm()
+ClearObject()

Figure 13-25

Try It Out   Building the clsContacts Class

Let's get started and build the clsContacts class module that will implement the object illustrated in Figure 13-25:

1. Create a new class module and name it clsContacts. Add the following code to the General Declarations section of the class:

```
Option Compare Database
Option Explicit

Const CLS_CONTACTS As String = "clsContacts"

Dim intContactIdVal As Integer
Dim strLastNameVal As String
```

```
Dim strFirstNameVal As String
Dim strMiddleNameVal As String
Dim strCompanyVal As String
Dim strAddress1Val As String
Dim strAddress2Val As String
Dim strCityVal As String
Dim strRegionVal As String
Dim strPostalCodeVal As String
Dim strWorkPhoneVal As String
Dim strHomePhoneVal As String
Dim strCellPhoneVal As String
Dim strEmailVal As String
```

2. Add the property procedures shown in the following code to the `clsProjects` class module:

```
Public Property Get ContactId() As Integer
    On Error Resume Next
    ContactId = intContactIdVal
End Property

    Public Property Let ContactId(ByVal Value As Integer)
    On Error Resume Next
    intContactIdVal = Value
End Property

Public Property Get LastName() As String
    On Error Resume Next
    LastName = strLastNameVal
End Property

    Public Property Let LastName(ByVal Value As String)
    On Error Resume Next
    strLastNameVal = Value
End Property

Public Property Get FirstName() As String
    On Error Resume Next
    FirstName = strFirstNameVal
End Property

    Public Property Let FirstName(ByVal Value As String)
    On Error Resume Next
    strFirstNameVal = Value
End Property

Public Property Get MiddleName() As String
    On Error Resume Next
    MiddleName = strMiddleNameVal
End Property

    Public Property Let MiddleName(ByVal Value As String)
    On Error Resume Next
    strMiddleNameVal = Value
```

```
    End Property

    Public Property Get Company() As String
        On Error Resume Next
        Company = strCompanyVal
    End Property
    Public Property Let Company(ByVal Value As String)
        On Error Resume Next
        strCompanyVal = Value
    End Property

    Public Property Get Address1() As String
        On Error Resume Next
        Address1 = strAddress1Val
    End Property

    Public Property Let Address1(ByVal Value As String)
        On Error Resume Next
        strAddress1Val = Value
    End Property

    Public Property Get Address2() As String
        On Error Resume Next
        Address2 = strAddress2Val
    End Property

    Public Property Let Address2(ByVal Value As String)
        On Error Resume Next
        strAddress2Val = Value
    End Property

    Public Property Get City() As String
        On Error Resume Next
        City = strCityVal
    End Property

    Public Property Let City(ByVal Value As String)
        On Error Resume Next
        strCityVal = Value
    End Property

    Public Property Get Region() As String
        On Error Resume Next
        Region = strRegionVal
    End Property

    Public Property Let Region(ByVal Value As String)
        On Error Resume Next
        strRegionVal = Value
    End Property

    Public Property Get PostalCode() As String
        On Error Resume Next
        PostalCode = strPostalCodeVal
```

```
    End Property

    Public Property Let PostalCode(ByVal Value As String)
        On Error Resume Next
        strPostalCodeVal = Value
    End Property
    Public Property Get WorkPhone() As String
        On Error Resume Next
        WorkPhone = strWorkPhoneVal
    End Property

    Public Property Let WorkPhone(ByVal Value As String)
        On Error Resume Next
        strWorkPhoneVal = Value
    End Property

    Public Property Get HomePhone() As String
        On Error Resume Next
        HomePhone = strHomePhoneVal
    End Property

    Public Property Let HomePhone(ByVal Value As String)
        On Error Resume Next
        strHomePhoneVal = Value
    End Property

    Public Property Get CellPhone() As String
        On Error Resume Next
        CellPhone = strCellPhoneVal
    End Property

    Public Property Let CellPhone(ByVal Value As String)
        On Error Resume Next
        strCellPhoneVal = Value
    End Property

    Public Property Get Email() As String
        On Error Resume Next
        Email = strEmailVal
    End Property

    Public Property Let Email(ByVal Value As String)
        On Error Resume Next
        strEmailVal = Value
    End Property
```

3. Add the RetrieveContacts function shown in the following code to the clsProjects class module:

```
Function RetrieveContacts() As ADODB.Recordset

    On Error GoTo HandleError
```

```
     Dim strSQLStatement As String
    Dim rsCont As New ADODB.Recordset

    'build the SQL statement to retrieve data
    strSQLStatement = BuildSQLSelectContacts

    'generate the recordset
    Set rsCont = ProcessRecordset(strSQLStatement)

    'return the populated recordset
    Set RetrieveContacts = rsCont

    Exit Function

HandleError:
    GeneralErrorHandler Err.Number, Err.Description, CLS_CONTACTS, _
            "RetrieveContacts"
    Exit Function

End Function
```

4. Add the `PopulatePropertiesFromRecordset` procedure shown in the following code to the `clsProjects` class module:

```
Sub PopulatePropertiesFromRecordset(rsCont As ADODB.Recordset)

    On Error GoTo HandleError

    'Populate the object with the current record in the
    'recordset
    Me.ContactId = rsCont!intContactId
    Me.LastName = rsCont!txtLastName
    Me.FirstName = rsCont!txtFirstName
    Me.MiddleName = rsCont!txtMiddleName
    Me.Company = rsCont!txtCompany
    Me.Address1 = rsCont!txtAddress1
    Me.Address2 = rsCont!txtAddress2
    Me.City = rsCont!txtCity
    Me.Region = rsCont!txtRegion
    Me.PostalCode = rsCont!txtPostalCode
    Me.WorkPhone = rsCont!txtWorkPhone
    Me.HomePhone = rsCont!txtHomePhone
    Me.CellPhone = rsCont!txtCellPhone
    Me.Email = rsCont!txtEmail
    Exit Sub

HandleError:
    GeneralErrorHandler Err.Number, Err.Description, CLS_CONTACTS, _
            "PopulatePropertiesFromRecordset"
    Exit Sub

End Sub
```

5. Add the `PopulatePropertiesFromForm` procedure shown in the following code to the `clsProjects` class module:

```
Sub PopulatePropertiesFromForm()

    On Error GoTo HandleError

    'Populate the object with the current record in the
    'form

    Me.LastName = Forms("frmContacts")!txtLName
    Me.FirstName = Forms("frmContacts")!txtFName
    Me.MiddleName = Forms("frmContacts")!txtMName
    Me.Company = Forms("frmContacts")!txtCompany
    Me.Address1 = Forms("frmContacts")!txtAddress1
    Me.Address2 = Forms("frmContacts")!txtAddress2
    Me.City = Forms("frmContacts")!txtCity
    Me.Region = Forms("frmContacts")!txtRegion
    Me.PostalCode = Forms("frmContacts")!txtPostalCode
    Me.WorkPhone = Forms("frmContacts")!txtWorkPhone
    Me.HomePhone = Forms("frmContacts")!txtHomePhone
    Me.CellPhone = Forms("frmContacts")!txtCellPhone
    Me.Email = Forms("frmContacts")!txtEmail

    Exit Sub

HandleError:
    GeneralErrorHandler Err.Number, Err.Description, CLS_CONTACTS, _
        "PopulatePropertiesFromForm"

    Exit Sub

End Sub
```

6. Add the `ClearObject` procedure shown in the following code to the `clsProjects` class module:

```
Sub ClearObject()

    On Error GoTo HandleError

    'clear the values in the contacts object
    Me.ContactId = 0
    Me.LastName = ""
    Me.FirstName = ""
    Me.MiddleName = ""
    Me.Company = ""
    Me.Address1 = ""
    Me.Address2 = ""
    Me.City = ""
    Me.Region = ""
    Me.PostalCode = ""
    Me.WorkPhone = ""
```

```
        Me.HomePhone = ""
        Me.CellPhone = ""
        Me.Email = ""

        Exit Sub

HandleError:
        GeneralErrorHandler Err.Number, Err.Description, CLS_CONTACTS,
                "ClearObject"
        Exit Sub

End Sub
```

7. Add the `Delete` procedure shown in the following code to the `clsProjects` class module:

```
Sub Delete(intCurContId As Integer, blnAddMode As Boolean, rsCont As _
        ADODB.Recordset)

    On Error GoTo HandleError

    Dim strSQLStatement As String
    Dim intResponse As Integer

    'make sure delete should be processed
    If Not ProceedWithDelete(blnAddMode) Then
      Exit Sub
    End If

    'build the SQL statement to delete the contact
    strSQLStatement = BuildSQLDeleteContacts(intCurContId)

    'perform the delete
    Call ProcessUpdate(strSQLStatement, rsCont)
    Exit Sub

HandleError:
    GeneralErrorHandler Err.Number, Err.Description, CLS_CONTACTS, "Delete"
    Exit Sub

End Sub
```

8. Add the `Save` procedure shown in the following code to the `clsProjects` class module:

```
Sub Save(blnAddMode As Boolean, rsCont As ADODB.Recordset)

    On Error GoTo HandleError

    Dim strSQLStatement As String

    'if adding a new record
    If blnAddMode = True Then
```

```
            strSQLStatement = BuildSQLInsertContacts(Me)
        Else
            'if updating a record
            strSQLStatement = BuildSQLUpdateContacts(Me)
        End If

        'perform the insert or update
        Call ProcessUpdate(strSQLStatement, rsCont)
        Exit Sub

HandleError:
        GeneralErrorHandler Err.Number, Err.Description, CLS_CONTACTS, "Save"
        Exit Sub

End Sub
```

9. Make sure to keep saving your changes periodically so they are not lost.

How It Works

The design of the clsContacts class module is similar to that of the clsProjects class module. You first added various local variables to the General Declarations section of the class for storing various property values:

```
Dim intContactIdVal As Integer
Dim strLastNameVal As String
Dim strFirstNameVal As String
Dim strMiddleNameVal As String
Dim strCompanyVal As String
Dim strAddress1Val As String
Dim strAddress2Val As String
Dim strCityVal As String
Dim strRegionVal As String
Dim strPostalCodeVal As String
Dim strWorkPhoneVal As String
Dim strHomePhoneVal As String
Dim strCellPhoneVal As String
Dim strEmailVal As String
```

Next, you added various Get and Let property procedures that are used to retrieve and assign values to the properties of the class:

```
Public Property Get ContactId() As Integer
    On Error Resume Next
    ContactId = intContactIdVal
End Property

Public Property Let ContactId(ByVal Value As Integer)
    On Error Resume Next
    intContactIdVal = Value
End Property

Public Property Get LastName() As String
```

```
         On Error Resume Next
         LastName = strLastNameVal
    End Property

    Public Property Let LastName(ByVal Value As String)
         On Error Resume Next
         strLastNameVal = Value
    End Property
```

Next, various sub procedures and functions were added to serve as methods for the object. For example, the RetrieveContacts function retrieves the contacts records from the database:

```
    Function RetrieveContacts() As ADODB.Recordset

         On Error GoTo HandleError
         Dim strSQLStatement As String
         Dim rsCont As New ADODB.Recordset

         'build the SQL statement to retrieve data
         strSQLStatement = BuildSQLSelectContacts

         'generate the recordset
         Set rsCont = ProcessRecordset(strSQLStatement)

         'return the populated recordset
         Set RetrieveContacts = rsCont
             Exit Function

    HandleError:
         GeneralErrorHandler Err.Number, Err.Description, CLS_CONTACTS, _
                 "RetrieveContacts"
         Exit Function

    End Function
```

The PopulatePropertiesFromRecordset procedure populated the properties of the object from the values in the rsCont recordset:

```
    Sub PopulatePropertiesFromRecordset(rsCont As ADODB.Recordset)

         On Error GoTo HandleError
         'Populate the object with the current record in the
         'recordset
         Me.ContactId = rsCont!intContactId
         Me.LastName = rsCont!txtLastName
         Me.FirstName = rsCont!txtFirstName
         Me.MiddleName = rsCont!txtMiddleName
         Me.Company = rsCont!txtCompany
         Me.Address1 = rsCont!txtAddress1
```

```
        Me.Address2 = rsCont!txtAddress2
        Me.City = rsCont!txtCity
        Me.Region = rsCont!txtRegion
        Me.PostalCode = rsCont!txtPostalCode
        Me.WorkPhone = rsCont!txtWorkPhone
        Me.HomePhone = rsCont!txtHomePhone
        Me.CellPhone = rsCont!txtCellPhone
        Me.Email = rsCont!txtEmail

        Exit Sub

HandleError:
        GeneralErrorHandler Err.Number, Err.Description, CLS_CONTACTS, _
                "PopulatePropertiesFromRecordset"
        Exit Sub

End Sub
```

Similarly, the `PopulatePropertiesFromForm` procedure populated the `contacts` object with the values currently displayed in the controls on the form:

```
Sub PopulatePropertiesFromForm()

        On Error GoTo HandleError
        'Populate the object with the current record in the
        'form

        Me.LastName = Forms("frmContacts")!txtLName
        Me.FirstName = Forms("frmContacts")!txtFName
        Me.MiddleName = Forms("frmContacts")!txtMName
        Me.Company = Forms("frmContacts")!txtCompany
        Me.Address1 = Forms("frmContacts")!txtAddress1
        Me.Address2 = Forms("frmContacts")!txtAddress2
        Me.City = Forms("frmContacts")!txtCity
        Me.Region = Forms("frmContacts")!txtRegion
        Me.PostalCode = Forms("frmContacts")!txtPostalCode
        Me.WorkPhone = Forms("frmContacts")!txtWorkPhone
        Me.HomePhone = Forms("frmContacts")!txtHomePhone
        Me.CellPhone = Forms("frmContacts")!txtCellPhone
        Me.Email = Forms("frmContacts")!txtEmail
        Exit Sub

HandleError:
        GeneralErrorHandler Err.Number, Err.Description, CLS_CONTACTS, _
                "PopulatePropertiesFromForm"
        Exit Sub


End Sub
```

A `ClearObject` procedure was added to reset the values in the object to the initial values so that a new contact record could be stored in the object:

```
Sub ClearObject()

    On Error GoTo HandleError

    'clear the values in the contacts object
    Me.ContactId = 0
    Me.LastName = ""
    Me.FirstName = ""
    Me.MiddleName = ""
    Me.Company = ""
    Me.Address1 = ""
    Me.Address2 = ""
    Me.City = ""
    Me.Region = ""
    Me.PostalCode = ""
    Me.WorkPhone = ""
    Me.HomePhone = ""
    Me.CellPhone = ""
    Me.Email = ""
    Exit Sub

HandleError:
    GeneralErrorHandler Err.Number, Err.Description, CLS_CONTACTS, _
         "ClearObject"
    Exit Sub

End Sub
```

Finally, `Delete` and `Save` procedures were added so that the user can delete and save contact records in the database. The `Delete` procedure first confirms that the user wishes to proceed with the deletion, and then, upon confirmation, proceeds with the delete:

```
Sub Delete(intCurContId As Integer, blnAddMode As Boolean, rsCont As _
         ADODB.Recordset)

    On Error GoTo HandleError

    Dim strSQLStatement As String
    Dim intResponse As Integer

    'make sure delete should be processed
    If Not ProceedWithDelete(blnAddMode) Then
      Exit Sub
    End If

    'build the SQL statement to delete the contact
    strSQLStatement = BuildSQLDeleteContacts(intCurContId)

    'perform the delete
```

```
        Call ProcessUpdate(strSQLStatement, rsCont)

        Exit Sub

HandleError:
        GeneralErrorHandler Err.Number, Err.Description, CLS_CONTACTS, "Delete"
        Exit Sub

End Sub
```

The Save procedure first checks to see if a new record is being added, and if so, generates the proper SQL insert statement. If an existing record is being updated, the proper SQL update statement is generated.

```
    Sub Save(blnAddMode As Boolean, rsCont As ADODB.Recordset)

        On Error GoTo HandleError

        Dim strSQLStatement As String

        'if adding a new record
        If blnAddMode = True Then
            strSQLStatement = BuildSQLInsertContacts(Me)
        Else
            'if updating a record
            strSQLStatement = BuildSQLUpdateContacts(Me)
        End If
```

The ProcessUpdate procedure is then called so the SQL insert or update statement is executed against the database.

```
        'perform the insert or update
        Call ProcessUpdate(strSQLStatement, rsCont)

        Exit Sub

HandleError:
        GeneralErrorHandler Err.Number, Err.Description, CLS_CONTACTS, "Save"
        Exit Sub

End Sub
```

Building the Standard Modules

In the previous section, you created the properties and methods for the Project and Contact objects. In this section, you begin writing the code in the standard modules that conduct a lot of the business logic and data access features for the application. Let's start with building the standard modules.

Try It Out · Building the modBusinessLogic and modDatabaseLogic Modules

The modBusinessLogic module is one of two standard modules you will be creating. The other one is the modDatabaseLogic that will contain calls that are specific to the database. The modBusinessLogic module will not contain any database access calls because you want to keep the data access code in a separate module to make maintenance and future growth easier. You will now turn to the task of creating these modules.

1. Insert a new standard module called modBusinessLogic. Add the following code to the General Declarations of the module:

```
Option Compare Database
Option Explicit

Public intContactProjectLookup As Integer
Public intContactProjectAdd As Integer

Const BUS_LOGIC As String = "modBusinessLogic"

Private Declare Function GetOpenFileName Lib "comdlg32.dll" Alias _
"GetOpenFileNameA" (pOpenfilename As OPENFILENAME) As Long

Private Type OPENFILENAME
    lStructSize As Long
    hwndOwner As Long
    hInstance As Long
    lpstrFilter As String
    lpstrCustomFilter As String
    nMaxCustFilter As Long
    nFilterIndex As Long
    lpstrFile As String
    nMaxFile As Long
    lpstrFileTitle As String
    nMaxFileTitle As Long
    lpstrInitialDir As String
    lpstrTitle As String
    flags As Long
    nFileOffset As Integer
    nFileExtension As Integer
    lpstrDefExt As String
    lCustData As Long
    lpfnHook As Long
    lpTemplateName As String
End Type
Public Declare Function ShellExecute _
    Lib "shell32.dll" _
    Alias "ShellExecuteA" ( _
    ByVal hwnd As Long, _
    ByVal lpOperation As String, _
    ByVal lpFile As String, _
    ByVal lpParameters As String, _
    ByVal lpDirectory As String, _
    ByVal nShowCmd As Long) _
    As Long
```

2. Add the following `OpenFileAttachment` procedure to the `modBusinessLogic` module:

```
Sub OpenFileAttachment(strFile As String)

    On Error GoTo HandleError

        Dim strAction As String
        Dim lngErr As Long

        'open the file attachment
        strAction = "OPEN"
        lngErr = ShellExecute(0, strAction, strFile, "", "", 1)

        Exit Sub

HandleError:
    GeneralErrorHandler Err.Number, Err.Description, BUS_LOGIC, _
        "OpenFileAttachment"
    Exit Sub
End Sub
```

3. Add the following `GetFileNameBrowse` function to the `modBusinessLogic` module:

```
Function GetFileNameBrowse() As String

    On Error GoTo HandleError

    Dim OpenFile As OPENFILENAME
    Dim lReturn As Long
    Dim sFilter As String
    OpenFile.lStructSize = Len(OpenFile)
    OpenFile.hwndOwner = Forms("frmProjects").hwnd

    sFilter = "All Files (*.*)" & Chr(0) & "*.*" & Chr(0)
    OpenFile.lpstrFilter = sFilter
    OpenFile.nFilterIndex = 1
    OpenFile.lpstrFile = String(257, 0)
    OpenFile.nMaxFile = Len(OpenFile.lpstrFile) - 1
    OpenFile.lpstrFileTitle = OpenFile.lpstrFile
    OpenFile.nMaxFileTitle = OpenFile.nMaxFile
    OpenFile.lpstrInitialDir = "C:"
    OpenFile.lpstrTitle = "Browse for an attachment"
    OpenFile.flags = 0
    lReturn = GetOpenFileName(OpenFile)
    If lReturn = 0 Then
        GetFileNameBrowse = ""
    Else
        'return the selected filename
        GetFileNameBrowse = Trim(OpenFile.lpstrFile)
    End If
```

```
        Exit Function

HandleError:
    GeneralErrorHandler Err.Number, Err.Description, BUS_LOGIC, _
        "GetFileNameBrowse"
    Exit Function

End Function
```

4. Add the following four recordset navigation procedures to the modBusinessLogic module:

```
Sub MoveToFirstRecord(intRecCounter As Integer, rsRecordset As ADODB.Recordset, _
                objObject As Object, blnAddMode As Boolean)

    On Error GoTo HandleError

    'move to the first record in the local disconnected recordset
    If Not rsRecordset.BOF And Not rsRecordset.EOF Then
        rsRecordset.MoveFirst
        intRecCounter = 1
        'add code to populate object with new current record
        objObject.PopulatePropertiesFromRecordset rsRecordset

        blnAddMode = False
    End If
    Exit Sub


HandleError:
        GeneralErrorHandler Err.Number, Err.Description, BUS_LOGIC, _
            "MoveToFirstRecord"
        Exit Sub

End Sub

Sub MoveToLastRecord(intRecCounter As Integer, rsRecordset As ADODB.Recordset, _
                objObject As Object, blnAddMode As Boolean)

    On Error GoTo HandleError
    'move to the last record in the local disconnected recordset
    If Not rsRecordset.BOF And Not rsRecordset.EOF Then
        rsRecordset.MoveLast
        intRecCounter = rsRecordset.RecordCount
        'add code to populate object with new current record
        objObject.PopulatePropertiesFromRecordset rsRecordset
        blnAddMode = False

    End If

    Exit Sub

HandleError:
```

```
        GeneralErrorHandler Err.Number, Err.Description, BUS_LOGIC, "MoveToLastRecord"
        Exit Sub

End Sub

Sub MoveToPreviousRecord(intRecCounter As Integer, rsRecordset As _
                ADODB.Recordset, objObject As Object, blnAddMode As Boolean)
        On Error GoTo HandleError
    'move to the previous record in the local disconnected recordset
    'if not already at the beginning
    If Not rsRecordset.BOF Then
        rsRecordset.MovePrevious
        intRecCounter = intRecCounter - 1

        blnAddMode = False

        'make sure not past beginning of recordset now
        If Not rsRecordset.BOF Then
            'add code to populate object with new current record
            objObject.PopulatePropertiesFromRecordset rsRecordset

        Else
            'at beginning of recordset so move to next record
            rsRecordset.MoveNext
                intRecCounter = intRecCounter + 1
        End If

    End If
        Exit Sub

HandleError:
    GeneralErrorHandler Err.Number, Err.Description, BUS_LOGIC, _
        "MoveToPreviousRecord"
    Exit Sub

End Sub

Sub MoveToNextRecord(intRecCounter As Integer, rsRecordset As ADODB.Recordset, _
                objObject As Object, blnAddMode As Boolean)

    On Error GoTo HandleError
    'move to the next record in the local disconnected recordset
    'if not already at the end
    If Not rsRecordset.EOF Then
        rsRecordset.MoveNext
        intRecCounter = intRecCounter + 1
        blnAddMode = False

        'make sure not past end of recordset
        If Not rsRecordset.EOF Then
            'add code to populate object with new current record
            objObject.PopulatePropertiesFromRecordset rsRecordset
        Else

            'at end of recordset so move back one
```

```
            rsRecordset.MovePrevious
            intRecCounter = intRecCounter - 1
        End If

    End If

    Exit Sub

HandleError:
    GeneralErrorHandler Err.Number, Err.Description, BUS_LOGIC, "MoveToNextRecord"
    Exit Sub

End Sub
```

5. Add the following `ProceedWithDelete` function to the `modBusinessLogic` module:

```
Function ProceedWithDelete(blnAddMode As Boolean) As Boolean

    On Error GoTo HandleError
    Dim blnProceed As Boolean
    Dim intResponse As Integer

    blnProceed = True

    'don't let the user issue a delete command if in add mode
    If blnAddMode = True Then
        blnProceed = False
        ProceedWithDelete = blnProceed
        Exit Function
    End If

    'confirm that user really wants to delete record
    intResponse = MsgBox("Are you sure you want to delete this record?", vbYesNo)

    'if the user cancels delete, then exit this procedure
    If intResponse = vbNo Then
        blnProceed = False

        ProceedWithDelete = blnProceed

        Exit Function
    End If

    ProceedWithDelete = blnProceed

    Exit Function

HandleError:
    ProceedWithDelete = False
    GeneralErrorHandler Err.Number, Err.Description, BUS_LOGIC, _
            "ProceedWithDelete"
    Exit Function

End Function
```

6. Add the following `GeneralErrorHandler` procedure to the `modBusinessLogic` module. This module will handle all errors for the application and will be referenced in each procedure or function:

```
Public Sub GeneralErrorHandler(lngErrNumber As Long, strErrDesc As String, _
                strModuleSource As String, strProcedureSource As String)

    On Error Resume Next
    Dim strMessage As String

    'build the error message string from the parameters passed in
    strMessage = "An error has occurred in the application."
    strMessage = strMessage & vbCrLf & "Error Number: " & lngErrNumber
    strMessage = strMessage & vbCrLf & "Error Description: " & strErrDesc
    strMessage = strMessage & vbCrLf & "Module Source: " & strModuleSource
    strMessage = strMessage & vbCrLf & "Procedure Source: " & strProcedureSource

    'display the message to the user
    MsgBox strMessage, vbCritical

    Exit Sub

End Sub
```

7. Save your changes to the `modBusinessLogic` module.

8. Insert a new standard module called `modDatabaseLogic`. Add the following code to the General Declarations of the module:

```
Option Compare Database
Option Explicit
Dim cnConn As ADODB.Connection
Dim strConnection As String
Const DB_LOGIC As String = "modDatabaseLogic"
```

9. Add the following `ExecuteSQLCommand` procedure to the `modDatabaseLogic` module:

```
Sub ExecuteSQLCommand(strSQL As String)

    On Error GoTo HandleError

    'the purpose of this procedure is to execute
    'a SQL statement that does not return any
    'rows against the database.

    Dim cmdCommand As ADODB.Command
    Set cmdCommand = New ADODB.Command

    'set the command to the current connection
    Set cmdCommand.ActiveConnection = cnConn
```

```
        'set the SQL statement to the command text
        cmdCommand.CommandText = strSQL
        'execute the command against the database
        cmdCommand.Execute

            Exit Sub

HandleError:
        GeneralErrorHandler Err.Number, Err.Description, DB_LOGIC, "ExecuteSQLCommand"
        Exit Sub

End Sub
```

10. Add the following procedures to the `modDatabaseLogic` module. You will need to modify the `strConnection` string, shown in the following code, to point to the path on your computer where the `ProjectTrackerDb` you created at the beginning of this chapter is located.

```
Sub OpenDbConnection()

    On Error GoTo HandleError

    strConnection = "Provider=Microsoft.ACE.OLEDB.12.0;" & _
                    "Data Source=" & CurrentProject.Path &
                    "ProjectTrackerDb.accdb;"

        'create an new connection instance and open it using the connection string
        Set cnConn = New ADODB.Connection
        cnConn.Open strConnection

    Exit Sub

HandleError:
    GeneralErrorHandler Err.Number, Err.Description, DB_LOGIC, "OpenDbConnection"
    Exit Sub

End Sub

Sub CloseDbConnection()

    On Error GoTo HandleError

    'close the database connection
    cnConn.Close
    Set cnConn = Nothing

    Exit Sub

HandleError:
    GeneralErrorHandler Err.Number, Err.Description, DB_LOGIC, "CloseDbConnection"
    Exit Sub

End Sub
```

11. Add the following `RequeryRecordset` procedure to the `modDatabaseLogic` module:

```
Sub RequeryRecordset(rsRecordset As ADODB.Recordset)

    On Error GoTo HandleError

    'repopulate the recordset to make sure it contains
    'the most current values from the database.  also
    'disconnect the recordset
    Set rsRecordset.ActiveConnection = cnConn
    rsRecordset.Requery
    Set rsRecordset.ActiveConnection = Nothing

        Exit Sub


HandleError:
    GeneralErrorHandler Err.Number, Err.Description, DB_LOGIC, "RequeryRecordset"
    Exit Sub

End Sub
```

12. Add the following procedures to the `modDatabaseLogic` module. These procedures build SQL statements that are used to make updates to the `tblContacts` table.

```
Function BuildSQLInsertContacts(objCurrContact As clsContacts) As String

    On Error GoTo HandleError

    Dim strSQLInsert As String

    'create SQL to insert a new record into the database
    'containing the values in the Contacts object
    strSQLInsert = "INSERT INTO tblContacts(" & _
        "txtLastName, txtFirstName, txtMiddleName, " & _
        "txtCompany, txtAddress1, txtAddress2, " & _
        "txtCity, txtRegion, txtPostalCode, " & _
        "txtWorkPhone, txtHomePhone, txtCellPhone, " & _
        "txtEmail) VALUES (" & _
        "'" & objCurrContact.LastName & "', " & _
        "'" & objCurrContact.FirstName & "', " & _
        "'" & objCurrContact.MiddleName & "', " & _
        "'" & objCurrContact.Company & "', " & _
        "'" & objCurrContact.Address1 & "', " & _
        "'" & objCurrContact.Address2 & "', " & _
        "'" & objCurrContact.City & "', " & _
        "'" & objCurrContact.Region & "', " & _
        "'" & objCurrContact.PostalCode & "', " & _
        "'" & objCurrContact.WorkPhone & "', " & _
        "'" & objCurrContact.HomePhone & "', " & _
        "'" & objCurrContact.CellPhone & "', " & _
        "'" & objCurrContact.Email & "') "
```

```
            BuildSQLInsertContacts = strSQLInsert

        Exit Function

HandleError:
    GeneralErrorHandler Err.Number, Err.Description, DB_LOGIC, _
"BuildSQLInsertContacts"
    Exit Function

End Function
Function BuildSQLUpdateContacts(objCurrContact As clsContacts) As String

        On Error GoTo HandleError

        Dim strSQLUpdate As String

    'create SQL to update the existing record in the
    'database with the values in the contact object
    strSQLUpdate = "UPDATE tblContacts SET " & _
        "txtLastName = '" & objCurrContact.LastName & "', " & _
        "txtFirstName = '" & objCurrContact.FirstName & "', " & -_
        "txtMiddleName = '" & objCurrContact.MiddleName & "', " & _
        "txtcompany = '" & objCurrContact.Company & "', " & _
        "txtAddress1 = '" & objCurrContact.Address1 & "', " & _
        "txtAddress2 = '" & objCurrContact.Address2 & "', " & _
        "txtCity = '" & objCurrContact.City & "', " & _
        "txtRegion = '" & objCurrContact.Region & "', " & _
        "txtPostalCode = '" & objCurrContact.PostalCode & "', " & _
        "txtWorkPhone = '" & objCurrContact.WorkPhone & "', " & _
        "txtHomePhone = '" & objCurrContact.HomePhone & "', " & _
        "txtCellPhone = '" & objCurrContact.CellPhone & "', " & _
        "txtEmail = '" & objCurrContact.Email & "' " & -_
        "WHERE intContactId = " & objCurrContact.ContactId

    BuildSQLUpdateContacts = strSQLUpdate
        Exit Function

HandleError:
    GeneralErrorHandler Err.Number, Err.Description, DB_LOGIC, _
        "BuildSQLUpdateContacts"
    Exit Function

End Function

Function BuildSQLDeleteContacts(intId As Integer) As String

    On Error GoTo HandleError
    'generate SQL command to delete current record
    Dim strSQLDelete As String
    strSQLDelete = "DELETE FROM tblContacts WHERE intContactId = " & intId
        BuildSQLDeleteContacts = strSQLDelete

    Exit Function

HandleError:
```

```
        GeneralErrorHandler Err.Number, Err.Description, DB_LOGIC, _
            "BuildSQLDeleteContacts"
    Exit Function

End Function

Function BuildSQLSelectContacts() As String

    On Error GoTo HandleError
    Dim strSQLRetrieve As String
    'if the intId is not included, retrieve all contacts
    If intContactProjectLookup = 0 Then
    'generate SQL command to retrieve contacts records
    strSQLRetrieve = "SELECT * FROM tblContacts " & _
            "ORDER BY txtLastName, txtFirstName, txtMiddleName"
    Else
    'look up particular contacts record
    strSQLRetrieve = "SELECT * FROM tblContacts " & _
            "WHERE intContactId = " & intContactProjectLookup & _
            " ORDER BY txtLastName, txtFirstName, txtMiddleName"
        End If

        BuildSQLSelectContacts = strSQLRetrieve

        Exit Function

HandleError:
    GeneralErrorHandler Err.Number, Err.Description, DB_LOGIC, _
            "BuildSQLSelectContacts"
    Exit Function

End Function
```

13. Add the following procedures to the modDatabaseLogic module. These procedures build SQL statements that are used to make updates to the tblProjects table.

```
Function BuildSQLInsertProjects(objCurrProject As clsProjects) As String

    On Error GoTo HandleError

        Dim strSQLInsert As String
        'create SQL to insert a new record into the database
    'containing the values in the Projects object
    strSQLInsert = "INSERT INTO tblProjects(" & _
        "txtProjectTitle, txtProjectDescription, txtPriority, " & _
        "txtReferenceNum, curMoneyBudget, curMoneyToDate, " & _
        "intHoursBudget, intHoursToDate, dtDateDue, " & _
        "txtStatus) VALUES (" & _
        "'" & objCurrProject.ProjectTitle & "', " & _
        "'" & objCurrProject.ProjectDescription & "', " & _
        "'" & objCurrProject.Priority & "', " & _
        "'" & objCurrProject.ReferenceNum & "', " & _
        objCurrProject.MoneyBudget & ", " & _
```

```
            objCurrProject.MoneyToDate & ", " & _
        "" & objCurrProject.HoursBudget & ", " & _
        "" & objCurrProject.HoursToDate & ", " & _
        "'" & objCurrProject.DateDue & "', " & _
        "'" & objCurrProject.Status & "') "

        BuildSQLInsertProjects = strSQLInsert

        Exit Function

HandleError:
    GeneralErrorHandler Err.Number, Err.Description, DB_LOGIC, _
        "BuildSQLInsertProjects"
    Exit Function

End Function

Function BuildSQLUpdateProjects(objCurrProject As clsProjects) As String

    On Error GoTo HandleError

        Dim strSQLUpdate As String

        'create SQL to update the existing record in the
    'database with the values in the Project object

    strSQLUpdate = "UPDATE tblProjects SET " & _
        "txtProjectTitle = '" & objCurrProject.ProjectTitle & "', " & _
        "txtProjectDescription = '" & objCurrProject.ProjectDescription & "', " & _
        "txtPriority = '" & objCurrProject.Priority & "', " & _
        "txtReferenceNum = '" & objCurrProject.ReferenceNum & "', " & _
        "curMoneyBudget = '" & objCurrProject.MoneyBudget & "', " & _
        "curMoneyToDate = '" & objCurrProject.MoneyToDate & "', " & _
        "intHoursBudget = " & objCurrProject.HoursBudget & ", " & _
        "intHoursToDate = " & objCurrProject.HoursToDate & ", " & _
        "dtDateDue = '" & objCurrProject.DateDue & "', " & _
        "txtStatus = '" & objCurrProject.Status & "' " & _
        "WHERE intProjectId = " & objCurrProject.ProjectId
        BuildSQLUpdateProjects = strSQLUpdate
        Exit Function

HandleError:
    GeneralErrorHandler Err.Number, Err.Description, DB_LOGIC, _
        "BuildSQLUpdateProjects"
    Exit Function

End Function

Function BuildSQLDeleteProjects(intId As Integer) As String

    On Error GoTo HandleError
        'generate SQL command to delete current record
    Dim strSQLDelete As String
    strSQLDelete = "DELETE FROM tblProjects WHERE intProjectId = " & intId
```

```
            BuildSQLDeleteProjects = strSQLDelete
        Exit Function

HandleError:
    GeneralErrorHandler Err.Number, Err.Description, DB_LOGIC, _
            "BuildSQLDeleteProjects"
    Exit Function

End Function

Function BuildSQLSelectProjects(blnAllRecords As Boolean) As String

    On Error GoTo HandleError
        'generate SQL command to retrieve projects records
    Dim strSQLRetrieve As String
        'if option to display all records is selected in toggle button
    If blnAllRecords Then

            strSQLRetrieve = "SELECT * FROM tblProjects " & _
            "ORDER BY intProjectId"

    Else
        'show only the unclosed projects
        strSQLRetrieve = "SELECT * " & _
            "FROM tblProjects WHERE txtStatus <> 'Closed' " & _
            "ORDER BY intProjectId "
                End If
        BuildSQLSelectProjects = strSQLRetrieve
        Exit Function

HandleError:
    GeneralErrorHandler Err.Number, Err.Description, DB_LOGIC, _
            "BuildSQLSelectProjects"
    Exit Function

End Function

Function BuildSQLSelectAll(strTableName) As String

    On Error GoTo HandleError

        Dim strSQLSelect As String

        'use this for selecting all records in a table
    strSQLSelect = "SELECT * FROM " & strTableName

        BuildSQLSelectAll = strSQLSelect
        Exit Function

HandleError:
    GeneralErrorHandler Err.Number, Err.Description, DB_LOGIC, "BuildSQLSelectAll"
    Exit Function

End Function
```

14. Add the following `ProcessRecordset` procedure to the `modDatabaseLogic` module:

```
Function ProcessRecordset(strSQLStatement As String) As ADODB.Recordset

    On Error GoTo HandleError

        'open the connection to the database
    Call OpenDbConnection

        'create a new instance of a recordset
    Dim rsCont As New ADODB.Recordset

        'set various properties of the recordset
    With rsCont
        'specify a cursortype and lock type that will allow updates

        .CursorType = adOpenKeyset
        .CursorLocation = adUseClient
        .LockType = adLockBatchOptimistic
        'populate the recordset based on SQL statement
        .Open strSQLStatement, cnConn
        'disconnect the recordset
        .ActiveConnection = Nothing
        'sort the recordset
    End With

        'close the connection to the database
    Call CloseDbConnection

        'return the recordset
    Set ProcessRecordset = rsCont
        Exit Function

HandleError:
    GeneralErrorHandler Err.Number, Err.Description, DB_LOGIC, "ProcessRecordset"
    Exit Function

End Function
```

15. Add the following `ProcessUpdate` procedure to the `modDatabaseLogic` module:

```
Sub ProcessUpdate(strSQLStatement As String, Optional rsRecordset As
ADODB.Recordset)

    On Error GoTo HandleError

        'This procedure is used to handle updates to the database

        'open the connection to the database
    Call OpenDbConnection

        'execute the command against the database
```

```
          Call ExecuteSQLCommand(strSQLStatement)

              If Not rsRecordset Is Nothing Then
              'repopulate the recordset with most current data
              Call RequeryRecordset(rsRecordset)
          End If
          'close the connection to the database
          Call CloseDbConnection

              Exit Sub

      HandleError:
          GeneralErrorHandler Err.Number, Err.Description, DB_LOGIC, "ProcessUpdate"
          Exit Sub

      End Sub
```

16. Add the following procedures to the `modDatabaseLogic` module that handle deleting records from the cross-reference tables that store comments, contacts, and file attachments for each project:

```
Function BuildSQLDeleteProjectsComments(intProjectId As Integer) As String

     'build SQL statement for deletion

         On Error GoTo HandleError

     Dim strSQLStatement As String

     strSQLStatement = "DELETE FROM tblProjectsComments WHERE intProjectId = " & _
                    intProjectId

     BuildSQLDeleteProjectsComments = strSQLStatement
     Exit Function

HandleError:
     GeneralErrorHandler Err.Number, Err.Description, DB_LOGIC, _
          "BuildSQLDeleteProjectsComments"
     Exit Function

End Function

Function BuildSQLDeleteProjectsContacts(intProjectId As Integer) As String

         'build SQL statement for deletion
         On Error GoTo HandleError

         Dim strSQLStatement As String

         strSQLStatement = "DELETE FROM tblProjectsContacts WHERE intProjectId = "& _
```

```
                        intProjectId

        BuildSQLDeleteProjectsContacts = strSQLStatement

        Exit Function

HandleError:
    GeneralErrorHandler Err.Number, Err.Description, DB_LOGIC, _
            "BuildSQLDeleteProjectsContacts"
    Exit Function

End Function

Function BuildSQLDeleteProjectsAttachments(intProjectId As Integer) As String

        'build SQL statement for deletion
            On Error GoTo HandleError


        Dim strSQLStatement As String

        strSQLStatement = "DELETE FROM tblProjectsFileAttachments WHERE " & _
                    "intProjectId = " & intProjectId
        BuildSQLDeleteProjectsAttachments = strSQLStatement

        Exit Function

HandleError:
    GeneralErrorHandler Err.Number, Err.Description, DB_LOGIC, _
            "BuildSQLDeleteProjectsAttachments"
    Exit Function

End Function
```

17. Add the following procedures to the `modDatabaseLogic` module that handle inserting records into the cross-reference tables that store comments, contacts, and file attachments for each project:

```
Function BuildSQLInsertProjectsComments(intProjectId As Integer, strComment _
        As String) As String

 'build SQL statement for insertion

 On Error GoTo HandleError

 Dim strSQLStatement As String

 strSQLStatement = "INSERT INTO tblProjectsComments(intProjectId, txtComment)" & _
        "VALUES(" & intProjectId & ", '" & strComment & "')"

 BuildSQLInsertProjectsComments = strSQLStatement
```

```
    Exit Function

HandleError:
    GeneralErrorHandler Err.Number, Err.Description, DB_LOGIC, _
        "BuildSQLInsertProjectsComments"
    Exit Function

End Function

Functionn BuildSQLInsertProjectsContacts(intContactId As Integer,intProjectId _
        As Integer) As String

    'build SQL statement for insertion
        On Error GoTo HandleError

        Dim strSQLStatement As String

        strSQLStatement = "INSERT INTO tblProjectsContacts(intContactId, " & _
        "intProjectId) VALUES(" & intContactId & ", " & intProjectId & ")"

    BuildSQLInsertProjectsContacts = strSQLStatement
        Exit Function

HandleError:
    GeneralErrorHandler Err.Number, Err.Description, DB_LOGIC, _
        "BuildSQLInsertProjectsContacts"
    Exit Function

End Function

Function BuildSQLInsertProjectsAttachments(intProjectId As Integer, _
        strFileDescription As String, strFileName As String) As String

    'build SQL statement for insertion
        On Error GoTo HandleError
        Dim strSQLStatement As String
        strSQLStatement = "INSERT INTO tblProjectsFileAttachments(intProjectId," & _
        "txtFileDescription, txtFileName) VALUES (" & _
        intProjectId & ", '" & strFileDescription & "', '" & strFileName & "')"
        BuildSQLInsertProjectsAttachments = strSQLStatement
        Exit Function

HandleError:
    GeneralErrorHandler Err.Number, Err.Description, DB_LOGIC, _
        "BuildSQLInsertProjectsAttachments"
    Exit Function

End Function
```

18.   Save your changes to the modDatabaseLogic module.

How It Works

You created the modBusinessLogic module for processing the business logic for the application, and the modDatabaseLogic module for communicating with the database. In the General Declarations section of the modBusinessLogic module, you added some declarations to external functions. The GetOpenFileName external function is used to display the File Open dialog box that allows you to browse the file system and select a file. This function is called later in the code to open the dialog box for selecting an attachment to associate with a particular project record.

```
Private Declare Function GetOpenFileName Lib "comdlg32.dll" Alias __
"GetOpenFileNameA" (pOpenfilename As OPENFILENAME) As Long

Private Type OPENFILENAME
  lStructSize As Long
  hwndOwner As Long
  hInstance As Long
  lpstrFilter As String
  lpstrCustomFilter As String
  nMaxCustFilter As Long
  nFilterIndex As Long
  lpstrFile As String
  nMaxFile As Long
  lpstrFileTitle As String
  nMaxFileTitle As Long
  lpstrInitialDir As String
  lpstrTitle As String
  flags As Long
  nFileOffset As Integer
  nFileExtension As Integer
  lpstrDefExt As String
  lCustData As Long
  lpfnHook As Long
  lpTemplateName As String
End Type
```

The ShellExecute external function is used to launch an external program:

```
Public Declare Function ShellExecute _
    Lib "shell32.dll" _
    Alias "ShellExecuteA" ( _
    ByVal hwnd As Long, _
    ByVal lpOperation As String, _
    ByVal lpFile As String, _
    ByVal lpParameters As String, _
    ByVal lpDirectory As String, _
    ByVal nShowCmd As Long) _
    As Long
```

The `OpenFileAttachment` procedure calls the `ShellExecute` external function in order to preview a particular attachment in its native application:

```
Sub OpenFileAttachment(strFile As String)

    On Error GoTo HandleError

        Dim strAction As String
        Dim lngErr As Long

        'open the file attachment
        strAction = "OPEN"
        lngErr = ShellExecute(0, strAction, strFile, "", "", 1)

        Exit Sub

HandleError:
    GeneralErrorHandler Err.Number, Err.Description, BUS_LOGIC, _
        "OpenFileAttachment"
    Exit Sub
End Sub
```

As I mentioned previously, the `GetOpenFileName` external function is used to open a file browser dialog box. This function is called from the `GetFileNameBrowse` function to allow a user to browse for a file attachment to associate with a project:

```
Function GetFileNameBrowse() As String

    On Error GoTo HandleError

    Dim OpenFile As OPENFILENAME
    Dim lReturn As Long
    Dim sFilter As String
    OpenFile.lStructSize = Len(OpenFile)
    OpenFile.hwndOwner = Forms("frmProjects").hwnd
    sFilter = "All Files (*.*)" & Chr(0) & "*.*" & Chr(0)
    OpenFile.lpstrFilter = sFilter
    OpenFile.nFilterIndex = 1
    OpenFile.lpstrFile = String(257, 0)
    OpenFile.nMaxFile = Len(OpenFile.lpstrFile) - 1
    OpenFile.lpstrFileTitle = OpenFile.lpstrFile
    OpenFile.nMaxFileTitle = OpenFile.nMaxFile
    OpenFile.lpstrInitialDir = "C:"
    OpenFile.lpstrTitle = "Browse for an attachment"
    OpenFile.flags = 0
    lReturn = GetOpenFileName(OpenFile)
    If lReturn = 0 Then
        GetFileNameBrowse = ""
    Else
```

```
    'return the selected filename
       GetFileNameBrowse = Trim(OpenFile.lpstrFile)
    End If

       Exit Function

HandleError:
    GeneralErrorHandler Err.Number, Err.Description, BUS_LOGIC, "GetFileNameBrowse"
    Exit Function

End Function
```

The code for these external functions is a little bit complicated. It is okay if you do not understand exactly how they work. I just wanted to include the functionality to show you how powerful your Access applications can be.

Next, you added four recordset navigation procedures to the `modBusinessLogic` module. For example, the `MoveToFirstRecord` procedure is responsible for moving to the first record in the local disconnected recordset:

```
Sub MoveToFirstRecord(intRecCounter As Integer, rsRecordset As ADODB.Recordset, _
                  objObject As Object, blnAddMode As Boolean)

    On Error GoTo HandleError


    'move to the first record in the local disconnected recordset
    If Not rsRecordset.BOF And Not rsRecordset.EOF Then
        rsRecordset.MoveFirst
        intRecCounter = 1
```

Once the record position changes, the object is populated with the new current record:

```
        'add code to populate object with new current record
        objObject.PopulatePropertiesFromRecordset rsRecordset

        blnAddMode = False
    End If

    Exit Sub
HandleError:
    GeneralErrorHandler Err.Number, Err.Description, BUS_LOGIC, _
        "MoveToFirstRecord"
    Exit Sub

End Sub
```

The `ProceedWithDelete` function prompts the user to confirm that she wishes to proceed with a delete operation, such as deleting a project record from `frmProjects` or deleting a contact record from `frmContacts`:

```
Function ProceedWithDelete(blnAddMode As Boolean) As Boolean

    On Error GoTo HandleError

        Dim blnProceed As Boolean
    Dim intResponse As Integer


        blnProceed = True
```

If the user is in add mode, that user cannot issue a delete command because the record has not even been added yet:

```
'don't let the user issue a delete command if in add mode
If blnAddMode = True Then
    blnProceed = False
    ProceedWithDelete = blnProceed
    Exit Function
End If
```

Then, the user is prompted to confirm that she wishes to proceed with the delete operation:

```
'confirm that user really wants to delete record
intResponse = MsgBox("Are you sure you want to delete this record?", vbYesNo)
```

The value returned from the `MsgBox` function is then analyzed to determine whether the user chose the option to proceed with the delete:

```
    'if the user cancels delete, then exit this procedure
    If intResponse = vbNo Then
        blnProceed = False
        ProceedWithDelete = blnProceed
        Exit Function
    End If

        ProceedWithDelete = blnProceed

        Exit Function

HandleError:
    ProceedWithDelete = False
    GeneralErrorHandler Err.Number, Err.Description, BUS_LOGIC, "ProceedWithDelete"
    Exit Function

End Function
```

The last procedure added to the modBusinessLogic module was the GeneralErrorHandler procedure. This module handles all errors for the application and is referenced in each procedure or function, as you have probably noticed by now.

```
Public Sub GeneralErrorHandler(lngErrNumber As Long, strErrDesc As String, _
                    strModuleSource As String, strProcedureSource As String)

    On Error Resume Next

        Dim strMessage As String
         'build the error message string from the parameters passed in
    strMessage = "An error has occurred in the application."
    strMessage = strMessage & vbCrLf & "Error Number: " & lngErrNumber
    strMessage = strMessage & vbCrLf & "Error Description: " & strErrDesc
    strMessage = strMessage & vbCrLf & "Module Source: " & strModuleSource
    strMessage = strMessage & vbCrLf & "Procedure Source: " & strProcedureSource

        'display the message to the user
    MsgBox strMessage, vbCritical
        Exit Sub

End Sub
```

Next, you created a standard module called modDatabaseLogic. You added various procedures to the module for interacting with the database. For example, the ExecuteSQLCommand procedure is responsible for executing a SQL statement against the database that does not return any rows. Examples of these types of statements include insert, update, and delete statements.

```
Sub ExecuteSQLCommand(strSQL As String)

    On Error GoTo HandleError

    'the purpose of this procedure is to execute
    'a SQL statement that does not return any
    'rows against the database.

        Dim cmdCommand As ADODB.Command
    Set cmdCommand = New ADODB.Command

        'set the command to the current connection
    Set cmdCommand.ActiveConnection = cnConn
    'set the SQL statement to the command text
    cmdCommand.CommandText = strSQL
    'execute the command against the database
    cmdCommand.Execute

        Exit Sub

HandleError:
    GeneralErrorHandler Err.Number, Err.Description, DB_LOGIC, _
```

```
          "ExecuteSQLCommand"

     Exit Sub

End Sub
```

Next, you added the `OpenDbConnection` and `CloseDbConnection` procedures for opening and closing database connections. In the `OpenDbConnection` procedure, you may have had to modify the `strConnection` string to point to the path where the `ProjectTrackerDb`, which you created at the beginning of this chapter, is located.

```
Sub OpenDbConnection()

    On Error GoTo HandleError

        strConnection = "Provider=Microsoft.ACE.OLEDB.12.0;" & _
                    "Data Source=" & CurrentProject.Path &
"ProjectTrackerDb.accdb;"

            'create a new connection instance and open it using the connection
string
        Set cnConn = New ADODB.Connection
        cnConn.Open strConnection

        Exit Sub

HandleError:
    GeneralErrorHandler Err.Number, Err.Description, DB_LOGIC, "OpenDbConnection"
    Exit Sub

End Sub
```

The `RequeryRecordset` procedure was then added to the `modDatabaseLogic` module to repopulate the values in the recordset with the current data in the underlying database:

```
Sub RequeryRecordset(rsRecordset As ADODB.Recordset)

    On Error GoTo HandleError

'repopulate the recordset to make sure it contains
    'the most current values from the database.  also
    'disconnect the recordset
    Set rsRecordset.ActiveConnection = cnConn
    rsRecordset.Requery
    Set rsRecordset.ActiveConnection = Nothing

        Exit Sub

HandleError:
    GeneralErrorHandler Err.Number, Err.Description, DB_LOGIC, "RequeryRecordset"
```

```
        Exit Sub

    End Sub
```

Next, you added various procedures for creating SQL statements for inserting, updating, deleting, and selecting records from the `tblContacts` table. For example, the `BuildSQLInsertContacts` procedure creates a SQL statement from the values in the `objCurrContact` object:

```
Function BuildSQLInsertContacts(objCurrContact As clsContacts) As String

    On Error GoTo HandleError

        Dim strSQLInsert As String

        'create SQL to insert a new record into the database
    'containing the values in the Contacts object
    strSQLInsert = "INSERT INTO tblContacts(" & _
        "txtLastName, txtFirstName, txtMiddleName, " & _
        "txtCompany, txtAddress1, txtAddress2, " & _
        "txtCity, txtRegion, txtPostalCode, " & _
        "txtWorkPhone, txtHomePhone, txtCellPhone, " & _
        "txtEmail) VALUES (" & _
        "'" & objCurrContact.LastName & "', " & _
        "'" & objCurrContact.FirstName & "', " & _
        "'" & objCurrContact.MiddleName & "', " & _
        "'" & objCurrContact.Company & "', " & _
        "'" & objCurrContact.Address1 & "', " & _
        "'" & objCurrContact.Address2 & "', " & _
        "'" & objCurrContact.City & "', " & _
        "'" & objCurrContact.Region & "', " & _
        "'" & objCurrContact.PostalCode & "', " & _
        "'" & objCurrContact.WorkPhone & "', " & _
        "'" & objCurrContact.HomePhone & "', " & _
        "'" & objCurrContact.CellPhone & "', " & _
        "'" & objCurrContact.Email & "') "

        BuildSQLInsertContacts = strSQLInsert
        Exit Function

HandleError:
    GeneralErrorHandler Err.Number, Err.Description, DB_LOGIC, _

            "BuildSQLInsertContacts"
    Exit Function

End Function
```

Similarly, you added various procedures for creating SQL statements. You created procedures for inserting, updating, and deleting project records, for selecting unclosed project records, and for selecting all project records. For example, the `BuildSQLInsertProjects` procedure creates a SQL statement from the values in the `objCurrProject` object:

```
Function BuildSQLInsertProjects(objCurrProject As clsProjects) As String

    On Error GoTo HandleError

        Dim strSQLInsert As String

        'create SQL to insert a new record into the database
    'containing the values in the Projects object
    strSQLInsert = "INSERT INTO tblProjects(" & _
        "txtProjectTitle, txtProjectDescription, txtPriority, " & _
        "txtReferenceNum, curMoneyBudget, curMoneyToDate, " & _
        "intHoursBudget, intHoursToDate, dtDateDue, " & _
        "txtStatus) VALUES (" & _
        "'" & objCurrProject.ProjectTitle & "', " & _
        "'" & objCurrProject.ProjectDescription & "', " & _
        "'" & objCurrProject.Priority & "', " & _
        "'" & objCurrProject.ReferenceNum & "', " & _
        objCurrProject.MoneyBudget & ", " & _
        objCurrProject.MoneyToDate & ", " & _
        "" & objCurrProject.HoursBudget & ", " & _
        "" & objCurrProject.HoursToDate & ", " & _
        "'" & objCurrProject.DateDue & "', " & _
        "'" & objCurrProject.Status & "') "

        BuildSQLInsertProjects = strSQLInsert
        Exit Function

HandleError:
    GeneralErrorHandler Err.Number, Err.Description, DB_LOGIC, _
            "BuildSQLInsertProjects"
    Exit Function

End Function
```

The `ProcessRecordset` procedure accepted a SQL statement as a parameter and executed that statement against the database. The database connection was opened, the SQL statement was executed, and the database connection was then closed. The recordset that was populated from the results of the SQL statement was returned to the calling function.

```
Function ProcessRecordset(strSQLStatement As String) As ADODB.Recordset

    On Error GoTo HandleError

    'open the connection to the database
    Call OpenDbConnection

        'create a new instance of a recordset
    Dim rsCont As New ADODB.Recordset

        'set various properties of the recordset
    With rsCont
        'specify a cursortype and lock type that will allow updates
```

```
            .CursorType = adOpenKeyset
            .CursorLocation = adUseClient
            .LockType = adLockBatchOptimistic
            'populate the recordset based on SQL statement
            .Open strSQLStatement, cnConn
            'disconnect the recordset
            .ActiveConnection = Nothing
        End With

            'close the connection to the database
        Call CloseDbConnection

            'return the recordset
        Set ProcessRecordset = rsCont

            Exit Function

    HandleError:
        GeneralErrorHandler Err.Number, Err.Description, DB_LOGIC, "ProcessRecordset"
        Exit Function

    End Function
```

Next, the ProcessUpdate procedure was added to the modDatabaseLogic module for processing various updates to the database. This procedure is similar to ProcessRecordset, only it does not return any values after executing the SQL statement.

```
    Sub ProcessUpdate(strSQLStatement As String, Optional rsRecordset As
    ADODB.Recordset)

        On Error GoTo HandleError

            'This procedure is used to handle updates to the database

            'open the connection to the database
        Call OpenDbConnection

            'execute the command against the database
        Call ExecuteSQLCommand(strSQLStatement)

            If Not rsRecordset Is Nothing Then
            'repopulate the recordset with most current data
            Call RequeryRecordset(rsRecordset)
        End If

    'close the connection to the database
        Call CloseDbConnection
            Exit Sub

    HandleError:
        GeneralErrorHandler Err.Number, Err.Description, DB_LOGIC, "ProcessUpdate"
        Exit Sub

    End Sub
```

Next, various functions were added to handle deleting records from the cross-reference tables that store comments, contacts, and file attachments for each project. For example, the `BuildSQLDelete ProjectsComments` function is responsible for creating the SQL statement used to delete comment records for a given project:

```
Function BuildSQLDeleteProjectsComments(intProjectId As Integer) As String

    'build SQL statement for deletion

        On Error GoTo HandleError

        Dim strSQLStatement As String

        strSQLStatement = "DELETE FROM tblProjectsComments WHERE intProjectId = " &
                    intProjectId

        BuildSQLDeleteProjectsComments = strSQLStatement

        Exit Function

HandleError:
        GeneralErrorHandler Err.Number, Err.Description, DB_LOGIC, _
            "BuildSQLDeleteProjectsComments"

    Exit Function

End Function
```

Various procedures were also added to handle inserting records into the cross-reference tables that store comments, contacts, and file attachments for each project. For example, the `BuildSQLInsertProject Comments` function is responsible for creating the SQL statement that inserts a new comment into the `tblProjectsComments` table in the database:

```
Function BuildSQLInsertProjectsComments(intProjectId As Integer, strComment _
        As String) As String

    'build SQL statement for insertion

        On Error GoTo HandleError
        Dim strSQLStatement As String

    strSQLStatement = "INSERT INTO tblProjectsComments(intProjectId, txtComment)" & _
        "VALUES(" & intProjectId & ", '" & strComment & "')"

    BuildSQLInsertProjectsComments = strSQLStatement
        Exit Function

HandleError:
        GeneralErrorHandler Err.Number, Err.Description, DB_LOGIC, _
            "BuildSQLInsertProjectsComments"

    Exit Function

End Function
```

Connecting the User Interface to the Code

So far, your application will probably not compile because some features used in the code have not been written yet. You're almost finished with the application anyway. You are now ready to tie everything together by adding the VBA code to the Project Tracker and Contacts forms. Most of this code will be event procedures that fire, for example, when certain buttons are clicked. Some of the code will be local procedures in the form that deal with user-interface-specific features that would not make sense to put in a standard or class module.

The Projects Form

An example of the Project Tracker form, called `frmProjects`, is shown in Figure 13-26 with some sample data populated. You will revisit this form in more detail at the end of the chapter, where you will explore its cool features. For now, just keep this form in mind to help you understand the purpose of the code that you are about to write (and have already written).

Try It Out   **Writing Code for the frmProjects Form**

As previously mentioned, you are now ready to write the VBA code that will finish up the application. You will start with the `frmProjects` form and will finish with the `frmContacts` form.

1. Open the `frmProjects` form and select the `Form_Load` event for the form to bring up the Visual Basic editor. Add the following code to the form:

```
Private Sub Form_Load()

    On Error GoTo HandleError

    Set objProjects = New clsProjects
    Set rsProjects = New ADODB.Recordset

        'load non-closed projects as default (open, on hold, etc.)
    blnAllRecords = False

    'make sure unclosed is enabled by default so only unclosed records load first
    togShowUnclosed.Value = True
    togShowAll.Value = False

    'lock project id field so no edits allowed (primary key assigned by database)
    txtProjectId.Locked = True

        'load the records in the recordset and display the first one on the form
    Call LoadRecords

        Exit Sub

HandleError:
    GeneralErrorHandler Err.Number, Err.Description, PROJECTS_FORM, "Form_Load"
    Exit Sub

End Sub
```

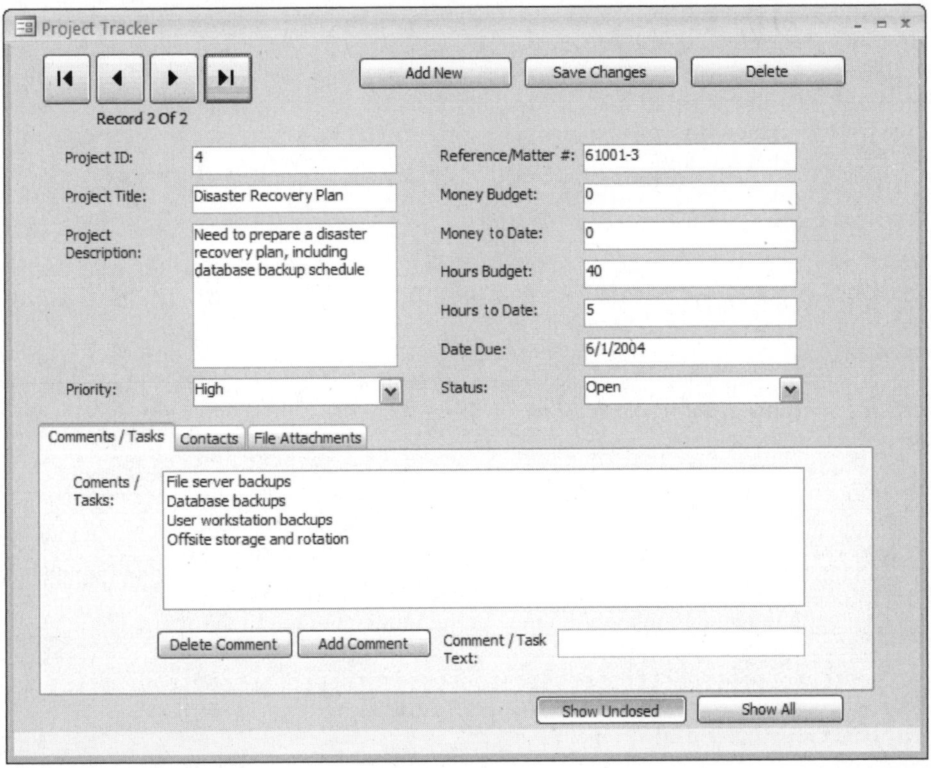

Figure 13-26

2. Add the following code to the General Declarations section of the form:

```
Option Compare Database
Option Explicit
Dim blnAddMode As Boolean
Dim blnAllRecords As Boolean
Dim rsProjects As ADODB.Recordset
Dim objProjects As clsProjects
Dim rsComments As ADODB.Recordset
Dim rsContacts As ADODB.Recordset
Dim rsAttachments As ADODB.Recordset
Const PROJECTS_FORM As String = "frmProjects"
Dim intCurrProjectRecord As Integer
```

3. Add Click event procedures to the form for making updates to the data:

```
Private Sub cmdAddNew_Click()

    On Error GoTo HandleError

        'clear the current controls to enable adding a new
```

```
        'Project record
        Call AddEmptyProjectRecord

            Exit Sub

HandleError:
    GeneralErrorHandler Err.Number, Err.Description, PROJECTS_FORM, _
            "cmdAddNew_Click"

    Exit Sub

End Sub

Private Sub cmdSave_Click()

    On Error GoTo HandleError

        Dim intCurProject As Integer

        'save the id of the current record if in update mode
    If Not blnAddMode Then
        intCurProject = objProjects.ProjectId
    Else
        intCurProject = 0
    End If

        'populate object with current info on form
    objProjects.PopulatePropertiesFromForm

    'save all changes to current record
    objProjects.Save blnAddMode, rsProjects

        'save changes in list boxes in tabs 1-3
    Call SaveComments
    Call SaveContacts
    Call SaveAttachments

    'move back to the project that was current before the requery
    If intCurProject > 0 Then

        'move back to the project that was just updated
        rsProjects.Find "[intProjectId] = " & intCurProject
    Else
        'if just added new record, move to the beginning of
        'the recordset
        Call MoveToFirstRecord(intCurrProjectRecord, rsProjects, objProjects, _
            blnAddMode)
    End If

Exit Sub

HandleError:
    GeneralErrorHandler Err.Number, Err.Description, PROJECTS_FORM, "cmdSave_Click"
```

```
        Exit Sub
    End Sub

    Private Sub cmdDelete_Click()

        On Error GoTo HandleError

            'delete the current record from the local disconnected recordset
        objProjects.Delete objProjects.ProjectId, blnAddMode, rsProjects

            'move to the first record in the recordset after the delete
        Call MoveToFirstRecord(intCurrProjectRecord, rsProjects, objProjects, _
            blnAddMode)

            'populate the controls on the form with the current record
        Call PopulateProjectsControls
            Exit Sub

    HandleError:
        GeneralErrorHandler Err.Number, Err.Description, PROJECTS_FORM, _
            "cmdDelete_Click"
        Exit Sub
    End Sub
```

4. Add the following `Click` event procedures to the form for navigating through the data:

```
    Private Sub cmdMoveFirst_Click()

        On Error GoTo HandleError

            'move to the first record in the local disconnected recordset
        Call MoveToFirstRecord(intCurrProjectRecord, rsProjects, objProjects, _
            blnAddMode)

            'populate the controls on the form with the current record
        Call PopulateProjectsControls

            Exit Sub

    HandleError:
        GeneralErrorHandler Err.Number, Err.Description, PROJECTS_FORM, _
            "cmdMoveFirst_Click"
        Exit Sub

    End Sub

    Private Sub cmdMoveLast_Click()

        On Error GoTo HandleError

            'move to the last record in the local disconnected recordset
        Call MoveToLastRecord(intCurrProjectRecord, rsProjects, objProjects, _
```

```
                                   blnAddMode)

            'populate the controls on the form with the current record
        Call PopulateProjectsControls

            Exit Sub

HandleError:
    GeneralErrorHandler Err.Number, Err.Description, PROJECTS_FORM, _
            "cmdMoveLast_Click"

    Exit Sub

End Sub

Private Sub cmdMoveNext_Click()

    On Error GoTo HandleError

        'move to the next record in the local disconnected recordset
        Call MoveToNextRecord(intCurrProjectRecord, rsProjects, objProjects, _
            blnAddMode)

        'populate the controls on the form with the current record
        Call PopulateProjectsControls

            Exit Sub

HandleError:
    GeneralErrorHandler Err.Number, Err.Description, PROJECTS_FORM, _
            "cmdMoveNext_Click"
    Exit Sub

End Sub

Private Sub cmdMovePrevious_Click()

On Error GoTo HandleError

'move to the previous record in the local disconnected recordset
Call MoveToPreviousRecord(intCurrProjectRecord, rsProjects, objProjects, _
    blnAddMode)

    'populate the controls on the form with the current record
    Call PopulateProjectsControls
    Exit Sub

HandleError:
    GeneralErrorHandler Err.Number, Err.Description, PROJECTS_FORM, _
            "cmdMovePrevious_Click"
    Exit Sub

End Sub
```

5. Add the following `Click` event procedures to the form for managing the contacts associated with a given project:

```
Private Sub cmdDeleteContact_Click()

    On Error GoTo HandleError

    'delete the selected contact from the list (not the database,
    'just the screen)
    If lstContacts.ListIndex >= 0 Then
        lstContacts.RemoveItem (lstContacts.ListIndex)
    End If

    Exit Sub

HandleError:
    GeneralErrorHandler Err.Number, Err.Description, PROJECTS_FORM, _
        "cmdDeleteContact_Click"
    Exit Sub

End Sub

Private Sub cmdManageContacts_Click()

    On Error GoTo HandleError

    'store the current projectid so a contact can be added
    intContactProjectAdd = objProjects.ProjectId

    'open contacts form so user can add contact to existing project
    DoCmd.OpenForm "frmContacts"

    Exit Sub

HandleError:
    GeneralErrorHandler Err.Number, Err.Description, PROJECTS_FORM, _
        "cmdManageContacts_Click"
    Exit Sub

End Sub

Private Sub cmdEmailContact_Click()

    On Error GoTo HandleError

    'create a new email to the selected contact using the email column
    DoCmd.SendObject acSendNoObject, , , lstContacts.Column(5), , , , , True, False
    Exit Sub

HandleError:
    GeneralErrorHandler Err.Number, Err.Description, PROJECTS_FORM, _
        "cmdEmailContact_Click"
```

```
        Exit Sub

End Sub

Private Sub cmdViewContact_Click()

    On Error GoTo HandleError

        'if there is a selected record in the list
    If lstContacts.ListIndex <> -1 Then

        'store the current projectid so a contact can be added
        intContactProjectAdd = objProjects.ProjectId
            'store the current contact so it can be retrieved
        'from the contacts form

        intContactProjectLookup = lstContacts.Column(6)
        DoCmd.OpenForm "frmContacts"
            intContactProjectLookup = 0

        End If

        Exit Sub

HandleError:
    GeneralErrorHandler Err.Number, Err.Description, PROJECTS_FORM, _
            "cmdViewContact_Click"
    Exit Sub
End Sub
```

6. Add the following Click event procedures to the form for managing the comments associated with a given project:

```
Private Sub cmdAddComment_Click()

    On Error GoTo HandleError

        'add comment/task to list box
    lstComments.AddItem (txtAddComment)

        'clear AddComment box since you just added it
    txtAddComment = ""

        Exit Sub

HandleError:
    GeneralErrorHandler Err.Number, Err.Description, PROJECTS_FORM, _
            "cmdAddComment_Click"
```

```
        Exit Sub

End Sub

Private Sub cmdDeleteComment_Click()

    On Error GoTo HandleError

        'remove the selected item from the list
    If lstComments.ListIndex >= 0 Then
        lstComments.RemoveItem (lstComments.ListIndex)
    End If
        Exit Sub

HandleError:
    GeneralErrorHandler Err.Number, Err.Description, PROJECTS_FORM, _
            "cmdDeleteComment_Click"
    Exit Sub

End Sub
```

7. Add the following `Click` event procedures to the form for managing the file attachments associated with a given project:

```
Private Sub cmdAddAttachment_Click()

    On Error GoTo HandleError
        'add file attachment to list box
    lstFileAttachments.AddItem (txtFileDesc & ";" & txtFileName)

        'clear text boxes since info was added to list
    txtFileDesc = ""
    txtFileName = ""

        Exit Sub

HandleError:
    GeneralErrorHandler Err.Number, Err.Description, PROJECTS_FORM, _
            "cmdAddAttachment_Click"
    Exit Sub

End Sub

Private Sub cmdFileBrowse_Click()

    On Error GoTo HandleError
        'show the open dialog and load
    'selected file name in text box
    txtFileName = GetFileNameBrowse

    Exit Sub

HandleError:
```

```
        GeneralErrorHandler Err.Number, Err.Description, PROJECTS_FORM, _
            "cmdFileBrowse_Click"
    Exit Sub

End Sub

Private Sub cmdOpenFile_Click()

    On Error GoTo HandleError

        Dim RetVal As Variant
    Dim strFile As String
        'if the user selected a value

    If lstFileAttachments.ListIndex >= 0 Then

            'retrieve the file name from the list box
        strFile = lstFileAttachments.Column(1)

            'open the selected file
        Call OpenFileAttachment(strFile)

        End If

        Exit Sub

HandleError:
    GeneralErrorHandler Err.Number, Err.Description, PROJECTS_FORM, _
            "cmdOpenFile_Click"

    Exit Sub

End Sub

Private Sub cmdRemoveAttachment_Click()

    On Error GoTo HandleError

        'remove the selected item from the list (if an item has been selected)
    If lstFileAttachments.ListIndex >= 0 Then
        lstFileAttachments.RemoveItem (lstFileAttachments.ListIndex)
    End If

Exit Sub

HandleError:
    GeneralErrorHandler Err.Number, Err.Description, PROJECTS_FORM, _
            "cmdRemoveAttachment_Click"
    Exit Sub

End Sub
```

8. Add the following `AddEmptyProject` procedure:

```
Sub AddEmptyProjectRecord()

    On Error GoTo HandleError
        'set add mode to true
    blnAddMode = True
        'clear the current values in the Projects object
    objProjects.ClearObject
        'clear the current controls on the form so the
    'user can fill in values for the new record
    Call ClearProjectsControls
    Exit Sub

HandleError:
    GeneralErrorHandler Err.Number, Err.Description, PROJECTS_FORM, _
        "AddEmptyProjectRecord"
    Exit Sub

End Sub
```

9. Add the following `PopulateProjectsControls` procedure:

```
Sub PopulateProjectsControls()

    On Error GoTo HandleError

            'Populate the controls on the Projects form with the values of the
        'current record in the Projects object.
        If Not rsProjects.BOF And Not rsProjects.EOF Then
            Me.txtProjectId = objProjects.ProjectId
            Me.txtProjectTitle = objProjects.ProjectTitle
            Me.txtProjectDesc = objProjects.ProjectDescription
            Me.cboPriority = objProjects.Priority
            Me.txtReferenceNum = objProjects.ReferenceNum
            Me.txtMoneyBudget = objProjects.MoneyBudget
            Me.txtMoneyToDate = objProjects.MoneyToDate
            Me.txtHoursBudget = objProjects.HoursBudget
            Me.txtHoursToDate = objProjects.HoursToDate
            If objProjects.DateDue = "1/1/1900" Then
                Me.txtDateDue = ""
            Else
                Me.txtDateDue = objProjects.DateDue
            End If
            Me.cboStatus = objProjects.Status

                    'populate the recordset for tab 1
            Set rsComments = New ADODB.Recordset

            Set rsComments = objProjects.RetrieveComments(objProjects.ProjectId)
            PopulateListFromRecordset Me.lstComments, rsComments, 1
```

```
                    rsComments.Close

                        'populate the recordset for tab 2
                Set rsContacts = New ADODB.Recordset
                Set rsContacts = objProjects.RetrieveContacts(objProjects.ProjectId)
                PopulateListFromRecordset Me.lstContacts, rsContacts, 7
                rsContacts.Close

                        'populate the recordset for tab 3
                Set rsAttachments = New ADODB.Recordset
                Set rsAttachments = _
                    objProjects.RetrieveAttachments(objProjects.ProjectId)
                PopulateListFromRecordset Me.lstFileAttachments, rsAttachments, 2
                rsAttachments.Close

                    'display the record count on the form
                lblRecordNum.Caption = "Record " & intCurrProjectRecord & " Of " & _
                    rsProjects.RecordCount
                        ElseIf rsProjects.BOF Then
            'past beginning of recordset so move to first record
            Call MoveToFirstRecord(intCurrProjectRecord, rsProjects, _
                objProjects, blnAddMode)

        ElseIf rsProjects.EOF Then
            'past end of recordset so move back to last record
            Call MoveToLastRecord(intCurrProjectRecord, rsProjects, _
                objProjects, blnAddMode)
        End If
    Exit Sub

HandleError:
    GeneralErrorHandler Err.Number, Err.Description, PROJECTS_FORM, _
            "PopulateProjectsControls"
    Exit Sub

End Sub
```

10. Add the following `ClearProjectControls` procedure:

```
Sub ClearProjectsControls()

    On Error GoTo HandleError

        'clear the values in the controls on the form
    Me.txtProjectId = ""
    Me.txtProjectTitle = ""
    Me.txtProjectDesc = ""
    Me.cboPriority = 0
    Me.txtReferenceNum = ""
    Me.txtMoneyBudget = ""
    Me.txtMoneyToDate = ""

    Me.txtHoursBudget = ""
```

```
        Me.txtHoursToDate = ""
        Me.txtDateDue = ""
        Me.cboStatus = 0
            'clear the values in the text box controls on the tab control pages
        Me.txtAddComment = ""
        Me.txtFileName = ""
        Me.txtFileDesc = ""
            Exit Sub


HandleError:
        GeneralErrorHandler Err.Number, Err.Description, PROJECTS_FORM, _
            "ClearProjectsControls"
        Exit Sub


End Sub
```

11. Add the following `PopulateComboBoxes` procedure:

```
Sub PopulateComboBoxes()

    On Error GoTo HandleError

            'populate the priority combo box
        cboPriority.RowSource = ""
        cboPriority.LimitToList = True
        cboPriority.ColumnCount = 1
        cboPriority.RowSourceType = "Value List"
        cboPriority.AddItem ("Normal")
        cboPriority.AddItem ("High")
        cboPriority.AddItem ("Low")


            'populate the status combo box
        cboStatus.RowSource = ""
        cboStatus.LimitToList = True
        cboStatus.ColumnCount = 1
        cboStatus.RowSourceType = "Value List"
        cboStatus.AddItem ("Open")
        cboStatus.AddItem ("Closed")
        cboStatus.AddItem ("On Hold")
        Exit Sub

HandleError:
        GeneralErrorHandler Err.Number, Err.Description, PROJECTS_FORM, _
            "PopulateComboBoxes"
        Exit Sub


End Sub
```

12. Add the following `PopulateListFromRecordset` procedure:

```
Sub PopulateListFromRecordset(lstList As ListBox, rsRecordset As _
        ADODB.Recordset, intNumCols As Integer)

    On Error GoTo HandleError
        Dim intCounter As Integer
    Dim strItem As String

        With lstList
        .RowSource = ""
        .ColumnCount = intNumCols
        .RowSourceType = "Value List"
    End With

        'add all of the values in the recordset to the list box

            Do Until rsRecordset.EOF
    'for each item in the current record, build string
    For intCounter = 0 To intNumCols - 1
        strItem = strItem & rsRecordset(intCounter).Value & ";"
    Next intCounter
    lstList.AddItem (strItem)
    strItem = ""
    rsRecordset.MoveNext
    Loop

        Exit Sub

HandleError:
    GeneralErrorHandler Err.Number, Err.Description, PROJECTS_FORM, _
        "PopulateListFromRecordset"
    Exit Sub

End Sub
```

13. Add the `Form_Unload` procedure for `frmProjects`:

```
Private Sub Form_Unload(Cancel As Integer)

    On Error GoTo HandleError

        'close the recordset and free the memory

    rsProjects.Close
    Set rsProjects = Nothing

        Exit Sub

HandleError:
    GeneralErrorHandler Err.Number, Err.Description, PROJECTS_FORM, "Form_Unload"
```

```
        Exit Sub

End Sub
```

14.   Add the `LoadRecords` procedure:

```
Sub LoadRecords()

    On Error GoTo HandleError

        intCurrProjectRecord = 0

        blnAddMode = False

        'populate the main recordset
    Set rsProjects = objProjects.RetrieveProjects(blnAllRecords)

        'if the recordset is empty
    If rsProjects.BOF And rsProjects.EOF Then
        Exit Sub
    Else

            'populate the status and priority combo boxes
        Call PopulateComboBoxes

                'populate the object with values in the recordset
        objProjects.PopulatePropertiesFromRecordset rsProjects

                Call MoveToFirstRecord(intCurrProjectRecord, rsProjects,
objProjects, _
            blnAddMode)

                    'populate the controls on the form with the current record
        Call PopulateProjectsControls

                End If
        Exit Sub

HandleError:
    GeneralErrorHandler Err.Number, Err.Description, PROJECTS_FORM, "LoadRecords"
    Exit Sub

End Sub
```

15. Add the following procedures for dealing with the toggle button allowing the user to switch from unclosed projects to all projects:

```
Private Sub togShowAll_Click()

    On Error GoTo HandleError

        If togShowAll.Value = True Then

            blnAllRecords = True

            'make sure Show Unclosed is not checked any more
        togShowUnclosed.Value = False

            'now, populate the form with all projects records
        LoadRecords

            End If

        Exit Sub

HandleError:
    GeneralErrorHandler Err.Number, Err.Description, PROJECTS_FORM, _
        "togShowAll_Click"
    Exit Sub

    End Sub

Private Sub togShowUnclosed_Click()

    On Error GoTo HandleError

        If togShowUnclosed.Value = True Then

            blnAllRecords = False

            'make sure Show All is not checked any more
        togShowAll.Value = False

            'now, populate the form with all unclosed projects records
        LoadRecords

            End If

        Exit Sub

HandleError:
    GeneralErrorHandler Err.Number, Err.Description, PROJECTS_FORM, _
        "togShowUnclosed_Click"
    Exit Sub

End Sub
```

16. Add the following procedures that deal with saving the records displayed on the tabs of the form to the database:

```
Sub SaveComments()

    On Error GoTo HandleError

        Dim strSQLStatement As String
    Dim intId As Integer
    Dim strComment As String
    Dim intCounter

        'remove all current comments in database for this project
    strSQLStatement = BuildSQLDeleteProjectsComments(objProjects.ProjectId)

    ProcessUpdate (strSQLStatement)

        'add back all comments based on current list (easier than tracking
    'changes, inserts, and deletes)
    For intCounter = 0 To lstComments.ListCount - 1
        intId = objProjects.ProjectId
        strComment = lstComments.Column(0, intCounter)
        strSQLStatement = BuildSQLInsertProjectsComments(intId, strComment)
        ProcessUpdate (strSQLStatement)
    Next intCounter

        Exit Sub

HandleError:
    GeneralErrorHandler Err.Number, Err.Description, PROJECTS_FORM, "SaveComments"
    Exit Sub

End Sub

Sub SaveContacts()

        On Error GoTo HandleError

        Dim strSQLStatement As String
    Dim intContId As Integer
    Dim intProjId As Integer
    Dim intCounter As Integer

        'remove all current contacts in database for this project
    strSQLStatement = BuildSQLDeleteProjectsContacts(objProjects.ProjectId)
    ProcessUpdate (strSQLStatement)

        'add back all contacts based on current list (easier than tracking
    'changes, inserts, and deletes)
    For intCounter = 0 To lstContacts.ListCount - 1
        intContId = lstContacts.Column(6, intCounter)
        intProjId = objProjects.ProjectId
        strSQLStatement = BuildSQLInsertProjectsContacts(intContId, intProjId)
```

```
            ProcessUpdate (strSQLStatement)
        Next intCounter

            Exit Sub

HandleError:
        GeneralErrorHandler Err.Number, Err.Description, PROJECTS_FORM, "SaveContacts"
        Exit Sub

End Sub

Sub SaveAttachments()

        On Error GoTo HandleError

        Dim strSQLStatement As String
        Dim intId As Integer
        Dim strDesc As String
        Dim strFile As String
        Dim intCounter As Integer

            'remove all current file attachments in database for this project
        strSQLStatement = BuildSQLDeleteProjectsAttachments(objProjects.ProjectId)
        ProcessUpdate (strSQLStatement)

            'add back all file attachments based on current list (easier than tracking
        'changes, inserts, and deletes)
        For intCounter = 0 To lstFileAttachments.ListCount - 1
            intId = objProjects.ProjectId
            strDesc = lstFileAttachments.Column(0, intCounter)
            strFile = lstFileAttachments.Column(1, intCounter)
            strSQLStatement = BuildSQLInsertProjectsAttachments(intId, strDesc, _
                            strFile)
            ProcessUpdate (strSQLStatement)
        Next intCounter

            Exit Sub

HandleError:
        GeneralErrorHandler Err.Number, Err.Description, PROJECTS_FORM, _
            "SaveComments"
        Exit Sub

End Sub
```

17. Add the following `RefreshContacts` procedure to `frmProjects`. This procedure gets called whenever the user clicks to add the contact to the current project.

```
Sub RefreshContacts()

        On Error GoTo HandleError

            'populate the recordset for tab 2
```

```
        Set rsContacts = New ADODB.Recordset
        Set rsContacts = objProjects.RetrieveContacts(objProjects.ProjectId)
        PopulateListFromRecordset Me.lstContacts, rsContacts, 7
        rsContacts.Close

            Exit Sub

HandleError:
        GeneralErrorHandler Err.Number, Err.Description, PROJECTS_FORM, _
                "RefreshContacts"
        Exit Sub

End Sub
```

How It Works

First, you added the code to the frmProjects form to tie it to the rest of the code created earlier in this chapter. As you have learned throughout this book, you typically tie the user interface to the rest of the code through various event procedures on the form. In the Form_Load event for the frmProjects form, you added a few startup settings, such as locking the ProjectId field to prevent editing and to load a project record onto the form.

```
Private Sub Form_Load()

    On Error GoTo HandleError
        Set objProjects = New clsProjects
    Set rsProjects = New ADODB.Recordset

        'load non-closed projects as default (open, on hold, etc.)
    blnAllRecords = False

        'make sure unclosed is enabled by default so only unclosed records load
first
    togShowUnclosed.Value = True
    togShowAll.Value = False

        'lock project id field so no edits allowed (primary key assigned by
database)
    txtProjectId.Locked = True

        'load the records in the recordset and display the first one on the form
    Call LoadRecords

            Exit Sub

HandleError:
    GeneralErrorHandler Err.Number, Err.Description, PROJECTS_FORM, "Form_Load"
    Exit Sub

End Sub
```

Next, you added various declarations to the General Declarations section of the form, in order to declare various recordsets that will store the projects and related records. You then added Click events for the cmdAddNew, cmdSave, and cmdDelete controls that fire when the user selects the respective button on the form. For example, the cmdAddNew_Click event procedure calls a procedure that adds an empty project record to allow the user to begin adding a new project record.

```
Private Sub cmdAddNew_Click()

    On Error GoTo HandleError

        'clear the current controls to enable adding a new
    'Project record
    Call AddEmptyProjectRecord


        Exit Sub

HandleError:
    GeneralErrorHandler Err.Number, Err.Description, PROJECTS_FORM, _
            "cmdAddNew_Click"
    Exit Sub

End Sub
```

The cmdSave_Click event saves a new or modified record to the database. When you click the cmdSave button, the ID of the current record is saved if the mode is Update Mode.

```
Private Sub cmdSave_Click()

    On Error GoTo HandleError

        Dim intCurProject As Integer

        'save the id of the current record if in update mode
    If Not blnAddMode Then
        intCurProject = objProjects.ProjectId
    Else
        intCurProject = 0
    End If
```

The objProjects object (created based upon the clsProject that you created earlier) is then populated with the values on the form:

```
'populate object with current info on form
objProjects.PopulatePropertiesFromForm
```

The changes to the current record are then saved to the database:

```
'save all changes to current record
objProjects.Save blnAddMode, rsProjects

    'save changes in list boxes in tabs 1-3
Call SaveComments
Call SaveContacts
Call SaveAttachments
```

If an existing record was updated, the updated record is reset to the current record. If Add Mode was activated, the first record now becomes the current record:

```
    'move back to the project that was current before the requery
    If intCurProject > 0 Then
        'move back to the project that was just updated
        rsProjects.Find "[intProjectId] = " & intCurProject
    Else
        'if just added new record, move to the beginning of
        'the recordset
        Call MoveToFirstRecord(intCurrProjectRecord, rsProjects, objProjects, _
            blnAddMode)
    End If
Exit Sub

HandleError:
    GeneralErrorHandler Err.Number, Err.Description, PROJECTS_FORM, _
"cmdSave_Click"
    Exit Sub
End Sub
```

Various Click event procedures were added to each of the command buttons to be used for record navigation. For example, the cmdMoveFirst_Click procedure calls a procedure to move to the first record and then populates the controls on the form with the data of the newly current record:

```
Private Sub cmdMoveFirst_Click()

    On Error GoTo HandleError

        'move to the first record in the local disconnected recordset
    Call MoveToFirstRecord(intCurrProjectRecord, rsProjects, objProjects, _
        blnAddMode)

        'populate the controls on the form with the current record
    Call PopulateProjectsControls

        Exit Sub

HandleError:
    GeneralErrorHandler Err.Number, Err.Description, PROJECTS_FORM, _
```

```
            "cmdMoveFirst_Click"
      Exit Sub

  End Sub
```

Next, several procedures were added to the form for managing contacts. For example, the cmdDeleteContacts_Click procedure deletes the selected contact from the list box on the form:

```
Private Sub cmdDeleteContact_Click()
      On Error GoTo HandleError

          'delete the selected contact from the list (not the database, just the
    screen)
      If lstContacts.ListIndex >= 0 Then
          lstContacts.RemoveItem (lstContacts.ListIndex)

      End If

        Exit Sub

HandleError:
      GeneralErrorHandler Err.Number, Err.Description, PROJECTS_FORM, _
            "cmdDeleteContact_Click"
      Exit Sub

  End Sub
```

The cmdManageContacts_Click event opens the frmContacts form so the user can add a contact to the existing project:

```
Private Sub cmdManageContacts_Click()

    On Error GoTo HandleError

        'store the current projectid so a contact can be added
    intContactProjectAdd = objProjects.ProjectId

        'open contacts form so user can add contact to existing project
    DoCmd.OpenForm "frmContacts"

          Exit Sub

HandleError:
      GeneralErrorHandler Err.Number, Err.Description, PROJECTS_FORM, _
            "cmdManageContacts_Click"
      Exit Sub

  End Sub
```

The cmdEmailContact_Click event procedure executes the SendObject method of the DoCmd object to generate an empty e-mail to the selected contact:

```
Private Sub cmdEmailContact_Click()

        On Error GoTo HandleError
        'create a new email to the selected contact using the email column
    DoCmd.SendObject acSendNoObject, , , lstContacts.Column(5), , , , ,       True,
False

        Exit Sub

HandleError:
    GeneralErrorHandler Err.Number, Err.Description, PROJECTS_FORM, _
        "cmdEmailContact_Click"
    Exit Sub

End Sub
```

The cmdViewContact_Click event opened the frmContacts form and displayed the contact record that was selected:

```
Private Sub cmdViewContact_Click()

    On Error GoTo HandleError

        'if there is a selected record in the list
    If lstContacts.ListIndex <> -1 Then
        'store the current projectid so a contact can be added
        intContactProjectAdd = objProjects.ProjectId

            'store the current contact so it can be retrieved
        'from the contacts form
        intContactProjectLookup = lstContacts.Column(6)
        DoCmd.OpenForm "frmContacts"

            intContactProjectLookup = 0

        End If

        Exit Sub

HandleError:
    GeneralErrorHandler Err.Number, Err.Description, PROJECTS_FORM, _
        "cmdViewContact_Click"
    Exit Sub
End Sub
```

Next, Click event procedures were created for adding and deleting comments from the lstComments list box. Event procedures were then added for managing file attachments associated with a given project. For example, the cmdAddAttachment_Click event added the value in the txtFileDesc and txtFileName fields to the lstFileAttachments list box:

```
Private Sub cmdAddAttachment_Click()

    On Error GoTo HandleError

        'add file attachment to list box
    lstFileAttachments.AddItem (txtFileDesc & ";" & txtFileName)

        'clear text boxes since info was added to list
    txtFileDesc = ""
    txtFileName = ""

        Exit Sub

HandleError:
    GeneralErrorHandler Err.Number, Err.Description, PROJECTS_FORM, _
        "cmdAddAttachment_Click"
    Exit Sub

End Sub
```

The `cmdFileBrowse_Click` event called the `GetFileNameBrowse` function, which then called the external function to open the File Browse dialog box:

```
Private Sub cmdFileBrowse_Click()

    On Error GoTo HandleError

    'show the open dialog and load

    'selected file name in text box
    txtFileName = GetFileNameBrowse

        Exit Sub

HandleError:
    GeneralErrorHandler Err.Number, Err.Description, PROJECTS_FORM, _
        "cmdFileBrowse_Click"

    Exit Sub

End Sub
```

The `cmdOpenFile_Click` event allows a user to preview a selected attachment in the native application. If the user selects an attachment from the list, the `OpenFileAttachment` procedure is executed to call the external function for opening another program associated with the attachment.

```
Private Sub cmdOpenFile_Click()

    On Error GoTo HandleError

        Dim RetVal As Variant
```

```
        Dim strFile As String
            'if the user selected a value
        If lstFileAttachments.ListIndex >= 0 Then

                'retrieve the file name from the list box
            strFile = lstFileAttachments.Column(1)

                'open the selected file
            Call OpenFileAttachment(strFile)

            End If

            Exit Sub

    HandleError:
        GeneralErrorHandler Err.Number, Err.Description, PROJECTS_FORM, _
                "cmdOpenFile_Click"

        Exit Sub

    End Sub
```

An `AddEmptyProjectRecord` procedure was added to clear the values in the object:

```
    Sub AddEmptyProjectRecord()

        On Error GoTo HandleError

            'set add mode to true
        blnAddMode = True

            'clear the current values in the Projects object
        objProjects.ClearObject
            'clear the current controls on the form so the
        'user can fill in values for the new record
        Call ClearProjectsControls
        Exit Sub

    HandleError:
        GeneralErrorHandler Err.Number, Err.Description, PROJECTS_FORM, _
                "AddEmptyProjectRecord"
        Exit Sub

    End Sub
```

The `PopulateProjectsControls` procedure populated the controls on the `frmProjects` form with the values of the current record in the `objProjects` object:

```
    Sub PopulateProjectsControls()

        On Error GoTo HandleError

                    'Populate the controls on the Projects form with the values of the
```

```
            'current record in the Projects object.
If Not rsProjects.BOF And Not rsProjects.EOF Then
    Me.txtProjectId = objProjects.ProjectId
    Me.txtProjectTitle = objProjects.ProjectTitle
    Me.txtProjectDesc = objProjects.ProjectDescription
    Me.cboPriority = objProjects.Priority
    Me.txtReferenceNum = objProjects.ReferenceNum
    Me.txtMoneyBudget = objProjects.MoneyBudget
    Me.txtMoneyToDate = objProjects.MoneyToDate
    Me.txtHoursBudget = objProjects.HoursBudget
    Me.txtHoursToDate = objProjects.HoursToDate
    If objProjects.DateDue = "1/1/1900" Then
        Me.txtDateDue = ""
    Else
        Me.txtDateDue = objProjects.DateDue
    End If
    Me.cboStatus = objProjects.Status
```

After the object was populated, the tab controls were populated with the values retrieved from the database:

```
            'populate the recordset for tab 1
    Set rsComments = New ADODB.Recordset
    Set rsComments = objProjects.RetrieveComments(objProjects.ProjectId)
    PopulateListFromRecordset Me.lstComments, rsComments, 1
    rsComments.Close

                'populate the recordset for tab 2
    Set rsContacts = New ADODB.Recordset
    Set rsContacts = objProjects.RetrieveContacts(objProjects.ProjectId)
    PopulateListFromRecordset Me.lstContacts, rsContacts, 7
    rsContacts.Close
                'populate the recordset for tab 3
    Set rsAttachments = New ADODB.Recordset
    Set rsAttachments = _
        objProjects.RetrieveAttachments(objProjects.ProjectId)
    PopulateListFromRecordset Me.lstFileAttachments, rsAttachments, 2
    rsAttachments.Close
```

The record count was also displayed, so the user could see how many records were available for viewing and updating:

```
    'display the record count on the form
    lblRecordNum.Caption = "Record " & intCurrProjectRecord & " Of " & _
        rsProjects.RecordCount
```

If no current record was available because the recordset was at the beginning or end, you moved to another record accordingly:

```
    ElseIf rsProjects.BOF Then
        'past beginning of recordset so move to first record
```

```
            Call MoveToFirstRecord(intCurrProjectRecord, rsProjects, _
                objProjects, blnAddMode)
        ElseIf rsProjects.EOF Then
            'past end of recordset so move back to last record
            Call MoveToLastRecord(intCurrProjectRecord, rsProjects, _
                objProjects, blnAddMode)
        End If
    Exit Sub


HandleError:
    GeneralErrorHandler Err.Number, Err.Description, PROJECTS_FORM, _
        "PopulateProjectsControls"
    Exit Sub

End Sub
```

The `ClearProjectControls` procedure was added to the `frmProjects` form. This procedure empties the various controls on the form.

```
Sub ClearProjectsControls()

    On Error GoTo HandleError

        'clear the values in the controls on the form
    Me.txtProjectId = ""
    Me.txtProjectTitle = ""
    Me.txtProjectDesc = ""
    Me.cboPriority = 0
    Me.txtReferenceNum = ""
    Me.txtMoneyBudget = ""
    Me.txtMoneyToDate = ""
    Me.txtHoursBudget = ""
    Me.txtHoursToDate = ""
    Me.txtDateDue = ""
    Me.cboStatus = 0
    'clear the values in the text box controls on the tab control pages
    Me.txtAddComment = ""
    Me.txtFileName = ""
    Me.txtFileDesc = ""

        Exit Sub


HandleError:
    GeneralErrorHandler Err.Number, Err.Description, PROJECTS_FORM, _
        "ClearProjectsControls"
    Exit Sub

End Sub
```

A procedure called `PopulateComboBoxes` was added to populate the values in the `cboPriority` and `cboStatus` combo boxes on the form:

```
Sub PopulateComboBoxes()

    On Error GoTo HandleError

            'populate the priority combo box
        cboPriority.RowSource = ""
        cboPriority.LimitToList = True
        cboPriority.ColumnCount = 1
        cboPriority.RowSourceType = "Value List"
        cboPriority.AddItem ("Normal")
        cboPriority.AddItem ("High")
        cboPriority.AddItem ("Low")

            'populate the status combo box
        cboStatus.RowSource = ""
        cboStatus.LimitToList = True
        cboStatus.ColumnCount = 1
        cboStatus.RowSourceType = "Value List"
        cboStatus.AddItem ("Open")
        cboStatus.AddItem ("Closed")
        cboStatus.AddItem ("On Hold")

        Exit Sub

HandleError:
    GeneralErrorHandler Err.Number, Err.Description, PROJECTS_FORM, _
            "PopulateComboBoxes"
    Exit Sub

End Sub
```

The `PopulateListFromRecordset` procedure populated a list box control with the values in a record-set. This procedure was used to populate the list boxes on the tab controls with the values from the database (for example, the comments, contacts, and attachments).

```
Sub PopulateListFromRecordset(lstList As ListBox, rsRecordset As _
        ADODB.Recordset, intNumCols As Integer)
    On Error GoTo HandleError

        Dim intCounter As Integer
    Dim strItem As String

        With lstList
        .RowSource = ""
        .ColumnCount = intNumCols
        .RowSourceType = "Value List"
    End With

        'add all of the values in the recordset to the list box

            Do Until rsRecordset.EOF
        'for each item in the current record, build string
```

```
        For intCounter = 0 To intNumCols - 1
            strItem = strItem & rsRecordset(intCounter).Value & ";"
        Next intCounter
        lstList.AddItem (strItem)
        strItem = ""
        rsRecordset.MoveNext
    Loop

        Exit Sub

HandleError:
    GeneralErrorHandler Err.Number, Err.Description, PROJECTS_FORM, _
        "PopulateListFromRecordset"
    Exit Sub

End Sub
```

The `Form_Unload` procedure for `frmProjects` closed the recordset and freed the memory associated with the recordset:

```
Private Sub Form_Unload(Cancel As Integer)

    On Error GoTo HandleError

        'close the recordset and free the memory
    rsProjects.Close
    Set rsProjects = Nothing

        Exit Sub

HandleError:
    GeneralErrorHandler Err.Number, Err.Description, PROJECTS_FORM, "Form_Unload"
    Exit Sub

End Sub
```

Next, you added the `LoadRecords` procedure, which is responsible for retrieving the project records from the database and displaying a record on the form:

```
Sub LoadRecords()

    On Error GoTo HandleError

        intCurrProjectRecord = 0

        blnAddMode = False

        'populate the main recordset
    Set rsProjects = objProjects.RetrieveProjects(blnAllRecords)
        'if the recordset is empty

    If rsProjects.BOF And rsProjects.EOF Then
```

```
            Exit Sub
        Else

                'populate the status and priority combo boxes
            Call PopulateComboBoxes

                    'populate the object with values in the recordset
            objProjects.PopulatePropertiesFromRecordset rsProjects

                    Call MoveToFirstRecord(intCurrProjectRecord, rsProjects,
        objProjects, _
                blnAddMode)

                    'populate the controls on the form with the current record
            Call PopulateProjectsControls

                    End If

            Exit Sub

    HandleError:
        GeneralErrorHandler Err.Number, Err.Description, PROJECTS_FORM, _
                "LoadRecords"

        Exit Sub

    End Sub
```

Two procedures were added to handle the toggle feature that enables the user to switch from displaying unclosed projects to all projects. For example, the togShowAll_Click event set the blnAllRecords flag to True because the user had indicated he wished to see all records. The records were then loaded based on the selected option.

```
    Private Sub togShowAll_Click()

        On Error GoTo HandleError

            If togShowAll.Value = True Then

                blnAllRecords = True

                'make sure Show Unclosed is not checked any more
            togShowUnclosed.Value = False
            'now, populate the form with all projects records
            LoadRecords

                    End If

        Exit Sub

    HandleError:
        GeneralErrorHandler Err.Number, Err.Description, PROJECTS_FORM, _
```

```
        "togShowAll_Click"
    Exit Sub


    End Sub
```

Various procedures were then added to deal with saving to the database the comments, contacts, and attachments records displayed on the tabs of the form. For example, the SaveComments procedure is responsible for removing all current comments in the database for the current project and then saving all comments in the list to the database. The delete and insert operations are performed because using these procedures is easier than keeping track of which comment records were changed, which ones were inserted, and which ones were deleted. Such a delete and reinsert operation is not appropriate in all circumstances. In the current situation, however, it works very well.

```
Sub SaveComments()

    On Error GoTo HandleError

        Dim strSQLStatement As String
    Dim intId As Integer
    Dim strComment As String
    Dim intCounter

        'remove all current comments in database for this project
    strSQLStatement = BuildSQLDeleteProjectsComments(objProjects.ProjectId)

        ProcessUpdate (strSQLStatement)

        'add back all comments based on current list (easier than tracking
    'changes, inserts, and deletes)
    For intCounter = 0 To lstComments.ListCount - 1
        intId = objProjects.ProjectId
        strComment = lstComments.Column(0, intCounter)
        strSQLStatement = BuildSQLInsertProjectsComments(intId, strComment)
        ProcessUpdate (strSQLStatement)
    Next intCounter

        Exit Sub

HandleError:
    GeneralErrorHandler Err.Number, Err.Description, PROJECTS_FORM, _
"SaveComments"

    Exit Sub

End Sub
```

To finish off the code for frmProjects, we added a RefreshContacts procedure that is called whenever the user clicks the button to add the contact to the current project. This feature ensures that the contacts tab is populated with the revised contact information.

```
Sub RefreshContacts()

    On Error GoTo HandleError

        'populate the recordset for tab 2
    Set rsContacts = New ADODB.Recordset
    Set rsContacts = objProjects.RetrieveContacts(objProjects.ProjectId)
    PopulateListFromRecordset Me.lstContacts, rsContacts, 7
    rsContacts.Close

        Exit Sub

HandleError:
    GeneralErrorHandler Err.Number, Err.Description, PROJECTS_FORM, _
            "RefreshContacts"

    Exit Sub

End Sub
```

The Contacts Form

The Contacts form, called `frmContacts`, is shown in Figure 13-27, so you can refresh your memory as to what it looks like. You are now going to add the code to implement the functionality of this form.

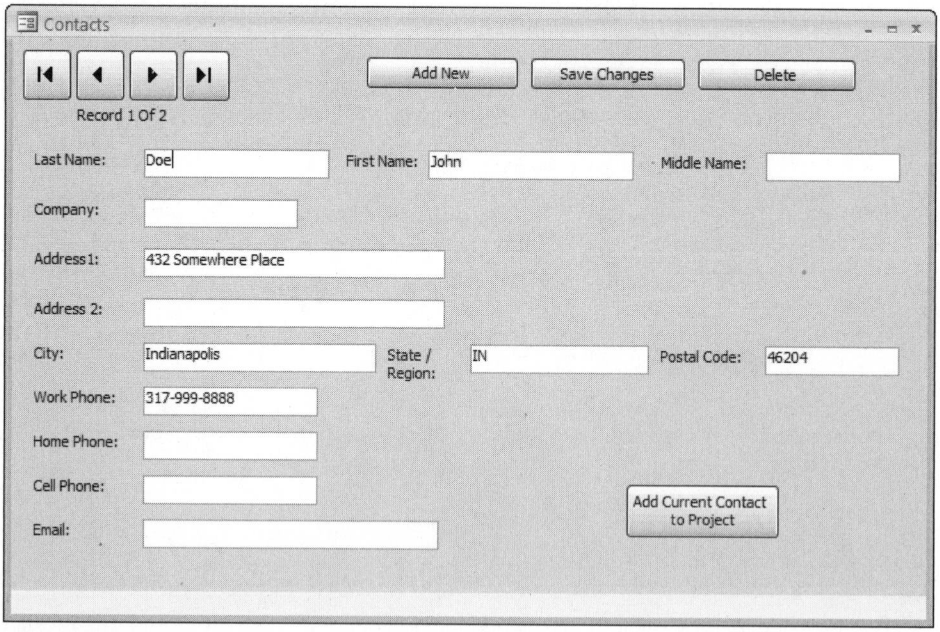

Figure 13-27

Try It Out **Writing Code for the frmContacts Form**

You're in the home stretch now. This is the last part of the application. You will now write the code behind the frmContacts form to finish the application.

1. Open the frmContacts form and select the Form_Load event for the form to bring up the Visual Basic Editor. Add the following code to the form:

```
Private Sub Form_Load()

    On Error GoTo HandleError

        Set objContacts = New clsContacts
    Set rsContacts = New ADODB.Recordset

        'not in add mode
    blnAddMode = False

        intCurrContactRecord = 0

        Set rsContacts = objContacts.RetrieveContacts
        'if the recordset is empty

    If rsContacts.BOF And rsContacts.EOF Then
        Exit Sub
    Else
        'populate the object with values in the recordset
        objContacts.PopulatePropertiesFromRecordset rsContacts
            Call MoveToFirstRecord(intCurrContactRecord, rsContacts, _
            objContacts, blnAddMode)
            'populate the controls on the form with the current record
        Call PopulateContactsControls
        End If
            Exit Sub

HandleError:
    GeneralErrorHandler Err.Number, Err.Description, CONTACTS_FORM, "Form_Load"
    Exit Sub

End Sub
```

2. Add the following to the General Declarations section of the frmContacts form:

```
Option Compare Database
Option Explicit
Dim blnAddMode As Boolean
Dim rsContacts As ADODB.Recordset
Dim objContacts As clsContacts
Const CONTACTS_FORM As String = "frmContacts"
Dim intCurrContactRecord As Integer
```

3. Add the following event procedure to the `frmContacts` form:

```
Private Sub cmdAddToProject_Click()

    On Error GoTo HandleError

        Dim strSQLStatement As String

        'build the SQL statement to insert a new contact for the current
    'project on frmProjects
    strSQLStatement = BuildSQLInsertProjectsContacts(objContacts.ContactId, _
                    intContactProjectAdd)

        'insert the record into the database
    ProcessUpdate (strSQLStatement)

        Call Forms("frmProjects").RefreshContacts

        'close the Contacts form to return the user to the Project streen
    DoCmd.Close acForm, "frmContacts"

        Exit Sub

HandleError:
    GeneralErrorHandler Err.Number, Err.Description, CONTACTS_FORM, _
            "cmdAddToProject_Click"
    Exit Sub

End Sub
```

4. Add the following event procedures to the `frmContacts` form to enable modification of records:

```
Private Sub cmdAddNew_Click()

    On Error GoTo HandleError

        'clear the current controls to enable adding a new
    'contact record
    Call AddEmptyContactRecord

        Exit Sub

HandleError:
    GeneralErrorHandler Err.Number, Err.Description, CONTACTS_FORM, _
```

```
                    "cmdAddNew_Click"

        Exit Sub

End Sub

Private Sub cmdSave_Click()

    On Error GoTo HandleError

    Dim intCurContact As Integer

        'save the id of the current record if in update mode
    If Not blnAddMode Then
        intCurContact = objContacts.ContactId
    Else
        intCurContact = 0
    End If

            'populate object with current info on form
        objContacts.PopulatePropertiesFromForm

            'save all changes to current record
        objContacts.Save blnAddMode, rsContacts

                'move back to the contact that was current before the requery
        If intCurContact > 0 Then
            'move back to the contact that was just updated
            rsContacts.Find "[intContactId] = " & intCurContact
        Else
            'if just added new record, move to the beginning of
            'the recordset
            Call MoveToFirstRecord(intCurrContactRecord, rsContacts, _
                objContacts, blnAddMode)
        End If

        Exit Sub

HandleError:
    GeneralErrorHandler Err.Number, Err.Description, CONTACTS_FORM, "cmdSave_Click"
    Exit Sub

End Sub

Private Sub cmdDelete_Click()

    On Error GoTo HandleError

        'delete the current record from the local disconnected recordset
```

```
        objContacts.Delete objContacts.ContactId, blnAddMode, rsContacts

            'move to the first record in the recordset after the delete
        Call MoveToFirstRecord(intCurrContactRecord, rsContacts, objContacts, _
            blnAddMode)

            'populate the controls on the form with the current record
        Call PopulateContactsControls

            Exit Sub

HandleError:
    GeneralErrorHandler Err.Number, Err.Description, CONTACTS_FORM, _
            "cmdDelete_Click"
    Exit Sub

End Sub
```

5.   Add the following event procedures to the `frmContacts` form that navigates through the records:

```
Private Sub cmdMoveFirst_Click()

    On Error GoTo HandleError

            'move to the first record in the local disconnected recordset
        Call MoveToFirstRecord(intCurrContactRecord, rsContacts, _
            objContacts, blnAddMode)

            'populate the controls on the form with the current record
        Call PopulateContactsControls

            Exit Sub

HandleError:
    GeneralErrorHandler Err.Number, Err.Description, CONTACTS_FORM, _
            "cmdMoveFirst_Click"

    Exit Sub

End Sub

Private Sub cmdMoveLast_Click()

    On Error GoTo HandleError

            'move to the last record in the local disconnected recordset
        Call MoveToLastRecord(intCurrContactRecord, rsContacts, _
            objContacts, blnAddMode)

            'populate the controls on the form with the current record
```

```
        Call PopulateContactsControls

        Exit Sub

HandleError:
    GeneralErrorHandler Err.Number, Err.Description, CONTACTS_FORM, _
        "cmdMoveLast_Click"

    Exit Sub

End Sub

Private Sub cmdMoveNext_Click()

    On Error GoTo HandleError

        'move to the next record in the local disconnected recordset
    Call MoveToNextRecord(intCurrContactRecord, rsContacts, objContacts, _
        blnAddMode)

        'populate the controls on the form with the current record
    Call PopulateContactsControls

        Exit Sub

HandleError:
    GeneralErrorHandler Err.Number, Err.Description, CONTACTS_FORM, _
        "cmdMoveNext_Click"
    Exit Sub

End Sub

Private Sub cmdMovePrevious_Click()

        On Error GoTo HandleError

        'move to the previous record in the local disconnected recordset
    Call MoveToPreviousRecord(intCurrContactRecord, rsContacts, _
        objContacts, blnAddMode)

        'populate the controls on the form with the current record
    Call PopulateContactsControls
        Exit Sub

HandleError:
    GeneralErrorHandler Err.Number, Err.Description, CONTACTS_FORM, _
        "cmdMovePrevious_Click"
    Exit Sub

End Sub
```

6. Add the following `AddEmptyContactRecord` procedure to the `frmContacts` form:

```
Sub AddEmptyContactRecord()

    On Error GoTo HandleError

        'set add mode to true
    blnAddMode = True

        'clear the current values in the contacts object
    objContacts.ClearObject

        'clear the current controls on the form so the
    'user can fill in values for the new record
    Call ClearContactsControls

        Exit Sub

HandleError:
    GeneralErrorHandler Err.Number, Err.Description, CONTACTS_FORM, _
        "AddEmptyContactRecord"
    Exit Sub

End Sub
```

7. Add the following `PopulateContactsControls` procedure to the `frmContacts` form:

```
Sub PopulateContactsControls()

        On Error GoTo HandleError

        'Populate the controls on the Contacts form with the values of the
    'current record in the contacts object.
    If Not rsContacts.BOF And Not rsContacts.EOF Then
        Me.txtLName = objContacts.LastName
        Me.txtFName = objContacts.FirstName
        Me.txtMName = objContacts.MiddleName
        Me.txtCompany = objContacts.Company
        Me.txtAddress1 = objContacts.Address1
        Me.txtAddress2 = objContacts.Address2
        Me.txtCity = objContacts.City
        Me.txtRegion = objContacts.Region
        Me.txtPostalCode = objContacts.PostalCode
        Me.txtWorkPhone = objContacts.WorkPhone
        Me.txtHomePhone = objContacts.HomePhone
        Me.txtCellPhone = objContacts.CellPhone
        Me.txtEmail = objContacts.Email

                'display the record count on the form
        lblRecordNum.Caption = "Record " & intCurrContactRecord & " Of " & _
```

```
                              rsContacts.RecordCount

                  ElseIf rsContacts.BOF Then
                      'past beginning of recordset so move to first record
                      Call MoveToFirstRecord(intCurrContactRecord, rsContacts, _
                                       objContacts, blnAddMode)
                  ElseIf rsContacts.EOF Then
                      'past end of recordset so move back to last record
                      Call MoveToLastRecord(intCurrContactRecord, rsContacts, _
                                       objContacts, blnAddMode)

              End If

              Exit Sub

      HandleError:
          GeneralErrorHandler Err.Number, Err.Description, CONTACTS_FORM, _
              "PopulateContactsControls"
          Exit Sub

      End Sub
```

8. Add the following `ClearContactsControls` procedure to the `frmContacts` form:

```
      Sub ClearContactsControls()

          On Error GoTo HandleError

              'clear the values in the controls on the form

          Me.txtLName = ""
          Me.txtFName = ""
          Me.txtMName = ""

          Me.txtCompany = ""
          Me.txtAddress1 = ""
          Me.txtAddress2 = ""
          Me.txtCity = ""
          Me.txtRegion = ""
          Me.txtPostalCode = ""
          Me.txtWorkPhone = ""
          Me.txtHomePhone = ""
          Me.txtCellPhone = ""
          Me.txtEmail = ""

              Exit Sub

      HandleError:
          GeneralErrorHandler Err.Number, Err.Description, CONTACTS_FORM, _
              "ClearContactsControls"
          Exit Sub

      End Sub
```

9. Add the following `Form_Unload` event to the `frmContacts` form:

```
Private Sub Form_Unload(Cancel As Integer)

    On Error GoTo HandleError

        'close the recordset and free the memory
    rsContacts.Close
    Set rsContacts = Nothing

        Exit Sub

HandleError:
    GeneralErrorHandler Err.Number, Err.Description, CONTACTS_FORM, _
"Form_Unload"
    Exit Sub

End Sub
```

10. Congratulations—that's all the code! Now take time to resolve any typographical errors, if you have not done so already. The next section will give you a tour of the most interesting features of the application.

How It Works

The last set of code you added for the project was for the `frmContacts` form. In the `Form_Load` event, you added code to initialize the form, for example, populating the contacts recordset with one or all contacts records:

```
Private Sub Form_Load()

    On Error GoTo HandleError

    Set objContacts = New clsContacts
    Set rsContacts = New ADODB.Recordset

        'not in add mode
    blnAddMode = False

        intCurrContactRecord = 0

        Set rsContacts = objContacts.RetrieveContacts

        'if the recordset is empty
    If rsContacts.BOF And rsContacts.EOF Then
        Exit Sub
    Else
        'populate the object with values in the recordset
        objContacts.PopulatePropertiesFromRecordset rsContacts

            Call MoveToFirstRecord(intCurrContactRecord, rsContacts, _
```

```
                objContacts, blnAddMode)

                    'populate the controls on the form with the current record
            Call PopulateContactsControls
            End If
                    Exit Sub

HandleError:
        GeneralErrorHandler Err.Number, Err.Description, CONTACTS_FORM, "Form_Load"
        Exit Sub


    End Sub
```

You also added the `cmdAddToProject_Click` event that is responsible for adding the selected contact to the current project record:

```
    Private Sub cmdAddToProject_Click()

        On Error GoTo HandleError

            Dim strSQLStatement As String
            'build the SQL statement to insert a new contact for the current
        'project on frmProjects
        strSQLStatement = BuildSQLInsertProjectsContacts(objContacts.ContactId, _
                        intContactProjectAdd)

            'insert the record into the database
        ProcessUpdate (strSQLStatement)

            Call Forms("frmProjects").RefreshContacts

            'close the Contacts form to return the user to the Project streen
        DoCmd.Close acForm, "frmContacts"

            Exit Sub
    HandleError:
        GeneralErrorHandler Err.Number, Err.Description, CONTACTS_FORM, _
            "cmdAddToProject_Click"

            Exit Sub

    End Sub
```

Similarly to what you did with `frmProjects`, you also added event procedures for the `cmdAddNew`, `cmdSave`, and `cmdDelete` buttons. For example, you added the `cmdAddNew_Click` event to put the form in add mode to allow the user to add a new contact to the database:

```
    Private Sub cmdAddNew_Click()

        On Error GoTo HandleError

            'clear the current controls to enable adding a new
```

```
        'contact record
        Call AddEmptyContactRecord

            Exit Sub

HandleError:
        GeneralErrorHandler Err.Number, Err.Description, CONTACTS_FORM, _
                "cmdAddNew_Click"

        Exit Sub

End Sub
```

Just as you did with the `frmProjects` form, you also added event procedures for navigating through the records. For example, the `cmdMoveFirst_Click` event moves to the first record in the local disconnected recordset and populates the controls on the form with the current record:

```
Private Sub cmdMoveFirst_Click()

    On Error GoTo HandleError

        'move to the first record in the local disconnected recordset
        Call MoveToFirstRecord(intCurrContactRecord, rsContacts, _
            objContacts, blnAddMode)

        'populate the controls on the form with the current record
        Call PopulateContactsControls

            Exit Sub

HandleError:
        GeneralErrorHandler Err.Number, Err.Description, CONTACTS_FORM, _
                "cmdMoveFirst_Click"
        Exit Sub

End Sub
```

You also created procedures for adding an empty contact record and for clearing the contacts controls on the form. Similarly, you added a procedure called `PopulateContactsControls` to populate the controls on the `frmContacts` form with the values of the current record in the `objContacts` object.

```
Sub PopulateContactsControls()

        On Error GoTo HandleError

        'Populate the controls on the Contacts form with the values of the
        'current record in the contacts object.
        If Not rsContacts.BOF And Not rsContacts.EOF Then
            Me.txtLName = objContacts.LastName
            Me.txtFName = objContacts.FirstName
            Me.txtMName = objContacts.MiddleName
```

```
                Me.txtCompany = objContacts.Company
                Me.txtAddress1 = objContacts.Address1
                Me.txtAddress2 = objContacts.Address2
                Me.txtCity = objContacts.City
                Me.txtRegion = objContacts.Region
                Me.txtPostalCode = objContacts.PostalCode
                Me.txtWorkPhone = objContacts.WorkPhone
                Me.txtHomePhone = objContacts.HomePhone
                Me.txtCellPhone = objContacts.CellPhone
                Me.txtEmail = objContacts.Email

                        'display the record count on the form
                lblRecordNum.Caption = "Record " & intCurrContactRecord & " Of " & _
                                rsContacts.RecordCount


                ElseIf rsContacts.BOF Then
                'past beginning of recordset so move to first record
                Call MoveToFirstRecord(intCurrContactRecord, rsContacts, _
                                objContacts, blnAddMode)

            ElseIf rsContacts.EOF Then
                'past end of recordset so move back to last record
                Call MoveToLastRecord(intCurrContactRecord, rsContacts, _
                                objContacts, blnAddMode)


            End If

            Exit Sub


    HandleError:
        GeneralErrorHandler Err.Number, Err.Description, CONTACTS_FORM, _
            "PopulateContactsControls"
        Exit Sub


    End Sub
```

Finally, the `Form_Unload` event was added to the `frmContacts` form to close the `rsContacts` recordset and free the memory taken up by the recordset.

```
    Private Sub Form_Unload(Cancel As Integer)

        On Error GoTo HandleError

        'close the recordset and free the memory
        rsContacts.Close
        Set rsContacts = Nothing
            Exit Sub

    HandleError:
        GeneralErrorHandler Err.Number, Err.Description, CONTACTS_FORM, "Form_Unload"
        Exit Sub

    End Sub
```

451

Touring the Finished Project Tracker Application

Now comes the fun part. You get to see the benefit of that hard work. Let's quickly look at each screen just to point out the most interesting features. You have already seen the screens in the design process, but it is always fun to see them working with real data in them.

> *You will have to click the Options button next to the security warning when you open the database and enable macros in the database, or none of the code you wrote will be allowed to execute.*

For starters, Figure 13-28 illustrates a sample project record on the Project Tracker screen. It shows details about this sample Project Tracking project and also comments that have been entered into the list on the first tab.

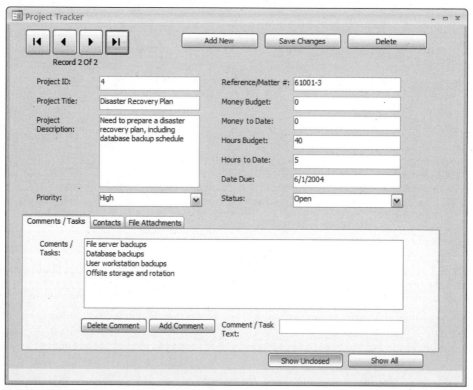

Figure 13-28

Figure 13-29 shows some contacts for the current project. You can view information such as name, phone numbers, and e-mail address. If you click the e-mail button, you will see a screen similar to that shown in Figure 13-30 with the e-mail address of the selected contact already filled in. The capability to integrate e-mail into your applications is really slick and will impress many users. You can also consult Chapter 7 on exporting and Chapter 10 on automation for more information on e-mail integration, for example, through Outlook.

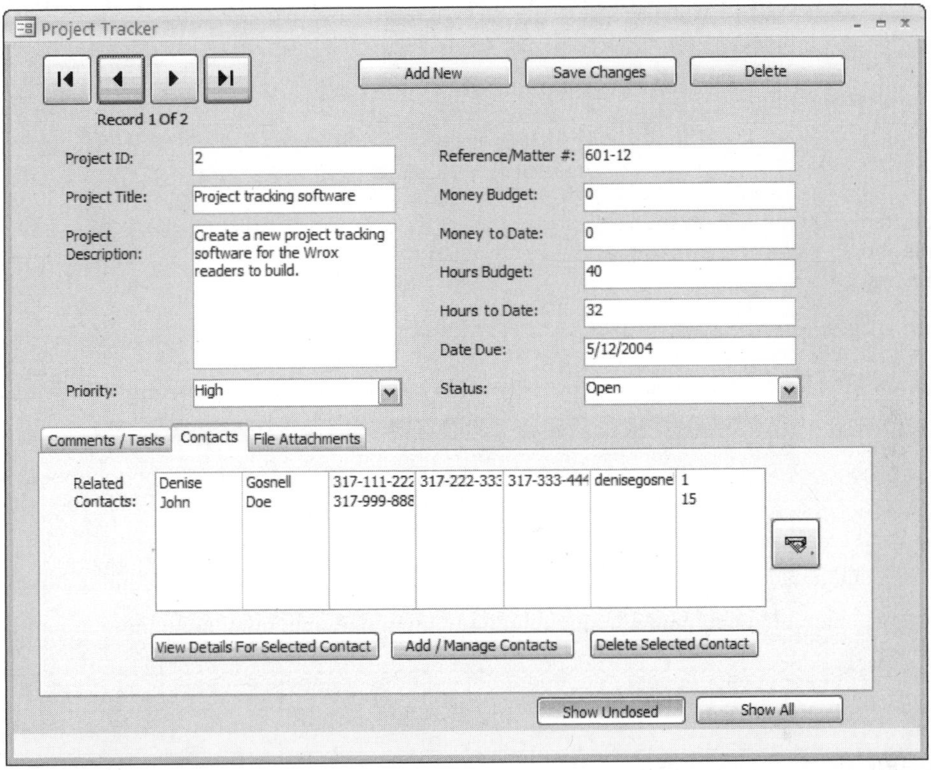

Figure 13-29

On the other hand, if you select the View Details for Selected Contact button, the Contacts screen opens with the record filtered to only the current one. This is shown in Figure 13-31.

If you want to manage contacts in general, add a contact to the existing project, or delete contacts from the database altogether, you should select the Add/Manage Contacts button shown in Figure 13-29. Figure 13-30 illustrates opening the Contacts form in general and, as you can see, more than just the one record was in the filtered version of Figure 13-31.

If you wish to add the current contact to the current project, select the Add Current Contact to Project button. You should not select this button if the current contact has already been added to the current project. If you do, you will receive a database error message indicating the change could not be made because of a duplicate value problem.

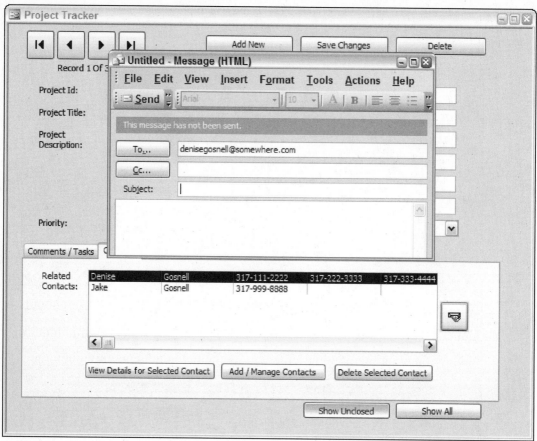

Figure 13-30

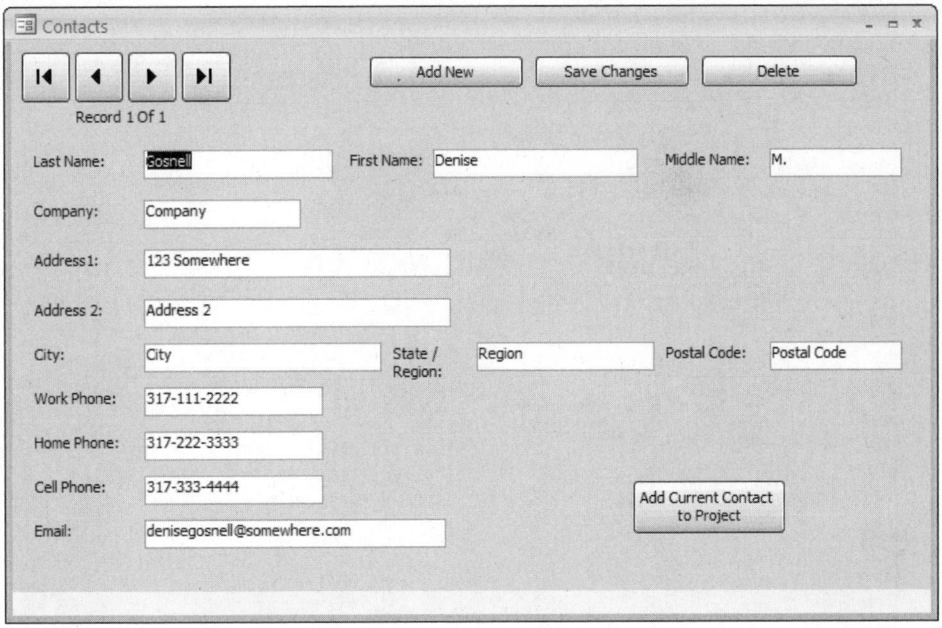

Figure 13-31

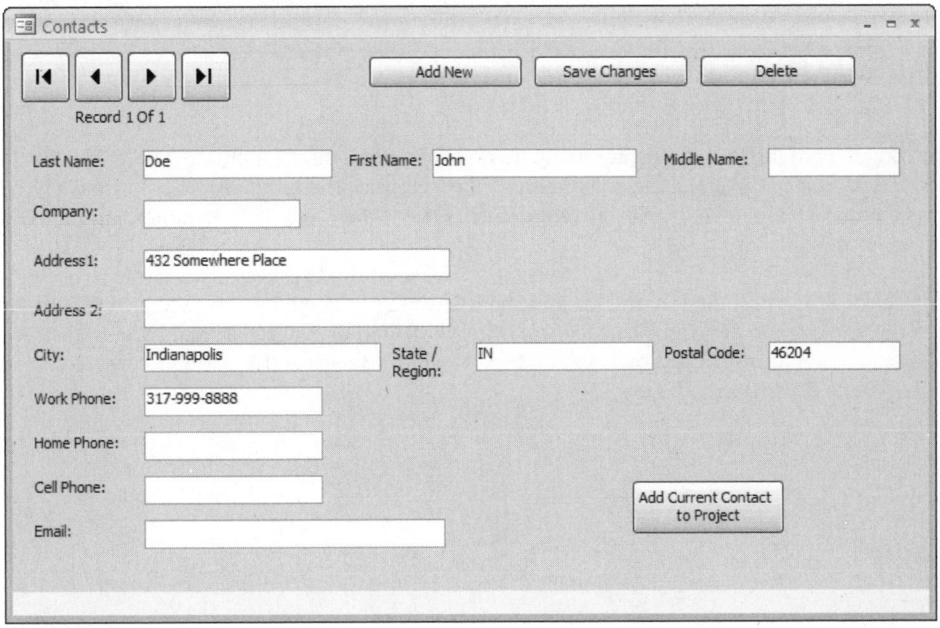

Figure 13-32

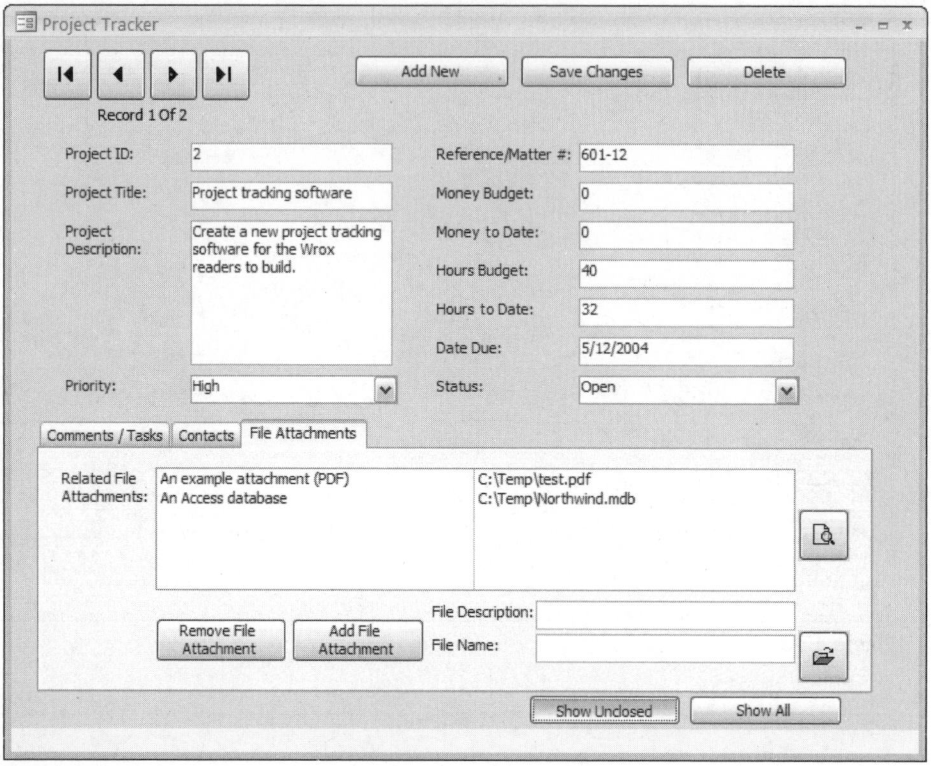

Figure 13-33

Returning now to the Project Tracker form, if you click on the third tab that contains file attachment information, you can manage file attachments. The example screen in Figure 13-33 shows two attachments that have been linked to the current project. One of them is a PDF document and the other is another Access database.

If you select a file attachment in the list and then select the Preview button, Access will actually open the file in the appropriate program. This feature is implemented using an external DLL function call to SHELLEXECUTE. Figure 13-34 shows what happens when you select the option to preview the example selected in the list shown in Figure 13-33.

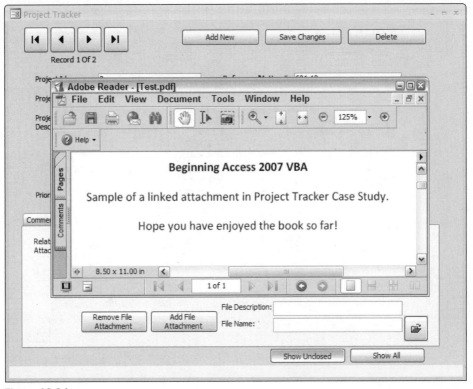

Figure 13-34

Notice how Adobe Acrobat is launched in a separate window. The procedures of the SHELLEXECUTE external function allow you to specify how the external program should open (for example, minimized, maximized, and so on).

Another interesting use of an external function call is to display a file open dialog box to help you search for an attachment. This is shown in Figure 13-35.

Figure 13-35

There is nothing special about the open dialog box itself. However, the fact that you can use this feature to locate file attachments is special. This is often a difficult task for most readers to implement, and you have just done so with relative ease. After you click the Open button on the dialog, the File Name field on the form is populated with the value. You then can fill in a file description and click the button to actually add the attachment to the list, as shown in Figure 13-36.

As I mentioned briefly earlier, the records you see on the screen and modify have not been saved back to the database yet. You are working with local disconnected records, and controls that are not updated in the database until you click the Save button. If you forget to save, you will lose your work.

A nice enhancement to this application is to keep track of whether changes have been made and then notify users when they are about to lose the changes, such as when they move to another record or close the form. This is beyond the scope of this chapter but is well worth exploring for any application that will be used extensively. Another option for you to consider is adding a dynamic web page that will display the currently pending projects in a web browser.

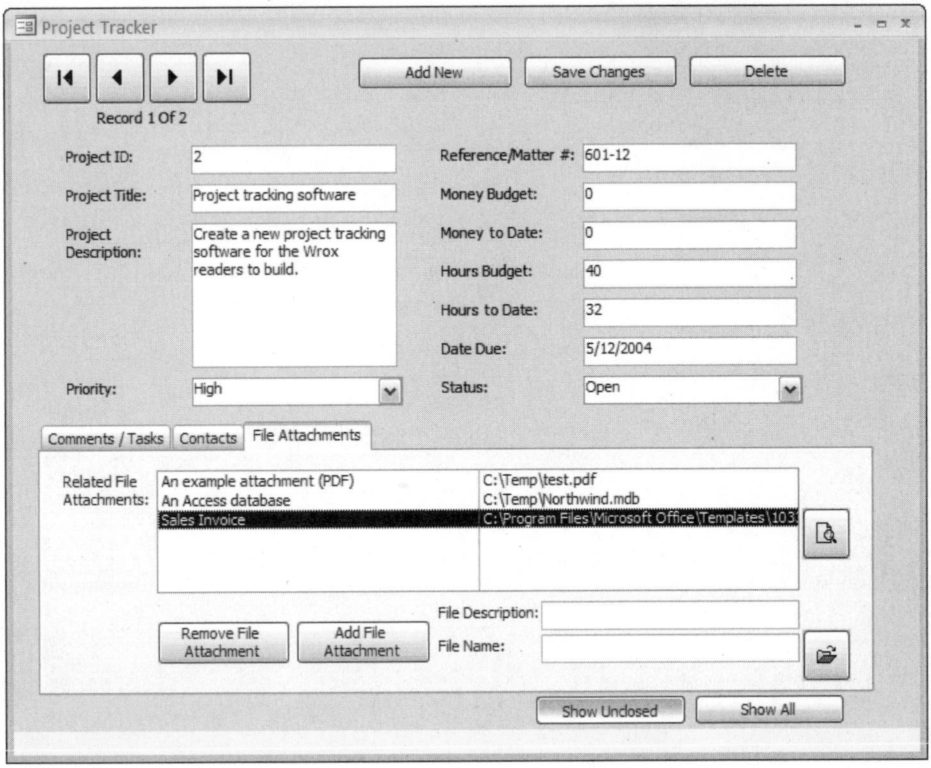

Figure 13-36

Summary

The fact that you have made it to the end of the chapter is worth a pat on the back. This was the most complicated chapter so far, both in topic and in sheer volume. Building Access applications in many ways can be quite complex. I hope you have also realized just how powerful Access can be as a development tool and how using it to implement some really slick features is easier than you thought.

At this point, you should have a much better understanding of the concepts presented in earlier chapters, especially the more complicated ones. Having a practical example is always useful. Just to make sure you get the full value out of the hard-earned money you spent on this book, I'm also including a second case study that deals with SQL Server so that you can get some experience with Access projects and SQL Server itself. Although the second case study uses SQL Server as the database, you can learn much that you can apply to other databases as well. Even if you are not a SQL Server database user, you will still solidify your understanding of the many programming concepts you've explored throughout the book.

Case Study 2: Customer Service Application

This chapter is the second of two case studies that will illustrate all the concepts covered to this point using a comprehensive real-world example. With the first case study under your belts, you now build a client-server customer service application with SQL Server storing the database and Access providing the user interface and business logic. This process includes:

❏ Using Access data projects with SQL Server databases

❏ Creating and executing stored procedures with and without parameters

❏ Creating search screens that dynamically build SQL statements from criteria entered by the user

You will create the customer service application from start to finish. For your convenience, I have included the Access project file and a text file containing the SQL stored procedures so that you can download all the source code from wrox.com. As in the earlier case study, I recommend that you work through the chapter yourself before using the source code I have provided.

For the sake of clarity, a "How It Works" section for the entire application is included at the end of this chapter.

Design Specifications

You learned in Chapter 1 and again in Chapter 13 that before you ever write a single line of code, you should carefully plan your application on paper. After detailed fact-finding regarding the purpose of the customer service application, you come up with a list of requirements. The application will be designed for use by customer service agents who receive incoming calls from customers. The application will allow the agent to retrieve the customer's account information quickly based on one or more pieces of information provided by the customer. For example, the customer may provide all or part of a home phone number, a first and last name, and/or a customer number. The Search screen will allow the agent to retrieve the customer's account record. The Search screen will implement ad hoc queries against the SQL Server database based upon the search criteria input by the agent. After the customer record is located and selected, it will be displayed containing such information as customer contact information, current service plan, and transaction history. Users also need the capability to open the View/Manage Customers screen independently of the search screen for all customers, not just for the selected customer.

Three use cases are shown in Figure 14-1. Users can execute a search to locate a particular customer (U.C. 1.1). Users can also clear the search results (U.C. 1.2). In addition, the application enables the user to open the View/Manage Customer Details screen for a selected customer (U.C. 1.3).

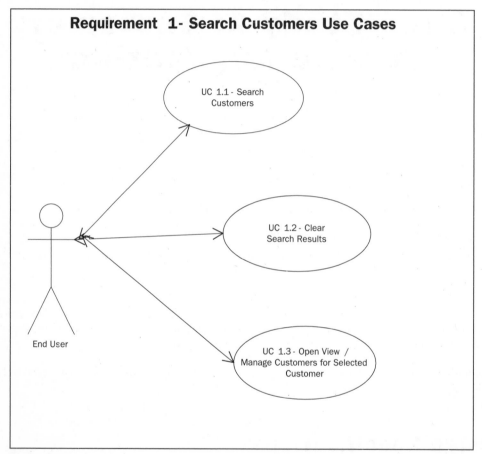

Figure 14-1

From the View/Manage Customer Details screen, you determine that the user should be able to view and manage customers using record navigation and update capabilities. However, users should not have the ability to delete user accounts, so we will not make that part of our use cases. Figure 14-2 shows these features represented in a Use Case Diagram.

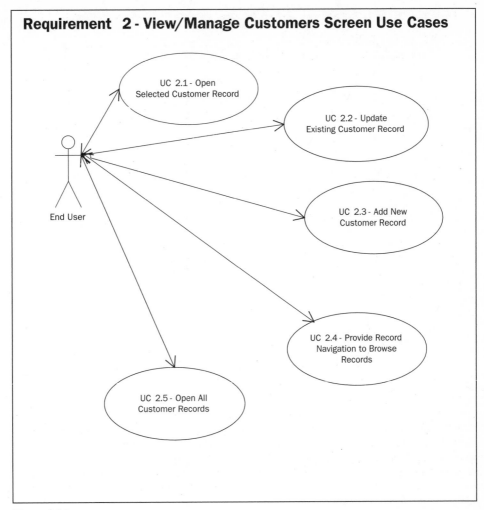

Figure 14-2

Five use cases are shown in Figure 14-2. Users can open the View/Manage Customer screen for a selected customer (U.C. 2.1). In addition, the application will enable the user to update existing (U.C. 2.2) and add new (U.C. 2.3) records. Navigation buttons are provided (U.C. 2.4) to allow the user to navigate among the records. These buttons are useful when the screen has been opened to view and manage all customer records (U.C. 2.5).

As you learned in Chapter 1 and again in Chapter 13, you have other ways to document the application, including activity diagrams, flow charts, network diagrams, and object diagrams. When you analyzed the requirements previously discussed, you determined that two main screens seem to make sense: a Customer Search screen and a View/Manage Customer Accounts screen. These designs are illustrated in Figures 14-3 and 14-4.

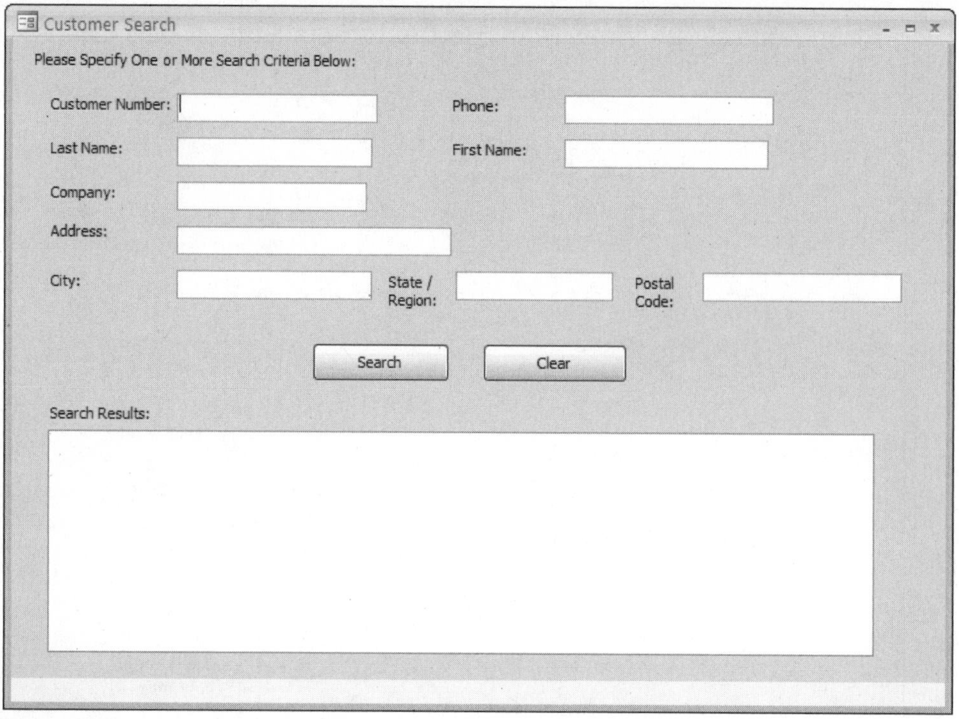

Figure 14-3

Figure 14-3 is a prototype screen for Customer Search. Notice how various data elements related to the customer are included, as well as Search and Clear buttons. The Search button allows a user to search the database for customer records that match the criteria specified in one or more fields. The matching is based on both partial and exact matches to make it quicker for the customer service representative to locate the correct record. The matching customer records are displayed in the Search Results list. If the user double-clicks a record in the Search Results list, the View/Manage Customer Accounts screen will appear for that selected customer.

Figure 14-4 is a prototype screen for View/Manage Customer Accounts. Various data elements related to the customer are included, such as name, address, and contact information. Navigation buttons plus buttons for saving changes to records are also included. Now that you have documented what you want the application to do, you can move on to creating the database and the code.

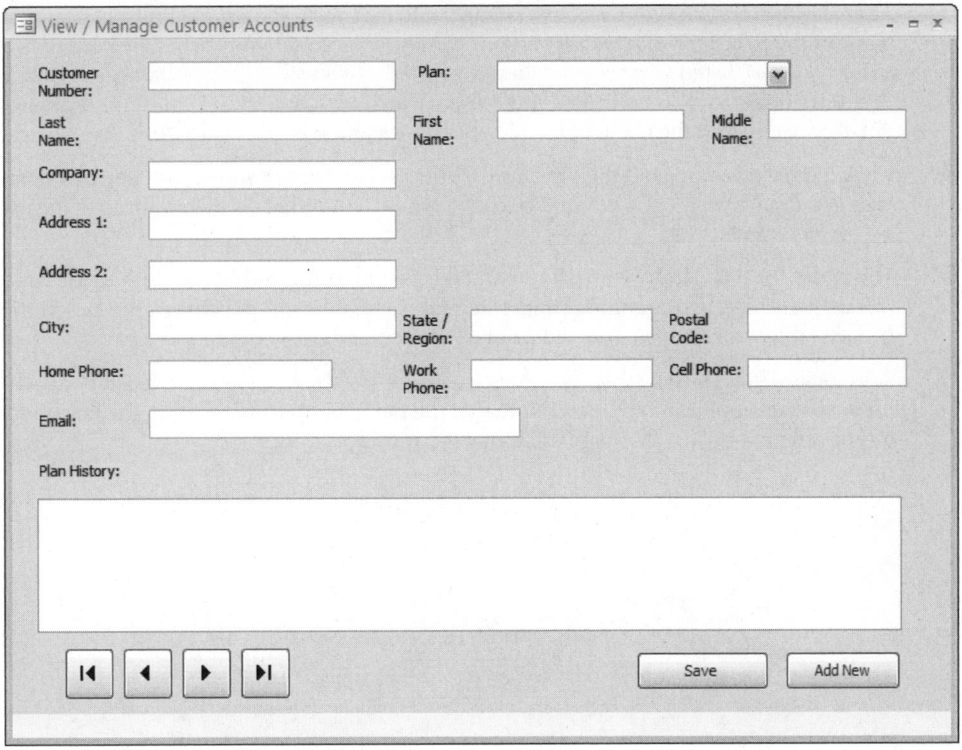

Figure 14-4

Building the Database and Database Objects

In this section, you will build the database in an Access project, which stores the data tables in SQL Server, and the user interface in the Access project itself.

You should have a version of Microsoft SQL Server installed in order to create this application. Please refer to Chapter 10 for more information on obtaining and setting up SQL Server.

Try It Out   **Building the CustomerServiceSQL Database**

Now, let's build the Access Project and SQL Server database that will store the data tables. You will also build the SQL Server stored procedures used by your application.

1.   Create a new Access project and SQL Server database by selecting the Office Button ⇨ New. Click on the Browse button. Specify a file name of CustomerService, in the Save As type dropdown list select the Microsoft Office Access Projects (*.adp) option, and press the OK button. You will be returned to the original window; press the Create button.

2.   Select "No" when Access asks you if you want to connect to an existing database.

3. The Microsoft SQL Server Database Wizard will appear, as shown in Figure 14-5. Specify the name of the SQL Server database on your computer. Also, identify whether Windows integrated security (Use Trusted Connection) should be used. If your SQL Server database is not set up for Windows integrated security, you must specify a valid SQL Server login ID and password. Finally, specify that the name of the SQL Server database is `CustomerServiceSQL`.

4. Click the Next button, and then the Finish button. The wizard shows a dialog box detailing its progress for a few seconds while it creates the new database and then returns to the newly created Access project file.

5. The tables for this database are shown in Figures 14-6 through 14-9. Note that, for your convenience, some details about the primary key for each table are specified in the Description field. In each table, you also need to add primary keys as indicated by the key icon.

6. Add the `tblCustomers` table, as shown in Figure 14-6. This table is the master customers table for storing customer information. Note that the fields in this table map to the fields on the prototype screen for View/Manage Customer Accounts.

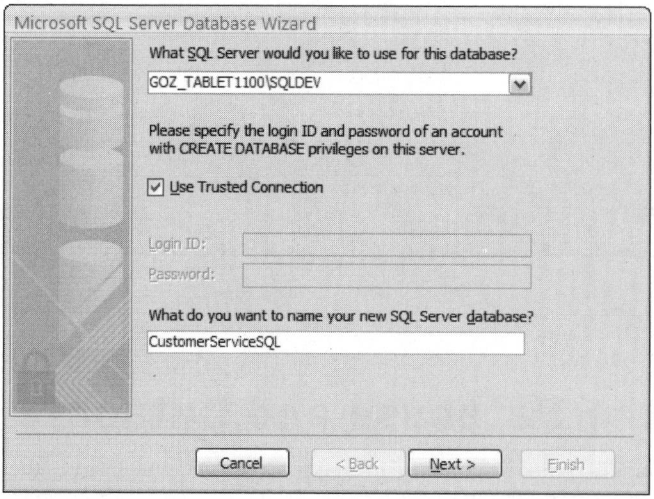

Figure 14-5

	Column Name	Data Type	Length	Allow Nulls	Description
🔑	CustomerID	int	4		Set Identity Property = YES
	LastName	nvarchar	50		
	FirstName	nvarchar	50		
	MiddleName	nvarchar	50	✓	
	Company	nvarchar	50	✓	
	Address1	nvarchar	100	✓	
	Address2	nvarchar	100	✓	
	City	nvarchar	50	✓	
	Region	nvarchar	50	✓	
	PostalCode	nvarchar	25	✓	
	WorkPhone	nvarchar	15	✓	
	HomePhone	nvarchar	15	✓	
	CellPhone	nvarchar	15	✓	
	Email	nvarchar	50	✓	
▶	CurrentPlanID	int	4		

Figure 14-6

7. Add the `tblCustomersPlanHistory` table as shown in Figure 14-7. This table maps to the plan history fields on the View/Manage Customer Accounts.

tblCustomerPlanHistory				
Column Name	Data Type	Length	Allow Nulls	Description
PlanHistoryID	int	4		Set Identity Property = YES
CustomerID	int	4		
PlanID	int	4		
RepName	nvarchar	50	✓	
DateChanged	datetime	8	✓	

Figure 14-7

tblPlans				
Column Name	Data Type	Length	Allow Nulls	Description
PlanID	int	4		Set Identity Property = YES
PlanName	nvarchar	25	✓	
PlanDescription	nvarchar	200	✓	
StatusID	int	4	✓	

Figure 14-8

tblPlanStatus				
Column Name	Data Type	Length	Allow Nulls	Description
StatusID	int	4		Set Identity Property = YES
StatusDesc	nvarchar	25		

Figure 14-9

8. Add the `tblPlans` table, as shown in Figure 14-8.

9. Add the `tblPlansStatus` table, as shown in Figure 14-9.

10. Add the data shown in Figure 14-10 to the `tblPlans` table. To do so, open the Database window, and select the table from the list of tables.

11. Add the data shown in Figure 14-11 to the `tblPlansStatus` table.

12. At this point, your `CustomerService` Access project should have the tables, as shown in Figure 14-12.

13. Select the Create ribbon in the Database window to add the stored procedures. Select the Stored Procedure option in the Other group.

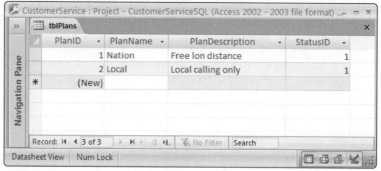

Figure 14-10

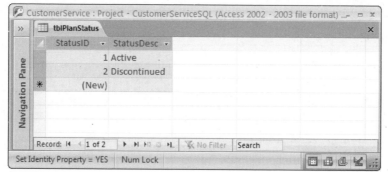

Figure 14-11

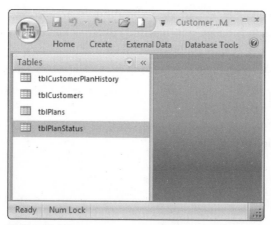

Figure 14-12

14. Select the Design ribbon ⇨ View ⇨ SQL View, as shown in Figure 14-13.

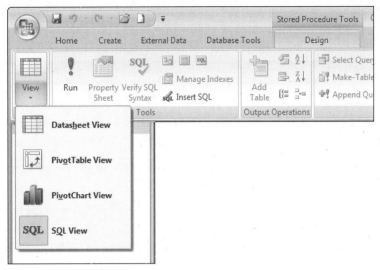

Figure 14-13

15. Replace the entire default text of the stored procedure with the following code. This stored procedure is called `spInsertCustomer` and is responsible for inserting a new record into the customer database based on the values passed to it. The procedure also inserts an entry into the `PlanHistory` table to keep track of the history of the new plan that was just added.

```
CREATE PROCEDURE dbo.spInsertCustomer
(@LastName nvarchar(50),
@FirstName nvarchar(50),
@MiddleName nvarchar(50),
@Company nvarchar(50),
@Address1 nvarchar(100),
@Address2 nvarchar(100),
@City nvarchar(50),
@Region nvarchar(50),
@PostalCode nvarchar(25),
@WorkPhone nvarchar(15),
@HomePhone nvarchar(15),
@CellPhone nvarchar(15),
@Email nvarchar(50),
@CurrentPlanId int,
@RepName nvarchar(50))
AS
DECLARE @CustomerId int

INSERT INTO dbo.tblCustomers
                (LastName, FirstName, MiddleName, Company, Address1,
Address2, City, Region, PostalCode, WorkPhone, HomePhone, CellPhone, Email,
                CurrentPlanID)
VALUES     (@LastName, @FirstName, @MiddleName, @Company, @Address1, @Address2,
@City, @Region, @PostalCode, @WorkPhone, @HomePhone,
```

```
                        @CellPhone, @Email, @CurrentPlanId)

SELECT @CustomerId = CustomerId FROM dbo.tblCustomers WHERE LastName = @LastName
and FirstName = @FirstName and CurrentPlanId = @CurrentPlanId

INSERT INTO tblCustomersPlanHistory (CustomerId, PlanId, RepName,
DateChanged) VALUES (@CustomerId, @CurrentPlanId, @RepName, CURRENT_TIMESTAMP)
```

Because there are multiple statements in the spInsertCustomer *stored procedure, you will not be able to view the stored procedure graphically from the Access Designer.*

16. The next time you open the procedure, the CREATE PROCEDURE statement will be changed to an ALTER PROCEDURE statement, as shown in Figure 14-14.

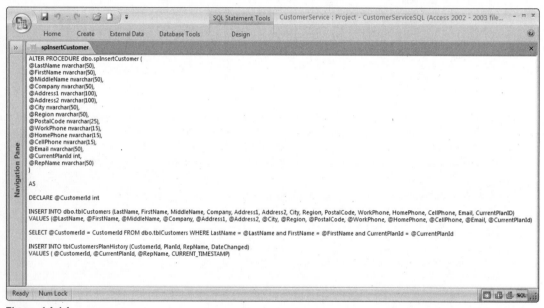

Figure 14-14

17. Add a stored procedure called spRetrieveAllCustomers. To do so, you can use either the designer or the SQL View. This procedure retrieves all customers from the database, such as when the View/Manage Customer Accounts is opened independently of the Customer Search screen.

18. To use the designer to create spRetrieveAllCustomers, from the Add Tables dialog box, select the tblCustomers table and click the Add button. Then, fill in the stored procedure design as illustrated in Figure 14-15.

19. To specify the SQL code in Design ribbon ➪ View ➪ SQL View, add the following code:

```
CREATE PROCEDURE dbo.spRetrieveAllCustomers
AS
SELECT     dbo.tblCustomers.*
FROM       dbo.tblCustomers
```

20. Add the stored procedure `spRetrieveCustomerHistory`, as shown in the Designer window of Figure 14-16 or in the code listing that follows. This procedure retrieves the customer history record that will be displayed on the View/Manage Customer Account screen in the Plan History list box.

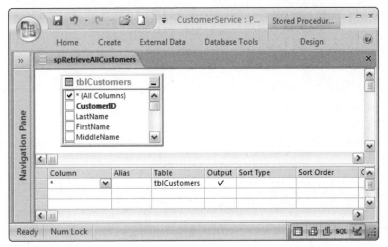

Figure 14-15

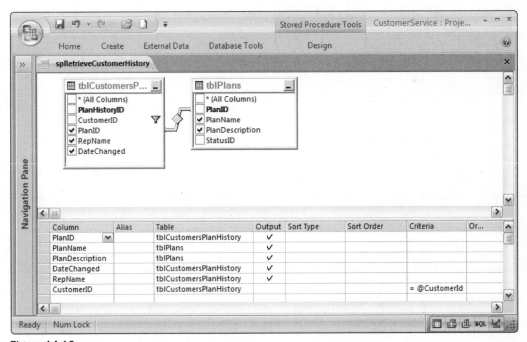

Figure 14-16

```
CREATE PROCEDURE dbo.spRetrieveCustomerHistory
(@CustomerID int)
AS
SELECT      dbo.tblCustomersPlanHistory.PlanID, dbo.tblPlans.PlanName,
dbo.tblPlans.PlanDescription, dbo.tblCustomersPlanHistory.DateChanged,
            dbo.tblCustomersPlanHistory.RepName
FROM        dbo.tblCustomersPlanHistory INNER JOIN
                dbo.tblPlans ON dbo.tblCustomersPlanHistory.PlanID =
dbo.tblPlans.PlanID
WHERE       (dbo.tblCustomersPlanHistory.CustomerID = @CustomerId)
```

21. Add the stored procedure `spRetrievePlans`, as shown in the Designer window of Figure
14-17 or in the code listing that follows. This procedure retrieves a list of the active plans from
the database to be displayed in the plan combo box on the View/Manage Customer Account
screen.

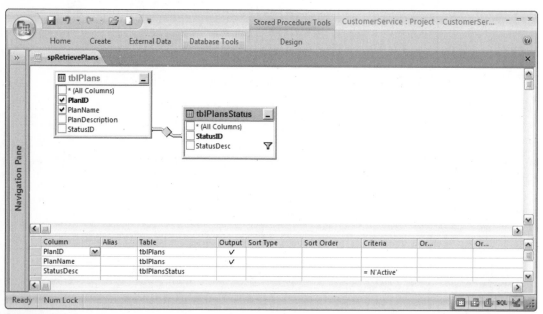

Figure 14-17

```
CREATE PROCEDURE dbo.spRetrievePlans
AS
SELECT      dbo.tblPlans.PlanID, dbo.tblPlans.PlanName
FROM        dbo.tblPlans INNER JOIN
                dbo.tblPlansStatus ON dbo.tblPlans.StatusID =
dbo.tblPlansStatus.StatusID
WHERE       (dbo.tblPlansStatus.StatusDesc = 'Active')
```

22. Add the stored procedure spRetrieveSelectedCustomer, as shown in the Designer window of Figure 14-18 or in the code listing that follows. This procedure retrieves information for the selected customer from the database.

```
CREATE PROCEDURE dbo.spRetrieveSelectedCustomer (@CustomerId as Integer)
AS SELECT      dbo.tblCustomers.*
FROM          dbo.tblCustomers
WHERE dbo.tblCustomers.CustomerID = @CustomerId
```

23. Add the stored procedure spUpdateCustomer, as shown in the code listing that follows. This procedure updates an existing customer record and also inserts a corresponding history record into the PlanHistory table if the plan has changed.

```
CREATE PROCEDURE dbo.spUpdateCustomer
(@CustomerId int,
@LastName nvarchar(50),
@FirstName nvarchar(50),
@MiddleName nvarchar(50),
@Company nvarchar(50),
@Address1 nvarchar(100),
@Address2 nvarchar(100),
@City nvarchar(50),
@Region nvarchar(50),
@PostalCode nvarchar(25),
@WorkPhone nvarchar(15),
@HomePhone nvarchar(15),
@CellPhone nvarchar(15),
@Email nvarchar(50),
@CurrentPlanId int,
@RepName nvarchar(50))
AS
DECLARE @OldPlanId  int

SELECT @OldPlanId = CurrentPlanId FROM dbo.tblCustomers WHERE CustomerId =
@CustomerId

UPDATE    dbo.tblCustomers
SET             LastName = @LastName, FirstName = @FirstName, MiddleName =
@MiddleName, Company = @Company, Address1 = @Address1,
Address2 = @Address2, City = @City, Region = @Region, PostalCode = @PostalCode,
WorkPhone = @WorkPhone, HomePhone = @HomePhone,                CellPhone =
@CellPhone, Email = @Email, CurrentPlanID = @CurrentPlanId
WHERE CustomerId = @CustomerId

IF @OldPlanId <> @CurrentPlanId
BEGIN
  INSERT INTO tblCustomersPlanHistory (CustomerId, PlanId, RepName, DateChanged)
VALUES (@CustomerId, @CurrentPlanId, @RepName, CURRENT_TIMESTAMP)
END
```

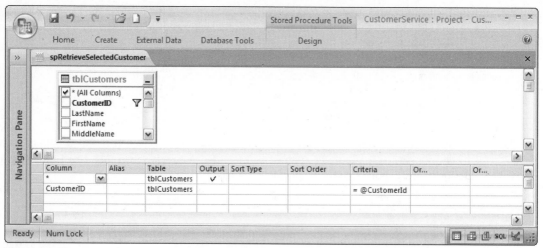

Figure 14-18

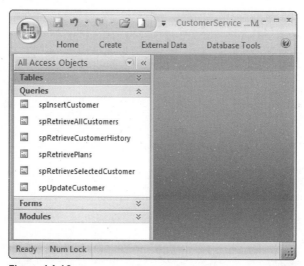

Figure 14-19

24. At this point, you should see the stored procedures listed in Figure 14-19 in the database window of the Access project.

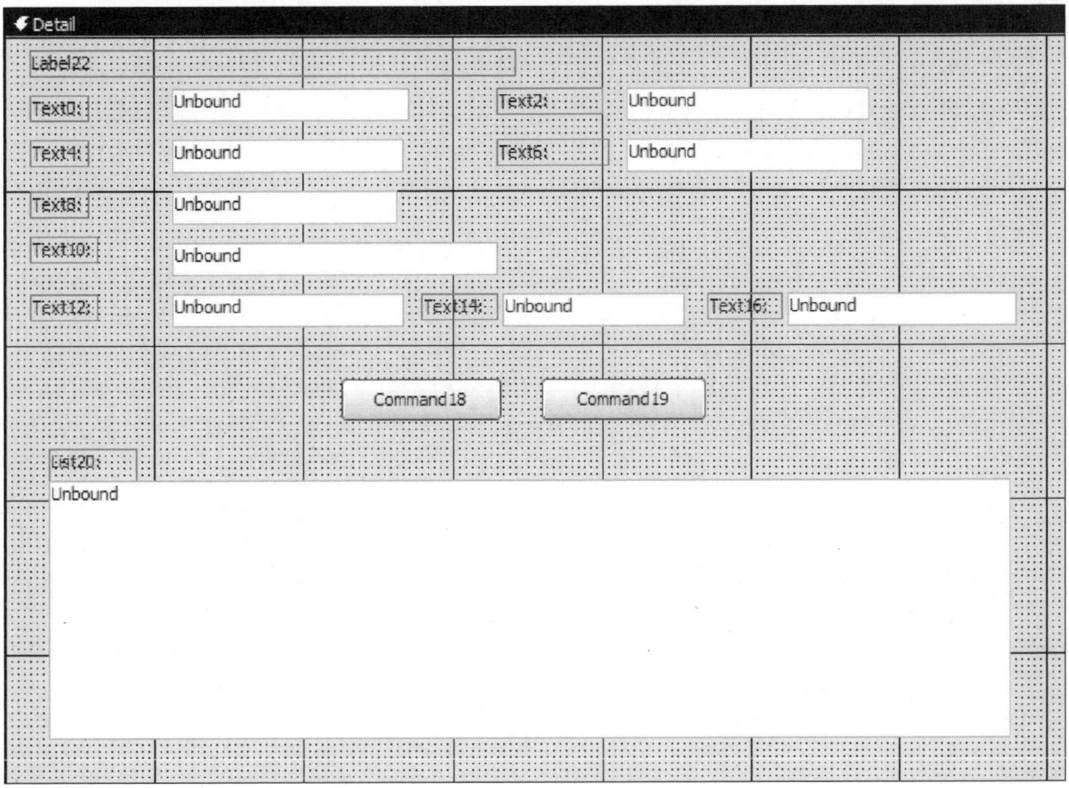

Figure 14-20

Building the User Interface

Let's create the empty forms for the user interface. You will then write the code in class modules and standard modules, and finish off by adding code to each form to call the class modules and standard modules.

Building the frmSearch and frmCustomers Forms

Let's create the two forms that will be used by the application.

1. Create a new form called `frmSearch`. Open the form in Design View. Next, drag the numerous controls onto the form and resize them, as shown in Figure 14-20.

2. The following table will help ensure you have all the correct objects on the form. Rename the controls and change other properties for each object as shown in the following table. If you placed items on the form in a different order than described, your column default names may not match with the exact numbers shown below.

Default Name on Figure 14-20	Name	Type of Control	Other Properties to Set from the Properties Dialog
Form1	frmSearch	Form	Record Selectors = No; Navigation Buttons = No; Dividing Lines = No; Auto Center = Yes; Pop up = Yes; Caption = "Customer Search''
Text0	txtCustomerNum	Text Box	Set corresponding label caption to "Customer Number:"
Text2	txtPhone	Text Box	Set corresponding label caption to "Phone:"
Text4	txtLName	Text Box	Set corresponding label caption to "Last Name:"
Text6	txtFName	Text Box	Set corresponding label caption to "First Name:"
Text8	txtCompany	Text Box	Set corresponding label caption to "Company:"
Text10	txtAddress	Text Box	Set corresponding label caption to "Address:"
Text12	txtCity	Text Box	Set corresponding label caption to "City:"
Text14	txtRegion	Text Box	Set corresponding label caption to "State / Region:"
Text16	txtPostalCode	Text Box	Set corresponding label caption to "Postal Code:"
Command18	cmdSearch	Command Button	Caption = "Search"
Command19	cmdClear	Command Button	Caption = "Clear"
List20	lstResults	List Box	Caption = "Search Results"
Label22	lblSearchInstr	Label	Caption = "Please Specify One Or More Search Criteria Below:"

3. Verify that each control on frmSearch has the correct name and other property settings as listed in the prior tables. If any of these are misspelled, later code referencing will produce an error you will have to fix. After setting all the properties, frmSearch should now appear as shown in Figure 14-21.

4. Make sure to save all the changes made to frmSearch.

5. Next, create a new form called frmCustomers. Drag the controls onto the form and resize them as shown in Figure 14-22.

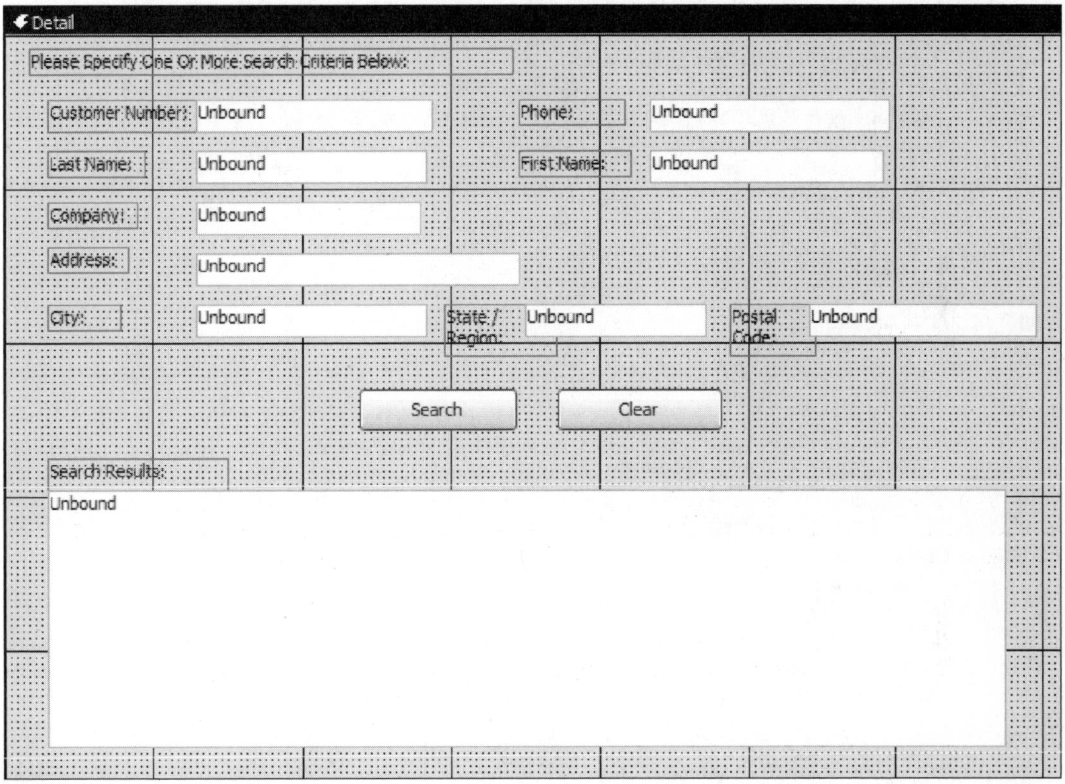

Figure 14-21

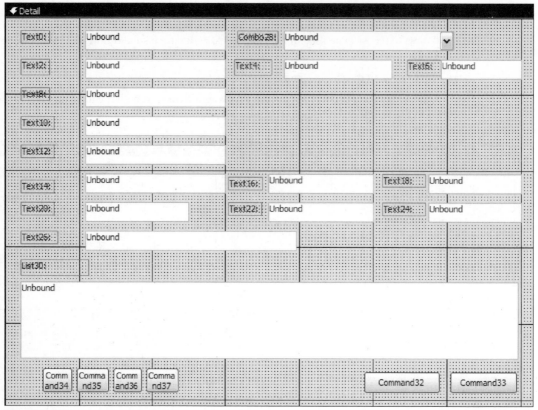

Figure 14-22

6. The following table will help ensure you have all the correct objects on the form. Rename the controls and change other properties for each object as shown in the table. If you placed items on the form in a different order than described, your default names may not match exactly as shown below.

Default Name (on Figure 14-22)	Name	Type of Control	Other Properties to Set from the Properties Dialog
Form2	frmCustomers	Form	Record Selectors = No; Navigation Buttons = No; Dividing Lines = No; Auto Center = Yes; Pop up = Yes; Caption = "View / Manage Customer Accounts"
Text0	txtCustomerNum	Text Box	Set corresponding label caption to "Customer Number:"
Text2	txtLName	Text Box	Set corresponding label caption to "Last Name:"
Text4	txtFName	Text Box	Set corresponding label caption to "First Name:"

Default Name (on Figure 14-22)	Name	Type of Control	Other Properties to Set from the Properties Dialog
Text6	txtMName	Text Box	Set corresponding label caption to "Middle Name:"
Text8	txtCompany	Text Box	Set corresponding label caption to "Company:"
Text10	txtAddress1	Text Box	Set corresponding label caption to "Address 1:"
Text12	txtAddress2	Text Box	Set corresponding label caption to "Address 2:"
Text14	txtCity	Text Box	Set corresponding label caption to "City:"
Text16	txtRegion	Text Box	Set corresponding label caption to "State / Region:"
Text18	txtPostalCode	Text Box	Set corresponding label caption to "Postal Code:"
Text20	txtHomePhone	Text Box	Set corresponding label caption to "Home Phone:"
Text22	txtWorkPhone	Text Box	Set corresponding label caption to "Work Phone:"
Text24	txtCellPhone	Text Box	Set corresponding label caption to "Cell Phone:"
Text26	txtEmail	Text Box	Set corresponding label caption to "Email:"
Combo28	cboPlan	Combo Box	Set corresponding label caption to "Plan:"
List30	lstPlanHistory	List Box	Set corresponding label caption to "Plan History:"
Command32	cmdSave	Command Button	Caption = "Save"
Command33	cmdAddNew	Command Button	Caption = "Add New"
Command34	cmdMoveFirst	Command Button	Caption = "Move First"; Picture = select Go To First 1 from list
Command35	cmdMovePrevious	Command Button	Caption = "Move Previous"; Picture = select Go To Previous 1 from list
Command36	cmdMoveNext	Command Button	Caption = "Move Next"; Picture = select Go To Next 1 from list
Command37	cmdMoveLast	Command Button	Caption = "Move Last"; Picture = select Go To Last 1 from list

7. After setting all the properties, frmCustomers should now appear as shown in Figure 14-23.

8. Save all the changes made to frmCustomers.

9. A database window of how the Customer Service Access project should appear at this point is illustrated in Figure 14-24.

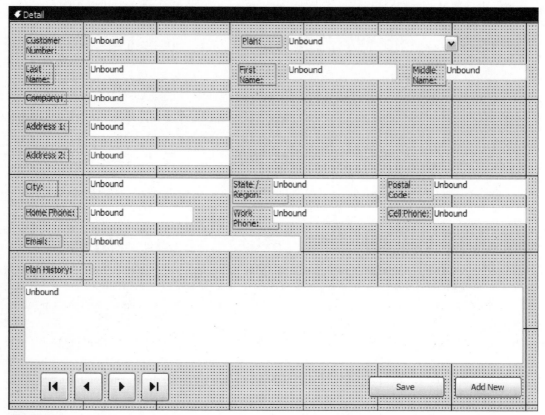

Figure 14-23

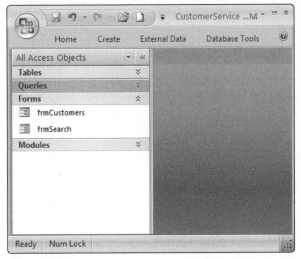

Figure 14-24

Building the Class Module for the Objects

Next, turn your attention to writing the code that will implement the desired features of your Customer Service application. VBA code can be written in various places, such as class modules that are independent or associated with a form, as well as in standard modules. Just as in the prior case study, you will create the custom class module first, then the standard modules, and finally the code for the forms to call the other modules. An example of how the Project Explorer will look in the Visual Basic Editor when you're finished is shown in Figure 14-25.

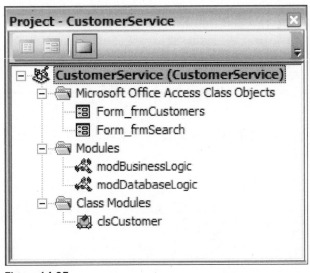

Figure 14-25

In this Customer Service application, you create one custom class module that will store the values for the current Customer.

An object diagram for the Customer class is shown in Figure 14-26.

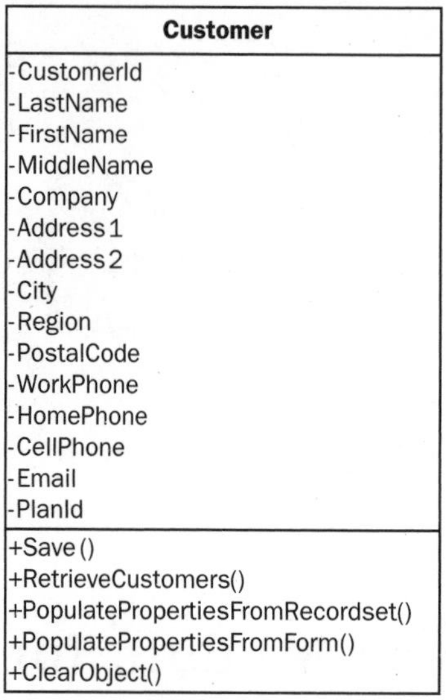

Customer
-CustomerId
-LastName
-FirstName
-MiddleName
-Company
-Address 1
-Address 2
-City
-Region
-PostalCode
-WorkPhone
-HomePhone
-CellPhone
-Email
-PlanId
+Save ()
+RetrieveCustomers()
+PopulatePropertiesFromRecordset()
+PopulatePropertiesFromForm()
+ClearObject()

Figure 14-26

The properties correspond to the data elements on the View/Manage Customer Accounts form for the most part, except that the values for the Plan History records are not shown here. The methods represent various actions that should be taken on the object. You will also write numerous other procedures that are not in the class module, as you will see later.

Try It Out   Building the clsCustomer Class

Let's get started and build the clsCustomer class module that will implement the object illustrated in Figure 14-26.

1. Add a new class module called clsCustomer. In the General Declarations section of the class, add the following code:

```
Option Compare Database
Option Explicit

Const CLS_CUSTOMER = "clsCustomer"

Dim intCustomerIdVal As Integer
Dim strLastNameVal As String
Dim strFirstNameVal As String
Dim strMiddleNameVal As String
Dim strCompanyVal As String
```

```
Dim strAddress1Val As String
Dim strAddress2Val As String
Dim strCityVal As String
Dim strRegionVal As String
Dim strPostalCodeVal As String
Dim strWorkPhoneVal As String
Dim strHomePhoneVal As String
Dim strCellPhoneVal As String
Dim strEmailVal As String
Dim intPlanIdVal As Integer
```

2. Add the various property procedures shown here to `clsCustomer` class module:

```
Public Property Get CustomerId() As Integer
    On Error Resume Next
    CustomerId = intCustomerIdVal
End Property
Public Property Let CustomerId(ByVal Value As Integer)
    On Error Resume Next
    intCustomerIdVal = Value
End Property

Public Property Get LastName() As String
    On Error Resume Next
    LastName = strLastNameVal
End Property
Public Property Let LastName(ByVal Value As String)
    On Error Resume Next
    strLastNameVal = Value
End Property

Public Property Get FirstName() As String
    On Error Resume Next
    FirstName = strFirstNameVal
End Property
Public Property Let FirstName(ByVal Value As String)
    On Error Resume Next
    strFirstNameVal = Value
End Property

Public Property Get MiddleName() As String
    On Error Resume Next
    MiddleName = strMiddleNameVal
End Property
Public Property Let MiddleName(ByVal Value As String)
    On Error Resume Next
    strMiddleNameVal = Value
End Property

Public Property Get Company() As String
    On Error Resume Next
    Company = strCompanyVal
```

```
    End Property


Public Property Let Company(ByVal Value As String)
    On Error Resume Next
    strCompanyVal = Value
End Property

Public Property Get Address1() As String
    On Error Resume Next
    Address1 = strAddress1Val
End Property
Public Property Let Address1(ByVal Value As String)
    On Error Resume Next
    strAddress1Val = Value
End Property

Public Property Get Address2() As String
    On Error Resume Next
    Address2 = strAddress2Val
End Property
Public Property Let Address2(ByVal Value As String)
    On Error Resume Next
    strAddress2Val = Value
End Property

Public Property Get City() As String
    On Error Resume Next
    City = strCityVal
End Property
Public Property Let City(ByVal Value As String)
    On Error Resume Next
    strCityVal = Value
End Property

Public Property Get Region() As String
    On Error Resume Next
    Region = strRegionVal
End Property
Public Property Let Region(ByVal Value As String)
    On Error Resume Next
    strRegionVal = Value
End Property

Public Property Get PostalCode() As String
    On Error Resume Next
    PostalCode = strPostalCodeVal
End Property
Public Property Let PostalCode(ByVal Value As String)
    On Error Resume Next
    strPostalCodeVal = Value
End Property


Public Property Get WorkPhone() As String
```

```
        On Error Resume Next
        WorkPhone = strWorkPhoneVal
    End Property
    Public Property Let WorkPhone(ByVal Value As String)
        On Error Resume Next
        strWorkPhoneVal = Value
    End Property
    Public Property Get HomePhone() As String
        On Error Resume Next
        HomePhone = strHomePhoneVal
    End Property
    Public Property Let HomePhone(ByVal Value As String)
        On Error Resume Next
        strHomePhoneVal = Value
    End Property

    Public Property Get CellPhone() As String
        On Error Resume Next
        CellPhone = strCellPhoneVal
    End Property
    Public Property Let CellPhone(ByVal Value As String)
        On Error Resume Next
        strCellPhoneVal = Value
    End Property

    Public Property Get Email() As String
        On Error Resume Next
        Email = strEmailVal
    End Property
    Public Property Let Email(ByVal Value As String)
        On Error Resume Next
        strEmailVal = Value
    End Property

    Public Property Get PlanId() As Integer
        On Error Resume Next
        PlanId = intPlanIdVal
    End Property
    Public Property Let PlanId(ByVal Value As Integer)
        On Error Resume Next
        intPlanIdVal = Value
    End Property
```

3. Add the RetrieveCustomers function shown here to the clsCustomer class module:

```
Function RetrieveCustomers() As ADODB.Recordset

    On Error GoTo HandleError

    Dim rsCust As New ADODB.Recordset


    If intCustomerLookupId > 0 Then
```

```
                'if form is being opened for selected customer from frmSearch
                Set rsCust = ExecuteSPRetrieveRS("spRetrieveSelectedCustomer", _
                    intCustomerLookupId)
            Else
                'if form is being opened for all customer records
                Set rsCust = ExecuteSPRetrieveRS("spRetrieveAllCustomers")
            End If
                'return the populated recordset
            Set RetrieveCustomers = rsCust
                Exit Function

    HandleError:
        GeneralErrorHandler Err.Number, Err.Description, CLS_CUSTOMER, _
                "RetrieveCustomers"
        Exit Function

    End Function
```

4. Add the `PopulatePropertiesFromRecordset` procedure shown here to the `clsProjects` class module:

```
Sub PopulatePropertiesFromRecordset(rsCust As ADODB.Recordset)

    On Error GoTo HandleError
        'Populate the object with the current record in the
    'recordset
    Me.CustomerId = rsCust!CustomerId
    Me.LastName = FixNull(rsCust!LastName)
    Me.FirstName = FixNull(rsCust!FirstName)
    Me.MiddleName = FixNull(rsCust!MiddleName)
    Me.Company = FixNull(rsCust!Company)
    Me.Address1 = FixNull(rsCust!Address1)
    Me.Address2 = FixNull(rsCust!Address2)
    Me.City = FixNull(rsCust!City)
    Me.Region = FixNull(rsCust!Region)
    Me.PostalCode = FixNull(rsCust!PostalCode)
    Me.WorkPhone = FixNull(rsCust!WorkPhone)
    Me.HomePhone = FixNull(rsCust!HomePhone)
    Me.CellPhone = FixNull(rsCust!CellPhone)
    Me.Email = FixNull(rsCust!Email)
    Me.PlanId = rsCust!currentplanid
        Exit Sub

HandleError:
    GeneralErrorHandler Err.Number, Err.Description, CLS_CUSTOMER, _
            "PopulatePropertiesFromRecordset"
    Exit Sub

End Sub
```

5. Add the `PopulatePropertiesFromForm` procedure shown here to the `clsCustomer` class module:

```
Sub PopulatePropertiesFromForm()

    On Error GoTo HandleError
        'Populate the object with the current record in the
    'form
        'if the customernum field is not empty (e.g. updating record)
    If Forms("frmCustomers")!txtCustomerNum <> "" Then
        Me.CustomerId = Forms("frmCustomers")!txtCustomerNum
    Else
        'adding new record so id not assigned yet
        Me.CustomerId = 0
    End If
    Me.LastName = Forms("frmCustomers")!txtLName
    Me.FirstName = Forms("frmCustomers")!txtFName
    Me.MiddleName = Forms("frmCustomers")!txtMName
    Me.Company = Forms("frmCustomers")!txtCompany
    Me.Address1 = Forms("frmCustomers")!txtAddress1
    Me.Address2 = Forms("frmCustomers")!txtAddress2
    Me.City = Forms("frmCustomers")!txtCity
    Me.Region = Forms("frmCustomers")!txtRegion
    Me.PostalCode = Forms("frmCustomers")!txtPostalCode
    Me.WorkPhone = Forms("frmCustomers")!txtWorkPhone
    Me.HomePhone = Forms("frmCustomers")!txtHomePhone
    Me.CellPhone = Forms("frmCustomers")!txtCellPhone
    Me.Email = Forms("frmCustomers")!txtEmail
    Me.PlanId = Forms("frmCustomers")!cboPlan
        Exit Sub

HandleError:
    GeneralErrorHandler Err.Number, Err.Description, CLS_CUSTOMER, _
            "PopulatePropertiesFromForm"
    Exit Sub
End Sub
```

6. Add the `ClearObject` procedure shown here to the `clsCustomer` class module:

```
Sub ClearObject()

    On Error GoTo HandleError
        'clear the values in the customer object
    Me.CustomerId = 0
    Me.LastName = ""
    Me.FirstName = ""
    Me.MiddleName = ""
    Me.Company = ""


    Me.Address1 = ""
    Me.Address2 = ""
    Me.City = ""
```

```
        Me.Region = ""
        Me.PostalCode = ""
        Me.WorkPhone = ""
        Me.HomePhone = ""
        Me.CellPhone = ""
        Me.Email = ""
        Me.PlanId = 0
            Exit Sub


HandleError:
        GeneralErrorHandler Err.Number, Err.Description, CLS_CUSTOMER, _
            "ClearObject"
        Exit Sub


End Sub
```

7. Add the `Save` procedure shown here to the `clsCustomer` class module:

```
Sub Save(blnAddMode As Boolean, rsCust As ADODB.Recordset)

    On Error GoTo HandleError

    Dim strSPname As String

    'if adding a new record
    If blnAddMode = True Then
        strSPname = "spInsertCustomer"
    Else
    'if updating a record
        strSPname = "spUpdateCustomer"
    End If

    'perform the insert or update
    Call ProcessUpdate(strSPname, Me, rsCust)

    Exit Sub

HandleError:
    GeneralErrorHandler Err.Number, Err.Description, CLS_CUSTOMER, "Save"
    Exit Sub

End Sub
```

8. Make sure to keep saving your changes periodically so they are not lost.

Building the Standard Modules

Now that you have created the properties and methods for the `Customer` objects, you are ready to begin writing the code in the standard modules.

Try It Out   Building the modBusinessLogic and modDatabaseLogic Modules

The modBusinessLogic module will contain business logic but will not contain any database access calls. The modDatabaseLogic module will contain calls that are specific to the database. Let's create these modules.

1. Insert a new standard module called modBusinessLogic. Add the following code to the General Declarations of the module:

```
Option Compare Database
Option Explicit
Const BUS_LOGIC = "modBusinessLogic"
Public intCustomerLookupId As Integer
```

2. Add the following FixNull function to the modBusinessLogic module:

```
Function FixNull(varIn As Variant) As String

'this procedure sets null values in the recordset
'to a null string so an error does not occur when
'trying to assign the value to a control for display

    'if the value is null
    If IsNull(varIn) Then
        FixNull = ""
    Else
        'return the value passed in
        FixNull = varIn
    End If

End Function
```

3. Add the following PopulateListFromRecordset procedure to the modBusinessLogic module:

```
Sub PopulateListFromRecordset(lstList As ListBox, rsRecordset As _
                        ADODB.Recordset, intNumCols As Integer)

    On Error GoTo HandleError

    Dim intCounter As Integer
    Dim strItem As String

    With lstList
        .RowSource = ""
        .ColumnCount = intNumCols
        .RowSourceType = "Value List"
    End With

    'add all of the values in the recordset to the list box

    Do Until rsRecordset.EOF
```

```
            'for each item in the current record, build string


        For intCounter = 0 To intNumCols - 1
            strItem = strItem & rsRecordset(intCounter).Value & ";"
        Next intCounter
        lstList.AddItem (strItem)
        strItem = ""
        rsRecordset.MoveNext
    Loop

    Exit Sub


HandleError:
    GeneralErrorHandler Err.Number, Err.Description, BUS_LOGIC, _
            "PopulateListFromRecordset"
    Exit Sub
End Sub
```

4. Add the following MoveToFirstRecord procedure to the modBusinessLogic module:

```
Sub MoveToFirstRecord(rsRecordset As ADODB.Recordset, objObject As Object, _
                blnAddMode As Boolean)

    On Error GoTo HandleError
        'move to the first record in the local disconnected recordset
    If Not rsRecordset.BOF And Not rsRecordset.EOF Then
        rsRecordset.MoveFirst
        'add code to populate object with new current record
        objObject.PopulatePropertiesFromRecordset rsRecordset
            blnAddMode = False
    End If
        Exit Sub
    HandleError:
        GeneralErrorHandler Err.Number, Err.Description, BUS_LOGIC, _
                "MoveToFirstRecord"
        Exit Sub

End Sub
```

5. Add the following MoveToLastRecord procedure to the modBusinessLogic module:

```
Sub MoveToLastRecord(rsRecordset As ADODB.Recordset, objObject As Object, _
                blnAddMode As Boolean)

    On Error GoTo HandleError
        'move to the last record in the local disconnected recordset
    If Not rsRecordset.BOF And Not rsRecordset.EOF Then
        rsRecordset.MoveLast

        'add code to populate object with new current record
```

```
            objObject.PopulatePropertiesFromRecordset rsRecordset
                    blnAddMode = False
            End If
            Exit Sub

HandleError:
        GeneralErrorHandler Err.Number, Err.Description, BUS_LOGIC, _
                "MoveToLastRecord"
        Exit Sub

End Sub
```

6. Add the following `MoveToPreviousRecord` procedure to the `modBusinessLogic` module:

```
Sub MoveToPreviousRecord(rsRecordset As ADODB.Recordset, objObject As Object, _
                    blnAddMode As Boolean)
        On Error GoTo HandleError
        'move to the previous record in the local disconnected recordset
      'if not already at the beginning
      If Not rsRecordset.BOF Then
            rsRecordset.MovePrevious
                    blnAddMode = False
                    'make sure not past beginning of recordset now
            If Not rsRecordset.BOF Then
                        'add code to populate object with new current record
                objObject.PopulatePropertiesFromRecordset rsRecordset
                Else
            'at beginning of recordset so move to next record
                rsRecordset.MoveNext
            End If
      End If
      Exit Sub

HandleError:
        GeneralErrorHandler Err.Number, Err.Description, BUS_LOGIC, _
                "MoveToPreviousRecord"
        Exit Sub

End Sub
```

7. Add the following `MoveToNextRecord` procedure to the `modBusinessLogic` module:

```
Sub MoveToNextRecord(rsRecordset As ADODB.Recordset, objObject As Object, _
                    blnAddMode As Boolean)

        On Error GoTo HandleError
            'move to the next record in the local disconnected recordset
      'if not already at the end
      If Not rsRecordset.EOF Then
            rsRecordset.MoveNext
                    blnAddMode = False
                    'make sure not past end of recordset
            If Not rsRecordset.EOF Then
```

```
                'add code to populate object with new current record
                objObject.PopulatePropertiesFromRecordset rsRecordset
         Else
                'at end of recordset so move back one
                rsRecordset.MovePrevious
         End If
         End If
         Exit Sub


HandleError:
      GeneralErrorHandler Err.Number, Err.Description, BUS_LOGIC, _
            "MoveToNextRecord"
      Exit Sub

End Sub
```

8. Add the following `GeneralErrorHandler` procedure to the `modBusinessLogic` module:

```
Public Sub GeneralErrorHandler(lngErrNumber As Long, strErrDesc As String, _
            strModuleSource As String, strProcedureSource As String)

      On Error Resume Next
          Dim strMessage As String
           'build the error message string from the parameters passed in
      strMessage = "An error has occurred in the application."
      strMessage = strMessage & vbCrLf & "Error Number: " & lngErrNumber
      strMessage = strMessage & vbCrLf & "Error Description: " & strErrDesc
      strMessage = strMessage & vbCrLf & "Module Source: " & strModuleSource
      strMessage = strMessage & vbCrLf & "Procedure Source: " &
strProcedureSource
          'display the message to the user
      MsgBox strMessage, vbCritical
          Exit Sub

End Sub
```

9. Save your changes to the `modBusinessLogic` module.

10. Insert a new standard module called `modDatabaseLogic`. Add the following code to the General Declarations of the module:

```
Option Compare Database
Option Explicit
Dim cnConn As ADODB.Connection
Dim strConnection As String
Const DB_LOGIC = "modDatabaseLogic"
```

11. Add the following `OpenDbConnection` procedure to the `modDatabaseLogic` module. You will need to modify the `strConnection` string to point to your SQL Server database. If you are not using integrated security, you must specify the user ID and password (`User Id=sa;` `Password=password;`) in place of the Integrated Security option (`Integrated Security=SSPI;`).

```
Sub OpenDbConnection()

    On Error GoTo HandleError
        strConnection = "Provider=sqloledb;Data Source=goz_tablet1100\sqldev;" & _
                "Integrated Security=SSPI;Initial Catalog=CustomerServiceSQL"

        'create a new connection instance and open it using the connection
         string
        Set cnConn = New ADODB.Connection
        cnConn.Open strConnection
        Exit Sub

HandleError:
    GeneralErrorHandler Err.Number, Err.Description, DB_LOGIC, _
            "OpenDbConnection"
    Exit Sub

End Sub
```

12. Add the following `CloseDbConnection` procedure to the `modDatabaseLogic` module:

```
Sub CloseDbConnection()
        On Error GoTo HandleError
        'close the database connection
    cnConn.Close
    Set cnConn = Nothing
        Exit Sub

HandleError:
    GeneralErrorHandler Err.Number, Err.Description, DB_LOGIC, _
            "CloseDbConnection"
    Exit Sub

End Sub
```

13. Add the following `ProcessRecordset` function to the `modDatabaseLogic` module:

```
Function ProcessRecordset(strSQLStatement As String) As ADODB.Recordset

    On Error GoTo HandleError
        'open the connection to the database
    Call OpenDbConnection
        'create a new instance of a recordset
    Dim rsCont As New ADODB.Recordset
        'set various properties of the recordset
    With rsCont
        'specify a cursortype and lock type that will allow updates
        .CursorType = adOpenKeyset
        .CursorLocation = adUseClient
        .LockType = adLockBatchOptimistic
        'populate the recordset based on SQL statement
        .Open strSQLStatement, cnConn
```

```
        'disconnect the recordset
        .ActiveConnection = Nothing
    End With
        'close the connection to the database
    Call CloseDbConnection
        'return the recordset
    Set ProcessRecordset = rsCont
        Exit Function

HandleError:
    GeneralErrorHandler Err.Number, Err.Description, DB_LOGIC, _
            "ProcessRecordset"
    Exit Function

End Function
```

14. Add the following `BuildSQLSelectFrom` function to the `modDatabaseLogic` module:

```
Function BuildSQLSelectFrom() As String

    On Error GoTo HandleError
        'create SELECT FROM part of SQL Statement
    BuildSQLSelectFrom = "SELECT CustomerID, FirstName, LastName, " & _
        " Company, Address1, City, Region, PostalCode, " & _
        " HomePhone, WorkPhone, CellPhone FROM tblCustomers "
        Exit Function

HandleError:
    GeneralErrorHandler Err.Number, Err.Description, DB_LOGIC, _
            "BuildSQLSelectFrom"
    Exit Function

End Function
```

15. Add the following `BuildSQLWhere` function to the `modDatabaseLogic` module:

```
Function BuildSQLWhere(blnPriorWhere As Boolean, strPriorWhere As String, _
                strValue As String, strDbFieldName As String) As String

    On Error GoTo HandleError
        Dim strWhere As String
        If blnPriorWhere Then
        'add to the existing where clause
        strWhere = strPriorWhere & " AND "
    Else
        'create the where clause for the first time
        strWhere = " WHERE "
    End If
        If strDbFieldName = "Phone" Then
        'search each of phone fields in the db for this value to see
        'if exact match or starts with this value for any one of the
        'phone fields
        strWhere = strWhere & "(HomePhone LIKE '" & PadQuotes(strValue) & "%'" & _
```

```
        " OR WorkPhone LIKE '" & PadQuotes(strValue) & "%'" & _
        " OR CellPhone LIKE '" & PadQuotes(strValue) & "%')"
    Else
        'build where clause using LIKE so will find both exact
        'matches and those that start with value input by user
        strWhere = strWhere & strDbFieldName & " LIKE '" & PadQuotes(strValue) & _
            "%' "
    End If
        blnPriorWhere = True
        'return where clause
    BuildSQLWhere = strWhere
        Exit Function

HandleError:
    GeneralErrorHandler Err.Number, Err.Description, DB_LOGIC, "BuildSQLWhere"
    Exit Function

End Function
```

16. Add the following `PadQuotes` function to the `modDatabaseLogic` module:

```
Function PadQuotes(strIn As String) As String

    'This function replaces the occurrence of single
    'quotes with two single quotes in a row.
    'This is to eliminate errors in SQL Server and other
    'databases when a user includes an apostrophe in the
    'data value, and helps to enhance application security.
        On Error GoTo HandleError
        PadQuotes = Replace(strIn, "'", "''")
        Exit Function

HandleError:
    GeneralErrorHandler Err.Number, Err.Description, DB_LOGIC, "PadQuotes"
    Exit Function

End Function
```

17. Add the following `ExecuteSPRetrieveRS` function to the `modDatabaseLogic` module:

```
Function ExecuteSPRetrieveRS(strSPname As String, Optional intCustomerId _
                    As Integer) As ADODB.Recordset
        On Error GoTo HandleError
        Dim parCustId As ADODB.Parameter
    Dim cmdCommand As ADODB.Command
    Dim rsCustomers As ADODB.Recordset
        'set up the command object for executing stored procedure
    Set cmdCommand = New ADODB.Command
    cmdCommand.CommandType = adCmdStoredProc
        Set rsCustomers = New ADODB.Recordset
        'if the customer id is specified and greater than 0
    If Not IsMissing(intCustomerId) And intCustomerId > 0 Then
        'Add parameter to be passed to stored procedure
        Set parCustId = cmdCommand.CreateParameter("CustomerId", _
```

```
                                adInteger, adParamInput)
            parCustId.Value = intCustomerId
            cmdCommand.Parameters.Append parCustId
        End If
            'set stored procedure name
        cmdCommand.CommandText = strSPname
            'open the database connection
        Call OpenDbConnection
            'set the command object to the current connection
        Set cmdCommand.ActiveConnection = cnConn


            'Create recordset by executing the command
        With rsCustomers
            .CursorLocation = adUseClient
            .CursorType = adOpenStatic
            .LockType = adLockBatchOptimistic
            Set .Source = cmdCommand
            .Open
        End With
            Set rsCustomers.ActiveConnection = Nothing
            'close the database connection
        Call CloseDbConnection
            'return the recordset
        Set ExecuteSPRetrieveRS = rsCustomers
            Exit Function

HandleError:
        GeneralErrorHandler Err.Number, Err.Description, DB_LOGIC, _
            "RetrieveCustomersDb"
        Exit Function

End Function
```

18.   Add the following ProcessUpdate procedure to the modDatabaseLogic module:

```
Sub ProcessUpdate(strSPname As String, objCust As clsCustomer, Optional _
                rsCust As ADODB.Recordset)

    On Error GoTo HandleError
        'This procedure is used to handle updates to the database
        'open the connection to the database
    Call OpenDbConnection
        'execute the stored procedure
    Call ExecuteStoredProcedure(strSPname, objCust)
        'close the connection to the database
    Call CloseDbConnection
        Exit Sub

HandleError:
    GeneralErrorHandler Err.Number, Err.Description, DB_LOGIC, "ProcessUpdate"
    Exit Sub


End Sub
```

19. Add the following `ExecuteStoredProcedure` procedure to the `modDatabaseLogic` module:

```
Sub ExecuteStoredProcedure(strSPname As String, objCust As clsCustomer)

    On Error GoTo HandleError
    'the purpose of this procedure is to execute
    'a stored procedure that does not return any
    'rows against the database.
    Dim cmdCommand As ADODB.Command
    Set cmdCommand = New ADODB.Command

    'set up the command object for executing stored procedure
    cmdCommand.CommandType = adCmdStoredProc
    Call AddParameters(strSPname, cmdCommand, objCust)

    'set the command to the current connection
    Set cmdCommand.ActiveConnection = cnConn

    'set the SQL statement to the command text
    cmdCommand.CommandText = strSPname

    'execute the command against the database
    cmdCommand.Execute
        Exit Sub

HandleError:
    GeneralErrorHandler Err.Number, Err.Description, DB_LOGIC, _
        "ExecuteStoredProcedure"
    Exit Sub

End Sub
```

20. Add the following `AddParameters` procedure to the `modDatabaseLogic` module:

```
Sub AddParameters(strSPname As String, cmdCommand As ADODB.Command, objCust _
                As clsCustomer)

    On Error GoTo HandleError
        Dim parParm As ADODB.Parameter

    'if updating existing record
    If strSPname = "spUpdateCustomer" Then
        'Add parameter for existing Customer Id to be passed to stored procedure
        Set parParm = cmdCommand.CreateParameter("CustomerId", adInteger, _
                adParamInput)
        cmdCommand.Parameters.Append parParm
        parParm.Value = objCust.CustomerId
    End If

    'Add parameter for Last Name to be passed to stored procedure
    Set parParm = cmdCommand.CreateParameter("LastName", adVarChar, _
```

```
                    adParamInput, 50)


parParm.Value = objCust.LastName
cmdCommand.Parameters.Append parParm
    'Add parameter for First Name to be passed to stored procedure
Set parParm = cmdCommand.CreateParameter("FirstName", adVarChar, _
             adParamInput, 50)
parParm.Value = objCust.FirstName
cmdCommand.Parameters.Append parParm

'Add parameter for Middle Name to be passed to stored procedure
Set parParm = cmdCommand.CreateParameter("MiddleName", adVarChar, _
             adParamInput, 50)
parParm.Value = objCust.MiddleName
cmdCommand.Parameters.Append parParm

'Add parameter for Company Name to be passed to stored procedure
Set parParm = cmdCommand.CreateParameter("Company", adVarChar, _
             adParamInput, 50)
parParm.Value = objCust.Company
cmdCommand.Parameters.Append parParm

'Add parameter for Address1 to be passed to stored procedure
Set parParm = cmdCommand.CreateParameter("Address1", adVarChar, _
             adParamInput, 100)
parParm.Value = objCust.Address1
cmdCommand.Parameters.Append parParm

'Add parameter for Address2 to be passed to stored procedure
Set parParm = cmdCommand.CreateParameter("Address2", adVarChar, _
             adParamInput, 100)
parParm.Value = objCust.Address2
cmdCommand.Parameters.Append parParm

'Add parameter for City to be passed to stored procedure
Set parParm = cmdCommand.CreateParameter("City", adVarChar, _
               adParamInput, 50)
parParm.Value = objCust.City
cmdCommand.Parameters.Append parParm

'Add parameter for Region to be passed to stored procedure
Set parParm = cmdCommand.CreateParameter("Region", adVarChar, _
               adParamInput, 50)
parParm.Value = objCust.Region
cmdCommand.Parameters.Append parParm

'Add parameter for Postal Code to be passed to stored procedure
Set parParm = cmdCommand.CreateParameter("PostalCode", adVarChar, _
             adParamInput, 25)
parParm.Value = objCust.PostalCode
cmdCommand.Parameters.Append parParm

'Add parameter for Work Phone to be passed to stored procedure
```

```
        Set parParm = cmdCommand.CreateParameter("WorkPhone", adVarChar, _
                adParamInput, 15)


    parParm.Value = objCust.WorkPhone
    cmdCommand.Parameters.Append parParm

    'Add parameter for Home Phone to be passed to stored procedure
    Set parParm = cmdCommand.CreateParameter("HomePhone", adVarChar, _
                adParamInput, 15)
    parParm.Value = objCust.HomePhone
    cmdCommand.Parameters.Append parParm

    'Add parameter for Cell Phone to be passed to stored procedure
    Set parParm = cmdCommand.CreateParameter("CellPhone", adVarChar, _
                adParamInput, 15)
    parParm.Value = objCust.CellPhone
    cmdCommand.Parameters.Append parParm

    'Add parameter for Email to be passed to stored procedure
    Set parParm = cmdCommand.CreateParameter("Email", adVarChar, _
                adParamInput, 50)
    parParm.Value = objCust.Email
    cmdCommand.Parameters.Append parParm

    'Add parameter for Current Plan Id to be passed to stored procedure
    Set parParm = cmdCommand.CreateParameter("CurrentPlanId", adInteger, _
                adParamInput)
    parParm.Value = objCust.PlanId
    cmdCommand.Parameters.Append parParm
        'Add parameter for RepName to be passed to stored procedure
    Set parParm = cmdCommand.CreateParameter("RepName", adVarChar, _
                adParamInput, 50)
    parParm.Value = Application.CurrentUser
    cmdCommand.Parameters.Append parParm

    Exit Sub

HandleError:
    GeneralErrorHandler Err.Number, Err.Description, DB_LOGIC, "AddParameters"
    Exit Sub

End Sub
```

21. Save your changes to the `modDatabaseLogic` module.

Connecting the User Interface to the Code

You are now ready to tie everything you have done so far together by adding the VBA code to the Customer Search and View/Manage Customer Accounts forms. Most of this code will be event procedures that fire when different buttons are clicked. Some of the code will also be local procedures that deal with user-interface-specific features. It just did not make sense to put these in a standard or class module.

The Customer Search Form

An example of the Customer Search form, called `frmSearch`, is shown in Figure 14-27 with some sample data populated. Keep it in mind as you write the code for the form.

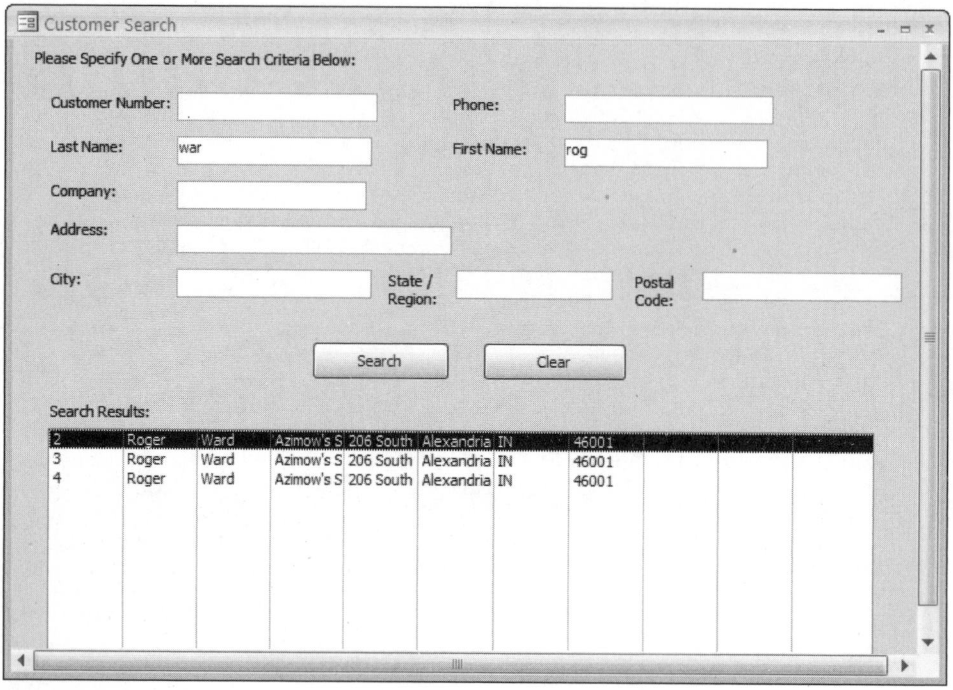

Figure 14-27

Try It Out   **Writing Code for the frmSearch**

As previously mentioned, you are now ready to write the VBA code that will finish up the application. Start with the `frmSearch` form, and finish with the `frmCustomers` form.

1.   Open the `frmSearch` form and select the `Form_Load` event for the form to bring up the Visual Basic Editor. Add the following code to the form:

```
Private Sub Form_Load()

    On Error GoTo HandleError
        'create new recordset
    Set rsSearch = New ADODB.Recordset
        Exit Sub


HandleError:
    GeneralErrorHandler Err.Number, Err.Description, SEARCH_FORM, "Form_Load"
```

```
        Exit Sub

End Sub
```

2. Add the following code to the General Declarations section of the form:

```
Option Compare Database
Option Explicit
Const SEARCH_FORM = "frmSearch"
Dim rsSearch As ADODB.Recordset
```

3. Add the following Click event procedures for running the search:

```
Private Sub cmdSearch_Click()

    On Error GoTo HandleError
        'run the search
    Call RunSearch
        Exit Sub

HandleError:
    GeneralErrorHandler Err.Number, Err.Description, SEARCH_FORM, _
        "cmdSearch_Click"
    Exit Sub

End Sub

Sub RunSearch()

    On Error GoTo HandleError
        Dim strSQL As String
        'get the SQL statement for the search
    strSQL = GetSQL
        'if the SQL statement was generated successfully
    If strSQL <> "ERROR" Then
        'execute the SQL statement against the
        'database and put results in recordset
        Set rsSearch = ProcessRecordset(strSQL)
            'load the search results into the list on the form
        PopulateListFromRecordset lstResults, rsSearch, 11
        End If
        Exit Sub


HandleError:
    GeneralErrorHandler Err.Number, Err.Description, SEARCH_FORM, "RunSearch"
```

```
    Exit Sub

End Sub

Function GetSQL() As String

On Error GoTo HandleError

    Dim strSQL As String
    Dim strSQLWhereClause As String
    Dim blnPriorWhere As Boolean
        blnPriorWhere = False
        'generate the first part of the SQL Statement
    strSQL = BuildSQLSelectFrom()
        'build the where criteria based on the criteria filled in
    'by the user in one or more of the search fields on the form
    If txtCustomerNum <> "" Then
        strSQLWhereClause = BuildSQLWhere(blnPriorWhere, strSQLWhereClause, _
                            txtCustomerNum, "CustomerID")
    End If
    If txtPhone <> "" Then
        strSQLWhereClause = BuildSQLWhere(blnPriorWhere, strSQLWhereClause, _
                            txtPhone, "Phone")
    End If
    If txtLName <> "" Then
        strSQLWhereClause = BuildSQLWhere(blnPriorWhere, strSQLWhereClause, _
                            txtLName, "LastName")
    End If
    If txtFName <> "" Then
        strSQLWhereClause = BuildSQLWhere(blnPriorWhere, strSQLWhereClause, _
                            txtFName, "FirstName")
    End If
    If txtCompany <> "" Then
        strSQLWhereClause = BuildSQLWhere(blnPriorWhere, strSQLWhereClause, _
                            txtCompany, "Company")
    End If
    If txtAddress <> "" Then
        strSQLWhereClause = BuildSQLWhere(blnPriorWhere, strSQLWhereClause, _
                            txtAddress, "Address1")
    End If

    If txtCity <> "" Then


        strSQLWhereClause = BuildSQLWhere(blnPriorWhere, strSQLWhereClause, _
                            txtCity, "City")
    End If
    If txtRegion <> "" Then
        strSQLWhereClause = BuildSQLWhere(blnPriorWhere, strSQLWhereClause, _
                            txtRegion, "Region")
    End If
    If txtPostalCode <> "" Then
        strSQLWhereClause = BuildSQLWhere(blnPriorWhere, strSQLWhereClause, _
                            txtPostalCode, "PostalCode")
    End If
```

```
        If blnPriorWhere Then
            'build the final SQL statement with the Select...From...and
            'Where clause
            strSQL = strSQL & strSQLWhereClause
        Else
            MsgBox "You must enter at least one search criteria!"
            strSQL = "ERROR"
        End If
            'return the SQL statement
        GetSQL = strSQL

        Exit Function

HandleError:
    GeneralErrorHandler Err.Number, Err.Description, SEARCH_FORM, "GetSQL"
    Exit Function

End Function
```

4.   Add the following procedures for clearing the search results:

```
Private Sub cmdClear_Click()

    On Error GoTo HandleError
        'clear the search fields
    Call ClearFields
        Exit Sub

HandleError:
    GeneralErrorHandler Err.Number, Err.Description, SEARCH_FORM, _
            "cmdClear_Click"
    Exit Sub

End Sub


Sub ClearFields()

    On Error GoTo HandleError
        'clear fields
    txtCustomerNum = ""
    txtLName = ""
    txtFName = ""
    txtCompany = ""
    txtAddress = ""
    txtCity = ""
    txtRegion = ""
    txtPostalCode = ""
    txtPhone = ""

    Exit Sub

HandleError:
    GeneralErrorHandler Err.Number, Err.Description, SEARCH_FORM, "ClearFields"
```

```
        Exit Sub

End Sub

Private Sub Form_Unload(Cancel As Integer)

    On Error GoTo HandleError
        'reset lookup id to 0
    intCustomerLookupId = 0
        If Not rsSearch Is Nothing Then
        'close recordset
        rsSearch.Close
        Set rsSearch = Nothing
    End If
            Exit Sub

HandleError:
    GeneralErrorHandler Err.Number, Err.Description, SEARCH_FORM, "Form_Unload"
    Exit Sub
    End Sub

Private Sub lstResults_DblClick(Cancel As Integer)

On Error GoTo HandleError

    'store the value of the selected customer id to be
    'used later by frmCustomers to open selected record
    intCustomerLookupId = lstResults.Column(0)
        'open frmCustomers
    DoCmd.OpenForm "frmCustomers"

    Exit Sub


HandleError:
    GeneralErrorHandler Err.Number, Err.Description, SEARCH_FORM, _
            "lstResults_DblClick"
    Exit Sub

End Sub
```

The View/Manage Customer Accounts Form

An example of the View/Manage Customer Accounts form, called `frmCustomers`, is shown in Figure 14-28 with some sample data populated. Keep this form in mind as you write the code.

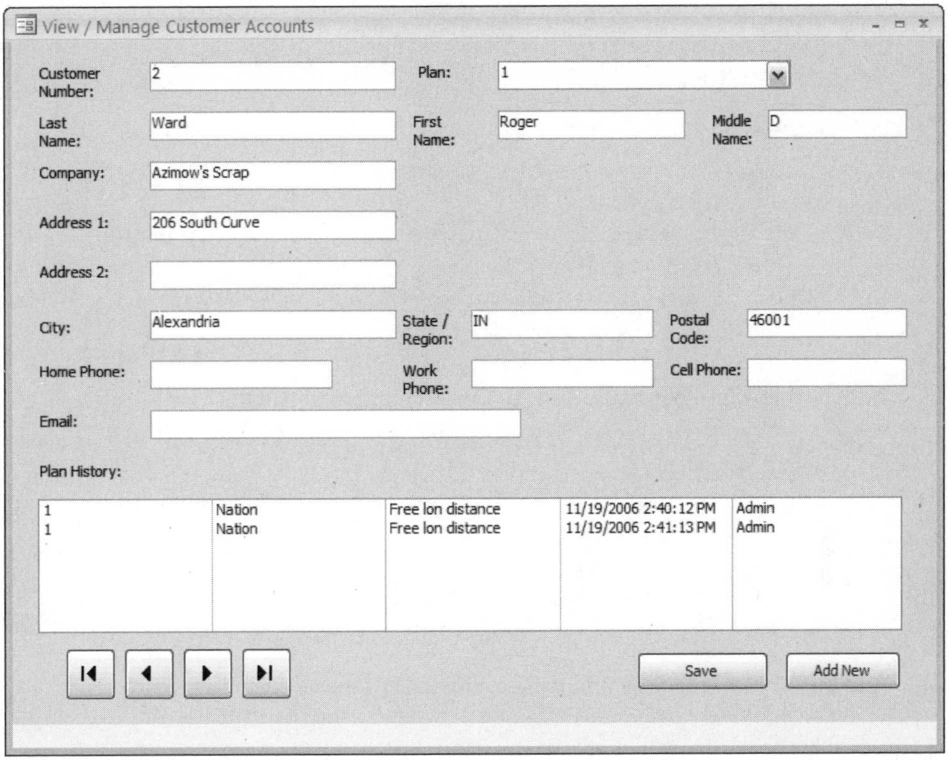

Figure 14-28

Try It Out   Writing Code for the frmCustomers

Now that you have finished with the VBA code for the frmSearch form, you can turn to the
frmCustomers form.

1. Open the frmCustomers form and select the Form_Load event for the form to bring up the
Visual Basic Editor. Add the following code to the form:

```
Private Sub Form_Load()

    On Error GoTo HandleError
        Set objCustomer = New clsCustomer
    Set rsCustomer = New ADODB.Recordset
        'lock the customer number field so user cannot modify it
    '(since assigned by the database)
    txtCustomerNum.Locked = True
        'set addmode to false since not adding yet
```

```
      blnAddMode = False
          'load the records from the database
      Call LoadRecords
          'populate plans combo box
      Call PopulatePlans
      Exit Sub

HandleError:
      GeneralErrorHandler Err.Number, Err.Description, CUSTOMERS_FORM, _
              "Form_Load"
      Exit Sub

End Sub
```

2. Add the following code to the General Declarations section of the form:

```
Option Compare Database
Option Explicit
Const CUSTOMERS_FORM = "frmCustomers"
Dim objCustomer As clsCustomer
Dim rsCustomer As ADODB.Recordset
Dim rsHistory As ADODB.Recordset
Dim blnAddMode As Boolean
```

3. Add the following code behind the form for adding a new customer record:

```
Private Sub cmdAddNew_Click()

    On Error GoTo HandleError
        'clear the current controls to enable adding a new
    'customer record
    Call AddEmptyCustomerRecord
        Exit Sub


HandleError:
    GeneralErrorHandler Err.Number, Err.Description, CUSTOMERS_FORM, _
            "cmdAddNew_Click"
    Exit Sub

End Sub

Sub AddEmptyCustomerRecord()

    On Error GoTo HandleError
        'set add mode to true
    blnAddMode = True
        'clear the current values in the contacts object
    objCustomer.ClearObject
        'clear the current controls on the form so the
    'user can fill in values for the new record
    Call ClearCustomerControls
```

```
        Exit Sub

HandleError:
    GeneralErrorHandler Err.Number, Err.Description, CUSTOMERS_FORM, _
        "AddEmptyCustomerRecord"
    Exit Sub

End Sub

Sub ClearCustomerControls()

    On Error GoTo HandleError
        'clear the values in the controls on the form
    Me.txtCustomerNum = ""
    Me.txtLName = ""
    Me.txtFName = ""
    Me.txtMName = ""
    Me.txtCompany = ""
    Me.txtAddress1 = ""
    Me.txtAddress2 = ""
    Me.txtCity = ""
    Me.txtRegion = ""
    Me.txtPostalCode = ""
    Me.txtWorkPhone = ""
    Me.txtHomePhone = ""
    Me.txtCellPhone = ""
    Me.txtEmail = ""
    Me.cboPlan = ""
        'clear the plan history list box
    lstPlanHistory.RowSource = ""
        Exit Sub


HandleError:
    GeneralErrorHandler Err.Number, Err.Description, CUSTOMERS_FORM, _
        "ClearCustomerControls"
    Exit Sub

End Sub
```

4.   Add the following procedures to the form for making updates to the data:

```
Private Sub cmdSave_Click()

    On Error GoTo HandleError
        Dim intCurCustomer As Integer
        'save the id of the current record if in update mode
    If Not blnAddMode Then
        intCurCustomer = objCustomer.CustomerId
    Else
        intCurCustomer = 0
    End If
            'populate object with current info on form
```

```
            objCustomer.PopulatePropertiesFromForm
                'save all changes to current record
            objCustomer.Save blnAddMode, rsCustomer
                    'move back to the customer that was current before the requery
            If intCurCustomer > 0 Then
                'move back to the contact that was just updated
                rsCustomer.Find "[CustomerId] = " & intCurCustomer
                'refresh the history list box for the record
                Call RefreshHistory
            Else
                'if just added new record, move to the beginning of
                'the recordset
                Call MoveToFirstRecord(rsCustomer, objCustomer, blnAddMode)
                'populate the controls on the form with the current record
                Call PopulateCustomerControls
            End If
                Exit Sub

HandleError:
    GeneralErrorHandler Err.Number, Err.Description, CUSTOMERS_FORM, _
            "cmdSave_Click"
    Exit Sub

End Sub
```

5. Add the following code to the form for navigating through the customer records:

```
Private Sub cmdMoveFirst_Click()

    On Error GoTo HandleError
        'move to the first record in the local disconnected recordset
    Call MoveToFirstRecord(rsCustomer, objCustomer, blnAddMode)
        'populate the controls on the form with the current record
    Call PopulateCustomerControls
        Exit Sub

HandleError:
    GeneralErrorHandler Err.Number, Err.Description, CUSTOMERS_FORM, _
            "cmdMoveFirst_Click"
    Exit Sub

End Sub

Private Sub cmdMoveLast_Click()

    On Error GoTo HandleError
        'move to the last record in the local disconnected recordset
    Call MoveToLastRecord(rsCustomer, objCustomer, blnAddMode)
        'populate the controls on the form with the current record
    Call PopulateCustomerControls
        Exit Sub

HandleError:
    GeneralErrorHandler Err.Number, Err.Description, CUSTOMERS_FORM, _
```

```
                       "cmdMoveLast_Click"
        Exit Sub

    End Sub

    Private Sub cmdMoveNext_Click()

        On Error GoTo HandleError
            'move to the next record in the local disconnected recordset
        Call MoveToNextRecord(rsCustomer, objCustomer, blnAddMode)
            'populate the controls on the form with the current record
        Call PopulateCustomerControls
            Exit Sub

    HandleError:
        GeneralErrorHandler Err.Number, Err.Description, CUSTOMERS_FORM, _
            "cmdMoveNext_Click"
        Exit Sub


    End Sub

    Private Sub cmdMovePrevious_Click()
            On Error GoTo HandleError
            'move to the previous record in the local disconnected recordset
        Call MoveToPreviousRecord(rsCustomer, objCustomer, blnAddMode)
            'populate the controls on the form with the current record
        Call PopulateCustomerControls
            Exit Sub

    HandleError:
        GeneralErrorHandler Err.Number, Err.Description, CUSTOMERS_FORM, _
            "cmdMovePrevious_Click"
        Exit Sub

    End Sub
```

6. Add the following code to the form for populating the fields on the form with the current customer record:

```
Sub PopulatePlans()

On Error GoTo HandleError

    'populate the Plans combo box with values from the database
    Dim rsPlans As New ADODB.Recordset
        'populate the list of plans from the database
    Set rsPlans = ExecuteSPRetrieveRS("spRetrievePlans", 0)

    cboPlan.RowSource = ""
    cboPlan.LimitToList = True
    cboPlan.ColumnCount = 2
    cboPlan.RowSourceType = "Value List"
    cboPlan.BoundColumn = 0
```

```
            Do While Not rsPlans.EOF
            'populate the plans combo box
            cboPlan.AddItem rsPlans!PlanId & ";" & rsPlans!PlanName
            rsPlans.MoveNext
        Loop
        Exit Sub

HandleError:
    GeneralErrorHandler Err.Number, Err.Description, CUSTOMERS_FORM, _
            "PopulatePlans"
    Exit Sub

End Sub


Sub LoadRecords()

    On Error GoTo HandleError
        'load the customer recordset
    Set rsCustomer = objCustomer.RetrieveCustomers
        'if the recordset is empty
    If rsCustomer.BOF And rsCustomer.EOF Then
        Exit Sub
    Else
        'populate the object with values in the recordset
        objCustomer.PopulatePropertiesFromRecordset rsCustomer

        Call MoveToFirstRecord(rsCustomer, objCustomer, blnAddMode)

        'populate the controls on the form with the current record
        Call PopulateCustomerControls
        End If
        Exit Sub

HandleError:
    GeneralErrorHandler Err.Number, Err.Description, CUSTOMERS_FORM, "LoadRecords"
    Exit Sub

End Sub

Sub PopulateCustomerControls()
        On Error GoTo HandleError
        'Populate the controls on the Customers form with the values of the
        'current record in the contacts object.
        If Not rsCustomer.BOF And Not rsCustomer.EOF Then
            Me.txtCustomerNum = objCustomer.CustomerId
            Me.txtLName = objCustomer.LastName
            Me.txtFName = objCustomer.FirstName
            Me.txtMName = objCustomer.MiddleName
            Me.txtCompany = objCustomer.Company
            Me.txtAddress1 = objCustomer.Address1
            Me.txtAddress2 = objCustomer.Address2
            Me.txtCity = objCustomer.City
            Me.txtRegion = objCustomer.Region
            Me.txtPostalCode = objCustomer.PostalCode
```

```
               Me.txtWorkPhone = objCustomer.WorkPhone
               Me.txtHomePhone = objCustomer.HomePhone
               Me.txtCellPhone = objCustomer.CellPhone
               Me.txtEmail = objCustomer.Email
               Me.cboPlan = objCustomer.PlanId
               'refresh the history list box
               Call RefreshHistory

           ElseIf rsCustomer.BOF Then
               'past beginning of recordset so move to first record
               Call MoveToFirstRecord(rsCustomer, objCustomer, blnAddMode)
           ElseIf rsCustomer.EOF Then
               'past end of recordset so move back to last record
               Call MoveToLastRecord(rsCustomer, objCustomer, blnAddMode)
           End If
           Exit Sub


HandleError:
       GeneralErrorHandler Err.Number, Err.Description, CUSTOMERS_FORM, _
               "PopulateCustomerControls"
       Exit Sub

End Sub
```

7. Add the following `RefreshHistory` procedure:

```
Sub RefreshHistory()

   On Error GoTo HandleError

   'populate the recordset for plan history list
   Set rsHistory = New ADODB.Recordset
   'get plan history for current customer
   Set rsHistory = ExecuteSPRetrieveRS("spRetrieveCustomerHistory", _
                   objCustomer.CustomerId)

   'Set rsHistory = objCustomer.RetrieveHistory(objCustomer.CustomerId)
   PopulateListFromRecordset Me.lstPlanHistory, rsHistory, 5
   rsHistory.Close
               Exit Sub

HandleError:
       GeneralErrorHandler Err.Number, Err.Description, CUSTOMERS_FORM, _
               "RefreshHistory"
       Exit Sub

End Sub
```

8. Add the following code to the `Form_Unload` event procedure:

```
Private Sub Form_Unload(Cancel As Integer)

   On Error GoTo HandleError
       'reset lookup id to 0
```

```
        intCustomerLookupId = 0
          If Not rsCustomer Is Nothing Then
          'close recordset


          rsCustomer.Close
          Set rsCustomer = Nothing
      End If
            Exit Sub

HandleError:
      GeneralErrorHandler Err.Number, Err.Description, CUSTOMERS_FORM, "Form_Unload"
      Exit Sub
      End Sub
```

9. That is all the code for the application. So, it's time now to resolve any typographical errors if you have not done so already.

Touring the Finished Customer Service Application

Now that you have written all the code for the application, let's walk through how it works in a bit more detail. Let's start with the frmSearch form, which builds a SQL statement dynamically based on the search criteria input by the user. To see how this SQL Statement is dynamically built, start by adding a breakpoint to the cmdSearch_Click event of frmSearch, as shown in Figure 14-29.

Next, open the frmSearch form to run the form. Enter some criteria into the form. It is okay at this point if you do not have any customer records in the database. You just want to see how the SQL statement gets built dynamically. When you click the Search button, code execution should stop at the breakpoint you set in Figure 14-29.

Step through the code by selecting Debug ➪ Step Into (or by pressing F8). The RunSearch procedure is called and then the GetSQL function is called to generate the SQL statement from the values you entered on the form. The GetSQL function is the heart of the code that builds the dynamic SQL statement. Let's see in more detail how it works.

```
Function GetSQL() As String

On Error GoTo HandleError

    Dim strSQL As String
    Dim strSQLWhereClause As String
    Dim blnPriorWhere As Boolean
```

After you declare some variables, you set the blnPriorWhere value to False because no WHERE clause added yet.

```
    blnPriorWhere = False
```

Next, the Select statement is generated based on the `BuildSQLSelectFrom` procedure.

```
'generate the first part of the SQL Statement
strSQL = BuildSQLSelectFrom()
```

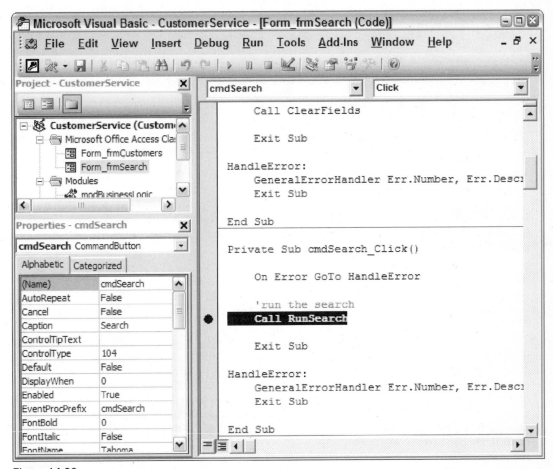

Figure 14-29

A series of statements for each of the search controls is located on the form. Each control is tested to see if a value is present. If some are present, the `BuildSQLWhere` procedure is called to add the criteria in the particular control to the WHERE clause of the SQL statement. In the following code, I list statements for only a few of these controls.

```
'build the where criteria based on the criteria filled in
'by the user in one or more of the search fields on the form

If txtCustomerNum <> "" Then
    strSQLWhereClause = BuildSQLWhere(blnPriorWhere, strSQLWhereClause, _
                    txtCustomerNum, "CustomerID")
```

```
        End If

    If txtPhone <> "" Then
        strSQLWhereClause = BuildSQLWhere(blnPriorWhere, strSQLWhereClause, _
                            txtPhone, "Phone")
    End If
    If txtLName <> "" Then
        strSQLWhereClause = BuildSQLWhere(blnPriorWhere, strSQLWhereClause, _
                            txtLName, "LastName")
    End If
```

Keep stepping through the code in the Visual Basic Editor until you are in the BuildSQLWhere function, as shown here.

```
Function BuildSQLWhere(blnPriorWhere As Boolean, strPriorWhere As String, _
        strValue As String, strDbFieldName As String) As String
    On Error GoTo HandleError

    Dim strWhere As String
```

If this is the first WHERE clause being added to the SQL statement (that is, it is the first control on the form that has criteria), then you must add the WHERE keyword to the SQL string. Otherwise, an AND statement is added to separate the existing WHERE clause correctly.

```
    If blnPriorWhere Then
        'add to the existing where clause
        strWhere = strPriorWhere & " AND "
    Else
        'create the where clause for the first time
        strWhere = " WHERE "
    End If
```

You must handle the Phone field in a special way, because you want the user to be able to type a single phone number for the customer but have the application search all the phone fields in the database. Thus, if the phone field is specified, you must add the WHERE clause that will search all three phone fields in the database.

```
    If strDbFieldName = "Phone" Then
        'search each of phone fields in the db for this value to see
        'if exact match or starts with this value for any one of the
        'phone fields
        strWhere = strWhere & "(HomePhone LIKE '" & PadQuotes(strValue) & "%'" & _
            " OR WorkPhone LIKE '" & PadQuotes(strValue) & "%'" & _
            " OR CellPhone LIKE '" & PadQuotes(strValue) & "%')"
```

Otherwise, you add the WHERE clause using the value that was passed in along with the LIKE keyword. The LIKE keyword will locate a match if the field begins with or matches the value input by the user. This saves time because the user does not have to type the entire field, although he can do so if he wants.

```
Else
        'build where clause using LIKE so will find both exact
        'matches and those that start with value input by user
        strWhere = strWhere & strDbFieldName & " LIKE '" & PadQuotes(strValue) & _
                "%' "
    End If
```

Now that there is a prior WHERE clause, the blnPriorWhere value is set to True:

```
        blnPriorWhere = True
```

The SQL statement is then returned to the calling procedure:

```
    'return where clause
    BuildSQLWhere = strWhere

    Exit Function

HandleError:
    GeneralErrorHandler Err.Number, Err.Description, DB_LOGIC, "BuildSQLWhere"
    Exit Function

End Function
```

If you press F5 to allow the code execution to continue, you see a Search Results screen similar to that shown in Figure 14-30.

In Figure 14-30, the search criteria that the user specified includes a portion of a last name and a company name. After you built the SQL string in the manner described previously, you executed the SQL statement against the database and the resulting records were displayed in the Search Results list. If you double-click an item in the Search Results list, the View/Manage Customer Account screen is displayed for that specific record, as illustrated in Figure 14-31.

In this instance, the only customer record open on the View/Manage Customer Accounts is the selected customer. This feature is useful in many scenarios, such as when the user works in a call center and needs to retrieve the customer's record quickly based on limited information. When he or she enters the search criteria and locates the correct customer record, the user can then open the customer account and view the information. In the example illustrated in Figure 14-31, the customer was first on a local plan but then switched to a national plan shortly thereafter.

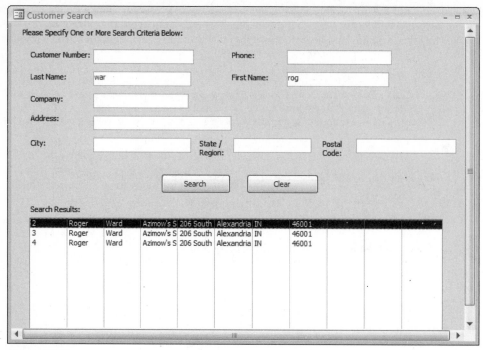

Figure 14-30

Figure 14-31

If the View/Manage Customer Accounts screen is opened independently of the Customer Search screen, multiple records are displayed and the navigation buttons allow the user to navigate through the customer records. The screen appears to be the same as the one shown in Figure 14-31, only the values in the screen change for the current customer record.

If changes are made to the customer information, the database is updated with the new data. The database updates to an existing customer record are made through the spUpdateCustomer stored procedure created earlier. Stored procedures are used to retrieve and update data for the entire application, except for the dynamic SQL statement executed from the Customer Search screen.

For those stored procedures that required parameters, you first had to add parameters to the ADO Command object that match the parameters expected by the stored procedure. An example of adding parameters using the CreateParameter method is shown in the following excerpt from the AddParameters procedure that performs an update to an existing customer record:

```
Sub AddParameters(strSPname As String, cmdCommand As ADODB.Command, _
        objCust As clsCustomer)

    On Error GoTo HandleError

    Dim parParm As ADODB.Parameter

    'if updating existing record
    If strSPname = "spUpdateCustomer" Then
        'Add parameter for existing Customer Id to be passed to stored
        procedure
        Set parParm = cmdCommand.CreateParameter("CustomerId", adInteger, _
                    adParamInput)
        cmdCommand.Parameters.Append parParm
        parParm.Value = objCust.CustomerId
    End If

    'Add parameter for Last Name to be passed to stored procedure
    Set parParm = cmdCommand.CreateParameter("LastName", adVarChar, _
                adParamInput, 50)
    parParm.Value = objCust.LastName
    cmdCommand.Parameters.Append parParm

    'Add parameter for First Name to be passed to stored procedure
    Set parParm = cmdCommand.CreateParameter("FirstName", adVarChar, _
                adParamInput, 50)
    parParm.Value = objCust.FirstName
    cmdCommand.Parameters.Append parParm
```

After all the required parameters are added, or if none is required for the stored procedure, the stored procedure can be executed using the Execute method of the Command object. The following example illustrates a portion of code from the ExecuteStoredProcedure procedure that runs the stored procedure after calling the AddParameters procedure:

```
'set the command to the current connection
Set cmdCommand.ActiveConnection = cnConn
```

```
'set the SQL statement to the command text
cmdCommand.CommandText = strSPname
'execute the command against the database
cmdCommand.Execute
```

After specifying any required parameters for the stored procedure, you just assign the `CommandText` property of the `Command` object to the name of the stored procedure and then run the `Execute` method. Learning how to retrieve data from SQL server databases and how to correctly execute SQL Server stored procedures from your VBA code are probably the two hardest parts of working with SQL Server from Access. You have just learned how to do so.

Summary

Congratulations! You have made your way through the entire book. This chapter is the most complicated in the entire book, so you deserve a special pat on the back for finishing it completely. You have no doubt learned from this book that Access is a powerful tool for building sophisticated applications. Some of the really cool features in Access enable you to implement using VBA code. You can even work with SQL Server databases from your Access applications today so that you can build interactive, multiuser applications that can serve all your multiuser purposes, or that may prepare you well for a future migration to another front-end language.

Exercise Answers

Chapter 1

1. The phases of the System Development Life Cycle methodology include requirements gathering, design, development, testing, and implementation. The purpose of the requirements gathering phase is to identify a list of features that the application should include. The design phase takes the requirements and determines how to design an application that meets the requirements. The development phase is where you create the application using forms for the screens and VBA code for the business logic and data access logic. The testing phase allows you to test and fix your application, and should be performed in various phases as the application is developed. The implementation phase is where you roll out the application to end users.

2. You can use Use Case Diagrams to list the various ways an end user might use the system. You can use Activity or other Flow Diagrams to illustrate the flow of activities in the system. You can use prototype screens to model how the user interface should look. These are just a few of numerous other documenting techniques that can be used.

3. A standalone application runs entirely on one computer. All of the user interface, business logic, and database elements run on the same computer. A standalone application in Access can be located on a network computer that multiple computers can access, but all computers will be opening the same file. A client-server application is one where the user interface is separated from the database, and the database is located on a server so that it is accessible from multiple computers.

4. By separating your code into different logical tiers, you can make migrating or improving your application easier in the future. For example, suppose that you include your business logic in one Access module and your data access logic in another Access module. If you need to change your data access code, such as to migrate to another database platform, you can find all code that interacts with the database in the data access layer in one place. This makes it much easier to upgrade different portions of your application without having to weed through the entire application to find the affected portions.

Chapter 2

1. A module is a storage container for your VBA code. Modules can either be standard modules or class modules. Standard modules are not associated with a particular object. Class modules can either be associated with forms or reports or be based on custom-defined objects.

2. A sub procedure performs a particular action. A function performs a particular action and also returns a particular result. When you need to obtain some type of result based on the action, such as a value that was calculated, you should use a function. An example of a function is one that calculates sales tax and returns the sales tax amount. An example of a procedure is one that displays a message to the user or runs a database update.

3. You can control the flow of code execution using `If . . . Then` statements, `Select . . . Case` statements, loops, conditional `If` statements, and `IIf` statements, as a few examples. Variables can be declared to store various values. Variables can then be used as part of the statements that control code execution to determine if certain conditions are met or whether certain actions should be taken.

4. Naming conventions involve naming your variables and objects in a particular way, such as with prefixes, which makes them easier to understand without tracking down the declaration or first use in code. Code documentation is important to illustrate how your program works and makes it much easier for you and others to debug and maintain the program in the future. Ideally, your code should be documented at the procedure level to describe how the procedure works, as well as with inline comments that explain how segments of code operate.

5. When writing VBA code, you will encounter various types of errors, such as syntax errors, runtime errors, compile errors, and logic errors. Syntax errors occur when you have not specified the correct language syntax. Compile errors occur when the program will not compile for some reason, although the syntax may be correct. Runtime errors occur when the program runs and encounters a scenario that is not allowed or expected. Logic errors are mistakes that are made in the logic itself such that the code does not perform the operation as intended. You can use various techniques from the Visual Basic Editor to eliminate most of these errors. A well-designed application should also include error handling that will capture and display informative error messages to users of the program so they do not get those nasty error messages.

Chapter 3

1. Properties are characteristics of the object, such as the caption, name, or size. Methods are actions that are taken upon an object, such as setting the focus to the object. Events are triggered by actions taken by the user and the application, such as changes to data, mouse movements, a form opening, and so on. Events allow you to link up your forms and reports with the VBA code that you write so that the code will execute at the appropriate time.

2. You can set properties and events for a given object from the Properties dialog box in the form or report designer. You can view and manipulate properties, methods, and events from within the code window in the Visual Basic Editor as you type the object name followed by the period. The Object Browser also allows you to view the properties, methods, and events available for a selected object.

3. The `Forms` collection of the `Application` object only works with currently open forms. The `AllForms` collection of the `Application.CurrentProject` object allows you to work with all forms in the application.

Chapter 4

1. A class diagram is a diagram that shows the classes and their relationships and how they should be structured in your application. The complete class diagram model for your system is critical to create, as it provides you with a roadmap for what your code structure needs to look like.

2. Custom properties can be created using public variable declarations in a class module. Or, a preferred way is to implement public `Property Get` and `Property Let` procedures in the class module. `Property Get` procedures specify what should happen when the property value is retrieved. `Property Let` procedures specify what should happen when the property is assigned. Custom methods can be created by adding public procedures or functions to the class module.

3. You can add additional properties and methods to existing objects in the same way that you create your own properties and methods for your own objects. The only difference is that you place the code in the class module for the existing object, such as a form.

Chapter 5

1. ADO stands for *ActiveX Data Objects* and is a data access methodology that allows you to manipulate data in underlying data sources for VBA code. You use ADO to insert, update, delete, and retrieve data in databases that you want to interact with in your Access applications.

2. A disconnected (unbound) recordset does not maintain a connection to the database like a connected (bound) recordset does. Disconnected recordsets are typically better for reducing the number of open connections and record locks in your application. Disconnected recordsets are typically better because the data is cached locally until an update is made to the database. Disconnected recordsets require a little extra effort because you have to write code to handle navigation and updates to the data. Connected recordsets maintain a constant connection to the database, and Access has a lot of navigation features built-in for working with connected recordsets.

3. SQL stands for *Structured Query Language* and is a language that you can use to retrieve, add, update, and delete data in databases. SQL can be used in conjunction with ADO, or separately from ADO as part of your Access solutions.

4. The ADOX object model provides a library of features that you can use to manipulate databases, tables, users, groups, and security from your VBA code. The `Catalog` object is at the highest level of the object model.

Chapter 6

1. The `AutoExec` macro is a macro that runs each time a particular database opens. This macro is a good place to add an `Open Form` command to specify which form should automatically open when the database opens. For example, you may want a switchboard form to open so the user can navigate among the available forms.

2. Combo boxes and list boxes both allow you to display data with single or multiple columns. Combo boxes can be programmed to allow a user to select a value from the drop-down list or to type in

a new value. List boxes, on the other hand, require a user to select a value from the list. Combo boxes use pattern matching to find the record matching the values as you type one or more letters. List boxes jump to the first item that starts with each value that you type. List boxes allow a user to select multiple items from the list, while combo boxes only allow selection of a single item.

3. You can use the MsgBox function to display a message box to the user. Message boxes are useful to inform the user of some error or other event, and also to ask the user questions, such as to confirm a delete action.

Chapter 7

1. Linking stores only a pointer to the location of the underlying data source, and updates are made to the original data itself. Linking is a good idea when the data resides on a database server that your application and others can use, the data is used by another program that requires the native file format, or the underlying data needs to be updated on a regular basis in its native format. Importing data actually brings a copy of the data into your Access database. Reasons for importing data include moving an existing system that is being migrated to a new application, and having numerous data operations that need to be run against the data from another source in a speedy fashion when you do not need to change that data.

2. TransferDatabase allows you to import, export, and link to various types of databases, such as Access and SQL Server. You specify various parameters to indicate which type of action should be performed. TransferSQLDatabase transfers the entire contents of a particular SQL Server database to your application.

3. You can use the SendObject method to generate an e-mail programmatically using VBA. This method allows you to generate an e-mail with or without attachments. You can use this method to create just one e-mail, or multiple e-mails, such as for a mailing list.

Chapter 8

1. A web service is an HTTP-based method for communicating with other applications. To consume a web service, you must create a reference to it, and then you can use it as you would any other object.

2. The acImportSharePointList actually imports the table and severs the link, whereas acLinkSharePointList creates a linked table.

3. You would use this method when you needed to connect only briefly and then needed to disconnect from the SharePoint instance.

Chapter 9

1. The CreateReport method is used to create a new report object. The CreateReportControl method is used to create new controls on a new or existing report. Using these two methods, you can create a new report from scratch.

2. Report events are basically the same as form events, except that there are fewer of them. As with form events, you can write VBA code that should execute when a particular report event occurs.

3. The `AutoStart` parameter is used to indicate whether the particular program associated with that type of file should be launched immediately after performing the `OutputTo` method. For example, if you are creating a web page, you could use this parameter to specify that a web browser should launch after the web page is output.

Chapter 10

1. A standard Access database (ACCDB file) contains the database tables and queries within the ACCDB file itself. An Access Project is a special type of Access file that uses SQL Server as the database. The database tables, queries (stored procedures, views, and functions), and database diagrams are physically stored on the SQL Server itself, although you can view them from Access.

2. If you use SQL Server as the database for your applications now, you will not have to go through the hassle of upgrading to SQL Server at a later date. If you anticipate that there is a good chance you will need to migrate to SQL Server in the future, you may be better served by using the free, but limited functionality, version of SQL Server now — the SQL Server Express Edition. If you need to migrate to SQL Server later, you will need to make changes to your database and/or code in order to work with SQL Server. In some cases, these changes are minimal, whereas in other cases the changes are substantial.

3. Stored procedures are procedures that are stored in the SQL Server database. They allow you to take frequently used SQL statements and save them in a procedure for reuse. Views are also stored in SQL Server and allow you to store frequently used SQL statements and can later be referenced just as you reference tables. Views are helpful for row- and column-level security, for example. Functions are also SQL statements stored in the SQL Server database and can be called from inline from another SQL statement. In many cases, the same functionality can be accomplished using any of these three.

Chapter 11

1. A standard library can be added using Tools ➪ References. You can then work with the objects of that library from within your code and have full access to the available properties, methods, and events as you type your code. An external library is more complicated to work with and requires an explicit declaration in the General Declarations section, as well as a procedure call from within your VBA code. External libraries must be declared with the exact syntax, or an error will occur.

2. Automation allows one application to control another application, such as Access controlling Word. You can use automation to create new Excel spreadsheets, to create new Word documents, or to manipulate Outlook objects such as e-mails, contacts, and calendar entries. These are just a few examples of using automation. In order to use automation, you must add a reference to the library that corresponds to the application you want to control.

3. A code library can be created by simply creating a new Access database that contains the code you want to have reused by other applications. Code libraries are a good idea for storing generic code that multiple applications might want to take advantage of, such as error-handling routines. Instead of copying the same procedures into every application and then having to update multiple locations, you can simply point each application to a single Access database. To add a reference to a library, you simply select Tools ⇨ References and then browse to the location of the Access database you want to use as a library. After the reference has been added, you can call the functions and sub procedures in the library just as if it were contained in your local module.

4. A transaction is a group of database actions that should succeed or fail together. You can use the `BeginTrans`, `CommitTrans`, and `RollbackTrans` methods of the ADO `Connection` object to implement transactions. If the updates all succeed, then all of the updates can be committed to the underlying database using the `CommitTrans` method. If any one of the updates fails, then all of the changes can be rolled back using the `RollbackTrans` method.

Chapter 12

1. One way to improve support for multiple users is to ensure that the proper type of record locking is being used. If your application is using page or table locks, for example, then more records than the one being accessed will be locked and other users will be unable to modify them. With bound forms, you can modify table locks in Tools ⇨ Options on the Advanced tab. With unbound forms, you specify the lock type in your code, for example by setting the lock type of your ADO recordset. Another way to improve support for multiple users is to separate standalone Access databases into two separate files: one database file that contains the tables and is shared on a network and another database file with the user-interface objects that is loaded onto each user's computer.

2. There are various ways to improve the performance of your Access applications. One way is to optimize the queries that retrieve data to ensure that they use the correct syntax, join to the correct tables, and use indexes so the retrieval will be faster. Another way to improve performance is to reduce the complexity of your forms, for instance by eliminating unnecessary controls and moving some code from forms to standard modules. Improving the code itself is another way to improve performance. For example, make sure to use the smallest data type you really need, make your procedures reusable to eliminate redundant code, and replace slower types of code statements with faster statements. If the user interface is separated into a separate database file than the tables, open the user-interface file exclusively to improve performance. Finally, the Performance Analyzer can help to identify areas for improvement.

3. To build a help system, you first create the content for the help system using any tool that can create HTML documents, such as Microsoft Word. You specify identifiers for the various topics so they can be retrieved later. After the help topics have been created and assigned identifiers, you then compile the help system into a help file and hook up the help system to your application. You assign your application to the help file just created. You then can set various properties in your application, for example at the form level or at a particular control level to point to a related help topic.

4. There are various ways to add security to your applications. For example, you can add a password to the database and a separate one to the source code. You can also add users and groups that have various security settings. For example, some users may have the ability to modify source code and data, while other users only have access to the data through the forms. By creating an ACCDE file, you can compile your application into a file that removes all source code. This is another way to add security to your application because it ensures that no one who opens that file can view or modify the source code.

5. ACCDE files are a special type of Access file that can be created to compile the database and remove all source code. An ACCDE file is one way you can distribute the application to end users. The Access runtime allows you to distribute your application to users who do not have a full version of Access installed on their computer. The Access runtime hides the database window from the users so they cannot modify the objects, such as the forms and reports. Built-in toolbars are not supported, so you have to build your own toolbars for the users. However, unlike ACCDE files, Access databases distributed with the runtime version still contain all of the code and could be opened by someone with the full version of Access.

Index

A

ACCDB file format, 2, 29
ACCDB files, 253, 278, 281
ACCDE file format, 2
ACCDE files, 331
Access 2007
changes from Access 2003, 2
as a front end to other databases, 132
three-tiered applications and, 15
Access 2007 VBA
changes from Access 2003, 2–3
programming concepts, 3–25
uses of, 1
Access database files. See ACCDB files
Access databases
attaching SharePoint lists to, 231
changes to existing prior to migration, 277
connecting to, 132
importing a SQL Server database, 203–204
importing data from, 201
separating into two database files, 319–322
upsizing, 277–284
Access designer, 271
Access field data types. See field data types
Access forms, generating prototype screens, 336–340
Access macros, VBA instead of or with, 1
Access Options, Advanced, 316–317
Access Project file, 278, 281

Access Projects
based on SQL Server databases, 260, 262–263
creating, 259–263
described, 253
displaying new, 278, 284
as a front end to SQL Server, 253–254
migrating existing Access databases to, 277–284
reusing code across multiple, 308
storage locations for objects seen from, 254
working with SQL Server objects, 264–277
Access runtime, 330
Access tables
checking dates in, 277
exporting contents to a spreadsheet, 205, 206
`ActionSuccess` **event, 116, 120–121**
`Activate` **event, 247**
active plans, retrieving, 472
`ActiveConnection` **property, 143, 147, 151, 155**
ActiveX controls, 305–308
ActiveX Data Objects. See ADO
Activity Diagrams, 7–8, 9, 10
actor in a Use Case Diagram, 5
Add Comment button, 337
Add Current Contact To Project button, 339, 340
`Add` **method, 112, 113**
add mode, 442–443, 449–450
Add mode flag, 169, 176
Add New navigation button, 137
Add Table dialog box, 275
Add Watch dialog box, 69, 71

AddEmptyProjectRecord **procedure, 419, 433**

Add-in Manager, 313

add-ins, 312–313

Add-Ins tab, 289

AddItem **method, 189, 190–191, 192–193**

AdditionalData **parameter, 209**

Add/Manage Contacts button, 453, 455

AddNew **method, 141–142**

AddParameters **procedure, 497–499, 517**

AddRecord **procedure**
  calling from OnClick, 144, 152
  indicating Add mode, 166, 172

adLockBatchOptimistic **value for the** LockType
  property, 134, 317

adLockOptimistic **value for the** LockType **property,**
  134, 317

adLockPessimistic **value for the** LockType
  property, 134, 317

adLockReadOnly **value for the** LockType **property,**
  134, 317

ADO (ActiveX Data Objects)
  adding a reference to, 358
  connecting to the ProjectTrackerDb, 344
  described, 129–130
  storing database errors, 75
  treating data sources as virtual tables, 163
  versions of, 130–131

ADO Command **object, 269**

ADO Connection **object, 313**

ADO object library, 130

ADO object model, 130–131

ADO Parameter **object, 269**

ADO recordsets
  based on SQL statements, 272
  binding a form to, 138
  specifying as a report's data source, 236–237

Adobe Acrobat, launching, 457

ADODB library. *See* **ADO object library**

ADO.NET, 130

adOpenDynamic **value for the** CursorType **property,**
  133

adOpenForwardOnly **value for the** CursorType
  property, 133

adOpenKeyset **value for the** CursorType **property,**
  133

adOpenStatic **value for the** CursorType **property,**
  133

ADOX library, 177–178

ADP file, opening, 278

ADPs. *See* **Access Projects**

All Object Types tab, 326

All Records option, 317

AllForms **collection, 97**

AllPrinters **collection, 247**

AllReports **collection, 238**

Analyze Performance, 326

And **statements in a** Where **clause, 161**

announcements in SharePoint, 221, 229–232

ANSI SQL, 159

application(s)
  determining the purpose of, 3
  distributing, 329–331
  elements of, 11–12
  exposing as a web service, 214
  finishing, 315–332
  identifying the objectives of, 3
  maintaining, 331
  modeling the design of, 4–11
  optimizing, 322–327
  securing, 327–329
  writing to handle multiple users, 315–322

application architecture, 11–18

application design, 4–11

application logic, 104

Application **object, 94**

architecture for applications, 11–18

arrays, 51–53

arrows in an Activity Diagram, 8, 9, 10

AS **predicate, 160**

ascending order, 162

Attachment data type, 50, 222

attachments
  database objects as, 210–211
  procedure for previewing, 385, 401
  procedures for saving, 439

Auto Order **option, 198**

AutoExec macro
  creating, 46–47, 185
  opening a switchboard form, 187
  specifying form to open, 182

automation, 294–305

automation client, 294

automation objects, 294–295

automation server, 294

AutoNumber (Long Integer) field data type, 51

AutoStart **parameter, 249**

B

backup copies of databases, **331**
batch optimistic recordset, **151**
BeforeUpdate **event, 196**
BeforeUpdate **procedure, 40, 41**
BeginTrans **method, 313, 314**
Blank Database section, **259**
bln **(Boolean) prefix, 55**
BOF **property of a recordset, 141**
Bookmark **property, 159**
bookmarks, **159**
Boolean data type, **50**
bound forms, **139, 316–317**
break mode, **70, 71**
breakpoints
    adding to code, 24
    adding to frmSearch, 512, 513
    stepping through code, 66–68
builder add-ins, **313**
BuildSQLDeleteProjectsComments **function,
    397–398, 409**
BuildSQLInsertContacts **procedure, 391–392, 406**
BuildSQLInsertProjectComments **function,
    398–399, 409**
BuildSQLSelectFrom **function, 494**
BuildSQLSelectFrom **procedure, 513**
BuildSQLWhere **function, 494–495, 514**
BuildSQLWhere **procedure, 513–514**
built-in constants, **54**
built-in functions, **45–46**
business logic, **14**
business logic layer, **17, 104**
business rules, **12**
buttons, adding to a command bar, **290**
byt **(Byte) prefix, 55**
Byte data type, **50**

C

Calculated data type, **222**
CalculateSalesTax **function, 43–45**
Calendar control, **306, 307**
call stack, **70**
Cancel **parameter, 90**
Caption **properties for command buttons, 115, 118**
Caption **property**
    changing at runtime, 81
    changing for a label, 115, 118
    changing for command buttons, 142
    of a command button, 86
    of a command button control, 95
    of a list box, 95
    setting for a form, 80
Catalog **object, 177**
CE devices, managing a SQL Server database, **255**
cells, assigning values to, **298**
Cells **property, 298**
child class, **122**
Choice data types, **222**
Choose Builder screen, **21, 22, 38**
class, **115, 121–122**
class diagrams, **102–105**
class hierarchies, **122**
class modules
    advanced techniques, 121–123
    building for objects in Project Tracker, 357
    creating custom objects, 101
    creating objects, 101–123
    for Customer Service application, 481–488
    defined, 101
    described, 29
    inserting new, 102
    public variable declarations, 105
    writing code in, 37–42
Classes list, limiting, **91, 92**
ClearContactsControls **procedure, 447**
ClearControlsOnForm **procedure, 146–147, 154**
ClearObject **procedure**
    adding to clsCustomer class module, 487–488
    adding to clsProjects class module, 365, 370,
        377–378, 382–383
ClearProjectControls **procedure, 420–421, 435**
Click **event**
    adding code for, 120
    adding to a class, 116
    for a command button, 90
Click **event procedures**
    adding to command buttons, 413–414, 429–431
    adding to frmProjects, 411–413, 428
    extracting data, 91
    managing comments, 416–417, 431
    managing contacts, 415–416, 430–431
    running a search, 501–503
client cursors, **134**
client machine, **13**
client-server applications, **13–14**

client-server architecture, example of, 253, 254
CloseDbConnection procedure, 390, 405, 493
cls prefix, 56
clsCar class
  methods for, 112–113
  properties for, 107–111
clsContacts class module, 372–383
clsCustomer class module, 482–488
clsProjects class module, 358–372
cmdAddAttachment_Click event, 417–418,
    431–432
cmdAddNew_Click event, 442–443, 449–450
cmdAddNew_Click event procedure, 411–412, 428
cmdAddToProject_Click event, 442, 449
cmdDeleteContacts_Click procedure, 415, 430
cmdEmailContact_Click procedure, 415–416, 431
cmdFileBrowse_Click event, 417–418, 432
cmdManageContacts_Click procedure, 415, 430
cmdMoveFirst_Click event, 444–445, 450
cmdMoveFirst_Click procedure, 413, 429–430
cmdOpenFile_Click event, 418, 432–433
cmdRun_Click event procedure, 40
cmdRun_Click procedure, 37, 39
cmdSave_Click event procedure, 412, 428
cmdViewContact_Click procedure, 416, 431
code
  debugging, 66–71
  documenting, 63–64
  encapsulating into objects, 101
  running and debugging, 24–25
  separating into logical tiers, 18, 103
  stepping through, 66–68, 512
Code Builder
  choosing, 84
  creating a procedure for an object, 37–40
  selecting, 95
  writing code for an event, 86–87
Code Builder option, 21, 22
code execution, 69
code library, 308–312
code modules. See modules
Code window
  adding code to, 21, 23
  creating additional procedures, 40–42
  in Visual Basic Editor, 19, 20
CodePage parameter, 206
coliections, 80, 94–100, 130

column-level security, 271
columns, selecting in a table, 160
combo boxes, 188–193
comma-delimited records, 207–208
command(s)
  displaying options for, 21, 23
  typing in the Code window, 21, 23
  writing within procedures, 56
command bar, creating a custom, 288–291
command button control, 94, 95
Command button, properties of, 86
command buttons
  adding to a form, 142, 150
  Click event for, 90
  creating a switchboard form, 186
  drawing on a form, 29, 30
command completion feature, 112
Command object
  assigning to an open connection, 132
  declaring and instantiating, 132
  declaring a new, 167, 173
  setting to the existing connection, 167, 173
CommandBar object, 100
CommandBars collection, 288
CommandBars property, 288
CommandText property
  assigning to a SQL statement, 167, 173
  assigning to the SQL statement, 169, 175
  of the Command object, 518
comments, saving to the database, 439
Comments/Tasks tab, 336, 337
CommitTrans method, 314
compacting Access databases, 331
comparison operators in a Where clause, 161
compile errors, 64, 65
compiling applications, 330
conditional If statements, 59
connected recordsets, 132
Connection object
  adding code for, 150
  in the ADO object model, 131
  declaring, 131, 138
  instantiating, 131
  opening, 131
connection string, 132, 138
connection string variable, 150

connections, opening, 138, 167, 173. *See also*
    database connections
Connectors in an Activity Diagram, 7
Const **statement, 53**
constants
  built-in, 54
  creating in VBA, 53–54
  declaring and using, 53
  defined, 53
  limiting a property value to, 122
  scope and lifetime of, 54–55
consuming program for web services, 214
Contact **object, class for, 357**
contacts
  adding to project records, 442, 449
  displaying, 452–453
  procedures for saving to the database, 439
  sending a letter to, 298–302
  as a SharePoint list, 221
Contacts **class, 372–383**
Contacts form
  building for Project Tracker, 440–451
  to connect and display data from a recordset, 134–140
  opening, 453, 455
Contacts list, 227–229
Contacts prototype form, 341
Contacts screen
  designing, 335–336
  with one filtered record, 453, 455
  prototype for, 339–340
Contacts tab, 338
ControlExcel **procedure, 296, 297**
ControlOutlook **procedure, 303–304**
controls
  adding to forms, 344–357
  adding to reports, 238–241
  aligning on forms, 197
  creating for reports, 245
  populating with the current record, 167, 174
  working with, 187–195
Controls ribbon, 306
ControlSource **property, 139**
ControlWord **procedure, 299–300**
copies, number for printing, 247
Create Back-End Database dialog box, 320, 321
Create New Database option, 277, 279
CREATE PROCEDURE **statement, 470**

Create ribbon
  Create Module option, 30, 32
  selecting Macro, 46, 47
  selecting Module, 19, 20
CreateCommandBar **function, 289**
CreateCommandBar **procedure, 290**
CreateComplaintsReport **procedure, 242–244**
CreateObject **method, 295**
CreateParameter **method, 517**
CreateReport **method, 238, 245**
CreateReportControl **method, 238–241, 245**
cross-reference tables
  deleting records from, 397–398, 409
  inserting records into, 398–399, 409
cur **(Currency) prefix, 55**
Currency data type, 43, 50, 221
CurrentProject **object, 97**
cursor, type of, 325
CursorLocation **property, 133–134**
CursorType **property, 133, 143, 151**
custom button, adding to a command bar, 291
custom class modules, 357, 482
custom event, 120–121
custom groupings, 2
custom lists in SharePoint, 221
custom methods, 125–126
custom objects, 102
custom properties, 124–125
custom ribbons, 2
custom toolbar, 247
Customer **class, 482**
customer history record, 471–472
customer records
  code for adding, 506–507
  code for navigating, 508–509
  code for populating, 509–511
  updating an existing, 473–474
Customer Search form, 500
Customer Search screen, prototype for, 464
Customer Service application
  building the class module for objects, 481–488
  building the database and database objects, 465–475
  connecting the user interface to the code, 499–512
  design specifications, 461–465
  standard modules, 488–499
  touring the finished, 512–518
  user interface, 475–480
customers, retrieving information on, 473

D

DAO (Data Access Objects), 129
data
deleting using SQL statements, 165–166
exporting from Access to other formats, 248
exporting to a spreadsheet, 205, 206
exporting using `OutputTo`, 211
importing from a text file, 206–208
importing from the Northwind database, 202–203
retrieving using SQL `Select` statements, 160–164
updating using SQL statements, 165
using from SharePoint lists, 222–232
using from web services, 214–220
data access
improving, 324–325
introduction to, 129–130
data access layer, 17, 104, 105
Data Access Objects (DAO), 129
data elements, determining, 11
data entry controls, emptying, 146–147, 154
data error, correcting up front, 196
data objects, manipulating, 177–178
data sources
linking to and importing from, 200
retrieving a set of records from, 132
specifying for a connection, 132
data tables, 318
data types
Access compared to SharePoint, 221
available in VBA, 49–50
changing from Access to equivalent SQL Server, 278, 282
user-defined, 52–53
data validation, adding, 196–197
database(s)
building for the Customer Service application, 465–475
building for the Project Tracker application, 340–343
compacting and repairing, 331
connecting to, 132
creating, 29–31
default format for, 29
encrypting, 329
making backup copies of, 331
updating from a disconnected recordset, 147, 155
database access code, isolating, 18
database calls, layer for, 16–17

database connections. *See also* connections, opening
closing and releasing from memory, 143, 151
maintaining open, 139–140
minimizing open, 324
database element, 12
database layer
in n-tier architecture, 17
in three-tier architecture, 15, 16
database location, making configurable, 340
database objects
attaching to an e-mail, 210
for the Customer Service application, 465–475
`Database` **parameter for the** `TransferSQLDatabase` **method, 204**
database password, 327–328
database server, 14
Database Splitter, 319
Database Splitter Wizard, 319–322
database tables
retrieving data from, 163
separating from the user interface, 319–322
Database Tools ribbon, 18, 19
database transfers, 201
database updates, 517
database window, replaced by the navigation pane, 2
`DatabaseName` **parameter, 201**
`DatabaseType` **parameter, 201**
`DataSource` **parameter, 209**
`DataSource` **property, 236**
`DataTarget` **parameter, 209**
Date data type, 50
Date of Birth text box, 87, 89
Date or Time data type, 221
dates, checking, 277
`dbl` **(Double) prefix, 55**
`Deactivate` **event, 247**
`Debug` **object, 82**
debugging
code, 66–71
errors, 64–71
`Debug.Print` **method, 82**
`Debug.Print` **statement, 68**
decision making in code, 56–61
Decision Points in Activity Diagrams, 8
Declarations/Procedure navigation box, 27, 28
default error messages, 72
Default File Format option, 29

default record locking, 317
Delete **command, 167, 173**
Delete Comment button, 337
Delete **method**
  adding to the clsCar class, 112–113
  of the Recordset object, 142
**delete operation, prompting the user to proceed,
    388, 403**
Delete **procedure, 365–366, 370–371, 378, 382–383**
Delete Selected Contact button, 338
Delete **statements, 165–166**
DeleteRecord **procedure, 144, 152, 166–167, 172**
delimited files, 208
demo CDs, creating, 256
descending order, 162
Description **property of the** Err **object, 74**
design guidelines, 322–323
design phase of SDLC, 4–18
Design ribbon
  adding controls to a form, 187, 188
  selecting and drawing controls, 115, 117
  SQL View, 468, 469
  ToolBox displayed on, 86
design specifications
  for the Customer Service application, 461–465
  for the Project Tracker application, 334–340
Design tab, enabling icons, 272
design time settings, 81
Design View
  accessing in hidden mode, 236
  retrieving data from multiple tables, 271, 272
  switching to from Layout View, 29
designer window for a stored procedure, 267, 268
Desktop Edition. See **SQL Server 2005 Express Edition**
Destination **parameter, 201**
detail section of a report, 245
developer extensions, 330
development methodology, 3
development phase of SDLC, 18–23
diagramming techniques, 5
Dim **statement**
  declaring a class, 115
  declaring variables, 51
disconnected recordsets
  building unbound forms, 142–156
  described, 132
  navigation procedures for, 145, 153
  as recommended, 156
  saving control values in, 147, 154–155

  updating databases from, 147, 155
  working with, 142
DisplayMessage **procedure, 291**
DisplaySystemInfo **procedure, 292, 293, 294**
DISTINCT **predicate, 160**
distribution options for applications, 329
divide by 0 error, 74
Dividing Lines **property, 142, 149**
DLLs (Dynamic Link Libraries)
  referencing external, 291–294
  standard, 287–291
  using, 287–294
Do...Loop **statement, 62–63**
Do...Until **loop, 62, 63**
Do...While **loop, 62**
Do...While **statement, 63**
docmd **command, 21, 23**
DoCmd **object**
  performing macro commands or menu options, 97–98
  programatically linking a list, 227–229
  TransferDatabase **method, 200–203**
documenting code, 63–64
Double data type, 50
DSN, 230
dt **(Date) prefix, 55**
dynamic arrays, 51, 52
Dynamic Link Libraries. See **DLLs**

E

early binding, 295, 324
Edited Record option, 317
elements
  of applications, 11–12
  running on different computers, 15
e-mails
  generating empty, 415–416, 431
  integrating into applications, 453, 454
  sending from VBA code, 210–211
  sending through Outlook from Access, 302–305
embedded macros, 2
empty forms for a user interface, 344, 475–481
empty record, adding to a recordset, 141–142
Enable this Content option, 34
Encode Database, 329
Encoding **parameter**
  for the ExportXML method, 209
  for the OutputTo method, 249
Encrypt with Password option, 327

encrypting a database, 329
end users, interviewing, 3–4
Ending Points in Activity Diagrams, 8
Enhanced Rich Text data type, 222
enumerated types, 122–123
EOF **property of a recordset, 141**
error handler, 73–74
error messages, 72, 77–78
ErrorHandlerLibrary **database, 308, 311**
error-handling code, writing, 71–78
error-handling procedure, 308
errors
  debugging, 64–71
  raising in code, 75
  types of, 64–66
Errors **collection, 75**
event(s)
  calling functions from, 45
  calling sub procedures from, 36
  common to objects, 84
  creating, 113–115
  declaring and raising, 114
  defined, 79
  described, 84–86
  example using, 86–91
  initializing and terminating, 115
  as a SharePoint list, 221
event handlers. *See* event procedures
Event Procedure option, 85
event procedures
  adding to a form, 143, 151
  adding to handle recordset navigation, 144, 152
  creating, 90
  navigating through records, 444–445, 450
event sub procedures, 114–115
Event tab
  from the cmdRun Properties window, 37
  of the Properties dialog box, 84, 95
Excel
  controlling from Access, 295–298
  creating a new instance of, 295
Execute **method, 132, 269, 517**
execute-only applications, 331
ExecuteSPRetrieveRS **function, 495–496**
ExecuteSQLCommand **procedure, 389–390, 404–405**
ExecuteStoredProcedure **procedure, 497**
ExecuteStoreProcedure **procedure, 517–518**

Exit **event, 86–87**
Exit **event procedure, 90**
exporting
  data using OutputTo, 211
  defined, 200
ExportXML **method, 208–209**
Express Edition. *See* **SQL Server 2005 Express Edition**
Expression Builder, 84
eXtensible Markup Language. *See* XML
external applications, automating, 294–295
external data sources, 199–211
External Data tab, 200, 222, 223
external DLLS, 291–294
external function calls, 456–458
external functions
  calling, 293
  declarations to, 400
external library, 293
Extreme Programming, 3

F

field data types, 50–51
fields
  specifying for sorting, 157
  viewing for a table, 134
file attachments, 456. *See also* attachments
File Attachments tab, 339
File Open button, 339
file-level security, 327
FileName **parameter**
  for the TransferSpreadsheet method, 205
  for the TransferText method, 206
Filter **property, 158–159**
FinalizeOrder **procedure, 35, 36**
Find **method, 157–158**
firing events. *See* raising events
fixed-size array, 52
FixNull **function, 489**
For Each...Next **loops, 61**
For Each **loops, 99–100**
For...Next **loops, 61–62**
For...Next **statement, 62**
form(s)
  adding to a database, 29
  binding to ADO recordsets, 138
  creating the user interface, 18

getting to the Visual Basic Editor from, 21
hiding to be reopened later, 325
loading, 47, 48
navigation and flow of, 181–187
obtaining a list of all open, 94–96
obtaining currently active, 98
opening from a switchboard form, 187
polishing, 197–198
properties of, 80
saving, 30, 87
form modules, 29
Form **object, 94**
Form_frmText **object, 40, 41**
Form_Load **event**
adding code to, 116, 119
adding to a form, 143, 150
code in, 138
ensuring changes are saved, 148, 156
for frmCustomers form, 505–506
for the frmProjects form, 410, 427
initializing frmContacts form, 441, 448–449
Form_Load **event procedure, 511–512**
Form_Load **procedure, 135–136**
Form_Unload **event, 448, 451**
Form_Unload **procedure, 422–423, 437**
Forms **collection, 94**
forward-only cursor, 133
frm **(Form) prefix, 56**
frmContacts **form**
building for Project Tracker, 440–451
creating, 351, 354–356, 357
writing code for, 441–451
frmCustomers **form, 477–480, 504–512**
frmProjects **form**
creating, 344–353, 357
example of, 410, 411
writing code for, 410–440
frmSearch **form**
adding a breakpoint to, 512, 513
creating, 475–477
writing code for, 500–504
frmTest **form**
Code Builder from, 40
creating a new procedure for, 37–40
displaying objects associated with, 40, 41
opening in View mode, 38
selecting from the Form Name field, 47, 48

FROM **clause, 160–161**
fsub **(SubForm) prefix, 56**
FullName **property, 97**
Function **keyword, 42**
function procedures, 42–44
functions
behind methods, 82–83
built-in, 45–46
built-in SQL Server, 275–277
calling from events, 45
calling from other procedures, 44–45
creating, 43–44, 114–115
defined, 33
scope and lifetime of, 45

G

general comment section, 63–64
General Declarations section, 54
GeneralErrorHandler **procedure**
adding, 75–76
adding to modBusinessLogic, 492
adding to the modBusinessLogic module, 389, 404
calling, 77
placing into a new database, 311
generic error handler, 75–78
Get External Data - SharePoint Site Wizard, 222–226
GetFileNameBrowse **function, 385–386, 401–402**
GetLookupDisplayValues **parameter, 226**
GetOpenFileName **external function, 384, 400**
GetPlaceFacts **method, 218–220**
GetSQL **function, 512**
GetSystemInfo **external library, 293**
global scope of the Err **object, 74**

H

HandleError **section, 74, 77**
HasFieldNames **parameter**
for TransferSpreadsheet method, 205
for TransferText method, 206
hidden mode, 236
hourglass, 325
HTML pages, creating static, 249–251
HTMLTableName **parameter, 206**
Hyperlink data type, 50, 222

I

icon
  for events, 92, 93
  for a method, 83
  for a property, 81, 82
ID data type, 221
ID of a SharePoint list, 227
`If` **statement, 34**
`If...Then` **statements, 56–59**
`If...Then...Else` **statement**
  as faster than `IIF` statements, 324
  syntax for, 57
`If...Then...ElseIf` **statement, 57**
`IIf` **function, 59**
`ImageTarget` **parameter, 209**
Immediate window
  calling `TestError2`, 76
  displaying the currently active form, 98
  running a new function in, 43
  running a procedure from, 34
  running the new `TestIfStatement` procedure, 58
  running the `TestCaseStatement` procedure, 60
  running the `TestError` procedure, 73
  running the `TestLoop` procedure, 62, 67, 68, 69
  seeing report names in, 97
  using, 68
  in the Visual Basic Editor, 24, 25
implementation phase of SDLC, 25
`implements` **keyword, 123**
importing
  defined, 200
  SharePoint lists, 222–226
  situations for, 200
`ImportOptions` **parameter, 208**
`ImportXML` **method, 208**
indexes, 325
infinite loop, 63
`Initialize` **event, 115**
in-line comments, 63, 64
inner join, 161
Insert ActiveX Control window, 306
`Insert` **statement, 164–165**
`int` **(Integer) prefix, 55**
`intCounter` **variable, 67**
Integer data type, 50
IntelliSense, 112

interactive forms, 181–198
interface inheritance, 123
interviewing end users, 3–4
intrinsic constants. *See* **built-in constants**
issues in SharePoint, 221
iterative process, testing as, 24

J

Jet SQL, 159
join syntax, 161

K

`KeyPress` **event, 85–86**

L

label
  changing properties of, 86
  selecting for a list box, 95
late binding, 295, 324
left join, 161
letters, creating Word from Access, 298–302
libraries
  available for use in Access applications, 100
  based on specific Access databases, 308–312
Libraries list, 93
life cycle
  of a procedure, 45
  of variables, 54
`LIKE` **keyword, 515**
`LimitToList` **property, 193**
`LinkChildFields` **property, 194**
linking
  to SharePoint lists within Access, 225–232
  situations for, 200
`LinkMasterFields` **property, 194**
links in SharePoint, 221
list box control
  dragging onto a new form, 94, 95
  populating, 422, 436–437
list boxes, versus combo boxes, 188–193
`ListID` **parameter, 226**
lists, choices in, 188
`lng` **(Long) prefix, 55**
`LoadRecords` **procedure, 423, 437–438**
local string variable, declaring, 219

local variables

adding for `clsProjects`, 372–373, 379

adding for Property Get and Property Set, 111

declaring and assigning values to, 40

declaring as `Report` objects, 97

declaring for `clsProjects`, 359, 366–367

in a procedure, 36

Local window, 24, 25

Locals Window, 68–69

Lock Project For Viewing option, 328

`LockType` **property**

of the `Recordset` object, 134, 317

setting, 143, 151

logic errors, 66

logical tiers, 18

`Login` **parameter, 204**

Long data type, 50

loops, declaring, 61–63

M

Macro Builder, 84

macros

embedded in Access 2007, 2

examples of, 46–48, 49

instead of procedures, 46

naming, 47, 49

versus procedures, 46–48, 49

responding to events, 84

saving, 47

"the Macros in this project are disabled" error message, 34

`mcr` **(Macro) prefix, 56**

MDB file format, 2

`Me` **keyword, 94, 125, 126**

Memo field data type, 51

memo fields, 2

menu add-ins, 312

menus, importing or linking data, 200

methods

adding to a class module, 111

adding to a form, 126

calling from within `Property Let`, 106

in a Class Diagram, 103

creating, 111–113

defined, 79

described, 82–83

example using, 86–91

implementing with interface inheritance, 123

Microsoft Access. *See* **Access 2007**

Microsoft Content Management Server 2002, 221

Microsoft Excel. *See* **Excel**

Microsoft IntelliSense, 112

Microsoft Office 12.0 Object Library, 288–291

Microsoft Office 2003 Web Services Toolkit, 214

Microsoft Outlook. *See* **Outlook**

Microsoft SharePoint Portal Server 2003, 221

Microsoft SQL Server. *See* **SQL Server**

Microsoft SQL Server Database Wizard, 262–263, 466

Microsoft Visio. *See* **Visio**

Microsoft Visual Basic, 1

Microsoft Word. *See* **Word**

middle (business) layer in three-tier architecture, 15, 16

`mod` **(Module) prefix, 56**

`modBusinessLogic` **module, 384–389, 400–404, 489–499**

`modDatabaseLogic` **module, 384, 389–399, 400, 404–408**

modeling, 4

`modError` **module, 308, 311**

Modify Columns and Settings link, 227

modules

authorizing to run, 34

creating, 27–28, 29

defined, 27

inserting into databases, 242

types of, 29, 101

Modules tab, 29

`MouseUp` **event, 92, 93**

`MouseWheel` **event, 92, 93**

Move Data ribbon, 319

`MoveToFirstRecord` **procedure, adding to** `modBusinessLogic`, **490**

`MoveToLastRecord` **procedure, adding to** `modBusinessLogic`, **490–491**

`MoveToNextRecord` **procedure, adding to** `modBusinessLogic`, **491–492**

`MoveToPreviousRecord` **procedure, adding to** `modBusinessLogic`, **491**

`msgbox` **command, 21, 23**

`msgbox` **function, 195–196, 293**

Multiple lines of text data type, 221

multiuser architecture considerations, 318–322

multiuser considerations for applications, 315–322

N

Name **properties**
  changing for command buttons, 115, 118
  changing for controls, 30, 31
  setting for command buttons, 142
Name **property**
  changing for a label, 115, 118
  changing for a text box, 86, 115, 118
  of a command button, 86, 95
  of a label, 86
  of a list box, 95
  modifying for text boxes, 135
naming conventions
  for objects, 55–56
  prefixes used as, 55–56
navigating through a recordset, 141
Navigation Buttons **property, 142, 149**
navigation pane, 2
navigation procedures, 145, 153
No Locks option, 317
nonvisual objects, 82
Northwind database, 202–203, 235
n-tier architecture. See three-tiered architecture
Number (Byte) field data type, 50
Number data type, 221
Number (Double) field data type, 50
Number (Integer) field data type, 51
Number (Long Integer) field data type, 51
Number (Single) field data type, 51

O

obj **(Object) prefix, 55**
object(s)
  building class modules for Project Tracker, 357
  characteristics of, 80
  class module for in Customer Service, 481–488
  creating custom methods for existing, 125–126
  creating custom properties for existing, 124–125
  creating your own, 101–127
  defined, 79
  elements of, 79–91
  instantiating at runtime, 295
  referring to, 93–94
  seeing methods available for, 83
  standardized way of naming, 55

  using, 94–100
  using class modules to create, 101–123
  viewing using the Object Browser, 91–93
Object Browser
  opening, 91, 92
  viewing objects using, 91–93
Object data type, 50
Object navigation box, 27, 28
object variables
  declaring and using, 53
  declaring for Excel, 294
  defined, 53
ObjectFormat **parameter, 210**
ObjectName **parameter**
  for OutputTo, 249
  for SendObject, 210
object-oriented programming. See OOP
object-oriented programming environment, 79–100
ObjectType **parameter**
  for the ExportXML method, 209
  for the OutputTo method, 249
  for SendObject, 210
  for the TransferDatabase method, 201
objProjects **object, populating, 412, 428–429**
ODBC database, importing data from, 201
ODBC data source name, 201
Office and Home Application Download Category, 214
Office Button, 79
Office SharePoint Server 2007, 221
On Click **event, 37, 38, 87**
On Click **event procedure, 95**
On Error **statement, 72, 77**
On Exit **event, 86–87**
On Load **event, 116**
1&1 Internet, 222
OOP (object-oriented programming), 79
Open Databases Using Record-Level Locking option, 317
Open Exclusive setting, 323
Open **method**
  of the Connection object, 131
  populating a recordset, 133
OpenDbConnection **procedure**
  adding to modDatabaseLogic module, 492–493
  adding to open database connections, 390, 405
OpenFileAttachment **procedure, 385, 401**
OpenForm action, 47, 48

optimistic locking, 317, 318

Option Explicit statement, 31, 32

Options parameter of the Recordset object, 134

OR, in an Activity Diagram, 8, 9, 10

Order By clause, 161–162

OtherFlags parameter, 209

Outlook, 302–305

Outlook Calendar, 163–164

OutputFile parameter for the OutputTo method, 249

OutputFormat parameter for the OutputTo method, 249

OutputQuality parameter for the OutputTo method, 249

OutputTo method, 211, 248–251

OutputToHTML procedure, 250

P

Packaging Wizard, 330

PadQuotes function, 495

page break, inserting into a Word document, 302

Parallel Activities in Activity Diagrams, 8

parameters, 33

parent-child class relationships, 122

password, 328–329

Password parameter, 204

Password Required dialog, 328

perceived performance, 325–326

percent meter, 325–326

performance

improving actual for applications, 322–325

improving perceived, 325–326

slowed by encryption, 329

Performance Analyzer, 326–327

period (.), referring to objects, 94

pessimistic locking, 317

Phone field, 514–515

physical tier, 18

Picture property, 142

PopulateComboBoxes procedure, 421, 435–436

PopulateContactsControls procedure, 446–447, 450–451

PopulateControlsOnForm procedure, 146, 153–154

PopulateListFromRecordset procedure, 422, 436–437, 489–490

PopulateProjectsControls procedure, 419–420, 433–434

PopulatePropertiesFromForm procedure

adding to clsCustomer class module, 487

adding to clsProjects class module, 364–365, 369–370, 377, 381

PopulatePropertiesFromRecordset procedure, 363–364, 368–369, 376, 380–381, 486

populating combo boxes and list boxes, 190–193

predicates, restricting records returned, 160

prefixes, as naming conventions, 55–56

presentation (user interface) layer

creating diagrams for, 104, 105

in n-tier architecture, 17

in three-tier architecture, 15, 16

PresentationTarget parameter, 209

Preserve statement, 52

Preview button, 339

preview mode, 245, 246

primary key for a SQL Server table, 265

printer devices, displaying in the Debug window, 98–100

printer margins, setting, 247

Printer object, 98, 246–247

Printers collection, 98–100, 246–247

private declarations of procedures, 45

private variable, 54

procedures

calling sub procedures from, 35–36

creating and calling, 33–46

declaring as private, 45

defined, 33

versus macros, 46–48, 49

for making updates to data, 507–508

making use of If...Then statements, 57–58

retrieving values for, 36

variables and constants in, 49

ProceedWithDelete function, 388, 403

process Flow Diagrams, 7

ProcessRecordset function, 493–494

ProcessRecordset procedure, 396, 407–408

ProcessUpdate procedure, 396–397, 408, 496

program flow, controlling, 56–63

progress bar, 325–326

Project class, 358–372

Project Explorer, 357

Project object, class for, 357

project records, creating procedures for, 393–395, 406–407

Project Tracker application
  building class modules for objects, 357–383
  building the database, 340–343
  building the user interface, 344–357
  connecting the user interface to the code, 410–451
  Contacts class, 372–383
  design specifications, 334–340
  opening, 335
  Project class, 358–372
  standard modules, 383–409
  touring the finished, 452–459
Project Tracker screen
  dividing into tabs, 336–339
  prototype, 342
  sample project record on, 452
Project window, 19, 20
ProjectId **field, 410, 427**
Projects form, 410–440
ProjectTrackerDb **database, 340–343**
ProjectTrackerUI **database, 344**
ProjectType **property, 97**
properties
  adding to forms, 124–125
  in a Class Diagram, 103
  creating, 105–111
  creating custom, 124–125
  creating for a class, 105
  creating for the Car class, 107–111
  described, 80–82
  of the Err object, 74
  example using, 86–91
  with interface inheritance, 123
  listing for an object, 81
  of objects, 79
  shared by objects, 81
Properties dialog box
  displaying for a form, 30
  Event tab, 84, 86, 116
  for a form, 80
  for a text box control, 86
Properties module, 19, 20
Properties window, 30, 32
Property Get **procedure**
  adding, 111
  creating properties for existing objects, 124
  syntax for, 106–107

  using, 106
  using SpecialFeaturesList enumeration, 122–123
Property Let **procedure**
  adding, 111
  creating properties for existing objects, 124
  general syntax for, 106
  using, 106
  using SpecialFeaturesList enumeration, 122–123
property procedures
  adding to clsCustomer class module, 483–485
  adding to clsProjects class module, 359–361, 367, 373–375, 380
Property Set **procedure, 106, 107, 124**
property value, limiting to specified constants, 122
Protection tab, selecting, 328, 329
prototype screens
  for the Customer Service application, 464–465
  generating with Access forms, 336–340
  generating with Visio, 336, 337
  for managing cars, 102, 103
public functions, 111
Public **keyword, 45, 54**
public sub procedures
  adding to a class, 111
  creating custom methods, 125–126
public variables
  creating properties for existing objects, 124
  declaring, 54–55
  implementing properties for custom classes, 105
  using, 105
PublicEvent **statement, 114**
purpose of an application, 3

Q

qry **(Query) prefix, 56**
queries
  errors in upsizing, 278, 283
  returning rows, 325
Queries category in the Navigation Pane, 267
Queries objects, 278, 284
Query Designer, 160
query processor for SQL Server, 259

R

Raise **method of the** Err **object, 74–75**
RaiseEvent **statement, 114**
raising events, 113
Range **parameter, 205**
Rapid Application Design (RAD), 3
read-only locks, 317
read-only properties, 107
record count, 434
record locking
  on bound forms, 316–317
  on unbound forms, 317–318
record navigation methods, 141
Record Selectors **property, 142, 149**
Recordcount **property, 140–141**
records
  adding to a table, 242
  counting in a recordset, 140–141
  deleting current from the recordset, 142
  deleting from cross-reference tables, 397–398, 409
  event procedures for navigating, 444–445, 450
  inserting into cross-reference tables, 398–399, 409
  navigating to particular, 157–158
  procedures for saving displayed, 425–426, 439
  sorting for the unbound contacts form, 156–157
  updating the current in a recordset, 142
recordset navigation procedures, 386–388, 402
Recordset **object**
  adding code for, 142, 150
  creating, 133–140
  declaring a new, 138
  instantiating a new, 138
  navigation methods, 141
  properties and methods of, 83, 156–159
  retrieving a set of records from a data source, 132
  setting properties of, 143, 151
Recordset **property, 138–139**
recordsets
  adding, editing, and deleting records in, 141–156
  counting records in, 140–141
  declaring in frmProjects, 428
  filtering to smaller subsets, 158–159
  navigating through, 141
  populating controls on a form, 143, 151
  procedures for navigating through, 144, 152
  reconnecting to underlying data sources, 147, 155

  repopulating values in, 405
  repopulating with the most current values, 169, 175
  sorting, finding, and filtering records in, 156–159
  storing in local memory, 143, 151
  using SQL and ADO to populate, 162–164
RecordSource **property**
  of CreateReport, 245
  of a report, 236
  specifying a SQL statement as, 160
ReDim **statement, 52**
references
  adding to the ADOX library, 177
  adding to web services, 215–218
References dialog box, 288
RefreshContacts **procedure, 426–427, 439–440**
RefreshHistory **procedure, 511**
registering add-ins, 313
repairing Access databases, 331
replication, removed for ACCDB files, 2
report events, 247–248
Report **object, 96–97**
report properties, changing, 236
reports
  adding controls to, 238–241
  creating programmatically, 237–248
  designating printing options for, 246–247
  manipulating from VBA code, 235–248
  opening in preview mode, 245, 246
  setting the data source for, 236–237
Reports **collection, 96–97**
Requery **method, 167, 173**
RequeryRecordset **procedure, 391, 405–406**
Require Variable Declaration option, 31
Requirement Number for a Use Case, 5
Resume Next **statement, 72**
Resume **statement, 72**
Retrieve **method, 112, 113**
RetrieveAttachments **function, 363, 368**
RetrieveComments **function, 362, 367–368**
RetrieveContacts **function, 362–363, 368, 375–376, 380**
RetrieveCustomers **function, 485–486**
RetrieveProjects **function, 361–367**
reusable modules, writing, 322
ribbons, 2
rich client, 16
Rich Text data type, 222

rich text in memo fields, 2
right join, 161
roadmap for building a system, 4–5
RollbackTrans method, 313, 314
row-level security, 271
RowSourceType property, 95
rpt (Report) prefix, 56
rsub (Subreport) prefix, 56
RunSearch procedure, 512
runtime, 330
runtime errors, 64, 66, 74
/runtime switch, 330

S

Save Changes button, 337
Save event, 116, 120
Save procedure
    adding to clsCustomer class module, 488
    adding to clsProjects class module, 366, 371,
        378–379, 383
SaveAllRecords procedure, 144, 147, 152, 155
SaveCurrentRecord procedure, 147, 154–155,
        168, 174
scaling up a database server, 14
SchemaTarget parameter, 209
scope
    of an Activity Diagram, 7
    defined, 45
    global, 74
    of a procedure, 45
    of a variable, 54
Screen object, 98
screen prototypes, 8–11
SDLC (Systems Development Life Cycle), 3
Search Inventory Screen
    Activity Diagram for, 8, 9
    designing for Wrox Auto Sales, 5
    mapping Use Cases to, 10–11
    prototype for, 11
    separate actions on, 5, 6
    Use Case Diagram requirements, 8
search results, clearing, 503–504
Search Results screen, 515, 516
securing applications, 327–329
security information, specifying, 278, 279
security model, 3
Select clause, 160

Select statements, 160–164
Select...Case statements, 59–61, 60–61
Send method, 305
SendObject method, 210–211
separation of tiers concept, 103–104
server cursors, 134
server machine, 13
Server parameter, 204
services, installed with SQL Server 2005 Express
        Edition, 257–259
Set statement, 115
SharePoint data types, 221
SharePoint DSN, 229, 230–231
SharePoint hosting, 222
SharePoint lists
    importing, 222–226
    introduction to, 221–222
    linking to, 225–232
    types of, 221
    using data from, 222–232
SHELLEXECUTE, external DLL function call to,
        456, 457
ShellExecute external function, 384, 400
Shift key, selecting multiple controls to align, 197
Single data type, 50
Single line of text data type, 221
single-tier applications, 12–13
SiteAddress parameter, 226
sng (Single) prefix, 55
sort order, 161–162
Sort property, 156–157
source argument, 134
Source parameter, 201
SourceObject property of a subform, 194
SourceTableName property, 229, 231
SpecialFeaturesList enumerated type, 122, 123
SpecificationName parameter, 206
spInsertCustomer stored procedure, 469–470
splash screen, 325
Split Database button, 320
spreadsheets, importing, linking, and exporting,
        204–205
SpreadsheetType parameter, 205
spRetrievalAllCustomers stored procedure,
        470, 471
spRetrieveCustomerHistory stored procedure,
        471–472

spRetrievePlans **stored procedure, 472**

spRetrieveSelectedCustomer **stored procedure, 473**

spUpdateCustomer **stored procedure, 473–474, 517**

SQL (Structured Query Language)

introduction to, 159–164

syntax of, 159–160

SQL code

adding, 470

for a stored procedure, 268

SQL Insert **statements, 164–165**

SQL queries, 324

SQL Server

Access as a front end to, 132

Access Projects as a front end to, 253–254

built-in functions, 275–277

setting up, 254–259

stored procedures, 267–271

versions of, 255

views, 271–274

SQL Server Browser Service, 259

SQL Server Configuration Manager, 257–258

SQL Server database

linking to, 253

modifying strConnection string to point to, 492–493

specifying, 466

specifying details necessary to connect to, 260, 261

transferring a complete, 203–204

using a new, 262–263

using an existing, 260–262

SQL Server Mobile Edition, 255

SQL Server objects, 264–277

SQL Server Service, 259

SQL Server storage engine, 259

SQL Server tables, 264–267

SQL Server 2005 Developer Edition, 255

SQL Server 2005 Enterprise Edition, 255

SQL Server 2005 Evaluation Edition, 255

SQL Server 2005 Express Edition, 255–259

SQL Server 2005 Standard Edition, 255

SQL Server 2005 Workgroup Edition, 255

SQL statements

adding procedures for creating, 391–393, 406–408

with and without ADO, 160

building dynamic, 512

deleting data using, 165–166

dialects of, 159

inserting current values on a form, 168, 174–175

modifying the unbound contacts form, 166–176

as a report's RecordSource property, 241

running against a database, 167, 173

setting changes and removing passwords, 327–328

as the source for the Open method, 162

specifying the DataSource of a report, 236

for stored procedures, 269

updating an existing record, 168–169, 175

updating data using, 165

updating tables, 393–395, 406–407

viewing in Query Designer, 160

SQL View on the Design ribbon, 468, 469

standalone application, 13

standard DLLs, 287–291

standard modules

building for Project Tracker, 383–409

for the Customer Service application, 488–499

defined, 101

described, 29

Starting Point for an Activity Diagram, 7

static arrays, 51

static HTML pages, 249–251

Static **keyword, 45, 54**

Step Into option, 66

Step Over option, 66

storage engine for SQL Server, 259

stored procedures

adding to the Customer Service application, 467

calling, 269

creating for SQL Server, 269–271

described for SQL Server, 267

running, 269, 271

StoreLogin **parameter, 201**

str **(String) prefix, 55**

String data type, 50

string variable, 60

structure variable, declaring, 219

Structured Query Language. See SQL

StructureOnly **parameter, 201**

sub procedures

behind methods, 82–83

calling from events, 36

calling from other procedures, 35–36

creating and calling new, 33–35

defined, 33

scope and lifetime of, 45

Subform control, 194
subforms
  described, 194
  example of, 194, 195
  minimizing the use of, 322
  tying to a parent form, 194
subqueries, 162
switchboard forms, 182–187
syntax errors, 64, 65
system information, from an external DLL, 292–294
SYSTEM_INFO type declaration, 293
Systems Development Life Cycle. See SDLC

T

tab controls, 193–195, 434
Tab Order screen, 197–198
tab stops, order of, 197
table(s)
  adding to the Customer Service application, 466–467
  adding to databases, 241–242
  combining data from two, 162
  creating in a database, 134
  creating with ADOX library, 177–178
  exporting to XML, 209
  inserting results from a Select statement, 165
  for Project Tracker, 341–343
  retrieving data from more than one, 161
  specifying to upsize, 278, 280
table alias, 160
table attributes, specifying to upsize, 278, 280
table names, removing spaces in, 277
table scans, reducing, 325
table view, 140
TableDef object
  creating, 229, 230
  programmatically linking a list, 229–232
  with a SharePoint list as its source, 229
TableName parameter
  for the TransferSharePointList method, 226
  for the TransferSpreadsheet method, 205
  for the TransferText method, 206
Tables category in Access Projects, 264
tabs
  controlling the visibility of, 194
  for the Project Tracker screen, 336–339
Tag property, 124

tags in an XML file, 209
tasks in SharePoint, 221
tbl (Table) prefix, 56
tblComplaints table, exporting to HTML, 249–251
tblContacts table, mapping to fields on, 341, 343
tblCustomers table, adding to the Customer Service application, 466
tblCustomersPlanHistory table, adding to the Customer Service application, 467
tblPlans table, adding to the Customer Service application, 467
tblPlansStatus table, adding to the Customer Service application, 467
tblProjects table, adding, 341, 343
tblProjectsComments table, adding to Project Tracker, 342, 343
tblProjectsContacts table, adding to Project Tracker, 342, 343
tblProjectsFileAttachments table, 342, 343
TemplateFile parameter for the OutputTo method, 249
templates, prebuilt, 2
Terminate event for a class, 115
TerraService web services, 215–216, 218–220
Test Connection button, 261
TestCaseStatement procedure, 60–61
TestError procedure, 73–74
TestError2 procedure, 76
TestIfStatement procedure, 57–58
testing phase of SDLC, 24–25
TestLibrary procedure, 311–312
TestLoop procedure, 61
TestMethod method, 111
TestPrinter procedure, 99
TestPrinter sub procedure, 99–100
TestTransferDatabase procedure, 202–203
TestWebService procedure, 218, 219
text box controls
  displaying a selected date, 307
  setting to current values, 146, 153–154
text boxes
  adding to a form, 135
  code displaying values in, 188
  drawing on a form, 29, 30
text box object variable, 53
Text field data type, 51

text files, 205–208
thin client, 16
three-tiered architecture, 15–17
tiers of an application architecture, 12
toggle button, 438–439
togShowAll_Click event, 424, 438–439
ToolBox, 86, 88
tooltip, 220
TOP predicate, 160
transactions, 313–314
transactions form, displaying, 194, 195
TransferCopyData parameter, 204
TransferDatabase method, 200–203
TransferSharePointList method, 225–229
TransferSpreadsheet method, 204–205, 206
TransferSQLDatabase method, 203–204
TransferText method, 205–208
TransferType parameter
    for the TransferDatabase method, 201
    for the TransferSharePointList method, 226
    for the TransferSpreadsheet method, 205
    for the TransferText method, 206
Trust Center, accessing, 47
T-SQL, 159
two-tier applications. See client-server applications
typ (User-Defined Type) prefix, 55
Type Mismatch error, 64, 66
typTripInfo user-defined type, 52–53

U

unbound contacts form
    building using a disconnected recordset, 142–156
    modifying to use SQL, 166–176
    sorting records for, 156–157
unbound forms
    better than bound, 324
    record locking on, 317–318
unhiding the switchboard form, 187
Union statement, 162
unique index number of each array element, 51
updatable, recordsets as, 134
update conflicts, 318
Update method
    adding the clsCar class, 112
    calling, 120
    committing a new empty record to the local
        disconnected recordset, 144, 152
    modifying in clsCar, 114
    of the Recordset object, 142
Update statements, 165
Upsizing Wizard, 277–284
URL, decoding, 227
Use Case Diagrams
    for the Customer Service application, 462–463
    for the Project Tracker application, 334, 335–336
    using, 5–7
Use Case Numbers, 5
Use Cases, 5, 8–11
UseOA parameter, 205
user ID, 194
user input, validating, 196–197
user interaction, 195–197
user interface
    of an application, 12
    building for Project Tracker, 344–357
    building for the Customer Service application, 475–480
    connecting to code, 410–451, 499–512
    determining properties and methods of an object,
        102, 103
    implementing a basic, 139
    separating from the data tables, 318
user interface database, opening exclusively, 323
user interface elements, mapping Use Cases to, 10–11
user interface objects, 344
user-defined data types, 50, 52–53
user-defined functions
    described, 275
    embedding within a basic SQL statement, 275
user-interface database, 322
user-interface objects, 319
user-level security, 2
users, interacting with controls, 195
UseTrustedConnection parameter, 204

V

validation checks, 106
ValidationRule property, 196
ValidationText property, 196
values
    calling a procedure with hard-coded, 58
    preserving after a procedure ends, 45
    returning from function procedures, 44
    using variables and constants to store, 49–56
var (Variant) prefix, 55

variables

declaring and using, 51–53

declaring in functions, 44

defined, 33

evaluating multiple times, 59

making visible in any module, 54–55

naming conventions for, 55–56

scope and lifetime of, 54–55

standardized way of naming, 55

storing the number of loop iterations, 62

types of, 49–51

Variant data type, 50

variants, minimizing the use of, 324

VB (Visual Basic), 1

VBA (Visual Basic for Applications), 1

VBA code

adding a password for, 328–329

basics of writing and testing, 27–78

handling data validation from, 196

linking to another database, 319

optimizing to improve performance, 323–324

responding to events, 84

sending an e-mail from, 210–211

using to link, import, and export, 199–211

working with controls, 187–195

working with reports from, 235–248

writing behind report events, 247

writing for the business logic and database access logic, 18

VBA data types, correspondence to field data types, 50–51

VBA Help documentation, obtaining a list of available functions, 45

VBA source code, securing separately, 328

VBA version 6.0, 1

VB.NET, 1

`VerifyCreditAvail` **procedure**

calling from another procedure, 35–36

creating, 33–35

View button, 273

View Details for Selected Contact button, 453

View mode, 139

`ViewID` **parameter for the** `TransferShare-PointList` **method, 226**

View/Manage Car Details Screen

Activity Diagram for, 8, 10

prototype for, 11, 12

Use Case Diagram for, 5, 7

View/Manage `CustomerAccounts` **form, 504–505**

View/Manage Customer Accounts screen

displaying a customer record on, 515, 516

opening independently of the Customer Search screen, 517

prototype for, 464–465

View/Manage Customer Details screen, 462–463

views

advantages of, 271

creating, 273–274

Views tab of the Add Table dialog box, 275

virtual tables, 163

`Visible` **property**

hiding and redisplaying forms, 325

of the `objExcel` object, 295

setting to `False`, 186

setting to `True`, 291

Visio

creating Activity Diagrams, 8

generating prototype screens, 336

Visual Basic, 1

Visual Basic Editor (VBE)

for Access 2007, 2

display of, 19, 20

opening, 37, 38

opening with a new empty procedure, 85

running and debugging code in, 24–25

sample module displayed, 27–28

writing VBA code in, 18–23

Visual Basic for Applications, 1

Visual Basic .NET, 1

visual objects, 82

Visual Studio Tools for Microsoft Office, 2

Visual Studio Tools for Office (VSTO), using ADO.NET, 130

W

Watch window, 69–70, 71

Watches window, 24, 25

Web browser interface. See thin client

Web formats, exporting Access data to, 248–251

web services

adding references to, 215–218

consuming, 214

others available, 218

using data from, 214–220

Web Services References option, 215

Web Services Toolkit, 214
Where clause, 161
Where keyword, 514
WhereCondition parameter, 209
While...Wend statement, 63
Windows integrated security, 466
With...EndWith, 323–324
WithEvents keyword
  declaring an object variable, 114
  as part of a declaration, 119
wizard add-ins, 312
Word
  controlling from Access, 298–302
  displaying in Print Preview mode, 302

Word Application object, 301
workstations in client-server architecture, 14
Wrox Auto Sales Application, 4

X

XML (eXtensible Markup Language), 208
XML files, importing and exporting, 208–210

Y

Yes/No data type in SharePoint, 222
Yes/No field data type, 50